CONTENTS

Edinburgh

Water of Leith

LANE
CUMBERLAND ST.
DUNDONALD ST.
Drummond Place
BARONY ST.
KERR ST.
ST. STEPHEN
GREAT KING ST.
DUNDAS ST.
PUBLIN ST.
ALBANY
INDIA PL.
Royal Circus
NORTHUMBERLAND
ABERCROMBY PL.
DOUNE TERR.
GLOUCESTER LN.
INDIA ST.
N. LANE
S. LANE
HERIOT ROW
Gardens
SCOTTISH NATIONAL PORTRAIT GALLERY **25**
BUS STATION
Moray Place
Queen Street
ANDREW LN.
HARVEY NICHOLS
ST. COLME ST.
QUEEN STREET
ST. ANDREW'S & ST. GEORGE'S CHURCH
St Andrew Square
T
SAINT ANDREW ST.
GEORGIAN HOUSE **8**
HILL ST.
POST
THISTLE ST.
NEW TOWN
SAINT DAVID ST.
WAVERLEY MALL
i
YOUNG ST.
N CASTLE STREET
FREDERICK STREET
HANOVER STREET
JENNERS DEP'T STORE
SCOTT MONUMENT
23
Charlotte Square
GEORGE STREET
ROSE STREET
ROYAL SCOTTISH ACADEMY
WAVERLEY BR.
To A-90, Forth Bridge & Inverness
PRINCES STREET
Princes St. (tram to Airport) T
THE MOUND
24
SCOTTISH NATIONAL GALLERY
MARKET
SHANDWICK PL.
West Princes Street Gardens
15
To A-8, Airport & Glasgow
ST. CUTHBERT †
ST. MARGARET'S CHAPEL
3
9
BANK
ROYAL
27 ST. GILES
28
4
NAT'L WAR MUSEUM
11
17
LOTHIAN RD.
CASTLE TERRACE
EDINBURGH CASTLE
ROYAL PALACE & CROWN JEWELS
6
Esplanade
WAR MEMORIAL
22
OLD
VICTORIA ST.
GEORGE IV BR.
APPROACH RD.
ST.
KING'S STABLES RD.
GRASSMARKET
TOWN
10
CANDLEMAKER
SPITTAL
LADY LAWSON ST.
WEST PORT
Greyfriars Cemetery
Greyfriars Cemetery †
MORRISON ST.
HERIOT PL.
GEORGE HERIOT'S SCHOOL
TEVIOT
LAURISTON PL.
MEADOW WALK
LONSDALE TERRACE
MELVILLE DRIVE

SIGHTS

1 To Arthur's Seat Trail
2 To *Britannia* (Yacht)
3 Camera Obscura
4 Deacon Brodie's Tavern
5 Dynamic Earth
6 Edinburgh Castle
7 Fringe Festival Tickets
8 Georgian House
9 Gladstone's Land
10 Greyfriars Bobby Statue
11 The Hub (Festival Tickets)
12 John Knox House
13 Museum of Childhood
14 Museum of Edinburgh

15 Museum on the Mound
16 National Museum of Scotland
17 Old Parliament House
18 Palace of Holyroodhouse
19 People's Story Museum
20 Queen's Gallery
21 Royal Mile
22 Scotch Whisky Experience
23 Scott Monument
24 Scottish National Gallery
25 Scottish Nat'l Portrait Gallery
26 Scottish Parliament
27 St. Giles' Cathedral
28 Writers' Museum at Lady Stair's House

Scotland's national dress: the kilt

Oban's harbor

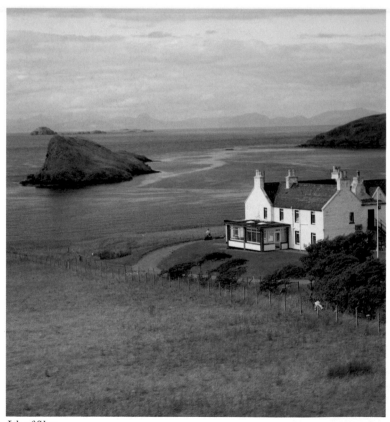

Isle of Skye

Rick Steves®

SCOTLAND

Welcome to Rick Steves' Europe

Travel is intensified living—maximum thrills per minute and one of the last great sources of legal adventure. Travel is freedom. It's recess, and we need it.

I discovered a passion for European travel as a teen and have been sharing it ever since—through tours, my public television and radio shows, and travel guidebooks. Over the years, I've taught thousands of travelers how to best enjoy Europe's blockbuster sights—and experience "Back Door" discoveries that most tourists miss.

This book offers a balanced mix of Scotland's rich cultural heritage and the rugged beauty of its countryside. And it's selective—rather than listing every windswept isle, I recommend only the best ones. My self-guided city walks and driving tours give insight into the country's vibrant history and today's living, breathing culture.

I advocate traveling simply and smartly. Take advantage of my money- and time-saving tips on sightseeing, transportation, and more. Try local, characteristic alternatives to expensive hotels and restaurants. In many ways, spending more money only builds a thicker wall between you and what you traveled so far to see.

We visit Scotland to experience it—to become temporary locals. Thoughtful travel engages us with the world, as we learn to appreciate other cultures and new ways to measure quality of life.

Judging from the positive feedback I receive from readers, this book will help you enjoy a fun, affordable, and rewarding vacation—whether it's your first trip or your tenth.

Happy travels!

Rick Steves

INTRODUCTION

Scotland is a little land that packs a big punch. From the yin-and-yang cities of Edinburgh and Glasgow to the rugged Highlands and remote islands, this fiercely proud country specializes in showing off its dramatic scenery and unique culture. Scotland's famous clichés—whisky distilleries, moody glens, golf links, bagpipes, kilts, and, yes, haggis—offer glimpses of a deeply engaging cultural feast.

This book breaks Scotland into its top big-city, small-town, and rural destinations. It gives you all the information and opinions necessary to wring the maximum value out of your limited time and money in each of these locations. If you plan a month or less for Scotland and have a normal appetite for information, this book is all you need. If you're a travel-info fiend, this book sorts through all the superlatives and provides a handy rack upon which to hang your supplemental information.

Experiencing Scottish culture, people, and natural wonders economically and hassle-free has been my goal for more than three decades of traveling, tour guiding, and travel writing. With this book, I pass on to you the lessons I've learned, updated for your trip.

While including the predictable biggies (such as Edinburgh, Glasgow, Stirling, and the Isle of Skye), this book also mixes in a healthy dose of Back Door intimacy (windswept moors, evocative glens, and small-town Highland Games). It is selective. Scotland has more than 790 islands, but I recommend just my favorites: Skye, Mull, Iona, Staffa, and Orkney.

The best is, of course, only my opinion. But after spending much of my life researching Europe, I've developed a sixth sense for what travelers enjoy. The places featured in this book will knock your spots off.

INTRODUCTION

ABOUT THIS BOOK

Rick Steves Scotland is a personal tour guide in your pocket. This book is organized by destinations. Each is a mini vacation on its own, filled with exciting sights, strollable neighborhoods, homey and affordable places to stay, and memorable places to eat. Within the destination chapters, you'll find these sections:

Planning Your Time suggests a schedule for how to best use your limited time.

Orientation has specifics on public transportation, helpful hints, local tour options, easy-to-read maps, and tourist information.

Sights describes the top attractions and includes their cost and hours.

Self-Guided Walks take you through interesting neighborhoods, pointing out sights and fun stops.

Sleeping describes my favorite hotels, from good-value deals to cushy splurges.

Eating serves up a buffet of options, from inexpensive pubs to fancy restaurants.

Connections outlines your options for traveling to destinations by train, bus, boat, and plane, plus route tips for drivers.

The **Scotland: Past & Present** chapter gives a quick overview of Scottish history and culture.

The **Practicalities** chapter near the end of this book is a traveler's tool kit, with my best advice about money, sightseeing, sleeping, eating, staying connected, and transportation (trains, buses, ferries, driving, and flights). Here you'll also find definitions of typically Scottish terms.

The **appendix** has the nuts and bolts: useful phone numbers and websites, a holiday and festival list, recommended books and films, a climate chart, a handy packing checklist, and a fun British-Yankee dictionary.

Throughout this book, you'll find money- and time-saving tips for sightseeing, transportation, and more. Some businesses—especially hotels and walking tour companies—offer special discounts to my readers, indicated in their listings.

Browse through this book, choose your favorite destinations, and link them up. Then have a brilliant trip! Traveling like a temporary local, you'll get the absolute most out of every mile, minute, and dollar. And, as you visit places I know and love, I'm happy that you'll be meeting my favorite Scottish people.

Top Destinations in Scotland

NORTHERN SCOTLAND

ISLE OF SKYE

INVERNESS & LOCH NESS

EASTERN SCOTLAND

GLENCOE & FORT WILLIAM

OBAN & THE INNER HEBRIDES

STIRLING & NEARBY

ST. ANDREWS

GLASGOW

EDINBURGH

SCOTLAND

North Sea

Irish Sea

ENGLAND

50 Kilometers

50 Miles

Planning

This section will help you get started on planning your trip—with advice on trip costs, when to go, and what you should know before you take off.

TRIP COSTS

Five components make up your trip costs: airfare, surface transportation, room and board, sightseeing and entertainment, and shopping and miscellany.

Airfare to Europe: A basic round-trip flight from the US to Edinburgh can cost, on average, about $1,000-2,000 total, depending on where you fly from and when (cheaper in winter). If your trip extends beyond Scotland, consider saving time and money by

Scotland at a Glance

This book's destinations are organized roughly south (the Lowlands) to north (the Highlands).

The Lowlands

▲▲▲Edinburgh Proud and endlessly entertaining Scottish capital, with an imposing castle, attraction-studded Royal Mile, excellent museums, and atmospheric neighborhoods.

▲▲Glasgow Scotland's fun and funky biggest city—gritty but gentrifying, and packed with gregarious locals, edgy culture, and a treasure trove of Art Nouveau architecture.

▲Stirling & Nearby Site of one of Scotland's top castles (home of the Stuart kings) overlooking a historic plain, with great sights nearby—from giant horse heads and a Ferris wheel for boats at Falkirk to Highland scenery in the Trossachs.

▲▲St. Andrews Beach town that hosts Scotland's top university and the world's most famous golf course, plus interesting industrial museums in nearby Dundee and charming coastal scenery in the East Neuk.

The Highlands

▲▲Oban & the Inner Hebrides Handy home-base town of Oban, with boat trips to the isles of Mull, Iona, and Staffa.

flying into one city and out of another—for instance, into Edinburgh and out of Amsterdam. Overall, Kayak.com is the best place to start searching for flights on a combination of mainstream and budget carriers.

Transportation in Europe: For a two-week whirlwind trip of all my recommended Scottish destinations, allow $250 per person for public transportation (train and bus tickets). If you'll be renting a car, allow at least $250 per week, not including gas and supplemental insurance. If you need the car for three weeks or more, leasing can save you money on insurance and taxes. A short flight can be cheaper than the train (check www.skyscanner.com for intra-European flights).

Room and Board: You can thrive in Scotland on $120 a day per person for room and board (more in big cities). This allows $15 for lunch, $35 for dinner, and $70 for lodging (based on two people splitting the cost of a $140 double room that includes breakfast). Students and tightwads can enjoy Scotland for as little as $60 ($30 for a bed, $30 for meals and snacks).

▲**Glencoe & Fort William** Stirring "Weeping Glen" of Glencoe offering some of the Highlands' best scenery and hikes, plus the transit-hub town of Fort William and the historic "Road to the Isles."

▲▲**Inverness & Loch Ness** Regional capital with easy access to more Highland sights, including Culloden Battlefield (Scotland's Alamo) and monster-spotting at the famous Loch Ness.

▲**Eastern Scotland** Grab-bag of sights between Inverness and Edinburgh, including the whisky and hillwalking mecca of Pitlochry, a look at early Iron Age crannog life on Loch Tay, the distilleries of Speyside, the Queen's Scottish retreat at Balmoral Castle, and cliff-capping Dunnottar Castle.

▲▲**Isle of Skye** Dramatically scenic island with craggy Cuillin Hills, jagged Trotternish Peninsula, castles, a distillery, dynamic clan history, and the colorful harbor town of Portree.

▲**Northern Scotland** Some of the Highlands' best get-away-from-it-all scenery along Wester Ross and the north coast, plus the fascinating Orkney Islands—with Scotland's best prehistoric sites, evocative Old Norse history, and WWI/WWII naval harbor.

Sightseeing and Entertainment: Figure about $12–25 per major sight (Edinburgh Castle-$22, Stirling Castle-$20, around $12-15 for whisky distillery tours), $7-10 for minor ones (Georgian House or Gladstone's Land in Edinburgh), and $35-80 for splurge experiences (e.g., bus tours and concerts). For information on various sightseeing passes, see page 443. An overall average of $30 a day works for most people. Don't skimp here. After all, this category is the driving force behind your trip—you came to sightsee, enjoy, and experience Scotland.

Shopping and Miscellany: Figure roughly $2 per postcard, $3 for tea or an ice-cream cone, and $5 per pint of beer. Shopping can vary in cost from nearly nothing to a small fortune. Good budget travelers find that this category has little to do with assembling a trip full of lifelong memories.

Scotland's Best Two-Week Trip by Car

Day	Plan	Sleep in
1	Arrive in Edinburgh	Edinburgh
2	Edinburgh	Edinburgh
3	Edinburgh	Edinburgh
4	More time in Edinburgh, then train to Glasgow	Glasgow
5	Glasgow	Glasgow
6	Pick up car, drive to Oban	Oban
7	Side-trip to Mull and Iona	Oban
8	Drive through Glencoe this morning, then to Isle of Skye	Isle of Skye
9	Isle of Skye	Isle of Skye
10	Drive along Caledonian Canal and Loch Ness to Inverness	Inverness
11	Inverness and side-trip to Culloden and other sights	Inverness
12	Head south, enjoying your choice of sights in Eastern Scotland or St. Andrews	Pitlochry, Ballater, or St. Andrews
13	More Eastern Scotland or St. Andrews sightseeing; spend evening in Stirling	Stirling
14	Stirling Castle and nearby sights	Stirling
15	Drive to Edinburgh for your flight home	

While this two-week itinerary is designed to be done by car after leaving Glasgow, most connections can be done by bus with a few modifications: You may want to rent a car for your day on Skye; consider a package tour for Highland side-tripping from Inverness; and at the end, go from Inverness straight to Stirling (skipping Eastern Scotland sights, which are out of the way by public transit).

If cities aren't your thing, consider skipping Glasgow (or

SIGHTSEEING PRIORITIES

So much to see, so little time. How to choose? Depending on the length of your trip, and taking geographic proximity into account, here are my recommended priorities:

- 3 days: Edinburgh
- 5 days, add: Glasgow, Stirling
- 7 days, add: Oban, Glencoe
- 9 days, add: Inverness, Loch Ness, Culloden

doing it at the end, as a side-trip from Stirling) to make more time for the countryside.

With more time, slow down and linger—or enjoy additional scenery by looping around the north of Scotland: Wester Ross, the north coast, and the Orkney Islands.

11 days, add: Isle of Skye
13 days, add: St. Andrews, Mull/Iona/Staffa
15 days, add: Your choice of sights near Stirling or
                  in Eastern Scotland
17 days, add: Orkney
21 days, add: More sights near Stirling, Wester Ross
                  and the north coast, and slow down

The top 15 days include everything on my "Scotland's Best

Two-Week Trip by Car" itinerary and map (see page 6). If you're traveling here in summer, check schedules for Highland Games in the areas you're visiting, and plan your time accordingly.

Build your itinerary to match your interests. Golfers make a pilgrimage to St. Andrews; nature lovers add extra time for hiking in Glencoe or the Isle of Skye; whisky aficionados appreciate Speyside and Pitlochry; royalists tour Balmoral and Glamis castles; prehistorians prioritize Orkney, Kilmartin Glen, and Clava Cairns; and those interested in Scotland's industrial heritage check out the Caledonian Canal, Falkirk Wheel, and museums in Dundee. If you're interested in castles, see page 426 for a rundown of Scotland's best.

WHEN TO GO

In most of Scotland, July and August are peak season—with very long days, the best weather, and the busiest schedule of tourist fun. (Edinburgh is especially swamped throughout August, during the city's festival season.) While it never quite feels "crowded," Scotland has a finite number of B&Bs and restaurants—and they are jam-packed in July and August.

Travel during "shoulder season" (May, early June, Sept, and early Oct) is easier and can be a bit less expensive. In fact, many travelers' favorite time to visit Scotland is May and June: smaller crowds, the full range of sights and tourist fun spots, and generally better room availability (and prices). Even in the peak of summer, Scotland's damp and chilly climate means that sunny weather is far from guaranteed—you may do just as well in shoulder season.

Winter travelers find absolutely no crowds and soft room prices, but sightseeing hours are shorter and the weather is reliably bad. Some attractions open only on weekends or close entirely in the winter (Nov-Feb). The weather can be cold and dreary, and nightfall draws the shades on sightseeing well before dinnertime. While rural charm falls with the leaves, city sightseeing is fine in the winter.

Plan for rain no matter when you go. Just keep traveling and take full advantage of bright spells. The weather can change several times in a day, but rarely is it extreme. As the locals say, "There is no bad weather, only inappropriate clothing." Bring a jacket and dress in layers. Temperatures below 32°F cause headlines, and days that break 80°F—while more frequent in recent years—are still rare in Scotland. (For more information, see the climate chart in the appendix.) While sunshine may be uncommon, summer days are very long. The midsummer sun is up from 6:30 until 22:30. It's not uncommon to have a gray day, eat dinner, and enjoy hours of sunshine afterward.

Before You Go

You'll have a smoother trip if you tackle a few things ahead of time. For more information on these topics, see the Practicalities chapter (and www.ricksteves.com, which has helpful travel tips and talks).

Make sure your passport is valid. If it's due to expire within six months of your ticketed date of return, you need to renew it. Allow up to six weeks to renew or get a passport (www.travel.state. gov).

Arrange your transportation. Book your international flights. Figure out your main form of transportation within Great Britain: It's worth thinking about buying train tickets online in advance, getting a rail pass, renting a car, or booking cheap European flights. (You can wing it once you're there, but it may cost more.)

Book rooms well in advance, especially if your trip falls during peak season or any major holidays or festivals (see list on page 493); those visiting Edinburgh in August or the Isle of Skye in peak season should book especially early.

Reserve or buy tickets ahead for major sights. Tickets to **Edinburgh's Military Tattoo** (Aug) sell out early—book as far ahead as possible (www.edintattoo.co.uk; for details, see page 96). If you'll be in **Edinburgh at festival time** (most of Aug), check the schedule for theater and music ahead of time. If there's something you just have to see, consider buying tickets before you go (for tips, see page 95, and for a current festival schedule, visit www.eif.co.uk and www.edfringe.com). Other good places for live shows are Glasgow and even little Pitlochry (with its hardworking Festival Theatre, www.pitlochryfestivaltheatre.com). To **golf at St. Andrews' famous Old Course,** you'll need to reserve the previous fall, or put your name in for the "ballot" two days before (see page 214). If you plan to hire a **local guide,** reserve ahead by email. Popular guides can get booked up.

Consider travel insurance. Compare the cost of the insurance to the cost of your potential loss. Check whether your existing insurance (health, homeowners, or renters) covers you and your possessions overseas.

Call your bank. Alert your bank that you'll be using your debit and credit cards in Europe. Ask about transaction fees, and get the PIN number for your credit card. You don't need to bring pounds for your trip; you can withdraw pounds from cash machines in Great Britain.

Use your smartphone smartly. Sign up for an international service plan to reduce your costs, or rely on Wi-Fi in Europe instead. Download any apps you'll want on the road, such as maps, translation, transit schedules, and Rick Steves Audio Europe (see sidebar).

INTRODUCTION

🎧 Stick This Guidebook in Your Ear!

 My free Rick Steves Audio Europe app makes it easy for you to download my audio tours of many of Europe's top attractions and listen to them offline during your travels. For Scotland, this includes my Edinburgh Royal Mile Walk. Sights covered by audio tours are marked in this book with this symbol: 🎧. The app also offers insightful travel interviews from my public radio show with experts from Scotland and around the globe. It's all free! You can download the app via Apple's App Store, Google Play, or Amazon's Appstore. For more info, see www.ricksteves.com/audioeurope.

Rip up this book! Turn chapters into mini guidebooks: Break the book's spine and use a utility knife to slice apart chapters, keeping gummy edges intact. Reinforce the chapter spines with clear, wide tape; use a heavy-duty stapler; or make or buy a cheap cover (see Travel Store at www.ricksteves.com), swapping out chapters as you travel.

Pack light. You'll walk with your luggage more than you think. Bring a single carry-on bag and a daypack. Use the packing checklist in the appendix as a guide.

Travel Smart

If you have a positive attitude, equip yourself with good information (this book), and expect to travel smart, you will.

Read—and reread—this book. To have an "A" trip, be an "A" student. Note opening hours of sights, closed days, crowd-beating tips, and whether reservations are required or advisable. Check the latest at www.ricksteves.com/update.

Be your own tour guide. As you travel, get up-to-date info on sights, reserve tickets and tours, reconfirm hotels and travel arrangements, and check transit connections. Visit local tourist information offices (TIs). Upon arrival in a new town, lay the groundwork for a smooth departure; confirm the train, bus, or road you'll take when you leave.

Outsmart thieves. Pickpockets abound in crowded places where tourists congregate. Treat commotions as smokescreens for theft. Keep your cash, credit cards, and passport secure in a money belt tucked under your clothes; carry only a day's spending money in your front pocket. Don't set valuable items down on counters or café tabletops, where they can be quickly stolen or easily forgotten.

Minimize potential loss. Keep expensive gear to a minimum. Bring photocopies or take photos of important documents (passport and cards) to aid in replacement if they're lost or stolen.

Guard your time and energy. Taking a taxi can be a good value if it saves you a long wait for a cheap bus or an exhausting walk across town. To avoid long lines, follow my crowd-beating tips, such as making advance reservations, or sightseeing early or late.

Be flexible. Even if you have a well-planned itinerary, expect changes, strikes, closures, sore feet, bad weather, and so on. Your Plan B could turn out to be even better.

Connect with the culture. Interacting with locals carbonates your experience. Enjoy the friendliness of the Scottish people. You speak the language—use it! Ask questions; most locals are happy to point you in their idea of the right direction. Set up your own quest for the best hike, castle, or whisky. When an opportunity pops up, make it a habit to say "yes."

Scotland...here you come!

SCOTLAND

One of the three countries that make up Great Britain, rugged, feisty, colorful Scotland stands apart. Whether it's the laid-back, less-organized nature of the people, the stony architecture, the unmanicured landscape, or simply the haggis, go-its-own-way Scotland is distinctive.

Scotland encompasses about a third of Britain's geographical area (30,400 square miles), but has less than a tenth of its population (about 5.4 million). This sparsely populated chunk of land stretches to Norwegian latitudes. Its Shetland Islands, at about 60°N (similar to Anchorage, Alaska), are the northernmost point of the British Isles. You may see Scotland referred to as "Caledonia" (its ancient Roman name) or "Alba" (its Gaelic name). Scotland's fortunes were long tied to the sea; all of its leading cities are located along firths (estuaries), where major rivers connect to ocean waters.

The southern part of Scotland, called the Lowlands, is relatively flat and urbanized. The northern area—the Highlands—features a wild, severely undulating terrain, punctuated by lochs (lakes) and fringed by sea lochs (inlets) and islands.

The Highland Boundary Fault that divides Scotland geologically also divides it culturally. Historically, there were two distinct identities: rougher Highlanders in the northern wilderness and the more refined Lowlanders in the southern

SCOTLAND

Scotland Almanac

Official Name: Scotland.

Population: About 5.4 million. Scotland is mostly English-speaking, though about 1.5 million people use the Scots "language," and about 60,000 speak Scottish Gaelic.

Latitude and Longitude: 57°N and 4°W. The Shetland Islands are Scotland's northernmost point, at 60°N (similar to Anchorage, Alaska).

Area: 30,400 square miles, about the size of South Carolina.

Geography: Scotland's flatter southern portion is the Lowlands; the Highlands to the north are more wild and hilly, and the country boasts over 6,000 miles of coastline and more than 790 islands (only about 130 are inhabited). Ben Nevis in western Scotland (at 4,406 feet) is Great Britain's highest peak.

Biggest Cities: Glasgow has 600,000 people, Edinburgh 490,000.

Economy: The gross domestic product is about $142 billion, and the GDP per capita is $26,500. The Scottish service sector (including retail and financial services) has become an increasingly significant part of its economy, producing over 60 percent of all economic activity in 2015.

Scotland's main exports include food and drink, as well as chemicals and petroleum products. Scotch whisky comprises a quarter of all UK food and drink exports; exports to the US represent the biggest market for Scotch by value, though France is the biggest market by volume.

Scotland uses the same currency as the other UK countries of England, Wales, and Northern Ireland: the pound sterling.

Government: Queen Elizabeth II officially heads the country—but for Scots she is simply Queen Elizabeth, not Queen Elizabeth II. (Scotland and England were separate monarchies when England had their first Elizabeth.) Theresa May is the UK's prime minister, and Nicola Sturgeon is Scotland's first minister.

Flag: The Saltire, with a diagonal, X-shaped white cross on a blue field, is meant to represent the crucifixion of Scotland's patron saint, the apostle Andrew.

The Average Scot: The average Scottish person will live to age 79 and doesn't identify with an organized religion. He or she has free health care, gets 28 vacation days a year (versus 16 in the US), lives within a five-minute walk of a park or green space, and gets outdoors at least once a week.

flatlands and cities. Highlanders represented the stereotypical image of "true Scots," speaking Gaelic, wearing kilts, and playing bagpipes, while Lowlanders spoke languages of Saxon origin and wore trousers. After the Scottish Reformation, the Lowlanders embraced Protestantism, while most Highlanders stuck to Catholicism. Although this Lowlands/Highlands division has faded over time, some Scots still cling to it.

The Lowlands are dominated by a pair of rival cities: Edinburgh (on the east coast's Firth of Forth) and Glasgow (on the west

coast's Firth of Clyde) mark the endpoints of Scotland's 75-mile-long "Central Belt," where three-quarters of the country's population resides. Edinburgh, the old royal capital, teems with Scottish history and is the country's most popular tourist attraction. Glasgow, once a gloomy industrial city, is becoming a hip, laid-back city of art, music, and architecture. In addition to these two cities—both of which warrant a visit—the Lowlands' highlights include the medieval university town and golf mecca of St. Andrews, the small city of Stirling (with its castle and many nearby historic sites), and selected countryside stopovers.

Generally, the Highlands are hungry for the tourist dollar, and everything overtly Scottish is exploited to the kilt; you need to spend some time here to get to know the area's true character. You can get a feel for the Highlands with a quick drive to Oban, through Glencoe, then up the Caledonian Canal to Inverness. With more time, the Isles of Iona, Staffa, and Mull (an easy day trip from Oban); the Isle of Skye; the handy distillery town of Pit-

lochry; and countless brooding countryside castles will flesh out your Highlands experience. And for those really wanting to get off the beaten path, continue north—all the way up the dramatic west coast (called Wester Ross) to John O'Groats, at Britain's northeastern tip. To go farther, cross the Pentland Firth to Orkney, with its own unique culture and history.

At these northern latitudes, cold and drizzly weather isn't uncommon—even in midsummer. The blazing sun can quickly be covered over by black clouds and howling wind. Your B&B host will warn you to prepare for "four seasons in one day." Because Scots feel personally responsible for bad weather, they tend to be overly optimistic about forecasts. Take any Scottish promise of "sun by the afternoon" with a grain of salt—and bring your raincoat, just in case.

Americans and Canadians of Scottish descent enjoy coming "home" to Scotland. If you're Scottish, your surname will tell you which clan your ancestors likely belonged to. The prefix "Mac" (or "Mc") means "son of"—so "MacDonald" means the same thing as "Donaldson." Tourist shops everywhere are happy to help you track down your clan's tartan (distinctive plaid pattern). For more on how these "clan tartans" don't go back as far as you might think, see the sidebar on page 33.

Scotland shares a monarchy with the rest of the United Kingdom, though to Scots, Queen Elizabeth II is just "Queen Elizabeth"; the first Queen Elizabeth ruled England, but not Scotland. (In this book, I use England's numbering.) Scotland is not a sovereign state, but it is a "nation" in that it has its own traditions, ethnic identity, languages (Gaelic and Scots), and football league. To some extent, it even has its own government.

Recently, Scotland has enjoyed its greatest measure of political autonomy in centuries—a trend called "devolution." In 1999, the

Scottish parliament convened in Edinburgh for the first time in almost 300 years; in 2004, it moved into its brand-new building near the foot of the Royal Mile. Though the Scottish parliament's powers are limited (most major decisions are still made in London), the Scots are enjoying the refreshing breeze of increased self-governance. In a 2014 independence referendum, the Scots favored staying in the United Kingdom by a margin of 10 percent. The question of independence will likely remain a pivotal issue in Scotland for many years to come. (For more on Scotland's rocky history with British rule and devolution, see page 429.)

Scotland even has its own currency...sort of. Scots use the same coins as England, Wales, and Northern Ireland, but Scotland also prints its own bills (featuring Scottish rather than English people and landmarks). Just to confuse tourists, three different banks print Scottish pound

SCOTLAND

Scotland

Orkney Islands
Durness
John O'Groats
Thurso
Wick

OUTER HEBRIDES
Lewis

Harris

Ullapool

50 Kilometers

50 Miles

North Atlantic

Isle of Skye
Portree
Applecross

Inverness
CULLODEN
CLAVA CAIRNS

Loch Ness

INNER HEBRIDES

Mallaig
Fort William
Ben Nevis
Glencoe

H I G H L A N D S

BALMORAL
Ballater

Aberdeen

North Sea

Iona
Mull

Oban

Pitlochry

Dundee

Loch Lomond

Stirling

FALKIRK WHEEL

St. Andrews

Glasgow
Edinburgh

Arran

L O W L A N D S

Irish Sea

Ayr

Jedburgh

NORTHERN IRELAND

Cairnryan

Dumfries

Newcastle

Belfast

ENGLAND

notes, each with a different design. In the Lowlands (around Edinburgh and Glasgow), you'll receive both Scottish and English pounds from ATMs and in change. But in the Highlands, you'll almost never see English pounds. Bank of England notes are legal and widely used; Northern Ireland bank notes are legal but less common.

The Scottish flag—a diagonal, X-shaped white cross on a blue field—represents the cross of Scotland's patron saint, the Apostle Andrew (who was crucified on an X-shaped cross). You may not realize it, but you see the Scottish flag every time you look at the Union Jack: England's flag (the red St. George's cross on a white field) superimposed on Scotland's (a blue field with a white diagonal cross). The diagonal red cross (St. Patrick's cross)

British, Scottish, and English

Scotland and England have been tied together politically for more than 300 years, since the Act of Union in 1707. For a century and a half afterward, Scottish nationalists rioted for independence in Edinburgh's streets and led rebellions ("uprisings") in the Highlands. In this controversial union, history is clearly seen through two very different filters.

If you tour a British-oriented sight, such as Edinburgh's National War Museum Scotland, you'll find things told in a "happy union" way, which ignores the long history of Scottish resistance—from the ancient Picts through the time of Robert the Bruce. The official line: In 1706-1707, it was clear to England and certain parties in Scotland (especially landowners from the Lowlands) that it was in their mutual interest to dissolve the Scottish government and fold it into the United Kingdom, to be ruled from London.

But talk to a cabbie or your B&B host, and you may get a different spin. Scottish independence is still a hot-button issue. Since 2007, the Scottish National Party (SNP) has owned the largest majority in the Scottish Parliament. During a landmark referendum in September 2014, the Scots voted to remain part of the union—but many polls, right up until election day, suggested that things could easily have gone the other way.

The rift shows itself in sports, too. While the English may refer to a British team in international competition as "English," the Scots are careful to call it "British." If a Scottish athlete does well, the English call him "British." If he screws up...he's a clumsy Scot.

over Scotland's white one represents Northern Ireland. (Wales gets no love on the Union Jack.)

Here in "English-speaking" Scotland, you may still encounter a language barrier. First is the lovely, lilting Scottish accent—which may take you a while to understand. You may also hear an impenetrable dialect of Scottish English that many linguists consider to be a separate language, called "Scots." You may already know several Scots words: lad, lassie, wee, bonnie, glen, loch, aye. On menus, you'll see neeps and tatties (turnips and potatoes). And in place names, you'll see ben (mountain), brae (hill), firth (estuary), and kyle (strait). Second is Gaelic (pronounced "gallic" here; Ireland's closely related Celtic language is pronounced "gaylic")—the ancient Celtic language of the Scots. While only one percent of the population speaks Gaelic, it's making a comeback—particularly in the remote and traditional Highlands. For more on the languages of Scotland—including a glossary of Scots words—see page 468.

While soccer ("football") is as popular here as anywhere, golf is Scotland's other national sport. But in Scotland, it's not necessarily considered an exclusively upper-class pursuit; you can generally play a round at a basic course for about £15. While Scotland's best scenery is along the west coast, its best golfing is on the east coast—home to many prestigious golf courses. Most of these are links courses, which use natural sand from the beaches for the bunkers. For tourists, these links are more authentic, more challenging, and more fun than the regular-style courses (with artificial landforms) farther inland. If you're a golfer, St. Andrews—on the east coast—is a pilgrimage worth making.

Outside of the main cities, Scotland's sights are subtle, but its misty glens, brooding countryside castles, and warm culture are plenty engaging. Whether toasting with beer, whisky, or Scotland's favorite soft drink, Irn-Bru, enjoy meeting the Scottish people. It's easy to fall in love with the irrepressible spirit and beautiful landscape of this faraway corner of Britain.

EDINBURGH

Edinburgh is the historical, cultural, and political capital of Scotland. For nearly a thousand years, Scotland's kings, parliaments, writers, thinkers, and bankers have called Edinburgh home. Today, it remains Scotland's most sophisticated city.

Edinburgh (ED'n-burah—only tourists pronounce it like "Pittsburgh") is Scotland's showpiece and one of Europe's most entertaining cities. It's a place of stunning vistas—nestled among craggy bluffs and studded with a prickly skyline of spires, towers, domes, and steeples. Proud statues of famous Scots dot the urban landscape. The buildings are a harmonious yellow-gray, all built from the same local sandstone.

Culturally, Edinburgh has always been the place where Lowland culture (urban and English) met Highland style (rustic and Gaelic). Tourists will find no end of traditional Scottish clichés: whisky tastings, kilt shops, bagpipe-playing buskers, and gimmicky tours featuring Scotland's bloody history and ghost stories.

Edinburgh is two cities in one. The Old Town stretches along the Royal Mile, from the grand castle on top to the palace on the bottom. Along this colorful labyrinth of cobbled streets and narrow lanes, medieval skyscrapers stand shoulder to shoulder, hiding peaceful courtyards.

A few hundred yards north of the Old Town lies the New Town. It's a magnificent planned neighborhood (from the 1700s). Here, you'll enjoy upscale shops, broad boulevards, straight streets, square squares, circular circuses, and Georgian mansions decked out in Greek-style columns and statues.

Today's Edinburgh is big in banking, scientific research, and scholarship at its four universities. Since 1999, when Scotland regained a measure of self-rule, Edinburgh reassumed its place as home of the Scottish Parliament. The city hums with life. Students and professionals pack the pubs and art galleries. It's especially lively in August, when the Edinburgh Festival takes over the town. Historic, monumental, fun, and well organized, Edinburgh is a tourist's delight.

PLANNING YOUR TIME

While the major sights can be seen in a day, I'd give Edinburgh two days and three nights.

Day 1: Tour the castle, then consider catching a city bus tour for a one-hour loop (departing from a block below the castle at the Hub/Tolbooth Church; you could munch a sandwich from the top deck if you're into multitasking). Back near the castle, take my self-guided Royal Mile walk, stopping in at shops and museums that interest you (Gladstone's Land is tops but you can only visit it by booking a tour). At the bottom of the Mile, consider visiting the Scottish Parliament, the Palace of Holyroodhouse, or both. If the weather's good, you could hike back to your B&B along the Salisbury Crags.

Day 2: Visit the National Museum of Scotland. After lunch (several great choices nearby, on Forrest Road), stroll through the Princes Street Gardens and the Scottish National Gallery. Then follow my self-guided walk through the New Town, visiting the Scottish National Portrait Gallery and the Georgian House—or squeeze in a quick tour of the good ship *Britannia* (check last entry time before you head out).

Evenings: Options include various "haunted Edinburgh" walks, literary pub crawls, or live music in pubs. Sadly, full-blown traditional folk performances are just about extinct, surviving only in excruciatingly schmaltzy variety shows put on for tour-bus groups. Perhaps the most authentic evening out is just settling down in a pub to sample the whisky and local beers while meeting the locals...and attempting to understand them through their thick Scottish accents (see "Nightlife in Edinburgh," page 102).

Orientation to Edinburgh

A VERBAL MAP

With 490,000 people (835,000 in the metro area), Edinburgh is Scotland's second-biggest city (after Glasgow). But the tourist's Edinburgh is compact: Old Town, New Town, and the B&B area south of the city center.

Edinburgh's **Old Town** stretches across a ridgeline slung be-tween two bluffs. From west to east, this "Royal Mile" runs from the Castle Rock—which is visible from anywhere—to the base of the 822-foot extinct volcano called Arthur's Seat. For visitors, this east-west axis is the center of the action. Just south of the Royal Mile are the university and the National Museum of Scotland; farther to the south is a handy B&B neighborhood that lines up along **Dalkeith Road** and **Mayfield Gardens.** North of the Royal Mile ridge is the **New Town,** a neighborhood of grid-planned streets and elegant Georgian buildings.

In the center of it all—in a drained lake bed between the Old and New Towns—sit the Princes Street Gardens park and Waverley Bridge, where you'll find the Waverley train station, TI, Waverley Mall, bus info office (starting point for most city bus tours), Scottish National Gallery, and a covered dance-and-music pavilion.

TOURIST INFORMATION

The crowded TI is as central as can be, on the rooftop of the Waverley Mall and Waverley train station (Mon-Sat 9:00-17:00, Sun from 10:00, June daily until 18:00, July-Aug daily until 19:00; tel. 0131-473-3868, www.visitscotland.com). While the staff is helpful, be warned that much of their information is skewed by tourism payola (and booking seats on bus tours seems to be a big priority). There's also a TI at the airport (tel. 0131-344-3120).

For more information than what's included in the TI's free map, buy the excellent *Collins Discovering Edinburgh* map (which comes with opinionated commentary and locates almost every major sight). If you're interested in evening music, ask for the comprehensive entertainment listing, *The List*. Also consider buying Historic Scotland's Explorer Pass, which can save you some money if you visit the castles at both Edinburgh and Stirling, or are also visiting the Orkney Islands (for details, see page 443).

ARRIVAL IN EDINBURGH

By Train: Arriving by train at Waverley Station puts you in the city center and below the TI. Taxis line up outside, on Market Street or Waverley Bridge. For the TI or bus stop, follow signs for Princes Street and ride up several escalators. From here, the TI is to your left, and the city bus stop is two blocks to your right (for bus directions from here to my recommended B&Bs, see "Sleeping in Edinburgh," later).

By Bus: Scottish Citylink, Megabus, and National Express buses use the bus station (with luggage lockers) in the New Town, two blocks north of the train station on St. Andrew Square.

EDINBURGH

Greater Edinburgh

To St. Andrews,
Inverness
& John O'Groats

To
Culross

Firth of Forth

2 km

2 miles

ROYAL YACHT
BRITANNIA

LEITH

FIRTH OF FORTH
BRIDGES

A-90

A-902

Water of Leith

WAVERLEY
TRAIN STN.

M-90

QUEENSFERRY ROAD

A-90

To
Falkirk
& Stirling

M-9

AIRPORT

CORSTORPHINE ROAD

See
Edinburgh
detail maps

CENTER

Holyrood
Park

Arthur's
Seat

M-8

A-8

See
South B&Bs
detail map

DALKEITH ROAD

To
Glasgow

A-720

E D I N B U R G H

A-71

To
Berwick-
upon-Tweed,
Newcastle & Durham
(England)

A-70

Water of Leith

HILLEND

A-720

MIDLOTHIAN
SKI CENTRE

A-702

Pentland Hills
Regional Park

ROSSLYN
CHAPEL

A-701

To
A-74,
Carlisle &
Lake District
(England)

Roslin

By Car: If you're arriving from the north, rather than drive through downtown Edinburgh to my recommended B&Bs, circle the city on the A-720 City Bypass road. Approaching Edinburgh on the M-9, take the M-8 (direction: Glasgow) and quickly get onto the A-720 City Bypass (direction: Edinburgh South). After four miles, you'll hit a roundabout. Ignore signs directing you into *Edinburgh North* and stay on the A-720 for 10 more miles to the next and last roundabout, named *Sheriffhall*. Exit the roundabout at the first left *(A-7 Edinburgh)*. From here it's four miles to the B&B neighborhood. After a while, the A-7 becomes Dalkeith Road (you'll pass the Royal Infirmary hospital complex). If you see the huge Royal Commonwealth Pool, you've gone a couple of blocks too far (avoid this by referring to the map on page 107).

If you're driving in on the A-68 from the south, first follow signs for *Edinburgh South & West* (A-720), then exit at *A-7(N)/Edinburgh* and follow the directions above.

By Plane: Edinburgh's airport is eight miles and a 25-minute taxi ride from downtown. For information, see "Edinburgh Connections," at the end of this chapter.

HELPFUL HINTS

Sunday Activities: Many Royal Mile sights close on Sunday (except in Aug), but other major sights and shops are open. Sunday is a good day to catch a guided walking tour along the Royal Mile or a city bus tour (buses go faster in light traffic). The slopes of Arthur's Seat are lively with hikers and picnickers on weekends.

Festivals: August is a crowded, popular month to visit Edinburgh thanks to the multiple festivals hosted here, including the official Edinburgh International Festival, the Fringe Festival, and the Military Tattoo. Book ahead for hotels, events, and restaurant dinners if you'll be visiting in August, and expect to pay significantly more for your room. Many museums and shops have extended hours in August. For more festival details, see page 193.

Baggage Storage: At the train station, you'll find pricey, high-security luggage storage near platform 2 (daily 7:00-23:00). There are also lockers at the bus station on St. Andrew Square, just two blocks north of the train station.

Laundry: The **Ace Cleaning Centre** launderette is located near my recommended B&Bs south of town. You can pay for full-service laundry (drop off in the morning for same-day service) or stay and do it yourself. For a small extra fee, they'll collect your laundry from your B&B and drop it off the next day (Mon-Fri 8:00-20:00, Sat 9:00-17:00, Sun 10:00-16:00, along bus route to city center at 13 South Clerk Street, opposite Queens Hall, tel. 0131/667-0549).

Bike Rental and Tours: The laid-back crew at **Cycle Scotland** happily recommends good bike routes with your rental (prices starting at £20/3 hours or £30/day, electric bikes available for extra fee, daily 10:00-18:00, may close for a couple of months in winter, just off Royal Mile at 29 Blackfriars Street, tel. 0131/556-5560, mobile 07796-886-899, www.cyclescotland. co.uk, Peter). They also run guided three-hour bike tours daily at 11:00 that start on the Royal Mile and ride through Holyrood Park, Arthur's Seat, Duddingston Village, Doctor Neil's (Secret) Garden, and along the Innocent railway path (£45/person, extra fee for e-bike, book ahead).

Car Rental: These places have offices both in the town center and at the airport: **Avis** (24 East London Street, tel. 0844-544-6059, airport tel. 0844-544-6004), **Europcar** (Waverley Station, near platform 2, tel. 0871-384-3453, airport tel. 0871-384-3406), **Hertz** (10 Picardy Place, tel. 0843-309-3026, airport tel. 0843-309-3025), and **Budget** (24 East London Street, tel. 0844-544-9064, airport tel. 0844-544-4605). Some downtown offices close or have reduced hours on Sunday, but the airport locations tend to be open daily. If you plan to rent a car, pick it up on your way out of Edinburgh—you won't need it in town.

EDINBURGH

Dress for the Weather: Weather blows in and out—bring your sweater and be prepared for rain.

GETTING AROUND EDINBURGH

Many of Edinburgh's sights are within walking distance of one another, but **buses** come in handy—especially if you're staying at a B&B south of the city center. Double-decker buses come with fine views upstairs. It's easy once you get the hang of it: Buses come by frequently (screens at bus stops show wait times) and have free, fast

Edinburgh at a Glance

▲▲▲**Royal Mile** Historic road—good for walking—stretching from the castle down to the palace, lined with museums, pubs, and shops. **Hours:** Always open, but best during business hours, with walking tours daily. See page 31.

▲▲▲**Edinburgh Castle** Iconic hilltop fort and royal residence complete with crown jewels, Romanesque chapel, memorial, and fine military museum. **Hours:** Daily 9:30-18:00, Oct-March until 17:00. See page 53.

▲▲▲**National Museum of Scotland** Intriguing, well-displayed artifacts from prehistoric times to the 20th century. **Hours:** Daily 10:00-17:00. See page 75.

▲▲**Gladstone's Land** Seventeenth-century Royal Mile merchant's residence. **Hours:** Daily 10:30-16:00 by tour only, closed Nov-March. See page 64.

▲▲**St. Giles' Cathedral** Preaching grounds of Scottish Reformer John Knox, with spectacular organ, Neo-Gothic chapel, and distinctive crown spire. **Hours:** Mon-Fri 9:00-19:00, Sat until 17:00; Oct-April Mon-Sat 9:00-17:00; Sun 13:00-17:00 year-round. See page 65.

▲▲**Scottish Parliament Building** Striking headquarters for parliament, which returned to Scotland in 1999. **Hours:** Mon-Sat 10:00-17:00, longer hours Tue-Thu when parliament is in session (Sept-June), closed Sun year-round. See page 72.

▲▲**Palace of Holyroodhouse** The Queen's splendid official residence in Scotland, with lavish rooms, 12th-century abbey, and gallery with rotating exhibits. **Hours:** Daily April-Oct 9:30-18:00, Nov-March until 16:30, closed during royal visits. See page 73.

▲▲**Scottish National Gallery** Choice sampling of European masters and Scotland's finest. **Hours:** Daily 10:00-17:00, Thu until 19:00; longer hours in Aug. See page 79.

▲▲**Scottish National Portrait Gallery** Beautifully displayed

Wi-Fi on board. The only hassle is that you must pay with exact change (£1.60/ride, £4/all-day pass). As you board, tell your driver where you're going (or just say "single ticket") and drop your change into the box. Ping the bell as you near your stop. You can pick up a route map at the TI or at the transit office at the Old Town end of Waverley Bridge (tel. 0131/555-6363, www.lothianbuses.com).

Who's Who of Scottish history. **Hours:** Daily 10:00-17:00. See page 84.

▲▲**Georgian House** Intimate peek at upper-crust life in the late 1700s. **Hours:** Daily 10:00-17:00, March and Nov 11:00-16:00, closed Dec-Feb. See page 87.

▲▲**Royal Yacht *Britannia*** Ship for the royal family with a history of distinguished passengers, a 15-minute trip out of town. **Hours:** Daily 9:30-16:30, Oct until 16:00, Nov-March 10:00-15:30 (these are last-entry times). See page 87.

▲**Scotch Whisky Experience** Gimmicky but fun and educational introduction to Scotland's most famous beverage. **Hours:** Generally daily 10:00-18:00. See page 63.

▲**The Real Mary King's Close** Tour of underground street and houses last occupied in the 17th century, viewable by guided tour. **Hours:** Daily 10:00-21:00, Nov-March Sun-Thu until 17:00 (these are last-tour times). See page 70.

▲**Museum of Childhood** Five stories of historic fun. **Hours:** Thu-Mon 10:00-17:00 except Sun from 12:00, closed Tue-Wed. See page 70.

▲**People's Story Museum** Everyday life from the 18th to 20th century. **Hours:** Wed-Sat 10:00-17:00 except Sun from 12:00, closed Mon-Tue. See page 71.

▲**Museum of Edinburgh** Historic mementos, from the original National Covenant inscribed on animal skin to early golf balls. **Hours:** Thu-Mon 10:00-17:00 except Sun from 12:00, closed Tue-Wed. See page 71.

▲**Rosslyn Chapel** Small 15th-century church chock-full of intriguing carvings a short drive outside of Edinburgh. **Hours:** Mon-Sat 9:30-17:00, June-Aug until 18:00, Sun 12:00-16:45 year-round. See page 89.

EDINBURGH

Edinburgh's single **tram** line (also £1.60/ride) is designed more for locals than tourists; it's most useful for reaching the airport (see "Edinburgh Connections" at the end of this chapter).

The 1,300 **taxis** cruising Edinburgh's streets are easy to flag down (ride between downtown and the B&B neighborhood costs about £7; rates go up after 18:00 and on weekends). They can turn on a dime, so hail them in either direction. **Uber** also works well here.

Tours in Edinburgh

Royal Mile Walking Tours

Walking tours are an Edinburgh specialty; you'll see groups trailing entertaining guides all over town. Below I've listed good all-purpose walks; for **literary pub crawls** and **ghost tours,** see "Nightlife in Edinburgh" on page 102.

Edinburgh Tour Guides offers a good historical walk (without all the ghosts and goblins). Their Royal Mile tour is a gentle two-hour downhill stroll from the castle to the palace (£16.50; daily at 9:30 and 19:00; meet outside Gladstone's Land, near the top of the Royal Mile—see map on page 35, must reserve ahead, mobile 0785-888-0072, www.edinburghtourguides.com, info@ edinburghtourguides.com).

Mercat Tours offers a 1.5-hour "Secrets of the Royal Mile" walk that's more entertaining than intellectual (£13; £30 includes optional, 45-minute guided Edinburgh Castle visit; daily at 10:00 and 13:00, leaves from Mercat Cross on the Royal Mile, tel. 0131/225-5445, www.mercattours.com). The guides, who enjoy making a short story long, ignore the big sights and take you behind the scenes with piles of barely historical gossip, bully-pulpit Scottish pride, and fun but forgettable trivia. They also offer other tours, such as ghost walks, tours of 18th-century underground vaults on the southern slope of the Royal Mile, and *Outlander* sights (see their website for a rundown).

Sandemans New Edinburgh runs "free" tours multiple times a day; you won't pay upfront, but the guide will expect a tip (check schedule online, 3 hours, meet in front of Starbucks by Tron Kirk on High Street, www.neweuropetours.eu).

The **Voluntary Guides Association** offers free two-hour walks, but only during the Edinburgh Festival. You don't need a reservation—just show up (check website for times, generally depart from City Chambers across from St. Giles' Cathedral on the Royal Mile, www.edinburghfestivalguides.org). You can also hire their guides (for a small fee) for private tours outside of festival time.

Blue Badge Local Guides

The following guides charge similar prices and offer half-day and full-day tours: **Jean Blair** (a delightful teacher and guide, £190/ day without car, £430/day with car, mobile 0798-957-0287, www. travelthroughscotland.com, scotguide7@gmail.com); **Sergio La Spina** (an Argentinean who adopted Edinburgh as his hometown more than 20 years ago, £250/day, tel. 0131/664-1731, mobile 0797-330-6579, www.vivaescocia.com, sergiolaspina@aol.com); **Ken Hanley** (who wears his kilt as if pants don't exist, £130/half-day, £250/day, extra charge if he uses his car—seats up to six, tel. 0131/666-1944, mobile 0771-034-2044, www.small-world-tours. co.uk, kennethhanley@me.com); and **Liz Everett** (walking tours only—no car; £165/half-day, £230/day, mobile 07821-683-837, liz. everett@live.co.uk).

Hop-On, Hop-Off Bus Tours

The following one-hour hop-on, hop-off bus tour routes, all run by the same company, circle the town center, stopping at the major

sights. **Edinburgh Tour** (green buses) focuses on the city center, with live guides. **City Sightseeing** (red buses, focuses on Old Town) has recorded commentary, as does the **Majestic Tour** (blue-and-yellow buses, includes a stop at the *Britannia* and Royal Botanic Garden). You can pay for just one tour (£15/24 hours), but most people pay a few pounds more for a ticket covering all buses (£20; buses run April-Oct roughly 9:00-19:00, shorter hours off-season; every 10-15 minutes, buy tickets on board, tel. 0131/220-0770, www.edinburghtour.com). On sunny days the buses go topless, but come with increased traffic noise and exhaust fumes. For £52, the Royal Edinburgh Ticket covers two days of unlimited travel on all three buses, as well as admission (and line-skipping privileges) at Edinburgh Castle, the Palace of Holyroodhouse, and *Britannia* (www.royaledinburghticket.co.uk).

The **3 Bridges Tour** combines a hop-on, hop-off bus to South Queensferry with a boat tour on the Firth of Forth (£20, 3 hours total).

Weekend Tour Packages for Students

Andy Steves (Rick's son) runs Weekend Student Adventures (WSA Europe), offering 3-day and 10-day budget travel packages across Europe including accommodations, skip-the-line sightseeing, and unique local experiences. Locally guided and DIY options are available for student and budget travelers in 13 of Europe's most popular cities, including Edinburgh (guided trips from €199, see www.wsaeurope.com for details). Check out Andy's tips, resources, and podcast at www.andysteves.com.

EDINBURGH

Day Trips from Edinburgh

Many companies run a variety of day trips to regional sights, as well as multiday and themed itineraries. (Several of the local guides listed earlier have cars, too.)

The most popular tour is the all-day **Highlands trip.** The standard Highlands tour gives those with limited time a chance to experience the wonders of Scotland's wild and legend-soaked Highlands in a single long day (about £50, roughly 8:00-20:00). Itineraries vary but you'll generally visit/pass through the Trossachs, Rannoch Moor, Glencoe, Fort William, Fort Augustus on Loch Ness (some tours offer an optional boat ride), and Pitlochry. To save time, look for a tour that gives you a short glimpse of Loch Ness rather than driving its entire length or doing a boat trip. (Once you've seen a little of it, you've seen it all.)

Larger outfits, typically using bigger buses, include **Timberbush Highland Tours** (tel. 0131/226-6066, www.timberbushtours.com), **Gray Line** (tel. 0131/555-5558, www.graylinescotland.com), **Highland Experience** (tel. 0131/226-1414, www.highlandexperience.com), **Highland Explorer** (tel. 0131/558-3738, www.highlandexplorertours.com), and **Scotline** (tel. 0131/557-0162, www.scotlinetours.co.uk). Other companies pride themselves on keeping group sizes small, with 16-seat minibuses; these include **Rabbie's** (tel. 0131/212-5005, www.rabbies.com) and **Heart of Scotland Tours: The Wee Red Bus** (10 percent Rick Steves discount on full-price day tours—mention when booking, does not apply to overnight tours or senior/student rates, occasionally canceled off-season if too few sign up—leave a contact number, tel. 0131/228-2888, www.heartofscotlandtours.co.uk, run by Nick Roche).

For young backpackers, **Haggis Adventures** runs day tours plus overnight trips of up to 10 days (tel. 0131/557-9393, www.haggisadventures.com).

At **Discreet Scotland,** Matthew Wight and his partners specialize in tours of greater Edinburgh and Scotland in spacious SUVs—good for families (£360/2 people, 8 hours, mobile 0798-941-6990, www.discreetscotland.com).

Walks in Edinburgh

I've outlined two walks in Edinburgh: along the Royal Mile, and through the New Town. Many of the sights we'll pass on these walks are described in more detail later, under "Sights in Edinburgh."

THE ROYAL MILE

The Royal Mile is one of Europe's most interesting historic walks—it's worth ▲▲▲. The following self-guided stroll is also available as a 🎧 downloadable Rick Steves audio tour; see page 10.

Overview

Start at Edinburgh Castle at the top and amble down to the Palace of Holyroodhouse. Along the way, the street changes names—Castlehill, Lawnmarket, High Street, and Canongate—but it's a straight, downhill shot totaling just over one mile. And nearly every step is packed with shops, cafés, and lanes leading to tiny squares.

The city of Edinburgh was born on the easily defended rock at the top, where the castle stands today. Celtic tribes (and maybe the Romans) once occupied this site. As the town grew, it spilled downhill along the sloping ridge that became the Royal Mile. Because this strip of land is so narrow, there was no place to build but up. So in medieval times, it was densely packed with multistory "tenements"—large edifices under one roof that housed a number of tenants.

As you walk, you'll be tracing the growth of the city—its birth atop Castle Hill, its Old Town heyday in the 1600s, its expansion in the 1700s into the Georgian New Town (leaving the old quarter an overcrowded, disease-ridden Victorian slum), and on to the 21st century at the modern Scottish parliament building (2004).

In parts, the Royal Mile feels like one long Scottish shopping mall, selling all manner of kitschy souvenirs (known locally as "tartan tat"), shortbread, and whisky. But the streets are also packed with history, and if you push past the postcard racks into one of the many side alleys, you can still find a few surviving rough edges of the old city. Despite the drizzle, be sure to look up—spires, carvings, and towering Gothic "skyscrapers" give this city its unique urban identity.

This walk covers the Royal Mile's landmarks, but skips the many museums and indoor attractions along the way. These and other sights are described in walking order under "Sights in Edinburgh" on page 53. You can stay focused on the walk (which takes about 1.5 hours, without entering sights), then return later to visit the various indoor attractions; or review the sight descriptions beforehand and pop into those that interest you as you pass them.

• *We'll start at the Castle Esplanade, the big parking lot at the entrance to...*

❶ Edinburgh Castle

Edinburgh was born on the bluff—a big rock—where the castle now stands. Since before recorded history, people have lived on this strategic, easily defended perch.

The **castle** is an imposing symbol of Scottish independence. Flanking the entryway are statues of the fierce warriors who battled English invaders, William Wallace (on the right) and Robert the Bruce (left). Between them is the Scottish motto, *Nemo me impune lacessit*—roughly, "No one messes with me and gets away with it." (For a self-guided tour of Edinburgh Castle, see page 54.)

The esplanade—built as a military parade ground (1816)—is now the site of the annual Military Tattoo. This spectacular massing of regimental bands fills the square nightly for most of August. Fans watch from temporary bleacher seats to see kilt-wearing bagpipers marching against the spectacular backdrop of the castle. TV crews broadcast the spectacle to all corners of the globe.

When the bleachers aren't up, there are fine views in both directions from the esplanade. Facing north, you'll see the body of water called the Firth of Forth, and Fife beyond that. (The Firth of Forth is the estuary where the River Forth flows into the North Sea.) Still facing north, find the lacy spire of the Scott Monument and two Neoclassical buildings housing art galleries. Beyond them, the stately buildings of Edinburgh's New Town rise. (For a self-guided walk of the New Town, see page 46.) Panning to the right, find the Nelson Monument and some faux Greek ruins atop Calton Hill (see page 93).

The city's many bluffs, crags, and ridges were built up by volcanoes, then carved down by glaciers—a city formed in "fire and ice," as the locals say. So, during the Ice Age, as a river of glaciers swept in from the west (behind today's castle), it ran into the super-hard volcanic basalt of Castle Rock and flowed around it, cutting valleys on either side and leaving a tail that became the Royal Mile you're about to walk.

At the bottom of the esplanade, where the square hits the road, look left to find a plaque on the wall above the tiny **witches' well** (now a planter). This memorializes 300 women who were accused of witchcraft and burned here. Below was the Nor' Loch, the swampy lake where those accused of witchcraft (mostly women) were tested: Bound up, they were dropped into the lake. If they

The Kilt

The kilt, Scotland's national dress, is intimately tied to the country's history. The six-foot-by-nine-foot bolt of fabric

originated in the 1500s as a multipurpose robe, toga, tent, poncho, and ground cloth. A wearer would lay it on the ground to scrunch up pleats, then wrap it around the waist and belt it. Extra fabric was thrown over the shoulder or tucked into the belt, creating both a rakish sash and a rucksack-like pouch.

The kilt was standard Highlands dress and became a patriotic statement during conflicts with England. After the tragic-for-Scotland Battle of Culloden in 1746, the British government wanted to end the Scottish clan system. Wearing the kilt, speaking Gaelic, and playing the bagpipes were all outlawed.

In 1782, kilts were permitted again, but had taken on an unrefined connotation, so many Scots no longer wanted to wear one. This changed in 1822 when King George IV visited Edinburgh, wearing a kilt to send the message that he was king of Scotland. Scottish aristocrats were charmed by the king's pageantry, and the kilt was in vogue once more.

During the king's visit, Sir Walter Scott organized a Highland festival that also helped change the image of traditional Scottish culture, giving it a newfound respectability. A generation later, Queen Victoria raised the image of Scottish culture even higher. She loved Scotland and wallpapered her palace at Balmoral with tartan patterns.

The colors and patterns of the original kilts were determined by what dyes were available and who wove them. Because members of one clan tended to live in the same areas, they often wore similar patterns—but the colors were muted, and the patterns weren't necessarily designed to represent a single clan. The "clan tartans" you'll see in Scottish souvenir shops—with a specific, brightly colored design for each family—started as a scam by fabric salesmen in Victorian times. Since then, tartanry has been embraced as if it were historic. (By the way, Scots use these key terms differently than Americans do: "Tartan" is the pattern itself, while "plaid" is the piece of cloth worn over the shoulder with a kilt.)

As Highlanders moved to cities and took jobs in factories, the smaller kilt, or philibeg, replaced the traditional kilt, which could become dangerously snagged by modern machinery. Half the weight of old-style kilts, the practical philibeg is more like a wraparound skirt.

Other kilt-related gear includes the sporran, the leather pouch worn around the waist, and the *sgian dubh* ("black knife"), the short blade worn in the top of the sock. If you're in the market for a kilt, see page 100.

EDINBURGH

sank and drowned, they were innocent. If they floated, they were guilty, and were burned here in front of the castle, providing the city folk a nice afternoon out. The plaque shows two witches: one good and one bad. Tickle the serpent's snout to sympathize with the witches. (I just made that up.)

• *Start walking down the Royal Mile. The first block is a street called...*

❷ Castlehill

You're immediately in the tourist hubbub. The big tank-like building on your left was the Old Town's **reservoir.** You'll see the wellheads it served all along this walk. While it once held 1.5 million gallons of water, today it's filled with the touristy Tartan Weaving Mill and Exhibition. While it's interesting to see the mill at work, you'll have to twist your way down through several floors of tartanry and Chinese-produced Scottish kitsch to reach it at the bottom level.

The black-and-white tower ahead on the

Royal Mile Walk

To Leith
DUGALD STEWART MONUMENT
NATIONAL MONUMENT
NELSON MONUMENT
WATERLOO PLACE
REGENT ROAD
MARTYRS' MONUMENT
Old Calton Cemetery
ST. ANDREW'S HOUSE
CALTON ROAD
CALTON RD.
PALACE OF HOLYROOD-HOUSE
ABBEYHILL CRES.
WALK ENDS
GATE
WHITE HORSE CLOSE
CANONGATE CHURCH
PEOPLE'S STORY MUSEUM
NEW ST.
(ROYAL MILE)
SCOTTISH PARLIAMENT
QUEEN'S GALLERY (WC, CAFE & TICKETS TO HOLYROOD-HOUSE)
EAST MARKET ST.
JEFFREY ST.
CANONGATE
ROBERT FERGUSSON MON.
MUSEUM OF EDINBURGH
JOHN KNOX HOUSE
CADENHEAD'S WHISKY SHOP
DYNAMIC EARTH
STREET
WORLD'S END
ST. JOHN ST.
BAKEHOUSE CL.
HOLYROOD ROAD
To Arthur's Seat & Trail to Top of Salisbury Crags
MUSEUM OF CHILDHOOD
GULLAN'S CLOSE
BIKE RENTAL
BLACKFRIARS ST.
ST. MARY'S ST.
CANONGATE
N
200 Meters
200 Yards
COWGATE
NIDDRY ST.
14, 30 & 33
SOUTH BRIDGE
INFIRMARY ST.
ROXBURGH ST.
S. COLLEGE ST.
To Dalkeith Road

EDINBURGH

❶ Edinburgh Castle
❷ Castlehill
❸ Lawnmarket
❹ Bank/High Streets Intersection
❺ St. Giles' Cathedral
❻ More of High Street
❼ John Knox House
❽ The World's End
❾ Canongate
❿ Scottish Parliament Building
⓫ Palace of Holyroodhouse

left has entertained visitors since the 1850s with its **camera obscura,** a darkened room where a mirror and a series of lenses capture live images of the city surroundings outside. (Giggle at the funny mirrors as you walk fatly by.) Across the street, filling the old Castlehill Primary School, is a gimmicky-if-intoxicating whisky-sampling exhibit called the **Scotch Whisky Experience** (a.k.a. "Malt Disney"). Both of these are described later, under "Sights in Edinburgh."

• *Just ahead, in front of the church with the tall, lacy spire, is the old market square known as...*

❸ Lawnmarket

During the Royal Mile's heyday, in the 1600s, this intersection was bigger and served as a market for fabric (especially "lawn," a linen-like cloth). The market would fill this space with hustle, bustle, and lots of commerce. The round white hump in the middle of the roundabout is all that remains of the official weighing beam called the Butter Tron—where all goods sold were weighed for honesty and tax purposes.

Towering above Lawnmarket, with the tallest spire in the

EDINBURGH

city, is the former **Tolbooth Church.** This impressive Neo-Gothic structure (1844) is now home to the Hub, Edinburgh's festival-ticket and information center. The world-famous Edinburgh Festival fills the month of August with cultural action. The various festivals feature classical music, traditional and fringe theater (especially comedy), art, books, and more. Drop inside the building to get festival info (see also page 95). This is a handy stop for its WC, café, and free Wi-Fi.

In the 1600s, this—along with the next stretch, called High Street—was the city's main street. At that time, Edinburgh was bursting with breweries, printing presses, and banks. Tens of thousands of citizens were squeezed into the narrow confines of the Old Town. Here on this ridge, they built **tenements** (multiple-unit residences) similar to the more recent ones you see today. These tenements, rising 10 stories and more, were some of the tallest domestic buildings in Europe. The living arrangements shocked class-conscious English visitors to Edinburgh because the tenements were occupied by rich and poor alike—usually the poor in the cellars and attics, and the rich in the middle floors.

• *Continue a half-block down the Mile.*

Gladstone's Land (at #477b, on the left), a surviving original tenement, was acquired by a wealthy merchant in 1617. Stand in front of the building and look up at this centuries-old skyscraper. This design was standard for its time: a shop or shops on the ground floor, with columns and an arcade, and residences on the floors above. Because window glass was expensive, the lower halves of window openings were made of cheaper wood, which swung out like shutters for ventilation—and were convenient for tossing out garbage. (Gladstone's Land can be seen by tour only and is closed Nov-March—consider dropping in and booking ahead for a spot. For details, see listing on page

64.) Out front, you may also see trainers with live birds of prey. While this is mostly just a fun way to show off for tourists (and raise donations for the Just Falconry center), docents explain the connection: The building's owner was named Thomas Gledstanes—and *gled* is the Scots word for "hawk."

Branching off the spine of the

Royal Mile are a number of narrow alleyways that go by various local names. A "wynd" (rhymes with "kind") is a narrow, winding lane. A "pend" is an arched gateway. "Gate" is from an Old Norse word for street. And a "close" is a tiny alley between two buildings (originally with a door that "closed" at night). A "close" usually leads to a "court," or courtyard.

To explore one of these alleyways, head into **Lady Stair's Close** (on the left, 10 steps downhill from Gladstone's Land). This alley pops out in a small courtyard, where you'll find the **Writers' Museum** (described on page 64). It's well worth a visit for fans of Scotland's holy trinity of writers (Robert Burns, Sir Walter Scott, and Robert Louis Stevenson), but it's also a free glimpse of what a typical home might have looked like in the 1600s. Burns actually lived for a while in this neighborhood, in 1786, when he first arrived in Edinburgh.

Opposite Gladstone's Land (at #322), another close leads to **Riddle's Court.** Wander through here and imagine Edinburgh in the 17th and 18th centuries, when tourists came here to marvel at its skyscrapers. Some 40,000 people were jammed into the few blocks between here and the World's End pub (which we'll reach soon). Visualize the labyrinthine maze of the old city, with people scurrying through these back alleyways, buying and selling, and popping into taverns.

No city in Europe was as densely populated—or perhaps as filthy. Without modern hygiene, it was a living hell of smoke, stench, and noise, with the constant threat of fire, collapse, and disease. The dirt streets were soiled with sewage from bedpans emptied out windows. By the 1700s, the Old Town was rife with poverty and cholera outbreaks. The smoky home fires rising from tenements and the infamous smell (or "reek" in Scottish) that wafted across the city gave it a nickname that sticks today. "Auld Reekie."

• *Return to the Royal Mile and continue down it a few steps to take in some sights at the...*

❹ Bank/High Streets Intersection

A number of sights cluster here, where Lawnmarket changes its name to High Street and intersects with Bank Street and George IV Bridge.

Begin with **Deacon Brodie's Tavern.** Read the "Doctor Jekyll and Mr. Hyde" story of this pub's

EDINBURGH

notorious namesake on the wall facing Bank Street. Then, to see his spooky split personality, check out both sides of the hanging signpost. Brodie—a pillar of the community by day but a burglar by night—epitomizes the divided personality of 1700s Edinburgh. It was a rich, productive city—home to great philosophers and scientists, who actively contributed to the Enlightenment. Meanwhile, the Old Town was riddled with crime and squalor. The city was scandalized when a respected surgeon—driven by a passion for medical research and needing corpses—was accused of colluding with two lowlifes, named Burke and Hare, to acquire freshly murdered corpses for dissection. (In the next century, in the late 1800s, novelist Robert Louis Stevenson would capture the dichotomy of Edinburgh's rich-poor society in his *Strange Case of Dr. Jekyll and Mr. Hyde*.)

In the late 1700s, Edinburgh's upper class moved out of the Old Town into a planned community called the New Town (a quarter-mile north of here). Eventually, most tenements were torn down and replaced with newer **Victorian buildings.** You'll see some at this intersection.

Look left down Bank Street to the green-domed **Bank of Scotland.** This was the headquarters of the bank, which had practiced modern capitalist financing since 1695. The building now houses the Museum on the Mound, a free exhibit on banking history (see page 65), and is also the Scottish headquarters for Lloyds Banking Group—which swallowed up the Bank of Scotland after the financial crisis of 2008.

If you detour left down Bank Street toward the bank, you'll find the recommended **Whiski Rooms Shop.** If you head in the opposite direction, down George IV Bridge, you'll reach the excellent **National Museum of Scotland,** the famous Greyfriars Bobby statue, restaurant-lined Forrest Road, and photogenic Victoria Street, which leads to the pub-lined Grassmarket square (all described later in this chapter).

Otherwise, continue along the Royal Mile. As you walk, be careful crossing the streets along the Mile. Edinburgh drivers—especially cabbies—have a reputation for being impatient with jaywalking tourists. Notice and heed the pedestrian crossing signals, which don't always turn at the same time as the car signals.

Across the street from Deacon Brodie's Tavern is a seated green statue of hometown boy **David Hume** (1711-1776)—one of the most influential thinkers not only of Scotland, but in all of Western philosophy. The atheistic Hume was one of the towering figures of the Scottish Enlightenment of the mid-1700s. Thinkers and scientists were using the experimental method to challenge and investigate everything, including religion. Hume questioned cause and effect in thought puzzles such as this: We can see that when one billiard ball strikes another, the second one moves, but how do we know the collision "caused" the movement? Notice his shiny toe: People on their way to trial (in the high court just behind the statue) or students on their way to exams (in the nearby university) rub it for good luck.

Follow David Hume's gaze to the opposite corner, where a **brass H** in the pavement marks the site of the last public execution in Edinburgh in 1864. Deacon Brodie himself would have been hung about here (in 1788, on a gallows whose design he had helped to improve—smart guy).

• *From the brass H, continue down the Royal Mile, pausing just before the church square at a stone wellhead with the pyramid cap.*

All along the Royal Mile, **wellheads** like this (from 1835) provided townsfolk with water in the days before buildings had plumbing. This neighborhood well was served by the reservoir up at the castle. Imagine long lines of people in need of water standing here, gossiping and sharing the news. Eventually buildings were retrofitted with water pipes—the ones you see running along building exteriors.

• *Ahead of you (past the Victorian statue of some duke), embedded in the pavement near the street, is a big heart.*

The **Heart of Midlothian** marks the spot of the city's 15th-century municipal building and jail. In times past, in a nearby open space, criminals were hanged, traitors were decapitated, and witches were burned. Citizens hated the rough justice doled out here. Locals still spit on the heart in the pavement. Go ahead...do as the locals do—land one right in the heart of the heart. By the way, Edinburgh has two soccer teams—Heart of Midlothian (known as "Hearts") and Hibernian ("Hibs"). If you're a Hibs fan, spit again.

• *Make your way to the entrance of the church.*

❺ St. Giles' Cathedral

This is the flagship of the Church of Scotland (Scotland's largest denomination)—called the "Mother Church of Presbyterianism." The interior serves as a kind of Scottish Westminster Abbey, filled with monuments, statues, plaques, and stained-glass windows dedicated to great Scots and moments in history.

A church has stood on this spot since 854, though this structure is an architectural hodgepodge, dating mostly from the 15th through 19th century. In the 16th century, St. Giles' was a kind of national stage on which the drama of the Reformation was played out. The reformer John Knox (1514-1572) was the preacher here. His fiery sermons helped turn once-Catholic Edinburgh into a bastion of Protestantism. During the Scottish Reformation, St. Giles' was transformed from a Catholic cathedral to a Presbyterian church. The spacious interior is well worth a visit, and described in my self-guided tour on page 65.

• *Facing the church entrance, curl around its right side, into a parking lot.*

Sights Around St. Giles'

The grand building across the parking lot from St. Giles' is the **Old Parliament House.** Since the 13th century, the king had ruled a rubber-stamp parliament of nobles and bishops. But the Protestant Reformation promoted democracy, and the parliament gained real power. From the early 1600s until 1707, this building evolved to become the seat of a true parliament of elected officials. That came to an end in 1707, when Scotland signed an Act of Union, joining what's known today as the United Kingdom and giving up their right to self-rule. (More on that later in the walk.) If you're curious to peek inside, head through the door at #11 (free, described on page 69).

The great reformer **John Knox** is buried—with appropriate austerity—under parking lot spot #23. The statue among the cars shows King Charles II riding to a toga party back in 1685.

• *Continue on through the parking lot, around the back end of the church.*

Every Scottish burgh (town licensed by the king to trade) had three standard features: a "tolbooth" (basically a Town Hall, with a courthouse, meeting room, and jail); a "tron" (official weighing scale); and a "mercat" (or market) cross. The **mercat cross** standing just behind St. Giles' Cathedral has a slender column decorated with a unicorn holding a flag with the cross of St. Andrew. Royal proclamations have been read at this mercat cross since the 14th century. In 1952, a town crier heralded the news that Britain had a new queen—three days after the actual event (traditionally the time it took for a horse to speed here from London). Today, Mercat Cross is the meeting point for many of Edinburgh's walking tours—both historic and ghostly.

• *Circle around to the street side of the church.*

The statue to **Adam Smith** honors the Edinburgh author of the pioneering *Wealth of Nations* (1776), in which he laid out the economics of free-market capitalism. Smith theorized that an "invisible hand" wisely guides the unregulated free market. Stand in front of Smith and imagine the intellectual energy of Edinburgh in the mid-1700s, when it was Europe's most enlightened city. Adam Smith was right in the center of it. He and David Hume were good friends. James Boswell, the famed biographer of Samuel Johnson, took classes from Smith. James Watt, inventor of the steam engine, was another proud Scotsman of the age. With great intellectuals like these, Edinburgh helped create the modern world. The poet Robert Burns, geologist James Hutton (who's considered the father of modern geology), and the publishers of the first *Encyclopedia Britannica* all lived in Edinburgh. Steeped in the inquisitive mindset of the Enlightenment, they applied cool rationality and a secular approach to their respective fields.

• *Head on down the Royal Mile.*

❻ More of High Street

A few steps downhill, at #188 (on the right), is the **Police Information Center.** This place provides a pleasant police presence (say that three times) and a little local law-and-order history to boot. Ask the officer on duty about the impact of modern technology and budget austerity on police work today. Seriously—drop in and discuss whatever law-and-order issue piques your curiosity.

Continuing down this stretch of the Royal Mile, which is traffic-free most of the day (notice the bollards that raise and lower for permitted traffic), you'll see the Fringe Festival office (at #180), street musicians, and another wellhead (with horse "sippies," dating from 1675).

Notice those **three red boxes.** In the 20th century, people used these to make telephone calls to each other. (Imagine that!) These cast-iron booths are produced for all of Britain here in Scotland. As phone booths are decommissioned, some are finding new use as tiny shops, ATMs, and even showing up in residential neighborhoods as nostalgic garden decorations.

At the next intersection, on the left, is **Cockburn Street** (pronounced "COE-burn"). This was cut through High Street's dense wall of medieval skyscrapers in the 1860s to give easy access to the Georgian New Town and the train station. Notice how the sliced buildings were thoughtfully capped with facades that fit the aesthetic look of the Royal Mile. In the Middle Ages, only tiny lanes (like Fleshmarket Close just uphill from Cockburn Street) interrupted the long line of Royal Mile buildings. These days, Cockburn Street has a reputation for its eclectic independent shops and string of trendy bars and eateries.

• *When you reach the* **Tron Church** *(17th century, currently housing shops), you're at the intersection of* **North and South Bridge** *streets. These major streets lead left to Waverley Station and right to the Dalkeith Road B&Bs. Several handy bus lines run along here.*

This is the halfway point of this walk. Stand on the corner diagonally across from the church. Look up to the top of the Royal Mile at the Hub and its 240-foot spire. Notwithstanding its turret and 16th-century charm, the **Radisson Blu Hotel** just across the street is entirely new construction (1990), built to fit in. The city is protecting its historic look. The **Inn on the Mile** next door was once a fancy bank with a lavish interior. As modern banks are moving away from city centers, sumptuous buildings like these are being converted into ornate pubs and restaurants.

In the next block downhill are three **characteristic pubs,** side by side, that offer free traditional Scottish and folk music in the evenings. Notice the chimneys. Tenement buildings shared stairways and entries, but held individual apartments, each with its own chimney. Take a look back at the spire of St. Giles' Cathedral—inspired by the Scottish crown and the thistle, Scotland's national flower.

• *Go down High Street another block, passing near the* **Museum of Childhood** *(on the right, at #42, and worth a stop; see page 70) and a fragrant* **fudge shop** *a few doors down, where you can sample various flavors (tempting you to buy a slab).*

Directly across the street, just below another wellhead, is the...

❼ John Knox House

Remember that Knox was a towering figure in Edinburgh's history, converting Scotland to a Calvinist style of Protestantism. His religious bent was "Presbyterianism," in which parishes are governed by elected officials rather than appointed bishops. This more democratic brand of Christianity also spurred Scotland toward political democracy. If you're interested in Knox or the Reformation, this sight is worth a visit (see page 70). Full disclosure: It's not certain that Knox ever actually lived here. Attached to the Knox House is the Scottish Storytelling Centre, where locals with the gift of gab perform regularly; check the posted schedule.

• *A few steps farther down High Street, at the intersection with St. Mary's and Jeffrey streets, you'll reach...*

❽ The World's End

For centuries, a wall stood here, marking the end of the burgh of

Edinburgh. For residents within the protective walls of the city, this must have felt like the "world's end," indeed. The area beyond was called Canongate, a monastic community associated with Holyrood Abbey. At the intersection, find the brass bricks in the street that trace the gate (demolished in 1764). Look to the right down St. Mary's Street about 200 yards to see a surviving bit of that old wall, known as the **Flodden Wall.** In the 1513 Battle of Flodden, the Scottish king James IV made the disastrous decision to invade northern England. James and 10,000 of his Scotsmen were killed. Fearing a brutal English counterattack, Edinburgh scrambled to reinforce its broken-down city wall. To the left, down Jeffrey Street, you'll see Scotland's top tattoo parlor, and a supplier for a different kind of tattoo (the Scottish Regimental Store).

• *Continue down the Royal Mile—leaving old Edinburgh—as High Street changes names to...*

❾ Canongate

About 10 steps down Canongate, look left down Cranston Street (past the train tracks) to a good view of the Calton Cemetery up on **Calton Hill.** The obelisk, called Martyrs' Monument, remembers a group of 18th-century patriots exiled by London to Australia for their reform politics. The round building to the left is the grave of philosopher David Hume. And the big, turreted building to the right was the jail master's house. Today, the main reason to go up Calton Hill is for the fine views (described on page 93).

The giant, blocky building that dominates the lower slope of the hill is **St. Andrew's House,** headquarters of the Scottish Government—including the office of the first minister of Scotland. According to locals, the building has also been an important base for MI6, Britain's version of the CIA. Wait a minute—isn't James Bond Scottish? Hmmm...

• *A couple hundred yards farther along the Royal Mile (on the right at #172) you reach **Cadenhead's,** a serious place to learn about and buy whisky (see page 97). About 30 yards farther along, you'll pass two worthwhile and free museums, the **People's Story Museum** (on the left, in the old tollhouse at #163) and the Museum of Edinburgh (on the right,* *at #142; for more on both, see page 71). But our next stop is the church just across from the **Museum of Edinburgh**.*

The 1688 **Canongate Kirk** (Church)—located not far from the royal residence of Holyroodhouse—is where Queen Elizabeth II and her family worship whenever they're in town. (So don't sit in the front pew, marked with her crown.) The gilded emblem at the top of the roof, high above the door, has the antlers of a stag from the royal estate of Balmoral (see page 345). The Queen's granddaughter married here in 2011.

The church is open only when volunteers have signed up to welcome visitors (and closed in winter). Chat them up and borrow the description of the place. Then step inside the lofty blue and red interior, renovated with royal money; the church is filled with light and the flags of various Scottish regiments. In the narthex, peruse the photos of royal family events here, and find the list of priests and ministers of this parish—it goes back to 1143 (with a clear break with the Reformation in 1561).

Outside, turn right as you leave the church and walk up into the graveyard. The large, gated grave (abutting the back of the People's Story Museum) is the affectionately tended tomb of **Adam Smith,** the father of capitalism. (Throw him a penny or two.)

Just outside the churchyard, the statue on the sidewalk is of the poet **Robert Fergusson.** One of the first to write verse in the Scots language, he so inspired Robert Burns that Burns paid for Fergusson's tombstone in the Canongate churchyard and composed his epitaph.

Now look across the street at the **gabled house** next to the Museum of Edinburgh. Scan the facade to see shells put there in the 17th century to defend against the evil power of witches yet to be drowned.

• *Walk about 300 yards farther along. In the distance you can see the Palace of Holyroodhouse (the end of this walk) and soon, on the right, you'll come to the modern Scottish parliament building.*

Just opposite the parliament building is **White Horse Close** (on the left, in the white arcade). Step into this 17th-century courtyard. It was from here that the Edinburgh stagecoach left for London. Eight days later, the horse-drawn carriage would pull into its destination: Scotland Yard. Note that bus #35 leaves in two directions from here—downhill for the Royal Yacht *Britannia*, and uphill along the Royal Mile (as far as South Bridge) and on to the National Museum of Scotland.

• *Now walk up around the corner to the flagpoles (flying the flags of Europe, Britain, and Scotland) in front of the...*

⑩ Scottish Parliament Building

Finally, after centuries of history, we reach the 21st century. And finally, after three centuries of London rule, Scotland has a parliament building...in Scotland.

When Scotland united with England in 1707, its parliament was dissolved. But in 1999, the Scottish parliament was reestablished, and in 2004, it moved into this striking new home. Notice how the eco-friendly building, by the Catalan architect Enric Miralles, mixes wild angles, lots of light, bold windows, oak, and native stone into a startling complex. (People from Catalunya—another would-be breakaway nation—have an affinity for Scotland.) From the front of the parliament building, look in the distance at the rocky Salisbury Crags, with people hiking the traverse up to the dramatic next summit called Arthur's Seat. Now look at the building in relation to the craggy cliffs. The architect envisioned the building as if it were rising right from the base of Arthur's Seat, almost bursting from the rock.

Since it celebrates Scottish democracy, the architecture is not a statement of authority. There are no statues of old heroes. There's not even a grand entry. You feel like you're entering an office park. Given its neighborhood, the media often calls the Scottish Parliament "Holyrood" for short (similar to calling the US Congress "Capitol Hill"). For details on touring the building and seeing parliament in action, see page 72.

• *Across the street is the* **Queen's Gallery,** *where she shares part of her amazing personal art collection in excellent revolving exhibits (see page 74). Finally, walk to the end of the road (Abbey Strand), and step up to the impressive wrought-iron gate of the Queen's palace. Look up at the stag with its holy cross, or "holy rood," on its forehead, and peer into the palace grounds. (The ticket office and palace entryway, a fine café, and a handy WC are just through the arch on the right.)*

⑪ Palace of Holyroodhouse

Since the 16th century, this palace has marked the end of the Royal Mile. An abbey—part of a 12th-century Augustinian monastery—originally stood in its place. While most of that old building is

EDINBURGH

gone, you can see the surviving nave behind the palace on the left. According to one legend, it was named "holy rood" for a piece of the cross, brought here as a relic by Queen (and later Saint) Margaret. (Another version of the story is that King David I, Margaret's son, saw the image of a cross upon a stag's head while hunting here and took it as a sign that he should build an abbey on the site.) Because Scotland's royalty preferred living at Holyroodhouse to the blustery castle on the rock, the palace grew over time. If the Queen's not visiting, the palace welcomes visitors (see page 73 for details).

• *Your walk—from the castle to the palace, with so much Scottish history packed in between—is complete. And, if your appetite is whetted for more, don't worry; you've just scratched the surface. Enjoy the rest of Edinburgh.*

BONNIE WEE NEW TOWN WALK

Many visitors, mesmerized by the Royal Mile, never venture to the New Town. And that's a shame. With some of the city's finest Georgian architecture (from its 18th-century boom period), the New Town has a completely different character than the Old Town. This self-guided walk—worth ▲▲—gives you a quick orientation in about one hour.

• *Begin on Waverley Bridge, spanning the gully between the Old and New towns; to get there from the Royal Mile, just head down the curved Cockburn Street near the Tron Church (or cut down any of the "close" lanes opposite St. Giles' Cathedral). Stand on the bridge overlooking the train tracks, facing the castle.*

View from Waverley Bridge: From this vantage point, you can enjoy fine views of medieval Edinburgh, with its 10-story-plus "skyscrapers." It's easy to imagine how miserably crowded this area was, prompting the expansion of the city during the Georgian period. Pick out landmarks along the Royal Mile, most notably the open-work steeple of St. Giles'.

A big lake called the **Nor' Loch** once was to the north (nor') of the Old Town; now it's a valley between Edinburgh's two towns. The lake was drained around 1800 as part of the expansion. Before that, the lake was the town's water reservoir...and its sewer. Much has been written about the town's infamous stink (a.k.a. the "flowers of Edinburgh"). The town's nickname, "Auld Reekie," referred to both the smoke of its industry and the stench of its squalor.

The long-gone loch was also a handy place for drowning witches. With their thumbs tied to their ankles, they'd be lashed to dunking stools. Those who survived the ordeal were considered "aided by the devil" and burned as witches. If they died, they were innocent and given a good Christian burial. Edinburgh was Europe's witch-burning mecca—any perceived "sign," including a small birthmark, could condemn you. Scotland burned more witches per capita than any other country—17,000 souls between 1479 and 1722.

EDINBURGH

Visually trace the train tracks as they disappear into a tunnel below the **Scottish National Gallery** (with lesser-known paintings by great European art-ists; you can visit it during this walk—see page 79). The two fine Neoclassical buildings of the National Gallery date from the 1840s and sit upon a mound that's called, well, **The Mound.** When the New Town was built, tons of rubble from the excavations were piled here

(1781-1830), forming a dirt bridge that connected the new development with the Old Town to allay merchant concerns about being cut off from the future heart of the city.

Turning 180 degrees (and facing the ramps down into the train station), notice the huge, turreted building with the clock tower. **The Balmoral** was one of the city's two grand hotels during its glory days (its opposite bookend, the **Waldorf Astoria Edinburgh**, sits at the far end of the former lakebed—near the end of this walk). Aristocrats arriving by train could use a hidden entrance to go from the platform directly up to their plush digs. (Today The Balmoral is known mostly as the place where J. K. Rowling completed the final Harry Potter book.)

• *Now walk across the bridge toward the New Town. Before the corner, enter the gated gardens on the left, and head toward the big, pointy monument. You're at the edge of...*

❶ **Princes Street Gardens:** This grassy park, filling the former lakebed, offers a wonderful escape from the bustle of the city. Once the private domain of the wealthy, it was opened to the public around 1870—not as a democratic gesture, but in hopes of increas-

Bonnie Wee New Town Walk

200 Meters
200 Yards

① Princes Street Gardens
② Scott Monument
③ Jenners Department Store
④ St. Andrew Square
⑤ George Street
⑥ St. Andrew's & St. George's Church
⑦ The Dome Restaurant
⑧ King George IV Statue
⑨ Thistle Street
⑩ William Pitt Statue
⑪ Rose Street
⑫ Charlotte Square
⑬ Georgian House

ing sales at the Princes Street department stores. Join the office workers for a picnic lunch break.

• *Take a seat on the bench indicated by the Livingstone (Dr. Livingstone, I presume?) statue. (The Victorian explorer is well equipped with a guidebook, but is hardly packing light—his lion skin doesn't even fit in his rucksack carry-on.)*

Look up at the towering...

❷ **Scott Monument:** Built in the early 1840s, this elaborate Neo-Gothic monument honors the great author Sir Walter Scott, one of Edinburgh's many illustrious sons. When Scott died in 1832, it was said that "Scotland never owed so much to one man." Scott almost singlehandedly created the Scotland we know. Just as the country was in danger of being assimilated into England, Scott celebrated traditional songs, legends, myths, architecture, and kilts, thereby reviving the Highland culture and cementing a national identity. And, as the father of the Romantic historical novel, he contributed to Western literature in general. The 200-foot monument shelters a marble statue of Scott and his favorite pet, Maida, a deerhound who was one of 30 canines this dog lover owned during his lifetime. They're sur-

EDINBURGH

rounded by busts of 16 great Scottish poets and 64 characters from his books. Climbing the tight, stony spiral staircase of 287 steps earns you a peek at a tiny museum midway, a fine city view at the top, and intimate encounters going up and down (£5, daily 10:00-19:00, Oct-March until 16:00, tel. 0131/529-4068). For more on Scott, see page 69.

• *Exit the gate near Livingstone and head across busy Princes Street to the venerable...*

❸ **Jenners Department Store:** As you wait for the light to change (and wait...and wait...), notice how statues of women support the building—just as real women support the business. The arrival of new fashions here was such a big deal in the old days that they'd announce it by flying flags on the Nelson Monument atop Calton Hill.

Step inside and head up-stairs into the grand, skylit

atrium. The central space—filled with a towering tree at Christmas—is classic Industrial Age architecture. The Queen's coat of arms high on the wall indicates she shops here.

• *From the atrium, turn right and exit onto South St. David Street. Turn left and follow this street uphill one block up to...*

❹ **St. Andrew Square:** This green space is dedicated to the patron saint of Scotland. In the early 19th century, there were no shops around here—just fine residences; this was a private garden for the fancy people living here. Now open to the public, the square is a popular lunch hangout for workers. The Melville Monument honors a powermonger member of parliament who, for four decades (around 1800), was nicknamed the "uncrowned king of Scotland."

One block up from the top of the park is the excellent **Scottish National Portrait Gallery,** which introduces you to all of the biggest names in Scottish history (described later, under "Sights in Edinburgh").

• *Follow the Melville Monument's gaze straight ahead out of the park. Cross the street and stand at the top of...*

❺ **George Street:** This is the main drag of Edinburgh's grid-planned New Town. Laid out in 1776, when King George III was busy putting down a revolution in a troublesome overseas colony, the New Town was a model of urban planning in its day. The architectural style is "Georgian"—British for "Neoclassical." And the street plan came with an unambiguous message: to celebrate the union of Scotland with England into the United Kingdom. (This was particularly important, since Scotland was just two decades removed from the failed Jacobite uprising of Bonnie Prince Charlie.)

St. Andrew Square (patron saint of Scotland) and Charlotte Square (George III's queen) bookend the New Town, with its three main streets named for the royal family of the time (George, Queen, and Princes). Thistle and Rose streets—which we'll see near the end of this walk—are named for the national flowers of Scotland and England.

The plan for the New Town was the masterstroke of the 23-year-old urban designer James Craig. George Street—20 feet wider than the others (so a four-horse carriage could make a U-turn)—was the main drag. Running down the high spine of the area, it afforded grand, unobstructed views (thanks to the parks on either side) of the River Forth in one direction and the Old Town in the other. As you stroll down the street, you'll notice that Craig's grid is a series of axes designed to connect monuments new and old; later architects made certain to continue this harmony. For example, notice that the Scott Monument lines up perfectly with this first intersection.

• *Halfway down the first block of George Street, on the right, is...*

❻ **St. Andrew's and St. George's Church:** Designed as part of the New Town plan in the 1780s, the church is a product of the Scottish Enlightenment. It has an elliptical plan (the first in Britain) so that all can focus on the pulpit. If it's open, step inside. A fine leaflet tells the story of the church, and a handy cafeteria downstairs serves cheap and cheery lunches.

Directly across the street from the church is another temple, this one devoted to money. This former bank building (now housing the recommended restaurant ❼ **The Dome**) has a pediment filled with figures demonstrating various ways to make money, which they do with all the nobility of classical gods. Consider scurrying across the street and ducking inside to view the stunning domed atrium.

Continue down George Street to the intersection with a ❽ statue commemorating the visit by **King George IV.** Notice the particularly fine axis formed by this cross-street: The National Gallery lines up perfectly with the Royal Mile's skyscrapers and the former Tolbooth Church, creating a Gotham City collage.

• *By now you've gotten your New Town bearings. Feel free to stop this walk here: If you were to turn left and head down Hanover Street, in a block you'd run into the Scottish National Gallery; the street behind it curves back up to the Royal Mile.*

But to see more of the New Town—including the Georgian House, offering an insightful look inside one of these fine 18th-century homes—stick with me for a few more long blocks, zigzagging through side streets to see the various personalities that inhabit this rigid grid.

Turn right on Hanover Street; after just one (short) block, cross over and go down...

❾ **Thistle Street:** Of the many streets in the New Town, this has perhaps the most vivid Scottish character. And that's fitting, as it's named after Scotland's national flower. At the beginning and end of the street, also notice that Craig's street plan included tranquil cul-de-sacs within the larger blocks. Thistle Street seems sleepy, but holds characteristic boutiques and good restaurants (see "Eating in Edinburgh," later). Halfway down the street on the left, Howie Nicholsby's shop, 21st Century Kilt, updates traditional Scottish menswear.

You'll pop out at Frederick Street. Turning left, you'll see a ❿ statue of **William Pitt,** prime minister under King George III. (Pitt's father gave his name to the American city of Pittsburgh— which Scots pronounce as "Pitts-burrah"...I assume.)

• *For an interesting contrast, we'll continue down another side street.*

Pass the statue of Pitt (heading toward Edinburgh Castle), and turn right onto...

❶ Rose Street: As a rose is to a thistle, and as England is to Scotland, so is brash, boisterous Rose Street to sedate, thoughtful

Thistle Street. This stretch of Rose Street feels more commercialized, jammed with chain stores; the second block is packed with pubs and restaurants. As you walk, keep an eye out for the cobbled Tudor rose embedded in the brick sidewalk. When you cross the aptly named Castle Street, linger over the grand views to Edinburgh Castle.

It's almost as if they planned it this way...just for the views.

• *Popping out at the far end of Rose Street, across the street and to your right is...*

❷ Charlotte Square: The building of the New Town started cheap with St. Andrew Square, but finished well with this stately

space. In 1791, the Edinburgh town council asked the prestigious Scottish architect Robert Adam to pump up the design for Charlotte Square. The council hoped that Adam's plan would answer criticism that the New Town buildings lacked innovation or ambition—and they got what they wanted. Adam's design, which raised the standard of New Town architecture to "international class," created Edinburgh's finest Georgian square.

• *Along the right side of Charlotte Square, at #7 (just left of the pointy pediment), you can visit the* **❸** *Georgian House, which gives you a great peek behind all of these harmonious Neoclassical facades (see page 87).*

When you're done touring the house, you can head back through the New Town grid, perhaps taking some different streets than the way you came. Or, for a restful return to our starting point, consider this...

Return Through Princes Street Gardens: From Charlotte Square, drop down to busy Princes Street (noticing the red building to the right—the grand Waldorf Astoria Hotel and twin sister of The Balmoral at the start of our walk). But rather than walking along the busy bus-and-tram-lined shopping drag, head into **Princes Street Gardens** (cross Princes Street and enter the gate on the left). With the castle looming overhead, you'll pass a playground, a fanciful Victorian fountain, more monuments to great Scots, war memorials, and a bandstand (which hosts Scottish country dancing—see page 103—as well as occasional big-name acts). Finally you'll reach a staircase up to the Scottish National Gallery; notice the oldest **floral clock** in the world on your left as you climb up.

• *Our walk is over. From here, you can tour the gallery; head up Bank Street just behind it to reach the Royal Mile; hop on a bus along Princes Street to your next stop (or B&B); or continue through another stretch of the Princes Street Gardens to the Scott Monument and our starting point.*

Sights in Edinburgh

▲▲▲EDINBURGH CASTLE

The fortified birthplace of the city 1,300 years ago, this imposing symbol of Edinburgh sits proudly on a rock high above you. The home of Scotland's kings and queens for centuries, the castle has witnessed royal births, medieval pageantry, and bloody sieges. Today it's a complex of various buildings, the oldest dating from the 12th century, linked by cobbled roads that survive from its more recent use as a military garrison. The castle—with expansive views, plenty of history, and the stunning crown jewels of Scotland—is a fascinating and multifaceted sight that deserves several hours of your time.

Cost and Hours: £17, daily 9:30-18:00, Oct-March until 17:00, last entry one hour before closing, tel. 0131/225-9846, www.edinburghcastle.gov.uk.

Avoiding Lines: The castle is usually less crowded after 14:00 or so; if planning a morning visit, the earlier the better. To avoid ticket lines (worst in Aug), book online and print your ticket at home. You can also pick up your prebooked ticket at machines just inside the entrance or at the visitor information desk a few steps uphill on the right. You can also skip the ticket line with a Historic Scotland Explorer Pass (see page 443 for details).

Getting There: Simply walk up the Royal Mile (if arriving by bus from the B&B area south of the city, get off at South Bridge and huff up the Mile for about 15 minutes). Taxis get you closer, dropping you a block below the esplanade at the Hub/Tolbooth Church.

Tours: Thirty-minute introductory **guided tours** are free with admission (2-4/hour, depart from Argyle Battery, see clock for next departure; fewer off-season). The infor- mative **audioguide** provides four hours of descriptions, including the National War Museum Scotland (£3 if you purchase with your ticket; £3.50 if you rent it once inside, pick up inside Portcullis Gate).

Eating: You have two choices within the castle. The **$ Redcoat Café**—just past the Argyle Battery—is a big, bright, ef- ficient cafeteria with great views. The **$$ Tea Rooms** in Crown Square serves sit-down meals and afternoon tea. A whisky shop, with tastings, is just through Foog's Gate.

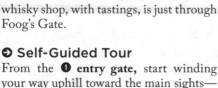

⊘ Self-Guided Tour

From the ❶ **entry gate,** start winding your way uphill toward the main sights— the crown jewels and the Royal Palace—located near the summit. Since the castle was protected on three sides by sheer cliffs, the main defense had to be here at the entrance. During the castle's heyday in the 1500s, a 100-foot tower loomed overhead, facing the city.

• *Passing through the portcullis gate, you reach the...*

❷ **Argyle (Six-Gun) Battery, with View:** These front-load- ing, cast-iron cannons are from the Napoleonic era (c. 1800), when the castle was still a force to be reck- oned with.

From here, look north across the valley to the grid of the New Town. The valley sits where the Nor' Loch once was; this lake was drained and filled in when the New Town was built in the late 1700s, its swamps replaced with gardens. Later the land provided sites for the Greek-temple-esque Scot-

tish National Gallery and Waverley Station. Looking farther north, you can make out the port town of Leith with its high-rises and cranes, the Firth of Forth, the island of Inchkeith, and—in the far, far distance (to the east)—the cone-like mountain of North Berwick Law, a former volcano.

Now look down. The sheer north precipice looks impregnable.

Edinburgh Castle

Princes St. Gardens

WALLS

AUDIOGUIDE PICKUP

Cliffs PORTCULLIS GATE

50 Meters

50 Yards

⑩

③ MIDDLE WARD

⑨

②

④

SHOP

Esplanade

TICKETS

DITCH

① TOUR BEGINS

⑫

ENTRY GATE

WALLS

FOOG'S GATE

⑧

EXHIBIT ENTRANCE WC

⑤

WC

DITCH

To Royal Mile

⑥

⑪

Crown Square

⑦

MAIN ENTRANCE

Cliffs

Gardens

Gardens

EDINBURGH

Tour
❶ Entry Gate
❷ Argyle Battery
❸ One O'Clock Gun
❹ St. Margaret's Chapel, Mons Meg & Dog Cemetery
❺ Crown Square
❻ Scottish Crown Jewels (Honours of Scotland)

❼ Royal Apartments
❽ Scottish National War Memorial
❾ National War Museum Scotland

Eateries & Other
❿ Redcoat Café
⓫ Tea Rooms
⓬ Whisky Shop

But on the night of March 14, 1314, 30 armed men silently scaled this rock face. They were loyal to Robert the Bruce and determined to recapture the castle, which had fallen into English hands. They caught the English by surprise, took the castle, and—three months later—Bruce defeated the English at the Battle of Bannockburn.

• *A little farther along, near the café, is the...*

❸ **One O'Clock Gun:** Crowds gather for the 13:00 gun blast, a tradition that gives ships in the bay something to set their navigational devices by. Before the gun, sailors set their clocks with help from the Nelson Monument—that's the tall pillar in the distance on Calton Hill. The monument has a "time ball" affixed to the cross on top, which drops precisely at the top of the hour. But on foggy days, ships couldn't see the ball, so the cannon shot was instituted instead (1861). The tradition stuck, every day at 13:00. (Locals joke that the frugal Scots don't fire it at high noon, as that would cost 11 extra rounds a day.)

• *Continue uphill, winding to the left and passing through Foog's Gate. At the very top of the hill, on your left, is...*

❹ **St. Margaret's Chapel:** This tiny stone chapel is Edinburgh's oldest building (around 1120) and sits atop its highest point

(440 feet). It represents the birth of the city.

In 1057, Malcolm III murdered King Macbeth (of Shakespeare fame) and assumed the Scottish throne. Later, he married Princess Margaret, and the family settled atop this hill. Their marriage united Malcolm's Highland Scots with Margaret's Lowland Anglo-Saxons—the cultural mix that would define Edinburgh.

Step inside the tiny, unadorned church—a testament to Margaret's reputed piety. The style is Romanesque. The nave is wonderfully simple, with classic Norman zigzags decorating the round arch that separates the tiny nave from the sacristy. You'll see a facsimile of St. Margaret's 11th-century gospel book. The small (modern) stained-glass windows feature St. Margaret herself, St. Columba, and St. Ninian (who brought Christianity to Scotland in A.D. 397), St. Andrew (Scotland's patron saint), and William Wallace (the defender of Scotland). These days, the place is popular for weddings. (As it seats only 20, it's particularly popular with brides' parents.)

Margaret died at the castle in 1093, and her son King David I built this chapel in her honor (she was sainted in 1250). David

expanded the castle and also founded Holyrood Abbey, across town. These two structures were soon linked by a Royal Mile of buildings, and Edinburgh was born.

Mons Meg, in front of the church, is a huge and once-upon-a-time frightening 15th-century siege cannon that fired 330-pound stones nearly two miles. Imagine. It was a gift from Philip the Good, duke of Burgundy, to his great-niece's husband King James II of Scotland.

Nearby, belly up to the banister and look down to find the **Dog Cemetery,** a tiny patch of grass with a sweet little line of doggie tombstones, marking the graves of soldiers' faithful canines in arms.

• *Continue on, curving downhill into...*

❺ **Crown Square:** This courtyard is the center of today's Royal Castle complex. Get oriented. You're surrounded by the crown jewels, the

Royal Palace (with its Great Hall), and the Scottish National War Memorial.

The castle has evolved over the centuries, and Crown Square is relatively "new." After the time of Malcolm and Margaret, the castle was greatly expanded by David II (1324-1371), complete with tall towers, a Great Hall, dungeon, cellars, and so on. This served as the grand royal residence for two centuries. Then, in 1571-1573, the Protestant citizens of Edinburgh laid siege to the castle and its Catholic/monarchist holdouts, eventually blasting it to smithereens. (You can tour the paltry remains of the medieval castle in nearby **David's Tower.**) The palace was rebuilt nearby—around what is today's Crown Square.

• *We'll tour the buildings around Crown Square. First up: the crown jewels. Look for two entrances. The one on Crown Square, only open in peak season, deposits you straight into the room with the crown jewels but usually comes with a line. The other entry, around the side (near the WCs), takes you—often at a shuffle—through the interesting, Disney-esque "Honours of Scotland" exhibition, which tells the story of the crown jewels and how they survived the harrowing centuries, but lacks any actual artifacts.*

❻ Scottish Crown Jewels (Honours of Scotland): For centuries, Scotland's monarchs were crowned in elaborate rituals involving three wondrous objects: a jewel-studded crown, scepter, and sword. These objects—along with the ceremonial Stone of Scone (pronounced "skoon")—are known as the "Honours of Scotland." Scotland's crown jewels may not be as impressive as England's, but they're treasured by locals as a symbol of Scottish nationalism. They're also older than England's; while Oliver Cromwell destroyed England's jewels, the Scots managed to hide theirs.

History of the Jewels: The Honours of Scotland exhibit that leads up to the Crown Room traces the evolution of the jewels, the ceremony, and the often-turbulent journey of this precious regalia. Here's the SparkNotes version:

In 1306, Robert the Bruce was crowned with a "circlet of gold" in a ceremony at Scone—a town 40 miles north of Edinburgh, which Scotland's earliest kings had claimed as their capital. Around 1500, King James IV added two new items to the coronation ceremony—a scepter (a gift from the pope) and a huge sword (a gift from another pope). In 1540, James V had the original crown augmented by an Edinburgh goldsmith, giving it the imperial-crown shape it has today.

William Wallace (c. 1270-1305)

In 1286, Scotland's king died without an heir, plunging the prosperous country into a generation of chaos. As Scottish nobles bickered over naming a successor, the English King Edward I—nicknamed "Longshanks" because of his long legs—invaded and assumed power (1296). He placed a figurehead on the throne, forced Scottish nobles to sign a pledge of allegiance to England (the "Ragman's Roll"), moved the British parliament north to York, and took the highly symbolic Stone of Scone to London, where it would remain for centuries.

A year later, the Scots rose up against Edward, led by William Wallace (popularized in the film *Braveheart*). A mix of history and legend portrays Wallace as the son of a poor-but-knightly family that refused to sign the Ragman's Roll. Exceptionally tall and strong, he learned Latin and French from two uncles, who were priests. In his teenage years, his father and older brother were killed by the English. Later, he killed an English sheriff to avenge the death of his wife, Marion. Wallace's rage inspired his fellow Scots to revolt.

WILLIAM WALLACE.

In the summer of 1297, Wallace and his guerrillas scored a series of stunning victories over the English. On September 11, a well-equipped English army of 10,000 soldiers and 300 horsemen began crossing Stirling Bridge. Wallace's men attacked, and in the chaos, the bridge collapsed, splitting the English ranks in two. The ragtag Scots drove the confused English into the river. The Battle of Stirling Bridge was a rout, and Wallace was knighted and appointed guardian of Scotland.

All through the winter, King Edward's men chased Wallace, continually frustrated by the Scots' hit-and-run tactics. Finally, at the Battle of Falkirk (1298), they drew Wallace's men out onto the open battlefield. The English with their horses and archers easily destroyed the spear-carrying Scots. Wallace resigned in disgrace and went on the lam, while his successors negotiated truces with the English, finally surrendering unconditionally in 1304. Wallace alone held out.

In 1305, the English tracked him down and took him to London, where he was convicted of treason and mocked with a crown of oak leaves as the "king of outlaws." On August 23, they stripped him naked and dragged him to the execution site. There he was strangled to near death, castrated, and dismembered. His head was stuck on a spike atop London Bridge, while his body parts were sent on tour to spook would-be rebels. But Wallace's martyrdom only served to inspire his countrymen, and the torch of independence was picked up by Robert the Bruce (see page 62). Despite the *Braveheart* movie, Robert the Bruce, not Wallace, was considered the original "Braveheart." (For the full story, see page 188.)

These Honours were used to crown every monarch: nine-month-old Mary, Queen of Scots (she cried); her one-year-old son James VI (future king of England); and Charles I and II. But the days of divine-right rulers were numbered.

In 1649, the parliament had Charles I (king of both England and Scotland) beheaded. Soon Cromwell's rabid English antiroyalists were marching on Edinburgh. Quick! Legend says two women scooped up the crown and sword, hid them in their skirts and belongings, and buried them in a church far to the northeast until the coast was clear.

When the monarchy was restored, the regalia were used to crown Scotland's last king, Charles II (1660). Then, in 1707, the Treaty of Union with England ended Scotland's independence. The Honours came out for a ceremony to bless the treaty, and were then locked away in a strongbox in the castle. There they lay for over a century, until Sir Walter Scott—the writer and great champion of Scottish tradition—forced a detailed search of the castle in 1818. The box was found...and there the Honours were, perfectly preserved. Within a few years, they were put on display, as they have been ever since.

The crown's most recent official appearance was in 1999, when it was taken across town to the grand opening of the reinstated parliament, marking a new chapter in the Scottish nation. As it represents the monarchy, the crown is present whenever a new session of parliament opens. (And if Scotland ever secedes, you can be sure that crown will be in the front row.)

The Honours: Finally, you enter the Crown Room to see the regalia itself. The four-foot steel **sword** was made in Italy under orders of Pope Julius II (the man who also commissioned Michelangelo's Sistine Chapel and St. Peter's Basilica). The **scepter** is made of silver, covered with gold, and topped with a rock crystal and a pearl. The gem- and pearl-encrusted **crown** has an imperial arch topped with a cross. Legend says the band of gold in the center is the original crown that once adorned the head of Robert the Bruce.

The **Stone of Scone** (a.k.a. the "Stone of Destiny") sits plain and strong next to the jewels. It's a rough-hewn gray slab of sandstone, about 26 by 17 by 10 inches. As far back as the ninth century, Scotland's kings were crowned atop this stone, when it stood at the medieval capital of Scone. But in 1296, the invading army of Edward I of England carried the stone off to Westminster Abbey. For the next seven centuries, English (and subsequently British) kings and queens were crowned sitting on a coronation chair with the Stone of Scone tucked in a compartment underneath.

In 1950, four Scottish students broke into Westminster Abbey on Christmas Day and smuggled the stone back to Scotland in an act of foolhardy patriotism. But what could they do with it? After three months, they abandoned the stone, draped in Scotland's national flag. It was returned to Westminster Abbey, where (in 1953) Queen Elizabeth II was crowned atop it. In 1996, in recognition of increased Scottish autonomy, Elizabeth agreed to let the stone go home, on one condition: that it be returned to Westminster Abbey for all British coronations. One day, the next monarch of the United Kingdom—Prince Charles is first in line—will sit atop it, re-enacting a coronation ritual that dates back a thousand years.

• *Exit the crown jewel display, heading down the stairs. But just before exiting into the courtyard, turn left through a door that leads into the...*

❼ Royal Apartments: Scottish royalty lived in the Royal Palace only when safety or protocol required it (they preferred the Palace of Holyroodhouse at the bottom of the Royal Mile). Here you can see several historic but unimpressive rooms. The first one, labeled **Queen Mary's Chamber,** is where Mary, Queen of Scots (1542-1587), gave birth to James VI of Scotland, who later became King James I of England. Nearby **Laich Hall** (Lower Hall) was the dining room of the royal family.

The **Great Hall** (through a separate entrance on Crown Square) was built by James IV to host the castle's official banquets and meetings. It's still used for such purposes today. Most of the

interior—its fireplace, carved walls, pikes, and armor—is Victorian. But the well-constructed wood ceiling is original. This hammer-beam roof (constructed like the hull of a ship) is self-supporting. The complex system of braces and arches distributes the weight of the roof outward to the walls, so there's no need for supporting pillars or long cross beams. Before leaving, look for the big iron-barred peephole above the fireplace, on the right. This allowed the king to spy on his subjects while they partied.

• *Across the Crown Square courtyard is the...*

❽ Scottish National War Memorial: This commemorates the 149,000 Scottish soldiers lost in World War I, the 58,000 who died in World War II, and the nearly 800 (and counting) lost in British battles since. This is a somber spot (stow your camera and phone). Paid for by public donations, each bay is dedicated to a particular Scottish regiment. The main shrine, featuring a green Italian-marble memorial that contains the original WWI rolls of honor, sits on an exposed chunk of the castle rock. Above you, the archangel Michael is busy slaying a dragon. The bronze frieze accurately shows the attire of various wings of Scotland's military. The stained glass starts with Cain and Abel on the left, and finishes with a celebration of peace on the right. To appreciate how important this place is, consider that Scottish soldiers died at twice the rate of other British soldiers in World War I.

• *Our final stop is worth the five-minute walk to get there. Backtrack to the café (and One O'Clock Gun), then head downhill to the War Museum. The statue in the courtyard in front of the museum is* **Field Marshall Sir Douglas Haig**—*the Scotsman who commanded the British Army through the WWI trench warfare of the Battle of the Somme and in Flanders Fields.*

❾ National War Museum Scotland: This thoughtful museum covers four centuries of Scottish military history. Instead of the usual musty, dusty displays of endless armor, there's a compelling mix of videos, uniforms, weapons, medals, mementos, and eloquent excerpts from soldiers' letters.

Here you'll learn the story of how the fierce and courageous Scottish warrior changed from being a symbol of resistance against Britain to being a champion of that same empire. Along the way, these military men received many decorations for valor and did more than their share of dying in battle. But even when fighting alongside—rather than against—England, Scottish regiments still promoted their romantic, kilted-warrior image.

Queen Victoria fueled this ideal throughout the 19th century. She was infatuated with the Scottish Highlands and the culture's untamed, rustic mystique. Highland soldiers, especially officers, went to great personal expense to sport all their elaborate regalia, and the kilted men fought best to the tune of their beloved bagpipes. For centuries the stirring drone of bagpipes accompanied Highland soldiers into battle—raising their spirits and announcing to the enemy that they were about to meet a fierce and mighty foe.

This museum shows the human side of war as well as the

Robert the Bruce (1274-1329)

In 1314, Robert the Bruce's men attacked Edinburgh's Royal Castle, recapturing it from the English. It was just one of many intense battles between the oppressive English and the plucky Scots during the Wars of Independence.

In this era, Scotland had to overcome not only its English foes but also its own divisiveness—and no one was more divided than Robert the Bruce. As earl of Carrick, he was born with blood ties to England and a long-standing family claim to the Scottish throne.

When England's King Edward I ("Longshanks") conquered Scotland in 1296, the Bruce family welcomed it, hoping Edward would defeat their rivals and put Bruce's father on the throne. They dutifully signed the "Ragman's Roll" of allegiance—and then Edward chose someone else as king.

Twentysomething Robert the Bruce (the "the" comes from his original family name of "de Bruce") then joined William Wallace's revolt against the English. As legend has it, he was the one who knighted Wallace after the victory at Stirling Bridge. When Wallace fell from favor, Bruce became a guardian of Scotland (caretaker ruler in the absence of a king) and continued fighting the English. But when Edward's armies again got the upper hand in 1302, Robert—along with Scotland's other nobles—diplomatically surrendered and again pledged loyalty.

In 1306, Robert the Bruce murdered his chief rival and boldly claimed to be king of Scotland. Few nobles supported him. Edward crushed the revolt and kidnapped Bruce's wife, the Church excommunicated him, and Bruce went into hiding on a distant North Sea island. He was now the king of nothing. Legend says he gained inspiration by watching a spider patiently build its web.

The following year, Bruce returned to Scotland and wove alliances with both nobles and the Church, slowly gaining acceptance as Scotland's king by a populace chafing under English rule. On June 24, 1314, he decisively defeated the English (now led by Edward's weak son, Edward II) at the Battle of Bannockburn. After a generation of turmoil (1286-1314), England was finally driven from Scotland, and the country was united under Robert I, king of Scotland.

As king, Robert the Bruce's priority was to stabilize the monarchy and establish clear lines of succession. His descendants would rule Scotland for the next 400 years, and even today, Bruce blood runs through the veins of Queen Elizabeth II, Prince Charles, princes William and Harry, and wee George and Charlotte.

cleverness of government-sponsored ad campaigns that kept the lads enlisting. Two centuries of recruiting posters make the same pitch that still works today: a hefty signing bonus, steady pay, and job security with the promise of a manly and adventurous life—all spiked with a mix of pride and patriotism.

Stepping outside the museum, you're surrounded by cannons that no longer fire, stony walls that tell an amazing story, dramatic views of this grand city, and the clatter of tourists (rather than soldiers) on cobbles. Consider for a moment all the bloody history and valiant struggles, along with British power and Scottish pride, that have shaped the city over which you are perched.

SIGHTS ON AND NEAR THE ROYAL MILE
Camera Obscura

A big deal when it was built in 1853, this observatory topped with a mirror reflected images onto a disc before the wide eyes of people

who had never seen a photograph or a captured image. Today, you can climb 100 steps for an entertaining 20-minute demonstration (3/hour). At the top, enjoy the best view anywhere of the Royal Mile. Then work your way down through five floors of illusions, holograms, and early photos. This is a big hit with kids, but very overpriced. (It's less impressive on cloudy days.)

Cost and Hours: £15, daily 9:30-19:00, July-Aug until 21:00, Sept-Oct until 20:00, tel. 0131/226-3709, www.camera-obscura. co.uk.

▲The Scotch Whisky Experience

This attraction seems designed to distill money out of your pocket. The 50-minute experience consists of a "Malt Disney" whisky-

barrel ride through the production process followed by an explanation and movie about Scotland's five main whisky regions. Though gimmicky, it does succeed in providing an entertaining yet informative orientation to the creation of Scottish firewater (things get pretty psychedelic when you hit the yeast stage). Your ticket also includes sampling a wee dram and the chance to stand amid the world's largest Scotch whisky collection (almost 3,500 bottles).

At the end, you'll find yourself in the bar, with a fascinating wall of unusually shaped whisky bottles. Serious connoisseurs should stick with the more substantial shops in town, but this place can be worthwhile for beginners. (For more on whisky and whisky tastings, see page 464).

Cost and Hours: £15 "silver tour" includes one sample, £26 "gold tour" includes samples from each main region, generally daily 10:00-18:00, tel. 0131/220-0441, www.scotchwhiskyexperience. co.uk.

▲▲Gladstone's Land

This is a typical 16th- to 17th-century merchant's "land," or tenement building. These multistory structures—in which merchants ran their shops on the ground floor and lived upstairs—were typical of the time (the word "tenement" didn't have the slum connotation then that it has today). At six stories, this one was still just half the height of the tallest "skyscrapers."

Gladstone's Land, which you'll visit via one-hour guided tour, comes complete with an almost-lived-in, furnished interior and 400-year-old Renaissance painted ceiling. The downstairs cloth shop and upstairs kitchen and living quarters are brought to life by your guide. Keep this place in mind as you stroll the rest of the Mile, imagining other houses as if they still looked like this on the inside. (For a comparison of life in the Old Town versus the New Town, also visit the Georgian House, described later.)

Cost and Hours: £7, tours run daily 10:30-16:00, 3-8 tours/ day, must book ahead by phone or in person; closed Nov-March, tel. 0131/226-5856, www.nts.org.uk/Visit/Gladstones-Land.

Writers' Museum at Lady Stair's House

This aristocrat's house, built in 1622, is filled with well-described manuscripts and knickknacks of Scotland's three greatest literary figures: Robert Burns, Robert Louis Stevenson, and Sir Walter Scott. If you'd like to see Scott's pipe and Burns' snuffboxes, you'll love this little museum. You'll wind up steep staircases through a maze of rooms as you peruse first editions and keepsakes of these celebrated writers. Edinburgh's high society gathered in homes like this in the 1780s to hear the great poet Robbie Burns read his work—it's meant to be read aloud rather than to oneself (stop in the Burns room to hear his poetry).

Cost and Hours: Free, Wed-Sat 10:00-17:00, Sun from 12:00, closed Mon-Tue, tel. 0131/529-4901, www.edinburghmuseums. org.uk.

Museum on the Mound

Located in the basement of the grand Bank of Scotland building, this exhibit tells the story of the bank, which was founded in 1695 (making it only a year younger than the Bank of England, and the longest operating bank in the world). Featuring displays on cash production, safe technology, and bank robberies, this museum struggles mightily to make banking interesting (the case holding £1 million is cool). It's worth popping in if you have extra time or find the subject appealing.

Cost and Hours: Free, Tue-Fri 10:00-17:00, closed Sat-Mon, down Bank Street from the Royal Mile—follow the street around to the left and enter through the gate, tel. 0131/243-5464, www.museumonthemound.com.

▲▲St. Giles' Cathedral

This is Scotland's most important church. Its ornate spire—the Scottish crown steeple from 1495—is a proud part of Edinburgh's skyline. The fascinating interior contains nearly 200 memorials honoring distinguished Scots through the ages.

Cost and Hours: Free but £3 donation encouraged; Mon-Fri 9:00-19:00, Sat until 17:00; Oct-April Mon-Sat 9:00-17:00; Sun 13:00-17:00 year-round; info sheet-£1, guidebook-£6, tel. 0131/225-9442, www.stgilescathedral.org.uk.

Concerts: St. Giles' busy concert schedule includes free organ recitals and visiting choirs (frequent events at 12:15 and concerts Sun at 18:00, also sometimes Wed, Thu, or Fri at 20:00, see schedule or ask for *Music at St. Giles'* pamphlet at welcome desk or gift shop).

◑ Self-Guided Tour: Today's facade is 19th-century Neo-Gothic, but most of what you'll see inside is from the 14th and 15th centuries. Engage the cathedral guides in conversation; you'll be glad you did.

Just inside the entrance, turn around to see the modern stained-glass **❶** Robert Burns window, which celebrates Scotland's favorite poet (see page 424). It was made in 1985 by the Icelandic artist Leifur Breidfjord. The green of the lower level symbolizes the natural world—God's creation. The middle zone with the circle shows the brotherhood of man—Burns was a great internationalist. The top is a rosy red sunburst of creativity,

St. Giles' Cathedral

←—Edinburgh Castle — *To*

To — Holyrood House—→

HIGH STREET (ROYAL MILE)

HEART OF
MIDLOTHIAN

SHOP ❾

❷ ❸

ENTRANCE→ ❶ NAVE ❹ CHANCEL

MERCAT
CROSS

❾

❻ ❼

Parliament
Square ❺ CAFÉ
(DOWN-
STAIRS) ❽

JOHN KNOX'S →
BURIAL SPOT ■KING CHARLES II
STATUE

20 Meters

20 Yards

PARKING LOT

❶ Robert Burns Window   ❻ Stained-Glass Window
❷ Pre-Raphaelite Window ❼ National Covenant
❸ John Knox Statue   ❽ Thistle Chapel
❹ Four Central Pillars   ❾ Down to Café & WC (2)
❺ Organ

EDINBURGH

reminding Scots of Burns' famous line, "My love is like a red, red rose"—part of a song near and dear to every Scottish heart.

To the right of the Burns window is a fine ❷ **Pre-Raphaelite window.** Like most in the church, it's a memorial to an important patron (in this case, John Marshall). From here stretches a great swath of war memorials.

As you walk along the north wall, find ❸ **John Knox's statue** (standing like a six-foot-tall bronze chess piece). Look into his eyes for 10 seconds from 10 inches away, and think of the Reformation struggles of the 16th century. Knox, the great religious reformer and founder of austere Scottish Presbyterianism, first preached here in 1559. His insistence that every person should be able to personally read the word of God—notice that he's pointing to a book—gave Scotland an educational system 300 years ahead of the rest of Europe (for more on Knox, see

"The Scottish Reformation" on page 208). Thanks partly to Knox, it was Scottish minds that led the way in math, science, medicine, and engineering. Voltaire called Scotland "the intellectual capital of Europe."

Knox preached Calvinism. Consider that the Dutch and the Scots both embraced this creed of hard work, frugality, and strict ethics. This helps explain why the Scots are so different from the English (and why the Dutch and the Scots—both famous for their thriftiness and industriousness—are so much alike).

The oldest parts of the cathedral—the **❹ four massive central pillars**—are Norman and date from the 12th century. They supported a mostly wooden superstructure that was lost when an invading English force burned it in 1385. The Scots rebuilt it bigger and better than ever, and in 1495 its famous crown spire was completed.

During the Reformation—when Knox preached here (1559-1572)—the place was simplified and whitewashed. Before this, when the emphasis was on holy services provided by priests, there were lots of little niches. With the new focus on sermons rather than rituals, the grand pulpit took center stage.

Knox preached against anything that separated you from God, including stained glass (considered the poor man's Bible, as illiterate Christians could learn from its pictures). Knox had the church's fancy medieval glass windows replaced with clear glass, but 19th-century Victorians took them out and installed the brilliantly colored ones you see today.

Cross over to the **❺ organ** (1992, Austrian-built, one of Europe's finest) and take in its sheer might. (To light it up, find the button behind the organ to the right of the glass.)

Immediately to the right of the organ (as you're facing it) is a tiny chapel for silence and prayer. The dramatic **❻ stained-glass**

window above shows the commotion that surrounded Knox when he preached. The bearded, fiery-eyed Knox had a huge impact on this community. Notice how there were no pews back then. The church was so packed, people even looked through clear windows from across the street. With his hand on the holy book, Knox seems to conduct divine electricity to the Scottish faithful.

Find a copy of the **❼ National Covenant** (in the corner to the far left of the organ as you face it). It was signed in blood in 1638 by Scottish heroes who refused to compromise their religion for the king's. Most who signed were martyred (their monument is nearby

EDINBURGH

Scotland's Literary Greats

Edinburgh was home to Scotland's three greatest literary figures, pictured above: Robert Burns (left), Robert Louis Stevenson (center), and Sir Walter Scott (right).

Robert Burns (1759-1796), known as "Rabbie" in Scotland and quite possibly the most famous and beloved Scot of all time, moved to Edinburgh after achieving overnight celebrity with his first volume of poetry (staying in a house on the spot where Deacon Brodie's Tavern now stands). Even though he wrote in the rough Scots dialect and dared to attack social rank, he was a favorite of Edinburgh's high society, who'd gather in fine homes to hear him recite his works. For more on Burns, see the sidebar on page 424.

One hundred years later, **Robert Louis Stevenson** (1850-1894) also stirred the Scottish soul with his pen. An avid traveler who always packed his notepad, Stevenson created settings that are vivid and filled with wonder. Traveling through Scotland, Europe, and around the world, he distilled his adventures into Romantic classics, including *Kidnapped* and *Treasure Island* (as well as *The Strange Case of Dr. Jekyll and Mr. Hyde*). Stevenson,

in Grassmarket). You can see the original National Covenant in the Edinburgh Museum, described later.

Head toward the east (back) end of the church, and turn right to see the Neo-Gothic ❽ **Thistle Chapel** (£3 donation requested, volunteer guide is a wealth of information). The interior is filled with intricate wood carving. Built in two years (1910-1911), entirely with Scottish materials and labor, it is the private chapel of the Order of the Thistle, the only Scottish chivalric order. It's used several times a year for the knights to gather (and, if one dies, to inaugurate a new member). Scotland recognizes its leading citizens by bestowing a membership upon them. The Queen presides over the ritual from her fancy stall, marked by her Scottish coat of arms—a heraldic zoo of symbolism. Are there bagpipes in heaven?

who was married in San Francisco and spent his last years in the South Pacific, wrote, "Youth is the time to travel—both in mind and in body—to try the manners of different nations." He said, "I travel not to go anywhere...but to simply go." Travel was his inspiration and his success.

Sir Walter Scott (1771-1832) wrote the *Waverley* novels, including *Ivanhoe* and *Rob Roy*. He's considered the father of the Romantic historical novel. Through his writing, he generated a worldwide interest in Scotland, and reawakened his fellow countrymen's pride in their heritage. His novels helped revive interest in Highland culture—the Gaelic language, kilts, songs, legends, myths, the clan system—and created a national identity. An avid patriot, he wrote, "Every Scottish man has a pedigree. It is a national prerogative, as unalienable as his pride and his poverty." Scott is so revered in Edinburgh that his towering Neo-Gothic monument dominates the city center. With his favorite hound by his side, Sir Walter Scott overlooks the city that he inspired, and that inspired him.

The best way to learn about and experience these literary greats is to visit the Writers' Museum at Lady Stair's House (see page 64) and to take Edinburgh's Literary Pub Tour (see page 102).

While just three writers dominate your Edinburgh sightseeing, consider also the other great writers with Edinburgh connections: J. K. Rowling (who captures the "Gothic" spirit of Edinburgh with her Harry Potter series); current resident Ian Rankin (with his "tartan noir" novels); J. M. Barrie (who attended University of Edinburgh and later created Peter Pan); Sir Arthur Conan Doyle (who was born in Edinburgh, went to medical school here, and is best known for inventing Sherlock Holmes); and James Boswell (who lived 50 yards away from the Writers' Museum, in James Court, and is revered for his biography of Samuel Johnson).

Find the tooting stone angel at the top of a window to the left of the altar, and the wooden one to the right of the doorway you came in.

❾ **Downstairs** you'll find handy public WCs and an inviting **$ café**—a good place for paupers to munch prayerfully (simple, light lunches, coffee and cakes; Mon-Sat 9:00-17:00, Sun from 11:00, in basement on back side of church, tel. 0131/225-5147).

Old Parliament House

The building now holds the civil law courts, so you'll need to go through security first. Peruse the info panels in the grand hall, with its fine 1639 hammer-beam ceiling and stained glass. This space housed the Scottish parliament until the Act of Union in 1707. The biggest stained-glass window depicts the initiation of the first Scottish High Court in 1532. The building now holds the civil law courts and is busy with wigged and robed lawyers hard at work in the old library (peek through the door) or pacing the hall deep in discussion. The basement café is literally their supreme court's restaurant (open to public until 14:30).

Cost and Hours: Free, public welcome Mon-Fri 9:00-16:30, closed Sat-Sun, no photos, enter behind St. Giles' Cathedral at door #11; open-to-the-public trials are just across the street at the High Court—the doorman has the day's docket.

▲The Real Mary King's Close

For an unusual peek at Edinburgh's gritty, plague-ridden past, join a costumed performer on an hour-long trip through an excavated underground street and buildings on the northern slope of the Royal Mile. Tours cover the standard goofy, crowd-pleasing ghost stories, but also provide authentic and historical insight into a part of town entombed by later construction. It's best to book ahead (online up to the day before, or by phone or in person for a same-day booking)—even though tours leave every 15-30 minutes, groups are small and the sight is popular.

Cost and Hours: £15; daily 10:00-21:00, Nov-March Sun-Thu until 17:00; these are last tour times, across from St. Giles' at 2 Warriston's Close—but enter through well-marked door facing High Street, tel. 0845-070-6244, www.realmarykingsclose.com.

▲Museum of Childhood

This five-story playground of historical toys and games is rich in nostalgia and history. Each well-signed gallery is as jovial as a Norman Rockwell painting, highlighting the delights and simplicity of childhood. The museum does a fair job of representing culturally relevant oddities, such as ancient Egyptian, Peruvian, and voodoo dolls, and displays early versions of toys it's probably best didn't make the final cut (such as a grim snake-centered precursor to the popular board game Chutes and Ladders).

Cost and Hours: Free, Thu-Mon 10:00-17:00 except Sun from 12:00, closed Tue-Wed, 42 High Street.

John Knox House

Intriguing for Reformation buffs, this fine medieval house dates back to 1470 and offers a well-explained look at the life of the great 16th-century reformer. Although most contend he never actually lived here, preservationists called it "Knox's house" to save it from the wrecking ball in the 1840s. Regardless, the place has good information on Knox and his intellectual sparring partner, Mary, Queen of Scots. Imagine the Protestant firebrand John Knox and the devout Catholic Mary sitting face-to-face in old rooms like these, discussing the most intimate matters of their spiritual lives as they decided the course of Scotland's religious future. The sparsely furnished house contains some period furniture, an early 1600s hand-painted ceiling, information on the house and its resident John Mossman (goldsmith to Mary, Queen of Scots), and exhibits on printing—an essential tool for early reformers.

Cost and Hours: £5, Mon-Sat 10:00-18:00, closed Sun except in July-Aug 12:00-18:00, 43 High Street, tel. 0131/556-9579, www.tracscotland.org.

▲People's Story Museum

This engaging exhibit traces the working and social lives of ordinary people through the 18th, 19th, and 20th centuries. You'll see tools, products, and objects related to important Edinburgh trades (printing, brewing), a wartime kitchen, and a circa-1989 trip to the movies. On the top floor, a dated but endearing 22-minute film offers insight into the ways people have lived in this city for generations. On the ground floor, peek into the former jail, an original part of the historic building (the Canongate Tolbooth, built in 1591).

Cost and Hours: Free, Wed-Sat 10:00-17:00 except Sun from 12:00, closed Mon-Tue, 163 Canongate, tel. 0131/529-4057, www.edinburghmuseums.org.uk.

▲Museum of Edinburgh

Another old house full of old stuff, this one is worth a stop for a look at its early Edinburgh history (and its handy ground-floor WC). Be sure to see the original copy of the National Covenant—written in 1638 on animal skin. Scottish leaders signed this, refusing to adopt the king's religion—and were killed because of it. Exploring the rest of the collection, keep an eye out for Robert Louis Stevenson's antique golf ball, James Craig's architectural plans for the Georgian New Town, an interactive kids' area with dress-up clothes, a sprawling top-floor exhibit on Edinburgh-born Field Marshall Sir David Haig (who led the British Western Front efforts in World War I and later became Earl Haig), and locally made glass and ceramics.

Cost and Hours: Free, Thu-Mon 10:00-17:00 except Sun from 12:00, closed Tue-Wed, 142 Canongate, tel. 0131/529-4143, www.edinburghmuseums.org.uk.

▲▲Scottish Parliament Building

Scotland's parliament originated in 1293 and was dissolved when Scotland united with England in 1707. But after the Scottish elec-

torate and the British parliament gave their consent, in 1997 it was decided that there should again be "a Scottish parliament guided by justice, wisdom, integrity, and compassion." Formally reconvened by Queen Elizabeth II in 1999, the Scottish parliament now enjoys self-rule in many areas (except for matters of defense, foreign policy, immigration, and taxation). The current government, run by the Scottish Nationalist Party (SNP), is pushing for even more independence.

The innovative building, opened in 2004, brought together all the functions of the fledgling parliament in one complex. It's a people-oriented structure (conceived by Catalan architect Enric Miralles. Signs are written in both English and Gaelic (the Scots' Celtic tongue).

For a peek at the building and a lesson in how the Scottish parliament works, drop in, pass through security, and find the visi-

tors' desk. You're welcome in the public parts of the building, including a small ground-floor exhibit on the parliament's history and function and, up several flights of stairs, a viewing gallery overlooking the impressive Debating Chambers.

Cost and Hours: Free; Mon-Sat 10:00-17:00, Tue-Thu 9:00-18:30 when parliament is in session (Sept-June), closed Sun year-round. For a complete list of recess dates or to book tickets for debates, check their website or call their visitor services line, tel. 0131/348-5200, www.parliament. scot.

Tours: Free worthwhile hour-long tours covering history, architecture, parliamentary processes, and other topics are offered by proud locals. Tours generally run throughout the day Mon and Fri-Sat in session (Sept-June) and Mon-Sat in recess (July-Aug). While you can try dropping in, these tours can book up—it's best to book ahead online or over the phone.

Seeing Parliament in Session: The public can witness the Scottish parliament's hugely popular debates (usually Tue-Thu 14:00-18:00; book ahead online, over the phone, or at the info desk).

On Thursdays from 11:40 to 12:45 the First Minister is on the hot seat and has to field questions from members across all parties (reserve ahead for this popular session over the phone a week in advance; spots book up quickly—call at 9:00 sharp on Thu for the following week).

▲▲Palace of Holyroodhouse

Built on the site of the abbey/monastery founded in 1128 by King David I, this palace was the true home, birthplace, and corona-

tion spot of Scotland's Stuart kings in their heyday (James IV; Mary, Queen of Scots; and Charles I). It's particularly memorable as the site of some dramatic moments from the short reign of Mary, Queen of Scots—including the murder of her personal secretary, David Rizzio, by agents of her jealous husband. Today,

it's one of Queen Elizabeth II's official residences. She usually manages her Scottish affairs here during Holyrood Week, from late June to early July (and generally stays at Balmoral in August). Holyrood is open to the public outside of the Queen's visits. Touring the interior offers a more polished contrast to Edinburgh Castle, and is particularly worth considering if you don't plan to go to Balmoral. The one-way audioguide route leads you through the fine apartments and tells some of the notable stories that played out here.

Cost: £12.50, includes quality one-hour audioguide; £17.50 combo-ticket includes the Queen's Gallery; £21.50 combo-ticket adds guided tour of palace gardens (April-Oct only); tickets sold in Queen's Gallery to the right of the castle entrance (see next listing).

Hours: Daily 9:30-18:00, Nov-March until 16:30, last entry 1.5 hours before closing, tel. 0131/556-5100, www.royalcollection.org.uk. It's still a working palace, so it's closed when the Queen or other VIPs are in residence.

Visiting the Palace: The building, rich in history and decor, is filled with elegantly furnished Victorian rooms and a few darker, older rooms with glass cases of historic bits and Scottish pieces that locals find fascinating. Bring the palace to life with the audioguide. The tour route leads you into the grassy inner courtyard, then up to the royal apartments: dining rooms, *Downton Abbey*-style drawing rooms, and royal bedchambers. Along the way, you'll learn the story behind the 96 portraits of Scottish leaders (some real, others imaginary) that line the Great Gallery; why the king never slept in his official "state bed"; why the exiled Comte d'Artois took refuge in the palace; and how the current Queen puts her Scottish subjects at ease when she receives them here. Finally, you'll twist up a tight spiral staircase to the private chambers of Mary, Queen of Scots, where conspirators stormed in and stabbed her secretary 56 times.

After exiting the palace, you're free to stroll through the evocative **ruined abbey** (destroyed by the English during the time of Mary, Queen of Scots, in the 16th century) and the **palace gardens** (closed Nov-March except some weekends). Some 8,000 guests—including many honored ladies sporting fancy hats—gather here every July when the Queen hosts a magnificent tea party. (She gets help pouring.)

Nearby: Hikers, note that the wonderful trail up Arthur's Seat starts just across the street from the gardens (see page 91 for details).

Queen's Gallery

This small museum features rotating exhibits of artwork from the royal collection. For more than five centuries, the royal family has

amassed a wealth of art treasures. While the Queen keeps most in her many private palaces, she shares an impressive load of it here, with exhibits changing about every six months. Though the gallery occupies just a few rooms, its displays can be exquisite. The entry fee includes an excellent audioguide, written and read by the curator.

Cost and Hours: £7, £17.50 combo-ticket includes Palace of Holyroodhouse, daily 9:30-18:00, Nov-March until 16:30, last entry one hour before closing, café, on the palace grounds, to the right of the palace entrance, www.royalcollection.org.uk. Buses #35 and #36 stop outside, saving you a walk to or from Princes Street/North Bridge.

Our Dynamic Earth

Located about a five-minute walk from the Palace of Holyroodhouse, this immense exhibit tells the story of our planet, filling several underground floors under a vast, white Gore-Tex tent. It's pitched, appropriately, at the base of the Salisbury Crags. The exhibit is designed for younger kids and does the same thing an American science exhibit would do—but with a charming Scottish accent. You'll learn about the Scottish geologists who pioneered the discipline, then step into a "time machine" to watch the years rewind, from cave dwellers to dinosaurs to the Big Bang. After viewing several short films on stars, tectonic plates, ice caps, and worldwide weather (in a "4-D" exhibit), you're free to wander past salty pools and a re-created rain forest.

Cost and Hours: £15, kids-£9.50, daily 10:00-17:30, July-Aug until 18:00, closed Mon-Tue Nov-March, last entry 1.5 hours before closing, on Holyrood Road, between the palace and mountain, tel. 0131/550-7800, www.dynamicearth.co.uk.

SIGHTS SOUTH OF THE ROYAL MILE

▲▲▲National Museum of Scotland

This huge museum has amassed more historic artifacts than every other place I've seen in Scotland combined. It's all wonderfully displayed, with fine descriptions offering a best-anywhere hike through the history of Scotland.

Cost and Hours: Free, daily 10:00-17:00; two long blocks south of St. Giles' Cathedral and the Royal Mile, on Chambers Street off George IV Bridge, tel. 0131/247-4422, www.nms.ac.uk.

Tours: Free one-hour general tours are offered daily at 11:00 and 13:00; themed tours at 15:00 (confirm tour schedule at info desk or on TV screens). The National Museum of Scotland Highlights app provides thin coverage of select items but is free and downloadable using their free Wi-Fi.

Eating: A **$$ brasserie** is on the ground floor near the information desks, and a **$ café** with coffee, tea, cakes, and snacks is on the level 3 balcony overlooking the Grand Gallery. On the museum's fifth floor, the dressy and upscale **$$$ Tower restaurant** serves good food with a castle view (lunch/early-bird special, afternoon tea, three course dinner specials; daily 10:00-22:00—use Tower entry if eating after museum closes, reservations recommended, tel. 0131/225-3003, www.tower-restaurant.com). A number of good eating options are within a couple of blocks of the museum (see page 115).

Overview: The place gives you two museums in one. One wing houses the Natural World galleries (T. Rex skeletons and other animals), the Science and Technology galleries, and a fashion exhibit. (The museum's Ancient Egypt and East Asia collections are currently under renovation.) With time and interest, these are all worth a look. But we'll focus on the other wing, which sweeps you through Scottish history covering Roman and Viking times, Edinburgh's witch-burning craze and clan massacres, the struggle for Scottish independence, the Industrial Revolution, and right up to Scotland in the 21st century.

◑ Self-Guided Tour: Get oriented on level 1, in the impressive glass-roofed Grand Gallery right above the entrance hall. Just outside the Grand Gallery is the **millennium clock,** a 30-foot high clock with figures that move to a Bach concerto on the hour from 11:00 to 16:00. The clock has four parts (crypt, nave, belfry, and spire) and represents the turmoil of the 20th century, with a pietà at the top.

• *To reach the Scottish history wing, exit the Grand Gallery at the far right end, under the clock and past the statue of James Watt.*

On the way, you'll pass through the science and technology wing. While walking through, look for **Dolly the sheep**—the world's first cloned mammal—born in Edinburgh and now stuffed and on display. Continue into Hawthornden Court (level 1), where our tour begins. (It's possible to detour downstairs from here to level -1 for Scotland's prehistoric origins—geologic formation, Celts, Romans, Vikings.)

• *Enter the door marked...*

Kingdom of the Scots (c. 1300-1700): From its very start, Scotland was determined to be free. You're greeted with proud quotes from what's been called the Scottish Declaration of Independence—the Declaration of Arbroath, a defiant letter written to the pope in 1320. As early as the ninth century, Scotland's patron saint, Andrew (see the small statue in the next room), had—according to legend—miraculously intervened to help the Picts and Scots of Scotland remain free by defeating the Angles of England. Andrew's X-shaped cross still decorates the Scottish flag today.

Enter the first room on your right, with imposing swords and other objects related to Scotland's most famous patriots—William Wallace and Robert the Bruce. Bruce's descendants, the Stuarts, went on to rule Scotland for the next 300 years. Eventually, James VI of Scotland (see his baby cradle) came to rule England as well (as King James I of England).

In the next room, a big guillotine recalls the harsh justice meted out to criminals, witches, and "Covenanters" (17th-century political activists who opposed interference of the Stuart kings in affairs of the Presbyterian Church of Scotland). Nearby, also check out the tomb (a copy) of Mary,

EDINBURGH

Queen of Scots, the 16th-century Stuart monarch who opposed the Presbyterian Church of Scotland. Educated and raised in Renaissance France, Mary brought refinement to the Scottish throne. After she was imprisoned and then executed by Elizabeth I of England in 1587, her supporters rallied each other by invoking her memory. Pendants and coins with her portrait stoked the irrepressible Scottish spirit (see display case near tomb).

Browse the rest of level 1 to see everyday objects from that age: carved panels, cookware, and clothes.

• *Backtrack to Hawthornden Court and head up to level 3.*

Scotland Transformed (1700s): You'll see artifacts related to Bonnie Prince Charlie and the Jacobite rebellions as well as the ornate Treaty of Union document, signed in 1707 by the Scottish parliament. This act voluntarily united Scotland with England under the single parliament of the United Kingdom. For some Scots, this move was an inevitable step in connecting to the wider world, but for others it symbolized the end of Scotland's existence.

Union with England brought stability and investment to Scotland. In this same era, the advances of the Industrial Revolution

were making a big impact on Scottish life. Mechanized textile looms (on display) replaced hand craftsmanship. The huge Newcomen steam-engine water pump helped the mining industry to develop sites with tricky drainage. Nearby is a model of a coal mine (or "colliery"); coal-rich Scotland exploited this natural resource to fuel its textile factories.

How the parsimonious Scots financed these new, large-scale enterprises is explained in an exhibit on the Bank of Scotland. Powered by the Scottish work ethic and the

new opportunities that came from the Industrial Revolution, the country came into relative prosperity. Education and medicine thrived. With the dawn of the modern age came leisure time, the concept of "healthful sports," and golf—a popular Scottish pastime. On display (near the back, behind the machinery) are some early golf balls, which date from about 1820, made of leather and stuffed with feathers.

• *Journey up to level 5.*

Industry and Empire (1800s): Turn right and do a counterclockwise spin around this floor to survey Scottish life in the 19th century. Industry had transformed the country. Highland farmers left their land to find work in Lowland factories and foundries. Modern inventions—the phonograph, the steam-powered train, the kitchen range—revolutionized everyday life. In Glasgow near the turn of the century, architect Charles Rennie Mackintosh helped to define Scottish Art Nouveau. Scotland was at the forefront of literature (Robert Burns, Sir Walter Scott, Robert Louis Stevenson), science (Lord Kelvin, James Watt, Alexander Graham Bell...he was born here, anyway!), world exploration (John Kirk in Africa, Sir Alexander Mackenzie in Canada), and whisky production.

• *Climb the stairs to level 6.*

Scotland: A Changing Nation (1900s): Turn left and do a clockwise spin through this floor to bring the story to the present day. The two world wars decimated the population of this already wee nation. In addition, hundreds of thousands emigrated, especially to Canada (where one in eight Canadians has Scottish origins). Other exhibits include Scots in the world of entertainment (from early boy-band Bay City Rollers to actor-comedian Billy Connolly); a look at the recent trend of devolution from the United Kingdom (1999 opening of Scotland's own parliament and the landmark 2014 referendum on Scottish independence); and a sports Hall of Fame (from golfer Tom Morris to auto racers Jackie Stewart and Jim Clark).

• *Finish your visit on level 7, the rooftop.*

Garden Terrace: The well-described roof garden features grasses and heathers from every corner of Scotland and spectacular views of the city.

Greyfriars Bobby Statue and Greyfriars Cemetery

This famous **statue** of Edinburgh's favorite dog is across the street from the National Museum of Scotland. Every business nearby, it seems, is named for this Victorian Skye terrier, who is reputed to have stood by his master's grave in Greyfriars Cemetery for 14 years. The story was immortalized in a 1960s Disney flick, but recent research suggests that 19th-century

business-men bribed a stray to hang out in the cemetery to attract sightseers. If it was a ruse, it still works.

Just behind Bobby is the entrance to his namesake **cemetery.** Stepping through the gate, you'll see the pink-marble grave of Bobby himself. The well-tended cemetery is an evocative place to stroll, and a nice escape from the city's bustle. Harry Potter fans could turn it into a scavenger hunt: J. K. Rowling sketched out her saga just around the corner at The Elephant House café—and a few of the cemetery's weather-beaten headstones bear familiar names, including McGonagall and Thomas Riddell. Beyond the cemetery fence are the frilly Gothic spires of posh George Heriot's School, said to have inspired Hogwarts. And just a few short blocks to the east is a street called...Potterrow.

Grassmarket

Once Edinburgh's site for hangings (residents rented out their windows—above the rudely named "Last Drop" pub—for the

view), today Grassmarket is a people-friendly piazza. It was originally the city's garage, a depot for horses and cows (hence the name). It's rowdy here at night—a popular place for "hen dos" and "stag dos" (bachelorette and bachelor parties). In the early evening, the Literary Pub Tour departs from here (see page 102). Some good shopping streets branch off from Grassmarket: Victoria Street, built in the Victorian Age, is lined with colorful little shops and eateries; angling off in the other direction, Candlemaker's Row has a few interesting artisan shops (and leads, in just a couple minutes' walk, up to Greyfriars Bobby and the National Museum; for more shopping tips in this area, see page 96).

At the top of Grassmarket is the round monument to the "Covenanters." These strict 17th-century Scottish Protestants were killed for refusing to accept the king's Episcopalian prayer book. To this day, Scots celebrate their national church's emphatically democratic government. Rather than big-shot bishops (as in the Anglican or Roman Catholic Church), they have a low-key "moderator" who's elected each year.

MUSEUMS IN THE NEW TOWN

These sights are linked by the "Bonnie Wee New Town Walk" on page 46.

▲▲Scottish National Gallery

This delightful, small museum has Scotland's best collection of paintings. In a short visit,

EDINBURGH

you can admire well-described works by Old Masters (Raphael, Rembrandt, Rubens), Impressionists (Monet, Degas, Gauguin), and a few underrated Scottish painters. (Scottish art is better at the National Portrait Gallery, described next.) Although there are no iconic masterpieces, it's a surprisingly enjoyable collection that's truly world-class.

Cost and Hours: Free; daily 10:00-17:00, Thu until 19:00, longer hours in Aug; café downstairs, The Mound (between Princes and Market streets), tel. 0131/624-6200, www.nationalgalleries.org.

Expect Changes: The museum is undergoing major renovation to increase the space of its Scottish collection and build a grand main entrance from Princes Street Gardens. As a result, certain exhibits may be closed, and pieces may be relocated, on loan, or in storage. Ask one of the friendly tartan-sporting attendants or at the info desk downstairs (near the WCs and gallery shop) if you can't find a particular item.

Next Door: The skippable **Royal Scottish Academy** hosts temporary art exhibits and is connected to the Scottish National Gallery at the Gardens level (underneath the gallery) by the Weston Link building (same hours as gallery, fine café and restaurant).

Visiting the Museum: Start at the gallery entrance (at the north end of the building). Climb the stairs to the upper level (north end), and take a left. You'll run right into...

Van der Goes, *The Trinity Panels*, c. 1473-1479: For more

than five centuries, these two double-sided panels have remained here—first in a church, then (when the church was leveled to build Waverley train station) in this museum. The panels likely were the wings of a triptych, flanking a central scene of the Virgin Mary that was destroyed by Protestant vandals during the Reformation.

In one panel is the Trinity: God the Father, in a rich red robe, cradles a spindly, just-crucified Christ, while the dove of the Holy Spirit hovers between them. (This is what would have been seen when the triptych was closed.) The flip side of the Christ panel depicts Scotland's king and queen, who are best known to history as the parents of the boy kneeling alongside them. He grew up to become James IV, the Renaissance king who made Edinburgh a cultural capital. On the other panel, the church's director (the man who commissioned the painting from the well-known Flemish painter) kneels and looks on while an angel plays a hymn on the church organ. On the opposite side is Margaret of Denmark, Queen of Scots, being presented by a saint.

In typically medieval fashion, the details are meticulous—expressive faces, intricate folds in the robes, Christ's pallid skin, observant angels. The donor's face is a remarkable portrait, with realistic skin tone and a five-o'clock shadow. But the painting lacks true 3-D realism—God's gold throne is overly exaggerated, and Christ's cardboard-cutout body hovers weightlessly.

• *Go back across the top of the skylight, to a room where the next two paintings hang.*

Botticelli, *The Virgin Adoring the Sleeping Christ Child,* c. 1485: Mary looks down at her baby, peacefully sleeping in a flower-filled garden. It's easy to appreciate Botticelli's masterful style: the precisely drawn outlines, the Virgin's pristine skin, the translucent glow. Botticelli creates a serene world in which no shadows are cast. The scene is painted on canvas—unusual at a time when wood panels were the norm. For the Virgin's rich cloak, Botticelli used ground-up lapis lazuli (a very pricey semiprecious stone), and her hem is decorated with gold leaf.

Renaissance-era art lovers would instantly catch the symbolism. Mary wears a wispy halo and blue cloak that recalls the sky blue of heaven. The roses without thorns and enclosed garden are both symbols of virginity, while the violet flowers (at bottom) represent humility. Darker symbolism hints at what's to come. The strawberries (lower right) signify Christ's blood, soon to be shed, while the roses—though thornless now—will become the Crown of Thorns. For now, Mary can adore her sleeping, blissful baby in a peaceful garden. But in a few decades she'll be kneeling again to weep over the dead, crucified Messiah.

Raphael, *Holy Family with a Palm Tree,* 1506-1507: Mary, Joseph, and the Christ Child fit snugly within a round frame (a tondo), their pose symbolizing geometric perfection and the perfect family unit. Joseph kneels to offer Jesus flowers. Mary curves toward him. Baby Jesus dangles in between, linking the family together. Raphael also connects the figures through eye contact: Mary eyes Joseph, who locks onto Jesus, who gazes precociously back. Like in a cameo, we see the faces incised in profile, while their bodies bulge out toward us.

• *Back downstairs at ground level is the main gallery space. Circle around the collection chronologically, watching for works by Bellini, Titian, Velázquez, and El Greco. In Room 7, look for the next two paintings.*

Rubens, *Feast of Herod*, c. 1635-1638: All eyes turn to watch the dramatic culmination of the story of John the Baptist. Salome (standing in center) presents John's severed head on a platter to a horrified King Herod, who clutches the tablecloth and buries his hand in his beard to stifle a gag. Meanwhile, Herod's wife—who cooked up the nasty plot—pokes spitefully at John's head with a fork. A dog tugs at Herod's foot like a nasty conscience. The canvas—big, colorful, full of motion and drama—is totally Baroque. Some have suggested that the features of Herod's wife and Salome are those of Rubens' wife and ex-wives, and the head is Rubens himself.

Rembrandt, *Self-Portrait, Aged 51*, c. 1657: It's 1657, and 51-year-old Rembrandt has just declared bankruptcy. Besides financial hardship and the auctioning-off of his personal belongings, he's also facing social stigma and behind-his-back ridicule. Once Holland's most renowned painter, he's begun a slow decline into poverty and obscurity.

His face says it all. Holding a steady gaze, he stares with matter-of-fact acceptance, with his lips pursed. He's dressed in dark clothes against a dark background, with the only spot of light shining on the worry lines of his forehead. Get close enough to the canvas to see the thick paste of paint he used for the wrinkles around his eyes—a study in aging.

• *In Room 11, find...*

Gainsborough, *The Honorable Mrs. Graham*, 1775-1777: The slender, elegant, lavishly dressed woman was the teenage bride of a wealthy Scottish landowner. She leans on a column, ostrich feather in hand, staring off to the side (Thoughtfully? Determinedly? Haughtily?). Her faultless face and smooth neck stand out from the elaborately ruffled dress and background foliage. This 18th-century woman wears a silvery dress that echoes 17th-century style—Gainsborough's way of showing how, though she was young, she was classy. Thomas ("Blue Boy") Gainsborough—the product of a clothes-making father and a flower-painting mother — uses aspects of both in this lush portrait.

The ruby brooch on her bodice marks the center of this harmonious composition.

• *Climb the stairs to the upper level (south end, opposite from where you entered) and turn right for the Impressionists and Post-Impressionists.*

Impressionist Collection: The gallery has a smattering of (mostly smaller-scale) works from all the main artists of the Impressionist and Post-Impressionist eras. You'll see Degas' ballet scenes, Renoir's pastel-colored family scenes, Van Gogh's peasants, and Seurat's pointillism.

• *Keep an eye out for these three paintings.*

Monet's *Poplars on the River Epte* (1891) was part of the artist's famous "series" paintings. He set up several canvases in a floating studio near his home in Giverny. He'd start on one canvas in the morning (to catch the morning light), then move to the next as the light changed. This particular canvas captures a perfect summer day, showing both the poplars on the riverbank and their mirror image in the still water. The subject matter begins to dissolve into a pure pattern of color, anticipating abstract art.

Gauguin's *Vision of the Sermon* (1888) shows French peasant women imagining the miraculous event they've just heard preached about in church—when Jacob wrestles with an angel. The painting is a watershed in art history, as Gauguin throws out the rules of "realism" that had reigned since the Renaissance. The colors are surreal, there are no shadows, the figures are arranged almost randomly, and there's no attempt to make the wrestlers appear distant. The diagonal tree branch is the only thing separating the everyday world from the miraculous. Later, when Gauguin moved to Tahiti (see his *Three Tahitians* nearby), he painted a similar world, where the everyday and magical coexist, with symbolic power.

Sargent's *Lady Agnew of Lochnaw* (1892) is the work that launched the career of this American-born portrait artist. Lady Agnew—the young wife of a wealthy old Scotsman—lounges back languidly and gazes out self-assuredly. The Impressionistic smudges of paint on her dress and the chair contrast with her clear skin and luminous eyeballs. Her relaxed pose (one arm hanging down the side) contrasts with her intensity: head tilted slightly down while she gazes up, a corner of her mouth askew, and an eyebrow cocked seductively.

Scottish Collection: The museum is undergoing a major renovation to build a larger and better

EDINBURGH

home for this collection. Until then, look for the following artists scattered around the main gallery.

Allan Ramsay, the son of the well-known poet of the same name, painted portraits of curly-wigged men of the Enlightenment era (the philosopher David Hume, King George III) as well as like-nesses of his two wives. Ramsay's portrait of the duke of Argyll—founder of the Royal Bank of Scotland—appears on the front of notes printed by this bank.

Sir Henry Raeburn chronicled the next generation: Sir Walter Scott, the proud kilt-wearing Alastair MacDonell, and the ice-skating Reverend Robert Walker, minister of the Canongate Church.

Sir David Wilkie's forte was small-scale scenes of everyday life. *The Letter of Introduction* (1813) captures Wilkie's own experience of trying to impress skeptical art patrons in London; even the dog is sniffing the Scotsman out. *Distraining for Rent* (1815) shows the plight of a poor farmer about to lose his farm—a common occurrence during 19th-century industrialization.

William Dyce's *Francesca da Rimini* (1837) depicts star-crossed lovers—a young wife and her husband's kid brother—who can't help but indulge their passion. The husband later finds out and kills her; at the far left, you see his ominous hand.

William McTaggart's impressionistic landscape scenes from the late 1800s provide a glimpse of the unique light, powerful clouds, and natural wonder of the Highlands.

▲▲Scottish National Portrait Gallery

Put a face on Scotland's history by enjoying these portraits of famous Scots from the earliest times until today. From its Neo-Gothic facade to a grand entry hall featuring a *Who's Who* of Scotland, to galleries highlighting the great Scots of each age, this impressive museum will fascinate anyone interested in Scottish culture. The gallery also hosts temporary exhibits highlighting the work of more contemporary Scots. Because of its purely Scottish focus, many travelers prefer this to the (pan-European) main branch of the National Gallery.

Cost and Hours: Free, daily 10:00-17:00, good $ cafeteria serving healthy meals, 1 Queen Street, tel. 0131/624-6490, www. nationalgalleries.org.

Visiting the Gallery: In the stirring **entrance hall** you'll find busts of great Scots and a full-body statue of Robbie "Rabbie" Burns, as well as (up above) a glorious frieze showing a parade of historical figures and murals depicting important events in Scottish history. (These are better viewed from the first floor and its mezzanine—described later.) We'll start on the **second floor,** right into the thick of the struggle between Scotland and England over who should rule this land.

Reformation to Revolution (gallery 1): The collection starts with a portrait of **Mary, Queen of Scots** (1542-1587), her cross and

rosary prominent. This controversial ruler set off two centuries of strife. Mary was born with both Stuart blood (the ruling family of Scotland) and the Tudor blood of England's monarchs (Queen Elizabeth I was her cousin). Catholic and French-educated, Mary felt alienated from her own increasingly Protestant homeland. Her tense conversations with the reformer John Knox must have been epic. Then came a series of scandals: She married unpopular Lord Darnley, then (possibly) cheated on him, causing Darnley to (possibly) murder her lover, causing Mary to (possibly) murder Darnley, then (possibly) run off with another man, and (possibly) plot against Queen Elizabeth.

Amid all that drama, Mary was forced by her own people to relinquish her throne to her infant son, **James VI.** Find his portraits as a child and as a grown-up. James grew up to rule Scotland, and when Queen Elizabeth (the "virgin queen") died without an heir, he also became king of England (James I). But James' son, **Charles I,** after a bitter civil war, was arrested and executed in 1649: See the large *Execution of Charles I* painting high on the far wall, his blood-dripping head displayed to the crowd; nearby is a portrait of Charles in happier times, as a 12-year-old boy. His son, Charles II, restored the Stuarts to power. He was then succeeded by his Catholic brother James VII of Scotland (II of England), who was sent into exile in France. There the Stuarts stewed, planning a return to power, waiting for someone to lead them in what would come to be known as the Jacobite rebellions.

The Jacobite Cause (gallery 4): One of the biggest paintings in the room is *The Baptism of Prince Charles Edward Stuart.* Born in 1720, this Stuart heir to the thrones of Great Britain and Ireland is better known to history as "Bonnie Prince Charlie." (See his bonnie features in various portraits nearby, as a child, young man, and grown man.) Charismatic Charles convinced France to invade Scotland and put him back on the throne there. In 1745, he entered Edinburgh in triumph. But he was defeated at the tide-turning Battle of Culloden (1746). The Stuart cause died forever, and Bonnie Prince Charlie went into exile, eventually dying drunk and wasted in Rome, far from the land he nearly ruled.

• *The next few rooms (galleries 5-6) contain special exhibits that swap out every year or two—they're worth a browse.*

The Age of Improvement (gallery 7): The faces portrayed here belonged to a new society whose hard work and public spirit achieved progress with a Scottish accent. Social equality and the Industrial Revolution "transformed" Scotland—you'll see portraits of the great poet Robert Burns, the son of a farmer (Burns was heralded as a "heaven-taught ploughman" when his poems were first published), and the man who perfected the steam engine, James Watt.

• *Check out the remaining galleries, with more special exhibits, then head back down to the first floor for a good look at the...*

Central Atrium (first floor): Great Scots! The atrium is decorated in a parade of late-19th-century Romantic Historicism. The **frieze** (working counterclockwise) is a visual encyclopedia, from an ax-wielding Stone Age man and a druid, to the early legendary monarchs (Macbeth), to warriors William Wallace and Robert the Bruce, to many kings (James I, II, III, and so on), to great think-ers, inventors, and artists (Allan Ramsay, Flora MacDonald, David Hume, Adam Smith, James Boswell, James Watt), the three greatest Scot-tish writers (Robert Burns, Sir Wal-ter Scott, Robert Louis Stevenson), and culminating with the historian Thomas Carlyle, who was the driv-ing spirit (powered by the fortune of

a local newspaper baron) behind creating this portrait gallery.

Around the first-floor mezzanine are large-scale **murals** de-picting great events in Scottish history, including the landing of St. Margaret at Queensferry in 1068, the Battle of Stirling Bridge in 1297, the Battle of Bannockburn in 1314, and the marriage procession of James IV and Margaret Tudor through the streets of Edinburgh in 1503.

• *Also on this floor you'll find the...*

Modern Portrait Gallery: This space is dedicated to rotating art and photographs highlighting Scots who are making an impact in the world today, such as Annie Lennox, Alan Cumming, and physicist Peter Higgs (theorizer of the Higgs boson, the so-called God particle). Look for the *Three Oncologists,* a ghostly painting depicting the anxiety and terror of cancer and the dedication of those working so hard to conquer it.

▲▲Georgian House

This refurbished Neoclassical house, set on Charlotte Square, is a trip back to 1796. It recounts the era when a newly gentrified and well-educated Edinburgh was nicknamed the "Athens of the North." Begin on the second floor, where you'll watch an interesting 16-minute video dramatizing the upstairs/downstairs lifestyles of the aristocrats and servants who lived here. Try on some Georgian outfits, then head downstairs to tour period rooms and even peek into the fully stocked medicine cabinet. Info sheets are available in each room, along with volunteer guides who share stories and trivia, such as why Georgian bigwigs had to sit behind a screen while enjoying a fire. A walk down George Street after your visit here can be fun for the imagination.

Cost and Hours: £7.50, daily 10:00-17:00, March and Nov 11:00-16:00, closed Dec-Feb, last entry 45 minutes before closing; 7 Charlotte Square, tel. 0131/226-3318, www.nts.org.uk.

SIGHTS NEAR EDINBURGH

▲▲Royal Yacht *Britannia*

This much-revered vessel, which transported Britain's royal family for more than 40 years on 900 voyages (an average of once around the world per year) before being retired in 1997, is permanently moored in Edinburgh's port of Leith. Queen Elizabeth II said of the ship, "This is the only place I can truly relax." Today it's open to the curious public, who have access to its many decks—from engine rooms to draw-

EDINBURGH

ing rooms—and offers a fascinating time-warp look into the late-20th-century lifestyles of the rich and royal. It's worth the 20-minute bus or taxi ride from the center; figure on spending about 2.5 hours total on the outing.

Cost and Hours: £15.50, includes 1.5-hour audioguide, daily 9:30-16:30, Oct until 16:00, Nov-March 10:00-15:30, these are last-entry times, tearoom; at the Ocean Terminal Shopping Mall, on Ocean Drive in Leith; tel. 0131/555-5566, www.royalyachtbritannia.co.uk.

Getting There: From central Edinburgh, catch Lothian bus #11 or #22 from Princes Street (just above Waverley Station), or #35 from the bottom of the Royal Mile (alongside the parliament building) to Ocean Terminal (last stop). From the B&B neighborhood, you can either bus to the city center and transfer to one of the buses above, or take bus #14 from Dalkeith Road to Mill Lane, then walk about 10 minutes. The Majestic Tour hop-on, hop-off bus stops here as well. Drivers can park free in the blue parking garage. Take the shopping center elevator to level E, then follow the signs.

Visiting the Ship: First, explore the **museum**, filled with engrossing royal-family-afloat history. You'll see lots of family photos that evoke the fine times the Windsors enjoyed on the *Britannia,* as well as some nautical equipment and uniforms. Then, armed with your audioguide, you're welcome aboard.

This was the last in a line of royal yachts that stretches back to 1660. With all its royal functions, the ship required a crew of more than 200. Begin in the captain's bridge, which feels like it's been preserved from the day it was launched in 1953. Then head down a deck to see the officers' quarters, then the garage, where a Rolls Royce was hoisted aboard to use in places where the local transportation wasn't up to royal standards. The Veranda Deck at the back of the ship was the favorite place for outdoor entertainment. Ronald Reagan, Boris Yeltsin, Bill Clinton, and Nelson Mandela all sipped champagne here. The Sun Lounge, just off the back Veranda Deck, was the Queen's favorite, with Burmese teak and the same phone system she was used to in Buckingham Palace. When she wasn't entertaining, the Queen liked it quiet. The crew wore sneakers, communicated in hand signals, and (at least near the Queen's quarters) had to be finished with all their work by 8:00 in the morning.

Take a peek into the adjoining his-and-hers bedrooms of the Queen and the Duke of Edinburgh (check out the spartan twin beds), and the honeymoon suite where Prince Charles and Lady Di began their wedded bliss.

Heading down another deck, walk through the officers' lounge (and learn about the rowdy games they played) and past the galleys (including custom cabinetry for the fine china and silver) on your way to the biggest room on the yacht, the state dining room. Now decorated with gifts given by the ship's many noteworthy guests, this space enabled the Queen to entertain a good-size crowd. The drawing room, while rather simple (the Queen

specifically requested "country house comfort"), was perfect for casual relaxing among royals. Princess Diana played the piano, which is bolted to the deck. Note the contrast to the decidedly less plush crew's quarters, mail room, sick bay, laundry, and engine room.

▲Rosslyn Chapel

This small but fascinating countryside church, about a 20-minute drive outside Edinburgh, is a riot of carved iconography. The patterned ceiling and walls have left scholars guessing about the symbolism for centuries.

Cost and Hours: £9, Mon-Sat 9:30-17:00, June-Aug until 18:00, Sun 12:00-16:45 year-round, located in Roslin Village, tel. 0131/440-2159, www.rosslynchapel.org.uk.

Getting There: Ride Lothian bus #37 from Princes Street (stop PJ), North Bridge, or Newington Road in the B&B neighborhood (1-2/hour, 45 minutes). By car, take the A-701 to Penicuik/Peebles, and follow signs for *Roslin;* once you're in the village, you'll see signs for the chapel.

Background: After it was featured in the climax of Dan Brown's 2003 bestseller *The Da Vinci Code,* the number of visitors to Rosslyn Chapel more than quadrupled. But the chapel's allure existed well before the books, and will endure long after they move from bargain bin to landfill. Founded in 1446 as the private mausoleum of the St. Clair family—who wanted to be buried close to God—the church's interior is carved with a stunning mishmash of Christian, pagan, family, Templar, Masonic, and other symbolism. After the Scottish Reformation, Catholic churches like this fell into disrepair. But in the 18th and 19th centuries, Romantics such as Robert Burns and Sir Walter Scott discovered these evocative old ruins, putting Rosslyn Chapel back on the map. Even Queen

Victoria visited, and gently suggested that the chapel be restored to its original state. Today, after more than a century of refits and refurbishments, the chapel transports visitors back to a distant and mysterious age.

Visiting the Chapel: From the ticket desk and visitors center, head to the chapel itself. Ask about docent lectures (usually at the top of the hour). If you have time to kill, pick up the good laminated descriptions for a clockwise tour of the carvings. In the crypt—where the stonemasons worked—you can see faint architectural drawings engraved in the wall, used to help them plot out their master design.

Elsewhere, look for these fun details: In the corner to the left of the altar, find the angels playing instruments—including one with bagpipes. Nearby, you'll see a person dancing with a skeleton. This "dance of death" theme—common in the Middle Ages—is a reminder of mortality: We'll all die eventually, so we might as well whoop it up while we're here. On the other side of the nave are carvings of the seven deadly sins and the seven acts of mercy. One inscription reads: "Wine is strong. Kings are stronger. Women are stronger still. But truth conquers all."

Flanking the altar are two carved columns that come with a legend: The more standard-issue column, on the left, was executed by a master mason, who soon after (perhaps disappointed in his lack of originality) went on a sabbatical to gain inspiration. While he was gone, his ambitious apprentice carved the beautiful corkscrew-shaped column on the right. Upon returning, the master flew into an envious rage and murdered the apprentice with his carving hammer.

Scattered throughout the church, you'll also see the family's symbol, the "engrailed cross" (with serrated edges). Keep an eye out for the more than one hundred "green men"—chubby faces with leaves and vines growing out of their orifices, symbolizing nature. This paradise/Garden of Eden theme is enhanced by a smattering of exotic animals (monkey, elephant, camel, dragon, and a lion fighting a unicorn) and some exotic foliage: aloe vera, trillium, and corn. That last one (framing a window to the right of the altar) is a mystery: It was carved well before Columbus sailed the ocean blue, at a time when corn was unknown in Europe. Several theories have been suggested—some far-fetched (the father of the man who built the chapel explored the New World before Columbus), and others more plausible (the St. Clairs were of Norse descent, and the Vikings are known to have traveled to the Americas well before Columbus). Others simply say it's not corn at all—it's stalks of wheat. After all these centuries, Rosslyn Chapel's mysteries still inspire the imaginations of historians, novelists, and tourists alike.

Royal Botanic Garden
Britain's second-oldest botanical garden (after Oxford) was established in 1670 for medicinal herbs, and this 70-acre refuge is now one of Europe's best. A visitors center has temporary exhibits.

Cost and Hours: Gardens-free, greenhouse-£6.50, daily

10:00-18:00, Feb and Oct until 17:00, Nov-Jan until 16:00, greenhouse last entry one hour before closing, café and restaurant, a mile north of the city center at Inverleith Row, tel. 0131/248-2909, www.rbge.org.uk.

Getting There: It's a 10-minute bus ride from the city center: Take bus #8 from North Bridge, or #23 or #27 from George IV Bridge (near the National Museum) or The Mound. The Majestic Tour hop-on, hop-off bus also stops here.

Scottish National Gallery of Modern Art

This museum, set in a beautiful parkland, houses Scottish and international paintings and sculpture from 1900 to the present, including works by Matisse, Duchamp, Picasso, and Warhol. The grounds include a pleasant outdoor sculpture park and a café.

Cost and Hours: Free, daily 10:00-17:00, 75 Belford Road, tel. 0131/624-6336, www.nationalgalleries.org.

Getting There: It's about a 20-minute walk west from the city center. Or take the shuttle bus, which runs about hourly between this museum and the Scottish National Gallery (£1 donation requested, confirm times on website).

Experiences in Edinburgh

URBAN HIKES

▲▲Holyrood Park: Arthur's Seat and the Salisbury Crags

Rising up from the heart of Edinburgh, Holyrood Park is a lush green mountain squeezed between the parliament/Holyroodhouse (at the bottom of the Royal Mile) and my recommended B&B neighborhood. For an exhilarating hike, connect these two zones with a moderately strenuous 30-minute walk along the Salisbury Crags—red-

dish cliffs with sweeping views over the city. Or, for a more serious climb, make the ascent to the summit of Arthur's Seat, the 822-foot-tall remains of an extinct volcano. You can run up like they did in *Chariots of Fire*, or just stroll—at the summit, you'll be rewarded with commanding views of the town and surroundings. On May Day, be on the summit at dawn and wash your face in the morning dew to commemorate the Celtic holiday of Beltane, the celebration of spring. (Morning dew is supposedly very good for your complexion.)

You can do this hike either from the bottom of the Royal Mile, or from the B&B neighborhood.

From the Royal Mile: Begin in the parking lot below the Palace of Holyroodhouse. Facing the cliff, you'll see two trailheads. For the easier hike along the base of the **Salisbury Crags,** take the trail to the right. At the far end, you can descend into the Dalkeith Road area or—if you're up for more hiking—continue steeply up the switchbacked trail to the Arthur's Seat summit. If you know you'll want to ascend **Arthur's Seat** from the start, take the wider path on the left from the Holyroodhouse parking lot (easier grade, through the abbey ruins and "Hunter's Bog").

From the B&B Neighborhood: If you're sleeping in this area, enjoy a pre-breakfast or late-evening hike starting from the other side (in June, the sun comes up early, and it stays light until nearly midnight). From the Commonwealth Pool, take Holyrood Park Road, bear left at the first roundabout, then turn right at the second roundabout (onto Queen's Drive). Soon you'll see the trailhead, and make your choice: Bear right up the steeper "Piper's Walk" to **Arthur's Seat** (about a 20-minute hike from here, up a steeply switchbacked trail), or bear left for an easier ascent up the "Radial Road" to the **Salisbury Crags,** which you can follow—with great views over town—all the way to Holyroodhouse Palace.

By Car: If you have a car, you can drive up most of the way to Arthur's Seat from behind (follow the one-way street from the palace, park safely and for free by the little lake, and hike up).

Duddingston Village and Dr. Neil's Garden

This low-key, 30-minute walk goes from the B&B neighborhood to Duddingston Village—a former village that got absorbed by the city but still retains its old, cobbled feel, local church, and great old-time pub, the recommended Sheep Heid Inn. Also here is Dr. Neil's Garden, a peaceful, free garden on a loch.

Walk behind the Commonwealth Pool along Holyrood Park Road. Before the roundabout, just after passing through the wall/gate, take the path to your right. This path runs alongside the Duddingston Low Road all the way to the village and garden. Ignore the road traffic and enjoy the views of Arthur's Seat, the golf course, and eventually, Duddingston Loch. When you reach the cobbled road, you're in Duddingston Village, with the church on your right and the Sheep Heid Inn a block down on your left. Another 100 feet down the main road is a gate labeled *"The Manse"* with the number 5—enter here for the garden.

Dr. Neil's Garden (also known as the Secret Garden) was started by doctors Nancy and Andrew Neil, who traveled throughout Europe in the 1960s gathering trees and plants. They brought them back here, planted them on this land, and tended to them with the help of their patients. Today it offers a quiet, secluded break from the city, where you can walk among flowers and trees and over quaint bridges, get inspired by quotes written on chalk-boards, or sit on a bench overlooking the loch (free, daily 10:00-dusk, mobile 07849-187-995, www.drneilsgarden.co.uk).

▲Calton Hill

For an easy walk for fine views over all of Edinburgh, head up to Calton Hill—the monument-studded bluff that rises up from the eastern end of the New Town. From the Waverley Station area, simply head east on Princes Street (which becomes Waterloo Place).

About five minutes after passing North Bridge, watch on the right for the gated entrance to the **Old Calton Cemetery**—worth a quick walk-through for its stirring monuments to great Scots. The can't-miss-it round monument honors the philosopher David Hume; just next to that is a memorial topped by Abraham Lincoln, honoring Scottish-American troops who were killed in combat. The obelisk honors political martyrs.

The views from the cemetery are good, but for even better ones, head back out to the main road and continue a few more minutes

on Waterloo Place. Across the street, steps lead up into **Calton Hill.** Explore. Informational plaques identify the key landmarks. At the summit of the hill is the giant, unfinished replica of the Parthenon, honoring those lost in the Napoleonic Wars. Donations to finish
it never materialized, leaving it with the nickname "Edinburgh's Disgrace." Nearby, the old observatory is filled with an avant-garde art gallery, and the back of the hillside boasts sweeping views over the Firth of Forth and Edinburgh's sprawl. Back toward the Old Town, the tallest tower celebrates Admiral Horatio Nelson—the same honoree of the giant pillar on London's Trafalgar Square. The best views are around the smaller, circular Dugald Stewart Monument, with postcard panoramas overlooking the spires of the Old Town and the New Town.

More Hikes

You can hike along the river (called the Water of Leith) through Edinburgh. Locals favor the stretch between Roseburn and Dean Village, but the 1.5-mile walk from Dean Village to the Royal Botanic Garden is also good. For more information on these and other hikes, ask at the TI or your B&B.

WHISKY AND GIN TASTING
Whisky Tasting

One of the most accessible places to learn about whisky is at the **Scotch Whisky Experience** on the Royal Mile, an expensive but informative overview to whisky, including a tasting (see page 63). To get more into sampling whisky, try one of the early-evening tastings at the recommended **Cadenhead's Whisky Shop** (see page 97).

Serious whisky drinkers can check out **The Scotch Malt Whisky Society** in the New Town. Formerly a private club, it recently opened the Kaleidoscope bar to the public, serving glasses from anonymous, numbered bottles of single malts from all over Scotland and beyond. In this "blind tasting" approach, you have to read each number's tasting notes to make your choice...or enlist the help of the bartender, who will probe you on what kind of flavor profile you like. While this place's shrouded-in-mystery pretense could get lost on novices, aficionados enjoy it (daily 11:00-23:00, bar serves light dishes, on-site restaurant, 28 Queen Street, tel. 0131/220-2044, www.smws.com).

Gin Distillery Tours

The residents of Edinburgh drink more gin per person than any other city in the United Kingdom, and the city is largely responsible for the recent renaissance of this drink, so it's only appropriate that you visit a gin distillery while in town. Two distilleries right in the heart of Edinburgh offer hour-long tours with colorful guides who discuss the history of gin, show you the stills involved in the production process, and ply you with libations. Both tours are popular and fill up; book ahead on their websites.

Pickering's is located in a former vet school and animal hospital at Summerhall, halfway between the Royal Mile and the B&B neighborhood—you'll still see cages lining the walls (£10, 3/day Thu-Sun, meet at the Royal Dick Bar in the central courtyard at 1 Summerhall, tel. 0131/290-2901, www.pickeringsgin.com).

Edinburgh Gin is in the New Town, next to the Waldorf Astoria Hotel. Besides the basic tour, there's a connoisseur tour with more tastings and a gin-making tour (basic tour £10, 3/day daily, 1A Rutland Place, tel. 0131/656-2810, www.edinburghgin.com). If you can't get on to one of their tours, visit their Heads & Tales bar to taste their gins (daily 17:00-24:00).

LEISURE ACTIVITIES

Several enjoyable activities cluster near the B&B area around Dalkeith Road. For details, check their websites.

The **Royal Commonwealth Pool** is an indoor fitness and activity complex with a 50-meter pool, gym/fitness studio, and kids' soft play zone (daily, tel. 0131/667-7211, www.edinburghleisure. co.uk).

The **Prestonfield Golf Club,** also an easy walk from the B&Bs, has golfers feeling like they're in a country estate (dress code, 6 Priestfield Road North, tel. 0131/667-9665, www.prestonfieldgolf. co.uk).

Farther out at **Midlothian Snowsports Centre** (a little south of town in Hillend; better for drivers), try skiing without any pesky snow. It feels like snow-skiing on a slushy day, even though you're schussing over matting misted with water. Four new tubing runs offer fun even for nonskiers (Mon-Fri 9:30-21:00, Sat-Sun until 19:00, tel. 0131/445-4433, http://ski.midlothian.gov.uk).

EDINBURGH'S FESTIVALS

Every summer, Edinburgh's annual festivals turn the city into a carnival of the arts. The season begins in June with the international film festival (www.edfilmfest.org.uk); then the jazz and blues festival in July (www.edinburghjazzfestival. com).

In August a riot of overlapping festivals known collectively as the **Edinburgh Festival** rages simultaneously—international, fringe, book, and art, as well as the Military Tattoo. There are enough music, dance, drama, and multicultural events to make even the most jaded traveler giddy with excitement. Every day is jammed with formal and spontaneous fun. Many city sights run on extended hours. It's a glorious time to be in Edinburgh...*if* you have (and can afford) a room.

If you'll be in town in August, book your room and tickets for major events (especially the Tattoo) as far ahead as you can lock in dates. Plan carefully to ensure you'll have time for festival activities as well as sightseeing. Check online to confirm dates; the best overall website is www.edinburghfestivals.co.uk. Several publications—including the festival's official schedule, the *Edinburgh Festivals Guide Daily, The List, Fringe Program,* and *Daily Diary*—list and evaluate festival events.

The official, more formal **Edinburgh International Festival** is the original. Major events sell out well in advance (ticket office at the Hub, in the former Tolbooth Church near the top of the Royal Mile, tel. 0131/473-2000, www.hubtickets.co.uk or www. eif.co.uk).

The less formal **Fringe Festival,** featuring edgy comedy and theater, is huge—with 2,000 shows—and has eclipsed the original festival in popularity (ticket/info office just below St. Giles' Cathedral on the Royal Mile, 180 High Street, bookings tel. 0131/226-0000, www.edfringe.com). Tickets may be available at the door, and half-price tickets for some events are sold on the day of the show at the Half-Price Hut, located at The Mound, near the Scottish National Gallery.

The **Military Tattoo** is a massing of bands, drums, and bagpipes, with groups from all over the former British Empire and beyond. Displaying military finesse with a stirring lone-piper finale, this grand spectacle fills the Castle Esplanade (nightly during most of Aug except Sun, performances Mon-Fri at 21:00, Sat at 19:30 and 22:30, £25-63, booking starts in Dec, Fri-Sat shows sell out first, all seats generally sold out by early summer, some scattered same-day tickets may be available; office open Mon-Fri 10:00-16:30, closed Sat-Sun, during Tattoo open until show time and closed Sun; 32 Market Street, behind Waverley Station, tel. 0131/225-1188, www.edintattoo.co.uk). Some performances are filmed by the BBC and later broadcast as a big national television special.

The **Festival of Politics,** adding yet another dimension to Edinburgh's festival action, is held in August in the Scottish parliament building. It's a busy weekend of discussions and lectures on environmentalism, globalization, terrorism, gender, and other issues (www.festivalofpolitics.org.uk).

Other summer festivals cover books (mid-late Aug, www.edbookfest.co.uk) and art (late July-Aug, www.edinburghartfestival.com).

Shopping in Edinburgh

Edinburgh is bursting with Scottish clichés for sale: kilts, shortbread, whisky...if they can slap a tartan on it, they'll sell it. Locals dismiss the touristy trinket shops, which are most concentrated along the Royal Mile, as "tartan tat." Your challenge is finding something a wee bit more authentic. If you want to be sure you are taking home local merchandise, check if the labels read: "Made in Scotland." "Designed in Scotland" actually means "Made in China." Shops are usually open around 10:00-18:00 (later on Thu, shorter hours or closed on Sun). Tourist shops are open longer hours.

SHOPPING STREETS AND NEIGHBORHOODS

Near the Royal Mile: The Royal Mile is intensely touristy, mostly lined with interchangeable shops selling made-in-China souvenirs. I've listed a few worthwhile spots along here later, under "What to

Shop For." But in general, the area near Grassmarket, an easy stroll from the top of the Royal Mile, offer more originality. **Victoria Street,** which climbs steeply downhill from the Royal Mile (near the Hub/Tolbooth Church) to Grassmarket, has a fine concentration of local chain shops, including I.J. Mellis Cheesemonger and Walker Slater for designer tweed (both described later), plus Calzeat (scarves, throws, and other textiles), a Harry Potter store, and more clothing and accessory shops. **Candlemaker Row,** exiting Grassmarket opposite Victoria Street, is a little more artisan, with boutiques selling hats (everything from dapper men's caps to outrageous fascinators), jewelry, art, design items, and even fossils. The street winds a couple of blocks up toward the National Museum; Greyfriars Bobby awaits you at the top of the street (see page 78).

In New Town: For mass-market shopping, you'll find plenty of big chain stores along **Princes Street.** In addition to Marks & Spencer, H&M, Zara, Primark, and a glitzy Apple Store, you'll also see the granddaddy of Scottish department stores, Jenners (generally daily 9:30-18:30, open later on Thu, shorter hours on Sun; described on page 49). Parallel to Princes Street, **George Street** has higher-end chain stores (including many from London, such as L.K. Bennett, Molton Brown, and Karen Millen). Just off St. Andrew Square is a branch of the high-end London department store Harvey Nichols.

For more local, artisan shopping, check out **Thistle Street,** lined with some fun eateries and a good collection of shops. You'll see some fun boutiques selling jewelry, shoes, and clothing. This is also the home of Howie Nicolsby's 21st Century Kilts, which attempts to bring traditional Scottish menswear into the present day (described later).

WHAT TO SHOP FOR
Whisky
You can order whisky in just about any bar in town, and whisky shops are a dime a dozen around the Royal Mile. But the places I've listed here distinguish themselves by their tradition and helpful staff. Before sampling or buying whisky, read all about Scotland's favorite spirit on page 464.

Cadenhead's Whisky Shop is not a tourist sight—don't expect free samples. Founded in 1842, this firm prides itself on bottling good whisky straight from casks at the distilleries, without all the compromises that come with profitable mass production (coloring with sugar to fit the expected look, watering down to reduce the alcohol tax, and so on). Those drinking from Cadenhead-bottled whiskies will enjoy the pure product as the distilleries' owners themselves do, not as the sorry public does. The staff explains the sometimes-complex whisky board and talks you through flavor profiles. Buy the right bottle to enjoy in your hotel room night after night (prices start around £14 for about 7 ounces)—unlike wine, whisky has a long shelf life after it's opened. The bottles are extremely durable; ask them to demonstrate (Mon-Sat 10:30-17:30, closed Sun, 172 Canongate, tel. 0131/556-5864, www.wmcadenhead.com). They host hour-

Edinburgh Shopping

To Leith

PICARDY PL.

LEITH WALK

ROYAL TERRACE

Royal Terrace Gardens

GREENSIDE ROW

CALTON

200 Meters

200 Yards

Calton Hill

Regent Gardens

NATIONAL MONUMENT

CARLTON TERR.

DUGALD STEWART MONUMENT

NELSON MONUMENT

WATERLOO PLACE

REGENT TERR.

REGENT ROAD

ABBEYHILL CRES.

ABBEYHILL RD.

MARTYRS' MONUMENT

ST. ANDREW'S HOUSE

PALACE OF HOLYROOD-HOUSE

Old Calton Cemetery

CALTON ROAD

CALTON RD.

GATE

EDINBURGH

NEW ST.

CANONGATE CHURCH

WHITE HORSE CLOSE

QUEEN'S GALLERY (WC, CAFE & TICKETS TO HOLYROOD-HOUSE)

EAST MARKET ST.

JEFFREY ST.

PEOPLE'S STORY MUSEUM

ROBERT FERGUSSON MON.

(ROYAL MILE)

SCOTTISH PARLIAMENT

❿ ⓮ ❾ ⓭

CANONGATE

JOHN KNOX HOUSE

MUSEUM OF EDINBURGH

❻

STREET

BLACKFRIARS ST.

CADENHEAD'S WHISKY SHOP

BAKEHOUSE CL.

DYNAMIC EARTH

MUSEUM OF CHILDHOOD

WORLD'S END

ST. JOHN ST.

ST. MARY'S ST.

⓯ ← GULLAN'S CLOSE

HOLYROOD ROAD

To Arthur's Seat & Trail to Top of Salisbury Crags

NIDDRY ST.

BIKE RENTAL

CANONGATE

❶ Victoria Street
❷ Candlemaker Row
❸ Princes Street
❹ George Street
❺ Thistle Street
❻ Cadenhead's Whisky Shop
❼ Whiski Rooms Shop
❽ The Scotch Malt Whisky Society
❾ Nicolson Kiltmakers
❿ The Scottish Regimental Store
⓫ Howie Nicholsby's 21st Century Kilts
⓬ Walker Slater Tweed
⓭ Jewelry Shops
⓮ Cranachan & Crowdie
⓯ Pinnies & Poppy Seeds
⓰ I.J. Mellis Cheesemonger

long whisky tastings during the week—a hit with aficionados (£25, Mon-Fri at 17:45, best to arrange in advance in peak season).

Whiski Rooms Shop, just off the Royal Mile, comes with a knowledgeable, friendly staff that happily assists novices and experts alike to select the right bottle. Their adjacent bar usually has about 400 open bottles: Serious purchasers can get a sample. Even better, try one of their tastings. You have two options: You can order a flight in the bar, which comes with written information about each whisky you're sampling (variety of options starting around £25, available anytime the bar is open). Or you can opt for a guided tasting (£22.50 introductory tasting, £40 premium tasting with the really good stuff, chocolate and cheese pairings also available; takes about one hour, reserve ahead). If you're doing a flight or a tasting, you'll get a small discount voucher for buying a bottle in the store (shop open daily 10:00-18:00, bar until 24:00, both open later in Aug, 4 North Bank Street, tel. 0131/225-1532, www. whiskirooms.com).

Near the B&B Neighborhood: Perhaps the most accessible place to learn about local whiskies is conveniently located in the

B&B area south of the city center. **Wood-Winters** has a passion both for traditional spirits and for the latest innovations in Edinburgh's booze scene. It's well stocked with 300 whiskies and gins (a trendy alternative to Scotch), as well as wines and local craft beers. Manager Rob invites curious browsers to sample a wee dram; he loves to introduce customers to something new (Mon-Tue 10:00-19:00, Wed-Sat until 21:00, Sun 13:00-17:00, 91 Newington Road, www.woodwinters.com, tel. 0131/667-2760). For location, see the map on page 107.

Kilts and Other Traditional Scottish Gear

Many of the kilt outfitters you'll see along the Royal Mile are selling cheap knock-offs, made with printed rather than woven tartan material. If you want a serious kilt—or would enjoy window-shopping for one—try one of the places below. These have a few off-the-rack options, but to get a kilt in your specific tartan and size, they'll probably take your measurements, custom-make it, and ship it to you. For a good-quality outfit (kilt, jacket, and accessories), plan on spending in the neighborhood of £1,000.

Nicolson Kiltmakers has a respect for tradition and quality. Owner Gordon enlists and trains local craftspeople who specialize in traditionally manufactured kilts and accessories. He prides himself on keeping the old ways alive (in the face of deeply discounted "tartan tat") and actively cultivates the next generation of kiltmakers (daily 9:30-17:30, 189 Canongate, tel. 0131/558-2887, www. nicolsonkiltmakers.co.uk).

The Scottish Regimental Store, run by Nigel, is the official outfitter for military regiments. They sell top-of-the-line, formal kiltwear, as well as medals and pins that can be a more affordable souvenir (Mon-Thu 10:00-16:00, Fri-Sat until 17:00, closed Sun,

9 Jeffrey Street, tel. 0131/557-0249, www.scottishregimentalstore. co.uk).

Howie Nicholsby's 21st Century Kilts, in the New Town, brings this traditional craft into the present day. It's fun to peruse his photos of both kilted celebrities (from Alan Cumming to Vin Diesel) and wedding albums—which make you wish you were Scottish, engaged, and wealthy enough to hire Howie to outfit your bridal party (Howie asks that you make an appointment, though you're welcome to drop in if he happens to be there; closed Sun-Mon and Wed, 48 Thistle Street, send text to 07774-757-222, www.21stcenturykilts.com, howie@21stcenturykilts.com).

Tweed

Several places around town sell the famous Harris Tweed (the authentic stuff is handwoven on the Isle of Harris). **Walker Slater** is the place to go for top-quality tweed at top prices. They have three locations on Victoria Street, just below the Royal Mile near Grassmarket: menswear (at #16), womenswear (#44), and a sale shop

(#5). You'll find a rich interior and a wide variety of gorgeous jackets, scarves, bags, and more. This place feels elegant and exclusive (Mon-Sat 10:00-18:00, Sun 11:00-17:00, www.walkerslater.com).

Jewelry

Jewelry with Celtic designs, mostly made from sterling silver, is a popular and affordable souvenir. While you'll see these sold around town, two convenient shops face each other near the bottom of the Royal Mile: **Hamilton and Young,** which has a line of *Outlander*-inspired designs (173 Canongate), and **Celtic Design** (156 Canongate).

Food and Treats

Cranachan & Crowdie collects products (mostly edibles, some crafts) from more than 200 small, independent producers all over Scotland. The selection goes well beyond the mass-produced clichés, and American Beth and Scottish Fiona love to explain the story behind each item. They also offer up Scottish gin samples upon request (daily 11:00-18:00, on the Royal Mile at 263 Canongate, tel. 07951/587-420).

Pinnies & Poppy Seeds is a small, artisan bakery selling handmade shortbread made fresh daily from local, organic ingredients. Besides traditional all-butter shortbread, they have a rotating selection of 35 other flavors including chocolate hazelnut, rose pistachio, and cardamom white chocolate. They can package it for you to take home (lasts a month). They also sell other Scottish-made treats, both their own and from other local artisans, such as their Ballantyne Toffee from an old family recipe, gourmet marsh-mallows, shortbread truffles, and scented candles to match their shortbread flavors (Mon-Sat 10:00-17:30, closed Sun and in Jan, 26 St Mary's Street, tel. 0131/261-7012, run by American Jennifer).

I.J. Mellis Cheesemonger, tucked down Victoria Street just off the top of the Royal Mile, stocks a wide variety of Scottish, English, and international cheeses. They're as knowledgeable about cheese as they are generous with samples (Mon-Sat 9:30-19:00, Sun 11:00-18:00, 30A Victoria Street, tel. 0131/226-6215).

Nightlife in Edinburgh

▲▲Literary Pub Tour

This two-hour walk is interesting even if you think Sir Walter Scott won an Oscar for playing General Patton. You'll follow the witty dialogue of two actors as they debate whether the great literature of Scotland was high art or the creative re-creation of fun-loving louts fueled by a passion for whisky. You'll wander from the Grassmarket over the Old Town and New Town, with stops in three pubs, as your guides share their takes on Scotland's literary greats. The tour meets at the Beehive Inn on Grassmarket (£14, book online and save £2, May-Sept nightly at 19:30, April and Oct Thu-Sun, Jan-March Fri and Sun, Nov-Dec Fri only, tel. 0800-169-7410, www.edinburghliterarypubtour.co.uk).

▲Ghost Walks

A variety of companies lead spooky walks around town, provid-ing an entertaining and affordable night out (offered nightly, most around 19:00 and 21:00, easy socializing for solo travelers). These two options are the most established.

The theatrical and creatively staged **The Cadies & Witchery Tours,** the most established outfit, offers two different 1.25-hour walks: "Ghosts and Gore" (April-Aug only, in daylight and follow-ing a flatter route) and "Murder and Mystery" (year-round, after dark, hillier, more surprises and scares). The cost for either tour is the same (£10, includes book of stories, leaves from top of Royal Mile, outside the Witchery Restaurant, near Castle Esplanade, res-ervations required, tel. 0131/225-6745, www.witcherytours.com).

Auld Reekie Tours offers a scary array of walks daily and nightly (£12-16, 60-90 minutes, leaves from front steps of the Tron Church building on Cockburn Street, tel. 0131/557-4700, www.auldreekietours.com). Auld Reekie focuses on the paranormal, witch covens, and pagan temples, taking groups into the "haunted vaults" under the old bridges "where it was so dark, so crowded, and so squalid that the people there knew each other not by how they looked, but by how they sounded, felt, and smelt." If you want more, there's plenty of it (complete with screaming Gothic "jumpers").

Scottish Folk Evenings

A variety of £35-40 dinner shows, generally for tour groups intent on photographing old cultural clichés, are held in the huge halls of expensive hotels. (Prices are bloated to include 20 percent commissions.) Your "traditional" meal is followed by a full slate of swirling kilts, blaring bagpipes, and Scottish folk dancing with an old-time music hall emcee. If you like Lawrence Welk, you're in for a treat. But for most travelers, these are painfully cheesy. You can sometimes see the show without dinner for about two-thirds the price. The TI has fliers on all the latest venues.

Prestonfield House, a luxurious venue near the Dalkeith Road B&Bs, offers its kitschy "Taste of Scotland" folk evening with or without dinner Sunday to Friday. For £50, you get the show with two drinks and a wad of haggis; £65 buys you the same, plus a three-course meal and a half-bottle of wine (be there at 18:45, dinner at 19:00, show runs 20:00-22:00, April-Oct only). It's in the stables of "the handsomest house in Edinburgh," which is now home to the recommended Rhubarb Restaurant (Priestfield Road, a 10-minute walk from Dalkeith Road B&Bs, tel. 0131/225-7800, www.scottishshow.co.uk).

For something more lowbrow—and arguably more authentic—in summer, you can watch the **Princes Street Gardens Dancers** perform a range of Scottish country dancing. The volunteer troupe will demonstrate each dance, then invite spectators to give it a try (£5, June-July Mon 19:30-21:30, at Ross Bandstand in Princes Street Gardens—in the glen just below Edinburgh Castle, tel. 0131/228-8616, www.princesstreetgardensdancing.org.uk). The same group offers summer programs in other parts of town (see website for details).

Theater

Even outside festival time, Edinburgh is a fine place for lively and affordable theater. Pick up *The List* for a complete rundown of what's on (free at TI; also online at www.list.co.uk).

▲▲Live Music in Pubs

While traditional music venues have been eclipsed by beer-focused student bars, Edinburgh still has a few good pubs that can deliver a traditional folk-music fix. The monthly *Gig Guide* (free at TI, accommodations, and various pubs, www.gigguide.co.uk) lists sev-

EDINBURGH

eral places each night that have live music, divided by genre (pop, rock, world, and folk).

South of the Royal Mile: Sandy Bell's is a tight little pub with live folk music nightly from 21:30 (near National Museum of Scotland at 25 Forrest Road, tel. 0131/225-2751). Food is very simple (toasted sandwiches and pies), drinks are cheap, tables are small, and the vibe is local. They also have a few sessions earlier in the day (Sat at 14:00, Sun at 16:00, Mon at 17:30).

Captain's Bar is a cozy, music-focused pub with live sessions of folk and traditional music nightly around 21:00—see website for lineup (4 South College Street, http://captainsedinburgh.webs. com).

The Royal Oak is another good—if small—place for a dose of folk and blues (just off South Bridge opposite Chambers Road at 1 Infirmary Street, tel. 0131/557-2976).

The **Grassmarket** neighborhood (below the castle) bustles with live music and rowdy people spilling out of the pubs and into what was (once upon a time) a busy market square. While it used to be a mecca for Scottish folk music, today it's more youthful with a heavy-drinking, rockin' feel. It's fun to just wander through this area late at night and check out the scene. Thanks to the music and crowds, you'll know where to go...and where not to. Have a beer and follow your ear to places like **Biddy Mulligans** or **White Hart Inn** (both on Grassmarket). **Finnegans Wake,** on Victoria Street (which leads down to Grassmarket), also has live music in a variety of genres each night.

On the Royal Mile: Three characteristic pubs within a few steps of each other on High Street (opposite Radisson Hotel) offer a fun setting, classic pub architecture and ambience, and live music for the cost of a beer: **Whiski Bar** (mostly trad and folk; nightly at 22:00), **Royal Mile** (variety of genres; nightly at 22:00), and **Mitre Bar** (acoustic pop/rock with some trad; Fri-Sun at 21:30).

Just a block away (on South Bridge) is **Whistlebinkies Live Music Bar.** While they rarely do folk or Scottish trad, this is the most serious of the music pubs, with an actual stage and several acts nightly (schedule posted inside the door makes the genre clear; most nights music starts at 19:00 or 21:30, young crowd, fun energy, sticky floors, no cover, tel. 0131/557-5114). **No. 1 High Street** is an accessible little pub with a love of folk and traditional music (Wed-Thu from about 21:00, 1 High Street, tel. 0131/556-5758). **World's End,** across the street, also has music starting about 21:00 (trad on Thu, other genres Fri-Sat, 4 High Street, tel. 0131/556-3628).

In the New Town: All the beer drinkers seem to head for the pedestrianized Rose Street, famous for having the most pubs per square inch anywhere in Scotland—and plenty of live music.

Pubs near the B&B Neighborhood

The pubs in the B&B area don't typically have live music, but some are fun evening hangouts. **Leslie's Bar,** sitting between a working-class and an upper-class neighborhood, has two sides. Originally, the gang would go in on the right to gather around the great hardwood bar, glittering with a century of *Cheers* ambience. Meanwhile, the more delicate folks would slip in on the left, with its discreet doors, plush snugs (cozy private booths), and ornate ordering windows. Since 1896, this Victorian classic has been appreciated for both its real ales and its huge selection of fine whiskies (listed on a lengthy menu). Dive into the whisky mosh pit on the right, and let them show you how whisky can become "a very good friend." (daily 12:00-24:00, 49 Ratcliffe Terrace, tel. 0131/667-7205.)

Other good pubs in this area include **The Old Bell** (uphill from Leslie's, popular and cozy, with big TV screens) and **The Salisbury Arms** (bigger, more sprawling, feels upscale); both are described later, under "Eating in Edinburgh."

Sleeping in Edinburgh

To stay in the city center, you'll likely have to stay in a larger hotel or more impersonal guesthouse. For the classic B&B experience, look to the area south of town. A number of B&Bs cluster along Dalkeith Road and on side streets just off of it (south of the Royal Commonwealth Pool), and also along the parallel street Mayfield Gardens (which leads directly to South Bridge in the center). From either area, it's a long walk to the city center (about 25 minutes) or a quick bus or taxi/Uber ride.

While many of my B&B listings are not cheap (generally around £90-130), most come with friendly hosts and great cooked breakfasts. And they're generally cheaper than staying at a city-center hotel.

Note that during the Festival in August, prices skyrocket and most places do not accept bookings for one- or even two-night stays. If coming in August, book far in advance. Conventions, rugby matches, school holidays, and weekends can make finding a room tough at other times of year, too. In winter, when demand is light, some B&Bs close, and prices at all accommodations get soft.

For some travelers, short-term Airbnb-type rentals can be a good alternative to hotels; search for places in my recommended hotel and B&B neighborhoods. See page 452 for more information.

B&BS SOUTH OF THE CITY CENTER

At these not-quite-interchangeable places, character is provided by the personality quirks of the hosts and sometimes the decor. In

EDINBURGH

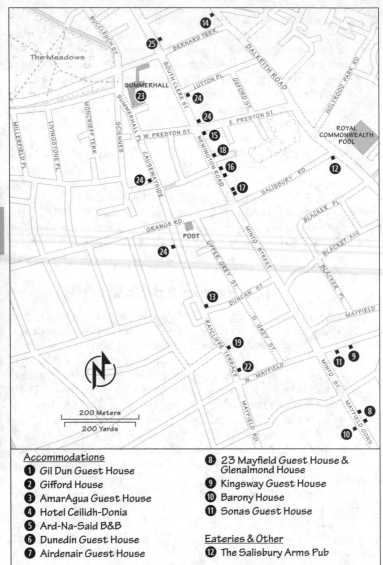

Accommodations
1 Gil Dun Guest House
2 Gifford House
3 AmarAgua Guest House
4 Hotel Ceilidh-Donia
5 Ard-Na-Said B&B
6 Dunedin Guest House
7 Airdenair Guest House
8 23 Mayfield Guest House & Glenalmond House
9 Kingsway Guest House
10 Barony House
11 Sonas Guest House

Eateries & Other
12 The Salisbury Arms Pub

general, cash is preferred and can lead to discounted rates. Book direct—you will pay a much higher rate through a booking service.

Near the B&Bs, you'll find plenty of fine eateries (see "Eating in Edinburgh," later) and some good, classic pubs (see "Nightlife in Edinburgh," earlier). A few places have their own private parking; others offer access to easy, free street parking (ask when booking—or better yet, don't rent a car for your time in Edinburgh). The near-

**B&Bs & Restaurants
South of the City Center**

To Duddingston Village, Dr. Neil's Garden & 21

QUEEN'S DRIVE

DUDDINGSTON LOW ROAD

Preston Field Golf Course

PRESTONFIELD HOUSE 20

1
2 4
MARCHHALL CRES
PRIESTFIELD RD
5
KIRKHILL RD
KIRKHILL GARDENS
KIRKHILL TERRACE
KILMAURS RD
6
7 KIRKHILL DRIVE
PRESTONFIELD TERR.
PRIESTFIELD ROAD

TERRACE
E. MAYFIELD
QUEEN'S CRESCENT
DALKEITH ROAD (A7)
3
PRESTONFIELD AVE.
B

Waverley Park

COPPER RD
MCLAREN RD
Newington Cemetery

To Cameron Toll Shopping Centre & England

EDINBURGH

13 The Old Bell Inn	20 Rhubarb Restaurant & Prestonfield House
14 Aizle	21 To The Sheep Heid Inn, Duddingston Village & Dr. Neil's Garden
15 Southpour	
16 Ristorante Isola & WoodWinters Whisky Shop	22 Leslie's Bar
17 Voujon & Edinburgh Bakehouse	23 Pickering's Gin Distillery
18 Aplary	24 Supermarket (4)
19 Earthy	25 Launderette

est launderette is Ace Cleaning Centre (which picks up and drops off; see page 23).

Taxi or Uber fare between the city center and the B&Bs is about £7. If taking the bus from the B&Bs into the city, hop off at the South Bridge stop for the Royal Mile (£1.60 single ride, £4 day ticket, use exact change; see the next page for more bus specifics).

Near Dalkeith Road

Most of my B&Bs near Dalkeith Road are located south of the Royal Commonwealth Pool. This comfortable, safe neighborhood is a ten-minute bus ride from the Royal Mile.

To get here from the train station, catch the bus around the corner on North Bridge: Exit the station onto Princes Street, turn right, cross the street, and walk up the bridge to the bus stop in front of the Marks & Spencer department store (#14, #30, or #33). About 10 minutes into the ride, after following South Clerk Street for a while, the bus makes a left turn, then a right. Depending on where you're staying, you'll get off at the first or second stop after the turn (confirm specifics with your B&B).

$$ Gil Dun Guest House, with eight rooms—some contemporary, others more traditional—is on a quiet cul-de-sac just off Dalkeith Road. It's comfortable, pleasant, and managed with care by Gerry and Bill; Maggie helps out and keeps things immaculate (family rooms, two-night minimum in summer preferred, limited off-street parking, 9 Spence Street, tel. 0131/667-1368, www.gildun.co.uk, gildun.edin@btinternet.com).

$$ Gifford House, on busy Dalkeith Road, is a bright, flowery retreat with six peaceful rooms (some with ornate cornices and views of Arthur's Seat) and compact, modern bathrooms (RS%, family rooms, cash preferred, street parking, 103 Dalkeith Road, tel. 0131/667-4688, www.giffordhouseedinburgh.com, giffordhouse@btinternet.com, David and Margaret).

$$ AmarAgua Guest House is an inviting Victorian home away from home, with five welcoming rooms, a Japanese garden, and eager hosts (one double has private bath down the hall, 2-night minimum, no kids under 12, street parking, 10 Kilmaurs Terrace, tel. 0131/667-6775, www.amaragua.co.uk, reservations@amaragua.co.uk, Lucia and Kuan).

$$ Hotel Ceilidh-Donia is bigger (17 rooms) and more hotel-like than other nearby B&Bs, with a bar and a small reception area, but managers Kevin and Susan and their staff provide a guesthouse warmth. The back deck is a pleasant place to sit on a warm day (family room, two-night minimum on peak-season weekends, 14 Marchhall Crescent, tel. 0131/667-2743, www.hotelceilidh-donia.co.uk, reservations@hotelceilidh-donia.co.uk).

$$ Ard-Na-Said B&B, in an elegant 1875 Victorian house, has seven bright, spacious rooms with modern bathrooms, including one ground-floor room with a pleasant patio (two-night minimum preferred in summer, off-street parking, 5 Priestfield Road, tel. 0131/283-6524, mobile 07476-606-202, www.ardnasaid.co.uk, info@ardnasaid.co.uk, Audrey Ballantine and her son Steven).

$$ Dunedin Guest House (dun-EE-din) is bright and plush, with seven well-decorated rooms, an angelic atrium, and a spacious breakfast room/lounge with TV (family rooms, one room with private bath down the hall, includes continental breakfast, extra charge for cooked breakfast, limited off-street parking, 8 Priestfield Road, tel. 0131/468-3339, www.dunedinguesthouse.co.uk, reservations@dunedinguesthouse.co.uk, Mary and Tony).

$ Airdenair Guest House is a hands-off guesthouse, with no formal host greeting (you'll get an access code to let yourself in) and a self-serve breakfast buffet. But the price is nice and the five simple rooms are well-maintained (29 Kilmaurs Road, tel. 0131/468-0173, http://airdenair-edinburgh.co.uk, contact@airdenair-edinburgh.co.uk, Duncan).

On or near Mayfield Gardens

These places are just a couple of blocks from the Dalkeith Road options, along the busy Newington Road (which turns in to Mayfield Gardens). All have private parking. To reach them from the center, hop on bus #3, #7, #8, #29, #31, #37, or #49. Note: Some of these buses depart from the second bus stop, a bit farther along North Bridge. To ride from these guesthouses to the city center, simply hop on any bus (except #47).

$$$ At 23 Mayfield Guest House, Ross and Kathleen (with their wee helpers Ethan and Alfie) rent seven splurge-worthy, thoughtfully appointed rooms complete with high-tech bathrooms (rain showers and motion-sensor light-up mirrors). Little extras—such as locally sourced gourmet breakfasts, an inviting guest lounge outfitted with leather-bound Sir Arthur Conan Doyle books, an "honesty bar," and classic black-and-white movie screenings—make you feel like royalty (RS% if you pay cash, family room for up to 4, two-night minimum preferred in summer, 23 Mayfield Gardens, tel. 0131/667-5806, www.23mayfield.co.uk, info@23mayfield.co.uk). They also rent an apartment (details on website).

$$$ Glenalmond House, run by Jimmy and Fiona Mackie, has nine elegantly decorated rooms featuring elaborately carved mahogany pieces (RS% if you pay cash, family room, no kids under 5, 25 Mayfield Gardens, tel. 0131/668-2392, www.glenalmondhouse.com, enquiries@glenalmondhouse.com).

$$ Kingsway Guest House, with seven stylish rooms, is owned by conscientious, delightful Gary and Lizzie, who have thought of all the little touches, such as a DVD library and in-room Internet radios, and offer good advice on neighborhood eats (RS% if you pay cash, family room, one room with private bath down

EDINBURGH

the hall, 5 East Mayfield, tel. 0131/667-5029, www.edinburgh-guesthouse.com, booking@kingswayguesthouse.com).

$$ Barony House is run with infectious enthusiasm by Aussies Paul and Susan. Their eight doubles are each named and themed, and lovingly decorated by Susan, who's made the beautiful fabric headboards and created some of the art (she also bakes welcome pastries for guests). Two of the rooms are next door, in a former servants quarters, now a peaceful retreat with access to a shared kitchen (three-night minimum preferred in summer, no kids under 9, 20 Mayfield Gardens, tel. 0131/662-9938, www.baronyhouse.co.uk, booknow@baronyhouse.co.uk).

$$ Sonas Guest House is nothing fancy—just a simple, easy-going place with seven rooms, six of which have bathtubs (family room, 3 East Mayfield, tel. 0131/667-2781, www.sonasguesthouse.com, info@sonasguesthouse.com, Irene and Dennis).

HOTELS IN THE CITY CENTER

While a B&B generally provides more warmth, character, and lower prices, a city-center hotel gives you more walkability and access to sights and Edinburgh's excellent restaurant and pub scene. Prices are very high in peak season and drop substantially in off-season (a good time to shop around). In each case, I'd skip the institutional breakfast and eat out. You'll generally pay about £10 a day to park near these hotels.

$$$$ Macdonald Holyrood Hotel is a four-star splurge, with 157 rooms up the street from the parliament building and Holyroodhouse Palace. With its classy marble-and-wood decor, fitness center, spa, and pool, it's hard to leave. On a gray winter day in Edinburgh, this could be worth it (pricey breakfast, elevator, pay valet parking, near bottom of Royal Mile, across from Dynamic Earth, 81 Holyrood Road, tel. 0131/528-8000, www.macdonaldhotels.co.uk, newres@macdonald-hotels.co.uk).

$$$$ The Inn on the Mile is your trendy, central option, filling a renovated old bank building right in the heart of the Royal Mile (at North Bridge/South Bridge). The nine bright and stylish rooms are an afterthought to the busy upmarket pub, which is where you'll check in. If you don't mind some noise (from the pub and the busy street) and climbing lots of stairs, it's a handy home base (breakfast extra, complimentary drink, 82 High Street, tel. 0131/556-9940, www.theinnonthemile.co.uk, info@theinnonthemile.co.uk).

$$$$ The Inn Place, part of a small chain, fills the zformer headquarters of *The Scotsman* newspaper—a few steep steps below the Royal Mile—with 41 characterless, minimalist rooms ("bunk rooms" for 6-8 people, best deals on weekdays, breakfast extra, elevator, 20 Cockburn Street, tel. 0131/526-3780, www.

theinnplaceedinburgh.co.uk, reception@theinnplaceedinburgh. co.uk).

$$$ Grassmarket Hotel's 42 rooms are quirky and fun, from the Dandy comic-book wallpaper to the giant wall map of Edinburgh equipped with planning-your-visit magnets. The hotel is in a great location right on Grassmarket overlooking the Covenanters Memorial and above Biddy Mulligans Bar (family rooms, two-night minimum on weekends, elevator only serves half the rooms, 94 Grassmarket, tel. 0131/220-2299, www.grassmarkethotel. co.uk).

$$$ The Place Hotel, sister of the Inn Place listed earlier, has a fine New Town location 10 minutes north of the train station. It occupies three grand Georgian townhouses, with no elevator and long flights of stairs leading up to the 47 contemporary, no-frills rooms. Their outdoor terrace with retractable roof and heaters is a popular place to unwind (save money with a smaller city double, 34 York Place, tel. 0131/556-7575, www.yorkplace-edinburgh.co.uk, frontdesk@yorkplace-edinburgh.co.uk).

$$ Motel One Edinburgh Royal, part of a stylish German budget-hotel chain, is between the train station and the Royal Mile; it feels upscale and trendy for its price range (208 rooms, pay more for a park view or less for a windowless "budget" room with skylight, breakfast extra, elevator, 18 Market Street, tel. 0131/220-0730, www.motel one.com, edinburgh-royal@motel-one.com; second location in the New Town/shopping zone at 10 Princes Street).

Chain Hotels in the Center: Besides my recommendations above, you'll find a number of cookie-cutter chain hotels close to the Royal Mile, including **Jurys Inn** (43 Jeffrey Street), **Ibis Hotel** (two convenient branches: near the Tron Church and another around the corner along the busy South Bridge), **Holiday Inn Express** (two locations: just off the Royal Mile at 300 Cowgate and one in the New Town), and **Travelodge Central** (just below the Royal Mile at 33 St. Mary's Street; additional locations in the New Town).

HOSTELS

¢ **Baxter Hostel** is your boutique hostel option. Occupying one floor of a Georgian townhouse (up several long, winding flights of stairs and below two more hostels), it has tons of ambience: tartan wallpaper, wood paneling, stone walls, decorative tile floors, and a beautifully restored kitchen/lounge that you'd want in your own house. Space is tight—hallways are snug, and five dorms (42 beds) share one bathroom. Another room, with four beds, has its own en-suite bathroom (includes scrambled-egg breakfast; small

EDINBURGH

1 Macdonald Holyrood Hotel
2 The Inn on the Mile
3 The Inn Place
4 Grassmarket Hotel
5 The Place Hotel
6 Motel One Edinburgh (2)

7 Baxter Hostel
8 To Edinburgh Central Youth Hostel
9 SafeStay Edinburgh Hostel
10 High Street Hostel
11 Royal Mile Backpackers Hostel
12 Castle Rock Hostel

Edinburgh Hotels

EDINBURGH

*Map labels:*

To ❽ & Leith
LEITH WALK
PICARDY PL.
GREENSIDE ROW
ROYAL TERRACE
Royal Terrace Gardens
CALTON
200 Meters
200 Yards
Calton Hill
Regent Gardens
CARLTON TERR.
N
NATIONAL MONUMENT
DUGALD STEWART MONUMENT
NELSON MONUMENT
REGENT TERR.
REGENT ROAD
ABBEY HILL RD.
ABBEYHILL CRES.
WATERLOO PLACE
MARTYRS' MONUMENT
Old Calton Cemetery
ST. ANDREW'S HOUSE
REGENT ROAD
PALACE OF HOLYROOD-HOUSE
GATE
CALTON ROAD
CALTON RD.
WHITE HORSE CLOSE
NEW ST.
CANONGATE CHURCH
PEOPLE'S STORY MUSEUM
ROBERT FERGUSSON MON.
(ROYAL MILE)
CANONGATE
SCOTTISH PARLIAMENT
QUEEN'S GALLERY (WC, CAFE & TICKETS TO HOLYROOD-HOUSE)
EAST MARKET ST.
JEFFREY ST.
JOHN KNOX HOUSE
STREET
WORLD'S END
MUSEUM OF EDINBURGH
CADENHEAD'S WHISKY SHOP
MUSEUM OF CHILDHOOD
GULLAN'S CLOSE
BIKE RENTAL
ST. MARY'S ST.
ST. JOHN ST.
BAKEHOUSE CL.
HOLYROOD ROAD
❶
DYNAMIC EARTH
To Arthur's Seat & Trail to Top of Salisbury Crags
❷
❶❶
BLACKFRIARS ST.
❶❶
❾
NIDDRY ST.
SOUTH BRIDGE
COWGATE
CANONGATE
VIEWCRAIG ST.
DUMBIEDYKES ST.
Salisbury Crags
Ⓑ
14, 30 & 33
S. COLLEGE ST.
INFIRMARY ST.
DRUMMOND ST.
FOXBURGH PL.
PLEASANCE
To Dalkeith Road
SOUTH SIDE
Holyrood Park
NICOLSON ST.
HILL PL.
BROWN ST.
200 Meters
200 Yards
To Arthur's Seat & Dalkeith Road B & B Area
POTTERROW
CRICHTON
CHAPEL ST.
W. RICHMOND
RICHMOND
To Dalkeith Road
W. RICHMOND ST.
ST. LEONARD'S ST.
ST. LEONARD'S HILL
QUEEN'S DRIVE
EAST CROSSCAUSEWAY
BOWMONT ST. PL.
BUCCLEUCH PL.
BUCCLEUCH ST.
CLERK ST.
BANKEILLOR ST.
MONTAGUE ST.
HERMITS CROFT

fee for towel, travel adapters, and locks; 5 West Register Street, tel. 0131/503-1001, www.thebaxter.eu, info@thebaxter.eu).

¢ **Edinburgh Central Youth Hostel** rents 251 beds in 72 rooms accommodating three to six people (all with private bathrooms and lockers). Guests can eat cheaply in the cafeteria, or cook for the cost of groceries in the members' kitchen (private rooms available, pay laundry, 15-minute downhill walk from Waverley Station—head down Leith Walk, pass through two roundabouts, hostel is on your left—or take Lothian bus #22 or #25 to Elm Rowe, 9 Haddington Place off Leith Walk, tel. 0131/524-2090, www.syha.org.uk, central@syha.org.uk).

¢ **SafeStay Edinburgh,** just off the Royal Mile, rents 272 bunks in pleasing purple-accented rooms. Dorm rooms have 4 to 12 beds, and there are also a few private singles and twin rooms (all rooms have private bathrooms). Bar 50 in the basement has an inviting lounge. Half of the rooms function as a university dorm during the school year, becoming available just in time for the tourists (breakfast extra, kitchen, laundry, free daily walking tour, 50 Blackfriars Street, tel. 0131/524-1989, www.safestay.com, reservations-edi@safestay.com).

¢ **Cheap and Scruffy Bohemian Hostels in the Center:** These three sister hostels—popular crash pads for young, hip backpackers—are beautifully located in the noisy center (some locations also have private rooms, www.macbackpackers.com): **High Street Hostel** (140 beds, 8 Blackfriars Street, just off High Street/Royal Mile, tel. 0131/557-3984); **Royal Mile Backpackers** (40 beds, 105 High Street, tel. 0131/557-6120); and **Castle Rock Hostel** (300 beds, just below the castle and above the pubs, 15 Johnston Terrace, tel. 0131/225-9666).

Eating in Edinburgh

Reservations for restaurants are essential in August and on weekends, and a good idea anytime. Children aren't allowed in many of the pubs.

THE OLD TOWN

Pricey places abound on the Royal Mile (listed later). While those are tempting, I prefer the two areas described first, each within a few minutes' walk of the Mile—just far enough to offer better value and a bit less touristy crush.

On Victoria Street, Near Grassmarket

$$$$ **Grainstore Restaurant,** a sedate and dressy world of wood, stone, and candles tucked away above busy Victoria Street, has served Scottish produce with a French twist for more than two

decades. While they have inexpensive £14 two-course lunch specials, dinner is à la carte. Reservations are recommended (daily 12:00-14:30 & 18:00-21:30, 30 Victoria Street, tel. 0131/225-7635, www.grainstore-restaurant.co.uk).

$$$ Maison Bleue Restaurant is popular for their à la carte French/Scottish/North African menu and dinner special before 18:30 (18:00 on Fri-Sat; open daily 12:00-22:00, 36 Victoria Street, tel. 0131/226-1900).

$ Oink carves from a freshly roasted pig each afternoon for sandwiches that come in "oink" or "grunter" sizes. Watch the pig shrink in the front window throughout the day (daily 11:00-18:00 or whenever they run out of meat, cash only, 34 Victoria Street, tel. 01890/761-355). There's another location at the bottom end of the Royal Mile, near the parliament building (at 82 Canongate).

Near the National Museum

These restaurants are happily removed from the Royal Mile melee and skew to a youthful clientele with few tourists. After passing the Greyfriars Bobby statue and the National Museum, fork left onto Forrest Road.

$ Union of Genius is a creative soup kitchen with a strong identity. They cook up a selection of delicious soups with fun foodie twists each morning at their main location in Leith, then deliver them to this shop by bicycle (for environmental reasons). These are supplemented with good salads and fresh-baked breads. The "flight" comes with three small cups of soup and three types of bread. Line up at the counter, then either take your soup to go or sit in the cramped interior, with a couple of tables and counter seating (Mon-Fri 10:00-16:00, Sat from 12:00, closed Sun, 8 Forrest Road, tel. 0131/226-4436).

$$ Mums is a kitschy diner serving up comfort food just like mum used to make. The menu runs to huge portions of heavy, greasy Scottish/British standards—bangers (sausages), meat pies, burgers, and artery-clogging breakfasts (served until 12:00)—all done with a foodie spin, including vegetarian options (Mon-Sat 9:00-22:00, Sun from 10:00, 4A Forrest Road, tel. 0131/260-9806).

$$ Ting Thai Caravan, just around the corner from the previous listings, is a casual, industrial-mod, food-focused eatery selling adventurous Thai street food (daily 11:30-22:00, Fri-Sat until 23:00, 8 Teviot Place, tel. 0131/225-9801).

Dessert: The **Frisky** frozen-yogurt shop, on Forrest Road, makes for a fun treat.

Along the Royal Mile

Though the eateries along this most-crowded stretch of the city are invariably touristy, the scene is fun. Sprinkled in this list are some

EDINBURGH

1. Grainstore, Maison Bleue & Oink
2. Union of Genius, Mums & Frisky
3. Ting Thai Caravan
4. The Witchery by the Castle
5. Angels with Bagpipes
6. Devil's Advocate
7. Wedgwood Restaurant
8. David Bann
9. Edinburgh Larder
10. Mimi's Bakehouse Picnic Parlour
11. Clarinda's Tea Room
12. Hendersons (3)
13. Café Royal
14. The Dome Restaurant
15. Dishoom
16. St. Andrew's & St. George's Church Undercroft Café
17. Marks & Spencer Food Hall
18. Sainsbury's

Edinburgh Eateries

EDINBURGH

200 Meters
200 Yards

CALTON

Royal Terrace Gardens
ROYAL TERRACE
PICARDY PL.
LEITH WALK
To Leith
GREENSIDE ROW
Calton Hill
Regent Gardens
NATIONAL MONUMENT
DUGALD STEWART MONUMENT
NELSON MONUMENT
WATERLOO PLACE
MARTYRS' MONUMENT
Old Calton Cemetery
ST. ANDREW'S HOUSE
CALTON ROAD
CALTON RD.
REGENT ROAD
REGENT TERR.
REGENT TERRACE
CARLTON TERR.
ABBEYHILL CRES.
ABBEYHILL RD.
PALACE OF HOLYROOD-HOUSE
GATE
QUEEN'S GALLERY (WC, CAFE & TICKETS TO HOLYROODHOUSE)
WHITE HORSE CLOSE
CANONGATE CHURCH
PEOPLE'S STORY MUSEUM
ROBERT FERGUSSON MON.
(ROYAL MILE)
SCOTTISH PARLIAMENT
❶❶
EAST MARKET ST.
JEFFREY ST.
NEW ST.
CANONGATE
MUSEUM OF EDINBURGH
CADENHEAD'S WHISKY SHOP
BAKEHOUSE CL.
❶❷
DYNAMIC EARTH
To Arthur's Seat & Trail to Top of Salisbury Crags
JOHN KNOX HOUSE
❸❷
STREET
❸❶
❸❶
❸❶
MUSEUM OF CHILDHOOD
❷❸
❼
❶❶
ST. MARY'S ST.
WORLD'S END
GULLAN'S CLOSE
ST. JOHN ST.
HOLYROOD ROAD
BIKE RENTAL
❾
❽
BLACKFRIARS ST.
COWGATE
NIDDRY ST.
CANONGATE
VIEWCRAIG ST.
DUMBIEDYKES ST.
Salisbury Crags
SOUTH BRIDGE
14, 30 & 33
❸
❷❻
INFIRMARY ST.
DRUMMOND ST.
PLEASANCE
S. COLLEGE ST.
ROXBURGH PL.
To Dalkeith Road
❷❺
NICOLSON ST.
HILL PL.
W. RICHMOND
RICHMOND
BROWN ST.
To Dalkeith Road
SOUTH SIDE
POTTERROW
Holyrood Park
To Arthur's Seat & Dalkeith Road B & B Area
200 Meters
200 Yards

❶❾ Le Café St. Honoré
❷⓿ The Bon Vivant
❷❶ El Cartel

Pubs & Nightlife
❷❷ Deacon Brodie's Tavern
❷❸ The World's End Pub
❷❹ Sandy Bell's Pub
❷❺ Captain's Bar

❷❻ The Royal Oak Pub
❷❼ Biddy Mulligans
❷❽ White Hart Inn
❷❾ Finnegans Wake
❸⓿ Whiski Bar, Royal Mile & Mitre Bar
❸❶ Whistlebinkies Bar
❸❷ No. 1 High Street Pub

places a block or two off the main drag offering better values and maybe fewer tourists.

Sit-Down Restaurants

These are listed roughly in downhill order, starting at the castle. You'll have more success getting into any of these with a reservation, especially on weekends.

$$$$ The Witchery by the Castle is set in a lushly decorated 16th-century building just below the castle on the Royal Mile, with wood paneling, antique candlesticks, tapestries, and opulent red-leather upholstery. Frequented by celebrities, tourists, and locals out for a splurge, the restaurant's emphasis is on pricey Scottish meats and seafood. Their Secret Garden dining room, in a separate building farther back, is also a special setting—down some steps and in a fanciful room with French doors opening on to a terrace. Reserve ahead for either space, dress smartly, and bear in mind you're paying a premium for the ambience (two-course lunch specials—also available before 17:30 and after 22:30, three-course dinner menu, daily 12:00-23:30, tel. 0131/225-5613, www. thewitchery.com).

$$$ Angels with Bagpipes, conveniently located across from St. Giles' Cathedral, serves sophisticated Scottish staples in its dark, serious, plush interior (two- and three-course lunches, tasting menus at dinner, daily 12:00-21:30, 343 High Street, tel. 0131/220-1111, www.angelswithbagpipes.co.uk).

$$$ Devil's Advocate is a popular gastropub that hides down the narrow lane called Advocates Close, directly across the Royal Mile from St. Giles'. With an old cellar setting—exposed stone and heavy beams—done up in modern style, it feels like a mix of old and new Edinburgh. Creative whisky cocktails kick off a menu that dares to be adventurous, but with a respect for Scottish tradition (daily 12:00-22:00, later for drinks, 8 Advocates Close, tel. 0131/225-4465).

$$$$ Wedgwood Restaurant is romantic, contemporary, chic, and as gourmet as possible with no pretense. Paul Wedgwood cooks while his wife Lisa serves with appetizing charm. The cuisine: creative, modern Scottish with an international twist and a whiff of Asia. The pigeon-and-haggis starter is scrumptious. Paul and Lisa believe in making the meal the event of the evening—don't come here to eat and run. I like the ground level with the Royal Mile view, but the busy kitchen ambience in the basement is also nice (fine wine by the glass, daily 12:00-15:00 & 18:00-22:00, reservations advised, 267 Canongate on Royal Mile, tel. 0131/558-8737, www.wedgwoodtherestaurant.co.uk).

$$$ David Bann is a worthwhile stop for well-heeled vegetarians in need of a break from the morning fry-up. While vegetarian as can be, this place doesn't have even a hint of hippie. It's upscale (it has a cocktail bar), sleek, minimalist, and stylish (gorgeously presented dishes), serious about quality, and organic. Reserve ahead (decadent desserts, Mon-Fri 12:00-22:00, Sat-Sun from 11:00, vegan and gluten-free options, just off the Royal Mile at 56 St. Mary's Street, tel. 0131/556-5888, www.davidbann.co.uk).

Quick, Easy, and Cheap Lunch Options

$ Edinburgh Larder promises "a taste of the country" in the center of the city. They focus on high-quality, homestyle breakfast and lunches made from seasonal, local ingredients. The café, with table service, is a convivial space with rustic tables filled by local families. The takeaway shop next door has counter service and a few dine-in tables (Mon-Fri 8:00-16:00, Sat-Sun from 9:00, 15 Blackfriars Street, tel. 0131/556-6922).

$ Mimi's Bakehouse Picnic Parlour, a handy Royal Mile outpost of a prizewinning bakery, serves up baked goods—try the scones—and sandwiches in their cute and modern shop (daily 9:00-18:00, 250 Canongate, tel. 0131/556-6632).

$ Clarinda's Tea Room, near the bottom of the Royal Mile, is a charming and girlish time warp—a fine and tasty place to relax after touring the Mile or the Palace of Holyroodhouse. Stop in for a quiche, salad, or soup lunch. It's also great for sandwiches and tea and cake anytime (Mon-Sat 9:00-16:30, Sun from 10:00, 69 Canongate, tel. 0131/557-1888).

$$ Hendersons is a bright and casual local chain with good vegetarian dishes to go or eat in (daily 9:00-17:00, 67 Holyrood Road—three minutes off Royal Mile near Scottish Parliament end, tel. 0131/557-1606; for more details, see the Hendersons listing later, under "The New Town").

Historic Pubs Along the Mile

To drink a pint or grab some forgettable pub grub in historic surroundings, consider one of the landmark pubs described on my self-guided walk: **$$ Deacon Brodie's Tavern,** at a dead-center location on the Royal Mile (a sloppy pub on the ground floor with a sloppy restaurant upstairs) or **$$ The World's End Pub,** farther down the Mile at Canongate (a colorful old place dishing up hearty meals from a creative menu in a fun, dark, and noisy space, 4 High Street). Both serve pub meals and are open long hours daily.

THE NEW TOWN

In the Georgian part of town, you'll find a bustling world of office workers, students, and pensioners doing their thing. All of these eateries are within a few minutes' walk of the TI and Waverley Station.

EDINBURGH

Elegant Spaces near Princes Street

These places provide a staid glimpse at grand old Edinburgh. The ambience is generally better than the food.

Café Royal is a movie producer's dream pub—the perfect *fin de siècle* setting for a coffee, beer, or light meal. (In fact, parts of *Chariots of Fire* were filmed here.) Drop in, if only to admire the 1880 tiles featuring famous inventors (daily 12:00-14:30 & 17:00-21:30, bar food available all day, two blocks from Waverley Mall on 19 West Register Street, tel. 0131/556-1884, www.caferoyaledinburgh.co.uk). There are two eateries here: the noisy **$$ pub** and the dressier **$$$ restaurant,** specializing in oysters, fish, and game (reserve for dinner—it's quite small and understandably popular).

$$$$ The Dome Restaurant, in what was a fancy bank, serves modern international cuisine around a classy bar and under the elegant 19th-century skylight dome. With soft jazz and chic, white-tablecloth ambience, it feels a world apart. Come here not for the food, but for the opulent atmosphere (daily 12:00-23:00, food served until 21:30, reserve for dinner, open for a drink any time under the dome; the adjacent, more intimate Club Room serves food Mon-Thu 10:00-16:00, Fri-Sat until 21:30, closed Sun; 14 George Street, tel. 0131/624-8624, www.thedomeedinburgh.com).

Casual and Cheap near St. Andrew Square

$$ Dishoom, in the New Town, is the first non-London outpost of this popular Bombay café. You'll enjoy upscale Indian cuisine in a bustling, dark, 1920s dining room on the second floor overlooking St. Andrew Square. You can also order from the same menu in the basement bar at night (daily 9:00-23:00, 3A St. Andrew Square, tel. 0131/202-6406).

$ St. Andrew's and St. George's Church Undercroft Café, in the basement of a fine old church, is the cheapest place in town for lunch. Your tiny bill helps support the Church of Scotland (Mon-Fri lunch only, closed Sat-Sun, at 13 George Street, just off St. Andrew Square, tel. 0131/225-3847).

Supermarkets: Marks & Spencer Food Hall offers an assortment of tasty hot foods, prepared sandwiches, fresh bakery items, a wide selection of wines and beverages, and plastic utensils at the checkout queue. It's just a block from the Scott Monument and the picnic-perfect Princes Street Gardens (Mon-Sat 8:00-19:00, Thu until 20:00, Sun 11:00-18:00, Princes Street 54—separate stairway next to main M&S entrance leads directly to food hall, tel. 0131/225-2301). **Sainsbury's** supermarket, a block off Princes Street, also offers grab-and-go items (daily 7:00-22:00, on corner of Rose Street on St. Andrew Square, across the street from Jenners).

Hip Eateries on and near Thistle Street

For something a little more modern and food-focused, head a few more minutes deeper into the New Town to find Thistle Street. This strip and its surrounding lanes are packed with more enticing eateries than the rest of the New Town put together. Browse the options here, but tune into these favorites.

$$$ Le Café St. Honoré, tucked away like a secret bit of old Paris, is a charming place with friendly service and walls lined with wine bottles. It serves French-Scottish cuisine in tight, Old World, cut-glass elegance to a dressy crowd (three-course lunch and dinner specials, daily 12:00-14:00 & 17:30-22:00, reservations smart—ask to sit upstairs, down Thistle Street from Hanover Street, 34 Northwest Thistle Street Lane, tel. 0131/226-2211, www.cafesthonore. com).

$$$ The Bon Vivant is woody, youthful, and candlelit, with a rotating menu of French/Scottish dishes, a good cocktail list, and a companion wine shop next door. They have fun tapas plates and heartier dishes, served either in the bar up front or in the restaurant in back (daily 12:00-22:00, 55 Thistle Street, tel. 0131/225-3275, www.bonvivantedinburgh.co.uk).

$$ Hendersons has fed a generation of New Town vegetarians hearty cuisine and salads. Even carnivores love this place for its delectable salads, desserts, and smoothies. Hendersons has two separate eateries: Their main restaurant, facing Hanover Street, is self-service by day but has table service after 17:00. Each evening after 19:00, they have pleasant live music—generally guitar or jazz (Mon-Sat 9:00-22:00, Sun 10:30-16:00, between Queen and George streets at 94 Hanover Street, tel. 0131/225-2131). Just around the corner on Thistle Street, **Hendersons Vegan** has a strictly vegan menu and feels a bit more casual (daily 12:00-21:30, tel. 0131/225-2605).

$ El Cartel is a youthful place serving up good tacos and other Mexican dishes in a cramped, edgy atmosphere. Enjoy a drink at their sister restaurant the Bon Vivant (listed earlier) while waiting for a table to open up (daily 12:00-22:00, 64 Thistle Street, tel. 0131/226-7171).

IN THE B&B NEIGHBORHOOD

Nearly all of these places (except for The Sheep Heid Inn) are within a 10-minute walk of my recommended B&Bs. For locations, see the map on page 107. For a cozy drink after dinner, visit the recommended pubs in the area (see "Nightlife in Edinburgh," earlier).

Pub Grub

$$ The Salisbury Arms Pub, with a nice garden terrace and separate restaurant area, serves upscale, pleasing traditional classics with yuppie flair in a space that exudes more Martha Stewart and Pottery Barn than traditional public house (book ahead for restaurant, food served daily 12:00-22:00, across from the pool at 58 Dalkeith Road, tel. 0131/667-4518, www.thesalisburyarmsedinburgh.co.uk).

$$ The Old Bell Inn, with an old-time sports-bar ambience—fishing, golf, horses, televisions—serves pub meals. This is a classic "snug pub"—all dark woods and brass beer taps, littered with evocative knickknacks. It comes with sidewalk seating and a mixed-age crowd (bar tables can be reserved, food served daily until 21:15, 233 Causewayside, tel. 0131/668-1573, http://oldbelledinburgh.co.uk).

Other Eateries

$$$$ Aizle is a delicious night out. They serve a set £45 five-course tasting menu based on what's in season—ingredients are listed on the chalkboard (with notice, they can accommodate dietary restrictions). The restaurant is intimate but unpretentious, and they only serve 36 people a night to keep the experience special and unrushed (dinner-only Wed-Sun, this is not a walk-in type of place—book at least a week ahead, 107 St. Leonard's Street—five minutes past the Royal Commonwealth Pool, tel. 0131/662-9349, www.aizle.co.uk).

$$ Southpour is a nice place for a local beer, craft cocktail, or a reliable meal from a menu of salads, sandwiches, meat dishes, and other comfort foods. The brick walls, wood beams, and giant windows give it a warm and open vibe (daily 10:00-22:00, 1 Newington Road, tel. 0131/650-1100).

$$ Ristorante Isola is a calm and casual place with 15 tables surrounding a bright yellow bar. They serve pizzas, pastas, and meat or seafood *secondi* with an emphasis on Sardinian specialties (Mon-Tue 17:00-22:30, Wed-Sun 12:00-22:30, 85 Newington Road, tel. 0131/662-9977).

$$ Voujon Restaurant serves a fusion menu of Bengali and Indian cuisines. Vegetarians appreciate the expansive yet inexpensive offerings (daily 17:00-23:00, 107 Newington Road, tel. 0131/667-5046).

$$ Apiary has an inviting, casual interior and a hit-or-miss, eclectic menu that mingles various international flavors (daily 10:00-15:00 & 17:30-21:00, 33 Newington Road, tel. 0131/668-4999).

Fast Eats

At **$ Edinburgh Bakehouse,** award-winning baker James Lynch makes £1-2 fresh breads, sweets, and meat pies from scratch in this laid-back, nondescript shop. Locals line up for his morning rolls—which earned him the title "baker of the year." Stop by to see the friendly staff and open kitchen in action and judge for yourself (cash only, daily 7:00-16:00 or whenever the goods sell out, open 24 hours from Fri until Sun afternoon to cater to the weekend pub crowd, 101 Newington Road).

$ Earthy is an organic, farm-fresh café and grocery store with a proudly granola attitude. Order from the counter, with its appealing display of freshly prepared salads, sandwiches, and baked goods. Sit in the industrial-mod interior, with rustic picnic benches, or out in the ragtag back garden. In the well-stocked store, assemble a pricey but top-quality picnic (café daily 9:00-17:00, store open until 19:00, 33 Ratcliffe Terrace, tel. 0131/667-2967).

Groceries: Several grocery stores are on the main streets near the restaurants, including Sainsbury's Local and Co-op on South Clerk Road, and Tesco Express and another Sainsbury's Local one block over on Causewayside (all open late—until at least 22:00). Cameron Toll Shopping Centre, about a half-mile south on your way out of town, houses a Sainsbury's superstore for more substantial supplies and gasoline.

Memorable Meals Farther Out

$$$$ Rhubarb Restaurant specializes in Old World elegance. It's in "Edinburgh's most handsome house"—an over-the-top riot of antiques, velvet, tassels, and fringes. The plush dark-rhubarb color theme reminds visitors that this was the place where rhubarb was first grown in Britain. It's a 10-minute walk past the other recommended eateries behind Arthur's Seat, in a huge estate with big, shaggy Highland cattle enjoying their salads al fresco. At night, it's a candlelit wonder. Most spend a wad here. Reserve in advance and dress up if you can (two-course lunch and three-course dinner, daily 12:00-14:00 & 18:00-22:00, afternoon tea served daily 12:00-19:00, in Prestonfield House, Priestfield Road, tel. 0131/662-2303, www.prestonfield.com). For details on their schmaltzy Scottish folk evening, see "Nightlife in Edinburgh," earlier.

$$ The Sheep Heid Inn, Edinburgh's oldest and most inviting public house, is equally notable for its history, date-night appeal, and hearty portions of affordable, classy dishes. It's either a short cab ride or pleasant 30-minute walk from the B&B neighborhood (see page 92), but it's worth the effort to dine in this dreamy setting in the presence of past queens and kings—choose between the bar downstairs, dining room upstairs, or outside in the classic garden courtyard (food served Mon-Fri 12:00-21:00, Sat-Sun 12:00-21:30, 43 The Causeway, tel. 0131/661-7974, www.thesheephcidedinburgh.co.uk).

Edinburgh Connections

BY TRAIN OR BUS

From Edinburgh by Train to: Glasgow (10/hour, 50 minutes), **St. Andrews** (train to Leuchars, 2/hour, 1 hour, then 10-minute bus into St. Andrews), **Stirling** (2/hour, 1 hour), **Pitlochry** (6/day direct, 2 hours), **Inverness** (6/day direct, 3.5 hours, more with transfer), **Oban** (5/day, 4.5 hours, change in Glasgow), **York** (3/hour, 2.5 hours), **London** (2/hour, 4.5 hours), **Durham** (hourly direct, 2 hours, less frequent in winter), **Newcastle** (3/hour, 1.5 hours), **Keswick/Lake District** (8/day to Penrith—more via Carlisle, 2 hours, then 40-minute bus ride to Keswick), **Birmingham** (hourly, 5 hours, less with transfer), **Crewe** (every 2 hours, 3 hours), **Bristol**, near Bath (hourly, 6.5 hours), **Blackpool** (2/hour, 3.5 hours, transfer in Preston). Train info: Tel. 0345-748-4950, www.nationalrail. co.uk.

By Bus: Edinburgh's bus station is in the New Town, just off St. Andrew Square, two blocks north of the train station. Direct buses go to **Glasgow** (Citylink bus #900, 4/hour, 1.5 hours), **Inverness** (express #G90, 2/day, 3.5 hours; slower #M90, 6/day, 4 hours), **Pitlochry** (Citylink #M90, 3/day, 2.5 hours), **Stirling** (every 2 hours on Citylink #909, 1 hour). To reach other destinations in the Highlands—including **Oban, Fort William, Glencoe,** or **Portree** on the Isle of Skye—you'll have to transfer. It's usually fastest to take the train to Glasgow and change to a bus there. For details, see "Getting Around the Highlands" on page 235. For bus info, stop by the station or call Scottish Citylink (tel. 0871-266-3333, www.citylink.co.uk). Additional long-distance routes may be operated by National Express (www.nationalexpress. com) or Megabus (www.megabus.com).

BY PLANE

Edinburgh Airport is located eight miles northwest of the center (airport code: EDI, tel. 0844-481-8989, www.edinburghairport. com). **Taxis** or **Uber rides** between the airport and city center are about £20-25 (25 minutes to downtown or Dalkeith Road). The airport is also well connected to central Edinburgh by tram and bus. Just follow signs outside; the tram tracks are straight ahead, and the bus stop is to the right, along the main road in front of the terminal. **Trams** make several stops in town, including along Princes Street and at St. Andrew Square (£5.50, buy ticket from machine, runs every 10 minutes from early morning until 23:30, 35 minutes, www.edinburghtrams.com).

The Lothian **Airlink bus #100** drops you at Waverley Bridge (£4.50, £7.50 round-trip, runs every 10 minutes, 30 minutes, tel. 0131/555-6363, http://lothianbuses.co.uk). Whether you take the tram or bus to the center, to continue on to my recommended B&Bs south of the city center, you can either take a taxi (about £7) or hop on a city bus (for directions, see "Sleeping in Edinburgh," earlier). To get from the B&Bs *to* the Airlink or tram stops downtown, you can take a taxi...or ride a city bus to North Bridge, turn left at the grand Balmoral Hotel, and walk a short distance down Princes Street. Turn right up St. Andrew Street to catch the tram at St. Andrew Square, or continue up to the next bridge, Waverley, for the Airlink bus.

ROUTE TIPS FOR DRIVERS HEADING SOUTH

It's 100 miles south from Edinburgh to Hadrian's Wall; to Durham, it's another 50 miles.

To Hadrian's Wall: From Edinburgh, Dalkeith Road leads south and eventually becomes the A-68 (handy Cameron Toll supermarket with cheap gas is on the left as you leave Edinburgh Town, 10 minutes south of Edinburgh; gas and parking behind store). The A-68 road takes you to Hadrian's Wall in 2.5 hours. You'll pass Jedburgh and its abbey after one hour. (For one last shot of Scotland shopping, there's a coach tour's delight just before Jedburgh, with kilt makers, woolens, and a sheepskin shop.) Across from Jedburgh's lovely abbey is a free parking lot, a good visitors center, and pay toilets. The England/Scotland border is a fun, quick stop (great view, ice cream, and tea caravan). Just after the turn for Colwell, turn right onto the A-6079, and roller-coaster four miles down to Low Brunton. Then turn right onto the B-6318, and stay on it by turning left at Chollerford, following the Roman wall westward.

To Durham: If you're heading straight to Durham, you can take the scenic coastal route on the A-1 (a few more miles than the A-68, but similar time), which takes you near Holy Island and Bamburgh Castle.

GLASGOW

Glasgow (GLAS-goh)—astride the River Clyde—is a surprising city. In its heyday, Glasgow was one of Europe's biggest cities and the second-largest in Britain, right behind London. A century ago it had 1.2 million people, twice the size (and with twice the importance) of today. It was an industrial powerhouse producing 25 percent of the world's oceangoing ships. But in the mid-20th century, tough times hit Glasgow, giving it a rough edge and a run-down image.

At the city's low point during the Margaret Thatcher years (1980s), its leaders embarked on a systematic rejuvenation designed to again make Glasgow appealing to businesses, tourists...and locals. Today the city feels revitalized and goes out of its way to offer a warm welcome. Glaswegians (rhymes with "Norwegians") are some of the chattiest people in Scotland—and have the most entertaining (and impenetrable) accent.

Many travelers give Glasgow a miss, but that's a shame: I consider it Scotland's most underrated destination. Glasgow is a workaday Scottish city as well as a cosmopolitan destination, with an unpretentious friendliness, an energetic dining and nightlife scene, topnotch museums (most of them free), and a unique flair for art and design. It's also a pilgrimage site for architecture buffs, thanks to a cityscape packed with Victorian facades, early

20th-century touches, and bold and glassy new construction. Most beloved are the works by hometown boy Charles Rennie Mackintosh, the visionary—and now very trendy—architect who left his mark all over Glasgow at the turn of the 20th century.

Many more tourists visit Edinburgh, a short train trip away. But for a more complete look at urban Scotland, be sure to stop off in Glasgow. Edinburgh may have the royal aura, but Glasgow has down-to-earth appeal. In Glasgow, there's no upper-crust history, and no one puts on airs. In Edinburgh, people identify with the quality of the school they attended; in Glasgow, it's their soccer team allegiance. One Glaswegian told me, "The people of Glasgow have a better time at a funeral than the people of Edinburgh have at a wedding." Here, friendly locals do their best to introduce you to the fun-loving, laid-back Glaswegian way of life.

PLANNING YOUR TIME

While many visitors blitz Glasgow as a day trip from Edinburgh or Stirling (and a single day in Glasgow is certainly more exciting than a fourth day in Edinburgh), the city can easily fill two days of sightseeing.

On a quick visit, follow my "Get to Know Glasgow" self-guided walk of the city center, tying together the most important sights in the city's core. If your time is short, the interiors most worth considering are the Tenement House and the Kelvingrove Museum.

With additional time, your options open up. Follow my West End Walk to get a taste of Glasgow's appealing residential zone, which has some of the city's best restaurants as well as a number of worthwhile sights. Fans of Art Nouveau and Charles Rennie Mackintosh can lace together a busy day's worth of sightseeing (the TI has a brochure laying it out). At a minimum, those interested in Mackintosh should visit the Mackintosh House at the Hunterian Gallery (in the West End) and the Mackintosh exhibit at the Kelvingrove Museum.

Regardless of how long you're staying, consider the two-hour hop-on, hop-off bus tour, which is convenient for getting the bigger picture and reaching three important sights away from the center (the Cathedral Precinct, the Riverside Museum, and the Kelvingrove Museum).

Day Trip from Edinburgh: For a full day, catch the 9:30 train to Glasgow (morning trains every 10 minutes; discount for same-day round-trip if leaving after 9:15 or on weekend); it arrives at Queen Street Train Station before 10:30. To fill your Glasgow hours smartly, I'd do the entire hop-on, hop-off bus tour circuit (two hours), then follow my self-guided walk through downtown (finishing with the Tenement House). Next, check out the Kelvingrove Museum and have dinner nearby (in the Finnieston area). Catch a train that leaves around 21:00 to return to Edinburgh (evening trains depart every 10-20 minutes).

Orientation to Glasgow

Although it's often thought of as a "second city," Glasgow is actually Scotland's biggest (pop. 600,000, swelling to 1.2 million within Greater Glasgow—that's one out of every five Scots).

The tourist's Glasgow has two parts: the businesslike downtown (train stations, commercial zone, and main shopping drag) and the residential West End (B&Bs, restaurants, and nightlife). Both areas have good sights, and both are covered in this chapter by self-guided walks.

Glasgow's **downtown** is a tight grid of boxy office buildings and shopping malls, making it feel more like a midsized American city than a big Scottish one—like Cincinnati or Pittsburgh, but with shorter skyscrapers made of Victorian sandstone rather than glass and steel. The walkable city center has two main drags, both lined with shops and crawling with shoppers: Sauchiehall Street (pronounced "Suckyhall," running west to east) and Buchanan Street (running north to south). These two pedestrian malls—part of a shopping zone nicknamed the Golden Zed—make a big zig and zag through the heart of town (the third street of the Zed, Argyle Street, is busy with traffic and less appealing).

The **West End** is a posh suburb, with big homes, upscale apartment buildings, and lots of green space. The area has three pockets of interest: near the Hillhead subway stop, with a lively restaurant scene and the Botanic Gardens; the University of Glasgow campus, with its stately buildings and fine museums; and, just downhill through a sprawling park, the area around the Kelvingrove Museum, with a lively nearby strip of trendy bars and restaurants (Finnieston).

TOURIST INFORMATION

The TI is inside the Gallery of Modern Art on Royal Exchange Square, downstairs. They hand out a good, free map and brochures on Glasgow and the rest of Scotland (daily 10:00-17:00, www.visitscotland.com).

ARRIVAL IN GLASGOW

By Train: Glasgow, a major Scottish transportation hub, has two main train stations, which arc just a few blocks apart in the heart of town: **Central Station** (with a grand, genteel interior under a vast

Greater Glasgow

To Stirling

To Edinburgh

Royal Botanic Garden

GREAT WESTERN ROAD

To Loch Lomond & Oban

WEST END

See West End detail map

TENEMENT HOUSE

M-8

To Stirling & Edinburgh

A-82

Kelvingrove Park

Kelvingrove Museum

See Glasgow Walk detail map

QUEEN ST. STN.

George Square

See Glasgow Center detail map

CATHEDRAL

The Necropolis

M-8

RIVERSIDE MUSEUM

River Clyde

CENTER

CENTRAL STN.

A-8

IBROX STADIUM (RANGERS)

EAST END

A-74

M-8

To Airport

To Celtic Park Stadium

M-77

To Ayr & Cairnryan

M 74

A-77

BURRELL COLLECTION

To Carlisle (England)

Pollok County Park

Pollokshaws West Stn.

N

1 kilometer

1/2 mile

GLASGOW

steel-and-glass Industrial Age roof) and **Queen Street Station** (more functional, with better connections to Edinburgh—take the exit marked *Buchanan Street* to reach the main shopping drag). Both stations have pay WCs and baggage storage. If going between the stations to change trains, you can walk five minutes or take the roundabout "RailLink" bus #398 (free with train ticket, otherwise £1.20, 5/hour; also goes to bus station).

By Bus: Buchanan bus station is at Killermont Street, two blocks up the hill behind Queen Street Station (luggage lockers; travel center open daily 9:00-17:00).

By Car: Glasgow's downtown streets are steep, mostly one-way, congested with buses and pedestrians, and a horrible place to drive. Parking downtown is a hassle: Metered street parking is expensive (£3/hour) and limited to two hours during the day; ga-

When the Great Ships of the World Were "Clyde-Built"

Glasgow's River Clyde shipyards were the mightiest in the world, famed for building the largest moving man-made objects on earth. The shipyards, once 50 strong, have dwindled to just three. Yet a few giant cranes still stand to remind locals and visitors that from 1880 to 1950, a quarter of the world's ships were built here and "Clyde-built" meant reliability and quality. For 200 years, shipbuilding was Glasgow's top employer—as many as 100,000 workers at its peak, producing a new ship every two days. The glamorous Cunard ships were built here—from the *Lusitania* in 1906 (infamously sunk by a German U-boat in World War I, which almost brought the US into the war) to the *Queen Elizabeth II* in 1967. People still talk about the day when over 200,000 Glaswegians gathered for the launch, the Queen herself smashed the champagne bottle on the prow, and the magnificent ship slid into the harbor. To learn lots more about shipbuilding in Glasgow, visit the excellent Riverside Museum (described under "Sights in Glasgow").

rages are even more expensive (figure £25 for 24 hours). Ideally, do Glasgow without a car—for example, tour Edinburgh and Glasgow by public transit, then pick up your rental car on your way out of town. If you are stuck with a car in Glasgow, try to sleep in the West End, where driving and parking are easier (and use public transportation or taxis as necessary).

The M-8 motorway, which slices through downtown Glasgow, is the easiest way in and out of the city. Ask your hotel for directions to and from the M-8, and connect with other highways from there.

By Plane: For information on Glasgow's two airports, see "Glasgow Connections," at the end of this chapter.

HELPFUL HINTS

Safety: The city center, which is packed with ambitious career types during the day, can feel deserted at night. While the area between Argyle Street and the River Clyde has been cleaned up in recent years, parts can still feel sketchy. As in any big city, use common sense and don't wander down dark, deserted alleys. The Golden Zed shopping drag, the Merchant City area (east of the train stations), and the West End all bustle with crowded restaurants well into the evening and feel well populated in the wee hours.

If you've picked up a football (soccer) jersey or scarf as a souvenir, don't wear it in Glasgow; passions run very high, and most drunken brawls in town are between supporters of

Glasgow's two rival soccer clubs: Celtic in green, and Rangers in blue and red. (For more on the soccer rivalry, see page 136.)

Sightseeing: Almost every sight in Glasgow is free, but request £3-5 donations (www.glasgowmuseums.com). While these donations are not required, I like to consider what the experience was worth and decide if and how much to donate as I leave. (Voluntary donations are a nice option—but will only work if people actually donate.) Note that most city sights have the same hours: Mon-Thu and Sat 10:00-17:00, Fri and Sun from 11:00, closed Monday.

Sunday Travel: Bus and train schedules are dramatically reduced on Sundays and in the off-season. (If you want to get to the Highlands by bus on a Sunday in winter, forget it.)

Laundry: Majestic Launderette will pick up and drop off at your B&B or hotel (call to arrange); they also have a launderette near the Kelvingrove Museum in the West End (self-serve or full-serve, Mon-Fri 8:00-18:00, Sat until 16:00, Sun 10:00-16:00, 1110 Argyle Street, tel. 0141/334-3433).

GETTING AROUND GLASGOW

By City Bus: Most city-center routes are operated by First Bus Company (£2.20/ride, £4.50 for all-day ticket on First buses, buy tickets from driver, exact change required). Buses run every few minutes down Glasgow's main thoroughfares (such as Sauchiehall Street) to the downtown core (train stations). You can also get around the city via hop-on, hop-off bus (see "Tours in Glasgow," next).

By Taxi: Taxis are affordable, plentiful, and often come with nice, chatty cabbies (if your driver has an impenetrable Glaswegian accent, just smile and nod). Most taxi rides within the downtown area cost about £6; to the West End is about £8.

By Uber: Uber works particularly well in Glasgow and lets you make quick connections for about £5.

By Subway: Glasgow's cute little single-line subway system, nicknamed The Clockwork Orange, makes a six-mile circle that has 15 stops. While simple today, when it opened in 1896 it was a wonder (it's the world's third-oldest subway system, after those in London and Budapest). Though the subway is useless for connecting city-center sightseeing (Buchanan Street and St. Enoch are the only downtown stops), it's ideal for reaching sights farther out, including the Kelvingrove Museum (Kelvinhall stop) and West End restaurant/nightlife neighborhood (Hillhead stop). Ticket options are: £1.65 single trip, £4 for all-day ticket, or frequent riders can get a £3 Bramble card, which is reloadable and reduces your single-ride cost to £1.45 (subway runs Mon-Sat 6:30-23:15, Sun 10:00-18:00, www.spt.co.uk/subway).

Central Glasgow

To Edinburgh ↗

TENEMENT HOUSE MUSEUM

REID BLDG SCHOOL OF ART

NAT'L PIPING CENTRE

WILLOW TEA ROOMS

CHARING CROSS STATION

Blythswood Square

Buchanan

CONCERT HALL

CENTRAL STATION

MURALS

GOMA

THE LIGHTHOUSE

CELTIC TEAM SHOP

St Enoch

ST. ENOCH CENTRE

See Glasgow Walk detail map

River Clyde

To Airport & Oban via A-82

To Riverside Museum

To Kelvingrove Museum

To West End

To Burrell Collection

GLASGOW

Tours in Glasgow

Hop-On, Hop-Off Bus

CitySightseeing connects Glasgow's far-flung historic sights in a two-hour loop and lets you hop on and off as you like for two days. Buses are frequent (every 10-20 minutes, 9:30-18:20, service ends earlier in off-season) and alternate between live guides and recorded narration (both are equally good). The route covers the city very well, and the guide does a fine job of describing activities at each stop. While the first stop is on George Square, you can hop on and pay the driver anywhere along the route (£15, tel. 0141/204-0444, www.citysightseeingglasgow.co.uk).

GLASGOW

Walking Tours

Walking Tours in Glasgow was started by Jenny and Liv, two recent University of Glasgow graduates who love their city. The city center tour starts in George Square and covers about 3.5 miles in 2.5 hours (daily 10:30 and 14:00; off-season tours by request). They also run a West End tour at 14:30 that requires advance booking (£10, www.walkingtoursin.com, walkingtoursinglasgow@gmail.com).

Trainspotters may enjoy the guided, behind-the-scenes tours of **Central Station,** including a spooky, abandoned Victorian train platform (book ahead, www.glasgowcentraltours.co.uk).

Those with a specific interest in **Mackintosh** architecture should consider the 2.25-hour Mackintosh-themed city walking tours given by students of the Glasgow School of Art (£20, 4/week, see page 150).

Local Guides

Joan Dobbie, a native Glaswegian and registered Scottish Tourist Guide, will give you the insider's take on Glasgow's sights (£135/half-day, £200/day, tours on foot or by public transit—no tours by car, tel. 01355/236-749, mobile 07773-555-151, joan.leo@lineone.net).

Ann Stewart is a former high-school geography teacher turned Blue Badge guide who is excited to show you around Glasgow or take you on an excursion outside the city (£150/4 hours, £220/8 hours, mobile 07716-358-997, www.comeseescotland.com, ann@comeseescotland.com).

Highlands Day Trips

Most of the same companies that do Highlands side-trips from Edinburgh also operate trips from Glasgow. If you'd like to spend an efficient day away from the city, skim the descriptions and listings on page 30, and then check each company's website or browse the brochures at the TI for details.

Glasgow Walks

These two self-guided walks introduce you to Glasgow's most interesting (and very different) neighborhoods: the downtown zone, and the residential and university sights of the West End.

GET TO KNOW GLASGOW: THE DOWNTOWN CORE

Glasgow isn't romantic, but it has an earthy charm, its people are a joy to chat with, and architecture buffs love it. The more time you spend here, the more you'll appreciate the edgy, artsy vibe and the quirky, fun-loving spirit. Be sure to look up—above the chain restaurants and mall stores—and you'll discover a wealth of imaginative facades, complete with ornate friezes and expressive sculptures. These buildings transport you to the heady days around the turn of the 20th century—when the rest of Britain was enthralled by Victorianism, but Glasgow set its own course, thanks largely to the artistic bravado of Charles Rennie Mackintosh and his Art Nouveau friends (the "Glasgow Four"). This walking tour takes about 1.5 hours (plus sightseeing stops along the way).

• *Start at the St. Enoch subway station, at the base of the pedestrian*

Downtown Walk

1. Argyle Street & Nearby
2. Buchanan Street
3. Royal Exchange Square
4. George Square
5. Nelson Mandela Place
6. Buchanan to Sauchiehall Streets
7. Willow Tea Rooms

shopping boulevard, Buchanan Street. (This is a short walk from Central Station, or a longer walk or quick cab ride from Queen Street Station.) Stand at the intersection of Argyle and Buchanan, where the square hits the street (with your back to the glassy subway entry). Take a moment to get oriented.

❶ Argyle Street and Nearby

The grand pedestrian boulevard, Buchanan Street, leads uphill to the Royal Concert Hall. This is the start of the "Golden Zed"—the nickname for a Z-shaped pedestrian boulevard made of three streets: Buchanan, Sauchiehall, and Argyle. Always coming up with marketing slogans to goose the shopping metabolism of the city, this district (with the top shops in town) is also called the "Style Mile."

Look left (a long block away) to where Central Station (with its huge glass facade) makes a bridge over Argyle Street. This bridge was nicknamed "The Highlanders' Umbrella" from the days when poor Highlanders, who came to Glasgow to find work, would gather here to connect with their community.

Before heading up Buchanan Street, take a quick detour down Argyle to see a couple slices of Glasgow life. About halfway to the Highlanders' Umbrella on the right, step into the extremely green sports store, the **Celtic Shop** (at #154).

Green is the color of Glasgow's dominant (for now) soccer team. It's hard for outsiders to fathom the intensity of the rivalry between Glasgow's Celtic and Rangers. Celtic, founded by an Irish Catholic priest to raise money for poor Irish immigrants in the East End, is—naturally—green and favored by Catholics. (For reasons no one can explain, the Celtic team name is pronounced "sell-tic"—like it is in Boston; in all other cases, such as when referring to music, language, or culture, this word is pronounced "kell-tic.") Rangers, with team colors of the Union Jack (red, white, and blue), are more likely to be supported by Unionist and Protestant families. Wander into the shop (minimizing or hiding any red or blue you might be wearing). Check out the energy in the photos and shots of the stadium filled with 60,000 fans. You're in a world where red and blue don't exist. Upstairs, tucked in a back room, is a trophy room with photos of the 1967 team, considered the best in club history.

Now head around the corner from the Celtic Shop and walk a few steps down the alley (Mitchell Street). While it seems a bit

seedy, it should be safe...but look out for giant magnifying glasses and taxis held aloft by balloons. City officials have cleverly co-opted street artists by sanctioning huge, fun, and edgy **graffiti murals** like these. (You'll see even more if you side-trip down alleys along the Style Mile.) The girl with the magnifying glass is painted by graffiti artist Smug (see the girl's necklace). In the taxi painting, the driver is actually the artist and the license plate alludes to his tag name: Rogue-One. (By the way, there are no actual bricks on that wall.) Glasgow produces a free booklet, called City Center Mural Trail (also available at www.citycentremuraltrail.co.uk), which explains all this fun art around town.

• *Now return to the base of...*

❷ Buchanan Street

Buchanan Street has a friendly Ramblas-style vibe with an abundance of street musicians. As you stroll uphill, keep an eye out for a

few big landmarks: **Frasers** (#45, on the left) is a vast and venerable department store, considered the "Harrods of Glasgow." The **Argyll Arcade** (#30, opposite Frasers), dating from 1827 with a proud red-sandstone façade, is the oldest arcade in town. It's filled mostly with jewelry and comes with security guards dressed in Victorian-era garb. **Princes Square** (at #48, just past Argyll Arcade) is a classic old building dressed with a modern steel peacock and foliage. Step inside to see the delightfully modernized Art Nouveau atrium.

At #97 (50 yards up, on the left) is one of two Mackintosh-designed **Willow Tea Rooms** (the other location, described later in this walk, is the original). This central location is designed to capitalize on the trendiness of Mackintosh.

• *Just past the tearooms, turn down the alley on the right, called Exchange Place. You'll pass the recommended Rogano restaurant on your right before emerging onto...*

❸ Royal Exchange Square

The centerpiece of this square—which marks the entrance to the shopping zone called Merchant City—is a stately, Neoclassical, bank-like building. This was once the **private mansion** of one of the tobacco lords, the super-rich businessmen who reigned here through the 1700s, stomping through the city with gold-tipped canes. During the port's heyday, these entrepreneurs helped Glasgow become Europe's sixth-biggest city—number two in the British Empire.

Today the mansion houses the **Glasgow Gallery of Modern Art,** nicknamed GoMA. Circle around the building to the main entry (at the equestrian statue of the Duke of Wellington, often creatively decorated as Glasgow's favorite conehead), and step back to take in the full Neoclassical facade. On the pediment, notice the funky, mirrored mosaic celebrating the miracles of St. Mungo—an example of how Glasgow

refuses to take itself too seriously. The temporary exhibits inside

GLASGOW

GoMA are generally forgettable, but the museum does have an unusual charter: It displays only the work of living artists (free, £2 suggested donation, daily 10:00-17:00, TI inside and downstairs).

• *Facing the fanciful GoMA facade, turn right up Queen Street. Within a block, you'll reach...*

❹ George Square

This square, the centerpiece of Glasgow, is filled with statues and lined with notable buildings, such as the Queen Street train station and the Glasgow City Chambers. (It's the big Neoclassical building standing like a secular church to the east; pop in to see its grand ground floor.) In front of the City Chambers stands a monument to Glaswegians killed fighting in the World Wars. The square is decorated with a *Who's Who* of statues depicting great Glaswegians. Find James Watt (the only

guy with a chair; he perfected the steam engine that helped power Europe into the Industrial Age), as well as Scotland's two top literary figures: Robert Burns and Sir Walter Scott (capping the tallest pillar in the center). The twin equestrian statues are of Prince Albert and a skinny Queen Victoria—a rare image of her in her more svelte youth.

• *Just past skinny Vic and Robert Peel, turn left onto West George Street, and cross Buchanan Street to the tall church in the middle of...*

❺ Nelson Mandela Place

This first public space named for Nelson Mandela honors the man who, while still in prison, helped bring down apartheid in South Africa. The square was renamed in the 1980s while apartheid was still in place— and when the South African consulate was on it. Subsequently, anyone sending the consulate a letter had to address it with the name of the man who embodied the anti-apartheid spirit: Mandela. (Glasgow, nicknamed Red Clyde Side for its socialist politics and empathy for the working class, has been quick to jump on progressive causes.)

The area around St. George's Church features some interesting bits of architectural detail. Facing the church's left side are the three circular friezes of the former

Stock Exchange (with a Neo-Gothic facade, built in 1875). These idealized heads represent the industries that made Glasgow prosperous during its prime: building, engineering, and mining.

Around the back of the church, find the **Athenaeum,** the sandy-colored building at #8 (notice the low-profile label over the door). Now a law office, this was founded in 1847 as a school and city library during Glasgow's Golden Age. (Charles Dickens gave the building's inaugural address.) Like Edinburgh, Glasgow was at the forefront of the 18th-century Scottish Enlightenment, a celebration of education and intellectualism. The Scots were known for their extremely practical brand of humanism; all members of society, including the merchant and working classes, were expected to be well educated. Look above the door to find the symbolic statue of a reader sharing books with young children, an embodiment of this ideal.

• *Return to the big, pedestrianized Buchanan Street in front of the church. Head uphill.*

❻ Buchanan Street to Sauchiehall Street (More of the Golden Zed)

A short distance uphill is the glass entry to Glasgow's subway. Soon after, on the right, you'll pass the Buchanan Galleries, an indoor mall that sprawls through several city blocks (filled with shopping temptations and offering a refuge in rainy weather).

Whisky Side-trip: For a fun education in whisky, take a little detour. At Buchanan Galleries, head left down Bath Street 1.5 blocks to #23, where stairs lead down into **The Good Spirits Company.** This happy world of whisky is run by two young aficionados (Shane and Matthew) and their booze-geek staff. They welcome you to taste and learn (Mon-Sat 10:00-19:00, Sun 12:00-17:00, tel. 0141/258-8427).

• *Returning to Buchanan Street, continue uphill to the top.*

At the top of Buchanan Street stands the **Glasgow Royal Concert Hall.** Its steps are a favorite perch where local office workers munch lunch and enjoy the street scene. The statue is of **Donald Dewar,** who served as Scotland's first-ever "First Minister" after the Scottish Parliament reconvened in 1999 (previously they'd been serving in London—as part of the British Parliament—since 1707).

• *From here, the Golden Zed zags left, Buchanan Street becomes Sauchiehall Street, and the shopping gets cheaper and less elegant. While*

GLASGOW

Charles Rennie Mackintosh (1868-1928)

Charles Rennie Mackintosh brought an exuberant Art Nouveau influence to the architecture of his hometown. His designs challenged the city planners of this otherwise practical, working-class port city to create beauty in the buildings they commissioned.

As a student traveling in Italy, Mackintosh ignored the paintings inside museums and set up his easel to paint the exteriors of churches and buildings instead. He rejected the architectural traditions of ancient Greece and Rome. In Venice and Ravenna, he fell under the spell of Byzantine design, and in Siena he saw a unified, medieval city design he would try to import—but with a Scottish flavor and palette—to Glasgow.

When Mackintosh was at the Glasgow School of Art, the Industrial Age dominated life. Factories belched black soot as they burned coal and forged steel. Mackintosh and his artist friends drew inspiration from nature and created some of the first Art Nouveau buildings, paintings, drawings, and furniture. His first commission came in 1893, to design an extension to the Glasgow Herald building. More work followed, including the Glasgow School of Art and the Willow Tea Rooms.

A radical thinker, Mackintosh shared credit with his artist wife, Margaret MacDonald (who specialized in glass and metalwork). He once famously said, "I have the talent...Margaret has the genius." The two teamed up with another husband-and-wife duo—Herbert MacNair and Margaret's sister, Frances MacDonald—to define a new strain of Scottish Art Nouveau, called the "Glasgow Style." These influential couples were known as "the Glasgow Four."

there's little of note to see, it's still an entertaining stroll. Walk a few blocks, passing "Pound Shops" (the equivalent of "dollar stores"), newspaper hawkers, beggars, buskers, souvenir shops, and a good bookstore. Enjoy the people-watching. Just before the end of the pedestrian zone, on the left side (at #217), are the...

❼ Willow Tea Rooms

Tearooms were hugely popular during the industrial boom of the late 19th century. As Glasgow grew, more people moved to the suburbs, meaning that office workers couldn't easily return home for lunch. And during this age of Victorian morals, the temperance movement was trying to discourage the consumption of alcohol.

Mackintosh's works show a strong Japanese influence, particularly in his use of black-and-white contrast to highlight the idealized forms of nature. He also drew inspiration from the Arts and Crafts movement, with an eye to simplicity, clean lines, respect for tradition, and an emphasis on precise craftsmanship over mass production. While some of his designs appear to be repeated, no two motifs are exactly alike—just as nothing is exactly the same in nature.

Mackintosh insisted on designing every element of his commissions—even the furniture, curtains, and cutlery. As a furniture and woodwork designer, Mackintosh preferred to use cheaper materials, then paint them with several thick coats, hiding seams and imperfections and making the piece feel carved rather than built. His projects often went past deadline and over budget, but resulted in unusually harmonious spaces.

Mackintosh inspired other artists, such as painter Gustav Klimt and Bauhaus founder Walter Gropius, but his vision was not appreciated in his own time as much as it is now; he died poor. Now, a century after Scotland's greatest architect set pencil to paper, his hometown is at last celebrating his unique vision.

In Glasgow, there are four main Mackintosh sights (listed in order of importance and all described in this chapter): The Mackintosh House (a reconstruction of his 1906 home filled with his actual furniture, on the University of Glasgow campus); the Kelvingrove Art Gallery (with a wonderful exhibit of his work along with the other three of the "Glasgow Four"); the Willow Tea Rooms (a functioning tea room entirely furnished in the Mackintosh style); and the Glasgow School of Art (the building is his design but it was gutted by fire and is closed until 2019). For the mildly interested traveler, the easiest way to "experience" Mackintosh is to focus on the Kelvingrove Art Gallery exhibit and perhaps pop into the Willow Tea Rooms.

Tearooms were designed to be an appealing alternative to eating in pubs.

These tearooms, opened in 1903, are also an Art Nouveau masterpiece by Charles Rennie Mackintosh. Mackintosh made his living from design commissions, including multiple tearooms for businesswoman Kate Cranston. Mackintosh designed everything here—down to the furniture, lighting, and cutlery. He took his theme for the café from the name of the street it's on—*saugh* is Scots for willow.

In the design of these tearooms, there was a meeting of the (very modern) minds. In addition to giving office workers an alternative to pubs, Cranston also wanted a place where women could gather while unescorted—in a time when traveling solo could give a woman a less-than-desirable reputation. An ardent women's rights supporter, Cranston requested that the rooms be bathed in white, the suffragettes' signature color.

At the Willows, you can have tea or just browse the exhibits showcasing his designs along with Mackintosh-inspired jewelry. The almost-hidden Room de Luxe dining room (upstairs) appears just as it did in Mackintosh's day, though most features are reproductions, such as the chairs and the doors, which were too fragile to survive (for details, see listing on page 154).

• *Our walk ends here. Within a few minutes' stroll are three more interesting sights. One of those is the Glasgow School of Art, which was gutted by a 2014 fire. Before the fire, this building, designed by 28-year-old Charles Rennie Mackintosh, attracted architects from far and wide. Now it's closed for a few years for repairs. Until it reopens, there are better Mackintosh sights for his fans to visit.*

*Two additional sights (described later) lie within a five-minute stroll (in different directions). The remarkably preserved **Tenement House** offers a fascinating glimpse into Glasgow lifestyles in the early 1900s. And the **National Piping Centre** goes beyond the clichés and provides a better appreciation for the history and musicality of Scotland's favorite instrument.*

WEST END WALK

Glasgow's West End—just a quick subway, bus, or taxi ride from downtown—is the city's top residential neighborhood. (Since this walk is most worthwhile as a scenic way to connect several important museums, be sure to do this when they're open.) As in so many British cities, the western part of town—upwind of industrial pollution—was the most desirable. This area has great restaurants and nightlife (see "Eating in Glasgow" and "Nightlife and Entertainment in Glasgow," later) and fine accommodations (see "Sleeping in Glasgow," later). This walk begins at the Hillhead subway stop, meanders through dining and residential zones, explores some grand old university buildings (and related museums), and ends with a wander through the park to the Kelvingrove Museum—Glasgow's top museum (walk route shown on page 144).

• *Start at the Hillhead subway station. Exiting the station, turn right and walk four short blocks up...*

Byres Road: A *byre* is a cowshed. So back when this was farmland outside the big city, cattle were housed along here. Today,

Byres Road is a main thoroughfare through a trendy district. A block before the big intersection, notice the **Waitrose** supermarket on the left. In Britain, this upscale grocery is a sure sign of a posh neighborhood.

Approaching the corner with Great Western Road, you'll see a church spire on the right. Dating from 1862, this church was converted into a restaurant and music venue called **Òran Mòr** (Gaelic for "The Great Music"). Step into the entryway to see the colorful murals (by Alasdair Gray, a respected Glaswegian artist and novelist). Consider a drink or meal in their pub (try some whisky—they have over 300 varieties). Also check what's on while you're in town, as this is a prime music and theater venue.

• *If the weather's good, cross Great Western Road and head into the...*

Glasgow Botanic Gardens: This inviting parkland is Glaswegians' favorite place to enjoy a break from the bustling city. And,

like so many things in Glasgow, it's free. Locals brag about their many parks, claiming that—despite their industrial reputation—they have more green space per capita than any other city in Europe. And even the city's name comes from the Gaelic for "the dear green place."

Before going into the park, pause at the red-brick entrance gate. On the gate on the left, look for Glasgow's quite-busy **city seal,** which honors St. Mungo, the near-legendary town founder. The jumble of symbols (a bird, a tree, a bell, and a salmon with a ring in its mouth) recall Mungo's four key miracles. Ask any Glaswegian to tell you the tales of St. Mungo—they learn it all by heart. The city motto, "Let Glasgow Flourish," is apt—particularly given its recent rejuvenation following a long, crippling period of industrial rot. Glasgow's current renaissance was kicked off with an ambitious 1989 garden festival in a disused former shipyard. Now the city is one of Europe's trendiest success stories. Let Glasgow flourish, indeed.

Head into the park. If the sun's out, it'll be jammed with people enjoying some rare rays. Young lads wait all winter for the day when they can cry, "Sun's oot, taps aff!" and pull off their shirts to make the most of it.

In addition to the finely landscaped gardens, the park has two inviting greenhouse pavilions—both free and open to the public. The big white one on the right (from 1873, open 10:00-18:00) is the most el-

Glasgow's West End

Glasgow Botanic Gardens

GREAT WESTERN
QUEEN MARGARET DRIVE

To ⑤

N

200 Meters
200 Yards

OBSERVATORY RD.

WAITROSE

ARHOLE LN.

ARHOLE GARDEN

RUTHVEN ST.

RUTHVEN LN.

DOWANSIDE RD.

⑧ ⑨

👣 WALK BEGINS

Hillhead M

ASHTON LANE

⑦

ASHTON RD.

ASHTON LANE

GREAT GEORGE LANE

STAIRS

HILLHEAD

⑫

⑪ ⑬

⑩

CRESSWELL ST.

CRESSWELL LANE

VINICOMBE ST.

CRAN.

KERSTAND ST.

SARDINIA LN.

CECIL ST.

GREAT GEORGE ST.

GRANBY LN.

HILLHEAD ST.

BUTE LN.

SOUTHPARK

⑥

④

HIGHBURGH RD.

DOWANHILL ST.

HAVELOCK ST.

LAWRENCE ST.

WHITE ST.

BYRES ROAD

UNIVERSITY AVE.

QUEEN MARGARET UNION

HUNTERIAN GALLERY

MACKINTOSH HOUSE

W E S T

UNIVERSITY

DECORATIVE GATE

MAIN GATE

HUNTERIAN MUSEUM

University of Glasgow

M Kelvinhall

CHURCH ST.

DUMBARTON RD.

AVE.

Kelvingrove Park

KELVIN STATUE

LISTER STATUE

KELVIN WAY

BENALDER ST.

FERRY RD.

To Riverside Museum of Transport & Travel

BUNHOUSE RD.

OLD DUMBARTON RD.

ARGYLE ST.

#77 SimpliCity #2 & 5

B

⑭

KELVINGROVE ART GALLERY & MUSEUM

DALNAIR ST.

BLANTYRE ST.

YORKHILL PARADE

NAIRN ST.

WALK ENDS

⑮

BOWLING GREEN

RADNOR ST.

SAUCHIEHALL ST.

GRAY ST.

ST.

①

⑯

②

⑳①

OVERNEWTON ST.

ARGYLE ST.

LYMBURN ST.

②②

CARFRAE ST.

HAUGH RD.

POINTHOUSE ROAD

EASTVALE PL.

SANDEFORD ST.

GILBERT ST.

KELVINHAUGH ST.

ST. VINCENT CRESCENT LN.

ST. VINCENT CRES.

GLASGOW

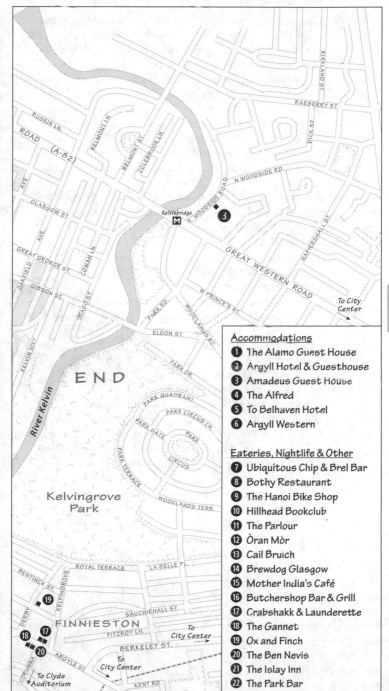

GLASGOW

Accommodations

1 The Alamo Guest House
2 Argyll Hotel & Guesthouse
3 Amadeus Guest House
4 The Alfred
5 To Belhaven Hotel
6 Argyll Western

Eateries, Nightlife & Other

7 Ubiquitous Chip & Brel Bar
8 Bothy Restaurant
9 The Hanoi Bike Shop
10 Hillhead Bookclub
11 The Parlour
12 Òran Mòr
13 Cail Bruich
14 Brewdog Glasgow
15 Mother India's Café
16 Butchershop Bar & Grill
17 Crabshakk & Launderette
18 The Gannet
19 Ox and Finch
20 The Ben Nevis
21 The Islay Inn
22 The Park Bar

egant, with classical statues scattered among the palm fronds (but beware the killer plants, to the left as you enter). When the clouds roll in and the weather turns rotten—which is more the status quo—these warm, dry areas become quite popular.

When you're done in the park, head back out the way you came in. Back on the street, before crossing Great Western Road, go right a few steps to find the blue **police call box.** Once an icon of British life, these were little neighborhood mini offices where bobbies could store paperwork and equipment, use the telephone, and catch up with each other. These days, some of the call boxes are being repurposed as coffee shops, ice-cream stands, and time machines.

• *Cross back over Great Western Road and backtrack (past the Òran Mòr church/restaurant) one block down Byres Road. Turn left down Vinicombe Street (across from the Waitrose). Now we'll explore...*

Back-Streets West End: Peek inside the **Hillhead Bookclub**—a former cinema that's been converted into a hipster bar/restaurant serving affordable food (described later, under "Eating in Glasgow"). A half-block after that, turn right and walk (on Crawnworth Street) along the row of red-sandstone **tenements.** While that word has negative connotations stateside, here a "tenement" is simply an apartment building. And judging from the grand size, bulging bay windows, and prime location of these, it's safe to say they're far from undesirable. Many are occupied by a single family, while others are subdivided into five or six rooms for students (the university is right around the corner). Across the street from this tenement row (at #12) is a **baths club**—a private swimming pool, like an exclusive health club back home. Historically, most people couldn't afford bathing facilities in their homes, so they came to central locations like this one to get clean every few days (or weeks). Today, it's the wealthy—not the poor—who come to places like this.

After the baths, turn right down Cresswell Street. A half-block down on the right, turn left down **Cresswell Lane**—an inviting, traffic-free, brick-floored shopping and dining zone. While the Golden Zed downtown is packed with chain stores, this is where you'll find charming one-off boutiques.

Browse your way to the end of the lane, cross the street, and continue straight to the even more appealing **Ashton Lane,** strung with fairy lights. Scout this street and pick a place to return for dinner tonight. Fancy a film? Halfway down the street on the right, the Grosvenor Cinema shows both blockbusters and art-house fare (see listing on page 161).

• *When you reach the end of the lane, take a very sharp left up the stairs (with the beer garden for Brel on your left). At the top of the stairs, turn right along the road. You're now walking through the modern part of the...*

University of Glasgow Campus: Founded in 1451, this is Scotland's second-oldest university (after St. Andrews). Its 24,000 students sprawl through the West End. Unlike the fancy "old university" buildings, this area is gloomy and concrete. The ugly, gray building on your left is the Queen Margaret Union, with a music venue that has hosted several big-name bands before they were famous—from Nirvana to Franz Ferdinand. (If you think Franz Ferdinand is an Austrian archduke rather than a Scottish alternative rock band...you've been out of college too long.)

• *Eventually you'll reach a wide cross street, University Avenue. Turn left up this street and walk two more blocks uphill. At the traffic light, the Hunterian Gallery and Mackintosh House are just up the hill on your left, and the Hunterian Museum is across the street on the right.*

Hunterian Gallery and Mackintosh House: First, stop in at the Hunterian Gallery to tour the Mackintosh House. In the morning, visits are by tour only; later you can free flow (admission is limited). Ask if there's a wait, and if so, spend your time either in the adjacent gallery, the wonderful university cafeteria (across the lane, cheap and cheery lunch), or the Hunterian Museum across the street. All three sights (the Mackintosh House, Hunterian Gallery, and Hunterian Museum) are important if you have the time and energy (for details, see page 154).

• *When you're done here, head for the Hunterian Museum in the university's big, old, main building across University Avenue. Instead of going through the main gate, go to the left end of the building facing the street to find a more interesting decorative gate.*

University of Glasgow Main Building: Take a good look at the gate, which is decorated with the names of illustrious alums. Pick out the great Scots you're familiar with: James Watt, King James II, Adam Smith, Lord Kelvin, William Hunter (the namesake of the university's museums), and Donald Dewar, a driving force behind devolution who became Scotland's first "First Minister" in 1999.

Go through the gate and face the main university building. Stretching to the left is Graduation Hall, where commencement takes place. Head straight into the building, ride the elevator to floor 4, and enjoy the **Hunterian Museum.**

After you visit the Hunterian Museum, find the grand stair-

case down (in the room with the Antonine Wall exhibit). You'll emerge into one of the twin quads enclosed by the enormous ensemble of univer-sity buildings. Veer right to find your way into the atmo-spheric, Neo-Gothic **cloisters** that support the wing separat-ing the two quads. These are modeled after the Gothic cloisters in the lower chapel of Glasgow Cathedral, across town. On the other side, you'll pop out into the adjoining quad. Enjoy pretending you're a student for a few minutes, then head out the door at the bottom of the quad.

Leaving the university complex, head for the tall flagpole on a bluff overlooking a grand view. The turreted building just below is the Kelvingrove Museum, where this walk ends. (If you get turned around in the park, just head for those spires.)

• *From the flagpole, turn left and head to the end of the big building. Head down the stairs leading through the woods on your right (marked* James Watt Building*). When you reach the busy road, turn right along it for a short distance, then—as soon as you can—angle to the right back into the green space of...*

Kelvingrove Park: Another of Glasgow's favorite parks, this originated in the Victorian period, when there was a renewed

focus on trying to get people out into green spaces. One of the first things you'll come to is a big statue of **Lord Kelvin** (1824-1907). Born William Thomson, he chose to take the name of the River Kelvin, which runs through Glasgow (and gives its name to many other things here, including the mu-seum we're headed to). One of the most re-spected scientists of his time, Kelvin was a pioneer in the field of thermodynamics, and gave his name (or, actually, the river's) to a new, absolute unit of temperature measure-

ment designed to replace Celsius and Fahrenheit.

Just past Kelvin, bear left at the statue of **Joseph Lister** (1827-1912, of "Listerine" fame—he pioneered the use of antiseptics to remove infection-causing germs from the surgical environment), and take the bridge across the River Kelvin. Once across the bridge, turn right toward the museum. You'll walk along a pleasant bowling green that was built for the Commonwealth Games that Glasgow hosted in 2014. They keep it free and open to anyone—hoping to create a popular interest in this very old and genteel sport (see page 157 for details).

Now's the time to explore the Kelvingrove Museum, described on page 156.

• *When you're finished at the museum, exit out the back end, toward the busy road. Several recommended restaurants are ahead and to the left, in the Finnieston neighborhood (see page 169). Or, if you'd like to hop on the subway, just turn right along Argyle Street and walk five minutes to the Kelvinhall station.*

Sights in Glasgow

DOWNTOWN
▲▲Tenement House

Here's a chance to drop into a perfectly preserved 1930s-era middle-class residence. The National Trust for Scotland bought this otherwise ordinary row home, located in a residential neighborhood, because of the peculiar tendencies of Miss Agnes Toward (1886-1975). For five decades, she kept her home essentially unchanged. The kitchen calendar is still set for 1935, and canisters of licorice powder (a laxative) still sit on the bathroom shelf. It's a time-warp experience, where Glaswegian old-timers enjoy coming to reminisce about how they grew up.

Cost and Hours: £6.50, April-Oct daily 13:00-17:00, July-Aug from 11:00, closed Nov-March, guidebook-£3, 145 Buccleuch Street (pronounced "ba-KLOO"), down from the top of Garnethill, tel. 0141/333-0183, www.nts.org.uk.

Visiting the House: Buy your ticket on the main floor, and poke around the little museum. You'll learn that in Glasgow, a "tenement" isn't a slum—it's simply an apartment house. In fact, tenements like these were typical for every class except the richest. Then head upstairs to the apartment, which is staffed by caring volunteers. Ring the doorbell to be let in. Explore the four little rooms. Imagine a world without electricity (Miss Toward was a late adapter, making the leap to electricity only in 1960). Ask about the utility of the iron stove. Ponder the importance of that drawer full of coal and how that stove heated her entire world. Ask why the bed is in the kitchen. As you look through the rooms laced with Victorian trinkets—such as the ceramic dogs on the living room's fireplace mantle—consider how different they are from Mackintosh's stark, minimalist designs from the same period.

▲National Piping Centre

If you consider bagpipes a tacky Scottish cliché, think again. At this small but insightful museum, you'll get a scholarly lesson in the proud and fascinating history of the bagpipe. For those with a healthy attention span for history or musical instruments—ideally both—it's fascinating. On Thursdays, Fridays, and Saturdays at 11:00 and 14:00 a piper is on hand to perform, answer questions, and show you around the collection. At other times, if it's quiet, ask the ticket-sellers to tell you more—some are bagpipe students at the music school across the street. The center also offers a shop, lessons, a restaurant, and accommodations.

Cost and Hours: £4.50, includes audioguide, Mon-Thu 9:00-19:00, Fri until 17:00, Sat until 15:00, closed Sun, 30 McPhater Street, tel. 0141/353-5551, www.thepipingcentre.co.uk.

Visiting the Museum: The collection is basically one big room packed with well-described exhibits, including several historic bagpipes. You'll learn that bagpipes from as far away as Italy, Spain, and Bohemia predated Scottish ones; that Lowlands bagpipes were traditionally bellows-blown rather than lung-powered; and why bagpipes started being used to inspire Scottish soldiers on the battlefield. At the back of the room, look for the hand-engraved,

backward printing plates for bagpipe sheet music (which didn't exist until the 19th century). The thoughtful, beautifully produced audioguide—which mixes knowledgeable commentary with sound bites of bagpipes being played and brief interviews with performers—feels like a 40-minute audio-documentary on the BBC. The 15-minute film shown at the end of the room sums up the collection helpfully. They also have a basket of chanters and a practice set of bagpipes in case you want to try your hand. The chanter fingering is easy if you play the recorder, but keeping the bag inflated is exhausting.

Glasgow School of Art

When he was just 28 years old—and still a no-name junior draughtsman for a big architectural firm—Charles Rennie Mackintosh won the contest to create a new home for the Glasgow School of Art. He threw himself into the project, designing every detail of the building, inside and out. Remember that this work was the Art Nouveau original, and that Frank Lloyd Wright, the Art Deco Chrysler Building, and everything that resembles it came well after Charles Rennie Mack's time.

Unfortunately, the building was badly damaged by a fire in

May 2014. It likely won't open again until 2019 at the earliest. For now, you can join the underwhelming tour of the **Reid Building,** which includes insight about the architecture of the School of Art and a visit to a small room full of furniture designed by Mackintosh and his wife, Margaret MacDonald. Or you can visit the small, free exhibition about Mackintosh, including an impressive model of the School of Art (shop, exhibition, and tour desk open daily during renovation 10:00-16:30).

Tours: Tours are £7 and last 45 minutes; 6/day in peak season, 4/day in off-season, check times online (tel. 0141/353-4526, www. gsa.ac.uk/tours). Serious admirers can ask about the 2.25-hour Mackintosh-themed city walking tours given by students (£20, 4/ week).

CATHEDRAL PRECINCT, WITH A HINT OF MEDIEVAL GLASGOW

Very little remains of medieval Glasgow, but a visit to the cathedral and the area around it is a visit to the birthplace of the city. The first church was built here in the seventh century. Today's towering cathedral is mostly 13th-century—the only great Scottish church to survive the Reformation intact. In front of the cathedral (near the street), you'll see an attention-grabbing statue of **David Livingstone** (1813-1873). Livingstone—the Scottish missionary/explorer/cartographer who discovered a huge waterfall in Africa and named it in honor of his queen, Victoria—was born eight miles from here.

Nearby, the Provand's Lordship is Glasgow's only secular building dating from the Middle Ages. The St. Mungo Museum of Religious Life and Art, built on the site of the old Bishop's Castle, is a unique exhibit covering the spectrum of religions. And the Necropolis, blanketing the hill behind the cathedral, provides an atmospheric walk through a world of stately Victorian tombstones. From there you can scan the city and look down on the brewery where Tennent's Lager (a longtime Glasgow favorite) has been made since 1885. And, if the spirit moves you, hike on down and tour the brewery (described later).

The following sights are within close range of each other. As you face the cathedral, the St. Mungo Museum is on your right (with handy public WCs), the Provand's Lordship is across the street from St. Mungo, and the Necropolis is behind the cathedral and to the right. The brewery is a 10-minute walk away.

To reach these sights from Buchanan Street, turn east on Bath Street, which soon becomes Cathedral Street, and walk about 15 minutes (or hop a bus along the main drag—try bus #38, or #57, confirm with driver that the bus stops at the cathedral). To head to the Kelvingrove Museum after your visit, from the cathedral, walk two blocks up Castle Street and catch bus #19 (on the cathedral side).

▲Glasgow Cathedral

This blackened, Gothic cathedral is a rare example of an intact pre-Reformation Scottish cathedral. (It was once known as "the

Pink Church" for the tone of its stone, but with Industrial Age soot and modern pollution, it blackened. Cleaning would damage the integrity of the stone structure, so it was left black.) The zealous Reformation forces of John Knox ripped out the stained glass and ornate chapels of the Catholic age, but they left the church standing. The church is aching to tell its long and fascinating story and volunteers are standing by to do just that.

Cost and Hours: Free, £3 suggested donation; Mon-Sat 9:30-17:30, Sun 13:00-17:00; Oct-March until 16:00; request a free tour or join one in progress; near junction of Castle and Cathedral Streets, tel. 0141/552-8198, www.glasgowcathedral.org.uk.

Visiting the Cathedral: Inside, look up to see the wooden barrel-vaulted ceiling, and take in the beautifully decorated section

over the choir ("quire"). The choir screen is the only pre-Reformation screen surviving in Scotland. It divided the common people from the priests and big shots of the day, who got to worship closer to the religious action. The cathedral's glass dates mostly from the 19th century. One window on the right side of the choir, celebrating the 14 trades of Glasgow (try to find them), dates from 1951. Left of that is a set of three windows that tell the story of St. Mungo retrieving a ring from the mouth of a fish (it's a long story).

Step into the choir and enjoy the east end with the four evangelists presiding high above in stained glass. Two seats (with high backs, right of altar) are reserved for Queen Elizabeth II and her husband Prince Philip, the Duke of Edinburgh.

Step into the lower church (down stairs on right as you face the choir), where the central altar sits upon St. Mungo's tomb. Mungo was the seventh-century Scottish monk and mythical founder of Glasgow who established the first wooden church on this spot and gave Glasgow its name. Notice the ceiling bosses (decorative caps where the ribs come together) with their colorfully carved demons, dragons, and skulls.

Nearby: On Cathedral Square, you'll find the cute Empire Coffee Box, where Rocco is ready to caffeinate you from this old-style police call box.

▲Necropolis

From the cathedral, a lane leads over the "bridge of sighs" into the park filled with grand tombstones. Glasgow's huge burial hill has a wistful, ramshackle appeal. A stroll among the tombstones of the eminent Glaswegians of the 19th century gives a glimpse of Victorian Glasgow and a feeling for the confidence and wealth of the second city of the British Empire in its glory days.

With the Industrial Age (in the early 1800s), Glasgow's population tripled to 200,000. The existing churchyards were jammed and unhygienic. The city needed a beautiful place in which to bury its beautiful citizens, so this grand necropolis was established. Because Presbyterians are more into simplicity, the statuary is simpler than in a Catholic cemetery. Wandering among the disintegrating memorials to once-important people, I thought about how, someday, everyone's tombstone will fall over and no one will care.

The highest pillar in the graveyard is a memorial to John Knox. The Great Reformer (who's actually buried in Edinburgh) looks down at the cathedral he wanted to strip of all art, and even tear down. (The Glaswegians rallied to follow Knox, but saved the church.) If the cemetery's main black gates are closed, see if you can get in and out through a gate off the street to the right.

▲St. Mungo Museum of Religious Life and Art

This secular, city-run museum, just in front of the cathedral, aims to promote religious understanding. Built in 1990 on the site of the old Bishop's Castle, it provides a handy summary of major and minor world religions, showing how each faith handles various rites of passage across the human life span: birth, puberty, marriage, death, and everything in between and after. Start with the 10-minute video overview on the first floor, and finish with a great view from the top floor of the cathedral and Necropolis. Ponder the Zen Buddhist garden out back as you leave.

Cost and Hours: Free, £3 suggested donation, Tue-Thu and Sat 10:00-17:00, Fri and Sun from 11:00, closed Mon, free WCs

GLASGOW

downstairs, cheap ground-floor café, 2 Castle Street, tel. 0141/276-1625, www.glasgowmuseums.com.

Nearby: To view a modern-day depiction of St. Mungo, walk two minutes down High Street from the museum to a building-sized mural by the artist Smug.

Provand's Lordship

With low beams and medieval decor, this creaky home—supposedly the "oldest house in Glasgow"—is the only secular building surviving in Glasgow from the Middle Ages. On three floors it displays the *Lifestyles of the Rich and Famous*...circa 1471. First, sit down and watch the 10-minute video (ground floor). The interior, while sparse and stony, shows off a few pieces of furniture from the 16th, 17th, and 18th centuries. Out back, explore the St. Nicholas Garden, which was once part of a hospital that dispensed herbal remedies. The plaques in each section show the part of the body each plant is used to treat.

Cost and Hours: Free, small donation requested, Tue-Thu and Sat 10:00-17:00, Fri and Sun from 11:00, closed Mon, across the street from St. Mungo Museum at 3 Castle Street, tel. 0141/552-8819, www.glasgowmuseums.com.

▲▲Tennent's Brewery Tour

Tennent's, founded in 1740, is now the biggest brewery in Scotland, spanning 18 acres. They give serious hour-long tours showing how they make "Scotland's favorite pint," and how they fill 700 kegs per hour and 1,000 bottles per minute (you'll see more action Mon-Fri). It's hot and sweaty inside, with 100 steps to climb on your tour. When you're done (surrounded by "the Lager Love-lies"—cans from 1965 to 1993 that were decorated with cover girls), you'll enjoy three samples followed by a pint of your choice (£10, tours depart daily at 10:00, 12:00, 14:00, 16:00, & 18:00; call or book online; 161 Duke Street, 0141/202-7145, www.tennentstours.com). To head back downtown, bus #41 stops in front of the brewery on Duke Street and goes to George Square.

THE WEST END

These sights are linked by my West End Walk on page 142.

▲Hunterian Gallery and Mackintosh House

Here's a sightseeing twofer: an art gallery offering a good look at some Scottish artists relatively unknown outside their homeland, and the chance to take a guided tour through the reconstructed home of Charles Rennie Mackintosh, decorated exactly the way he liked it. For Charles Rennie Mack fans—or anyone fascinated by the unique habitats of artists—it's well worth a visit.

Cost and Hours: Gallery-free, Tue-Sat 10:00-17:00, Sun 11:00-16:00, closed Mon, across University Avenue from the main university building, tel. 0141/330-4221, www.gla.ac.uk/hunterian. Mackintosh House-£5, same hours as gallery, last entry 45 minutes before closing. The Mackintosh House is open weekday mornings by 30-minute tour only (Tue-Fri 10:00-12:30, departs every 30 minutes). After 13:00, and all day Sat-Sun, the house is open without a tour, but only 12 people are allowed at a time, so there may be a short wait.

Visitor Information: First, check in at the reception desk to sign up for a tour of the Mackintosh House or see if there's a wait to get in. You'll also need to check any bags (free lockers available). Spend your waiting time visiting the gallery, or, with a longer wait, head across the street to the Hunterian Museum (described later). If it's lunchtime, eat at **$ Food,** a cheap, healthy, fast, and modern student cafeteria across the lane from the museum that's open to the public.

Mackintosh House: In 1906, Mackintosh and his wife, Margaret MacDonald, moved into the end unit of a Victorian row house. Mackintosh gutted the place and redesigned it to his own liking—bathing the interior in his trademark style, a mix of curving, organic lines and rigid, proto-Art Deco functionalism. They moved out in 1914, and the house was demolished in the 1960s—but the university wisely documented the layout and carefully removed and preserved all of Mackintosh's original furnishings. In 1981, when respect for Mackintosh was on the rise, they built this replica house and reinstalled everything just as Mackintosh had designed it. You'll see the entryway, dining room, drawing room, and bedroom—each one offering glimpses into the minds of these great artists. You'll see original furniture and decorations by Mackintosh and MacDonald, providing insight into their creative process.

Hunterian Art Gallery: The adjacent gallery is manageable and worth exploring. Circling one floor, you'll enjoy three thoughtfully described sections. One highlight is the modern Scottish art (1850-1960), focusing on two groups: the "Glasgow Boys," who traveled to France to study during the waning days of Realism (1880s), and, a generation later, the Scottish Colourists, who found a completely different inspiration in circa-1910 France—bright, bold, with an almost Picasso-like exuberance. The gallery also has an extensive collection of portraits by American artist James Whistler—Whistler's wife was of Scottish descent, as was Whistler's mother. (Hey, that has a nice ring to it.) The painter always found great support in Scotland, and his heir donated his estate to the University of Glasgow.

▲Hunterian Museum

The oldest public museum in Scotland was founded by William Hunter (1718-1783), a medical researcher. Today his natural sci-

ence collection is housed in a huge and gorgeous space inside the university's showcase building. Everything is well presented and well explained. You'll see a perceptive exhibit on the Antonine Wall (the lesser-known cousin of Hadrian's Wall), built in A.D. 142 to seal off the Picts from the Roman Empire. Ancient Roman artifacts on display include leather shoes, plumbing, weapons, and carved reliefs. The eclectic collection also includes musical instruments, a display on the Glasgow-built *Lusitania,* and a fine collection of fossils, including the aquatic dinosaur called plesiosaur (possibly a distant ancestor of the Loch Ness monster). But to some, most fascinating are the many examples of deformities—two-headed animals, body parts in jars, and so on (main hall, left of Romans). Ever the curious medical researcher, Hunter collected these for study, and these intrigue, titillate, and nauseate visitors to this day.

Cost and Hours: Free, Tue-Sat 10:00-17:00, Sun 11:00-16:00, closed Mon, Gilbert Scott Building, University Avenue, tel. 0141/330-4221, www.gla.ac.uk/hunterian.

▲▲Kelvingrove Art Gallery and Museum

This "Scottish Smithsonian" displays everything from a stuffed ele-

phant to paintings by the great masters and what, for me, is the city's best collection of work by Charles Rennie Mackintosh. The well-described contents are impressively displayed in a grand, 100-year-old, Spanish Baroque-style building. The Kelvingrove claims to be one of the most-visited museums in Britain—presumably because of all the field-trip groups you'll see here. Watching all the excited Scottish kids—their imaginations ablaze—is as much fun as the collection itself.

Cost and Hours: Free, £5 suggested donation, Mon-Thu and Sat 10:00-17:00, Fri and Sun from 11:00, free tours at 11:00 and 14:30, Argyle Street, tel. 0141/276-9599, www.glasgowmuseums.com.

Getting There: My self-guided West End Walk leads you here from the Hillhead subway stop, or you can ride the **subway** to the Kelvinhall stop. When you exit, turn left and walk five minutes. **Buses** #2 and #3 run from Hope Street downtown to the museum. It's also on **the hop-on, hop-off bus** route. No matter how you arrive, just look for the huge, turreted red-brick building.

Organ Concerts: At the top of the main hall, the huge pipe organ booms with a daily 30-minute recital at 13:00 (15:00 on Sunday).

Visiting the Museum: Built in 1901 to house the city collection, the museum is divided into two sections: Art ("Expression") and Natural ("Life"), each with two floors. The symmetrical floor plan can be confusing. Pick up a map and plan your strategy.

The "Expression" section, in the East Court, is marked by a commotion of heads—each with a different expression—raining down from the ceiling. This half of the museum focuses on artwork, including Dutch, Flemish, French, and Scottish Romanticism from the late 19th century. The exhibits on "Scottish Identity in Art" let you tour the country's scenic wonders and its history on canvas. The Mackintosh section, a highlight for many, demonstrates the Art Nouveau work of the "Glasgow Four," including Charles Rennie Mackintosh. Unfortunately, the museum's star painting, Salvador Dalí's *Christ of St. John of the Cross*, will be on the road until 2020.

The "Life" section, in the West Court, features a menagerie of stuffed animals (including a giraffe, kangaroo, ostrich, and moose) with a WWII-era Spitfire fighter plane hovering overhead. Branching off are halls with exhibits ranging from Ancient Egypt to "Scotland's First People" to weaponry ("Conflict and Consequence").

Kelvingrove Lawn Bowling

For a fun and free activity surrounded by relaxed locals, try your hand at lawn bowling. There's a mission behind the perfectly manicured greens next to the Kelvingrove Museum (made beautiful to host the 2014 Commonwealth Games): Keep young people interested in the traditional sport. They'll provide balls (4 per person) and a court time. It's all free and tourists are welcome. While sunny weekends may be too busy, you'll always find a court on a cloudy weekday. It's a fine evening activity; you can bowl rain or shine (April-Sept Mon-Fri 9:00-21:00, Sat-Sun until 18:00, mobile 07920-048-945). Lawn bowling is a lot like *petanque* (popular in France); the object and scoring are the same. The balls are bigger and "biased" (lopsided on purpose to let experts throw curves). Let the attendant explain the rules if necessary. (They also rent tennis gear for the adjacent courts.) An efficient plan would be to end your sightseeing day at the huge Kelvingrove Museum (closes at 17:00), play an hour of "bowls," and have dinner a couple blocks away at a recommended Finnieston restaurant of your choice. You could cap your night with a beer and live music at a Gaelic pub.

AWAY FROM THE CENTER
▲▲Riverside Museum

Located along the River Clyde, this high-tech, extremely kid-friendly museum—nostalgic and modern at the same time—is dedicated to all things transportation-related. Named the European museum of the year in 2013, visiting is a must for anyone interested in transportation and how it has shaped society.

Cost and Hours: Free, £5 suggested donation, Mon-Thu and Sat 10:00-17:00, Fri and Sun from 11:00, ground-floor café with £6-9 meals, upstairs coffee shop with basic drinks and snacks, 100 Pointhouse Place, tel. 0141/287-2720, www.glasgowmuseums.com.

Getting There: It's on the riverfront promenade, two miles west of the city center. **Bus** #100 runs between the museum and George Square (2/hour, last departure from George Square at 15:02, operated by McColl's), or you can take a **taxi** (£6-8, 10-minute ride from downtown). The museum is also included on the **hop-on, hop-off sightseeing bus** route (described on page 132, under "Tours in Glasgow").

Visiting the Museum: Most of the collection is strewn across one huge, wide-open floor. Upon entering, visit the info desk (to the right as you enter, near the shop) to ask about today's free tours and activities—or just listen for announcements. Also pick up a map from the info desk, as the museum's open floor plan can feel a bit like a traffic jam at rush hour.

Diving in, explore the vast collection: stagecoaches, locomotives,

GLASGOW

double-decker trolleys, and an entire wall stacked with vintage automobiles and another with motorcycles. Learn about the opening of Glasgow's old-timey subway (Europe's third oldest). Explore the collections of old toys and prams, and watch a film about 1930s cinema. Stroll the re-creation of a circa-1900 main street, with video clips bringing each shop to life (there's one about a little girl who discovers her daddy was selling things to the pawn shop to pay the rent).

Don't miss the much-smaller upstairs section, with great views over the River Clyde (cross the footbridge over the trains), additional exhibits about ships built here in Glasgow, and what may be the world's oldest bicycle. The description explains how two different inventors have tried to take credit for the bike—and both of them are Scottish.

Nearby: Be sure to head to the River Clyde directly behind the museum (just step out the back door). The *Glenlee,* one of five remaining tall ships built in Glasgow in the 19th century (1896), invites visitors to come aboard (free, daily 10:00-17:00, Nov-Feb until 16:00, tel. 0141/357-3699, www.thetallship.com). Good exhibits illustrate what it was like to live and work aboard the ship. Explore the officers' living quarters, then head below deck to the cafe and more exhibits. Below that, the cargo hold has kids' activities and offers the chance to peek into the engine room. As you board, note the speedboat river tour that leaves from here each afternoon (£10, 20 minutes).

Burrell Collection

This eclectic art collection of a wealthy local shipping magnate—which includes sculpture from Roman to Rodin, stained glass, tapestries, furniture, Asian and Islamic works, and halls of paintings starring Cézanne, Renoir, Degas, and a Rembrandt self-portrait—is closed for renovation until at least 2020 (three miles outside the city center in Pollok Country Park, tel. 0141/287-2550, www.glasgowmuseums.com).

Shopping in Glasgow

Downtown, the **Golden Zed**—a.k.a. "Style Mile"—has all the predictable chain stores, with a few Scottish souvenir stands mixed in. For more on this, see the start of my self-guided "Get to Know Glasgow" walk. The Glasgow Modern Art Museum (GoMA) has a quirky gift shop that many find enticing.

The West End also has some appealing shops. Many are concentrated on **Cresswell Lane** (covered in my self-guided West End Walk). Browsing here, you'll find an eclectic assortment of gifty shops, art galleries, design shops, hair salons, record stores, home-decor shops, and lots of vintage bric-a-brac. Be sure to poke into De Courcy's Arcade, a two-part warren of tiny offbeat shops.

Nightlife and Entertainment in Glasgow

Glasgow has a youthful vibe, and its nightlife scene is renowned. The city is full of live music acts and venues. Walking through the city center, you'll pass at least one club or bar on every block.

PUBS AND CLUBS

Downtown: Glasgow's central business and shopping district is pretty sleepy after hours, but there are a few pockets of activity—each with its own personality. **Bath Street**'s bars and clubs are focused on young professionals as well as students; the recommended Pot Still is a perfect place to sample Scotch whisky (see "Eating in Glasgow," later). Nearby, running just below the Glasgow School of Art, **Sauchiehall Street** is younger, artsier, and more student-oriented. The recently revitalized **Merchant City** zone, stretching just east of the Buchanan Street shopping drag, has a slightly older crowd and a popular gay scene.

West End: You'll find fun bars and music venues in **Hillhead**, on Ashton Lane and surrounding streets. **Finnieston**, just below the Kelvingrove Museum, is packed with trendy bars and restaurants. But it also has an old-school selection of spit-and-sawdust Gaelic pubs, some of which have live music in the evenings (see next).

LIVE MUSIC

Glasgow has a great music scene, on its streets (talented buskers) and in its bars and clubs (including trad sessions). For the latest, *The Skinny* is Glasgow's information-packed alternative weekly (www.theskinny.co.uk). Or check out *The List* (www.list.co.uk) or the *Gig Guide* (www.gigguide.co.uk). All three are also available in print around town. Or check out what's going on at these bars:

Finnieston

The following pubs line up along Argyle Street.

The Ben Nevis hosts lively, toe-tapping sessions three times a week. It's a good scene—full of energy but crowded. Show up early to grab a seat in this tiny pub, or be ready to stand (Wed, Thu, and Sun at 21:00, no food service—just snacks, #1147).

The Islay Inn has bands twice weekly—some traditional, some doing contemporary covers. On nonmusic nights you'll find televisions blasting sports (music Fri and Sat at 21:00, food available, #1256, at corner with Radnor).

At **The Park Bar,** you'll find live music several nights a week, including traditional Scottish bands and sessions on Thursdays (Thu-Sun around 21:00, food available, #1202).

Hillhead

The **Òran Mòr** (a former church, www.oran-mor.co.uk) and **Hillhead Bookclub** (a former cinema, www.hillheadbookclub.co.uk) are popular live music venues (both recommended later, under "Eating in Glasgow").

Jinty McGuinty's has acoustic music every night, ranging from chart hits to Irish classics to soul and blues (daily at 21:30, 29 Ashton Lane).

Downtown

Twice weekly at **Babbity Bowster,** musicians take over a corner of this cute pub (under a recommended B&B) for a trad session. The music, energy, and atmosphere are top-notch (Wed and Sat at 15:00, solid pub grub, 16 Blackfriars Street).

Sloans, hidden away through a muraled tunnel off Argyle Street, is a fun pub with outdoor tables filling an alley. They have live traditional music on Wednesdays (21:00) and *ceilidh* dancing instruction on Fridays (£10, starts at 20:30, book ahead, food available, 108 Argyle Street, www.sloansglasgow.com).

Waxy O'Connor's is a massive, multilevel Irish bar featuring a maze of dark, atmospheric rooms, a tree climbing up a wall, and lots of live music (usually acoustic—check their website for days/times) and trad sessions on Sundays at 15:00 (food available, 44 West George Street, www.waxyoconnors.co.uk).

MOVIES

The Grosvenor Cinema, right on Ashton Lane in the heart of the bustling West End restaurant scene, is an inviting movie theater, with cushy leather seats in two theaters showing films big and small (most movies £10) and lots of special events. Wine and beer are available at the theater, or you can order cocktails and warm food at the bar next door and have it delivered to your seat (21 Ashton Lane, tel. 0845-166-6002, www.grosvenorcinema.co.uk).

GLASGOW

Sleeping in Glasgow

For accommodations, choose between downtown (bustling by day, nearly deserted at night, close to main shopping zone and some major sights, very expensive parking and one-way streets that cause headaches for drivers) and the West End (neighborhoody, best variety of restaurants, easier parking, easy access to West End sights and parks but a bus or subway ride from the center and train station).

DOWNTOWN

These accommodations are scattered around the city center. For locations, see the map on page 164. Glasgow also has all the predictable chains—**Ibis, Premier Inn, Travelodge, Novotel, Mercure, Jurys Inn, EasyHotel**—check online for deals.

$$$ Pipers' Tryst has eight simple rooms enthusiastically done up in good tartan style above a restaurant in the National Piping Centre (described on page 150). It's in a grand, old former church building overlooking a busy intersection, across the street from the downtown business, shopping, and entertainment district. The location is handy, if not romantic, and it's practically a pilgrimage for fans of bagpipes (30 McPhater Street, tel. 0141/353-5551, www.thepipingcentre.co.uk, hotel@thepipingcentre.co.uk).

$$$ Z Hotel, part of a small "compact luxury" chain, offers 104 sleek, stylish rooms (some are very small and don't have windows). It's welcoming and handy to Queen Street Station, just a few steps off George Square (breakfast extra, air-con, elevator, free wine-and-cheese buffet each afternoon, 36 North Frederick Street, tel. 0141/212-4550, www.thezhotels.com, glasgow@thezhotels.com).

$$ Grasshoppers is a cheerful, above-it-all retreat on the sixth floor of a building overlooking Central Station. The street-level entry is minimal, but popping out of the elevator, you know you've arrived. The 29 rooms are tight, with small "efficiency" bathrooms, but the welcome is warm and there's 24-hour access to fresh cupcakes, shortbread, and ice cream (free breakfast to those booking direct, optional buffet dinner, elevator, 87 Union Street, tel. 0141/222-2666, www.grasshoppersglasgow.com, info@grasshoppersglasgow.com).

$$ Motel One, part of a stylish German budget hotel chain, has 374 rooms and is conveniently located right next to Central Station (corner of Oswald and Argyle streets, www.motel-one.com).

$ Babbity Bowster, named for a traditional Scottish dance, is a pub and restaurant renting five simple, mod rooms up top. It's located in the trendy Merchant City area on the eastern fringe of downtown, near several clubs and restaurants (no breakfast, lots

of stairs and no elevator, 10-minute walk from either station, 16
Blackfriars Street, tel. 0141/552-5055, www.babbitybowster.
com, info@babbitybowster.com). The ground-floor **$$** pub serves
good grub (daily 12:00-22:00) and has twice-weekly sessions (see
"Nightlife and Entertainment in Glasgow").

¢ The huge **Euro Hostel** (over 400 beds) is a well-run and
well-located option for those on a tight budget (private rooms,
family rooms, all rooms have en-suite bathrooms, breakfast extra,
kitchen, bar, very central on the River Clyde near Central Station,
318 Clyde Street, tel. 0845-539-9956, www.eurohostels.co.uk,
glasgow@eurohostels.co.uk).

IN THE WEST END

For a more appealing neighborhood experience, bunk in the West
End—the upper-middle-class neighborhood just a few subway
stops (or a 15-minute, £8 taxi ride) from downtown. As this is also
one of the city's best dining zones, you'll likely come here for din-
ner anyway—so why not sleep here? My favorites in this area are
the Alamo and Amadeus, which have the most personality. For
locations, see the map on page 164.

Finnieston

These places are in an inviting residential area near the Kelvingrove
Museum (not as handy to the subway, but easy by bus). They're
close to the lively Argyle Street scene, with good restaurants and
fun Gaelic pubs.

$$ The Alamo Guest House, energetically run by Steve and
Emma, faces the bowling green and tennis court. It has rich, lav-
ishly decorated public spaces and 10 comfortable rooms, including
two luxury suites with bathtubs (family room, some rooms with
bathroom down the hall, 2- or 3-night minimum stay on weekends in peak season, 46 Gray Street, tel. 0141/339-2395, www.
alamoguesthouse.com, info@alamoguesthouse.com).

At the **$$ Argyll Hotel and Guesthouse** you won't forget
you're in Scotland. Each room is accessorized with a different tar-
tan and has info on the associated clan, while the halls are adorned
with symbols of Scotland (bagpipes, thistle, local landmarks, etc.).
The hotel has an elevator, breakfast room, and higher prices than
the guesthouse (guesthouse customers must cross the street for
breakfast and deal with stairs). Otherwise the rooms are just as
nice and a bit larger in the guesthouse (family rooms, save money
by skipping breakfast, 973 Sauchiehall Street, tel. 0141/337-3313,
www.argyllhotelglasgow.co.uk, info@argyllhotelglasgow.co.uk).

Near Kelvinbridge

$$ Amadeus Guest House, a classy refuge just north of the large

Central Glasgow Hotels & Restaurants

Kelvingrove Park, has nine modern rooms and artistic flourishes. It hides down a quiet street yet is conveniently located near the Kelvinbridge subway stop—just a 10-minute walk or one subway stop from the restaurant zone (includes continental breakfast, 411 North Woodside Road, tel. 0141/339-8257, www.amadeusguesthouse. co.uk, reservations@amadeusguesthouse.co.uk, Alexandra).

Hillhead

These places, overlooking the busy Great Western Road, are close to the Botanic Gardens and Hillhead restaurant scene but farther from the center (10-minute walk to Hillhead subway stop or catch bus to center from Great Western Road).

$$ The Alfred, run by the landmark Òran Mòr restaurant/pub (located in the former church just up the street), brings a con-

Accommodations
1. Pipers' Tryst
2. Z Hotel
3. Grasshoppers
4. Motel One
5. Babbity Bowster
6. Euro Hostel

Eateries & Nightlife
7. Martha's
8. Mussel Inn
9. Willow Tea Rooms
10. Rogano
11. Tabac
12. Two Fat Ladies
13. CCA Saramago Bar & Courtyard Vegetarian Café
14. The Vic
15. The Pot Still
16. Sloans
17. Waxy O'Connor's

temporary elegance to the neighborhood, with 14 new-feeling, stylish rooms (family room, includes continental breakfast, 1 Alfred Terrace, tel. 0141/357-3445, www.thealfredhotelglasgow. co.uk, alfred@thealfredhotelglasgow.co.uk).

$$ Belhaven Hotel, a little farther out (about 10 minutes past Byres Road), has 18 rooms in an elegant four-floor townhouse with a pretty, tiled atrium (save money by skipping breakfast, bar in breakfast room serves drinks to guests, no elevator, 15 Belhaven Terrace, tel. 0141/339-3222, www.belhavenhotel.com, info@belhavenhotel.com).

$ Argyll Western, with 17 sleek and tartaned Scottish-themed rooms, feels modern, efficient, and a bit impersonal (breakfast extra, 6 Buckingham Terrace, tel. 0141/339-2339, www.

argyllwestern.co.uk, info@argyllwestern.co.uk; same family runs the Argyll Hotel, listed earlier).

Eating in Glasgow

DOWNTOWN

$ Martha's is ideal for hungry, hurried sightseers (and local office workers) in search of a healthy and satisfying lunch. They serve a seasonal menu of wraps, rice boxes, soups, and other great meals made with Scottish ingredients but with eclectic, exotic, international flavors (Indian, Thai, Mexican, and so on). It's understandably popular: Just line up (it moves fast), order at the counter, and then find a table or take your food to go (Mon-Fri 7:30-18:00, closed Sat-Sun, 142A St. Vincent Street, tel. 0141/248-9771).

$$$ Mussel Inn offers light, good-value fish dinners and seafood plates in an airy, informal environment. The restaurant is a cooperative, owned and run by shellfish farmers. Their "kilo pot" of Scottish mussels is popular with locals and big enough to share ("lunchtime quickie" deals, daily specials, daily 12:00-14:30 & 17:00-22:00, 157 Hope Street, tel. 0141/572-1405).

$$ The **Willow Tea Rooms,** designed by Charles Rennie Mackintosh, has a diner-type eatery and a classy Room de Luxe. The cheap and cheery menu covers both dining areas (afternoon tea, Mon-Sat 9:00-17:00, Sun from 10:30, reservations smart, 217 Sauchiehall Street, tel. 0141/332-0521, www.willowtearooms.co.uk).

Rogano is a time-warp Glasgow institution that retains much of the same classy Art Deco interior it had when it opened in 1935. The restaurant has three distinct sections: **$$ The Rogano Bar** in front is an Art Deco diner with dressy outdoor seating and serves soups, sandwiches, and simple dishes; **$$$$ The Rogano Restaurant,** a fancy dining room at the back of the main floor that smacks of the officers' mess on the *Queen Mary,* focuses on seafood, classic Scottish dishes, and afternoon tea (their early menu—until 19:00—is a good deal); **$$$ The Rogano Café,** a more casual yet still dressy bistro in the cellar, is filled with 1930s-Hollywood posters and offers a similar menu to the fancy restaurant, but cheaper (daily 12:00-16:00 & 18:00-21:30, 11 Exchange Place—just before giant Merchant City archway just off Buchanan Street, reservations smart, tel. 0141/248-4055, www.roganoglasgow.com).

$$ Tabac is a dark, mod, and artsy cocktail bar with spacious seating on a narrow lane just off Buchanan Street. They serve pizza, burgers, and big salads (daily 12:00-24:00, food served until 21:00, across from "The Lighthouse" at 10 Mitchell Lane, tel. 0141/572-1448).

$$$ Two Fat Ladies is a hardworking and dressy little place with a focus on food rather than atmosphere and a passion for white fish (early-bird menu until 18:15 a great value, daily 12:00-14:30 & 17:00-22:00, 118 Blythswood Street, tel. 0141/847-0088).

$$ CCA Saramago Bar and Courtyard Vegetarian Café, located on the first floor of Glasgow's edgy contemporary art museum, charges art-student prices for its designer, animal-free food. An 18th-century facade, discovered when the site was excavated to build the gallery, looms over the atrium restaurant (food served daily 12:00-22:00, free Wi-Fi, 350 Sauchiehall Street, tel. 0141/332-7959).

$ The Vic is a student hangout within the Glasgow School of Art itself. Face the modern Reid Building and hook around the left side to find the easy-to-miss entrance to this funky bar/café with starving-artist fare from an eclectic, international menu (Mon-Sat 12:00-21:00, closed Sun).

For Your Whisky: The Pot Still is an award-winning malt whisky bar dating from 1835 that's also proud of its meat pies. You'll see locals of all ages sitting in its leathery interior, watching football (soccer), and discussing their drinks. Give the friendly bartenders a little background on your beverage tastes, and they'll narrow down a good choice for you from their long list (daily 11:00-24:00, 154 Hope Street, tel. 0141/333-0980, Frank has the long beard).

IN THE WEST END

This hip, lively residential neighborhood/university district is worth exploring, particularly in the evening. The restaurant scene focuses on two areas (at opposite ends of my West End Walk): near the Hillhead subway stop and, farther down, in the Finnieston neighborhood near the Kelvingrove Museum. For locations, see the map on page 144. It's smart to book ahead at any of these places for weekend evenings.

Near Hillhead

There's a fun concentration of restaurants on the streets that fan out from the Hillhead subway stop (£8 taxi ride from downtown).

If it's a balmy evening, several have convivial gardens designed to catch the evening sun. Before choosing a place, take a stroll and scout the Ashton Lane scene, which has the greatest variety of places (including Ubiquitous Chip and Brel Bar, recommended next). Tucked away on Ruthven Lane (opposite the subway station) are Bothy Restaurant and The Hanoi Bike Shop. And a

GLASGOW

couple blocks away (near the Botanic Gardens) are Hillhead Book-club, The Parlour, Òran Mòr, and Cail Bruich.

$$$$ Ubiquitous Chip, aka "The Chip," is a beloved local landmark with a couple inviting pubs and two great restaurant options. On the ground floor is their fine restaurant with beautifully presented contemporary Scottish dishes in a garden atrium. Their early-bird menu (order by 18:30) is a great value. Upstairs (looking down on the scene) is the less-formal, less-expensive, but still very nice brasserie (daily 11:00-22:00, 12 Ashton Lane, tel. 0141/334-5007, www.ubiquitouschip.co.uk).

$$ Brel Bar is a fun-loving place with a happy garden and a menu with burgers, mussels, and quality bar food. On a nice evening, its backyard beer garden is hard to beat (daily 12:00-24:00, 37 Ashton Lane, tel. 0141/342-4966).

$$$ Bothy Restaurant is a romantic place offering tasty, traditional Scottish fare served by waiters in kilts. Sit outside in the inviting alleyway or in the rustic-contemporary dining room (daily 12:00-22:00, down the lane opposite the subway station to 11 Ruthven Lane, tel. 0141/334-4040).

$$ The Hanoi Bike Shop, a rare-in-Scotland Vietnamese "street food" restaurant, serves Asian tapas that are healthy and tasty, using local produce. With tight seating and friendly service, the place has a fun energy (daily 12:00-23:00, 8 Ruthven Lane, tel. 0141/334-7165).

$$ Hillhead Bookclub is a historic cinema building cleared out to make room for fun, disco, pub grub, and lots of booze. It's a youthful and quirky art-school scene, with lots of beers on tap, creative cocktails, retro computer games, ping-pong, and theme evenings like "drag queen bingo" night. The menu: meat pies, fish-and-chips, burgers, and salads (daily 10:00-21:30, 17 Vinicombe Street, tel. 0141/576-1700).

$$ The Parlour, across from the Hillhead Bookclub, gets all the evening sun on its terrace seating. In bad weather, the spacious interior is warmed by an open fire. It's young, fun, and pub-like, with pizza, tacos, burgers, and creative cocktails (daily 11:00-21:30, 28 Vinicombe Street, mobile 07943-852-973).

$$ Òran Mòr fills a converted church from the 1860s with a classic pub. They offer basic pub grub either inside or on the front-porch beer garden (daily 10:00-21:00, later on weekends, across from the Botanic Gardens at 731 Great Western Road, tel. 0141/357-600).

$$$$ Cail Bruich serves award-winning classic Scottish dishes with an updated spin in an elegant and romantic setting. Reservations are smart (classy tasting menus for £35-45, lunch Wed-Sun 12:00-14:00, dinner Mon-Sat 18:00-21:00, 725 Great Western Road, tel. 0141/334-6265, www.cailbruich.co.uk).

Facing the Kelvingrove Museum

These three places are immediately across from the Kelvingrove Museum (which is likely to leave you hungry). They're more basic and less trendy than the Finnieston places (a few blocks away, listed next) that will leave you with better memories.

$$ Brewdog Glasgow is a beer-and-burgers joint. It's a great place to sample Scottish microbrews—from their own brewery in Aberdeen, as well as guest brews—in an industrial-mod setting reminiscent of American brewpubs (daily 12:00-24:00, 1397 Argyle Street, tel. 0141/334-7175, www.brewdog.com).

$$ Mother India's Café serves basic Indian and is a good stop if you crave Scotland's national dish: "a good curry." The menu features small plates designed to enjoy family-style (about two plates per person makes a meal, daily 12:00-22:30, 1355 Argyle Street, tel. 0141/339-9145).

$$$ Butchershop Bar & Grill is a casual, rustic, American-style steakhouse, but featuring Scottish products—focusing on dry-aged Scottish steaks (lunch and early-bird deals, daily 12:00-22:00, 1055 Sauchiehall Street, tel. 0141/339-2999, www.butchershopglasgow.com).

Trendy Finnieston Eateries on and near Argyle Street

This trendy, up-and-coming neighborhood—with a hipster charm in this hipster city—stretches east from in front of the Kelvingrove Museum (a 10-minute walk from the Kelvinhall or Kelvinbridge subway stops). Each of these is likely to require a reservation. The Crabshakk started things off here and today it anchors a strip of similarly funky, foodie eateries.

$$ Crabshakk, specializing in fresh, beautifully presented seafood, is a foodie favorite, with a very tight bar-and-mezzanine seating area and tables spilling out onto the sidewalk. It's casual but still respectable, and worth reserving ahead (daily 12:00-22:00, 1114 Argyle Street, tel. 0141/334-6127, www.crabshakk.com).

$$$ The Gannet emphasizes Scottish ingredients with a modern spin. It's relaxed and stylish but the owners/chefs are serious about the food (lunch Thu-Sat 12:00-14:00, dinner Tue-Sat 17:00-21:30, Sun 13:00-19:30, closed Mon, 1155 Argyle Street, tel. 0141/204-2081, www.thegannetgla.com).

$$ Ox and Finch, with a romantic setting, open kitchen, and smart clientele, serves modern international cuisine. It features small plates in an upscale, rustic, wood-meets-industrial atmosphere (daily 12:00-22:00, 920 Sauchiehall Street, tel. 0141/339-8627, www.oxandfinch.com).

GLASGOW

Glasgow Connections

Traveline Scotland has a journey planner that's linked to all of Scotland's train and bus schedule info. Go online (www.travelinescotland.com), call them at tel. 0871-200-2233, or use the individual websites listed below. If you're connecting with Edinburgh, note that the train is faster but the bus is cheaper.

BY TRAIN

From Glasgow's Queen Street Station by Train to: Oban (5/day, 3 hours), **Fort William** (3/day, 4 hours), **Inverness** (5/day direct, 3 hours, more with change in Perth), **Edinburgh** (6/hour, 50 minutes), **Stirling** (3/hour, 45 minutes), **Pitlochry** (4/day direct, 1.5 hours, more with change in Perth).

From Glasgow's Central Station by Train to: Keswick in England's Lake District (hourly, 1.5 hours to Penrith, then catch a bus to Keswick, 45 minutes), **Cairnryan** for ferry to Belfast (take train to Ayr, 2/hour, 1 hour; then ride bus to Cairnryan, 1 hour), **Liverpool** (2/hour, 4 hours, change in Wigan or Preston), **Durham** (2/hour, 3 hours, may require change in Edinburgh), **York** (hourly, 4 hours, more with change in Edinburgh), **London** (2/hour, 5 hours direct). Train info: Tel. 0345-748-4950, www.nationalrail.co.uk.

BY BUS

Glasgow's Buchanan bus station is a hub for reaching the Highlands. If you're coming from Edinburgh, you can take the bus to Glasgow and transfer here. Or, for a speedier connection, zip to Glasgow on the train, then walk a few short blocks to the bus station. (Ideally, try to arrive at Glasgow's Queen Street Station, which is closer to the bus station.) For more details on these connections, see "Getting Around the Highlands" on page 235.

From Glasgow by Bus to: Edinburgh (Citylink bus #900, 4/hour, 1.5 hours), **Oban** (Citylink buses #976 and #977; 5/day, 3 hours), **Fort William** (Citylink buses #914, #915, and #916; 8/day, 3 hours), **Glencoe** (Citylink buses #914, #915, and #916; 8/day, 2.5 hours), **Inverness** (5/day on Citylink express bus #G10, 3 hours; 1/day direct on National Express #588, 4 hours), **Portree** on the Isle of Skye (Citylink buses #915 and #916, 3/day, 7 hours), **Pitlochry** (1/day direct on National Express #588, 5/day on Megabus to Perth, then transfer to Citylink bus for Pitlochry, 2.5 hours—train is faster), **Stirling** (hourly on Citylink #M8, 45 minutes). Citylink: tel. 0871-266-3333, www.citylink.co.uk. National Express: tel. 0871-781-8181, www.nationalexpress.com.

BY PLANE

Glasgow International Airport: Located eight miles west of the city, this airport (code: GLA) has currency-exchange desks, a TI, luggage storage, and ATMs (tel. 0844-481-5555, www. glasgowairport.com). Taxis connect downtown to the airport for about £25. Your hotel can likely arrange a private taxi service for £15, or you can take Uber.

Bus #500 zips to central Glasgow (every 10 minutes, 5:00-23:00, £7.50 one-way, £10 round-trip, 25 minutes to both train stations and the bus station, catch at bus stop #1). Slow bus #77 goes to the West End, stopping at the Kelvingrove Museum and rolling along Argyle Street (departs every 30 minutes, £5 one-way, 50 minutes).

Prestwick Airport: A hub for Ryanair, this airport is 30 miles southwest of the city center (code: PIK, tel. 0871-223-0700, ext. 1006, www.glasgowprestwick.com). The best connection is by train, which runs between the airport and Central Station (3/ hour, 50 minutes, half-price with Ryanair ticket, trains also run to Edinburgh Waverley Station—about 2/hour, 2 hours). Stagecoach buses link the airport with Buchanan Bus Station (£10, 1-2/hour, 50 minutes, www.stagecoachbus.com).

ROUTE TIPS FOR DRIVERS

From England's Lake District to Glasgow: From Keswick, take the A-66 for 18 miles to the M-6 and speed north nonstop (via Penrith and Carlisle), crossing Hadrian's Wall into Scotland. The road becomes the M-74 just north of Carlisle. To slip through Glasgow quickly, leave the M-74 at Junction 4 onto the M-73, following signs to *M-8/Glasgow*. Leave the M-73 at Junction 2, exiting onto the M-8. Stay on the M-8 west through Glasgow, exit at Junction 30, cross Erskine Bridge, and turn left on the A-82, following signs to *Criunlarich* and *Loch Lomond*. (For a scenic drive through Glasgow, take exit 17 off the M-8 and stay on the A-82 toward Dumbarton.)

GLASGOW

STIRLING & NEARBY

Stirling • Wallace Monument • Bannockburn • Falkirk • Culross • Doune • Loch Lomond and the Trossachs

The historic city of Stirling is the crossroads of Scotland: Equidistant from Edinburgh and Glasgow (less than an hour from both), and rising above a plain where the Lowlands meet the Highlands, it's no surprise that Stirling has hosted many of the biggest names (and biggest battles) of Scottish history. Everyone from Mary, Queen of Scots to Bonnie Prince Charlie has passed through the gates of its stately, strategic castle.

From the cliff-capping ramparts of Stirling Castle, you can see where each of the three pivotal battles of Scotland's 13th- and 14th-century Wars of Independence took place: the Battle of Stirling Bridge, where against all odds, the courageous William Wallace defeated the English army; the Battle of Falkirk, where Wallace was toppled by a vengeful English king; and the Battle of Bannockburn, when—in the wake of Wallace's defeat—Robert the Bruce rallied to kick out the English once and for all (well, at least for a few generations). The Wallace Monument and Bannockburn Heritage Centre—on the outskirts of Stirling, in opposite directions—are practically pilgrimage sites for patriotic Scots.

Stirling itself is sleepy, but it's a good home base for a variety of side-trips. In Falkirk, take a spin in a fascinating Ferris wheel for boats, and ogle the gigantic horse heads called The Kelpies. Sitting on the nearby estuary known as the Firth of Forth—on the way to Edinburgh or St. Andrews—is the gorgeously preserved time-warp village of Culross. To the north, fans of Monty Python and *Outlander* flock to Doune Castle. And drivers seeking a quick and easy peek at the Highlands make a loop through the Trossachs and along the bonnie, bonnie banks of Loch Lomond.

PLANNING YOUR TIME

You'll likely pass near Stirling at least once as you travel through Scotland. Skim this chapter to learn about your options and select the stops that interest you. If you can't fit it all in on a pass-through, spend the night. Just as Stirling was ideally situated for monarchs and armies of the past, it's handy for present-day visitors: It's much smaller, and arguably even more conveniently located, than Edinburgh or Glasgow, and it has a variety of good accommodations. You'd need a solid three days to see all the big sights within an hour's drive of Stirling—but most people are (and should be) more selective.

Stirling

Every Scot knows the city of Stirling (pop. 41,000) deep in their bones. This patriotic heart of Scotland is like Bunker Hill, Gettysburg, and the Alamo, all rolled into one. Stirling perches on a ridge overlooking Scotland's most history-drenched plain: a flat expanse—cut through by the twisting River Forth and the meandering stream called Bannockburn—that divides the Lowlands from the Highlands. And capping that ridge is Stirling's formidable castle, the seat of the final kings of Scotland.

From a traveler's perspective, Stirling is a pleasant mini-Edinburgh, with a steep spine leading up to that grand castle. It's busy with tourists by day, but sleepy at night. The town, and its castle, may lack personality—but both are striking and strategic.

Orientation to Stirling

Stirling's old town is situated along a long, narrow, steep hill. At its base are the train and bus stations and a thriving (but characterless) commercial district; at its apex is the castle. The old town feels like a steeper, shorter, less touristy, and far less characteristic version of Edinburgh's Royal Mile.

Tourist Information: The TI is a five-minute walk below the castle, just inside the gates of the Old Town Jail (daily 10:00-17:00, free Wi-Fi, St. Johns Street, tel. 01786/475-019).

Getting Around: While the sights within Stirling nestle together at the top of the town, the Wallace Monument and Bannockburn Heritage Centre are an easy bus or taxi ride, or short drive away.

Sights in Stirling

▲▲STIRLING CASTLE

"He who holds Stirling, holds Scotland." These fateful words have been proven, more often than not, to be true. Stirling Castle's prized position—perched on a volcanic crag overlooking a bridge over the River Forth, the primary passage between the Lowlands and the Highlands—has long been the key to Scotland. This castle was the preferred home of Scottish kings and queens in the Middle Ages; today it's one of the most historic—and most popular—castles in Scotland. While its interiors are pretty empty and new-feeling, the castle still has plenty to offer: spectacular views over a gentle countryside, tales of the dynamic Stuart monarchs, and several exhibits that try to bring the place to life.

Cost and Hours: £15, daily April-Sept 9:30-18:00, Oct-March until 17:00, last entry 45 minutes before closing, Regimental Museum closes one hour before castle, good café, tel. 01786/450-000, www.stirlingcastle.gov.uk.

Tours: The included 40-minute **guided tour** helps you get your bearings—both to the castle, and to Scottish history (gener-

Stirling

To University of Stirling

EASTER CORNTON RD.

2

DUMYAT RD.

CAUSEWAYHEAD ROAD

1

P

🚲

WALLACE MONUMENT

B-823

River Forth

A-9

To A-91

DRIP ROAD

SITE OF BATTLE OF STIRLING BRIDGE

To Park & Ride, Doune, Callander & The Trossachs

A-84

BURGH MUIR RD.

To Loch Lomond

STIRLING CASTLE

STIRLING KIRKYARD

ARGYLL'S LODGING

A-811

STIRLING SMITH ART GALLERY & MUSEUM

TOWN CENTER

i

OLD TOWN JAIL

TRAIN STATION

GOOSECROFT RD.

FORTHSIDE WAY

BUS STN.

King's Park

VICTORIA PL.

Victoria Square

ST. NINIANS RD.

A-905

To A-91

KING'S PARK RD.

See Stirling Center detail map

To Perth & Pitlochry

BURGHMUIR RD.

M-9

A-91

N

800 Meters

800 Yards

To Falkirk, Edinburgh & Glasgow

To M-9, Falkirk, Edinburgh & Glasgow

ROBERT THE BRUCE STATUE

HERITAGE CENTRE

BANNOCKBURN BATTLE SITE

P

FAIRHILL RD.

STIRLING & NEARBY

1 The Old Tramhouse & Craigard B&B

2 Springfield Lodge

ally on the hour 10:00-16:00, often on the half-hour too, departs from inside the main gate near the well). Docents posted throughout can tell you more, and you can rent a £3 **audioguide.**

Getting There: Stirling Castle sits at the very tip of a steep old town. Drivers should follow the *Stirling Castle* signs uphill through town to the esplanade and park at the £4 lot just outside the castle gate. Without a car, you can hike the 20-minute uphill route from the train or bus station to the castle, or take a taxi (about £5).

Background: The first real castle was built here in the 12th century by King David I. But Stirling Castle's glory days were in the 16th century, when it became the primary residence of the Stuart (often spelled "Stewart") monarchs, who turned it into a showpiece of Scotland—and a symbol of one-upmanship against England.

The 16th century was a busy time for royal intrigues here: James IV married the sister of England's King Henry VIII, thereby knitting together the royal families of Scotland (the Stuarts) and England (the Tudors). Later, James V further expanded the castle. Mary (who became the Queen of Scots) spent her early childhood at the castle before being raised in France. As queen and as a Catholic, she struggled against the rise of Protestantism in her realm. But when Mary's son, King James VI, was crowned King James I of England, he took his royal court with him away from Stirling to London—never to return.

During the Jacobite rebellions of the 18th century, the British military took over the castle—bulking it up and destroying its delicate beauty. Even after the Scottish threat had subsided, it remained a British garrison, home base of the Argyll and Sutherland regiments. (You'll notice the castle still flies the Union Jack of the United Kingdom.) Today, while Stirling Castle is fully restored and gleaming, it feels new and fairly empty—with almost no historic artifacts.

➋ Self-Guided Tour

Begin on the esplanade, just outside the castle entrance, with its grand views.

The Esplanade: The castle's esplanade, a military parade ground in the 19th century, is a tour-bus parking lot today. As you survey this site, remember that Stirling Castle bore witness to some of the most important moments in Scottish history. To the right as you face the castle, **King Robert the Bruce** looks toward the plain called Bannockburn, where he defeated the English army in 1314. Squint off to the horizon on Robert's left to spot the pointy stone monument capping the hill called Abbey Craig. This is the **Wallace Monument,** marking the spot where the Scottish warrior

William Wallace surveyed the battlefield before his victory in the Battle of Stirling Bridge (1297).

These great Scots helped usher in several centuries of home rule. In 1315, Robert the Bruce's daughter married into an on-the-rise noble clan called the Stuarts, who had distinguished themselves fighting at Bannockburn. When their son Robert became King Robert II of Scotland in 1371, he kicked off the Stuart dynasty. Over the next few generations, their headquarters—Stirling Castle—flourished. The fortified grand entry showed all who approached that James IV (r. 1488-1513) was a great ruler with a powerful castle.

• *Head through the first gate into Guardroom Square, where you can buy your ticket, check tour times, and consider renting the audioguide. Then continue up through the inner gate.*

Gardens and Battlements: Once through the gate, follow the passage to the left into a delightful grassy courtyard called the **Queen Anne Garden.** This was the royal family's playground in the 1600s. Imagine doing a little lawn bowling with the queen here.

In the casemates lining the garden is the **Castle Exhibition.** Its "Come Face to Face with 1,000

Years of History" exhibit provides an entertaining and worthwhile introduction to the castle. You'll meet each of the people who left their mark here, from the first Stuart kings to William Wallace and Robert the Bruce. The video leaves you thinking that re-enactors of Jacobite struggles are even more spirited than our Civil War re-enactors.

Leave the garden the way you came and make a sharp U-turn up the ramp to the top of the **battlements.** From up here, this castle's strategic position is evident: Defenders had a 360-degree view of enemy armies approaching from miles away. These battlements were built in 1710, long after the castle's Stuart glory days, in response to the early Jacobite rebellions (from the Latin word for "James"). By this time, the successes of William Wallace and Robert the Bruce were a distant memory; and through the 1707 Act of Union, Scotland had become welded to England. Bonnie Prince Charlie—descendant of those original Stuart "King Jameses" who built this castle—later staged a series of uprisings to try to reclaim the throne of Great Britain for the Stuart line, frightening England enough for it to further fortify the castle. And sure enough, Bonnie Prince Charlie found himself—ironically—laying siege to the fortress that his own ancestors had built: Facing the main gate (with its two round towers below the UK flag), notice the pockmarks from Jacobite cannonballs in 1746.

• *Now head back down to the ramp and pass through that main gate, into the...*

Outer Close: As you enter this courtyard, straight ahead is James IV's yellow **Great Hall.** To the left is his son **James V's royal palace,** lined with finely carved Renaissance statues. In 1540, King James V, inspired by French Renaissance châteaux he'd seen, had the castle covered with about 200 statues and busts to "proclaim the peace, prosperity, and justice of his reign" and to validate his rule. Imagine the impression all these classical

gods and goddesses made on visitors. The message: James' rule was a Golden Age for Scotland.

The **guided tours** of the castle depart from just to your right, near the well. Beyond that is the Grand Battery, with its cannons and rampart views and, underneath that, the Great Kitchens. We'll see both at the end of this tour.

• *Hike up the ramp between James V's palace and the Great Hall (under the crenellated sky bridge connecting them). You'll emerge into the...*

Inner Close: Standing at the center of Stirling Castle, you're surrounded by Scottish history. This courtyard was the core of the 12th-century castle. From here, additional buildings were added—each by a different monarch. Facing downhill, you'll see the Great Hall. To the left is the Chapel Royal—where Mary, Queen of Scots was crowned in 1543. Opposite that, to the right, is the royal palace (containing the Royal Apartments)—notice the "I5" monogram above the windows (for the king who built it: James, or Iacobus in Latin, V). Upstairs in this same palace is the Stirling Heads Gallery. And behind you is the Regimental Museum.

• *We'll visit each of these in turn. First, at the far-left end of the gallery with the coffee stand, step into...*

The Great Hall: This is the largest secular space in medieval Scotland. Dating from 1503, this was a grand setting for the great banquets of Scotland's Renaissance kings. One such party, to which all the crowned heads of Europe were invited, reportedly went on for three full days. This was also where kings and queens would hold court, earning it the nickname "the parliament." The impressive hammerbeam roof is a modern reconstruction, modeled on the early 16th-century roof at Edinburgh Castle. It's made of 400 local oak trees, joined by wooden pegs. If you flipped it over, it would float.

• *At the far end of the hall, climb a few stairs and walk across the sky bridge into James V's palace. Here you can explore...*

The Royal Apartments: Six ground-floor apartments are colorfully done up as they might have looked in the mid-16th century, when James V and

his queen, Mary of Guise, lived here. Costumed performers play the role of palace attendants, happy to chat with you about medieval life. You'll begin in the King's Inner Hall, where he received guests. Notice the 60 carved and colorfully painted oak medallions on the ceiling. The medallions are carved with the faces of Scottish and European royalty. These are copies, painstakingly reconstructed after expert research. You'll soon see the originals up close (and upstairs) in the Stirling Heads Gallery.

Continue (left of the fireplace) into the other rooms (each with actors in costumes who love to interact): the King's Bedchamber, with a four-poster bed supporting a less-than-luxurious rope mattress; and then the Queen's Bedchamber, the Inner Hall, and the Outer Hall, offering a more vivid example of what these rich spaces would have looked like.

• *From the queen's apartments, you'll exit into the top corner of the Inner Close. Directly to your left, up the stairs, is the...*

Stirling Heads Gallery: This is, for me, the castle's highlight—a chance to see the originals of the elaborately carved and painted portrait medallions that

decorated the ceiling of the king's presence chamber. Each one is thoughtfully displayed and lovingly explained. Don't miss the video at the end of the hall.

• *If you were to leave this gallery through the intended exit, you'd wind up back down in the Queen Anne Garden. Instead, backtrack and exit the way you came in to return to the Inner Close, and visit the two remaining sights.*

The Chapel Royal: One of the first Protestant churches built in Scotland, the Chapel Royal was constructed in 1594 by James VI for the baptism of his first son, Prince Henry. The faint painted frieze high up survives from Charles I's coronation visit to Scotland in 1633. Clearly the holiness of the chapel ended in the 1800s when the army moved in.

Regimental Museum: At the top of the Inner Close, in the King's Old Building, is the excellent **Argyll and Sutherland Highlanders Museum.** Another highlight of the castle, it's barely mentioned in castle promotional material because it's run by a different organization. With lots of tartans, tassels, and swords, it shows how the fighting spirit of Scotland was absorbed by Britain. The two regiments, established in the 1790s to defend Britain in the Napoleonic age and combined in the 1880s, have served with distinction in British military campaigns for more than two centuries. Their pride shows here in the building that has served as their headquarters since 1881. The "In the Trenches" exhibit is a powerful look at World War I, with accounts from the battlefield. Up the spiral stairs, the exhibit continues through World War II and conflicts in the Middle East to the present day.

• *When you're ready to move on, consider the following scenic route back to the castle exit.*

Rampart Walk to the Kitchen: The skinny lane between church and museum leads to the secluded Douglas Garden at the rock's highest point. Belly up to the ramparts for a commanding view, including the Wallace Monument. From here you can walk the ramparts downhill to the Grand Battery, with its cannon rampart back at the Outer Close. The Outer Close was the service zone, with a well and the kitchen (below the cannon rampart). The great banquets of James VI didn't happen all by themselves, as you'll appreciate when you explore the fine medieval kitchen exhibit (where mannequin cooks oversee medieval recipes); to find it, head down the ramp and look for the *Great Kitchens* sign.

• *Your castle visit ends here, but your castle ticket includes Argyll's Lodging, a fortified noble mansion. Or, for a scenic route down into town, consider a detour through an old churchyard cemetery (both described next).*

MORE SIGHTS IN STIRLING
Old Kirkyard Stroll
Stirling has a particularly evocative old cemetery in the kirkyard (churchyard) just below the castle. For a soulful stroll, sneak down the stairs where the castle meets the esplanade parking lot (near the statue of the Scotsman fighting in the South African War).

Stirling Center

To Wallace Monument,
A-1036/A-64
& Malton

A-9

BACK O'HILL ROAD

A-84

River Forth

To Park & Ride,
Doune,
Callander &
The Trossachs

A-84

UNION ST.

A-9

BURGHMUIR ROAD

❸

STIRLING CASTLE

GREAT HALL

CHAPEL ROYAL

KINGS OLD BUILDING (MUSEUM)

❹

CASTLE WYND

← ROBERT THE BRUCE STATUE

ROYAL PALACE

MAIN GATE

P

Castle Esplanade

❺

ARGYLL'S LODGING

GOOSECROFT RD.

To Loch Lomond

OLD KIRKYARD

❻ STIRLING BAGPIPES

Royal Gardens

HOLY RUDE CHURCH

BROAD ST.

DUMBARTON ROAD

A-811

ℹ

ST. JOHN STREET

BAKER ST.

BARNTON ROAD

GREY FRIARS ST.

TRAIN STATION

T

OLD TOWN JAIL

❿ ❾

STN. RD.

STIRLING SMITH ART GALLERY & MUSEUM

SPITTAL ST.

❶

Victoria Square

ALBERT PLACE

ABERCROMBIE PL.

❽

PORT STREET

MURRAY

BUS STATION

A-9

QUEEN'S RD.

VICTORIA RD.

CLARENDON PL.

GLEBE AVE.

❼

UPPER CRAIGS

GOOSECROFT RD.

Stirling Golf Club

To Bannockburn Battle Site, M-9, Falkirk, Edinburgh & Glasgow

King's Park

KING'S PARK ROAD

DRUMMOND PL.

GLADSTONE PL.

❷

ST. NINIAN'S ROAD

N

300 Meters
300 Yards

SNOWDON PL.

STIRLING & NEARBY

Accommodations
❶ Victoria Square Guest House
❷ Number Ten
❸ Castlecroft B&B

Eateries
❹ Unicorn Cafeteria

❺ The Portcullis
❻ Hermann's
❼ Blue Lagoon Fish & Chips
❽ Maharaja
❾ Brea
❿ Nicky-Tams Bar & Bothy

From here, you can wander through the tombstones—Celtic crosses, Victorian statues, and faded headstones—from centuries gone by. The rocky crag in the middle of the graveyard is a fine viewpoint. Work your way over to the Church of the Holy Rude (well worth a visit), where you can re-enter the town. From here, Argyll's Lodging and the castle parking lot are just to the left, and the Old Town Jail (also housing the TI) is just to the right.

Argyll's Lodging

Just below the castle esplanade is this 17th-century nobleman's fortified mansion. European aristocrats wanted to live near power—making this location, where the Earl of Argyll's family resided for about a century, prime real estate. You'll get oriented with a historical display on the first floor, then see the kitchens, dining room, drawing room, and bedchambers. Pick up the descriptions in each room, or ask the docents if you have any questions. Argyll's Lodging is less sterile than the castle and worth a few minutes.

Cost and Hours: Included in castle ticket, daily 12:45-17:30.

▲Historic and Haunted Walks

David Kinnaird, a local actor/historian, gives history walks by day and haunted walks by night in Stirling. Each walk meets at the TI (inside the gates of the Old Town Jail), lasts 75 minutes, and cost £4 for readers of this book (tel. 01592/874-449, www. stirlingghostwalk.com). Just show up and pay him directly. David's historic walks (May-Sept Fri-Sun at 12:00, 14:00, and 16:00) tell the story of Stirling as you wander through town. His "Happy Hangman" haunted walks through the old kirkyard cemetery involve more storytelling (July-Aug Tue-Sat at 20:30, Sept-June Fri-Sat at 20:00).

Old Town Jail

Stirling's jail was built during the Victorian Age, when the purpose of imprisonment was shifting from punishment to rehabilitation. While there's little to see today, theatrical 30-minute tours entertain families with a light and funny walk through one section of the jail. You'll end at the top of the tower for a Q&A with a commanding view of the surrounding countryside.

Cost and Hours: £6.50, July-Sept only, tours every 30 minutes daily 10:15-17:15, St. John Street, www.destinationstirling.com.

▲Stirling Bagpipes

This fun little shop, just a block below the castle on Broad Street, is worth a visit for those curious about bagpipes. Owner Alan refurbishes old bagpipes here, but also makes new ones from scratch, in a workshop on the premises. The pleasantly cluttered shop, which is a bit of a neighborhood hangout, is littered with bagpipe components—chanters, drones, bags, covers, and cords. If he's not too busy, Alan can answer your questions. He'll explain how the most expensive parts of the bagpipe are the "sticks"—the chanter and drones, carved from blackwood—while the bag and cover are cheap. A serious set costs £700...beginners should instead consider a £40 starter kit that includes a practice chanter (like a recorder) with a book of sheet music and a CD. Alan hopes to open a wee museum next door to show off his collection of historic bagpipes.

Cost and Hours: Free, Mon-Sat 10:00-18:00, closed Sun, 8 Broad Street, tel. 01786/448-886, www.stirlingbagpipes.com.

Nearby: On the wide street in front of the shop, look for Stirling's **mercat cross** ("market cross"). A standard feature of any medieval Scottish market town, this was the place where townsfolk would gather for the market, and where royal proclamations were read and executions took place. Today the commercial metabolism of this once-thriving street is at a low ebb. Locals joke that every 100 years, the shopping bustle moves one block farther down the road. These days, it's squeezed into the modern shopping mall between the old town and the river.

Stirling Smith Art Gallery and Museum

Tucked at the edge of the grid-planned, Victorian Age neighborhood just below the castle, this endearing and eclectic museum is a hodgepodge of artifacts from Stirling's past: art gallery (where you can meet historical figures with connections to this proud little town), pewter collection, local history exhibits, a steam-powered carriage, the mutton bone shard removed in the world's first documented tracheotomy (1853), and a 19th-century executioner's cloak and ax. The museum's prized piece is what they claim is the world's oldest surviving soccer ball—a 16th-century stitched-up pig's bladder that restorers found stuck in the rafters of Stirling Castle. The building is surrounded by a garden filled with public art.

Cost and Hours: Free, Tue-Sat 10:30-17:00, Sun from 14:00, closed Mon, Dumbarton Road, tel. 01786/471-917.

Sleeping in Stirling

NEAR THE TOWN CENTER

These places are all in large, spacious homes with easy parking.

In the Victorian Town, South of the Castle

When Stirling expanded beyond its old walls during the Victorian Age, a modern, grid-planned town sprouted just to the south. Today, this posh-feeling area holds a few B&Bs that are within a (long) walk of Stirling's old town and castle.

$$$ Victoria Square Guest House has 10 plush rooms in a beautiful location facing a big, grassy park. While the prices are high, it's neat as a pin, and Kari and Phil keep things running smoothly. It's about a 10-minute walk to the lower part of town, or 20 minutes up to the castle (no kids under 12, minifridges, 12 Victoria Square, tel. 01786/473-920, www.victoriasquareguesthouse. com, info@vsgh.co.uk).

$ Number Ten rents three nice, traditional rooms in a Scottish-feeling home with tartan carpets blanketing the halls and a lovely garden out back (no kids under 5, 10 Gladstone Place, tel. 01786/472-681, www.cameron-10.co.uk, cameron-10@tinyonline. co.uk, Carol and Donald Cameron).

Just Under the Castle

$$ Castlecroft B&B is well cared for by Laura, who keeps everything immaculate, bakes her own bread, and welcomes guests with tea/coffee and shortbread upon arrival. Just under the castle and overlooking a field with "hairy coos," it's a 10-minute walk down a path to the town center. Two of the five rooms come with their own patios, and anyone can make use of the living room and deck (Ballengeich Road, tel. 01786/474-933, www.castlecroft-uk.co.uk, castlecroft@gmail.com).

ALONG AND NEAR CAUSEWAYHEAD ROAD, NORTH OF THE CASTLE

A number of B&Bs offering slightly lower prices line Causewayhead Road, a busy thoroughfare that connects Stirling to the Wallace Monument. From here, it's a long walk into town (or the Wallace Monument), but the location is handy for drivers (each place has free parking). While this modern residential area lacks charm, it's convenient.

$$ The Old Tramhouse is the frilliest of the bunch, with five rooms elegantly decorated with a delicate charm (family room, 42 Causewayhead Road, tel. 01786/449-774, mobile 0759-054-0604, www.theoldtramhouse.com, enquiries@theoldtramhouse.com, Alison Cowie). They also have an apartment for up to five people.

$ Craigard B&B has three small, modern, tidy, and proper rooms that offer good value and a shared breakfast table (40 Causewayhead Road, tel. 01786/460-540, mobile 0784-040-1551, www. craigardstirling.co.uk, craigard@hotmail.co.uk, Liz).

$ Springfield Lodge sits at the back end of the residential zone that lines up along Causewayhead Road. It's across the street from farm fields, giving it a countryside feeling. The four neat rooms fill a spacious modern house (no kids under 6, Easter Cornton Road, tel. 01786/474-332, mobile 0795-469-2412, www.springfieldlodgebandb.co.uk, springfieldlodgebandb@gmail.com, Kim and Kevin).

Eating in Stirling

Stirling isn't a place to go looking for high cuisine; eateries here tend to be barely satisfying but functional. All of these are open daily unless otherwise noted.

UP NEAR THE CASTLE

$$ Unicorn Cafeteria, tucked under the casemates inside the castle, is a decent place for lunch if touring the grounds (same hours as castle).

$$ The Portcullis, just below the castle esplanade, is a pub that aches with history, from its dark, wood-grained bar area to its stony courtyard. The food, like the setting, is old-school. If the restaurant is full, you can also eat at the bar (01786/472-290, 12:00-15:00 & 17:30-20:30).

$$$$ Hermann's, a block below the castle esplanade, is more dressy, spacious, and homey with a sunny conservatory out back. It serves a mix of Scottish and Austrian food—perfect when you've got a hankering for haggis, but your travel partner wants Wiener schnitzel (lunch and dinner, top of Broad Street, tel. 01786/450-632, www.hermanns-restaurant.co.uk).

LOWER DOWN IN THE TOWN

Dumbarton Road, at the bottom of town, has a line of cheap eateries (Indian, Asian, cheap buffets) including **Blue Lagoon Fish & Chips** (11:00-23:00, at Port Street). Among a group of chain pubs and ethnic eateries (Thai and Italian), these three are within about a block of Stirling's clock tower near King Street in the old town center:

$$ Maharaja is popular for its "authentic Indian cuisine" served in a dressy dining room (39 King Street, tel. 01786/470-728).

$$$ Brea, which means "love" in Gaelic, has a nice Scottish theme, from the menu to the decor to the pop music playing. It's unpretentious and popular for its modern and tasty dishes. Consider treating first courses like tapas and eating family-style (12:00-21:00, closed for lunch Mon, 5 Baker Street, tel. 01786/446-277).

$$ Nicky-Tams Bar and Bothy is a fun little hangout with an Irish-pub ambience, providing a great place to chat up a local and enjoy some good, basic pub grub. They serve meals from 12:00 to 20:00, then make way for drinking and, often, live music (29 Baker Street, tel. 01786/472-194).

Stirling Connections

From Stirling by Train to: Edinburgh (2/hour, 1 hour), **Glasgow** (3/hour, 45 minutes), **Pitlochry** (5/day direct, 1 hour, more with transfer in Perth), **Inverness** (6/day direct, 3 hours, more with transfer in Perth). Train info: Tel. 0345-748-4950, www. nationalrail.co.uk.

By Bus to: Glasgow (hourly on #M8, 45 minutes), **Edinburgh** (every 2 hours on #909, 1 hour). Citylink: tel. 0871-266-3333, www.citylink.co.uk.

Near Stirling

The Wallace Monument and the Bannockburn Heritage Centre are just outside of town. Sights within side-trip distance include The Kelpies horse-head sculptures, the Falkirk Wheel boat "elevator," the stuck-in-time village of Culross, Doune Castle, and the Trossachs National Park.

JUST OUTSIDE OF STIRLING
▲Wallace Monument
Commemorating the Scottish hero better known to Americans as "Braveheart," this sandstone tower—built during a wave of Scottish nationalism in the mid-19th century—marks the Abbey Craig hill on the outskirts of Stirling. This is where, in 1297, William Wallace gathered forces and secured his victory against England's King Edward I at the Battle of Stirling Bridge. The victory was a huge boost to the Scottish cause, but England came back to beat the Scots the next year. (For more on Wallace, see page 58.)

Cost and Hours: £10, daily July-Aug 9:30-18:00, April-June and Sept-Oct until 17:00, Nov-March 10:30-16:00, last entry 45 minutes before closing, café at visitors center, tel. 01786/472-140, www. nationalwallacemonument.com. The £1 audioguide basically repeats the posted information.

Getting There: The monument is two miles northeast of Stirling on the A-9, signposted from the city center. Frequent public buses go from the Stirling bus station to the roundabout below the monument (15-minute ride). From there, it's about a 15-minute hike up to the visitors center, then an additional hike up to the monument. Taxis cost about £8 one-way. From the visitors center parking lot, you'll need to hike (a steep 10 minutes) or hop on the shuttle bus up the hill to the monument itself (free, departs every 10 minutes).

Visiting the Monument: Buy your ticket either at the visitors center below or the monument above. Then hike or ride the shuttle bus up to the monument's base. Gazing up, think about how this fanciful 19th-century structure, like so many around Europe in that age, was created and designed to evoke (and romanticize) earlier architectural styles—in this case, medieval Scottish castles. The crown-shaped top—reminiscent of St. Giles' on the Royal Mile in Edinburgh—and the dynamic sculpture of William Wallace are patriotic to the max.

Climb the tight, stone spiral staircases a total of 246 steps, stopping at each of the three levels to see museum displays. The first level, the Hall of Arms, tells the story of William Wallace and the Battle of Stirling Bridge. Second is the Hall of Heroes, adorned with busts of great Scots—suggesting the debt this nation owes to Wallace. In the middle of the room, ogle Wallace's five-foot-long broadsword. But it's not all just hero worship: A thoughtful video presentation on the first level considers the role of Wallace in both Scottish and English history, and raises the point that one person's freedom fighter is another person's terrorist. The third level's exhibits are about the monument itself: why and how it was built.

Finally, you reach the top with stunning views over Stirling, its castle, the winding River Forth, and Stirling Bridge—a 500-year-old stone version that re-placed the original wooden one. Looking out from the same vantage point as Wallace, imagine how the famous battle played out. But if you find yourself picturing *Braveheart*—with berserker Scots, their

faces painted blue, running across a field to take on the English cavalry—you have the wrong idea. While that portrayal was cinematically powerful, in reality the battle took place on a bridge in a narrow valley (see sidebar).

Bannockburn Heritage Centre

Just south of Stirling is the Bannockburn Heritage Centre, commemorating what many Scots view as their nation's most signifi-

STIRLING & NEARBY

Debunking *Braveheart*

The 1995 multiple-Oscar-winner movie *Braveheart* informs many travelers' impressions of William Wallace and the battles near Stirling. But Mel Gibson's much-assailed Scottish accent may very well be the most authentic thing about the film.

In the 1297 Battle of Stirling Bridge, William Wallace and his ragtag Scottish forces hid out in the forest overlooking the bottleneck bridge, waiting until the perfect moment to ambush the English. Thanks to the tight quarters and the element of surprise, the Scots won an unlikely victory. *Braveheart* serves up an entirely different version of events: armies lining up across an open field, with blue-faced, kilted Highlanders charging at top speed toward heavily armored English troops. The filmmakers left out the bridge entirely, calling it simply "The Battle of Stirling." And the blue face paint? Never happened. A millennium before William Wallace, the ancient Romans did encounter war-painted fighters in Scotland, whom they called the Picts ("painted ones"). But painting faces in the late 13th century would be like WWII soldiers suiting up in chain mail.

Braveheart takes many other liberties with history. William Wallace was *not* the rugged-born Highlander depicted in the movie—he was born in Elderslie, next to Paisley, in the Lowlands. Wallace did *not* vengefully kill Andrew de Moray for deserting him at Falkirk (Moray fought valiantly by Wallace's side at Stirling, and died from battle wounds). Robert the Bruce did *not* betray Wallace to the English. And William Wallace most certainly did

STIRLING & NEARBY

cant military victory over the invading English: the Battle of Bannockburn, won by a Scottish army led by Robert the Bruce against England's King Edward II in 1314. The battle memorial is free and always open. The Heritage Centre "Battle Game" is an interactive techy experience, with 3-D screens and a re-creation that basically reduces the battle to a video game.

Cost and Hours: Memorial-free, always open, Heritage Centre and "Battle Game"-£11.50, daily 10:00-17:30, Nov-Feb until 17:00, café, tel. 0844/493-2139, www.battleofbannockburn.com. If interested in the 3D experience, call or visit the website to book a time.

Getting There: Bannockburn is two miles south of Stirling on the A-872, off the M-80/M-9. For non-drivers, it's an easy bus ride from the Stirling bus station (8/hour, 15 minutes).

Background: In simple terms, Robert the Bruce—who was first and foremost a politician—found himself *not* impregnate the future King Edward II's French bride...who was 10 years old, not yet married to Edward, and still living in France at the time of Wallace's death.

Also, the modern concept of national "Freee-dooooom!" was essentially unknown during the divine-right Middle Ages. Wallace wasn't fighting for "democracy" or "liberty"; he simply wanted to trade one authoritarian, aristocratic ruler (from London) for another authoritarian, aristocratic ruler (from Scotland).

Even the film's title is a falsehood: No Scottish person ever referred to Wallace as "Braveheart," which was actually the nickname of one of the film's villains, Robert the Bruce. After Robert's death, his heart was taken (in a small casket) on a crusade to the Holy Land by his friend Sir James Douglas. During one battle, Douglas threw the heart at an oncoming army and shouted, "Lead on, brave heart, I will follow thee!" Gibson's title is a bit like naming a film about Abraham Lincoln *Old Hickory*.

Scottish people have mixed feelings about *Braveheart*. They appreciate the boost it gave to their underdog nation's profile—and to its tourist industry—juuust enough that they're willing to overlook the film's historical gaffes. For travelers, it can be enjoyable to watch *Braveheart* to prep for your trip...as entertainment. Then go to Stirling and get the real story. (For a fact-based account of Wallace's life, see the sidebar on page 58.)

out of political options after years of failed diplomatic attempts to make peace with the strong-arming English. William Wallace's execution left a vacuum in military leadership, and eventually Robert stepped in, waging a successful guerrilla campaign that came to a head as young Edward's army marched to Stirling. Although the Scots were greatly outnumbered, their strategy and use of terrain at Bannockburn—with its impossibly twisty stream presenting a natural barrier for the invading army—allowed them to soundly beat the English and drive Edward out of Scotland...for the time being. (For more about Robert the Bruce, see page 62.)

Visiting the Heritage Centre: There are no historic artifacts here. First, you'll spend 30 minutes learning about the emerging battle from the perspective of both sides, and getting familiar with the characters and weaponry. Then, when your time arrives, you enter the "battle room," huddling with a dozen or so others (divided into two sides—English and Scots) around a large, interactive 3D map of the battleground. On screen, the "Battle Master" leads the group, but you get to call the shots as the battle unfolds.

Monument and Statue of Robert the Bruce: Leaving the center, hike out into the field behind, where you can see a mon-

STIRLING & NEARBY

ument to those lost in the fight. Nearby, on a plinth, stands an equestrian statue of Robert the Bruce.

FALKIRK

Two engaging landmarks sit just outside the town of Falkirk, 12 miles south of Stirling. Taken together, The Kelpies and the Falkirk Wheel offer a welcome change of pace from Scottish countryside kitsch. These flank Falkirk's otherwise unexciting town center, about a 5-mile, 20-minute drive apart. Driving between the two is a riddle of roundabouts. Think of it as fun: Carefully follow the brown signs and you'll eventually get there. (Ask for a flier illustrating directions between them at either site.)

▲The Kelpies

Unveiled in 2014 and standing over a hundred feet tall, these two giant steel horse heads have quickly become a symbol of this town and region. They may seem whimsical, but they're rooted in a mix of mythology and real history: Kelpies are magical, waterborne, shape-shifting sprites of Scottish lore, who often took the form of a horse. And historically, horses—the ancestors of today's Budweiser Clydesdales—were used as beasts of burden to power Scotland's industrial output. These statues stand over old canals where hardworking horses towed heavily laden barges. But if you prefer, you can just forget all that and ogle the dramatic, energy-charged statues (particularly thrilling to Denver Broncos fans) that make for an entertaining photo op. A café nearby sells drinks and light meals, and a free visitors center shows how the heads were built. A 30-minute guided tour through the inside of one of the great beasts shows how they're supported by a sleek steel skeleton: 300 tons of steel apiece, sitting upon a foundation of 1,200 tons of steel-reinforced concrete, and gleaming with 990 steel panels.

Cost and Hours: Always open and free to view (£3 to park); visitors center open daily 9:30-17:00. Tours-£7.50, daily at the bottom of every hour 10:30-16:30, fewer tours Oct-March, tel. 01324/506-850, www.thehelix.co.uk.

Getting There: The Kelpies are in a park called The Helix, just off the M-9 motorway—you'll spot them looming high over the motorway as if inviting you to exit. For a closer look, exit the M-9 for the A-905 (Falkirk/Grangemouth), then follow *Falkirk/A-904* and brown *Helix Park & Kelpies* signs.

▲▲Falkirk Wheel

At the opposite end of Falkirk stands this remarkable modern incarnation of Scottish technical know-how. You can watch the beautiful, slow-motion contraption as it spins—like a nautical Ferris wheel—to efficiently shuttle ships between two canals separated by 80 vertical feet.

Cost and Hours: Wheel is free to view, visitors center open daily 10:00-17:30, park open until 20:00, shorter hours Nov-mid-March; cruises run about hourly and cost £13, call or go online to check schedule and book your seat, tel. 0870-050-0208, www.thefalkirkwheel.co.uk.

Getting There: Exit the M-876 motorway for *A-883/ Falkirk/Denny,* then follow brown *Falkirk Wheel* signs. Parking is free and a short walk from the wheel.

Background: Scotland was a big player in the Industrial Revolution, thanks partly to its network of shipping canals (including the famous Caledonian Canal—see page 323). Using dozens of locks to lift barges up across Scotland's hilly spine, these canals were effective...but slow.

The 115-foot-tall Falkirk Wheel, opened in 2002, is a modern take on this classic engineering challenge: linking the Forth and Clyde Canal below with the aqueduct of the Union Canal, 80 feet above. Rather than using rising and lowering water through several locks, the wheel simply picks boats up and—ever so slowly—takes them where they need to go, like a giant waterborne elevator. In the 1930s, it took half a day to ascend or descend through 11 locks; now it takes only five minutes.

The Falkirk Wheel is the critical connection in the Millennium Link project, an ambitious £78 million initiative to restore the long-neglected Forth and Clyde and Union canals connecting Edinburgh and Glasgow. Today this 70-mile-long aquatic connection between Scotland's leading cities is a leisurely traffic jam of pleasure craft, and canalside communities have been rejuvenated.

Visiting the Wheel: Twice an hour, the wheel springs (silently) to life: Gates rise up to seal off each of the water-filled gondolas, and then the entire structure slowly rotates a half-turn to swap the positions of the lower and upper boats—each of which stays comfortably upright. The towering structure is not only functional, but beautiful: The wheel's elegantly sweeping shape—with grace-

STIRLING & NEARBY

ful cogs and pointed tips that slice into the water as they spin. It's strangely exciting to witness this.

The **visitors center** has a cafeteria (with a fine view of the wheel) and a shop, but no information about the wheel. The Falkirk **TI** is just steps away. The park around the canal is cluttered with trampolines, laser tag, and other family amusements.

Riding the Wheel: Each hour, a barge takes 96 people (listening to a recorded narration explaining everything) into the Falkirk Wheel for the slow and graceful ride. Once at the top, the barge cruises a bit of the canal. The slow-motion experience lasts 50 minutes.

▲CULROSS

This time warp of a village, sitting across the Firth of Forth from Edinburgh (about a 30-minute drive from Stirling), is a perfectly preserved artifact from the 17th and 18th centuries. If you're looking to let your pulse slow, stroll through a steep and sleepy village, and tour a creaky old manor house, Culross is your place. Filmmakers often use Culross to evoke Scottish villages of yore (you've seen it in everything from *Captain America: The First Avenger* to *Outlander*). While not worth a long detour, it's a workable stop for drivers connecting Edinburgh to either the Stirling area or St. Andrews (free parking lots flank the town center—an easy, 5-minute waterfront stroll away).

The story of Culross (which locals pronounce KOO-russ) is the story of Sir George Bruce, who, in the late 16th century, figured out a way to build coal mines beneath the waters of the Firth of Forth. The hardworking town flourished, Bruce built a fine mansion, and the town was granted coveted "royal burgh" status by the king. But several decades later, with Bruce's death and the flooding of the mines, the town's fortunes tumbled—halting its development and trapping it as if in amber for centuries. Rescued and rehabilitated by the National Trust for Scotland, today the entire village feels like one big open-air folk museum.

The main sightseeing attraction here is the misnamed **Culross "Palace,"** the big-but-creaky, half-timbered home of George Bruce (£10.50, daily 11:00-17:00 in summer, Sat-Mon only in off-season, closed

Nov-March, tel. 01383/880-359, www.nts.org.uk/culross). Buy your ticket at the office under the Town Hall's clock tower, pick up the included audioguide, then head a few doors down to the ochre-colored palace. Following a 10-minute orientation film, you'll walk through several creaky floors to see how a small town's big shots lived four centuries ago. Docents in each room are happy to answer questions. You'll see the great hall, the "principal stranger's bedchamber" (guest room for VIPs), George Bruce's bedroom and stone strong room (where he stored precious—and flammable—financial documents), and the highlight, the painted chamber. The wood slats of its barrel-arched ceiling are painted with whimsical scenes illustrating Scottish virtues and pitfalls. You can also poke around the densely planted, lovingly tended garden out back.

A 45-minute **guided town walk** takes place for a small fee (3/day, check palace website for schedule).

The only other real sight, a steep hike up the cobbled lanes to the top of town, is the partially ruined **abbey.** While there are far more evocative ruins in Scotland, it's fun to poke into the stony, mysterious-feeling interior of this church. But the stroll up the town's cobbled streets past pastel houses, with their carefully tended flower boxes, is even better than the church itself.

DOUNE, BETWEEN STIRLING AND THE TROSSACHS

The village of Doune (pronounced "doon") is just a 15-minute drive north of Stirling. While there's not much to see in town, on its outskirts is a pair of attractions: a castle and a distillery. In the village of Doune itself, notice the town seal: a pair of crossed pistols. Aside from its castle and whisky, the town is known for its historic pistol factory. Locals speculate that the first shot of the American Revolution was fired with a Doune pistol.

Getting There: Bus #59 runs from Stirling to Doune and the distillery (just outside Doune). Drivers head to Doune, then follow castle signs on pretty back roads from there.

Doune Castle

Doune Castle is worth considering for its pop-culture connections: Most recently, Doune stands in for Castle Leoch in the TV series *Outlander*. But well before that, parts of *Monty Python and the Holy Grail* were filmed here. And, while the castle may underwhelm *Outlander* fans (only some ex-

STIRLING & NEARBY

terior scenes were shot here), Python fans—and anyone who appreciates British comedy—will be tickled by the included audioguide, narrated by Python troupe member Terry Jones (featuring sound clips from the film). The audioguide also has a few stops featuring Sam Heughan of *Outlander*. (If you're not into Python or *Outlander*, Scotland has better castles to visit.)

Cost and Hours: £6, daily April-Sept 9:30-17:30, Oct-March 10:00-16:00, tel. 01786/841-742.

Visiting the Castle: Buy your ticket and pick up the 45-minute audioguide, which explains that the castle's most important resident was not Claire Randall or the Knights Who Say Ni, but Robert Stewart, the Duke of Albany (1340-1420)—a man so influential he was called the "uncrowned king of Scotland." You'll see the cellars, ogle the empty-feeling courtyard, then scramble through the two tall towers and the great hall that connects them. The castle rooms are almost entirely empty, but they're brought to life by the audioguide. You'll walk into the kitchen's ox-sized fireplace to peer up the gigantic chimney, and visit the guest room's privy to peer down the medieval toilet. You'll finish your visit at the top of the main tower, with 360-degree views that allow you to fart in just about anyone's general direction.

Deanston Distillery

This big, attractive red-brick industrial complex (formerly a cotton mill) sits facing the river just outside of Doune. While Deanston has long been respected for its fruity, slightly spicy Highland single-malt whisky, the 2012 movie *The Angels' Share*, filmed partly at this distillery, helped put it on the map for tourists. The complex boasts a slick visitors center that's open for tours. On the 50-minute visit, you'll see the equipment used to make the whisky and enjoy a sample. (For more on whisky and the distillation process, see page 464.) A bit more corporate-feeling than some of my favorite Scottish distilleries, Deanston has the advantage of being handy to Stirling.

Cost and Hours: £9 or £12 depending on number of tastings, tours depart at the top of each hour daily 10:00-16:00 (last tour), best to call ahead to reserve, tel. 01786/843-010, www.deanstonmalt.com.

LOCH LOMOND AND THE TROSSACHS NATIONAL PARK

Within about an hour's drive of half the population of Scotland is the country's most popular national park. Though it's a single park, it takes its name from two separate areas: The famous lake called Loch Lomond and, just to the east, the Trossachs—a hilly terrain that pleases hikers and joyriders. The Highland Boundary Fault—

the geologic line separating the flat Lowlands from the rugged Highlands—runs right through the middle of this area, and in several places you can actually see the terrain in transition.

To be honest, the charms of Loch Lomond and the Trossachs are subtle. Scottish scenery crescendos dramatically as you head north (at Glencoe, the Cairngorms, and the Isle of Skye, for starters). But this area's proximity to Stirling and Glasgow—and its many entertaining connections to Scottish history, literature, and folk culture—make it worth knowing about. For those on a quick visit to Scotland's Central Belt, Loch Lomond and the Trossachs offer a glimpse of "the Highlands in miniature."

Loch Lomond

Twenty-four miles long and speckled with islands, Loch Lomond is Great Britain's biggest lake by surface area, and second in volume only to Loch Ness. Thanks largely to its easy proximity to Glasgow (about 15 miles away), this scenic lake is a favorite retreat for Scots as well as foreign tourists. The southernmost of the Munros, Ben Lomond (3,196 feet), looms over the eastern bank.

Loch Lomond's biggest claim to fame is its role in a beloved folk song: "Ye'll take the high road, and I'll take the low road, and I'll be in Scotland afore ye... For me and my true love will never meet again, on the bonnie, bonnie banks of Loch Lomond." As you'll now be humming that all day (you're welcome), here's one interpretation of the song's poignant meaning: Celtic culture believes that fairies return the souls of the deceased to their homeland through the soil. After the disastrous Scottish loss at the Battle of Culloden, Jacobite ringleaders were arrested and taken for trial in faraway London. In some cases, accused pairs were given a choice: One of you will die, and the other will live. The song is a bittersweet reassurance, sung from the condemned to the survivor, that the soon-to-be-deceased will take the spiritual "low road" back to his Scottish homeland—where his soul will be reunited with the living, who will return on the physical "high road" (over land).

Visiting Loch Lomond: There's not much to see, aside from some lochside scenery. You can get a fair dose simply driving by. People traveling from Glasgow toward Oban (or other points north) will get a good look at the loch's **west bank** as they follow the A-82 north (see "Glasgow to Oban Drive" on page 265).

To see the **east bank** of the lake, it's an easy detour from the

Trossachs loop described next, or from Glasgow. Take the A-811 west from Stirling, or the A-809 north from Glasgow, to the village of Drymen (DRIM-men). From here, carry on westward (along the B-837) to Balmaha. In this wide spot in the road, you'll find a visitors center with free geology and wildlife exhibits and advice about various hikes in the region. One easy and popular option is the ascent to Craigie Fort viewpoint (1 mile, 45 minutes round-trip), offering views over the southern part of the lake. For a more ambitious hike, you can follow part of the West Highland Way up to Conic Hill (2.5 miles, 3 hours round-trip).

▲The Trossachs

The hills-and-lochs terrain of the Trossachs, just northwest of Stirling (and due north of Glasgow), is a gently scenic, tourist-clogged corner of Highlands beauty. While the views here pale in comparison to more scenic areas farther north, this well-trod route is packed with interesting footnotes in Scottish history—from Rob Roy to Sir Walter Scott to the Beatles. The Trossachs makes for an easy, pretty spin close to Glasgow or Stirling, but can also be used as a slow-but-scenic connection to points in northern and eastern Scotland (see the options at the end of this drive). I've lightly narrated this loop in a clockwise order, coming from Stirling. But you can go in either direction, and begin or end wherever you like. I've focused on real history rather than silly legends...but sometimes the myths are hard to resist.

◐ Self-Guided Driving Tour: From Stirling, head west on the A-84, then turn off to the left onto the A-873 (marked for *Thornhill;* watch for brown *Trossachs* signs). Carry on through Thornhill and then, in the village of Blairhoyle, turn left onto the A-81.

Soon you'll pass the **Lake of Menteith.** Many Scots are quick to point out that this is the only "lake" (as opposed to "loch") in all of Scotland, and have cooked up an explanation: Its namesake, Sir John Menteith, was a Scot who betrayed William Wallace, leading to his arrest and execution. To punish the traitor, "loch" became "lake." But, like most trumped-up Trossachs legends, this is bogus: The "lake" is likely derived from the Lowland Scots word *laich*—meaning simply "low place."

Continue along the A-81, then bear right onto the A-821 to **Aberfoyle.** Approaching the town, notice the landscape heaving up just beyond it—you can actually see where the Highland Boundary Fault marks the start of the Highlands. The town itself is attractive, if something of a tour bus hell—with more parking lot than town. But it's a convenient place to take a break and grab picnic supplies. At the corner of the parking lot, the Scottish Wool Centre is a tacky tourist mall with a few free attractions out front

Rob Roy MacGregor (1671-1734)

The Trossachs region is Rob Roy country. This near-mythic Scottish folk hero was wounded fighting for the Jacobite cause, then became a trader of Highland cattle. He borrowed money from the Duke of Montrose (for whom Duke's Pass is named), but when one of his men ran off with the cash, Rob Roy had to resort to stealing cattle and harassing the duke, who now called for his head. In his new life as a lovable Robin Hood-type rogue, who stole from the rich and kept for himself, Rob Roy embodied the Scottish suspicion of authority. Immortalized in novels, verse, music, and film by everyone from Sir Walter Scott and William Wordsworth to Hector Berlioz and Liam Neeson, Rob Roy's reputation looms larger than his actual life. And today, visitors enjoy seeing his former stomping grounds, from Loch Katrine to his grave in Balquhidder.

that are worth a peek: sheep, noisy goats, birds of prey, and a fun little sheepdog demonstration, in which the clever dogs herd geese on a virtual "tour of Scotland." Across the parking lot, the TI has free Wi-Fi and a small exhibit touting Aberfoyle's literary connections: Sir Walter Scott's *The Lady of the Lake* was inspired by nearby Loch Katrine (which we'll reach soon). This was also the home of Robert Kirk, who (in 1691) wrote *The Secret Commonwealth of Elves, Fauns, and Fairies*, which remains the definitive compendium of Scottish superstition. Soon after, Kirk died mysteriously in a forest glen supposedly inhabited by fairies. (Locals love to share stories, theories, and superstitions about Kirk.)

Leaving Aberfoyle, carry on north along the A-821, following a twisty road called the **Duke's Pass.** This was built by the Duke of Montrose (the villain of the Rob Roy story) to access his mountain estates and to levy tolls. You'll wind your way up into a thickly forested hillscape; watch on the right for the turnoff for the Queen Elizabeth Forest Park visitors center. Here you can get maps and hiking advice, and peruse good exhibits on local geology and wildlife—including live cameras showing osprey nests. They share a parking lot with Go Ape, a popular zip-line and high-ropes course (best to book ahead, full course takes 2-3 hours, www.goape.co.uk).

As you crest the Duke's Pass, you'll get a small taste of the **Highland moor** terrain. For a good look at this landscape (and a parking lot with a handy viewpoint), pull off on the right at the start of the Three Lochs Forest Drive. You're surrounded by heather—the scrubby plant (with vibrant purple flowers in the late summer) that blankets much of the Highlands. The oldest pines around you are mostly Scotch (or "Scots") pines; more recently, these have been replaced by faster-growing pines that are better for harvesting. Meanwhile, the deciduous trees (with red berries or white flowers, depending on the season) are rowan trees, also called "mountain ash." Superstitious Highlanders believe that rowans keep witches away and prevent fairies from switching out babies for changelings. If you're bothered by the distant sight of wind farms from this viewpoint, you can commiserate with Donald Trump—before he became president he lobbied the Scottish government to outlaw these structures within sight of his Scottish golf courses.

Back on the main road, you'll start working your way downhill. On your right are glimpses of **Loch Drunkie.** Just ignore tour guides who tell you this was named for the practice of chugging and dumping illegal homebrew whisky here when the police showed up.

Farther down, you'll pass briefly along the banks of **Loch Achray.** Across the lake is the former Trossachs Hotel, which has hosted everyone from Queen Victoria to the Beatles. In the Fab Four's landmark 1964 tour around the UK, they'd do big shows in cities, then retreat to countryside getaways like this one.

At the end of Loch Achray, turn off on the left for **Loch Katrine.** Park in the big pay lot and stretch your legs. While this corner of the loch is nothing special, the scenery opens up if you follow its shore. You have several options: You can walk along the easy, paved lochside trail; you can pay for a boat trip (www.lochkatrine.com); or you can rent a bike (but be warned that the 14-mile path to the end of the lake gets increasingly hillier—consider taking a bike on the boat one way, and pedaling back; www.katrinewheelz.co.uk). Loch Katrine has various claims to fame. Sir Walter Scott's epic poem *The Lady of the Lake* was set here, and extols the beauties of this corner of the Trossachs. *Sir Wal-*

ter Scott is also the name of the steamship that does sightseeing cruises around the loch; while steamships like this were once a common sight on Scottish lochs, this is the last one still in operation. At the boat dock, big displays explain how Loch Katrine was the home of Rob Roy (see sidebar). Loch Katrine is also a primary water supply for Glasgow. In 1885, engineers harnessed the power of gravity to pipe the clean mountain waters into the big city. (Glaswegians of the time—accustomed to extremely polluted well water—were unimpressed. As one joke goes, a Glaswegian poured his first glass of water, eyed it suspiciously, and said, "It's got nae color, nae taste—nae good!") And finally, the US president's theme song also has a connection to this unassuming Scottish loch: "Hail to the Chief" came from a musical based on Scott's *Lady of the Lake*. In 1815, it was played to commemorate George Washington and to celebrate the end of the War of 1812, and the tradition stuck.

When you're done at Loch Katrine, return to the main A-821 and head toward Callander. You'll go along the other bank of **Loch Achray** (and get a closer look at the former Tros sachs Hotel—now a timeshare). Then you'll pass through **Brig O'Turk** (Gaelic for "Bridge of the Wild Boar") and drive along **Loch Venachar** before reaching a junction with the A-84. It's time to make your decision: Head north for more scenery and access to Loch Tay (Crannog Centre, Kenmore), Pitlochry, and other sights. Or head south for a speedy return to Stirling, by way of Callander and Doune Castle. Both options are outlined next.

To the North: If you head north on the A-84, you'll pass another pretty loch (Lubnaig), and soon after, you'll see the turn-off for **Balquhidder.** Fans of Rob Roy—or anyone named Mac-Gregor—may want to take the two-mile detour (on single-track roads) to Balquhidder's humble stone church. In the kirkyard, look for the grave of the famous MacGregor clan chieftain. Rob Roy lived most of his life in these hills overlooking Loch Voil (visible in the distance). Back on the main A-84, carry on north (in Lochearnhead, it becomes the A-85); eventually you'll reach the junction with the A-827. From here, you can stick with the main A-85 all the way to **Oban.** Or you can turn right onto the A-827 (toward Killin) to reach the dramatic **Falls of Dochart,** which tumble through a tiny village, and then follow the north bank of Loch Tay to **Kenmore** and the **Crannog Centre;** farther along the A-827, you'll rejoin the main A-9 highway, which heads north to **Pitlochry** and several other attractions on the way up to **Inverness.** (For details on all of these sights, see the Eastern Scotland chapter.) Turning south on the A-9 zips you back toward Perth, then Stirling.

To the South: To complete our loop more directly, head south on the A-84. Just after you make the turn, watch on the left for the Wool Center, with a pair of hairy coos (shaggy Highland cattle) around back who love to pose for photos. Soon after, you'll pass through **Callander,** which feels like a very slightly less touristy version of Aberfoyle. Carrying on through town on the A-84, you'll pass through the village of Doune, where you can stop off for a tour of **Doune Castle** and/or the **Deanston Distillery** (both described earlier in this chapter). **Stirling** is just down the road.

ST. ANDREWS

St. Andrews • Dundee • Glamis Castle • The East Neuk

St. Andrews is synonymous with golf. But there's much more to this charming town than its famous links. Dramatically situated at the edge of a sandy bay, St. Andrews is the home of Scotland's most important university—think of it as the Scottish Cambridge. And centuries ago, the town was the religious capital of the country.

In its long history, St. Andrews has seen two boom periods. First, in the early Middle Ages, the relics of St. Andrew made the town cathedral one of the most important pilgrimage sites in Christendom. The faithful flocked here from all over Europe, leaving the town with a medieval all-roads-lead-to-the-cathedral street plan that survives today. But after the Scottish Reformation, the cathedral rotted away and the town became a forgotten backwater. A new wave of visitors arrived in the mid-19th century, when a visionary mayor (with the on-the-nose surname Playfair) began to promote the town's connection with the newly in-vogue game of golf. Most buildings in town date from this Victorian era.

Today St. Andrews remains a popular spot for students, golf devotees (from amateurs to professional golfers to celebrities), and occasionally Britain's favorite royal couple, Will and Kate (college sweethearts, U. of St. A. class of '05). With vast sandy beaches, golfing opportunities for pros and novices alike, playgrounds of castle and cathedral ruins, and a fun-loving student vibe, St. Andrews is an appealing place to take a vacation from your busy vacation. It's also a handy home base for a variety of worthwhile sidetrips: interesting museums in the big city of Dundee, the castle home of the late Queen Mother, and a string of relaxing fishing villages (the East Neuk).

PLANNING YOUR TIME

St. Andrews, hugging the east coast of Scotland, is a bit off the main tourist track. But it's well connected by train to Edinburgh (via bus from nearby Leuchars), making it a worthwhile day trip from the capital. Better yet, spend a night (or more, if you're a golfer) to enjoy this university town after dark.

If you're not here to golf, this is a good way to spend a day:

Accommodations
1. Glenderran Guest House & Cameron House
2. Hoppity House
3. Montague Guest House & Lorimer House
4. Doune Guest House
5. St. Andrews Tourist Hostel
6. Agnes Blackadder Hall
7. McIntosh Hall

Eateries & Other
8. Forgan's
9. Playfair's
10. The Doll's House
11. The Seafood Ristorante
12. Little Italy
13. Kazoku
14. Cromars
15. Tailend
16. Aikmans
17. The Central
18. Greyfriars
19. Taste
20. Luvians Bottle Shop
21. I. J. Mellis Cheesemonger
22. Fisher and Donaldson
23. B. Jannettas
24. Supermarket (2)
25. Tom Morris & Old Course Shops

Follow my self-guided walk, which connects the golf course, the university quad, the castle, and the cathedral. Dip into the Golf Museum, watch the golfers on the Old Course, and play a round at "the Himalayas" putting green. With more time, walk along the West Sands beach, take a spin by car or bus to the nearby East Neuk, or drive up to the museums in Dundee. Dundee and Glamis Castle are also fine stops for those connecting St. Andrews to points north.

Orientation to St. Andrews

St. Andrews (pop. 16,000, plus several-thousand more students during term) is situated at the tip of a peninsula next to a broad bay. The town retains its old medieval street plan: Three main streets (North, Market, and South) converge at the cathedral, which overlooks the sea at the tip of town. The middle street—Market Street—has the TI and many handy shops and eateries. North of North Street, the seafront street called The Scores connects the cathedral with the golf scene, which huddles along the West Sands beach at the base of the old town. St. Andrews is compact: You can stroll across town—from the cathedral to the historic golf course—in about 15 minutes.

TOURIST INFORMATION

St. Andrews' helpful TI is on Market Street, about two blocks in front of the cathedral (Mon-Sat 9:15-17:00, Sun from 10:00, closed Sun in winter; free Wi-Fi, 70 Market Street, tel. 01334/472-021, www.visitscotland.com).

ARRIVAL IN ST. ANDREWS

By Train and Bus: The nearest train station is in the village of Leuchars, five miles away. From there, a 10-minute bus ride takes you right into St. Andrews (buy ticket from driver, buses meet most trains—see schedule at bus shelter for next bus to St. Andrews; while waiting, read the historical info under the nearby flagpole). St. Andrews' bus station is near the base of Market Street—a short walk from most B&Bs and the TI. A taxi from Leuchars into St. Andrews costs about £14.

By Car: For a short stay, drivers can park anywhere along the street in the town center (pay-and-display, coins only, 2-hour limit, monitored Mon-Sat 9:00-17:00, Sun from 13:00). For longer stays, you can park for free along certain streets near the center (such as the small lot near the B&B neighborhood around Murray Place, and along The Scores), or use one of the pay-and-display lots near the entrance to town.

HELPFUL HINTS

Golf Events: Every five years, St. Andrews is swamped with about 100,000 visitors when it hosts the British Open (officially called "The Open Championship"; the next one will be the 150th in 2021). The town also fills up every year in early October for the Alfred Dunhill Links Championship. Unless you're a golf pilgrim, avoid the town at these times (as room rates skyrocket).

School Term: The University of St. Andrews has two terms: spring semester ("Candlemas"), from mid-February through May; and fall semester ("Martinmas"), from mid-September until December. St. Andrews has a totally different vibe in the summer, when most students leave and are replaced by upper-crust golfers and tourists.

Sand Surfing and Adventure Activities: Nongolfers who want to stay busy while their travel partners play the Old Course may enjoy some of the adventure activities offered by **Blown Away**—including "land yachting" (zipping across the beach in wind-powered go-carts), kayaking, and paddle boarding. Brothers Guy and Jamie McKenzie set up shop at the northern tip of the West Sands beach (sporadic hours—call first, mobile 07784-121-125, www.blownaway.co.uk, ahoy@blownaway.co.uk).

Theater: The **Byre Theatre** regularly hosts concerts, shows, dance, and opera. Check their website or stop in to see what's on (tickets about £10-25, Abbey Street, tel. 01334/475-000, www.byretheatre.com).

Ghost Tours: Richard Falconer, who has researched and written books on paranormal activity in the area, gives 1.5-hour tours mixing St. Andrews history with ghost stories (£12, tours at 16:00, 17:30, 19:30, and 21:00, must book ahead, text 0746-296-3163 or visit www.standrewsghosttours.com).

St. Andrews Walk

This walk links all of St. Andrews' must-see sights and takes you down hidden medieval streets. Allow a couple of hours, or more if you detour for the sights along the way.

• *Start at the base of the seaside street called The Scores, overlooking the famous golf course.*

▲The Old Course

You're looking at the mecca of golf. The 18th hole of the world's first golf course is a few yards away, on your left (for info on playing the course, see "Golfing in St. Andrews," later).

The gray Neoclassical building to the right of the 18th hole is the clubhouse of the **Royal and Ancient Golf Club**—"R&A" for short. R&A is a private club with membership by invitation only; it was men-only until 2014, but

*Sidebar:* ST. ANDREWS

now—finally!—women are also allowed to join. (In Scotland, men-only clubs lose tax benefits, which is quite costly, but they generally don't care about expenses because their membership is wealthy.) The shop (across the street from the 18th hole, next to Tom Morris—the oldest golf shop in the world) is a great spot to buy a souvenir for the golf lover back home. Even if you're not golfing, watch the action for a while. (Serious fans can walk around to the low-profile stone bridge across the creek called the Swilken Burn, with golf's single most iconic view: back over the 18th hole and the R&A Clubhouse.)

Overlooking the course is the big red-sandstone **Hamilton Grand,** an old hotel that was turned into university dorms and then swanky apartments (rumor has it Samuel L. Jackson owns one). According to town legend, the Hamilton Grand was originally built to upstage the R&A Clubhouse by an American upset over being declined membership to the exclusive club.

Between Hamilton Grand and the beach is the low-profile British Golf Museum (described on page 216).

• *Now turn your back to the golf course and walk through the park toward the obelisk (along the street called The Scores). Stop at the top of the bluff.*

Beach Viewpoint

The broad, two-mile-long sandy beach that stretches below the golf course is the **West Sands.** It's a wonderful place for a relaxing and/or invigorating walk. Or do a slo-mo jog, humming the theme to *Chariots of Fire*—this is the beach on which the characters run in the movie's famous opening scene.

From the bluff, look at the **cliffs** on your right. The sea below was once called "Witches' Lake" because of all the women and men pushed off the cliff on suspicion of witchcraft.

The big obelisk is a **martyrs' monument,** commemorating all those who died for their Protestant beliefs during the Scottish Reformation. (We'll learn more about that chapter of St. Andrews history farther along this walk.)

The Victorian bandstand **gazebo** (between here and the Old Course) recalls the town's genteel heyday as a seaside resort, when the train line ran all the way to town.

• *Just opposite the obelisk, across The Scores and next to Alexander's Restaurant, walk down the tiny alley called...*

Gillespie Wynd

This winds through the back gardens of the city's stone houses. Notice how the medieval platting gave each landowner a little bit of street front and a long back garden. St. Andrews' street plan typifies that of a medieval pilgrimage town: All main roads lead to the cathedral; only tiny lanes, hidden alleys, and twisting "wynds" (rhymes with "minds") such as this one connect the main east-west streets.

• *The wynd pops you out onto North Street. Head left, past the cinema toward the church tower with the red clock face. It's on the corner of North Street and Butts Wynd. For some reason, this street sign often goes missing.*

St. Salvator's College

The tower with the red clock marks the entrance to St. Salvator's College. If you're a student, be careful not to stand on the **initials PH** in the reddish cobbles in front of the gate. These mark the spot where St. Andrews alum and professor Patrick Hamilton—the Scottish Reformation's most famous martyr—was burned at the stake. According to student legend, as he suffered in the flames, Hamilton threatened that any students who stood on this spot would fail their exams.

Now enter the grounds by walking through the arch under the tower. (If the entrance is closed, you can go halfway down Butts Wynd and enter, or at least look, through the gate to the green square.) This grassy square, known to students as **Sally's Quad,** is the heart of the university. As most of the university's classrooms, offices, and libraries are spread out across the medieval town, this quad is the one focal point for student gather-

ings. It's where graduation is held every July, where the free-for-all food fight of Raisin Monday takes place in November (see sidebar on page 210), and where almost the entire student body gathered on the wedding day of their famous alumni couple Prince William and Kate Middleton for a celebration complete with military flybys.

On the outside wall of St. Salvator's Chapel, under the arcade, are **display cases** holding notices and university information; if you're here in spring, you might see students nervously clustered here, looking to see if they've passed their exams.

Go through the simple wooden door and into the **chapel.** Dating from 1450, this is the town's most beautiful medieval church. It's a Gothic gem, with a wooden ceiling, 19th-century stained glass, a glorious organ, and what's supposedly the pulpit of reformer John Knox.

Stroll around Sally's Quad counterclockwise. On the east (far) side, stop to check out the crazy faces on the heads above the second-

The Scottish Reformation

It's easy to forget that during the 16th-century English Reformation—when King Henry VIII split with the Vatican and formed the Anglican Church (so he could get an officially recognized divorce)—Scotland was still its own independent nation. Like much of northern Europe, Scotland eventually chose a Protestant path, but it was more gradual and grassroots than Henry VIII's top-down, destroy-the-abbeys approach. While the English Reformation resulted in the Church of England (a.k.a. the Anglican Church, called "Episcopal" outside of England), with the monarch at its head, the Scottish Reformation created the Church of Scotland, which had groups of elected leaders (called "presbyteries" in church jargon).

One of the leaders of the Scottish Reformation was John Knox (1514-1572), who studied under the great Swiss reformer John Calvin. Returning to Scotland, Knox hopped from pulpit to pulpit, and his feverish sermons incited riots of "born-again" iconoclasts who dismantled or destroyed Catholic churches and abbeys (including St. Andrew's Cathedral). Knox's newly minted Church of Scotland gradually spread from the Lowlands to the Highlands. The southern and eastern part of Scotland, around St. Andrews—just across the North Sea from the Protestant countries of northern Europe—embraced the Church of Scotland long before the more remote and Catholic-oriented part of the country to the north and west. Today about 40 percent of Scots claim affiliation with the Church of Scotland, compared with 20 percent who are Catholic (still mostly in the western Highlands). Glasgow and western Scotland are more Catholic partly because of the Irish immigrants who settled there after fleeing the potato famine in the 1840s.

floor windows. Find the **university's shield** over the door marked *School 6*. The diamonds are from the coat of arms of the bishop who issued the first university charter in 1411; the crescent moon is a shout-out to Pope Benedict XIII, who gave the OK in 1413 to found the university (his given name was Peter de Luna); the lion is from the Scottish coat of arms; and the X-shaped cross is a stylized version of the Scottish flag (a.k.a. St. Andrew's Cross). On the next building to the left, facing the chapel, is St. Andrew himself (above door of building labeled *Lower & Upper College Halls*).

• *Exit the square and make your way back to Butts Wynd. Walk to the end; you're back at The Scores. Across the street and a few steps to the right is the...*

Museum of the University of St. Andrews (MUSA)

This free museum is worth a quick stop. The first room has some well-explained medieval artifacts. Find the copy of the earliest-known map of the town, made in 1580—back when the town walls led directly to the countryside and the cathedral was intact. Notice that the street plan within the town walls has remained the same—but no golf course. The next room has some exhibits on student life, including the "silver arrow competition" (which determined the best archer on campus from year to year) and several of the traditions explained in the "Student Life in St. Andrews" sidebar. The next room displays scientific equipment, great books tied to the school, and an exhibit on the Scottish Reformation. The final room has special exhibits. For a great view of the West Sands, climb to the rooftop terrace.

Cost and Hours: Free; Mon-Sat 10:00-17:00, Sun 12:00-16:00, shorter hours and closed Mon-Wed in winter; 7 The Scores, tel. 01334/461-660, www.st-andrews.ac.uk/musa.

• *Leaving the museum, walk left toward the castle. The turreted stone buildings along here (including one fine example next door to the museum) are built in the Neo-Gothic Scottish Baronial style, and most are academic departments. About 100 yards farther along, the grand building on the right is St. Salvator's Hall, the most prestigious of the university residences and former dorm of Prince William.*

Just past St. Salvator's Hall on the left are the remains of...

St. Andrews Castle

Overlooking the sea, the castle is an evocative empty shell—another casualty of the Scottish Reformation. With a small museum and good descriptions, it offers a quick king-of-the-castle experience in a striking setting.

Cost and Hours: £6, £9 combo-ticket includes cathedral exhibit, daily April-Sept 9:30-17:30, Oct-March 10:00-16:00, tel. 01334/477-196, www. historic-scotland.gov.uk.

Visiting the Castle: Your visit starts with a colorful, kid-friendly exhibit about the history of the castle. Built by a bishop to entertain visiting diplomats in the late 12th century, the castle was home to the powerful bishops, archbishops, and cardinals of St. Andrews. In 1546, the cardinal burned a Protestant preacher at the stake in front of the castle. In retribution, Protestant reformers took the castle and killed the cardinal. In 1547, the French came to attack the castle on behalf of their Catholic ally, Mary, Queen of Scots. During the ensuing siege, a young Protestant refugee named John Knox was captured and sent to France to row on a galley ship.

Student Life in St. Andrews

St. Andrews is first and foremost a university town. Scotland's most prestigious university, founded in 1411, is the third-oldest in the English-speaking world after Oxford and Cambridge. While U. of St. A. is sometimes called "England's northernmost university" due to the high concentration of English students—as numerous as the Scottish ones—a quarter of the 6,000 undergrads and 1,000 grad students hail from overseas.

Some Scots resent the preponderance of upper-crust English students (disparagingly dubbed "Yahs" for the snooty way they say "yes"). However, these southerners pay the bills—they are on the hook for tuition, unlike Scots and most EU citizens. And no one seems to mind that the school's most famous graduates, Prince William and Kate Middleton (class of '05), are the definition of upper-class. Soon after "Wills" started studying art history here, the number of female art history majors skyrocketed. (He later switched to geography.)

As with any venerable university, St. Andrews has its share of quirky customs. Most students own traditional red academic "gowns" (woolen robes) to wear on special occasions, such as graduation. In medieval times, however, they were the daily uniform—supposedly so students could be easily identified in brothels and pubs. (In a leap of faith, divinity students—apparently beyond temptation—wear black.) The way the robe is worn indicates the student's status: First-year students (called "bejants") wear them normally, on the shoulders; second-years ("semi-bejants") wear them slightly off the shoulders; third-years ("tertians") wear them off one shoulder (right for "scientists," left for "artists"); and fourth-years ("magistrands") wear them off both shoulders.

The best time to see these robes is during the Pier Walk on Sundays during the university term. After church services (around noon), gown-clad students parade out to the end of the lonesome pier beyond the cathedral ruins. The tradition dates so far back that no one's sure how it started (probably to bid farewell to a visiting dignitary). Today, students just enjoy being a part of the visual spectacle of a long line of red robes flapping in the North Sea wind.

Another age-old custom is a social-mentoring system in which underclass students choose an "academic family." On Raisin Monday, in mid-November, students give their upper-class "parents" treats—traditionally raisins, but these days more often indulgences like wine and lingerie. Then the "parents" dress up their "children" in outrageous costumes and parade them through town. The underclass students are obliged to carry around "receipts" for their gifts—written on unlikely or unwieldy objects like plastic dinosaurs, microwave ovens, or even refrigerators—and to sing the school song in Latin on demand. This oddball scenario invariably degenerates into a free-for-all food fight on Sally's Quad.

ST. ANDREWS

Eventually he traveled to Switzerland and met the Swiss Protestant ringleader, John Calvin. Knox brought Calvin's ideas back home and became Scotland's greatest reformer.

Next, head outside to explore. The most interesting parts are underground: the "bottle dungeon," where prisoners were sent, never to return (peer down into it in the Sea Tower); and the tight "mine" and even tighter "counter-mine" tunnels (follow the signs; crawling is required to reach it all—go in as far as your claustrophobia allows). This shows how the besieging pro-Catholic Scottish government of the day dug a mine to take (or "undermine") the castle—but were followed at every turn by the Protestant counterminers.

Nearby: Just below the castle is a small beach called the **Castle Sands,** where university students take a traditional and chilly morning dip on May 1. Supposedly, doing this May Day swim is the only way to reverse the curse of having stepped on Patrick Hamilton's initials (explained earlier).

• *Leaving the castle, turn left and continue along the bluff on The Scores, which soon becomes a pedestrian lane leading directly to the gate to the cathedral graveyard. Enter it to stand amid the tombstone-strewn ruins of...*

▲St. Andrews Cathedral

Between the Great Schism and the Reformation (roughly the 14th-16th centuries), St. Andrews was the ecclesiastical capital of Scotland—and this was its showpiece church. Today the site features the remains of the cathedral and cloister (with walls and spires pecked away by centuries of scavengers), a graveyard, and a small exhibit and climbable tower.

Cost and Hours: Cathedral ruins-free, exhibit and tower-£5, £9 combo-ticket includes castle; daily April-Sept 9:30-17:30, Oct-March 10:00-16:00, tel. 01334/472-563, www.historic-scotland. gov.uk.

Background: It was the relics of the Apostle Andrew that first put this town on the map and gave it its name. There are numerous legends associated with the relics. According to one version, in the fourth century, St. Rule was directed in a dream to bring the relics northward from Constantinople. When the ship wrecked offshore from here, it was clear that this was a sacred place. Andrew's bones (an upper arm, a kneecap, some fingers, and a tooth) were kept on this site, and starting in 1160, the cathedral was built and pilgrims began to arrive. Since St. Andrew had a direct connection to Jesus, his relics were believed to possess special properties, making them worthy of pilgrimages on par with St. James' relics in Santiago de Compostela, Spain (of Camino de Santiago fame). St. Andrew became Scotland's patron saint; in fact, the white "X" on the blue

ST. ANDREWS

Scottish flag evokes the diagonal cross on which St. Andrew was crucified (he chose this type of cross because he felt unworthy to die as Jesus had).

Visiting the Cathedral: You can stroll around the cathedral **ruins**—the best part of the complex—for free. First, walk between

the two ruined but still-towering ends of the church, which used to be the apse (at the sea end, where you entered) and the main entry (at the town end). Visually trace the gigantic footprint of the former church in the ground, including the bases of columns—like giant sawed-off tree trunks. Plaques identify where elements of the church once stood.

Looking at the one wall that's still standing, you can see the architectural changes that were made over the 150 years the cathedral was built—from the rounded, Romanesque windows at the front to the more highly decorated, pointed Gothic arches near the back. Try to imagine this church in its former majesty, when it played host to pilgrims from all over Europe.

The church wasn't destroyed all at once, like all those ruined abbeys in England (demolished in a huff by Henry VIII when he broke with the pope). Instead, because the Scottish Reformation was more gradual, this church was slowly picked apart over time. First just the decorations were removed from inside the cathedral. Then the roof was pulled down to make use of its lead. Without a roof, the cathedral fell further and further into disrepair, and was quarried by locals for its handy precut stones (which you'll still find in the walls of many old St. Andrews homes). The elements—a big storm in the 1270s and a fire in 1378—also contributed to the cathedral's demise.

The surrounding **graveyard,** dating from the post-Reformation Protestant era, is much more recent than the cathedral. In this

golf-obsessed town, the game even infiltrates the cemeteries: Many notable golfers from St. Andrews are buried here, including four-time British Open winner Young Tom "Tommy" Morris.

Go through the surviving wall into the former **cloister,** marked by a gigantic grassy square in the center. You can still see the cleats up on the wall, which once supported beams. Imagine the cloister back in its heyday, its passages filled with strolling monks.

At the end of the cloister is a small **exhibit** (entry fee required), with a relatively dull collection of old tombs and other carved-stone relics that have been unearthed on this site. Your ticket also includes entry to the surviving **tower of St. Rule's Church** (the rectangular tower beyond the cathedral ruins that was built to hold the precious relics of St. Andrew about a thousand years ago). If you feel like hiking up the 157 very claustrophobic steps for the view over St. Andrews' rooftops, it's worth the price. Up top, you can also look out to sea to find the pier where students traditionally parade in their robes (see sidebar on page 210).

• *Leave the cathedral grounds on the town side of the cathedral. Angling right, head down North Street. Just ahead, on the left, is the adorable...*

▲St. Andrews Preservation Trust Museum and Garden

Filling a 17th-century fishing family's house that was protected from developers, this museum is a time capsule of an earlier, simpler era. The house itself seems built for Smurfs, but it once housed 20 family members. The ground floor features replicas of a grocer's shop and a "chemist's" (pharmacy), using original fittings from actual stores. Upstairs are temporary exhibits. Out back is a tranquil garden (dedicated to the memory of a beloved professor) with "great-grandma's washhouse," featuring an exhibit about the history of soap and washing. Lovingly presented, this quaint, humble house provides a nice contrast to the big-money scene around the golf course at the other end of town.

Cost and Hours: Free but donation requested, generally open June-Sept daily 14:00-17:00, closed off-season, 12 North Street, tel. 01334/477-629, www.standrewspreservationtrust.org.

• *From the museum, hang a left around the next corner to South Castle Street. Soon you'll reach...*

Market Street

At the top of Market Street—one of the most atmospheric old streets in town—look for the tiny white house on your left, with the cute curved staircase. What's that chase scene on the roof?

Now turn right down Market Street (which leads directly to the town's center, but we'll take a curvier route). Notice how the streets and even the buildings are smaller at this oldest end of town, as if the whole city is shrinking as the streets close in on the cathedral. Homeowners along Market Street are particularly proud of their address, and recently pooled their money to spiff up the cobbles and sidewalks.

Passing an antique bookstore on your right, take a left onto Baker Lane, a.k.a. Baxter Wynd. You'll pass a tiny and inviting public garden on your right before landing on South Street.

• *Turn right and head down South Street. After 50 yards, cross the street and enter a gate marked by a cute gray facade and a university insignia.*

St. Mary's College

This is the home of the university's School of Divinity (theology). If the gate's open, find the peaceful quad, with its gnarled tree that was purportedly planted by Mary, Queen of Scots. To get a feel of student life from centuries past, try poking your nose into one of the old classrooms.

• *Back on South Street, continue to your left. Some of the plainest buildings on this stretch of the street have the most interesting history—several of them were built to fund the Crusades. Turn right on Church Street. You can end this walk at charming Church Square—perhaps while enjoying a decadent pastry from the recommended Fisher and Donaldson bakery. Or if you continue a few more yards down Church Street, you'll spill onto Market Street and the heart of town.*

Golfing in St. Andrews

St. Andrews is the Cooperstown of golf. While St. Andrews lays claim to founding the sport (the first record of golf being played here was in 1553), nobody knows exactly where and when people first hit a ball with a stick for fun. In the Middle Ages, St. Andrews traded with the Dutch; some historians believe they picked up a golf-like Dutch game played on ice and translated it to the bonnie rolling hills of Scotland's east coast. Since the grassy beachfront strip just outside St. Andrews was too poor to support crops, it was used for playing the game—and, centuries later, it still is. Why do golf courses have 18 holes? Because that's how many fit at the Old Course—golf's single most famous site. When you putt-er around, keep in mind this favorite Scottish say-it-aloud joke: "Balls," said the queen. "If I had two, I'd be king." The king laughed—he had to.

The Old Course

The Old Course hosts the British Open every five years (next in 2021). At other times it's open to the public for golfing. The famous Royal and Ancient Golf Club (R&A) doesn't actually own the course, which is public and managed by the St. Andrews Links Trust. Drop by the St. Andrews Links Clubhouse, overlooking the beach near the Old Course (open long hours daily). They have a well-stocked shop, a restaurant, and a rooftop garden with nice views over the Old Course.

Old Course Tours: One-hour guided tours visit the 1st, 17th, and 18th holes (£10, daily April-May at 11:00, June-Sept at 11:00 and 14:00, leaves from the St. Andrews Links Clubhouse, tel. 01334/466-666, www.standrews.com).

Teeing Off at the Old Course: Playing at golf's pinnacle course is pricey (£175/person, less off-season), but open to the public—subject to lottery drawings for tee times and reserved spots by club members. You can play the Old Course only if you have a handicap of 24 (men) or 36 (women and juniors) or better; bring along your certificate or card. If you don't know your handicap—or don't know what "handicap" means—then you're not good enough to play here (they want to keep the game moving). If you play, you'll do nine holes out, then nine more back in—however, all but four share the same greens.

Reserving a Tee Time: To ensure a specific tee time at the Old Course, reserve a year ahead during a brief window between late August and early September (fill out form at www.standrews.com). Otherwise, some tee times are determined each day by a lottery called the "daily ballot." Enter your name on their website, in person, or by calling 01334/466-666—by 14:00 two days before (2 players minimum, 4 players max). They post the results online at 16:00. Note that no advance reservations are taken on Saturdays or in September, and the courses are closed on Sundays—which is traditionally the day reserved for townspeople to stroll.

Singleton Strategies: Single golfers aren't eligible to reserve or ballot. If you're golfing solo, you could try to team up with someone (ask your B&B for tips). Otherwise, each day, a few single golfers fill out a two- or three-golfer group by showing up in person at the Old Pavilion (in front of the R&A Clubhouse). It's first-come, first-served, and a very long shot, so get there early. The starter generally arrives at 6:00, but die-hard golfers start lining up several hours before or even camp out overnight (especially in peak season). Swing by the day before, when they should have a sense of how likely a spot is to open up and can recommend just how early to arrive.

Other Courses: Two of the seven St. Andrews Links courses are right next to the Old Course—the New Course and the Jubilee Course. And the modern cliff-top Castle Course is just outside the city. These are cheaper, and it's much easier to get a tee time (£75 for New and Jubilee, £120 for Castle Course, much less for others). It's usually possible to get a tee time for the same day or next day (if you want a guaranteed reservation, make it at least 2 weeks in advance). The Castle Course has great views overlooking the town, but even more wind to blow your ball around.

Club Rental: You can rent decent-quality clubs around town for about £30. The **Auchterlonies** shop has a good reputation (on Golf Place—a few doors down from the R&A Clubhouse, tel. 01334/473-253, www.auchterlonies.com); you can also rent clubs from the St. Andrews Links Clubhouse for a few pounds more.

▲The Himalayas

The St. Andrews Ladies' Putting Club, better known as "The Himalayas" (for its dramatically hilly terrain), is basically a very classy (but still relaxed) game of minigolf. The course presents the perfect opportunity for nongolfers (female or male) to say they've played the links at St. Andrews—for less than the cost of a Coke. It's remarkable how this cute little patch of undulating grass can present even more challenging obstacles than the tunnels, gates, and distractions of a miniature golf course back home. Flat shoes are required (no high heels). You'll see it on the left as you walk toward the St. Andrews Links Clubhouse from the R&A Clubhouse.

Cost and Hours: £3 for 18 holes. The putting green is open to nonmembers (tourists like you) Mon-Fri 10:30-18:30, Sat until 18:00, Sun from 12:00, weekends-only Oct and March, closed in winter, tel. 01334/475-196, www.standrewsputtingclub.com.

British Golf Museum

This exhibit, which started as a small collection in the R&A Clubhouse across the street, is the best place in Britain to learn about the Scots' favorite sport. It's fascinating for golf lovers.

Cost and Hours: £8, April-Oct Mon-Sat 9:30-17:00, Sun from 10:00; Nov-March daily 10:00-16:00; last entry 45 minutes before closing; café upstairs; Bruce Embankment, in the blocky modern building squatting behind the R&A Clubhouse by the Old Course, tel. 01334/460-046, www.britishgolfmuseum.co.uk.

Visiting the Museum: The compact, one-way exhibit reverently presents a meticulous survey of the game's history. Start with the film, then follow the counterclockwise route to learn about the evolution of golf—from the monarchs who loved and hated golf (including the king who outlawed it because it was distracting men from church and archery practice), to Tom Morris and Bobby Jones, all the way up to the "Golden Bear" and a randy Tiger. Along the way, you'll see plenty of old clubs, balls, medals, and trophies, and learn about how the earliest "feathery" balls and wooden clubs were made. Touchscreens invite you to learn more, and you'll also see a "hall of fame" with items donated by today's biggest golfers. Finally, you'll have a chance to dress up in some old-school golfing duds and try out some of that antique equipment for yourself.

Sleeping in St. Andrews

Owing partly to the high-roller golf tourists flowing through the town, St. Andrews' accommodations are quite expensive. During graduation week in June, hotels often require a four-night stay and book up quickly. All of the guesthouses I've listed are on the streets called Murray Park and Murray Place, between North Street and The Scores in the old town. If you need to find a room on the fly, look around in this same neighborhood, which has far more options than just the ones I've listed below.

$$$ Glenderran Guest House offers five plush rooms (including two true singles) and a few nice breakfast extras (no kids under 12, pay same-day laundry, 9 Murray Park, tel. 01334/477-951, www.glenderran.com, info@glenderran.com, Ray and Maggie).

$$ Hoppity House is a bright and contemporary place, with attention to detail and fun hosts Gordon and Heather, who are helpful and generous with travel tips. There's a lounge and kitchen for guest use and a storage closet for golf equipment. You may find a stuffed namesake bunny or two hiding out among its four impeccable rooms (cash or PayPal only, fridges in rooms, 4 Murray Park, tel. 01334/461-116, mobile 07701-099-100, www.hoppityhouse.co.uk, enquiries@hoppityhouse.co.uk).

$$ Cameron House has five clean and simple rooms around a beautiful stained-glass atrium (two-night minimum in summer, 11 Murray Park, tel. 01334/472-306, www.cameronhouse-sta.co.uk, info@cameronhouse-sta.co.uk, Donna).

$$ Montague Guest House has richly furnished public spaces—with a cozy, leather-couches lounge/breakfast room—and eight nice rooms (21 Murray Park, tel. 01334/479-287, www.montaguehouse.com, info@montagueguesthouse.com, Raj and Judith).

$$ Lorimer House has six comfortable, tastefully decorated rooms, including one on the ground floor (two-night minimum preferred, no kids under 12, 19 Murray Park, tel. 01334/476-599, www.lorimerhouse.com, info@lorimerhouse.com, Mick and Chris).

$$ Doune Guest House's seven rooms provide a more impersonal but perfectly comfortable place to stay in St. Andrews (breakfast extra, two-night minimum preferred in summer, 5

Murray Place, tel. 01334/475-195, www.dounehouse.com, info@ dounehouse.com).

¢ **St. Andrews Tourist Hostel** has 44 beds in colorful 5- to 8-bed rooms about a block from the base of Market Street. The high-ceilinged lounge is a comfy place for a break, and the friendly staff is happy to recommend their favorite pubs (kitchen, St. Mary's Place, tel. 01334/479-911, www.hostelsstandrews.com, info@ hostelsstandrews.com).

UNIVERSITY ACCOMMODATIONS

In the summer (early June-Aug), some of the University of St. Andrews' student-housing buildings are tidied up and rented out to tourists. I've listed the most convenient options below (website for both: www.discoverstandrews.com; pay when reserving). Both of these include breakfast and Wi-Fi. Because true single rooms are rare in St. Andrews' B&Bs, these dorms are a good option for solo travelers.

$ **Agnes Blackadder Hall** has double beds and private bathrooms; it's more comfortable, but also more expensive and less central (North Haugh, tel. 01334/467-000, agnes.blackadder@st-andrews.ac.uk).

$ **McIntosh Hall** is cheaper and more central, but it only has twin beds and shared bathrooms (Abbotsford Crescent, tel. 01334/467-035, mchall@st-andrews.ac.uk).

Eating in St. Andrews

RESTAURANTS

$$$ **Forgan's** is tempting and popular, tucked back in a huge space behind Market Street in what feels like a former warehouse. It's done up country-kitschy, with high ceilings, cool lanterns, and a fun energy. It serves up hearty food and offers a tempting steak selection (daily 12:00-22:00, reservations smart, 110 Market Street, tel. 01334/466-973, www.forgansstandrews.co.uk). On Friday and Saturday nights after 22:30, they have live *ceilidh* (traditional Scottish) music, and everyone joins in the dancing; consider reserving a booth for a late dinner, then stick around for the show. They also have live acoustic music on Thursday evenings.

$$$ **Playfair's,** a restaurant and steakhouse downstairs in the Ardgowan Hotel between the B&B neighborhood and the Old Course, has a cozy/classy interior and outdoor seating at rustic tables set just below the busy street. Their bar next door also serves food (daily 12:00-22:00, off-season weekdays open for dinner only, 2 Playfair Terrace on North Street, tel. 01334/472-970).

$$$ **The Doll's House** serves dressed-up Scottish cuisine in a stone-and-wood interior or at tables on the square in front, com-

plete with fur throws on the chairs (daily 10:00-22:00, across from Holy Trinity Church at 3 Church Square, tel. 01334/477-422).

$$$$ The Seafood Ristorante, in a modern glassy building overlooking the beach near the Old Course, is like dining in an aquarium. They serve high-end Italian with a focus on seafood in a formal space with floor-to-ceiling windows providing unhindered views (minimum £20/person food order at dinner, daily 12:00-14:30 & 18:00-21:30, reservations a must on weekends and in summer, The Scores, tel. 01334/479-475, www.theseafoodristorante. com).

$$ Little Italy is a crowded Italian joint with all the clichés—red-and-white checkered tablecloths, replica Roman busts, a bit of freneticism, and even a moped in the wall. But the food is authentically good and the menu is massive. It's popular—make reservations (daily 12:30-22:30, 2 Logies Lane, tel. 01334/479-299).

$$ Kazoku is a casual and satisfying sushi bar that also serves some hot Japanese dishes (seared scallops on a bed of haggis, anyone?). It's a family business—the name means "family" in Japanese (daily 12:00-14:30 & 17:00-21:30, 6A Greyfriars Gardens, tel. 01334/477-750).

Fish-and-Chips: $ Cromars is a local favorite for takeaway fish-and-chips (and burgers). At the counter, you can order yours to go, or—in good weather—enjoy it at the sidewalk tables; farther in is a small **$$** sit-down restaurant with more choices (both open daily 11:00-22:00, at the corner of Union and Market, tel. 01334/475-555). **Tailend** also has a **$** takeaway counter up front (fish-and-chips) and a **$$** restaurant with a bigger selection in the back (daily 11:30-22:00, 130 Market Street, tel. 01334/474-070).

BEER, COFFEE, AND WHISKY

Pubs: There's no shortage in this college town. These aren't "gastropubs," but they all serve straightforward pub fare (all open long hours daily).

Aikmans, run by Barbara and Malcolm (two graduates from the university who couldn't bring themselves to leave), features a cozy wood-table ambience, a focus on ales, live music (usually Fri-Sat), and simple soups, sandwiches, and snacks (32 Bell Street, tel. 01334/477-425). **The Central,** right along Market Street, is a St. Andrews standby, with old lamps and lots of brass (77 Market Street, tel. 01334/478-296). **Greyfriars,** with forgettable food, is in a classy, modern hotel near the Murray Park B&Bs (129 North Street, tel. 01334/474-906).

Coffee: $ Taste, a little café just across the street from the B&B neighborhood, has the best coffee in town and a laid-back, borderline-funky ambience that feels like a big-city coffeehouse back home. It also serves cakes and light food (daily 7:00-18:00 in

summer, open later when students are back, 148 North Street, tel.
01334/477-959).

Whisky: Luvians Bottle Shop—run by three brothers
(Luigi, Vincenzo, and Antonio)—is a friendly place to talk, taste,
and purchase whisky. Distilleries bottle unique single-cask vintag-
es exclusively for this shop to celebrate the British Open every five
years (ask about the 21-year-old Springbank they received in 2015
to commemorate the tournament). With nearly 50 bottles open
for tastings, a map of Scotland's whisky regions, and helpful team
members, this is a handy spot to learn about whisky. They also sell
fine wines and a wide range of microbrews (Mon-Sat 10:00-22:00,
Sun from 12:30, 66 Market Street, tel. 01334/477-752).

PICNIC FOOD AND SWEETS
Cheese: I.J. Mellis Cheesemonger, the excellent Edinburgh
cheese shop with a delectable array of Scottish, English, and international cheeses, has a St. Andrews branch (Mon-Sat 9:00-19:00,
Sun 10:00-17:00, 149 South Street, tel. 01334/471-410).

Pastries: Fisher and Donaldson is beloved for its rich, affordable pastries and chocolates. Listen as the straw-hatted bakers chat
with their regular customers, then try their Coffee Tower—like a
giant cream puff filled with lightly coffee-flavored cream—or their
number-one seller, the fudge doughnut (Mon-Sat 6:00-17:00,
closed Sun, just around the corner from the TI at 13 Church Street,
tel. 01334/472-201).

Gelato: You'll see many people walking around licking cones
from **B. Jannettas,** which has been around for more than a century. While waiting in line, ponder what you want from their range
of 50-plus gelato flavors (daily 9:00-22:00, 31 South Street, tel.
01334/473-285).

Supermarkets: You can stock up for a picnic at **Tesco** or
Sainsbury's Local on Market Street.

St. Andrews Connections

Trains don't go into St. Andrews—instead, use the Leuchars station (5 miles from St. Andrews, connected by buses coordinated to
meet most trains, 2-4/hour, see "Arrival in St. Andrews" on page
204).

From Leuchars by Train to: Edinburgh (1-2/hour, 1 hour),
Glasgow (2/hour, 2 hours, transfer in Haymarket), **Inverness**
(roughly hourly, 3.5 hours, 1-2 changes). Trains run less frequently
on Sundays. Train info: Tel. 0345-748-4950, www.nationalrail.
co.uk. To reach **Dundee,** take bus #99 from St. Andrews bus station
near the base of Market Street (every 10 minutes, 30 minutes).

Near St. Andrews

Two starkly different destinations are within a half-hour's drive of St. Andrews, in opposite directions. To the north is the up-and-coming city of Dundee, with a pair of excellent museums (offering more-interesting-than-they-sound, in-depth exhibits on the local jute industry and Antarctic exploration); just beyond is Glamis Castle, the childhood home of Queen Elizabeth's late mother, known as the Queen Mother. And to the south is the charming string of seaside villages called the East Neuk. Either one makes a good half-day side-trip, or you can squeeze them in on your way between St. Andrews and other destinations.

DUNDEE

The once-prosperous, then decrepit, and now steadily rejuvenating city of Dundee (Scotland's fourth-largest, with about 150,000 people) sits at the mouth of the River Tay. In its heyday, Dundee was known for the "Three J's": jute (turning the raw fiber into rope, burlap, and canvas), jam (importing that orange marmalade that's on every B&B breakfast table), and journalism (being the home of D. C. Thomson & Co., the respected publishing company responsible for the *Sunday Post* and for creating many beloved Scottish cartoon characters).

Then, like many Industrial Age British boomtowns, Dundee fell on hard times in the 20th century. Today, thanks to some promising rejuvenation through the tech industry, Dundee is working to reinvent its downtown core and its waterfront (where a huge mess of construction will eventually become a £80-million branch of the Victoria & Albert Museum—due to open in 2018). But the city still has a ways to go, and for now it merits only a quick stop for two interesting museums.

Getting There: Drivers can take advantage of nearby parking for a strategic visit to one or both of Dundee's museums. The Discovery Point museum along the waterfront is well signed and easy to find. The Verdant Works Jute Museum is buried in a mostly deserted industrial area higher up in town (look for brown signs), but it's more reliably found by using GPS or an app. **Train** travelers find that Discovery Point is easy (it's right across the street from the train station), but the Verdant Works Jute Museum, just under a mile away, isn't well connected by public transit; walk or take a taxi from Discovery Point.

▲Discovery Point and the RRS *Discovery*

At the turn of the 20th century—long after the Age of Discovery—Antarctica was the world's last great mystery. With fervor matched a half-century later in the Space Race, ambitious countries set out

ST. ANDREWS

St. Andrews Area

To Ballater
To Dunnottar Castle & Aberdeen
Montrose
Kirriemuir
Forfar
Inverkeilor
Alyth
GLAMIS
A-928
Marywell
Blairgowrie
Meigle
Dean Water
Arbroath
Muirdrum
A-90
A-92
Carnoustie
To Pitlochry & Inverness
A-90
Dundee
Tayport
Newport-on-Tay
A-9
Perth
Firth of Tay
Leuchars
Bridge of Earn
St. Andrews
A-91
A-917
Cupar
Kingsbarns
B-9131
SECRET BUNKER
M-90
A-91
A-915
Crail
To Stirling
Falkland
FIFE
EAST NEUK
Milnathort
Glenrothes
A-917
Anstruther
Pittenweem
Leslie
Methil
Elie
Loch Leven
To Falkirk & Glasgow
A-92
Kirkcaldy
To Falkirk
Dunfermline
M-90
Kinghorn
North Berwick
FORTH BRIDGES
To Edinburgh
Firth of Forth
Aberlady
Whitekirk

10 Kilometers
10 Miles

Inverness
SCOTLAND
Edinburgh
ENGLAND

to learn more about the unexplored continent. This museum tells the story of the Royal Research Ship (RRS) *Discovery,* which was built in Dundee and set sail for Antarctica in 1901. It was one of the most successful scientific expeditions of its time. This attraction, on Dundee's riverfront, has two parts: a museum about the ship and the expeditions that it undertook, and the

actual ship, restored to how it was in 1924.

Cost and Hours: £9.25, £16 combo-ticket with Verdant Works Jute Museum; Mon-Sat 10:00-18:00, Sun 11:00-18:00, off-season daily until 17:00, last entry one hour before closing; audioguide-£3, Riverside Drive, closest parking is next door at Discovery Car Park, tel. 01382/309-060, www.rrsdiscovery.com.

Visiting the Museum: Begin by touring the **museum** (all well-described) to better appreciate the ship and the role it played in navigation history. You'll learn how the *Discovery* was built and provisioned, and how the crew (led by Commander Robert Falcon Scott, who died a decade later in a race to the South Pole) planned and perilously executed their icy journey. The exhibit explains that when the ship set sail in 1901, less was known about Antarctica than was known about the moon when the first Apollo mission landed in 1969. A good 10-minute film helps provide historical context.

Head outside to the ship itself (with a few brief informational plaques) to walk across the decks and delve below to see the engine room, galley, sick bay, mess deck, and living quarters. The photographic darkroom, drawing table, and vials for scientific samples illustrate the ship's mission: opening up a new continent to human understanding.

▲Verdant Works Jute Museum

Hardworking, industrious Scotland has several fine museums about how things are made—and this is one of the best. Filling a former jute-processing factory called Verdant Works, it's located in a run-down but gentrifying zone of brick factories. This museum explores every facet of the jute industry that put Dundee on the map. Especially worthwhile for those with a healthy interest in engineering, the well-presented museum accomplishes the remarkable task of making jute interesting even to those less mechanically inclined.

Cost and Hours: £9.25, £16 combo-ticket with Discovery Point, same hours as Discovery Point, West Henderson's Wynd, free parking lot in back, tel. 01382/309-060, www.verdantworks. com.

Background: Starting in the 1830s, Dundee businessmen—who came to be known as "jute barons"—developed a local industry around processing the fiber of a plant called jute, which could be used to make rope, burlap sacks, sails, canvases, carpeting, and even clothing. In an age before plastics, versatile jute was a prized material...and virtually all of the world's supply came through Dundee. Great Britain's nautical expansion further boosted the industry: Dundee-made materials sailed to every corner of the earth. Coinciding with the Highland Clearances and the decline of traditional rural lifestyles, the jute boom lured many floundering farmers and peasants into urban factories. By century's end, Dundee's population had tripled.

ST. ANDREWS

In Dundee, as in other Industrial Age cities, rapid changes created a sharply stratified society, with a tiny and obscenely wealthy upper class and a huge, desperately poor lower class. But before long, the jute industry fell victim to "outsourcing," a century before our time: By 1875, a jute factory opened in India (where the raw materials were harvested), and by 1900, more jute products were produced in Calcutta than in Dundee. The rise of plastics and other synthetic fibers in the 1970s drove the final nail into the industry's coffin; Dundee's last remaining jute factory closed in 1999.

Visiting the Museum: Try to start your visit with the 15-minute *Juteopolis* film (which sets the stage for the museum and helps explain why you're spending your vacation learning about jute) in a theater behind the ticket desk. But if it's not starting soon, you can keep going with your tour because you'll come to the theater again later in your visit.

Head across the courtyard to the Works Office and follow the one-way route through the exhibit. The highlight is the machine hall, where you'll see working (but much smaller) versions of the machinery used for each of the steps required to turn this tropical fiber into practical products. On some days, docents are standing by to explain more and demonstrate some of the century-old equipment.

Upstairs (access from outside, in the courtyard) is an exhibit about the social history of the city, showing different walks of life relating to the jute industry. The cavernous High Mill has more exhibits delving into different facets of the industry and a huge Boulton and Watt steam engine from 1801, still in working order.

Downtown Dundee

With a little time to spare, it's worth walking 10 minutes from Discovery Point to the town center. In front of the city's landmark Caird Hall concert venue (with the TI next door), you'll find a bustling, traffic-free people zone, with cafés, public tables, fountains, and a glitzy shopping mall. Find the life-sized statues of Desperate Dan and Minnie the Minx (Dundee-born cartoon characters who are as beloved among Scots as they are unknown to Americans). A quick walk here offers a peek into the Dundee of the future.

North of Dundee
▲Glamis Castle

A 20-minute drive north of Dundee (or 45 minutes north of St. Andrews) is the residence of the Earls of Strathmore—best known as the childhood-home castle of the Queen Mother (a.k.a. Elizabeth Bowes-Lyon, 1900-2002). Glamis (pronounced "glahms") is a proper castle inside and out: You'll drive down a grand, tree-lined driveway to a majestic palace bristling with turrets and filled with elaborately decorated rooms that drip with history and blue-blood quirk. Coming here just seems the right way to pay respects to the Queen Mother, who gave birth to the longest-reigning monarch in British history and supported her husband, King George VI, as he rallied Britain through World War II (as depicted in *The King's Speech*). Their second daughter, Princess Margaret, was born right here at Glamis—the first royal baby born in Scotland in 300 years. The "Queen Mum" always had a deep affection for her home at Glamis and was often clad in a distinctive hue that she liked to call "Strathmore blue."

Cost and Hours: £12.50, daily 10:00-16:30 (last tour time), weekends-only Nov-early Dec, closed early Dec-Easter, tel. 01307/840-393, www.glamis-castle.co.uk.

Getting There: From Dundee, head north on the A-90 expressway (toward Aberdeen); the exit is well marked with brown *Glamis Castle* signs (also marked for *Kirriemuir*). From the exit, follow the A-928 seven miles to the castle.

Visiting the Castle: You can only visit the interior on a 50-minute guided tour. You'll see both grand state rooms and intimate quarters—including the private rooms of the Queen Mother, which her parents installed after she married the prince to ensure she'd keep coming home for visits. The tour is packed with fun insights into aristocratic eccentricities, from the paintings of one earl who simply adored his leather body armor (painted to resemble a sculpted Greek god), to a rare painting of Jesus wearing a hat. Glamis also loves to tout its title as the "most haunted castle in Scotland"—though the ghost tales your guide imparts are more silly than scary. (Even more suspect are boasts that Glamis inspired Shakespeare as the setting for *Macbeth*—a claim also made by Cawdor Castle.) After your tour, you can visit a few more exhibits and explore the grounds on your own—a handout suggests several walking routes.

THE EAST NEUK

On the lazy coastline meandering south from St. Andrews, the cute-as-a-pin East Neuk (pronounced "nook") is a collection of tidy fishing villages. While hardly earth-shattering, the East Neuk is a pleasant detour if you've got the time. The villages of Crail and Pittenweem have their fans, but Anstruther is worth most of your attention. The East Neuk works best as a half-day side-trip (by either car or bus) from St. Andrews, though drivers can use it as a scenic detour between Edinburgh and St. Andrews.

Getting There: It's an easy **drive** from St. Andrews. For the scenic route, follow the A-917 south of town along the coast, past Crail, on the way to Anstruther and Pittenweem. For a shortcut directly to Anstruther, take the B-9131 across the peninsula (or return that way after driving the longer coastal route there). **Buses** connect St. Andrews to the East Neuk: Bus #95 goes hourly from St. Andrews to Crail and Anstruther (50 minutes to Anstruther, catch bus at St. Andrews bus station or from Church Street, around the corner from the TI). The hourly #X60 bus goes directly to Anstruther, then on to Edinburgh (25 minutes to Anstruther, 2 hours more to Edinburgh). Bus info: Tel. 0871-200-2233, www.travelinescotland. com.

▲Anstruther

Stretched out along its harbor, colorful Anstruther (AN-stru-ther; pronounced ENT-ster by locals) is the centerpiece of the East Neuk. The main parking lot and bus stop are both right on the harbor. Anstruther's handy **TI,** which offers lots of useful information for the entire East Neuk area, is located next door to the town's main sight, the Scottish Fisheries Museum (open daily in summer, closed Nov-March, tel. 01333/311-073). Stroll the harborfront to the end, detouring inland around the little cove (or crossing the causeway at low tide) to reach some colorful old houses, including one encrusted with seashells.

Anstruther's **Scottish Fisheries Museum** is true to its slogan: "We are bigger than you think!" The endearingly hokey exhibit sprawls through several harborfront buildings, painstakingly tracing the history of Scottish seafaring from primitive dugout dinghies to modern vessels. You'll learn the story of Scotland's "Zulu" fishing boats and walk through vast boat-filled rooms. For a glimpse at humble fishing lifestyles, don't miss the Fisherman's Cottage, hiding upstairs from the courtyard (open daily, tearoom, Harbourhead, tel. 01333/310-628, www.scotfishmuseum.org).

Eating in Anstruther: Anstruther's claim to fame is its fish-and-chips. Though there are several good chippies in town, the famous one is the **Anstruther Fish Bar,** facing the harbor just a block from the TI and Fisheries Museum (take out or dine in for a few pounds more, open long hours daily, 42 Shore Street, tel. 01333/310-518).

Scotland's Secret Bunker

Among the rolling farm fields between St. Andrews and the East Neuk, a blink-and-you'll-miss-it stone farmhouse conceals a sprawling network of corridors: 24,000 square feet, 100 feet under the ground, protected by 10-foot-thick reinforced concrete walls. You'll climb down the stairs and hike through a long tunnel to explore a warren of Cold War-era control rooms, dormitories, and telecommunications centers, plus a chapel and the office of the Minister of State of Scotland (who would command the military in the event of an attack). Black-and-white films calmly explain to homeowners how to prepare for—and cope with—a nuclear attack.

The exhibit itself is overpriced and frustratingly hokey—a jumble of 1970s technology, scarcely explained other than by the melodramatic audioguide. But for those interested in the Cold War, simply exploring this space can be a powerful experience.

The most striking part of the experience is watching the 46-minute BBC-produced film *The War Game,* a harrowing dramatization of what would happen in the event of a nuclear attack. Its "Keep Calm and Carry On," pull-no-punches straightforwardness is a haunting reminder of an age when global nuclear holocaust seemed not only possible, but likely. (Produced in 1965, the film was immediately branded too disturbing to broadcast, and was not shown on the BBC for 20 years.)

Cost and Hours: £12, daily 10:00-18:00, closed Nov-Feb, last entry one hour before closing, audioguide-£2, tel. 01333/310-301, www.secretbunker.co.uk.

Getting There: Head out of St. Andrews toward Crail, but just outside of town, turn off on the right toward *Dunino* and *Anstruther* (on the B-9131). Then follow brown *Secret Bunker* signs about six miles through farmland.

THE SCOTTISH HIGHLANDS

Filled with more natural and historical mystique than people, the Highlands are where Scottish dreams are set. Legends of Bonnie Prince Charlie linger around crumbling castles as tunes played by pipers in kilts swirl around tourists. Intrepid Munro baggers scale bald mountains, grizzled islanders man the drizzly ferry crossings, and midges make life miserable (bring bug spray). The Highlands are the most mountainous, least inhabited, and—for many—most scenic and romantic part of Scotland.

The Highlands are covered with mountains, lochs, and glens, scarcely leaving a flat patch of land for building a big city. Geographically, the Highlands are defined by the Highland Boundary Fault, which slashes 130 miles diagonally through the middle of Scotland just north of the big cities of the more densely populated "Central Belt" (Glasgow and Edinburgh).

This geographical and cultural fault line is clearly visible on maps, and you can even see it in the actual landscape—especially around Loch Lomond and the Trossachs, where the transition from rolling Lowland hills to bald Highland mountains is almost too on-the-nose. Just beyond the fault, the Grampian Mountains curve across the middle of Scotland; beyond that, the Caledonian Canal links the east and west coasts (slicing diagonally through the Great Glen, another geological fault, from Oban to Inverness), with even more mountains to the north.

Though the Highlands' many "hills" are technically too short to be called "mountains," they do a convincing imitation. (Just don't say that to a Scot.) Scotland has 282 hills over 3,000 feet. A list of these was first compiled in 1891 by Sir Hugh Munro, and to this day the Scots still call their high hills "Munros." (Hills

Hiking the Highlands

Scotland is a hiker's paradise...as long as you bring rain gear. I've recommended a few hikes of varying degrees of difficulty throughout this book. Remember: Wear sturdy (ideally waterproof) shoes, and be prepared for any weather. For serious hikes, pick up good maps and get advice at local TIs or from a knowledgeable resident (such as your B&B host). A good resource for hiking route tips is www.walkhighlands.co.uk.

For a more in-depth experience, consider one of Scotland's famous multiday walks. These are the most popular:

West Highland Way: 95 miles, 5-10 days, Milngavie to Fort William by way of Loch Lomond, Glencoe, and Rannoch Moor

Great Glen Way: 79 miles, 5-6 days, Fort William to Inverness along the Caledonian Canal, Fort Augustus, and Loch Ness

John Muir Way: 134 miles, 9-10 days, newer route—from 2014—that runs coast to coast through the Central Belt of Scotland, from Helensburgh to Dunbar via Falkirk, the Firth of Forth, and Edinburgh

from 2,500-3,000 feet are known as "Corbetts," and those from 2,000-2,500 are "Grahams.") Avid hikers—called "Munro baggers"—love to tick these minimountains off their list. According to the Munro Society, more than 5,000 intrepid hikers can brag that they've climbed all of the Munros. (To get started, you'll find lots of good information at www.walkhighlands.co.uk/munros).

The Highlands occupy more than half of Scotland's area, but are populated by less than five percent of its people—a population density comparable to Russia's. Scotland's Hebrides Islands (among them Skye, Mull, Iona, and Staffa), while not, strictly speaking, in the Highlands, are often included simply because they share much of the same culture, clan history, and Celtic ties. (Orkney and Shetland, off the north coast of Scotland, are a world apart—they feel more Norwegian than Highlander.)

Inverness is the Highlands' de facto capital, and often claims to be the region's only city. (The east coast port city of Aberdeen—Scotland's third largest, and quadruple the size of Inverness—has its own Doric culture and dialect, and is usually considered its own animal.)

The Highlands are where you'll most likely see Gaelic—the old Celtic language that must legally accompany English on road signs. While few Highlanders actually speak Gaelic—and virtually no one speaks it as a first language—certain Gaelic words are used as a nod of respect to their heritage. *Fàilte* (welcome), *Slàinte mhath!* (cheers!—literally "good health"), and *tigh* (house—featured in many business names) are all common. If you're making friends in a Highland pub, ask your new mates to teach you some Gaelic words.

The Highlands are also the source of many Scottish superstitions, some of which persist in remote communities, where mischievous fairies and shape-shifting kelpies are still blamed for trouble. Many superstitions surround babies. New parents were gripped with a fear that their newborn could be replaced by a devilish imposter called a changeling. Well into the 20th century, a midwife called a "howdie" would oversee key rituals: Before a birth, doors and windows would be unlocked and mirrors would be covered. And the day of the week a baby is born was charged with significance ("Monday's child is fair of face, Tuesday's child is full of grace...").

Many American superstitions and expressions originated in Scotland (such as "black sheep," based on the idea that a black sheep was terrible luck for the flock). Just as a baseball player might refuse to shave during a winning streak, many perfectly modern Highlanders carry a sprig of white heather for good luck at their wedding (and are careful not to cross two knives at the dinner table). And let's not even start with the Loch Ness monster...

In the summer, the Highlands swarm with tourists...and midges. These miniature mosquitoes—like "no-see-ums"—are bloodthirsty and determined. They can be an annoyance from late May through September, depending on the weather. Hot sun or a stiff breeze blows the tiny buggers away, but they thrive in damp, shady areas. Locals suggest blowing or brushing them off, rather than swatting them—since killing them only seems to attract more (likely because of the smell of fresh blood). Scots say, "If you kill one midge, a million more will come to his funeral." Even if you don't usually travel with bug spray, consider bringing or buying some for a summer visit. Locals recommend Avon's Skin So Soft, which is effective against midges, but less potent than DEET-based bug repellants.

Keep an eye out for another Scottish animal: shaggy Highland cattle called "hairy coos." They're big and have impressive horns, but are best known for their adorable hair falling into their eyes (the hair protects them from Scotland's troublesome insects and unpredictable weather). Hairy coos graze on sparse vegetation that other animals ignore, and, with a heavy coat (rather than fat) to keep them in-

sulated, they produce a lean meat that resembles venison. (Highland cattle meat is not commonly eaten, and the relatively few hairy coos you'll see are kept around mostly as a national symbol.)

While the prickly, purple thistle is the official national flower, heather is the unofficial national shrub. This scrubby vegetation blankets much of the Highlands. It's usually a muddy reddish-brown color, but it bursts with purple flowers in the late summer; the less common bell heather blooms in July. Heather is one of the few things that will grow in the inhospitable terrain of a moor, and it can be used to make dye, rope, thatch, and even beer (look for Fraoch Heather Ale).

Highlanders are an outdoorsy bunch. For a fun look at local athletics, check whether your trip coincides with one of the Highland Games that enliven Highland communities in summer (see the sidebar on page 236). And keep an eye out for the unique Highland sport of shinty: a brutal, fast-paced version of field hockey played for keeps. Similar to Irish hurling, shinty is a full-contact sport that encourages tackling and fielding airborne balls, with players swinging their sticks (called camans) perilously through the air. The easiest place to see shinty is at Bught Park in Inverness (see page 296), but it's played across the Highlands.

PLANNING YOUR TIME

Here are three recommended Highland itineraries: two days, four days, or a full week or more. These plans assume you're driving, but can be done (with some modifications) by bus.

Two- to Three-Day Highland Highlights Blitz

This ridiculously fast-paced option squeezes the maximum Highland experience out of a few short days, and assumes you're starting from Glasgow or Edinburgh.

The Scottish Highlands

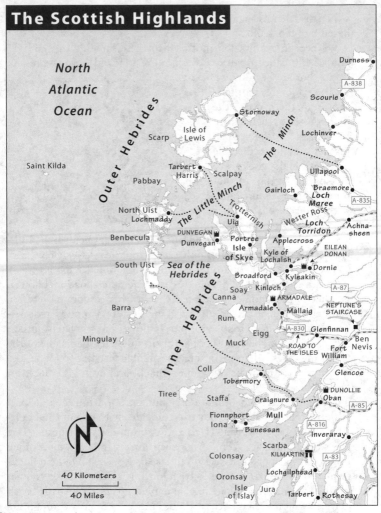

Day 1: In the morning, head up to the Highlands. (If coming from Edinburgh, consider a stop at Stirling Castle en route.) Drive along Loch Lomond and pause for lunch in Inveraray. Try to get to Oban in time for the day's last distillery tour (see hours on page 245; smart to book ahead). Have dinner in Oban.

Day 2: Get an early start from Oban and make a beeline for Glencoe, where you can visit the folk museum and enjoy a quick, scenic drive up the valley. Then drive to Fort William and follow the Caledonian Canal to Inverness, stopping at Fort Augustus to see the locks (and have a late lunch). Drive along Loch Ness to search for monsters, then wedge in a visit to the Culloden Battlefield (just outside Inverness) in the late afternoon. Finally, make

good time southward on the A-9 back to Edinburgh (3 hours, arriving late).

Day 3: To extend this plan a bit, take your time getting to Inverness on Day 2 and spend the night there. Follow my self-guided
Inverness Walk either that evening or the next morning. Leaving
Inverness, tour Culloden Battlefield, visit Clava Cairns, then head
south, stopping off at any place that appeals: The best options near
the A-9 are Pitlochry and the Scottish Crannog Centre on Loch
Tay, or take the more rugged eastern route to see the Speyside
whisky area, Balmoral Castle and Ballater village, and Cairngorms
mountain scenery. Or, if this is your best chance to see Stirling

Castle or the Falkirk sights (Falkirk Wheel, Kelpies sculptures), fit them in on your way south.

Six-Day Highlands and Islands Loop

While you'll see the Highlands on the above itinerary, you'll whiz past the sights in a misty blur. This more reasonably paced plan is for those who want to slow down a bit.

Day 1: Follow the plan for Day 1, above, sleeping in Oban (2 nights).

Day 2: Do an all-day island-hopping tour from Oban, with visits to Mull, Iona, and (if you choose) Staffa.

Day 3: From Oban, head up to Glencoe for its museum and valley views. Consider lingering for a (brief) hike. Then zip up to Fort William and take the "Road to the Isles" west (pausing in Glenfinnan to see its viaduct) to Mallaig. Take the ferry over the sea to Skye, then drive to Portree to sleep (2 nights).

Day 4: Spend today enjoying the Isle of Skye. In the morning, do the Trotternish Peninsula loop; in the afternoon, take your pick of options (Talisker Distillery, Dunvegan Castle, multiple hiking options).

Day 5: Leaving Portree, drive across the Skye Bridge for a photo-op pit stop at Eilean Donan Castle. The A-87 links you over to Loch Ness, which you'll follow to Inverness. If you get in early enough, consider touring Culloden Battlefield this evening. Sleep in Inverness (1 night).

Day 6: See the Day 3 options for my Highlands Highlights Blitz, earlier.

10-Day (or More) Highlands Explorer Extravaganza

Using the six-day Highlands and Islands Loop as a basis, pick and choose from these possible modifications (listed in order of where they'd fit into the itinerary):

- Add an overnight in **Glencoe** to make more time for hiking there.
- Leaving the Isle of Skye, drive north along **Wester Ross** (the scenic northwest coast). Go as far as Ullapool, then cut back down to Inverness, or...
- Take another day or two (after spending the night in Ullapool) to carry on northward through remote and rugged scenery to Scotland's **north coast.** Drive east along the coast all the way to John O'Groats; then either take the ferry from Scrabster across to Orkney, or shoot back down to Inverness on the A-9 (about 3 hours).
- Visit **Orkney** (2-night minimum). This can fit into the above plan after John O'Groats. Or, to cut back on the remote driving,

simply zip up on the A-9 from Inverness (about 3 hours)—or fly up from Inverness, Edinburgh, or Aberdeen.

• On the way south from Inverness, follow the **Speyside whisky trail,** cut through the **Cairngorms,** visit **Balmoral Castle,** and sleep in **Ballater.** Between Balmoral and Edinburgh, consider visiting Glamis Castle (Queen Mum's childhood home), Dundee (great industrial museums), or Culross (scenic firth-side village).

• Add an overnight wherever you'd like to linger; the best options are the **Isle of Skye** (to allow more island explorations) or **Inverness** (to fit in more side-trips).

GETTING AROUND THE HIGHLANDS

By Car: The Highlands are made for joyriding. There are a lot of miles, but they're scenic, the roads are good, and the traffic is light. Drivers enjoy flexibility and plenty of tempting stopovers. Be careful, but don't be too timid about passing; otherwise, diesel fumes and large trucks might be your main memory of driving in Scotland. The farther north you go, the more away-from-it-all you'll feel, with few signs of civilization. Even on a sunny weekend, you can go miles without seeing another car. Don't wait too long to gas up—village gas stations are few and far between, and can close unexpectedly. Get used to single-lane roads: While you can make good time when they're empty (as they often are), don't let your guard down, and slow down on blind corners—you never know when an oncoming car (or a road-blocking sheep) is right around the bend. If you do encounter an oncoming vehicle, unspoken rules of the road dictate that the driver closest to a pullout will use it—even if they have to back up. A little "thank-you" wave (or even just an index finger raised off the steering wheel) is the customary end to these encounters.

By Public Transportation: Glasgow is the gateway to this region (so you'll most likely have to transfer there if coming from Edinburgh). The **train** zips from Glasgow to Fort William, Oban, and Kyle of Lochalsh in the west; and up to Stirling, Pitlochry, and Inverness in the east. For more remote destinations (such as Glencoe), the bus is better.

Most of the **buses** are operated by Scottish Citylink. You can pay the driver in cash when you board. But in peak season—when these buses fill up—it's smart to buy tickets at least a day in advance: Book at www.citylink.co.uk, call 0871-216-3333, or stop by a bus station or TI.

Glasgow's Buchanan Station is the main Lowlands hub for reaching Highlands destinations. From Edinburgh, it's best to transfer in Glasgow (fastest by train, also possible by bus)—though there are direct buses from Edinburgh to Inverness, where you

Scottish Highland Games

Throughout the summer, Highland communities host traditional festivals of local sport and culture. These Highland Games (sometimes called Highland Gatherings) combine the best elements of a track meet and a county fair. They range from huge and glitzy (such as Braemar's world-famous games, which the Queen attends, or the Cowal Highland Gathering, Scotland's biggest) to humble and small-town. Some of the more modern games come with loud pop music and corporate sponsorship, but still manage to celebrate the Highland spirit.

Most Highland Games take place between mid-June and late August (usually on Saturdays, but occasionally on weekdays). The games are typically a one-day affair, kicking off around noon and winding down in the late afternoon. At smaller games, you'll pay a nominal admission fee (typically around £5-7). Events are rain or shine (so bring layers) and take place in a big park ringed by a running track, with the heavy events and Highland dancing stage at opposite ends of the infield. Surrounding the whole scene are junk-food stands, a few test-your-skill carnival games, and local charities raising funds by selling hamburgers, fried sausage sandwiches, baked goods, and bottles of beer and Irn-Bru. The emcee's running commentary is a delightful opportunity to just sit back and enjoy a lilting Scottish accent.

The day's events typically kick off with a **pipe band** parading through town—often led by the local clan chieftain—and ending with a lap around the field. Then the sporting events begin.

In the **heavy events**—or feats of Highland strength—brawny, kilted athletes test their ability to hurl various objects of awkward shapes and sizes as far as possible. In the weight throw, competitors spin like ballerinas before releasing a 28- or 56-pound ball on a chain. The hammer throw involves a similar technique with a 26-pound ball on a long stick, and the stone put (with a 20- to 25-pound ball) has been adopted in American sports as the shot put. In the "weight over the bar" event, Highlanders swing a 56-pound weight over a horizontal bar that begins at 10 feet high and ends at closer to 15 feet. (That's like tossing a 5-year-old child over a double-decker bus.) And, of course, there's the caber toss: Pick up a giant log (the caber), get a running start, and release it end-over-end with enough force to (ideally) make the caber flip all the way over and land at the 12 o'clock position. (Most competitors up closer to 6.)

Meanwhile, the **track events** run circles around the muscle:

the 90-meter dash, the 1,600-meter, and so on. The hill race adds a Scottish spin: Combine a several-mile footrace with the ascent of a nearby summit. The hill racers begin with a lap in the stadium before disappearing for about an hour. Keep an eye on nearby hillsides to pick out their colorful jerseys bobbing up and down a distant peak. This custom supposedly began when an 11th-century king staged a competition to select his personal letter carrier. After about an hour—when you've forgotten all about them—the hill racers start trickling back into the stadium to cross the finish line.

The **Highland dancing** is a highlight. Accompanied by a lone piper, the dancers (in groups of two to four) toe their routines

with intense concentration. Dancers remain always on the balls of their feet, requiring excellent balance and stamina. While some men participate, most competitors are female—from wee lassies barely out of nappies, all the way to poised professionals. Common steps are the Highland fling (in which the goal is to keep the feet as close as possible to one spot), sword dances (in which the dancers step gingerly over crossed swords on the stage), and a variety of national dances.

Other events further enliven the festivities. The pipe band periodically assembles to play a few tunes, often while marching around the track (giving the runners a break). Larger games may have a massing of multiple pipe bands, or bagpipe and drumming competitions. You may also see re-enactments of medieval battles, herd-dog demonstrations, or dog shows (grooming and obedience). Haggis hurling—a relatively new event in which participants stand on a whisky barrel and attempt to throw a cooked haggis as far as possible—has caught on recently. And many small-town events end with the grand finale of a town-wide tug-of-war, during which everybody gets bruised, muddy, and hysterical.

If you're traveling to Scotland in the summer, check online schedules to **see** if you'll be near any Highland Games before locking in your itinerary. Rather than target the big, famous gatherings, I make a point of visiting the smaller clan games. One helpful website—listing dates for most but not all of the games around Scotland—is www.shga.co.uk. For many travelers to Scotland, attending a Highland Games can be a trip-capping highlight. And, of course, many communities in the US and Canada also host their own Highland Games.

connect to Highlands buses. Once in the Highlands, Inverness and Fort William serve as the main bus hubs.

Note that bus frequency can be substantially reduced on Sundays and in the off-season (Oct-mid-May). Unless otherwise noted, I've listed bus information for summer weekdays. Always confirm schedules locally.

These buses are particularly useful for connecting the sights in this book:

Buses **#976** and **#977** connect Glasgow with Oban (5/day, 3 hours).

Buses **#914, #915,** and **#916** go from Glasgow to Fort William, stopping at Glencoe (8/day, 2.5 hours to Glencoe, 3 hours total to Fort William). From Fort William, these buses continue all the way up to Portree on the Isle of Skye (3/day, 7 hours for the full run).

Bus **#918** goes from Oban to Fort William, stopping en route at Ballachulish near Glencoe (2/day, 1 hour to Ballachulish, 1.5 hours total to Fort William).

Bus **#44** (operated by Stagecoach) is a cheaper alternative for connecting Glencoe to Fort William (hourly Mon-Sat, fewer on Sun, www.stagecoachbus.com).

Buses **#19** and **#919** connect Fort William with Inverness (7/day, 2 hours).

Buses **#M90** and **#G90** run from Edinburgh to Inverness (express #G90, 2/day, 3.5 hours; slower #M90, some stop in Pitlochry, 6/day, 4 hours).

Bus **#917** connects Inverness with Portree, on the Isle of Skye (3/day, 3 hours).

Bus **#G10** is an express connecting Inverness and Glasgow (5/day, 3 hours). National Express **#588** also goes direct (1/day, 4 hours, www.nationalexpress.com).

OBAN & THE INNER HEBRIDES

Oban • Isles of Mull, Iona and Staffa • Near Oban
(Inveraray and Kilmartin Glen)

For a taste of Scotland's west coast, the port town of Oban is equal parts endearing and functional. This busy little ferry-and-train terminal has no important sights, but makes up the difference in character, in scenery (with its low-impact panorama of overlapping islets and bobbing boats), and with one of Scotland's best distillery tours. But Oban is also convenient: It's midway between the Lowland cities (Glasgow and Edinburgh) and the Highland riches of the north (Glencoe, Isle of Skye). And it's the "gateway to the isles," with handy ferry service to the Hebrides Islands.

If time is tight and serious island-hopping is beyond the scope of your itinerary, Oban is ideally situated for a busy and memorable full-day side-trip to three of the most worthwhile Inner Hebrides: big, rugged Mull; pristine little Iona, where buoyant clouds float over its historic abbey; and Staffa, a remote, grassy islet inhabited only by sea birds. (The best of the Inner Hebrides—the Isle of Skye—is covered in its own chapter.) Sit back, let someone else do the driving, and enjoy a tour of the Inner Hebrides.

This chapter also includes a few additional sights near Oban, handy for those connecting the dots: the most scenic route between Glasgow and Oban (along the bonnie, bonnie banks of Loch Lomond and through the town of Inveraray, with its fine castle); and the faint remains of Kilmartin Glen, the prehistoric homeland of the Scottish people.

PLANNING YOUR TIME

If you're on a speedy blitz tour of Scotland, Oban is a strategic and pleasant place to spend the night. But you'll need two nights to enjoy Oban's main attraction: the side-trip to Mull, Iona, and

Staffa. There are few actual sights in Oban itself, beyond the distillery tour, but—thanks to its manageable size, scenic waterfront setting, and great restaurants—the town is an enjoyable place to linger.

Oban

Oban (pronounced OH-bin) is a low-key resort. Its winding promenade is lined by gravel beaches, ice-cream stands, fish-and-chip joints, a tourable distillery, and a good choice of restaurants. Everything in Oban is close together, and the town seems eager to please its many visitors: Wool and tweed are perpetually on sale, and posters announce a variety of day tours to Scotland's wild and wildlife-strewn western islands. When the rain clears, sun-starved Scots sit on benches along the Esplanade, leaning back to catch some rays. Wind, boats, gulls, layers of islands, and the promise of a wide-open Atlantic beyond give Oban a rugged charm.

Orientation to Oban

Oban, with about 10,000 people, is where the train system of Scotland meets the ferry system serving the Hebrides Islands. As "gateway to the isles," its center is not a square or market, but its harbor. Oban's business action, just a couple of streets deep, stretches along the harbor and its promenade.

TOURIST INFORMATION
Oban's TI, located at the North Pier, sells bus and ferry tickets, is well stocked with brochures, and has free Wi-Fi (generally daily July-Aug 9:00-19:00; April-June 9:00-17:30; Sept-March 10:00-17:00; 3 North Pier, tel. 01631/563-122, www.oban.org.uk).

HELPFUL HINTS
Bookstore: Waterstones, a huge bookstore overlooking the harborfront, offers maps and a fine collection of books on Scotland (Mon-Sat 9:00-17:30, Sun 11:00-17:00, longer hours in July-Aug, 12 George Street, tel. 0843/290-8529).

Baggage Storage: The train station has pay luggage lockers, but is open limited hours (Mon-Sat 5:00-20:30, Sun 10:45-18:00)—confirm the closing time before committing.

Laundry: You'll find **Oban Quality Laundry** tucked a block behind the main drag just off Stevenson Street (same-day drop-off service, no self-service, Mon-Fri 9:00-17:00, Sat until 13:00, closed Sun, tel. 01631/563-554). The recommended **Backpackers Plus Hostel** (page 251) will also do laundry for nonguests.

Supermarket: The giant **Tesco** is a five-minute walk from the train station (Mon-Sat until 24:00, Sun until 20:00, walk through Argyll Square and look for entrance to large parking lot on right, Lochside Street.

Bike Rental: Oban Cycles is on the main drag (£25/day, Tue-Sat 10:00-17:00, closed Sun-Mon, 87 George Street, tel. 01631/566-033).

Bus Station: The "station" is just a pullout, marked by a stubby clock tower, at the roundabout in front of the train station. In peak season, it's wise to book bus tickets the day before—either at the TI, or at the West Coast Tours office (see next).

Bus and Island Tour Tickets: West Coast Tours, a block from the train station in the bright-red building along the harbor, sells bus- and island-tour tickets (Tue-Sat 6:30-17:30, Sun-Mon 8:30-17:30, 17 George Street, tel. 01631/566-809, www.westcoasttours.co.uk).

Highland Games: Oban hosts its touristy Highland Games every August (www.obangames.com), and the more local-oriented Lorne Highland Games each June (www.lorne-highland-games.org.uk). Nearby Taynuilt, a 20-minute drive east, hosts their sweetly small-town Highland Games in mid-July (www.taynuilthighlandgames.com).

Tours from Oban

For the best day trip from Oban, tour the islands of Mull, Iona, and/or Staffa (offered daily Easter-Oct, described later)—or consider staying overnight on remote and beautiful Iona. With more time or other interests, consider one of many other options you'll see advertised.

Wildlife Tours

If you just want to go for a boat ride, the easiest option is the one-hour seal-watching tour (£10, various companies—look for signs at the harbor). But to really get a good look at Scottish coastal wildlife, several groups—including **Coastal Connection** (based in Oban) and **Scalife Adventures** and **SeaFari** (based in nearby coastal towns)—run whale-watching tours that seek out rare minke

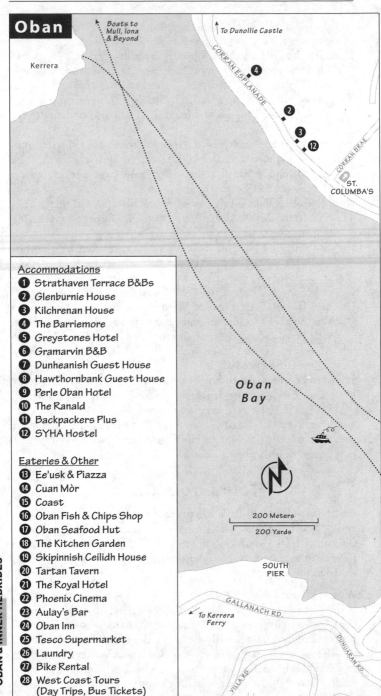

Oban

Kerrera

Boats to Mull, Iona & Beyond

To Dunollie Castle

CORRAN ESPLANADE

4

2

3

12

CORRAN BRAE

ST. COLUMBA'S

Oban Bay

200 Meters

200 Yards

SOUTH PIER

GALLANACH RD.

← *To Kerrera Ferry*

DUNUARAN RD.

VILLA RD.

Accommodations
1. Strathaven Terrace B&Bs
2. Glenburnie House
3. Kilchrenan House
4. The Barriemore
5. Greystones Hotel
6. Gramarvin B&B
7. Dunheanish Guest House
8. Hawthornbank Guest House
9. Perle Oban Hotel
10. The Ranald
11. Backpackers Plus
12. SYHA Hostel

Eateries & Other
13. Ee'usk & Piazza
14. Cuan Mòr
15. Coast
16. Oban Fish & Chips Shop
17. Oban Seafood Hut
18. The Kitchen Garden
19. Skipinnish Ceilidh House
20. Tartan Tavern
21. The Royal Hotel
22. Phoenix Cinema
23. Aulay's Bar
24. Oban Inn
25. Tesco Supermarket
26. Laundry
27. Bike Rental
28. West Coast Tours (Day Trips, Bus Tickets)

OBAN & INNER HEBRIDES

To Fort William
& Inverness

CROFT RD.

DUNOLLIE ROAD

LONGSDALE RD.

BREADALBANE ST.

DALRIACH RD.

ATLANTIS
SPORTS &
LEISURE
CENTRE

BENVOULIN RD.

OBAN
LAWN
BOWLING
CLUB

CORRAN ESPLANADE

DUNOLLIE TER.

NURSERY LN.

ALBERT RD.

CRAIGARD RD.

ARDCONNEL RD.

LAUREL RD.

LAUREL RD.

PULPIT DR.

PINCSAGGAN RD.

POST

OBAN
WAR & PEACE
MUSEUM

GEORGE ST.

OBAN
WHISKY
DISTILLERY

MC CAIG'S
TOWER

LONGSDALE RD.

NORTH
PIER

ARDCONNEL TERRACE

TWEEDDALE ST.

ROCKFIELD RD.

ROCKFIELD RD.

HILL ST.

STEVENSON ST.

TRAIN
STATION

AIRD'S CRES.

ROCKFIELD RD.

FERRY
TERMINAL

Argyll
Square

SHORE ST.

HIGH ST.

COMBIE ST.

ALBANY ST.

MARKET ST.

LOCHSIDE ST.

COMBIE ST.

GLENSHELLACH TERRACE

GLENCRUITTEN RD.

OBAN & INNER HEBRIDES

whales, basking sharks, bottlenose dolphins, and porpoises. For an even more ambitious itinerary, the holy grail is Treshnish Island (out past Staffa), which brims with puffins, seals, and other sea critters. Options abound—check at the TI for information.

Open-Top Bus Tours

If the weather is good and you don't have a car, you can go by bus for a spin out of Oban for views of nearby castles and islands, plus a stop near McCaig's Tower with narration by the driver (£7, departs train station 4/day June-Sept only, 1.5 hours, www.citysightseeingoban.com).

Sights in Oban

▲The Burned-Out Sightseer's Visual Tour from the Pier

If the west-coast weather permits, get oriented to the town while taking a break: Head out to the North Pier, just past the TI, and find the benches that face back toward town (in front of the recommended Piazza restaurant). Take a seat and get to know Oban.

Scan the harborfront from left to right, surveying the mix of grand Victorian sandstone buildings and humbler modern storefronts. At the far-right end of town is the **ferry terminal** and—very likely—a huge ferry loading or unloading. Oban has always been on the way to somewhere, and today is no different. (A recent tourism slogan: Oban...it's closer than you think.) The townscape seems dominated by Caledonian-MacBrayne, Scotland's biggest ferry company. CalMac's 30 ships serve 24 destinations and transport over 4 million passengers a year. The town's port has long been a lifeline to the islands.

Hiding near the ferry terminal is the **train station.** With the arrival of the train in 1880, Oban became the unofficial capital of Scotland's west coast and a destination for tourists. Close by is the former Caledonian Hotel, the original terminus hotel (now the Perle Oban Hotel) that once served those train travelers.

Tourism aside, herring was the first big industry. A dozen boats still fish commercially—you'll see them tucked around the ferry terminal. The tourist board, in an attempt to entice tourists to linger longer, is trying to rebrand Oban as a "seafood capital" rather than just the "gateway to the isles." As the ocean's supply has become depleted, most local fish is farmed. There's still plenty of shellfish.

After fishing, big industries here historically included tobacco (imported from the American colonies), then whisky. At the left end of the embankment, find the building marked *Oban Whisky Distillery*. It's rare to find a distillery in the middle of a town, but Oban grew up around this one. With the success of its whisky, the town enjoyed an invigorating confidence, optimism, and, in 1811, a royal charter. Touring Oban's distillery is the best activity in Oban.

Above the distillery, you can't miss the odd mini-Colosseum. This is **McCaig's Tower,** an employ-the-workers-and-build-me-a-fine-memorial project undertaken by an Oban tycoon in 1900. McCaig died before completing the structure, so his complete vision for it remains a mystery. This is an example of a "folly"—that uniquely British notion of an idiosyncratic structure erected by a colorful aristocrat. Building a folly was an in-your-face kind of extravagance many extremely wealthy people enjoyed when surrounded by struggling working-class people (an urge that survives among some of the one percent to this day). While the building itself is nothing to see up close, a 10-minute hike through a Victorian residential neighborhood leads you to a peaceful garden and a commanding view (nice at sunset).

Now turn and look out to sea, and imagine this: At the height of the Cold War, Oban played a critical role when the world's first two-way transatlantic telephone cable was laid from Gallanach Bay to Newfoundland in 1956—a milestone in global communication. This technology later provided the White House and the Kremlin with the "hotline" that was created after the Cuban Missile Crisis to avoid a nuclear conflagration.

▲▲Oban Whisky Distillery Tours

Founded in 1794, Oban Whisky Distillery produces more than 25,000 liters a week, and exports much of that to the US. Their exhibition (upstairs, free to all) gives a quick, whisky-centric history of Oban and Scotland.

The distillery offers serious and fragrant one-hour tours explaining the process from start to finish, with two smooth samples of their signature product: Oban whisky is moderately smoky ("peaty") and characterized by notes of sea salt, citrus, and honey. You'll also receive a whisky glass and a discount coupon for the shop. This is the handiest whisky tour you'll encounter—just a block off the harbor—and one of the best. Come 10 minutes before your tour starts to check out the exhibition upstairs. Then your guide will walk you through each step of the process: malting, mashing, fermentation, distillation, and maturation. Photos are not allowed inside. For details on the distilling process and tips on tasting whisky, see page 464.

Cost and Hours: Tours cost £10, are limited to 16 people and depart every 20 to 30 minutes. Tours fill up, so book in advance by phone, online, or in person to get a firm spot. Unless it's really a busy day, you should be able to drop in and pay for a tour leaving in the next hour or so, then easily pass time in the town center. Generally open July-Sept Mon-Fri 9:30-19:30, Sat-Sun until

17:00; March-June and Oct-Nov daily 9:30-17:30; Dec-Feb daily 12:30-16:00; last tour 1.25 hours before closing, Stafford Street, tel. 01631/572-004, www.discovering-distilleries.com.

Serious Tasting: Connoisseurs can ask about their "exclusive tour," which adds a visit to the warehouse and four premium tastings in the manager's office (£40, 2 hours, likely July-Sept, Mon, Wed, and Fri at 16:00 only, reservation required).

Oban War & Peace Museum
Opened in 1995 on the 50th anniversary of Victory in Europe Day, this charming little museum focuses on Oban's experience during World War II. But it covers more than just war and peace. Photos show Oban through the years, and a 15-minute looped video gives a simple tour around the town and region. Volunteer staffers love to chat about the exhibit—or anything else on your mind (free; May-Oct Mon-Sat 10:00-18:00, Sun until 16:00; off-season daily until 16:00; next to Regent Hotel on the promenade, tel. 01631/570-007, www.obanmuseum.org.uk).

Dunollie Castle and Museum
In a park just a mile up the coast, a ruined castle and an old house hold an intimate collection of clan family treasures. This spartan, stocky castle with 10-foot walls offers a commanding, windy view of the harbor—a strategic spot back in the days when transport was mainly by water. For more than a thousand years, clan chiefs ruled this region from this ancestral home of Clan MacDougall, but the castle was abandoned in 1746. The adjacent house, which dates from 1745, shows off the MacDougall clan's heritage with a handful of rooms filled with a humble yet fascinating trove of treasures. While the exhibit won't dazzle you, the family and clan pride in the display, their "willow garden," and the walk from Oban make the visit fun.

To get there, head out of town along the harborfront promenade. At the war memorial (with inviting seaview benches), cross the street. A gate leads to a little lane, lined with historic and nature boards along the way to the castle.

Cost and Hours: £5.50, April-Oct Mon-Sat 10:00-16:00, Sun from 13:00, closed Nov-March, free tours given most days at 11:00 and 14:00, tel. 01631/570-550, www.dunollie.org.

ACTIVITIES IN OBAN
Atlantis Leisure Centre
This industrial-type sports center is a good place to get some exercise on a rainy day or let the kids run wild for a few hours. It has a rock-climbing wall, tennis courts, indoor "soft play centre" (for kids under 5), and an indoor swimming pool with a big water slide. The outdoor playground is free and open all the time (pool only-

£4.20, no rental towels or suits, fees for other activities; open Mon-Fri 6:30-21:30, Sat-Sun 9:00-18:00; on the north end of Dalriach Road, tel. 01631/566-800, www.atlantisleisure.co.uk).

Oban Lawn Bowling Club

The club has welcomed visitors since 1869. This elegant green is the scene of a wonderfully British spectacle of old men tiptoeing wishfully after their balls. It's fun to watch, and—if there's no match scheduled and the weather's dry—anyone can rent shoes and balls and actually play (£5/person; informal hours, but generally daily 10:00-12:00 & 14:00-16:00 or "however long the weather lasts"; just south of sports center on Dalriach Road, tel. 01631/570-808, www.obanbowlingclub.com).

ISLANDS NEAR OBAN

The isles of Mull, Iona, and Staffa are farther out, require a full day to visit, and are described later in this chapter. For a quicker glimpse at the Inner Hebrides, consider these two options.

Isle of Kerrera

Functioning like a giant breakwater, the Isle of Kerrera (KEH-reh-rah) makes Oban possible. Just offshore from Oban, this stark but very green island offers a quick, easy opportunity to get that romantic island experience. While it has no proper roads, it offers nice hikes, a ruined castle, and a few sheep farms. It's also a fine place to bike (ask for advice at bike-rental shop). You may see the Kerrera ferry filled with sheep heading for Oban's livestock market.

Getting There: You have two options for reaching the island. A boat operated by the Oban Marina goes from Oban's North Pier to the Kerrera Marina in the northern part of the island (£5 round-trip, every two hours, book ahead at tel. 01631/565-333, www.obanmarina.com).

A ferry departs from Gallanach (two miles south of Oban) and goes to the middle of the island. This is the best option if you want to hike to Kerrera's castle (passengers only, £4.50 round-trip, bikes free, runs 10:30-18:00 with a break 12:30-14:00, none in off-season, 5-minute ride, tel. 01475/650-397, www.calmac.co.uk. To reach Gallanach, drive south, following the coast road past the ferry terminal (parking available).

Eating and Sleeping on Kerrera: $$ Waypoint Bar & Grill has a laid-back patio with a simple menu of steak, burgers, and seafood; on a nice day the open-air waterside setting is unbeatable (late May-Sept Tue-Sun 18:00-21:00, bar opens at 17:00, closed Mon and in winter, reservations highly recommended, tel. 01631/565-333, www.obanmarina.com). For lodging, your only option is the **$ Kerrera Bunkhouse,** a refurbished 18th-century stable that can sleep up to seven people in a small, cozy space (1 double and 5 single bunks, 2-night minimum, includes bedding but not towels, open Easter-Oct but must book ahead, kitchen, tel. 01631/566-367, www.kerrerabunkhouse.co.uk, info@kerrerabunkhouse.co.uk, Martin and Aideen). They also run a tea garden that serves meals (Easter-Sept daily 10:30-16:30, closed Oct-Easter).

Isle of Seil

Enjoy a drive, a walk, some solitude, and the sea. Drive 12 miles south of Oban on the A-816 to the B-844 to the Isle of Seil (pronounced "seal"), connected to the mainland by a bridge (which, locals like to brag, "crosses the Atlantic"...well, maybe a small part of it).

Just over the bridge on the Isle of Seil is a pub called **Tigh-an-Truish** ("House of Trousers"). After the Jacobite rebellions, a new law forbade the wearing of kilts on the mainland. Highlanders on the island used this pub to change from kilts to trousers before they made the crossing. The pub serves great meals and good seafood dishes to those either in kilts or pants (pub generally open daily—call ahead, tel. 01852/300-242).

Seven miles across the island, on a tiny second island and facing the open Atlantic, is **Easdale,** a historic, touristy, windblown little slate-mining town—with a slate-town museum and an egomaniac's incredibly tacky "Highland Arts" shop (shuttle ferry goes the 300 yards). Expensive wildlife/nature tours plus tours to Iona and Staffa also run from Easdale (www.seafari.co.uk).

Nightlife in Oban

Little Oban has a few options for entertaining its many visitors; check www.obanwhatson.co.uk. Fun low-key activities may include open-mic, disco, or quiz theme nights in pubs; occasional Scottish folk shows; coffee meetings; and—if you're lucky—duck races. On Wednesday nights, the Oban Pipe Band plays in the square by the train station. Here are a few other ways to entertain yourself while in town.

Music and Group Dancing: On many summer nights, you can climb the stairs to the **Skipinnish Ceilidh House,** a sprawling venue on the main drag for music and dancing (the owners are professional musicians Angus and Andrew). There's *ceilidh* (KAY-lee) dancing a couple of times per week, where you can learn some group dances to music performed by a folk band (including, usually, a piper). These group dances are a lot of fun—wallflowers and bad dancers are warmly welcomed, and the staff is happy to give you pointers (£8, May-Sept Mon & Thu at 21:00). They also host concerts by folk and traditional bands (check website for schedule, 34

George Street, tel. 01631/569-599, www.skipinnishceilidhhouse. com).

Traditional Music: Various pubs and hotels in town have live traditional music in the summer; as specifics change from year to year, ask your B&B host or the TI for the latest. Try the **Tartan Tavern,** a block off the waterfront at 3 Albany Terrace or **The Royal Hotel,** just above the train station on Argyll Square.

Cinema: The **Phoenix Cinema** closed down for two years and then was saved by the community. It's now volunteer-run and booming (140 George Street, tel. 01631/562-905, www. obanphoenix.com).

Characteristic Pubs: Aulay's Bar, with decor that shows off Oban's maritime heritage, has two sides, each with a different personality (I like the right-hand side). Having a drink here invariably comes with a good "blether" (conversation), and the gang is local (daily 11:00-24:00, 8 Airds Crescent, just around the corner from the train station and ferry terminal). The **Oban Inn,** right on the harborfront, is also a fun and memorable place for a pint and possibly live music.

Sleeping in Oban

Oban's B&Bs offer a much better value than its hotels.

ON STRATHAVEN TERRACE

The following B&Bs line up on a quiet, flowery street that's nicely located two blocks off the harbor, three blocks from the center, and a 10-minute walk from the train station. Rooms here are more compact than those on the Esplanade and don't have views, but the location can't be beat.

By car, as you enter town from the north, turn left immediately after King's Knoll Hotel, and take your first right onto Breadalbane Street. ("Strathaven Terrace" is actually just the name for this row of houses on Breadalbane Street.) The alley behind the buildings has tight, free parking for all of these places.

$$ Rose Villa Guest House has six crisp and cheery rooms (at #5, tel. 01631/566-874, stuartcameronsmith@yahoo.co.uk, Stuart and Jacqueline).

$ Raniven Guest House has five simple, tastefully decorated rooms and gracious, fun-loving hosts Moyra and Stuart (cash only, 2-night minimum in summer, continental breakfast, at #1, tel. 01631/562-713, www.ranivenoban.com, bookings@ranivenoban. com).

$ Sandvilla B&B rents five pleasant, polished rooms (2-night minimum in summer, at #4, tel. 01631/564-483, www.

holidayoban.co.uk, sandvilla@holidayoban.co.uk, Josephine and Robert).

ALONG THE ESPLANADE

These are along the Corran Esplanade, which stretches north of town above a cobble beach; they are a 10-minute walk from the center. For the most part, they offer much more spacious rooms than places in town (and many rooms have beautiful bay views). Walking from town, you'll reach them in this order: Kilchrenan, Glenburnie, and Barriemore.

$$ Glenburnie House, a stately Victorian home, has an elegant breakfast room overlooking the bay. Its 12 spacious, comfortable, classy rooms feel like plush living rooms. There's a nice lounge and a tiny sunroom with a stuffed "hairy coo" head (closed mid-Nov-March, tel. 01631/562-089, www.glenburnie.co.uk, stay@glenburnie.co.uk, Graeme).

$$ Kilchrenan House, the turreted former retreat of a textile magnate, has 16 large rooms, most with bay views. The stunning rooms #5, #9, and #15 are worth the few extra pounds, while the "standard" rooms in the newer annex are a good value (2-night minimum in summer, welcome drink of whisky or sherry, different "breakfast special" every day, family rooms, closed Nov-Feb, tel. 01631/562-663, www.kilchrenanhouse.co.uk, info@kilchrenanhouse.co.uk, Colin and Frances).

$$ The Barriemore, at the very end of Oban's grand waterfront Esplanade, is a welcome refuge after a day of exploration. Its 14 well-appointed rooms come with robes, sherry, etc. It has a nice front patio, spacious breakfast room, and glassed-in sun porch with a view of the water (family suite, tel. 01631/566-356, www.barriemore.co.uk, info@barriemore.co.uk, Jan and Mark).

ABOVE THE TOWN CENTER

These places perch on the hill above the main waterfront zone—a short (but uphill) walk from all of the action. Many rooms come with views, and are priced accordingly.

$$$ Greystones is an enticing splurge. It fills a big, stately, turreted mansion at the top of town with five spacious rooms that mix Victorian charm and sleek gray-and-white minimalism. Built as the private home for the director of Kimberley Diamond Mine, it later became a maternity hospital, and today Mark and Suzanne have turned it into a stylish and restful retreat. The lounge and breakfast room offer stunning views over Oban and the offshore isles (closed Nov-mid-Feb, 13 Dalriach Road, tel. 01631/358-653, www.greystonesoban.co.uk, stay@greystonesoban.co.uk).

$$ Gramarvin B&B feels a little more homey and personal, with just two rooms and warm host Mary. Window seats in each room provide a lovely view over Oban, but be warned—the climb up from town and then up their stairs is steep (skip breakfast to save a few pounds, cash only, 2-night minimum in summer preferred, on-street parking, Benvoulin Road, tel. 01631/564-622, www.gramarvin.co.uk, mary@gramarvin.co.uk, Mary and Joe).

$$ Dunheanish Guest House offers six pleasant rooms (two on the ground floor) and wide-open views from its perch above town, which you can enjoy from the front stone patio, breakfast room, and several guest rooms (parking, Ardconnel Road, tel. 01631/566-556, www.dunheanish.com, info@dunheanish.com, William and Linda).

$ Hawthornbank Guest House fills a big Victorian sandstone house with seven traditional-feeling rooms. Half of the rooms face bay views, and the other half overlook the town's lawn bowling green (2-night minimum in summer, Dalriach Road, tel. 01631/562-041, www.hawthornbank.co.uk, info@hawthornbank.co.uk).

HOTELS IN THE TOWN CENTER

A number of hotels are in the center of town along or near the main drag—but you'll pay heavily for the convenience.

$$$$ Perle Oban Hotel is your luxury boutique splurge. Right across from the harbor, it has 59 super sleek rooms with calming sea-color walls, decorative bath tile floors, and rain showers (suites, fancy restaurant, bar with light bites, pay parking, Station Square, tel. 01631/700-301, www.perleoban.com, stay@perleoban.com).

$$$ The Ranald is a modern change of pace from the B&B scene in Oban. This narrow, 17-room, three-floor hotel has a budget-boutique vibe going (family rooms, bar, no elevator, street or off-site parking, a block behind the Royal Hotel at 41 Stevenson Street, tel. 01631/562-887, www.theranaldhotel.com, info@theranaldhotel.com).

HOSTELS

¢ **Backpackers Plus** is central, laid-back, and fun. It fills part of a renovated old church with a sprawling public living room, 47 beds, and a staff generous with travel tips. Check out the walls as you go up to the reception desk—they're covered with graffiti messages from guests (includes breakfast, great shared kitchen, pay laundry service, 10-minute walk from station, on Breadalbane Street, tel. 01631/567-189, www.backpackersplus.com, info@backpackersplus.com, Peter). They have two other locations nearby with private rooms.

¢ The official **SYHA hostel**, on the scenic waterfront Esplanade, is in a grand building with 87 beds and smashing views of the harbor and islands from the lounges and dining rooms. While institutional, this place is quite nice (all rooms en suite, private rooms available, also has family rooms and 8-bed apartment with kitchen, breakfast extra, pay laundry, kitchen, tel. 01631/562-025, www.syha.org.uk, oban@syha.org.uk).

Eating in Oban

Oban brags that it is the "seafood capital of Scotland," and indeed its sit-down restaurants (listed first) are surprisingly high quality for such a small town. For something more casual, consider a fish-and-chips joint.

SIT-DOWN RESTAURANTS

These fill up in summer, especially on weekends. To ensure getting a table, you'll want to book ahead. The first four are generally open daily from 12:00-15:00 and 17:30-21:00.

$$$ Ee'usk (Scottish Gaelic for "fish") is a popular, stylish place on the waterfront. It has a casual-chic, yacht-clubby atmosphere, with a bright and glassy interior and sweeping views on three sides—fun for watching the ferries come and go. They sometimes offer an early-bird special until 18:45, and their seafood platters are a hit. Reservations are recommended (no kids under age 12 at dinner, North Pier, tel. 01631/565-666, www.eeusk.com, MacLeod family).

$$$ Cuan Mòr is a popular, casual restaurant that combines traditional Scottish food with modern flair—both in its crowd-pleasing cuisine and in its furnishings, made of wood, stone, and metal scavenged from the beaches of Scotland's west coast (brewery in back, 60 George Street, tel. 01631/565-078). Its harborside tables on the sidewalk are popular when it's warm.

$$$$ Coast proudly serves fresh local fish, meat, and veggies in a mod pine-and-candlelight atmosphere. As everything is cooked to order and presented with care by husband-and-wife team Richard and Nicola—who try to combine traditional Scottish elements in innovative new ways—this is no place to dine and dash (two- and three-course specials, closed Sun for lunch, 104 George Street, tel. 01631/569-900, www.coastoban.co.uk).

$$ Piazza, next door to Ee'usk, is a casual, family-friendly place serving basic Italian dishes with a great harborfront location. They have some outdoor seats and big windows facing the sea (smart to reserve ahead July-Aug, tel. 01631/563-628, www.piazzaoban.com).

$$ Oban Fish and Chips Shop—run by Lewis, Sammy, and their family—serves praiseworthy haddock and mussels among other tasty options in a cheery cabana-like dining room. Consider venturing away from basic fish-and-chips into a world of more cre-ative seafood dishes—like their tiny squat lobster. You can bring your own wine for no charge (daily, sit-down restaurant closes at 21:00, takeaway available later, 116 George Street, tel. 01631/567-000).

LUNCH

$ Oban Seafood Hut, in a green shack facing the ferry dock, is a finger-licking festival of cheap and fresh seafood. John and Marion regularly get fresh deliveries from local fishermen—this is the best spot to pick up a seafood sandwich or a snack. They sell smaller bites (such as cold sandwiches), as well as some bigger cold platters and a few hot dishes (picnic tables nearby, daily from 10:00 until the boat unloads from Mull around 18:00).

$ The Kitchen Garden is fine for soup, salad, or sandwiches. It's a deli and gourmet-foods store with a charming café upstairs (daily 9:00-17:30, 14 George Street, tel. 01631/566-332).

Oban Connections

By Train from Oban: Trains link Oban to the nearest transpor-tation hub in **Glasgow** (6/day, fewer on Sun, 3 hours); to get to **Edinburgh,** you'll have to transfer in Glasgow (5/day, 4.5 hours). To reach **Fort William** (a transit hub for the Highlands), you'll take the same Glasgow-bound train, but transfer in Crianlarich (3/day, 4 hours)—the direct bus is easier (see next). Oban's small train station has a ticket window and lockers (both open Mon-Sat 5:00-20:30, Sun 10:45-18:00, train info tel. 0845-748-4950, www.nationalrail.co.uk).

By Bus: Bus #918 passes through Ballachulish—a half-mile from **Glencoe**—on its way to **Fort William** (2/day, 1 hour to Bal-lachulish, 1.5 hours total to Fort William). Take this bus to Fort William, then transfer to reach **Inverness** (4 hours) or **Portree** on the Isle of Skye (5 hours)—see page 290 for onward bus informa-tion. A different bus (#976 or #977) connects Oban with **Glasgow** (5/day, 3 hours), from where you can easily connect by bus or train to **Edinburgh** (figure 4.5 hours). Buses arrive and depart from a roundabout, marked by a stubby clock tower, just before the en-trance to the train station (tel. 0871-266-3333, www.citylink.co.uk). You can buy bus tickets at the West Coast shop near the bus stop, or at the TI across the harbor. Book in advance during peak times.

By Boat: Ferries fan out from Oban to the **southern Hebrides** (see information on the islands of Iona and Mull, later). Caledo-nian MacBrayne Ferry info: Tel. 01631/566-688, free booking tel. 0800-066-5000, www.calmac.co.uk.

OBAN & INNER HEBRIDES

ROUTE TIPS FOR DRIVERS

From Glasgow to Oban via Loch Lomond and Inveraray: For details on the most scenic route from Glasgow to Oban, see "Near Oban" at the end of this chapter.

From Oban to Glencoe and Fort William: It's an easy one-hour drive from Oban to Glencoe. From Oban, follow the coastal A-828 toward Fort William. After about 20 miles—as you leave the village of Appin—you'll see the photogenic **Castle Stalker** marooned on a lonely island (you can pull over at the Castle Stalker View Café for a good photo from just below its parking lot). At North Ballachulish, you'll reach a bridge spanning Loch Leven; rather than crossing the bridge, turn off and follow the A-82 into the Glencoe Valley for about 15 minutes. (For tips on the best views and hikes in Glencoe, see the next chapter.) After exploring the dramatic valley, make a U-turn and return through Glencoe village. To continue on to Fort William, backtrack to the bridge at North Ballachulish (great view from bridge) and cross it, following the A-82 north.

For a scenic shortcut directly back to Glasgow or Edinburgh, continue south on the A-82 after Glencoe via Rannoch Moor and Tyndrum. Crianlarich is where the road splits, and you'll either continue on the A-82 toward Loch Lomond and Glasgow or pick up the A-85 and follow signs for Stirling, then Edinburgh.

Isles of Mull, Iona, and Staffa

For the easiest one-day look at a good sample of the dramatic and historic Inner Hebrides (HEB-rid-eez) islands, take a tour from Oban to Mull, Iona, and Staffa. Though this trip is spectacular when it's sunny, it's worthwhile in any weather (but if rain or rough seas are expected, I'd skip the Staffa option). For an even more in-depth look at the Inner Hebrides, head north to Skye.

GETTING AROUND THE ISLANDS
Visiting Mull and Iona

To visit Mull and ultimately Iona, you'll take a huge ferry run by Caledonian MacBrayne (CalMac) from Oban to the town of Craignure on Mull (45 minutes). From there, you'll ride a bus or drive across Mull to its westernmost ferry terminal, called Fionnphort (1.25 hours), where you can catch the ferry to Iona (10 minutes). It's a long journey, but it's all incredibly scenic; you also get about two hours of free time on Iona. There are several ways to do this.

By Tour (Easiest): If you book a tour with **West Coast Tours,**

all of the transportation is taken care of. The Cal-Mac ferry leaves from the Oban pier daily at 9:50 (as schedule can change from year to year, confirm times locally; board at least 20 minutes before departure). You can buy tickets online at www.westcoasttours.co.uk, from the West Coast Tours office, or from the Tour Shop Oban at the ferry building (tel. 01631/562-244, tourshop@calmac.co.uk). Book as far in advance as possible for July and August (tickets can sell out). When you book their tour, you'll receive a strip of tickets—one for each leg; if you book online, you must go to the West Coast Tours office and collect tickets in person (£35; April-Oct only, no tours Nov-March).

Tour Tips: The best inside seats on the **Oban-Mull ferry**—with the biggest windows—are in the sofa lounge on the "observation deck" (level 4) at the back end of the boat. (Follow signs for the toilets, and look for the big staircase to the top floor). The ferry has a fine cafeteria with hot meals and packaged sandwiches, a small snack bar on the top floor (hot drinks and basic sandwiches), and a bookshop. If it's a clear day, ask a local or a crew member to point out Ben Nevis, the tallest mountain in Britain. Five minutes before landing on Mull, you'll see the striking 13th-century Duart Castle on the left.

Walk-on passengers disembark from deck 3, across from the bookshop (port side). Upon arrival in Mull, find your **bus** for the entertaining and informative ride across the Isle of Mull. The right (driver's) side offers better sea views during the second half of the journey to Fionnphort, while the left side has fine views of Mull's rolling wilderness. The driver spends the entire ride chattering away about life on Mull, slowing to point out wildlife, and sharing adages like, "If there's no flowers on the gorse, snogging's gone out of fashion." These hardworking locals make historical trivia fascinating—or at least fun. At Fionnphort, you'll board a small, rocking **ferry to Iona.** You'll have about two hours to roam freely around the island before returning to Oban (arrives around 18:00).

By Public Transit: If you want an early start (and want to avoid some crowds), have more time on Iona (including spending the night—see "Sleeping and Eating on Iona"), or don't get a space on the tour described earlier, you can take the early ferry and public bus across Mull, paying individually per leg (Tue-Sat only; ap-

OBAN & INNER HEBRIDES

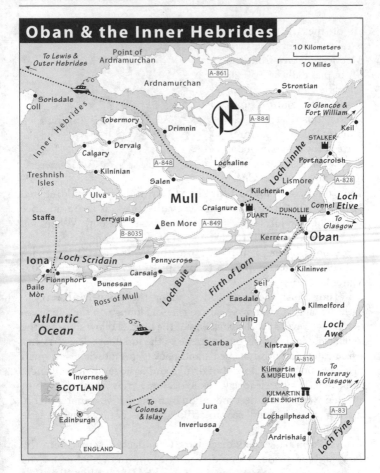

Oban & the Inner Hebrides

proximate round-trip prices: £7 for Oban-Mull ferry, £15 for public bus across Mull, £3.50 for Mull-Iona ferry).

Take the first boat of the day (departs about 7:30, buy ticket at Oban ferry terminal), then connect at Mull to bus #496 to Fionnphort (departs 8:25, 80 minutes, buy ticket from driver, no tour narration, no guarantee you'll get to sit), then hop on the Iona ferry (every 30 minutes, buy ticket from small trailer ferry office; if closed, purchase ticket from ferry worker at the dock; cash or credit/debit cards accepted; leaving Iona, do the same, as there's no ferry office). You'll have about four hours on Iona and will need to return to Fionnphort in time for the bus back (15:15). It's important to confirm all of these times locally (just pop in to the West Coast Tours office or the ferry terminal Tour Shop).

By Car: You can do this trip on your own by driving your car onto the ferry to Mull, but space is limited so book way in advance.

Because of tight ferry timings, you'll wind up basically following the tour buses anyway, you'll miss all of the commentary, and no visitor cars are allowed on Iona (£26 round-trip for the car, plus passengers, www.calmac.co.uk).

Visiting Staffa

With two extra hours, you can add a side-trip to Staffa along with your Mull/Iona visit. You'll ferry from Oban to Mull, take a bus across Mull to Fionnphort, then board a **Staffa Tours** boat (35-minute trip, about an hour of free time on Staffa). From Staffa you'll head to Iona for about two hours before returning to Mull for the bus then ferry back to Oban. You can either depart on the 9:50 ferry, returning around 20:05 (£60) or do the "early bird" tour (£55, Tue-Sat only, depart at 7:30, return 18:00; book through West Coast Tours or Staffa Tours—mobile 07831 885 985, www. staffatours.com).

For a bit more relaxed schedule, **Staffa Trips** offers a guided tour with the same route as the one above, but with more time on Staffa and Iona (£60, Tue-Sat only, depart at 7:30, return 19:10, tel. 01681/700-358, www.staffatrips.co.uk).

Turus Mara offers nature/wildlife tours to just Staffa or Staffa and the small island of Ulva, departing from Oban (book at Tour Shop at Oban ferry terminal or contact Turus Mara—tel. 01688/400-242, www.turusmara.com).

Mull

The Isle of Mull, the second largest of the Inner Hebrides (after Skye), has nearly 300 scenic miles of coastline and castles and a

3,169-foot-high mountain, one of Scotland's Munros. Called Ben More ("Big Mountain" in Gaelic), it was once much bigger. At 10,000 feet tall, it made up the entire island of Mull— until a volcano erupted. Things are calmer now, and, similarly, Mull has a noticeably laidback population. My bus driver reported that there are no deaths from stress, and only a few from boredom.

With steep, fog-covered hillsides topped by cairns (piles of stones, sometimes indicating graves) and ancient stone circles, Mull has a gloomy, otherworldly charm. Bring plenty of rain protection and wear layers in case the sun peeks through the clouds.

As my driver said, Mull is a place of cold, wet, windy winters and mild, wet, windy summers.

On the far side of Mull, the caravan of tour buses unloads at Fionnphort, a tiny ferry town. The ferry to the island of Iona takes about 200 walk-on passengers. Confirm the return time with your bus driver, then hustle to the dock to make the first trip over (otherwise, it's a 30-minute wait; on very busy days, those who dillydally may not fit on the first ferry). At the dock, there's a small ferry-passenger building with a meager snack bar and a pay WC; a more enticing seafood bar is across the street. After the 10-minute ride, you wash ashore on sleepy Iona (free WC on this side), and the ferry mobs that crowded you on the boat seem to disappear up the main road and into Iona's back lanes.

The **About Mull Tours and Taxi** service can get you around Mull (tel. 01681/700-507 or mobile 0788-777-4550, www.aboutmull.co.uk). They also do day tours of Mull, focusing on local history and wildlife (half-day tours also available, or ask about shorter Mull tour combined with drop-off and pick-up at Fionnphort ferry dock for quick Iona trip, minimum 2 people, must book ahead).

Iona

The tiny island of Iona, just 3 miles by 1.5 miles, is famous as the birthplace of Christianity in Scotland. If you're on a day trip, you'll have about two hours here on your own before you retrace your steps (your bus driver will tell you which return ferry to take back to Mull).

A pristine quality of light and a thoughtful peace pervades the stark, (nearly) car-free island and its tiny community. With buoyant clouds bouncing play-fully off distant bluffs, sparkling-white crescents of sand, and lone tourists camped thoughtfully atop huge rocks just looking out to sea, Iona is a place that's perfect for meditation. To experience Iona, it's important to get out and take a little hike; you can follow some or all of my self-guided walk outlined later. And you can easily climb a peak—nothing's higher than 300 feet above the sea.

History of Iona

St. Columba (521-597), an Irish scholar, soldier, priest, and founder of monasteries, got into a small war over the posses-

sion of an illegally copied psalm book. Victorious but sickened by the bloodshed, Columba left Ireland, vowing never to return. According to legend, the first bit of land out of sight of his homeland was Iona. He stopped here in 563 and established an abbey.

Columba's monastic community flourished, and Iona became the center of Celtic Christianity. Missionaries from Iona spread the gospel throughout Scotland and northern England, while scholarly monks established Iona as a center of art and learning. The *Book of Kells*—perhaps the finest piece of art from Dark Ages Europe—was probably made on Iona in the eighth century.

The island was so important that it was the legendary burial place for ancient Scottish clan chieftains and kings (including Macbeth, of Shakespeare fame) and even some Scandinavian monarchs.

Slowly, the importance of Iona ebbed. Vikings massacred 68 monks in 806. Fearing more raids, the monks evacuated most of Iona's treasures to Ireland (including the *Book of Kells*, which is now in Dublin). Much later, with the Reformation, the abbey was abandoned, and most of its finely carved crosses were destroyed. In the 17th century, locals used the abbey only as a handy quarry for other building projects.

Iona's population peaked at about 500 in the 1830s. In the 1840s, a potato famine hit, and in the 1850s, a third of the islanders emigrated to Canada or Australia. By 1900, the population was down to 210, and today it's only around 200.

But in our generation, a new religious community has given the abbey fresh life. The Iona Community is an ecumenical gathering of men and women who seek new ways of living the Gospel in today's world, with a focus on worship, peace and justice issues, and reconciliation (http://iona.org.uk).

Orientation to Iona

The ferry arrives at the island's only real village, Baile Mòr, with shops, a restaurant/pub, a few accommodations, and no bank (get cash back with a purchase at the grocery store). The only taxi on Iona is **Iona Taxi** (mobile 07810-325-990, www.ionataxi.co.uk). Up the road from the ferry dock is a little **Spar** grocery with free island maps. Iona's official website (www.isle-of-iona.net) has good information about the island.

Iona Walk

Here's a basic self-guided route for exploring Iona on foot (since no private cars are permitted unless you're a resident or have a permit). With the standard two hours on Iona that a day trip allows, you will have time for a visit to the abbey (with a guided tour and/or audioguide) and then a light stroll; or do the entire walk described below, but skip the abbey (unless you have time for a quick visit on your way back).

Nunnery Ruins: From the ferry dock, head directly up the single paved road that passes through the village and up a small hill to visit one of Britain's best-preserved medieval nunneries (free).

Immediately after the nunnery, turn right on North Road. You'll curve up through the fields—passing the parish church.

Heritage Center: This little museum, tucked behind the church (watch for signs), is small but well done, with displays on local and natural history and a tiny tearoom (free but donation requested, closed Sun and in off-season, tel. 01681/700-576, www. ionaheritage.co.uk).

St. Oran's Chapel and Iona Abbey: Continue on North Road. After the road swings right, you'll soon see **St. Oran's Chapel,** in the graveyard of the Iona Abbey. This chapel is the oldest church building on the island. Inside you'll find a few grave slabs carved in the distinctive Iona School style, which was developed by local stone-carvers in the 14th century. On these tall, skinny headstones, look for the depictions of medieval warrior aristocrats with huge swords. Many more of these carvings have been moved to the abbey, where you can see them in its cloister and museum.

It's free to see the graveyard and chapel; the ▲**Iona Abbey** itself has an admission fee, but it's worth the cost just to sit in the stillness of its lovely, peaceful interior courtyard (£7.50, tel. 01681/700-512, www.historicenvironment.scot—search for "Iona Abbey").

The abbey marks the site of Christianity's arrival in Scotland.

You'll see Celtic crosses, the original shrine of St. Columba, a big church slathered with medieval carvings, a tranquil cloister, and an excellent museum with surviving fragments of this site's fascinating layers of history. While the present abbey, nunnery, and graveyard go back to the 13th century, much of what you'll see was rebuilt in the 20th century. Be sure to read the "History of Iona" sidebar to prepare for your visit.

At the entrance building, pick up your included audioguide, and ask about the good 30-minute guided tours (4/day and worthwhile). Then head toward the church. You'll pass two faded **Celtic crosses** (and the base of a third); the originals are in the museum at the end of your visit. Some experts believe that Celtic crosses—with their distinctive shape so tied to Christianity on the British Isles—originated right here on Iona.

Facing the entrance to the church, you'll see the original **shrine to St. Columba** on your left—a magnet for pilgrims.

Head inside the **church.** It feels like an active church—with hymnals neatly stacked in the pews—because it is, thanks to the Iona Community. While much of this space has been rebuilt, take a moment to look around. Plenty of original medieval stone carving (especially the capitals of many columns) still survives. To see a particularly striking example, stand near the pulpit in the middle of the church and look back to the entrance. Partway up the left span of the pointed arch framing the transept, look for the eternally screaming face. While interpretations vary, this may have been a reminder for the priest not to leave out the fire-and-brimstone parts of his message. Some of the newer features of the church—including the base of the baptismal font near the entrance, and the main altar—are carved from locally quarried Iona marble: white with green streaks. In the right/south transept is the tomb of George Campbell—the Eighth Duke of Argyll, who donated this property in 1900, allowing it to be restored.

When you're ready to continue, find the poorly marked door into the **cloister.** (As you face the altar, it's about half-way down the nave on the left, before the transept.) This space is filled with harmonious light, additional finely carved capitals (these are modern re-creations), and—displayed along the walls—several more of the tall, narrow tombstones like the ones displayed in St. Oran's Chapel. On these, look for a couple of favorite motifs: the long, intimidating sword (indicating a warrior of the Highland clans) and the ship with billowing sails (a powerful symbol of this seafaring culture).

Around the far side of the cloister is the shop. But before leaving, don't overlook the easy-to-miss **museum.** (To find it, head outside and walk around the left side of the abbey complex, toward the sea.) This modern, well-presented space exhibits a remarkable collection of original stonework from the abbey—including what's left of the three Celtic crosses out front—all eloquently described.

Take some time to linger and make sure you've seen all you want to see. Then go in peace.

Iona Community's Welcome Centre: Just beyond and across the road from the abbey is the Iona Community's Welcome Centre (free WCs), which runs the abbey with Historic Scotland and hosts modern-day pilgrims who come here to experience the birthplace of Scottish Christianity. (If you're staying longer, you could attend a worship service at the abbey—check the schedule here; tel. 01681/700-404, www.iona.org.uk.) Its gift shop is packed with books on the island's important role in Christian history.

Views: A 10-minute walk on North Road past the welcome center brings you to the footpath for **Dùn Ì,** a steep but short climb with good views of the abbey looking back toward Mull.

North Beach: Returning to the main road, walk another 20-25 minutes to the end of the paved road, where you'll arrive at a gate leading through a sheep- and cow-strewn pasture to Iona's pristine white-sand beach. Dip your toes in the Atlantic and ponder what this Caribbean-like alcove is doing in Scotland. Be sure to allow at least 40 minutes to return to the ferry dock.

Sleeping and Eating on Iona

For a chance to really experience peaceful, idyllic Iona, spend a night or two (Scots bring their kids and stay on this tiny island for a week). To do so, you'll have to buy each leg of the ferry-bus-ferry (and return) trip separately (see "By Public Transit," earlier). These accommodations are listed roughly in the order you'll reach them as you climb the main road from the ferry dock. The first two hotels listed have **$$$** restaurants that are open to the public for lunch, tea, and dinner and closed in winter. For more accommodation options, see www.isle-of-iona.net/accommodation.

$$ Argyll Hotel, built in 1867, proudly overlooks the waterfront, with 17 cottage-like rooms and pleasingly creaky hallways lined with bookshelves. Of the two hotels, this one feels classier (reserve far in advance for summer, comfortable lounge and sunroom, tel. 01681/700-334, www.argyllhoteliona.co.uk, reception@argyllhoteliona.co.uk).

$$$$ St. Columba Hotel, a bit higher up in town and situated in the middle of a peaceful garden with picnic tables, has 27 institutional rooms and spacious lodge-like common spaces—such as a big, cushy seaview lounge (closed Nov-March, next door to abbey on road up from dock, tel. 01681/700-304, www.stcolumba-hotel.co.uk, info@stcolumba-hotel.co.uk).

$ Calva B&B, a five-minute walk past the abbey, has three spacious rooms (second house on left past the abbey, look for sign in window and gnomes on porch, tel. 01681/700-340; friendly Janetta and Ken).

Staffa

Those more interested in nature than in church history will enjoy the trip to the wildly scenic Isle of Staffa. Completely uninhabited (except for seabirds), Staffa is a knob of rock draped with a vibrant green carpet of turf. Remote and quiet, it feels like a Hebrides nature preserve.

Most day trips give you an hour on Staffa—barely enough time to see its two claims to fame: The basalt columns of Fingal's

Cave, and (in summer) a colony of puffins. To squeeze in both, be ready to hop off the boat and climb the staircase. Partway up to the left, you can walk around to the cave (about 7 minutes). Or continue up to the top, then turn right and walk across the spine of the grassy island (about 10-15 minutes) to the cove where the puffins gather. (Your captain should point out both options and let you know how active the puffins have been.)

▲▲Fingal's Cave

Staffa's shore is covered with bizarre, mostly hexagonal basalt columns that stick up at various heights. It's as if the earth were offering God his choice of thousands of six-sided cigarettes. (The island's name likely came from the Old Norse word for "stave"—the building timbers these columns resemble.) This is the other end of Northern Ireland's popular Giant's Causeway. You'll walk along the uneven surface of these columns, curling around the far side of the island, until you can actually step inside the gaping mouth of a cave—where floor-to-ceiling columns and crashing waves combine to create a powerful experience. Listening to

Puffins

The Atlantic puffin (Fratercula arctica) is an adorably stout, tuxedo-clad seabird with a too-big orange beak and beady black eyes. Puffins live most of their lives on the open Atlantic, coming to land only to breed. They fly north to Scotland between mid-May and early June, raise their brood, then take off again late in August. Puffins mate for life and typically lay just one egg each year, which the male and female take turns caring for. A baby puffin is called—wait for it—a puffling.

To feed their pufflings, puffins plunge as deep as 200 feet below the sea's surface to catch sand eels, herring, and other small fish. Their compact bodies, stubby wings, oil-sealed plumage, and webbed feet are ideal for navigating underwater. Famously, puffins can stuff several small fish into their beaks at once, thanks to their agile tongues and uniquely hinged beaks. This evolutionary trick lets puffins stock up before returning to the nest.

Stocky, tiny-winged puffins have a distinctive way of flying. To take off, they either beat their wings like crazy (on sea) or essentially hurl themselves off a cliff (on land). Once aloft, they beat their wings furiously—up to 400 times per minute—to stay airborne. Coming in for a smooth landing on a rocky cliff is a challenge (and highly entertaining to watch): They choose a spot, swoop in at top speed on prevailing currents, then flutter their wings madly to brake as they try to touch down. At the moment of truth, the puffin decides whether to attempt to stick the landing; more often than not, he bails out and does another big circle on the currents...and tries again...and again...and again.

the water and air flowing through this otherworldly space inspired Felix Mendelssohn to compose his overture, *The Hebrides*.

While you're ogling the cave, consider this: Geologists claim these unique formations were created by volcanic eruptions more than 60 million years ago. As the surface of the lava flow quickly cooled, it contracted and crystallized into columns (resembling the caked mud at the bottom of a dried-up lakebed, but with deeper cracks). As the rock later settled and eroded, the columns broke off into the many stair-like steps that now honeycomb Staffa.

Of course, in actuality, these

formations resulted from a heated rivalry between a Scottish giant named Fingal, who lived on Staffa, and an Ulster warrior named Finn MacCool, who lived across the sea on Ireland's Antrim Coast. Knowing that the giant was coming to spy on him, Finn had his wife dress him as a sleeping infant. The giant, shocked at the infant's size, fled back to Scotland in terror of whomever had sired this giant baby. Breathing a sigh of relief, Finn tore off the baby clothes and prudently knocked down the bridge.

▲▲Puffin Watching

A large colony of Atlantic puffins settles on Staffa each spring and summer during mating season (generally early May through early August). The puffins tend to scatter when the boat arrives. But after the boat pulls out and its passengers hike across the island, the very tame puffins' curiosity gets the better of them. First you'll see them flutter up from the offshore rocks, with their distinctive, bobbing flight. They'll zip and whirl around, and finally they'll start

to land on the lip of the cove. Sit quietly, move slowly, and be patient, and soon they'll get close. (If any seagulls are nearby, shoo them away—puffins are undaunted by humans, who do them no harm, but they're terrified of predator seagulls.)

In the waters around Staffa—on your way to and from the other islands—also keep an eye out for a variety of **marine life,** including seals, dolphins, porpoises, and the occasional minke whale, fin whale, or basking shark (a gigantic fish that hinges open its enormous jaw to drift-net plankton).

Near Oban

The following sights are worth considering for drivers. The first section outlines the best driving route from Glasgow to Oban, including the appealing pit stop at Inveraray. And the second section covers a longer route through one of Scotland's most important prehistoric sites, Kilmartin Glen.

GLASGOW TO OBAN DRIVE

The drive from Glasgow (or Edinburgh) to Oban via Inveraray provides dreamy vistas and your first look at the dramatic landscapes of the Highlands, as well as historic sites and ample opportunity to stop for a picnic.

• *Leaving Glasgow on the A-82, you'll soon be driving along the west bank of...*

Loch Lomond

The first picnic turnout has the best views of this famous lake (described on page 194), benches, a park, and a playground. You're driving over an isthmus between Loch Lomond and a sea inlet. Halfway up the loch, you'll find the town of Tarbet—the Viking word for isthmus, a common name on Scottish maps. Imagine, a thousand years ago, Vikings dragging their ships across this narrow stretch of land to reach Loch Lomond.

• *At Tarbet, the road forks. The signs for Oban keep you on the direct route along A-82. For the scenic option that takes you past Loch Fyne to Inveraray (about 30 minutes longer to drive), keep left for the A-83 (toward Campbeltown).*

Highland Boundary Fault

You'll pass the village of **Arrochar,** then drive along the banks of Loch Long. The scenery crescendos as you pull away from the loch and twist up over the mountains and through a pine forest, getting your first glimpse of bald Highlands mountains—it's clear that you've just crossed the **Highland Boundary Fault.** Enjoy the waterfalls, and notice that the road signs are now in English as well as Gaelic. As you climb into more rugged territory—up the valley called Glen Croe—be mindful that the roads connecting the Lowlands with the Highlands (like the one down in the glen below) were originally a military project designed to facilitate government quelling of the Highland clans.

• *At the summit, watch for the large parking lot with picnic tables on your left (signed for Argyll Forest Park). Stretch your legs at what's aptly named...*

Rest-and-Be-Thankful Pass

The colorful name comes from the 19th century, when just reaching

ing this summit was exhausting. At the top of the military road, just past the last picnic table, there's actually a stone dated 1814 put there by the military with that phrase.

As you drive on, enjoy the dramatic green hills. You may see little bits of hillside highlighted by sunbeams. Each of

The Irish Connection

The Romans called the people living in what is now Ireland the "Scoti" (meaning pirates). When the Scoti crossed the narrow Irish Sea and invaded the land of the Picts 1,500 years ago, that region became known as Scoti-land. Ireland and Scotland were never fully conquered by the Romans, and they retained similar clannish Celtic traits. Both share the same Gaelic branch of the linguistic tree.

On clear summer days, you can actually see Ireland—just 17 miles away—from the Scottish coastline. The closest bit to Scotland is the boomerang-shaped Rathlin Island, part of Northern Ireland. Rathlin is where Scottish leader Robert the Bruce retreated in 1307 after defeat at the hands of the English. Legend has it that he hid in a cave on the island, where he observed a spider patiently rebuilding its web each time a breeze knocked it down. Inspired by the spider's perseverance, Bruce gathered his Scottish forces once more and finally defeated the English at the decisive battle of Bannockburn (see page 62).

Flush with confidence from his victory, Robert the Bruce decided to open a second front against the English...in Ireland. In 1315, he sent his brother Edward over to enlist their Celtic Irish cousins in an effort to thwart the English. After securing Ireland, Edward hoped to move on and enlist the Welsh, thus cornering England with their pan-Celtic nation. But Edward's timing was bad: Ireland was in the midst of famine. His Scottish troops had to live off the land and began to take food and supplies from the starving Irish. Some of Ireland's crops may have been intentionally destroyed to keep it from being used as a colonial "breadbasket" to feed English troops. The Scots quickly wore out their welcome, and Edward the Bruce was eventually killed in battle near Dundalk in 1318.

It's interesting to imagine how things might be different today if Scotland and Ireland had been permanently welded together as a nation 700 years ago. You'll notice the strong Scottish influence in Northern Ireland when you ask a local a question and he answers, "Aye, a wee bit." And in Glasgow—on Scotland's west coast, closest to Ireland—an Ireland-like

division between royalist Protestants and republican Catholics survives today in the form of soccer team allegiances. In big Scottish cities (like Glasgow and Edinburgh), you'll even see "orange parades" of protesters marching in solidarity with their Protestant Northern Irish cousins. The Irish—always quick to defuse tension with humor—joke that the Scots are just Irish people who couldn't swim home.

these is a "soot" (Sun's Out Over There). Look for soots as you drive further north into the Highlands.

• *Continue twisting down the far side of the pass. You'll drive through Glen Kinglas and soon reach...*

Loch Fyne

This saltwater "sea loch" is famous for its shellfish (keep an eye out for oyster farms and seafood restaurants). In fact, Loch Fyne is the namesake of a popular UK restaurant chain with 40 locations across the UK. While a chain restaurant is a chain restaurant, this is different: **$$$$ Loch Fyne Seafood Restaurant and Deli** in the big white building at the end of the loch is the original. It's a famous stop for locals—an elegant seafood restaurant and oyster bar worth traveling for (open daily from noon, last order 18:45, no reservations, tel. 01499/600-482, www.lochfyne.com). Even if you're not eating, it's fun to peruse their salty deli (tasty treats to go, picnic tables outside, good coffee).

• *Looping around Loch Fyne, you approach Inveraray. As you get close, keep an eye on the right (when crossing the bridge, have your camera ready) for the dramatic...*

▲Inveraray Castle

This residence of the Duke of Argyll comes with a dramatic, turreted exterior (one of Scotland's most striking) and a lavishly decorated interior that feels spacious, neatly tended, and lived in. Historically a stronghold of one of the more notorious branches of the Campbell clan, it's filled with precious-if-you're-a-Campbell artifacts and fun to tour.

Roam from room to room, reading the laminated descriptions and asking questions of the gregarious docents. The highlight is the Armory Hall that fills the main atrium, where swords and rifles are painstakingly arrayed in starburst patterns. The rifles were actually used when the Campbells fought with the British at the Battle of Culloden in 1746.

Upstairs is a room dedicated to *Downton Abbey*. Public television fans may recognize this as "Duneagle Castle" (a.k.a. Uncle Shrimpy's pad) from one of the *Downton Abbey* Christmas specials—big photos of the Grantham and MacClare clans decorate the genteel rooms.

As with many such castles, the aristocratic clan still lives here (*private* signs mark rooms where the family resides). Another upstairs room is like an Argyll family scrapbook; for example, see photos of the duke playing elephant polo—the ultimate aristocratic sport. The kids attend school in London, but spend a few months here each year; in the winter, the castle is closed to the public and they have the run of the place. After touring the interior, do a loop through the finely manicured gardens (£11, April-Oct daily 10:00-17:45, closed Nov-March, last entry 45 minutes before closing, nice café in the basement, buy tickets at the car park booth, tel. 01499/302-203, www.inveraray-castle.com).

• *After visiting the castle, spend some time exploring...*

▲Inveraray Town

Nearly everybody stops at this lovely, seemingly made-for-tourists town on Loch Fyne. Browse the main street—lined with touristy shops and cafés all the way to the church at its top. As this is the geological and demographic border between the Highlands and the Lowlands, traditionally church services here were held in both Scots and Gaelic. Just before the church is Loch Fyne Whiskies with historic bottles on its ceiling.

There's free parking on the main street and plenty of pay-and-display parking near the pier (TI open daily, on Front Street, tel. 01499/302-063; public WCs at end of nearby pier).

The **Inveraray Jail** is the main site in town—an overpriced, corny, but mildly educational former jail converted into a museum. This "living 19th-century prison" includes a courtroom where mannequins argue the fate of the accused. Then you'll head outside and explore the various cells of the outer courtyard. The playful guards may lock you up for a photo op, while they explain how Scotland reformed its prison system in 1839—you'll see both "before" and "after" cells in this complex (£11.50, includes 75-minute audioguide, open daily, tel. 01499/302-381, www.inverarayjail.co.uk).

• *To continue directly to Oban from Inveraray (about an hour), leave town through the gate at the woolen mill and get on the A-819, which takes you through Glen Aray and along Loch Awe. A left turn on the A-85 takes you into Oban.*

But if you have a healthy interest in prehistoric sites, you can go to Oban by way of Kilmartin Glen (described next, adds about 45 minutes of driving).

KILMARTIN GLEN

Except for the Orkney Islands, Scotland isn't as rich with prehistoric sites as South England is, but the ones in Kilmartin Glen, while faint, are some of Scotland's most accessible—and most important. This wide valley, clearly imbued with spiritual and/or strategic power, contains reminders of several millennia worth of inhabitants. Today it's a playground for those who enjoy tromping through grassy fields while daydreaming about who moved these giant stones here so many centuries ago. This isn't worth a long detour, unless you're fascinated by prehistoric sites.

Four to five thousand years ago, Kilmartin Glen was inhabited by Neolithic people who left behind fragments of their giant, stony monuments. And 1,500 years ago, this was the seat of the kings of the Scoti, who migrated here from Ireland around A.D. 500, giving rise to Scotland's own branch of Celtic culture. From this grassy valley, the Scoti kings ruled their empire, called Dalriada (also sometimes written Dál Riata), which encompassed much of Scotland's west coast, the Inner Hebrides, and the northern part of Ireland. The Scoti spoke Gaelic and were Christian; as they overtook the rest of the Highlands—eventually absorbing their rival Picts—theirs became a dominant culture, which is still evident in pockets of present-day Scotland. Today, Kilmartin Glen is scattered with burial cairns, standing stones, and a hill called Dunadd—the fortress of the Scoti kings.

• *To get here from Inveraray, head straight up Inveraray's main street and get on the waterfront A-83 (marked for Campbeltown); after a half-hour, in Lochgilphead, turn right onto the A-816, which takes you through Kilmartin Glen and all the way up to Oban. (To avoid backtracking, be ready to stop at the prehistoric sites lining the A-816 between Lochgilphead and Kilmartin village.)*

Visiting Kilmartin Glen

Sites are scattered throughout the valley, including some key locations along or just off the A-816 south of Kilmartin village. If you're coming from Inveraray, you'll pass these *before* you reach the village and museum itself. Each one is explained by good informational signs.

Dunadd: This bulbous hill sits just west of the A-816, about four miles north of Lochgilphead and four miles south of Kilmartin village (watch for blue, low-profile *Dunadd Fort* signs). A fort had stood here since the time of Christ, but it was the Scoti kings—who made it their primary castle from the sixth to ninth centuries—that put Dunadd on the map. Park in the big lot at its base and hike through the faint outlines of terraces to the top, where you can enjoy sweeping views over all of Kilmartin Glen; this southern stretch is a marshland called "The Great Moss" (Moine Mhor). Look for carvings in the rock: early Celtic writing, the image of a boar, and a footprint (carved into a stone crisscrossed with fissures). This "footprint of fealty" (a replica) recalls the inauguration ceremony in which the king would place his foot into the footprint, symbolizing the marriage between the ruler and the land.

Dunchraigaig Cairn: About two miles farther north on the A-816, brown *Dunchraigaig* signs mark a parking lot where you can cross the road to the 4,000-year-old, 100-foot-in-diameter Dunchraigaig Cairn—the burial place for 10 Neolithic VIPs. Circle around to find the opening, where you can still crawl into a small recess. This is one of at least five such cairns that together created a mile-and-a-half-long "linear cemetery" up the middle of Kilmartin Glen.

From this cairn, you can walk five minutes to several more prehistoric structures: Follow signs through the gate, and walk to a farm field with **Ballymeanoch**—an avenue of two stone rows (with six surviving stones), a disheveled old cairn, and a stone circle.

Sites near Kilmartin Burn: About one more mile north on the A-816, just off the intersection with the B-8025 (toward *Tayvallich*), is the small Kilmartin Burn parking lot. From here, cross the stream to a field where the five **Nether Largie Standing Stones** have stood in a neat north-south line for 3,200 years. Were these stones designed as an astronomical observatory? Burial rituals or other religious ceremonies? Sporting events? Or just a handy place for sheep to scratch themselves? From here, you can hike the rest of the way through the field (about 10 minutes) to the **Nether Largie South Cairn** and the **Temple Wood Stone Circles** (which don't have their own parking). The larger, older of these circles dates to more than 5,000 years ago, and both were added onto and modified over the millennia.

Kilmartin Museum: To get the big picture, head for the Kilmartin Museum, in the center of Kilmartin village. The cute stone house has a ticket desk, bookshop, and café; the museum—with exhibits explaining this area's powerful history—fills the basement of the adjacent building (though a new home for the exhibit is in the works). The modest but modern museum features handy explanations, a few original artifacts, and lots of re-creations (£6.50, daily except closed Christmas-Feb, tel. 01546/510-278, www.kilmartin.org).

From the museum, you can look out across the fields to see **Glebe Cairn,** one of the five cairns of the "linear cemetery."

Another one, the **Nether Largie North Cairn,** was reconstructed in the 1970s and can actually be entered (a half-mile
south of the museum; ask for directions at museum).

Many more prehistoric sites fill Kilmartin Glen (more than
800 within a six-mile radius); the museum sells in-depth guidebooks for the curious, and can point you in the right direction for
what you're interested in.

GLENCOE & FORT WILLIAM

Glencoe • Fort William • The Road to the Isles

Scotland is a land of great natural wonders. And some of the most spectacular—and most accessible—are in the valley called Glencoe, just an hour north of Oban and on the way to Fort William, Loch Ness, Inverness, or the Isle of Skye. The evocative "Weeping Glen" of Glencoe aches with both history and natural beauty. Beyond that, Fort William anchors the southern end of the Caledonian Canal, offering a springboard to more Highlands scenery. This is where Britain's highest peak, Ben Nevis, keeps its head in the clouds, and where you'll find a valley made famous by a bonnie prince...and (later) by a steam train carrying a young wizard named Harry.

PLANNING YOUR TIME

On a quick visit, this area warrants just a few hours between Oban and either Inverness or Skye: Wander through Glencoe village, tour its modest museum, then drive up Glencoe valley for views before continuing on your way north. But if you have only a day or two to linger in the Highlands, Glencoe is an ideal place to do it. Settle in for a night (or more) to make time for a more leisurely drive and to squeeze in a hike or two—I give an overview of the best options, from easy strolls to challenging ascents.

Beyond Glencoe, Fort William—a touristy and overrated transportation hub—is skippable, but can be a handy lunch stop. The Road to the Isles, stretching west from Fort William to the coast, isn't worth a detour, but it's very handy for those connecting to the Isle of Skye. Along the way, the only stop worth more than a quick photo is Glenfinnan, with its powerful ties to Bonnie Prince Charlie and Jacobite history.

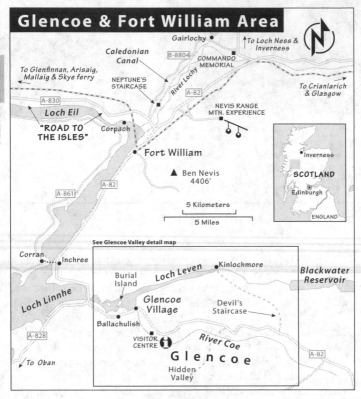

Glencoe & Fort William Area

This valley is the essence of the wild, powerful, and stark beauty of the Highlands. Along with its scenery, Glencoe offers a good dose of bloody clan history: In 1692, government Redcoats (led by a local Campbell commander) came to the valley, and they were sheltered and fed for 12 days by the MacDonalds—whose leader had been late in swearing an oath to the British monarch. Then, on the morning of February 13, the soldiers were ordered to rise

up early and kill their sleeping hosts, violating the rules of Highland hospitality and earning the valley the nickname "The Weeping Glen." Thirty-eight men were killed outright; hundreds more fled through a blizzard, and some 40 additional villagers (mostly women and children) died from exposure. It's fitting that such an epic, dramatic incident should be set in this equally epic, dramatic

Harry Potter Sights

Harry Potter's story is set in a magical, largely fictional Britain, but you can visit real locations used in the film series. **Glencoe** was the main location for outdoor filming in *The Prisoner of Azkaban* and *The Half-Blood Prince,* and many shots of the Hogwarts grounds were filmed in the Fort William and Glencoe areas. The Hogwarts Express that carries Harry, Ron, and Hermione to school each year runs along the actual **Jacobite Steam Train** line (between Fort William and Mallaig).

In *The Prisoner of Azkaban* and *The Goblet of Fire,* **Loch Shiel, Loch Eilt,** and **Loch Morar** (near Fort William) were the stand-ins for the Great Lake. **Steal Falls,** at the base of Ben Nevis, is the locale for the Triwizard Tournament in *The Goblet of Fire.*

valley, where the cliffsides seem to weep (with running streams) when it rains.

Aside from its tragic history, this place has captured the imaginations of both hikers and artists. Movies filmed here include everything from *Monty Python and the Holy Grail* and *Highlander* to *Harry Potter and the Prisoner of Azkaban* and the James Bond film *Skyfall.* When filmmakers want a stunning, rugged backdrop; when hikers want a scenic challenge; and when Scots want to remember their hard-fought past...they all think of Glencoe.

Orientation to Glencoe

The valley of Glencoe is an easy side-trip just off the main A-828/A-82 road between Oban and points north (such as Fort William and Inverness). If you're coming from the north, the signage can be tricky—at the roundabout south of Fort William, follow signs to *Crianlarich* and *A-82.* The most appealing town here is the sleepy one-street village of Glencoe, worth a stop for its folk museum and its status as the gateway to the valley. The town's hub of activity is its grocery store, which has an ATM (daily 8:00-19:30). The slightly larger and more modern town of Ballachulish (a half-mile away) has more services, including a Co-op grocery store (daily 7:00-22:00).

In the loch just outside Glencoe (near Ballachulish), notice the burial island—where the souls of those who "take the low road" are piped home. (For an explanation of "Ye'll take the high road, and I'll take the low road," see page 195.) The next island was the Island of Discussion—where those in dispute went until they found agreement.

TOURIST INFORMATION

Your best source of information (especially for walks and hikes) is the **Glencoe Visitor Centre,** described later. The nearest **TI** is in the next town, Ballachulish (buried inside a huge gift shop, daily 9:00-17:00, Nov-Easter 10:00-16:00, tel. 01855/811-866, www.glencoetourism.co.uk). For more information on the area, see www.discoverglencoe.com.

Bike Rental: At **Crank It Up Gear,** Davy rents road and mountain bikes, and can offer plenty of suggestions for where to pedal in the area (£15/half-day, £25/all day, just off the main street to the left near the start of town, 20 Lorn Drive, mobile 07746-860-023, www.crankitupgear.com, best to book ahead in summer).

Sights in Glencoe

Glencoe Village

Glencoe village is just a line of houses sitting beneath the brooding mountains. The only real sight in town is the folk museum (described later). But walking the main street gives a good glimpse of village Scotland. From the free parking lot at the entrance to town, go for a stroll. You'll pass lots of little B&Bs renting two or three rooms, the stony Episcopal church, the folk museum, the town's grocery store, and the village hall.

At the far end of the village, on the left just before the bridge, a Celtic cross **World War I** memorial stands on a little hill. Even this

wee village lost 11 souls during that war—a reminder of Scotland's disproportionate contribution to Britain's war effort. You'll see memorials like this (usually either a Celtic cross or a soldier with bowed head) in virtually every town in Scotland.

If you were to cross the little bridge, you'd head up into Glencoe's wooded parklands, with some easy hikes (described later). But for one more landmark, turn right just before the bridge and walk about five minutes. Standing on a craggy bluff on your right is another memorial—this one to the **Glencoe Massacre,** which still haunts the memories of people here and throughout Scotland.

Glencoe and North Lorn Folk Museum

This gathering of thatched-roof, early 18th-century croft houses is a volunteer-run community effort. It's jammed with local his-

tory, creating a huggable museum filled with humble exhibits gleaned from the town's old closets and attics. When one house was being rethatched, its owner found a cache of 200-year-old swords and pistols hidden there from the government Redcoats after the disastrous Battle of Culloden. You'll also see antique toys, boxes from old food products, sports paraphernalia, a cabinet of curiosities, evocative old black-and-white photos, and plenty of information on the MacDonald clan. Be sure to look for the museum's little door that leads out back, where additional, smaller buildings are filled with everyday items (furniture, farm tools, and so on) and exhibits on the Glencoe Massacre and a beloved Highland doctor. You can listen to an interview with the late Arthur Smith, a local historian, about the valley and its story in the "Scottish Highlands" program available on my Rick Steves Audio Europe app—for details, see page 10 (£3, Easter-Sept Mon-Sat 10:00-16:30, closed Sun and off-season, tel. 01855/811-664, www.glencoemuseum.com).

Glencoe Visitor Centre

This modern facility, a mile past Glencoe village up the A-82 into the dramatic valley, is designed to resemble a *clachan*, or traditional Highland settlement. The information desk inside the shop at the ranger desk is your single best resource for advice (and maps or guidebooks) about local walks and hikes (several of which are outlined later in this chapter). At the back of the complex you'll find a viewpoint with a handy 3-D model of the hills for orientation. There's also a pricey exhibition about the surrounding landscape, the region's history, wildlife, mountaineering, and conservation. It's worth the time to watch the more-interesting-than-it-sounds two-minute video on geology and the 14-minute film on the Glencoe Massacre, which thoughtfully traces the events leading up to the tragedy rather than simply recycling romanticized legends (free, exhibition-£6.50; April-Oct daily 9:30-17:30; Nov-March Thu-Sun 10:00-16:00, closed Mon-Wed; free Wi-Fi, café, tel. 01855/811-307, www.glencoe-nts.org.uk).

GLENCOE & FORT WILLIAM

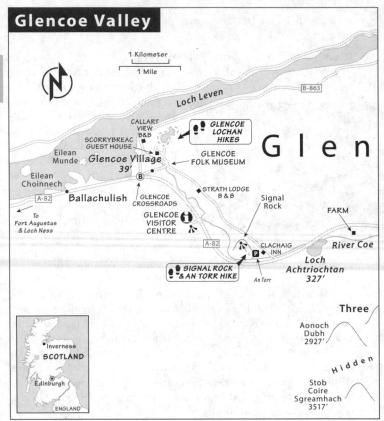

Glencoe Valley Driving Tour

If you have a car, spend an hour or so following the A-82 through the valley, past the Glencoe Visitor Centre, up into the desolate moor beyond, and back again. You'll enjoy grand views, dramatic craggy hills, and, if you're lucky, a chance to hear a bagpiper in the wind: Roadside Highland buskers often set up here on good-weather summer weekends. (If you play the recorder—and the piper's not swarmed with other tourists—ask to finger a tune while he does the hard work.)

Here's a brief explanation of the route. Along the way, I've pointed out sometimes easy-to-miss trailheads, in case you're up for a hike (hikes described in the next section).

● **Self-Guided Driving Tour:** Leaving Glencoe village on the A-82, it's just a mile to the **Glencoe Visitor Centre** (on the right, described earlier). Soon after, the road pulls out of the forest-ed hills and gives you unobstructed views of the U-shaped valley.

Kinlochmore

Kinlochleven

Loch Treig

WEST HIGHLAND WAY

c o e

Stob Mhic Mhartuin 2320'

Pass 1800'

THREE SISTERS TRAILHEAD & VIEWPOINT

The Study Viewpoint 451'

👣 *THE STUDY HIKE*

👣 *DEVIL'S STAIRCASE HIKE*

Coffin Cairn

THE STUDY TRAILHEAD

Waterfall

DEVIL'S STAIRCASE TRAILHEAD

A-82

To Ski Centre & Rannoch Moor

B-863

Gearr Aonach 2270'

👣 *HIDDEN VALLEY HIKE*

Sisters

Beinn Fhada 2700'

Stob Dearg 3350'

Valley 1226'

Glen Etive

About a mile after the visitors center, on the left, is a parking lot for **Signal Rock and An Torr,** a popular place for low-impact forested hikes. Just beyond, also on the left, is a single-track road leading to the recommended **Clachaig Inn,** a classic hikers' pub. The hillsides above the inn were the setting for Hagrid's hut in the third Harry Potter movie (though nothing remains from filming).

Continuing along the A-82, you'll hit a straight stretch, passing a lake (Loch Achtriochtan), and then a small farm, both on the

right. After the farm, the valley narrows a bit as you cut through Glencoe Pass. On the right, you'll pass two small parking lots. Pull into the second one for perhaps the best viewpoint of the entire valley, with point-blank views (directly ahead) of the steep ridge-like mountains known as the **Three Sisters.** Hike about 100 feet away from the pullout to your own private bluff to enjoy the view alone—it makes a big difference. This is also the starting point for the challenging **Hidden Valley hike,** which leads between the first and second sisters.

As you continue, you'll pass a raging waterfall in a canyon—the Tears of the MacDonalds—on the right. After another mile or so—through more glorious waterfall scenery—watch on the left for the **Coffin Cairn,** which looks like a stone igloo (parking is just across the road if you want a photo op). Just after the cairn, look on the left for pullout parking for the **hike to The Study,** a viewpoint overlooking the road you just drove down (described later).

After this pullout, you'll hit a straightaway for about a mile, followed by an S-curve. At the end of the curve, look for the pullout parking on the left, just before the stand of pine trees. This is the trailhead for the **Devil's Staircase** hike, high into the hills.

Continuing past here, you're nearing the end of the valley. The intimidating peak called the Great Shepherd of Etive (on the right) looms like a dour watchman, guarding the far end of the valley. Soon you'll pass the turnoff (on the right) for **Glen Etive,** an even more remote-feeling valley. (This was the setting for the final scenes of *Skyfall.* Yes, this is where James Bond grew up.) Continuing past that, the last sign of civilization (on the right) is the Glencoe Ski Centre. And from here, the terrain flattens out as you enter the vast **Rannoch Moor**—50 bleak square miles of heather, boulders, and barely enough decent land to graze a sheep. Robert Louis Stevenson called it the "Highland Desert."

You could keep driving as far as you like—but the moor looks pretty much the same from here on out. Turn around and head back through Glencoe...it's scenery you'll hardly mind seeing twice.

Hiking in Glencoe

Glencoe is made for hiking. Many routes are not particularly well marked, so it's essential to get very specific instructions (from the rangers at the Glencoe Visitor Centre, or other knowledgeable locals) and equip yourself with a good map (the Ordnance Survey Explorer Map #384, sold at the center). Next, I've suggested a few of the most enticing walks and hikes. These vary from easy, level strolls to challenging climbs. Either way, equip yourself with proper footwear (even the easy trails can get swamped in wet weather) and rain gear—you never know when a storm will blow in.

I've listed these roughly in order of how close they are to Glencoe village, and given a rough sense of difficulty for each. Some of them (including the first two) are more forested, but the ones out in the open—which really let you feel immersed in the wonders of Glencoe—are even better.

While you can walk to the first two areas from Glencoe village, the rest are best for drivers. Some of these trailheads are tricky to find; remember, I've designed the driving commentary in the previous section to help you find the hikes off the A-82.

Glencoe Lochan (Easy)

Perched on the forested hill above Glencoe village is an improbable slice of the Canadian Rockies. A century ago, this was the personal playground of Lord Strathcona, a local boy done good when he moved to Canada and eventually became a big Canadian Pacific Railway magnate. In 1894, he returned home with his Canadian wife and built the Glencoe House (which was recently restored into an exclusive, top-of-the-top hotel, with suites starting around £500 a night). His wife was homesick for the Rockies, so he had the grounds landscaped to represent the lakes, trees, and mountains of her home country. They even carved out a man-made lake (Glencoe Lochan), which looks like a slice of Canada tucked under a craggy Scottish backdrop. (She was still homesick—they eventually returned to Canada.)

Today, the house and immediate surroundings are off-limits, but the rest of the area is open for exploration. Head to the end of Glencoe village, cross the bridge, and continue straight up (following signs for *Glencoe Lochan*)—it's a 20-minute uphill walk, or 5-minute drive, from the village center. Once there, a helpful orientation panel in the parking lot suggests three different, color-coded, one-mile walking loops—mostly around that beautiful lake, which reflects the hillsides of Glencoe.

From this area, a good trail network called the **Orbital Recreational Track** follows the river through the forest up the valley, all the way to the Clachaig Inn (about 45 minutes one-way). This links you to the Signal Rock and An Torr areas (described next). Eventually they hope to extend this trail system across the valley and back to the Glencoe Visitor Centre, which would allow a handy loop hike around the valley floor.

Signal Rock and An Torr (Easy to Moderate)

This forested area has nicely tended trails and gives you a better chance of spotting wildlife than the more desolate hikes described later. To explore this area, park at the well-marked lot just off of the A-82 and go for a walk. A well-described panel at the trailhead narrates three options: easy yellow route to the Clachaig Inn; longer blue route to Signal Rock; and strenuous black route along the hillsides of An Torr. The Signal Rock route brings you to a panoramic point overlooking the valley—so named because a fire could be lit here to alert others in case of danger.

Hidden Valley (Challenging)

Three miles east of Glencoe village, this aptly named glen is tucked between two of the dramatic Three Sisters mountains. Also called the Lost Valley (Coire Gabhail in Gaelic), this was supposedly where the MacDonalds hid stolen cattle from their rivals, the Campbells (who later massacred them). This is the most challenging of the hikes I describe—it's strenuous and has stretches with uneven footing. Expect to scramble a bit over rocks, and to cross a river on stepping stones (which may be underwater after a heavy rain). As the rocks can be slippery when wet, skip this hike in bad weather. Figure about two-and-a-half to three hours round-trip (with an ascent of more than 1,000 feet).

Begin at the second parking lot at Glencoe Pass (on the right when coming from Glencoe), with views of the Three Sisters. You're aiming to head between the first and second Sisters (counting from the left). Hike down into the valley between the road and the mountains. Bear left, head down a metal staircase, and cross the bridge over the river. (Don't cross the bridge to the right of the parking lots—a common mistake.) Once across, you'll start the treacherous ascent up a narrow gorge. Some scrambling is required, and at one point a railing helps you find your way. The next tricky part is where you cross the river. You're looking for a pebbly beach and a large boulder; stepping stones lead across the river, and you'll see the path resume on the other side. But if the water level is high, the stones may be covered—though still passable with good shoes and steady footing. (Don't attempt to scramble over the treacherous slopes on the side of the river with the loose rocks called scree.) Once across the stepping stones, keep on the trail, hiking further up into the valley.

Much Easier Alternative: If you'd simply enjoy the feeling of walking deep in Glencoe valley—with peaks and waterfalls overhead—you can start down from the parking lot toward the Hidden Valley trail, and then simply stroll the old road along the valley floor as far as you want in either direction.

The Study (Easy to Moderate)

For a relatively easy, mostly level hike through the valley with a nice viewpoint at the end, consider walking to the flat rock called "The Study" and back. It takes about 45-60 minutes round-trip. The walk essentially parallels the main highway, but on the old road a bit higher up. You'll park just beyond the Three Sisters and the Coffin Cairn. From there, cut through the field of stone and marshy turf to the old road—basically two gravel tire ruts—and follow them to your left. You'll hike above the modern road, passing several modest waterfalls, until you reach a big, flat rock with stunning views of the Three Sisters and the valley beyond. (Fellow hikers have marked the spot with a pile of stones.)

The Devil's Staircase (Strenuous but Straightforward)
About eight miles east of Glencoe village, near the end of the valley, you can hike this brief stretch of the West Highland Way. It was built by General Wade, the British strategist who came to Scotland after the 1715 Jacobite rebellion to help secure government rule here. Designed to connect Glencoe valley to the lochside town of Kinlochmore, to the north, it's named for its challenging switchbacks. Most hikers simply ascend to the pass at the top (an 800-foot gain), then come back down to Glencoe. It's challenging, but easier to follow and with more comfortable footing than the Hidden Valley hike. Figure about 45-60 minutes up, and 30 minutes back down (add 45-60 minutes for the optional ascent to the summit of 2,320-foot Stob Mhic Mhartuin).

From the parking lot, a green sign points the way. It's a steep but straightforward hike up, on switchback trails, until you reach the pass—marked by a cairn (pile of stones). From here, you can return back down into the valley. Or, if you have stamina left, consider continuing higher—head up to the peak on the left, called **Stob Mhic Mhartuin.** The 30-40 minute hike to the top (an additional gain of 500 feet) earns you even grander views over the entire valley.

For an even longer hike, it is possible to carry on down the other side of the staircase to **Kinlochmore** (about 2 hours descent)—but your car will still be in Glencoe. Consider this: Leave your car in Glencoe village. Take a taxi to the trailhead. Hike across to Kinlochmore. Then take the hourly Stagecoach bus #44 back to Glencoe and your car (see "Glencoe Connections," later).

Sleeping in Glencoe

Glencoe is an extremely low-key place to spend the night between Oban or Glasgow and the northern destinations. You'll join two kinds of guests: one-nighters just passing through and outdoorsy types settling in for several days of hiking.

B&BS IN GLENCOE VILLAGE

The following B&Bs are along or just off the main road through the middle of the village.

$$ Beechwood Cottage B&B is a shoes-off, slippers-on, whisky-honor-bar kind of place where Jackie rents three lovely rooms and Ian pursues his rock-garden dreams in the yard (look for the sign at the church on Main Street, tel. 01855/811-062, www.beechwoodcottage.scot, stay@beechwoodcottage.scot).

$$ Heatherlea B&B is at the far end of the village, with a relaxed atmosphere, hotel-meets-country-home rooms, and a serene grassy garden with berry bushes (which they harvest for homemade jam). Hosts Jo and Helen are fun, outdoorsy types who opened a guesthouse because they "wanted to get out of the rat race" (four rooms—one a single with private bath down the hall, sack lunches available for small fee, tel. 01855/811-519, mobile 07815-042-505, www.heatherleaglencoe.com, info@heatherleaglencoe.com).

$ Ghlasdruim B&B, behind the Glencoe Café and set back from the A-82, has three large and cozy ground-floor rooms, spacious bathrooms, a homey dining room with a fireplace, and one big table for conversational breakfasts (cash only, closed in winter, tel. 01855/811-593, http://ghlasdruim.co.uk, ghlasdruim@gmail.com, Maureen and Ken).

OUTSIDE OF TOWN

These options are a bit outside of town, with good proximity to both the village and the valley. Strath Lodge and Clachaig Inn are on the back road that runs through the forest parallel to the A-82 (best-suited for drivers). Scorrybreac is on a hill above the village, and Callart View is along the flat road that winds past Loch Leven. Strathassynt Guest House is in the center of Ballachulish.

$$ Strath Lodge, energetically run by Ann and Dan (who are generous with hiking tips and maps), brings a fresh perspective to Glencoe's sometimes-stodgy accommodations scene. Their four rooms, in a modern, light-filled, lodge-like home, are partway down the road to the Clachaig Inn (2-3 night minimum preferred, no kids under 16, tel. 01855/811-337, www.strathlodgeglencoe.com, stay@strathlodgeglencoe.com). Take the road up through the middle of Glencoe village, cross the bridge, and keep right following the river for a few minutes; it's on the right.

$$ Clachaig Inn, which runs two popular pubs on site, also rents 23 rooms, all with private bath. It's a family-friendly place surrounded by a dramatic setting that works well for hikers seeking a comfy mountain inn (recommended pub, tel. 01855/811-252, 3 miles from Glencoe, www.clachaig.com, frontdesk@clachaig.com). Follow the directions for the Strath Lodge earlier, and drive another three miles past campgrounds and hostels—the Clachaig Inn is on the right.

$ Scorrybreac Guest House enjoys a secluded forest setting and privileged position next to the restored Glencoe House (now an exclusive luxury hotel). From here, walks around the Glencoe Lochan wooded lake park are easy, and it's about a 10-minute walk down into the village. Emma and Graham rent five homey rooms and serve a daily breakfast special that goes beyond the usual offerings (family room, 2-3 nights preferred in peak season, tel. 01855/811-354, www.scorrybreacglencoe.com, scorrybreac@btinternet.com). After crossing the bridge at the end of the village, head left up the hill and follow signs.

$ Callart View B&B offers four rooms, quilted-home comfort, and a peaceful spot overlooking Loch Leven, less than a mile outside the village and close to the wooded trails of the Glencoe Lochan. You'll be spoiled by Lynn's homemade shortbread (family room, self-catering cottages, pack lunches available, tel. 01855/811-259, www.callart-view.co.uk, callartview@hotmail.com, Lynn and Geoff). Turn off from the main road for Glencoe village but instead of turning right into the village, keep left and drive less than a mile along the loch.

$ Strathassynt Guest House sits in the center of Ballachulish, across from the recommended Laroch Bar & Bistro. Some parts of the house may feel dated (it's a work in progress—they call it "modern vintage"), but the six bedrooms are all fresh and nicely modernized (family rooms, closed Nov-Feb, tel. 01855/811-261, www.strathassynt.com, info@strathassynt.com, Neil and Katya).

Eating in Glencoe

Choices around Glencoe are slim—this isn't the place for fine dining. But the following options offer decent food a short walk or drive away. For evening fun, take a walk or ask your B&B host where to find music and dancing.

In Glencoe: The only real restaurant is **$$$ The Glencoe Gathering,** with lovely dining areas and a large outdoor deck, and specializing in seafood with a Scottish twist. Choose between the quirky, fun pub or the fancier restaurant (food served daily 8:00-22:00, at junction of A-82 and Glencoe village, tel. 01855/811-265). The adjacent hotel has a more subdued and formal restaurant called **The Glencoe Inn.**

The **$ Glencoe Café,** also in the village, is just right for soups and sandwiches, and Deirdre's homemade baked goods—especially the carrot loaf—are irresistible (soup and panini lunch combo, daily 10:00-17:00, last order at 16:15, free Wi-Fi, Alan).

Near Glencoe: Set in a stunning valley a few miles from

Glencoe village, **$$ Clachaig Inn** serves solid pub grub all day long to a clientele that's half locals and half tourists. This unpretentious and very popular social hub features billiards, live music, and a wide range of whiskies and hand-pulled ales. There are two areas, sharing the same menu: The Bidean Lounge feels a bit like an upscale ski lodge while the Boots Bar has a spit-and-sawdust, pub-around-an-open-fire atmosphere (open daily for lunch and dinner, music Sat from 21:00, Sun open-mike folk music, see hotel listing earlier for driving directions, tel. 01855/811-252, no reservations).

In Ballachulish: Trying to bring some modern class to this sleepy corner of Scotland, **$$$$ The Laroch Bar & Bistro** offers a choice between the fancier bistro (pricey, more sophisticated menu, reservations smart) or the cozy bar (lighter fare, no reservations) with big-screen TVs and video games (Tue-Sun 12:00-15:00 & 18:00-21:00, closed Mon, tel. 01855/811-940, www.thelarochrestaurantandbar.co.uk). Drive three minutes from Glencoe into Ballachulish village, and you'll see it on the left. There's also a simple **$ fish-and-chips** joint next door (open until 21:30).

Glencoe Connections

Buses don't actually drive down the main road through Glencoe village, but they stop nearby at a place called **"Glencoe Crossroads"** (a short walk into the village center). They also stop in the town of **Ballachulish,** which is just a half-mile away (or a £3 taxi ride). Tell the bus driver where you're going ("Glencoe village") and ask to be let off as close as possible.

Citylink buses #914, #915, or #916 stop at Glencoe Crossroads and Ballachulish, heading north to **Fort William** (8/day, 30 minutes) or south to **Glasgow** (3 hours). Another option is Stagecoach bus #44, which runs from either Glencoe Crossroads or Ballachulish to **Fort William** (hourly, fewer on Sun). From Ballachulish, you can take Citylink bus #918 to **Oban** (2/day, 1 hour).

To reach **Inverness** or **Portree** on the Isle of Skye, transfer in Fort William. To reach **Edinburgh,** transfer in Glasgow.

Bus info: Citylink tel. 0871-266-3333, www.citylink.co.uk; Stagecoach tel. 01397/702-373, www.stagecoachbus.com.

Fort William

Fort William—after Inverness, the second biggest town in the Highlands (pop. 10,000)—is Glencoe's opposite. While Glencoe is a humble one-street village, appealing to hikers and nature-lovers, Fort William's glammed-up car-free main drag feels like one big

Scottish shopping mall (with souvenir stands and outdoor stores touting perpetual "70 percent off" sales). The town is clogged with a United Nations of tourists trying to get out of the rain. Big bus tours drive through Glencoe...but they sleep in Fort William.

While Glencoe touches the Scottish soul of the Highlands, Fort William was a steely and intimidating headquarters of the British

counter-insurgency movement—in many ways designed to crush that same Highland spirit. After the English Civil War (early 1650s), Oliver Cromwell built a fort here to control his rebellious Scottish subjects. This was beefed up (and named for King William III) in 1690. And following the Jacobite uprising in 1715, King George I dispatched General George Wade to coordinate and fortify the crown's Highland defenses against further Jacobite dissenters. Fort William was the first of a chain of intimidating bastions (along with Fort Augustus on Loch Ness, and Fort George near Inverness) stretching the length of the Great Glen. But Fort William's namesake fortress is long gone, leaving precious little tangible (except a tiny bit of rampart in a park near the train station) to help today's visitors imagine its militaristic past.

With the opening of the Caledonian Canal in 1822, the first curious tourists arrived. Many more followed with the arrival of the train in 1894, and grand hotels were built. Today, sitting at the foot of Ben Nevis, the tallest peak in Britain, Fort William is considered the outdoors capital of the United Kingdom.

Orientation to Fort William

Given its strategic position—between Glencoe and Oban in the south, Inverness in the east, and the Isle of Skye in the west—you're likely to pass through Fort William at some point during your Highlands explorations. And, while "just passing through" is the perfect plan here, Fort William can provide a good opportunity to stock up on whatever you need (last supermarket before Inverness), grab lunch, and get any questions answered at the TI.

Arrival in Fort William: You'll find pay parking lots flanking the main pedestrian zone, High Street. The train and bus stations sit side by side just north of the old town center, where you'll find a handy pay parking lot.

Tourist Information: The TI is on the car-free main drag (daily July-Aug 9:30-18:30, Sept-June 9:00-17:00; free Wi-Fi,

15 High Street, tel. 01397/701-801). Free public WCs are up the street, next to the parking lot.

Sights in Fort William

Fort William's High Street

Enjoy an hour-long stroll up and down the length of Fort William's main street for lots of Scottish clichés, great people watching, and a shop at #125 (near the south end) called Aye2Aye, which favors a new referendum on Scottish independence.

▲West Highland Museum

Fort William's only real sight is its humble but well-presented museum. It's a fine opportunity to escape the elements, and—if you take the time to linger over the exhibits—genuinely insightful about local history and Highland life (free, £3 suggested donation, guidebook-£1.50, Mon-Sat 10:00-17:00, and maybe Sun in high season; Nov-Dec and March until 16:00, closed Sun; closed Jan-Feb; midway down the main street on Cameron Square, tel. 01397/702-169, www.westhighlandmuseum.org.uk).

Follow the suggested one-way route through exhibits on two floors. You'll begin by learning about the WWII green beret commandos, who were trained in secrecy near here (see "Commando Memorial" listing, later). Then you'll see the historic Governor's Room, decorated with the original paneling from the room in which the order for the Glencoe Massacre was signed. The ground floor also holds exhibits on natural history (lots of stuffed birds and other critters), mountaineering (old equipment), and archaeology (stone and metal tools).

Upstairs, you'll see a selection of old tartans and a salacious exhibit about Queen Victoria and John Brown (her Scottish servant... and, possibly, suitor). The Jacobite exhibit gives a concise timeline of that complicated history, from Charles I to Bonnie Prince Charlie, and displays a selection of items emblazoned with the prince's bonnie face—including a clandestine portrait that you can only see by looking in a cylindrical mirror. Finally, the Highland Life exhibit collects a hodgepodge of tools, musical instruments (some fine old harps that were later replaced by the much louder bagpipes as the battlefield instrument of choice), and other bric-a-brac.

NEAR FORT WILLIAM

Ben Nevis

From Fort William, take a peek at Britain's highest peak, Ben Nevis (4,406 feet). Thousands walk to its summit each year. On a clear day, you can admire it from a distance. Scotland's only mountain cable cars—at the **Nevis Range Mountain Experience**—can take you to a not-very-lofty 2,150-foot perch on the slopes of Aonach Mòr for a closer look (£14, 15-minute ride, generally open daily but closed in high winds and winter—call ahead, signposted on the A-82 north of Fort William, tel. 01397/705-825, www.nevisrange. co.uk).

▲Commando Memorial

This powerful bronze ensemble of three stoic WWII commandos, standing in an evocative mountain setting, is one of Britain's most

beloved war memorials. During World War II, Winston Churchill decided that Britain needed an elite military corps. He created the British Commandos, famous for wearing green berets (an accessory—and name—later borrowed by elite fighting forces in the US and other countries). The British Commandos trained in the Lochaber region near Fort William, in the windy shadow of Ben Nevis. Many later died in combat, and this memorial—built in 1952—remembers those fallen British heroes.

Nearby is the Garden of Remembrance, honoring British Commandos who died in more recent conflicts, from the Falkland Islands to Afghanistan. It's also a popular place to spread Scottish military ashes. Taken together, these sights are a touching reminder that the US is not alone in its distant wars. Every nation has its share of honored heroes willing to sacrifice for what they believe to be the greater good.

Getting There: The memorial is about nine miles outside of Fort William, on the way to Inverness (just outside Spean Bridge); see "Route Tips for Drivers" on page 290.

Sleeping and Eating in Fort William

Sleeping: The Hobbit-cute **$ Gowan Brae B&B** ("Hill of the Big Daisy") has an antique-filled dining room and three rooms with loch or garden views (one room has private bath down the hall, cash only, 2-night minimum July-Aug, on Union Road—a 5-minute walk up the hill above High Street, tel. 01397/704-399, www. gowanbrae.co.uk, gowan_brae@btinternet.com, Jim and Ann Clark).

Eating: These places are on traffic-free High Street, near the start of town. For lunch and picnics, try **$ Deli Craft,** with good, made-to-order deli sandwiches and other prepared foods (61 High Street, tel. 01397/698-100), or **$ Hot Roast Company,** which sells beef, turkey, ham, or pork sandwiches topped with some tasty extras, along with soup, salad, and coleslaw (127 High Street, tel. 01397/700-606).

For lunch or dinner, **$$ The Grog & Gruel** serves real ales, good pub grub, and Tex-Mex and Cajun dishes, with some unusual choices such as burgers made from boar and haggis or Highland venison. There's also a variety of "grog dogs" (66 High Street, tel. 01397/705-078).

Fort William Connections

Fort William is a major transit hub for the Highlands, so you'll likely change buses here at some point during your trip.

From Fort William by Bus to: Glencoe or **Ballachulish** (all Glasgow-bound buses—#914, #915, and #916; 8/day, 30 minutes; also Stagecoach bus #44, hourly, fewer on Sun), **Oban** (bus #918, 2/day, 1.5 hours), **Portree** on the Isle of Skye (buses #914, #915, and #916, 3/day, 3 hours), **Inverness** (buses #19 and #919, 7/day, 2 hours), **Glasgow** (buses #914, #915, and #916; 8/day, 3 hours). To reach **Edinburgh,** take the bus to Glasgow, then transfer to a train or bus (figure 5 hours total). Citylink: tel. 0871-266-3333, www.citylink.co.uk. Stagecoach: tel. 01397/702-373, www.stagecoachbus.com.

From Fort William by Train to: Glasgow (3/day, 4 hours), **Mallaig** and ferry to Isle of Skye (4/day, 1.5 hours). Also see the listing for the Jacobite Steam Train on page 294.

ROUTE TIPS FOR DRIVERS
From Fort William to Loch Ness and Inverness: Head north out of Fort William on the A-82. After about eight miles, in the village of Spean Bridge, take the left fork (staying on the A-82). About a mile later, on the left, keep an eye out for the **Commando Memorial** (described earlier and worth a quick stop). From here, the A-82 sweeps north and follows the Caledonian Canal, passing through **Fort Augustus** (a good lunch stop, with its worthwhile Caledonian Canal Visitor Centre), and then follows the north side of Loch Ness on its way to Inverness. Along the way, the A-82 passes **Urquhart Castle** and two **Loch Ness Monster exhibits** in Drumnadrochit (described in the Inverness & Loch Ness chapter).

From Oban to Fort William via Glencoe: See page 254 in the Oban chapter.

From Fort William to the Isle of Skye: You have two options: Head west on the A-830 through **Glenfinnan,** then catch the ferry from Mallaig to Armadale on the Isle of Skye (this "Road to the Isles" area is described in the next section). Or, head north on the A-82 to Invergarry, and turn left (west) on the A-87, which you'll follow (past **Eilean Donan Castle**) to Kyle of Lochalsh and the

Skye Bridge to the island. Consider using one route one way, and the other on the return trip.

The Road to the Isles

Between Fort William and the Isle of Skye lies a rugged landscape with close ties to the Jacobite rebellions. It was here that Bonnie Prince Charlie first set foot on Scottish soil in 1745, in his attempt to regain the British throne for his father. The village of Glenfinnan, about 30 minutes west of Fort William, is where he first raised the Stuart family standard—and an army of Highlanders. Farther west, the landscape grows even more rugged, offering off-shore glimpses of the Hebrides. It's all tied together by a pretty, meandering road—laid out by the great Scottish civil engineer Thomas Telford—that's evocatively (and aptly) named "The Road to the Isles." While these sights aren't worth going out of your way to see, they're ideal for those heading to the Isle of Skye (via the Mallaig-Armadale ferry), or for those who'd enjoy taking the so-called "Harry Potter train" through a Hogwartian landscape.

If you're driving, be sure you allow enough time to make it to Mallaig at least 20 minutes before the Skye ferry departs (figure at least 90 minutes of driving time from Fort William to the ferry, not including stops). In summer it's smart to reserve a spot on the ferry the day before, either online or by phone. For more tips on the Mallaig-Armadale ferry, see "Getting to the Isle of Skye" on page 352.

Sights on the Road to the Isles

I've connected these sights with some commentary for those driving from Fort William to Mallaig for the Skye ferry. (If you're interested in the Jacobite Steam Train instead, see the end of this chapter.) In addition to the sights at Glenfinnan, this route is graced with plenty of loch-and-mountain views and, near the end, passes along a beautiful stretch of coast with some fine sandy beaches.

• *From Fort William, head north on the A-82 (signed Inverness and Mallaig). At the big roundabout (where you'll see the tempting Ben Nevis Whisky Distillery with a visitors center), turn left onto the A-830 (marked for Mallaig and Glenfinnan). You'll pass a big sign listing the next Skye ferry departure. Just after, you'll cross a bridge; look up and to the right to see Neptune's Staircase. There's a park-like viewing zone on the right.*

Neptune's Staircase

This network of eight stair-step locks, designed by Thomas Telford in the early 19th century, offers a handy look at the ingenious locks of the Caledonian Canal.

For more on this remarkable engineering accomplishment—which combined natural lochs with man-made locks and canals to connect Scotland's east and west coasts—see the sidebar on page 323. Engineers might want to pull over just after the bridge (well marked) to stroll around the locks for a closer look, but the rest of us can pretty much get the gist from the road.

• *Continue west on the A-830 for another 14 miles, much of it along Loch Eil. Soon you'll reach a big parking lot and visitors center at...*

▲Glenfinnan

In the summer of 1745, Bonnie Prince Charlie—grandson of James VII of Scotland (and II of England), who was kicked off the British throne in 1688—arrived at Glenfinnan...and waited. He had journeyed a long way to this point, sailing from France by way of the Scottish Isle of Eriskay, and finally making landfall at Loch nan Uamh (just west of here). For the first time in his life, he set foot on his ancestral homeland...the land he hoped that, with his help, his father would soon rule. But to reclaim the thrones of England and Scotland for the Stuart line, the fresh-faced, 24-year-old prince would need the support of the Highlanders. And here at Glenfinnan, he held his breath at the moment of truth. Would the Highland clans come to his aid?

As Charlie waited, gradually he began to hear the drone of bagpipes filtering through the forest. And then, the clan chiefs appeared: MacDonalds. Camerons. MacDonnells. McPhees. They had been holding back—watching and waiting, to make sure they weren't the only ones. Before long, the prince felt confident that he'd reached a clan quorum. And so, here at Glenfinnan, on August 19, 1745, Bonnie Prince Charlie raised his royal standard—officially kicking off the armed Jacobite rebellion that came to be known as "The '45." Two days later, Charlie and his 1,500 clansmen compatriots headed south to fight for control of Scotland. (Sadly, Glenfinnan is also the place where Bonnie Prince Charlie retreated eight months later, after his campaign's crushing defeat at Culloden—see page 313.)

Today Glenfinnan, which still echoes with history, is a wide spot in the road with a big visitors center and two landmarks: a monument to Bonnie Prince Charlie's raising of the standard, and a railroad viaduct made famous by the Hogwarts Express.

Visiting Glenfinnan: Pay £2 to park your car, then head into the **visitors center** (free, daily July-Aug 9:30-17:30, April-June and Sept-Oct 10:00-17:00, closed Nov-March, café, WCs, tel. 0844-493-2221).

The **Jacobite Exhibit** inside the visitors center is small but enlightening, using modern exhibits to explain the story of Bonnie Prince Charlie and "The '45."

The **Glenfinnan Viaduct,** with 416 yards of raised track over 21 supporting arches, is visible from the parking lot. But if you have time, it's worth hiking 10 minutes up the adjacent hill for much better views. Find the well-marked, steeply switch-backed path behind the visitors center and huff on up. From the viewpoint, you'll enjoy sweeping (if distant) views of the viaduct in one direction, and the monument and banks of Loch Shiel in the other. You may even catch a glimpse of the Jacobite Steam Train chugging along (described later).

The **Glenfinnan Monument,** between the visitors center and the loch, is a pillar capped with a stirring statue of a kilted "Unknown Highlander" standing below the standard. (From here you can see the viaduct and the viewpoint above the visitors center.)

• *Carrying on west along the A-830, the scenery grows more rugged. Shortly you'll begin to catch glimpses of silver sand beaches at the heads of the rocky lochs. (If catching a ferry, figure 50 minutes' drive from Glenfinnan to Mallaig.) Soon you'll reach the village of...*

Arisaig

While there's not much to see in this village, it has an interesting history. Gaelic for "safe place," Arisaig has provided shelter for many seafarers—including the real Long John Silver (Robert Louis Stevenson was inspired by tales from his father, who was an engineer who built lighthouses here). In the 20th century, remote Arisaig was a secret training ground for WWII-era spies. The "Special Operations Executive" prepared brave men and women here for clandestine operations in Nazi-occupied Europe.

• *Around Arisaig, signs for the Alternative Coastal Route direct you to the B-8008, which parallels the A-830 highway the rest of the way (7 miles) to Mallaig. If you've got ample time to kill, consider taking these* *back roads for a more scenic approach to the end of the road. Either way, you'll end up at **Mallaig** and the **Skye Ferry**.*

The Jacobite Steam Train

The West Highland Railway Line chugs 42 miles from Fort William west to the ferry port at Mallaig. This train (they don't actually call it the "Hogwarts Express") offers a small taste of the Harry Potter experience...but it may be a letdown for those who take this trip only for its wizarding connections. Although one of the steam engines and some of the coaches were used in the films, don't expect a Harry Potter theme ride. However, you can expect beautiful scenery. Along the way, the train stops for 20 minutes at Glenfinnan Station (just after the Glenfinnan Viaduct), and then gives you too much time (1.75 hours) to poke around the dull port town of Mallaig before heading back to Fort William.

Cost and Hours: One-way-£30; round-trip-£35; more for first class, tickets must be purchased in advance—see details next, 1/day Mon-Fri mid-May-Oct, 2/day Mon-Fri early June-Aug, also 1/day Sat-Sun late-June-late-Sept, departs Fort William at 10:15 and returns at 16:00, afternoon service in summer departs Fort William at 14:30 and returns at 20:30, about a 2-hour ride each way, tel. 0844-850-4680, www.jacobitetrain.com. Pay lockers for storing luggage are at the Fort William train station (station open long hours daily).

Prebooking Tickets: Trains leave from Fort William's train station, but you must book ahead online or by phone—you cannot buy tickets for this train at ticket offices. A limited number of seats may be available each day on a first-come, first-served basis (cash only, buy from conductor at coach D), but in summer, trips are often sold out. Rail passes are not accepted.

Cheaper Alternative: The 84-mile round-trip from Fort William takes the better part of a day to show you the same scenery twice. Modern "Sprinter" trains follow the same line and accept rail passes. Consider taking the steam train one-way to Mallaig, then speeding back on a regular train to avoid the long Mallaig layover and slow return (£12.50 one-way between Fort William and Mallaig, 4/day, 1.5 hours, to ensure a seat in peak season book by 18:00 the day before, tel. 0845-755-0033, www.nationalrail.co.uk).

Skye Connection: Note that you can use either the steam train or the Sprinter to reach the Isle of Skye: Take the train to Mallaig, walk onto the ferry to Armadale (on Skye), then catch a bus in Armadale to your destination on Skye (bus #52, www.stagecoachbus.com).

INVERNESS & LOCH NESS

*Inverness • Culloden Battlefield • Clava Cairns •
Loch Ness*

Inverness, the Highlands' de facto capital, is an almost-unavoidable stop on the Scottish tourist circuit. It's a pleasant town and an ideal springboard for some of the country's most famous sights. Hear the music of the Highlands in Inverness and the echo of muskets at Culloden, where government troops drove Bonnie Prince Charlie into exile and conquered his Jacobite supporters. Ponder the mysteries of Scotland's murky prehistoric past at Clava Cairns, and enjoy a peek at Highland aristocratic life at Cawdor Castle. Just to the southwest of Inverness, explore the locks and lochs of the Caledonian Canal while playing hide-and-seek with the Loch Ness monster.

PLANNING YOUR TIME

Though it has little in the way of sights, Inverness does have a workaday charm and is a handy spot to spend a night or two between other Highland destinations. With two nights, you can find a full day's worth of sightseeing nearby.

Note that Loch Ness is between Inverness and Oban, Glencoe, and the Isle of Skye. If you're heading to or from one of those places, it makes sense to see Loch Ness en route, rather than as a side-trip from Inverness.

GETTING AROUND THE HIGHLANDS

With a car, the day trips around Inverness are easy. Without a car, you can get to Inverness by train (better from Edinburgh, Stirling, Glasgow, or Pitlochry) or by bus (better from Skye, Oban, and Glencoe), then side-trip to Loch Ness, Culloden, and other nearby sights by public bus or with a package tour.

Inverness

Inverness is situated on the River Ness at the base of a castle (now

used as a courthouse, but with a public viewpoint). Inverness' charm is its normalcy—it's a nice, midsize Scottish city that gives you a palatable taste of the "urban" Highlands and a contrast to cutesy tourist towns. It has a disheveled, ruddy-cheeked grittiness and is well located for enjoying the surrounding countryside sights. Check out the bustling, pedestrianized downtown, or meander the picnic-friendly riverside paths and islands—best at sunset, when the light hits the castle and couples hold hands while strolling along the water and over its footbridges.

Orientation to Inverness

Inverness, with about 70,000 people, has been one of the fastest-growing areas of Scotland in recent years. Marked by its castle,

Inverness clusters along the River Ness. The TI is on High Street, an appealing pedestrian shopping zone a few blocks away from the river; nearby are the train and bus stations. Most of my recommended B&Bs huddle atop a gentle hill behind the castle (a 10-minute uphill walk from the city center).

TOURIST INFORMATION

At the TI, you can pick up the self-guided *City Centre Trail* walking-tour leaflet and the *What's On* weekly events sheet (June-Sept Mon-Sat 8:45-18:30, shorter hours on Sun and off-season, free Wi-Fi, 36 High Street, tel. 01463/252-401, www.inverness-scotland.com).

HELPFUL HINTS

Charity Shops: Inverness is home to several pop-up charity shops. Occupying vacant rental spaces, these are staffed by volunteers who are happy to talk about their philanthropy. You can pick up a memorable knickknack, adjust your wardrobe for the weather, and learn about local causes.

Festivals and Events: The summer is busy with special events, which can make it tricky to find a room. Book far ahead during these times, including the Etape Loch Ness bike race (early June), Highland Games (late June), Belladrum Tartan Heart Festival (music, late July), Black Isle farm show (early Aug), and Loch Ness Marathon (late Sept). The big RockNess Music Festival has been on hiatus due to budget cuts, but may return.

For a real Highland treat, catch a **shinty match** (a combination of field hockey, hurling, and American football—but without pads). Inverness Shinty Club plays at Bught Park, along Ness Walk (the TI or your B&B can tell you if there are any matches on, or search online for the Inverness Shinty Club.

Bookstore: Leakey's Bookshop, located in a converted church built in 1649, is the place to browse through teetering towers of musty old books and vintage maps, warm up by the wood-burning stove, and climb the spiral staircase to the loft for views over the stacks (Mon-Sat 10:00-17:30, closed Sun, Church Street, tel. 01463/239-947, Charles Leakey).

Baggage Storage: The train station has lockers (open Mon-Sat 6:40-20:30, Sun from 10:40), or you can leave your bag at the bus station's ticket desk (small fee, daily until 17:30).

Laundry: New City Launderette is near the west end of the Ness Bridge (self-service or same-day full-service, Mon-Sat 8:00-18:00, until 20:00 Mon-Fri in summer, Sun 10:00-16:00 year-round, last load one hour before closing, 17 Young Street, tel. 01463/242-507). **Thirty Degrees Laundry** on Church Street is another option (full-service only, drop off before 10:00 for same-day service, Mon-Sat 8:30-17:30, closed Sun, a few blocks beyond Victorian Market at 84 Church Street, tel. 01463/710-380).

Tours in Inverness

IN TOWN

Skip the City Sightseeing hop-on, hop-off bus tour (this format doesn't work in Inverness).

Inverness Bike Tours

Hardworking Alison leads small groups on two-hour bike tours. Her six-mile route is nearly all on traffic-free paths along canals and lochs outside of the city and comes with light guiding along the way. You'll pedal through Ness Island, stop at the Botanical

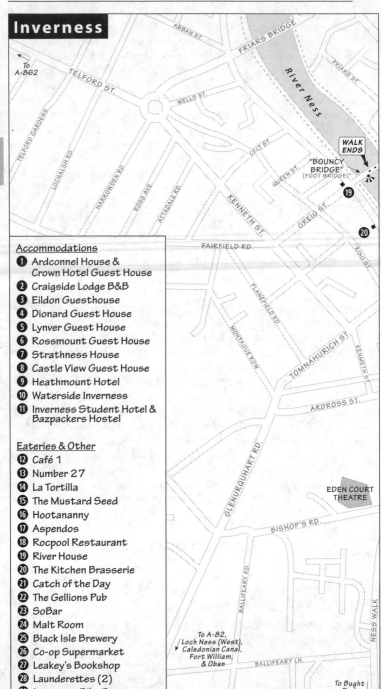

INVERNESS & LOCH NESS

Inverness

ABBAN ST.

FRIARS BRIDGE

To A-862

TELFORD ST.

WELLS ST.

River Ness

FRIARS ST.

TELFORD GARDENS

LOCHALSH RD.

HARROWDEN RD.

ROSS AVE.

ATTADALE RD.

CELT ST.

WALK ENDS

"BOUNCY BRIDGE" (FOOT BRIDGE)

QUEEN ST.

KENNETH ST.

GREIG ST.

19

20

KING ST.

FAIRFIELD RD.

PLANEFIELD RD.

MONTAGUE ROW

TOMNAHURICH ST.

KENNETH ST.

ARDROSS ST.

EDEN COURT THEATRE

GLENURQUHART RD.

BISHOP'S RD.

BALLIFEARY RD.

NESS WALK

To A-82, Loch Ness (West), Caledonian Canal, Fort William, & Oban

BALLIFEARY LN.

To Bught Park

Accommodations

1. Ardconnel House & Crown Hotel Guest House
2. Craigside Lodge B&B
3. Eildon Guesthouse
4. Dionard Guest House
5. Lynver Guest House
6. Rossmount Guest House
7. Strathness House
8. Castle View Guest House
9. Heathmount Hotel
10. Waterside Inverness
11. Inverness Student Hotel & Bazpackers Hostel

Eateries & Other

12. Café 1
13. Number 27
14. La Tortilla
15. The Mustard Seed
16. Hootananny
17. Aspendos
18. Rocpool Restaurant
19. River House
20. The Kitchen Brasserie
21. Catch of the Day
22. The Gellions Pub
23. SoBar
24. Malt Room
25. Black Isle Brewery
26. Co-op Supermarket
27. Leakey's Bookshop
28. Launderettes (2)
29. Inverness Bike Tours

INVERNESS & LOCH NESS

Gardens, ride along the Caledonian Canal with its system of locks (you may even catch a boat passing through the locks), and cycle through a nature preserve (£21, no kids under 14, 10-person max; daily in season at 10:00, 13:00, and 16:00; best to book a spot in advance online, goes even in light rain, meet near west end of Ness Bridge at Riva Restaurant at 5 Ness Walk, call or text mobile 07443-866-619, www.invernessbiketours.co.uk, info@invernessbiketours.co.uk). Arrive a bit early to size up your bike and helmet.

EXCURSIONS FROM INVERNESS

While thin on sights of its own, Inverness is a great home base for day trips. A variety of tour companies offer day trips—details and tickets are available at the TI. While the big sellers among Inverness day-trips are the many Loch Ness tours (because the monster is on every bucket list), I far prefer an Isle of Skye all-day joyride—which gives you a good look at Loch Ness and its famous castle along the way. Study the various websites for comparative details. For Isle of Skye and Orkney Island tours in summer, it's a good idea to book about a week in advance.

Loch Ness

The famous lake is just a 20-minute drive from Inverness. Tours will often include a short boat ride, a visit to the Urquhart Castle, and a stop at the Loch Ness monster exhibits. The lake is not particularly scenic. The castle, while scenic, is just a shell. And the monster is mostly a promotional gimmick. Still, if you have no car, this can be the most efficient way to check this off your list. **Jacobite Tours** focuses on trips that include Loch Ness, from a one-hour basic boat ride to a 6.5-hour extravaganza. Their four-hour "Sensation" tour includes a guided bus tour with live narration, a half-hour Loch Ness cruise, and visits to Urquhart Castle and the Loch Ness exhibits (£35, for more options see www.jacobite.co.uk, tel. 01463/233-999).

Isle of Skye

Several companies do good day tours to the Isle of Skye. They travel 110 miles (a 2.5-hour drive) to the heart of Skye (Portree). With about six hours of driving, and one hour for lunch in Portree, that leaves two or three hours for a handful of quick and scenic photo stops. All travel along Loch Ness so you can see Urquhart Castle and try for a monster sighting. And all stop for a view of Eilean Donan Castle. The longer rides loop around the Trotternish Peninsula. Websites explain the exact itineraries.

Wow Scotland's ambitious 12-hour itinerary goes in a big bus. They depart at 8:30 from the Inverness bus station and include short but smart and adequate stops all along the way (£77, 5/week June-Aug, fewer departures in April-May and Sept, none

Oct-March, tel. 01808/511-773, www.wowscotlandtours.com). I'd pay the extra for the £99 front row.

Highland Experience Tours runs another, shorter Isle of Skye itinerary in 24-seat buses (daily April-Oct, less off-season, 10 hours) but doesn't make it as far north as the Trotternish Peninsula (£55, tel. 01463/719-222, www.highlandexperience.com). They offer a variety of other daylong tours, including to the far north with John O'Groats, or a trip to Royal Deeside and the Speyside Whisky Trail.

Happy Tours Scotland organizes daily minibus tours on a 10-hour joy ride (getting all the way to Quiraing) with top-notch guides (£70, 8 people per minibus, daily at 8:30, leaves from 7 Ness Walk at Columba Hotel, mobile 07828-154-683, book at www.happy-tours.biz, run by Cameron). They also do other tours including itineraries focusing on Loch Ness, the *Outlander* books and TV series, a Speyside whisky tour, and private minibus tours.

Rabbie's Small Group Tours does 12-hour trips to Skye in its 16-seater buses for £52 nearly daily from Inverness. Their website explains their busy program (www.rabbies.com).

Iona Highland Tours takes eight people on several different Isle of Skye itineraries, including one that allows hiking time at the Fairy Pools (£70, 9 hours, tel. 01463/250-457, www.ionahighlandtours.com).

By Train Then Tour: To avoid a long bus ride or skip the sights along the way to Skye, take the train from Inverness to Kyle of Lochalsh, where a Skye-based tour company will pick you up and take you around. Try **Skye Tours** (tel. 01471/822-716, www.skye-tours.co.uk) or **Tour Skye** (tel. 01478/613-514, www.tourskye.com). The train leaves Inverness before 9:00 and arrives around 11:30; the return train is around 17:15 (covered by BritRail Pass).

The Orkney Islands

For a very ambitious itinerary, John O'Groats Ferries offers an all-day tour that departs Inverness at 7:15, drives you up to John O'Groats to catch the 40-minute passenger ferry, then a second bus takes you on a whistle-stop tour of Orkney's main attractions (with an hour in the town of Kirkwall) before returning you to Inverness by 21:00. While it's a long day, it's an efficient use of your time if you're determined to see Orkney (£74, daily June-Aug only, tel. 01955/611-353, www.jogferry.co.uk).

Inverness Walk

Humble Inverness has meager conventional sights, but its fun history and quirky charm become clear as you take this short self-guided walk (walk route shown on map earlier in this chapter).

INVERNESS & LOCH NESS

• *Start at the clock tower.*

Clock Tower: Notice the **Gaelic language** on directional and street signs all around you. While nobody speaks Gaelic as a first language (and only about 60,000 Scottish people speak it fluently), this old Celtic language symbolizes the strength of Scottish Highland culture.

The clock tower looming 130 feet above you is all that remains of a tollbooth building erected in 1791. This is the highest spire in town, and for generations was a collection point for local taxes. Here, four streets—Church, Castle, Bridge, and High—come together, integrating God, defense, and trade—everything necessary for a fine city.

About 800 years ago, a castle was built on the bluff overhead and the town of Inverness coalesced right about here. For centuries, this backwater town's economy was based on cottage industries. Artisans who made things also sold them. In 1854, the train arrived, injecting energy and money from Edinburgh and Glasgow, and the Victorian boom hit. With the Industrial Age came wholesalers, distributors, mass production, and affluence. Much of the city was built during this era, in Neo-Gothic style—over-the-top and fanciful, like the City Hall (from 1882, kitty-corner to the clock tower). With the Victorian Age also came tourism.

Look for the **Bible quotes** chiseled into the wall across the street from the City Hall. A civic leader, tired of his council members being drunkards, edited

these Bible verses for maximum impact, especially the bottom two.

Hiding just up the hill (behind the eyesore concrete home of the Inverness Museum and Art Gallery) is **Inverness Castle.** While the "castle" is now a courthouse, there is a small exhibition and a chance to climb to the top of the tower (£5). It's worth hiking up to the castle at some point during your visit to enjoy some of the best views of Inverness and its river. The courthouse in the castle doesn't see a lot of action. In the last few decades, there have been only two murders to prosecute. As locals like to say, "no guns, no problems." While hunters can own a gun, gun ownership in Scotland is complicated and tightly regulated.

• *Walk a few steps away from the river (toward McDonald's)...*

Mercat Cross and Old Town Center: Standing in front of the City Hall is a well-worn mercat cross, which designated the market in centuries past. This is where the townspeople gathered to hear important proclamations, share news, watch hangings, gossip, and so on. The scant remains of a prehistoric stone at the base of the cross are what's left of Inverness' "Stone of Destiny." According to tradition, whenever someone moved away from Inverness, they'd take a tiny bit of home with them in the form of a chip of this stone—so it's been chipped and pecked almost to oblivion.

The yellow **Caledonian** building faces McDonald's at the base of High Street. (Caledonia was the ancient Roman name for Scotland.) It was built in 1847, complete with Corinthian columns and a Greek-style pediment, as the leading bank in town, back when banks were designed to hold the money of the rich and powerful... and intimidate working blokes. Notice how nicely pedestrianized High Street welcomes people and seagulls...but not cars.

• *Next we'll head up Church Street, which begins between the clock tower and The Caledonian.*

Church Street: The street art you'll trip over at the start of Church Street is called *Earthquake*— a reminder of the quake that hit Inverness in 1816. As the slabs explain, the town's motto is "Open Heartedness, Insight, and Perseverance."

Stroll down Church Street. Look up above the modern store fronts to see Old World facades. **Union Street** (the second corner on the right)—stately, symmetrical, and Neoclassical—was the fanciest street in the Highlands when it was built in the 19th century. Its buildings had indoor toilets. That was big news.

Midway down the next block of Church Street (on the right), an alley marked by an ugly white canopy leads to the **Victorian**

Market. Venturing down the alley, you'll pass **The Malt Room** (a small and friendly whisky bar eager to teach you to appreciate Scotland's national tipple; see "Nightlife in Inverness") and **The Old Market Bar** (a dive bar worth a peek). Stepping into the Victorian Market, you'll find a gallery of shops under an iron-and glass domed roof dating from 1876. The first section seems abandoned, but delve deeper to find some more active areas, where local shops mix with tacky "tartan tat" souvenir stands. If you're seriously into bagpipes, look for **Cabar Fèidh,** where American expat

Brian sells CDs and sheet music, and repairs and maintains the precious instruments of local musicians.

Go back out of the market the way you came in, and continue down Church Street. At the next corner you come to **Hootananny,** famous locally for its live music (pop in to see what's on tonight). Just past that is **Abertarff House,** the oldest house in Inverness. It was the talk of the town in 1593 for its "turnpike" (spiral staircase) connecting the floors.

Continue about a block farther along Church Street. The lane on the left leads to the **"Bouncy Bridge"** (where we'll finish this walk). Opposite that lane (on the right) is **Dunbar's Hospital,** with four-foot-thick walls. In 1668, Alexander Dunbar was a wealthy landowner who built this as a poor folks' home. You can almost read the auld script in his coat of arms above the door.

A few steps farther up Church Street, walk through the iron gate on the left and into the churchyard (we're focusing on the shorter church on the right—ignore the bigger one on the left). Looking at the WWI and WWII memorials on the church's wall, it's clear which war hit Scotland harder. While no one famous is buried here, many tombstones go back to the 1700s. Being careful not to step on a rabbit, head for the bluff overlooking the river and turn around to see...

Old High Church: There are a lot of churches in Inverness (46 Protestant, 2 Catholic, 2 Gaelic-language, and one offering a Mass in Polish), but these days, most are used for other purposes. This one, dating from the 11th century, is the most historic (but is generally closed). It was built on what was likely the site of a pagan holy ground. Early Christians called upon St. Michael to take the fire out of pagan spirits, so it only made sense that the first Christians would build their church here and dedicate the spot as St. Michael's Mount.

In the sixth century, the Irish evangelist monk St. Columba brought Christianity to northern England, the Scottish islands (at Iona), and the Scottish Highlands (in Inverness). He stood here amongst the pagans and preached to King Brude and the Picts.

Study the bell tower from the 1600s. The small door to nowhere (one floor up) indicates that back before the castle offered protection, this tower was the place of last refuge for townsfolk under attack. They'd gather inside and pull up the ladder. The church became a prison for Jacobites after the Battle of Culloden, and executions were carried out in the churchyard.

Every night at 20:00, the bell in the tower rings 100 times. It has rung like this since 1730 to remind townsfolk that it's dangerous to be out after dinner.

• From here, you can circle back to the lane leading to the "Bouncy Bridge" and then hike out onto the bridge. Or you can just survey the countryside from this bluff.

The River Ness: Emptying out of Loch Ness and flowing seven miles to the sea (a mile from here), this is one of the shortest rivers in the country. While it's shallow (you can almost walk across it), there are plenty of fish in it. A 64-pound salmon was once pulled out of the river right here. In the 19th century, Inverness was smaller, and across the river stretched nothing but open fields. Then, with the Victorian boom, the suspension footbridge (a.k.a. "Bouncy Bridge") was built in 1881 to connect new construction across the river with the town.

• Your tour is over. Inverness is yours to explore.

Sights in Inverness

Inverness Museum and Art Gallery

This free, likable town museum is worth poking around on a rainy day to get a taste of Inverness and the Highlands. The ground-floor exhibits on geology and archaeology peel back the layers of Highland history: Bronze and Iron ages, Picts (including some carved stones), Scots, Vikings, and Normans. Upstairs you'll find the "social history" exhibit (everything from Scottish nationalism to hunting and fishing) and temporary art exhibits.

Cost and Hours: Free, April-Oct Tue-Sat 10:00-17:00, shorter hours off-season, closed Sun-Mon year-round, cheap café, in the ugly modern building on the way up to the castle, tel. 01463/237-114, www.highlifehighland.com.

Inverness Castle

Aside from nice views from the front lawn, a small exhibition on the ground floor, and a tower climb, Inverness' biggest nonsight is not open to the public. A wooden fortress that stood on this spot was replaced by a stone structure in the 15th century. In 1715, that castle was named Fort George to assert English control over the area. In 1745, it was destroyed by Bonnie Prince Charlie's Jacobite army and remained a ruin until the 1830s, when the present castle was built. The statue outside (from 1899) depicts Flora MacDonald, who helped Bonnie Prince Charlie escape from the English (see page 372). The castle was built as the courthouse, and when trials are in session, loutish-looking men hang out here, waiting for their bewigged barristers to arrive. For £5 you can climb to the top of the tower for a commanding city view. In a few years, the castle will host what promises to be a top-notch new museum.

River Walks

As with most European cities, where there's a river, there's a walk. Inverness, with both the River Ness and the Caledonian Canal, does not disappoint. Consider an early-morning stroll along the Ness Bank to capture the castle at sunrise, or a post-dinner jaunt to Bught Park for a local shinty match (see "Helpful Hints—Festivals and Events," earlier). The path is lit at night. The forested islands in the middle of the River Ness—about a 10-minute walk south of the center—are a popular escape from the otherwise busy city.

Here's a good plan for your Inverness riverside constitutional: From the Ness Bridge, head along the riverbank under the castle (along the path called "Ladies Walk"). As you work your way up the river, you'll see the architecturally bold Eden Court Theatre (across the river), pass a white pedestrian bridge, see a WWI memorial, and peek into the gardens of several fine old Victorian sandstone riverfront homes. Nearing the tree-covered islands, watch for fly-fishers in hip waders on the pebbly banks. Reaching the first, skinny little island, take the bridge with the wavy, wrought-iron railing and head down the path along the middle of the island. Notice that this is part of the Great Glen Way, a footpath that stretches from here all the way to Fort William (79 miles). Enjoy this little nature break, with gurgling rapids—and, possibly, a few midges. Reaching the bigger bridge, cross it and enjoy strolling through tall forests. Continue upriver. After two more green-railinged bridges, traverse yet another island, and find one last white-iron bridge that takes you across to the opposite bank. You'll pop out at the corner of Bught Park, the site of shinty practices and games—are any going on today?

From here, you can simply head back into town on this bank. If you'd like to explore more, you could continue farther south. It's not as idyllic or as pedestrian-friendly, but in this zone you'll find minigolf, a skate park, the Highland Archive building, the free Botanic Gardens (daily 10:00-17:00, until 16:00 Nov-March), and the huge Active Inverness leisure center, loaded with amusements including a swimming pool with adventure slides, a climbing wall, a sauna and steam area, and a gymnasium (www.invernessleisure. co.uk).

Continuing west from these leisure areas, you'll eventually hit the Caledonian Canal; to the south, this parallels the River Ness, and to the north is where it meets Beauly Firth, then Moray Firth and the North Sea. From the Tomnahurich Bridge, paths on either bank allow you to walk along the Great Glen Way until you're ready to turn around.

Nightlife in Inverness

Scottish Folk Music

While you can find traditional folk-music sessions in pubs and hotel bars anywhere in town, two places are well established as *the* music pubs. Neither charges a cover for the music, unless a bigger-name band is playing.

The Gellions has live folk and Scottish music nightly (from 21:30). It has local ales on tap and brags it's the oldest bar in town (14 Bridge Street, tel. 01463/233-648, www.gellions.co.uk).

Hootananny is an energetic place with several floors of live rock, blues, or folk music, and drinking fun nightly. It's rock (upstairs) and reel (ground floor). Music in the main bar (ground floor) usually begins about 21:30 (traditional music sessions Sun-Wed, trad bands on weekends; also a daytime session on Sat afternoon at 14:30). On Friday and Saturday nights only, upstairs is the Mad Hatter's nightclub, complete with a cocktail bar (67 Church Street, tel. 01463/233-651, www.hootananny.co.uk).

Billiards and Darts

SoBar is a sprawling pub with dart boards (free but £5 deposit), pool tables (£7.50 per hour), a museum's-worth of sports memorabilia, and the biggest TV screens in town (popular on big game nights). It's a fine place to hang out and meet locals if you'd rather not have live music (just across from the castle at 55 Castle Street, tel. 01463/229-780).

Whisky Tastings and Brew Pubs

For a whisky education, or just a fine cocktail, drop in to the intimate **Malt Room,** with whiskies ranging from £4 to £75. The whisky-plus-chocolate flight makes for a fun nightcap (just off Church Street in the alley leading to the Victorian Market, 34 Church Street, tel. 01463/221-888, Lee and Matt).

At the **Black Isle Brewery,** you can sample their local organic beers and ciders. Choose from 26 beers on tap (including some non-Black Isle brews), all listed on the TV screen over the bar (wood-fired pizzas, 68 Church Street, tel. 01463/229-920).

Sleeping in Inverness

B&BS NEAR THE TOWN CENTER

These B&Bs are popular; book ahead for June through August (and during the peak times listed in "Helpful Hints," earlier), and be aware that some require a two-night minimum during busy times. The places I list are a 10-15-minute walk from the train station and town center. To get to the B&Bs, either catch a taxi (£5) or walk: From the train and bus stations, go left on Academy Street. At the first stoplight (the second if you're coming from the bus station), veer right onto Inglis Street in the pedestrian zone. Go up the Market Brae steps. At the top, turn right onto Ardconnel Street.

On or near Ardconnel Street
These places line up above Castle Street (with several recommended restaurants).

$$ Ardconnel House is a classic, traditional place offering a nice, large guest lounge, along with six spacious and comfortable rooms (family room, two-night minimum preferred in summer, no children under 10, 21 Ardconnel Street, tel. 01463/240-455, www.ardconnel-inverness.co.uk, ardconnel@gmail.com, John and Elizabeth).

$ Craigside Lodge B&B has five large rooms with tasteful modern flair, nice tartan touches, and fun stuffed-animal doorstoppers. The breakfast room is a nice place to soak up city views (family room, no kids under 8, just above Castle Street at 4 Gordon Terrace, tel. 01463/231-576, www.craigsideguesthouse.co.uk, enquiries@craigsideguesthouse.co.uk, hospitable Paul and Mandy).

$ Crown Hotel Guest House has seven pleasant rooms (two with private bath down the hall) and is a bargain if you're willing to put up with a few quirks—some dated elements and owners who are still learning the ins and outs of running a guesthouse (family room, 19 Ardconnel Street, tel. 01463/231-135, www.crownhotel-inverness.co.uk, crownhotelguesthouse@gmail.com, Munawar and Asia).

Around Old Edinburgh Road and Southside Road
These places are just a couple of minutes farther out from Castle Street and the places on Ardconnel.

$$ Eildon Guesthouse, set on a quiet corner, offers five tranquil rooms with spacious baths. The cute-as-a-button 1890s countryside brick home exudes warmth and serenity from the moment you open the gate (family rooms, 2-night minimum in summer, no kids under 10, in-room fridges, parking, 29 Old Edinburgh Road, tel. 01463/231-969, www.eildonguesthouse.co.uk, eildonguesthouse@yahoo.co.uk, Jacqueline).

$$ Dionard Guest House, wrapped in a fine hedged-in garden, has cheerful common spaces, six lovely rooms, some fun stag art, and lively hosts Gail and Anne—best friends turned business partners (family suite, in-room fridges, they'll do guest laundry for free, 39 Old Edinburgh Road, tel. 01463/233-557, www. dionardguesthouse.co.uk, enquiries@dionardguesthouse.co.uk).

$$ Lynver Guest House will make you feel spoiled, with three large, boutique-y rooms (all with sitting areas), a backyard stone patio that catches the sun, and veggie and fish options at breakfast (2-night minimum preferred in summer, no kids under 10, in-room fridges, 30 Southside Road, tel. 01463/242-906, www. lynver.co.uk, info@lynver.co.uk, Michelle and Brian).

$$ Rossmount Guest House feels like home, with its curl-up-on-the-couch lounge space, unfussy rooms (five in all), and friendly hosts (two rooms share a bath and are cheaper, 2-night minimum in summer, Argyle Street, tel. 01463/229-749, www. rossmount.co.uk, mail@rossmount.co.uk, Ruth and Robert).

B&BS ACROSS THE RIVER

$$$ Strathness House has a prime spot on the river a block from Ness Bridge. Formerly a hotel, it's a bigger place, with 12 rooms and a large ground-floor lounge, but comes with the same intimate touches of a guesthouse. They cater to all diets at breakfast, including vegan, gluten-free, halal, and kosher (family room for 3, no kids under 5, street or off-site parking, 4 Ardross Terrace, tel. 01463/232-765, www.strathnesshouse.co.uk, info@strathnesshouse.com, Joan and Javed).

$$ Castle View Guest House sits right along the River Ness at the Ness Bridge—and, true to its name, it owns smashing views of the castle. Its five big and comfy rooms (some with views) are colorfully furnished, and the delightful place is lovingly run by Eleanor (2A Ness Walk, tel. 01463/241-443, www.castleviewguesthouseinverness. com, enquiries@castleviewguesthouseinverness.com).

HOTELS

Inverness has a number of big chain hotels. These tend to charge a lot when Inverness is busy but may be worth a look if the B&Bs are full or if it's outside the main tourist season. Options include the Inverness Palace Hotel & Spa (a Best Western fancy splurge right on the river with a pool and gym), Premier Inn (River Ness location), and Mercure. The following hotels are smaller and more local.

$$$ Heathmount Hotel's understated facade hides a chic retreat for comfort-seeking travelers. Its eight elegant rooms come with unique decoration, parking, and fancy extras (family room, no elevator, restaurant, Kingsmill Road, tel. 01463/235-877, www. heathmounthotel.com, info@heathounthotel.com,).

$$$ Waterside Inverness, in a nice, peaceful location along the River Ness, has 35 crisp rooms and a river-view restaurant (parking, 19 Ness Bank, tel. 01463/233-065, www. thewatersideinverness.co.uk, info@thewatersideinverness.co.uk).

HOSTELS

For funky and cheap dorm beds near the center and the recommended Castle Street restaurants, consider these friendly side-by-side hostels, geared toward younger travelers. They're about a 12-minute walk from the train station.

¢ **Bazpackers Hostel,** a stone's throw from the castle, has a quieter, more private feel for a hostel. There are 34 beds in basic dorms (private rooms with shared bath available, reception open 7:30-23:00, no curfew, pay laundry service, 4 Culduthel Road, tel. 01463/717-663, www.bazpackershostel.co.uk, info@ bazpackershostel.co.uk). They also rent a small apartment nearby (sleeps up to 4).

¢ **Inverness Student Hotel** has 57 thin-mattressed beds in nine brightly colored rooms and a laid-back lounge with a bay window overlooking the River Ness. The knowledgeable, friendly staff welcomes any traveler over 18. Dorms are a bit grungy, but each bunk has its own playful name (breakfast extra, free tea and coffee, pay laundry service, kitchen, 8 Culduthel Road, tel. 01463/236-556, www.invernessstudenthotel.com, info@invernessstudenthotel.com).

Eating in Inverness

BY THE CASTLE

The first three eateries line Castle Street, facing the back of the castle.

$$$ **Café 1** serves up high-quality modern Scottish and international cuisine with trendy, chic bistro flair. Fresh meat from their own farm adds to an appealing menu (lunch and early-bird dinner specials until 18:45, open Mon-Fri 12:00-14:30 & 17:00-21:30, Sat from 13:00 & 18:00, closed Sun, reservations smart, 75 Castle Street, tel. 01463/226-200, www.cafe1.net).

$$ **Number 27** has a straightforward, crowd-pleasing menu that offers something for everyone—burgers, pastas, and more. The food is surprisingly elegant for this price range (daily 12:00-15:00 & 17:00-21:00, generous portions, local ales on tap, 27 Castle Street, tel. 01463/241-999).

$$ **La Tortilla** has Spanish tapas, including spicy king prawns (the house specialty). It's an appealing, colorfully tiled, and vivacious dining option that feels like Spain. With the tapas format, three family-style dishes make about one meal (daily 12:00-22:00, 99 Castle Street, tel. 01463/709-809).

IN THE TOWN CENTER

$$$$ The Mustard Seed serves Scottish food with a modern twist in an old church with a river view. It's a lively place with nice outdoor tables over the river when sunny (early specials before 19:00, daily 12:00-15:00 & 17:30-22:00, reservations smart, on the corner of Bank and Fraser Streets, 16 Fraser Street, tel. 01463/220-220, www.mustardseedrestaurant.co.uk, Matthew).

$$ Hootananny is a spacious pub with a hardwood-and-candlelight vibe and a fun menu featuring dishes one step above pub grub (food served Mon-Sat 12:00-15:00 & 17:00-20:30, dinneronly on Sun). The kitchen closes early to make way for the live music scene that takes over each night after 21:30 (see "Nightlife in Inverness," earlier).

$$ Aspendos serves up freshly prepared, delicious Turkish dishes in a spacious, dressy, and exuberantly decorated dining room (daily 12:00-21:30, 26 Queensgate, tel. 01463/711-950).

Picnic: There's a **Co-op** market with plenty of cheap picnic grub at 59 Church Street (daily until 22:00).

ACROSS THE RIVER

$$$$ Rocpool Restaurant is a hit with locals, good for a splurge, and perhaps the best place in town. Owner/chef Steven Devlin serves creative modern European food to a smart clientele in a sleek, contemporary dining room (early-bird weekday special until 18:45, open Mon-Sat 12:00-14:30 & 17:45-22:00, closed Sun, reservations essential; across Ness Bridge at 1 Ness Walk, tel. 01463/717-274, www.rocpoolrestaurant.com).

$$$$ River House, a classy, sophisticated, but unstuffy riverside place, is the brainchild of Cornishman Alfie—who prides himself on melding the seafood know-how of both Cornwall and Scotland, with a bit of Mediterranean flair (Mon-Sat 15:00-21:30, closed Mon off-season and Sun year-round, reservations smart, 1 Greig Street, tel. 01463/222-033, www.riverhouseinverness.co.uk).

$$$ The Kitchen Brasserie is a modern building overlooking the river, popular for their homemade comfort food—pizza, pasta, and burgers (early-bird special until 19:00, daily 12:00-15:00 & 17:00-22:00, 15 Huntly Street, tel. 01463/259-119, www.kitchenrestaurant.co.uk, Christine).

Fish-and-Chips: Consider the **$ Catch of the Day** chippy for a nicely presented sit-down meal or to go (daily 12:00-14:00 & 16:30-22:00, closed Sun at lunch, a block over Ness Bridge on Young Street, mobile 07909-966-525).

Inverness Connections

From Inverness by Train to: Pitlochry (hourly, 1.5 hours), **Stirling** (every 1-2 hours, 3 hours, some transfer in Perth), **Kyle of Lochalsh** near Isle of Skye (4/day, 2.5 hours), **Edinburgh** (hourly, 4 hours, some with change in Perth), **Glasgow** (11/day, 3 hours, 4 direct, others change in Perth), **Thurso** (for ferries to Orkney; 4/day, 4 hours). The Caledonian Sleeper provides overnight service to **London** (www.sleeper.scot). Train info: tel. 0345-748-4950, www.nationalrail.co.uk.

By Bus: Inverness has a handy direct bus to **Portree** on the Isle of Skye (bus #917, 3/day, 3 hours), but for other destinations in western Scotland, you'll first head for **Fort William** (bus #19 or #919, 8/day, 2 hours). For connections onward to **Oban** (figure 4 hours total) or **Glencoe** (3 hours total), see "Fort William Connections" on page 290. Inverness is also connected by direct bus to **Edinburgh** (express bus #G90, 2/day, 3.5 hours; slower bus #M90, 6/day, 4 hours) and **Glasgow** (5/day on Citylink express bus #G10, 3 hours; 1/day direct on National Express #588, 4 hours). Scottish Citylink: www.citylink.co.uk.

Tickets are sold in advance online, by phone at tel. 0871-266-3333, or in person at the Inverness bus station (daily 7:45-18:15, baggage storage, 2 blocks from train station on Margaret Street, tel. 01463/233-371). For bus travel to England, check National Express (www.nationalexpress.com) or Megabus (http://uk.megabus.com).

ROUTE TIPS FOR DRIVERS

Inverness to Edinburgh (160 miles, 3.25 hours minimum): Leaving Inverness, follow signs to the A-9 (south, toward Perth). If you haven't seen the Culloden Battlefield yet (described later), it's an easy detour: Just as you leave Inverness, head four miles east off the A-9 on the B-9006. Back on the A-9, it's a wonderfully speedy, scenic highway (A-9, M-90, A-90) all the way to Edinburgh. If you have time, consider stopping en route in Pitlochry (just off the A-9; see the Eastern Scotland chapter).

Inverness to Portree, Isle of Skye (110 miles, 2.5 hours): The drive from Inverness to Skye is pretty but much less so than the valley of Glencoe or the Isle of Skye itself. You'll drive along boring Loch Ness and then follow signs to Portree and Skye on A-87 along Loch Cluanie (a loch tamed by a dam built to generate hydroelectric power). This valley was once a "drovers' route" for the cattle drive from the islands to the market—home of the original Scottish cowboys.

Inverness to Fort William (65 miles, 1.5 hours): This city, southwest of Inverness via the A-82, is a good gateway to Oban and Glencoe. See page 290.

Near Inverness

Inverness puts you in the heart of the Highlands, within easy striking distance of several famous and worthwhile sights: Commune with the Scottish soul at the historic Culloden Battlefield, where British history reached a turning point. Wonder at three mysterious Neolithic cairns, which remind visitors that Scotland's story goes back thousands of years. And enjoy a homey country castle at Cawdor. Loch Ness—with its elusive monster—is another popular and easy day trip.

In addition to the sights in this section, note that the Speyside Whisky Trail, the Leault Working Sheepdogs farm show, and the Highland Folk Museum are also within side-tripping distance of Inverness (all are covered in the Eastern Scotland chapter).

CULLODEN BATTLEFIELD

Jacobite troops under Bonnie Prince Charlie were defeated at Culloden (kuh-LAW-dehn) by supporters of the Hanover dynasty (King George II's family) in 1746. Sort of the "Scottish Alamo," this last major land battle fought on British soil spelled the end of Jacobite resistance and the beginning of the clan chiefs' fall from power. Wandering the desolate, solemn battlefield, you sense that something terrible occurred here. Locals still bring white roses and speak of "The '45" (as Bonnie Prince Charlie's entire campaign is called) as if it just happened. The battlefield at Culloden and its high-tech visitors center together are worth ▲▲▲.

Orientation to Culloden

Cost and Hours: £11, £5 guidebook; daily April-Oct 9:00-17:30, June-Aug until 18:00, Nov-Dec and Feb-March 10:00-16:00, closed Jan, café, tel. 01463/796-090, http://www.nts.org.uk/culloden.

Tours: The included **audioguide** leads you through both the exhibition and the battlefield. There are several free tours daily along with costumed events (see schedule posted at entry).

Getting There: It's a 15-minute **drive** east of Inverness. Follow signs to *Aberdeen*, then *Culloden Moor*—the B-9006 takes you right there (well-signed on the right-hand side). Parking is £2. Public **buses** leave from Inverness' Queensgate Street and drop you off in front of the entrance (£5 round-trip ticket, bus #5, roughly hourly, 40 minutes, ask at TI for route/schedule updates). A **taxi** costs around £15 one-way.

Length of This Tour: Allow 2 hours.

Background

The Battle of Culloden (April 16, 1746) marks the steep decline of the Scottish Highland clans and the start of years of cruel repression of Highland culture by the British. It was the culmination of a year's worth of battles, and at the center of it all was the charismatic, enigmatic Bonnie Prince Charlie (1720-1788).

Charles Edward Stuart, from his first breath, was raised with a single purpose—to restore his family to the British throne. His grandfather was King James II (VII of Scotland), deposed in 1688 by the English Parliament for his tyranny and pro-Catholic bias. The Stuarts remained in exile in France and Italy, until 1745, when young Charlie crossed the Channel from France to retake the throne in the name of his father (James VIII and III to his supporters). He landed on the west coast of Scotland and rallied support for the Jacobite cause. Though Charles was not Scottish-born, he was the rightful heir directly down the line from Mary, Queen of Scots—and why so many Scots joined the rebellion out of resentment at being ruled by a "foreign" king (King George II, who was born in Germany, couldn't even speak English).

Bagpipes droned, and "Bonnie" (handsome) Charlie led an army of 2,000 tartan-wearing, Gaelic-speaking Highlanders across Scotland, seizing Edinburgh. They picked up other supporters of the Stuarts from the Lowlands and from England. Now 6,000 strong, they marched south toward London—quickly advancing as far as Derby, just 125 miles from the capital—and King George II made plans to flee the country. But anticipated support for the Jacobites failed to materialize in the numbers they were hoping for (both in England and from France). The Jacobites had so far been victorious in their battles against the Hanoverian government forces, but the odds now turned against them. Charles retreated to the Scottish Highlands, where many of his men knew the terrain and might gain an advantage when outnumbered. The English government troops followed closely on his heels.

Against the advice of his best military strategist, Charles' army faced the Hanoverian forces at Culloden Moor on flat, barren terrain that was unsuited to the Highlanders' guerrilla tactics. The Jacobites—many of them brandishing only broadswords, targes (wooden shields covered in leather and studs), and dirks (long daggers)—were mowed down by King George's cannons and horsemen. In less than an hour, the government forces routed the Jacobite army, but that was just the start. They spent the next weeks methodically hunting down ringleaders and sympathizers (and many others in the Highlands who had nothing to do with the battle), ruthlessly killing, imprisoning, and banishing thousands.

Charles fled with a £30,000 price on his head (an equivalent of millions of today's pounds). He escaped to the Isle of Skye, hidden by a woman named Flora MacDonald (her grave is on the Isle of Skye, and her statue is outside Inverness Castle). Flora dressed Charles in women's clothes and passed him off as her maid. Later, Flora was arrested and thrown in the Tower of London before being released and treated like a celebrity.

Charles escaped to France. He spent the rest of his life wandering Europe trying to drum up support to retake the throne. He drifted through short-lived romantic affairs and alcohol, and died in obscurity, without an heir, in Rome.

Though usually depicted as a battle of the Scottish versus the English, in truth Culloden was a civil war between two opposing dynasties: Stuart (Charlie) and Hanover (George). However, as the history has faded into lore, the battle has come to be remembered as a Scottish-versus-English standoff—or, in the parlance of the Scots, the Highlanders versus the Strangers.

The Battle of Culloden was the end of 60 years of Jacobite rebellions, the last major battle fought on British soil, and the final stand of the Highlanders. From then on, clan chiefs were deposed; kilts, tartans, and bagpipes were outlawed; and farmers were cleared off their ancestral land, replaced by more-profitable sheep. Scottish culture would never fully recover from the events of the campaign called "The '45."

❷ Self-Guided Tour

Your tour takes you through two sections: the exhibit and the actual battlefield.

The Exhibit

As you pass the ticket desk, note the **family tree:** Bonnie Prince Charlie ("Charles Edward Stuart") and George II were distant cousins. Then the exhibit's shadowy-figure **touchscreens** connect you with historical figures who give you details from both the Hanoverian and Jacobite perspectives. A **map** shows the other power struggles happening in and around Europe, putting this fight for political control of Britain in a wider context. This battle was no small regional skirmish, but rather a key part of a larger struggle between Britain and its neighbors, primarily France, for control over trade and colonial power. In the display case are **medals** from the early 1700s, made by both sides as propaganda.

From here, your path through this building is cleverly designed to echo the course of the Jacobite army. Your short march

(with lots of historic artifacts) gets under way as Charlie sails from France to Scotland, then finagles the support of Highland clan chiefs. As he heads south with his army to take London, you, too, are walking south. Along the way, maps show the movement of troops, and wall panels cover the buildup to the attack, as seen from both sides. Note the clever division of information: To the left and in red is the story of the "government" (a.k.a. Hanoverians/Whigs/English, led by the Duke of Cumberland); to the right, in blue, is the Jacobites' perspective (Prince Charlie and his Highlander/French supporters).

But you, like Charlie, don't make it to London—in the dark room at the end, you can hear Jacobite commanders arguing over whether to retreat back to Scotland. Pessimistic about their chances of receiving more French support, they decide to U-turn, and so do you. Heading back up north, you'll get some insight into some of the strategizing that went on behind the scenes.

By the time you reach the end of the hall, it's the night before the battle. Round another bend into a dark passage, and listen to the voices of the anxious troops. While the English slept soundly in their tents (recovering from celebrating the Duke's 25th birthday), the scrappy and exhausted Jacobite Highlanders struggled through the night to reach the battlefield (abandoning their plan of a surprise night attack at Nairn and instead retreating back toward Inverness).

At last the two sides meet. As you wait outside the theater for the next showing, study the chart depicting how the forces were arranged on the battlefield. Once inside the theater, you'll soon be surrounded by the views and sounds of a windswept moor. An impressive four-minute **360° movie** projects the re-enacted battle with you right in the center of the action. The movie drives home just how outmatched the Jacobites were.

The last room has **period weapons,** including ammunition and artifacts found on the battlefield, as well as **historical depictions** of the battle. You'll also find a section describing the detective work required to piece together the story from historical evidence. Be sure to tour the **aftermath corridor,** which talks about the nearly genocidal years following the battle and the cultural wake of this event to this day. Be sure to examine the **huge map,** with narration explaining the combat you've just experienced while giving you a bird's-eye view of the field through which you're about to roam.

The Battlefield

Leaving the visitors center, survey the battlefield (which you'll tour with the help of your audioguide). In the foreground is a cottage used as a makeshift hospital during the conflict. Red flags show the front line of the government army (8,000 troops). This is where most of the hand-to-hand fighting took place. The blue flags in the distance are where the Jacobite army (5,500 troops) lined up.

As you explore the battlefield, notice how uneven and boggy the ground is in parts, and imagine trying to run across this hummocky terrain with all your gear, toward almost-certain death.

The old stone memorial cairn, erected in 1881, commemorates

the roughly 1,500 Jacobites buried in in this field. It's known as the Graves of the Clans. As you wander the battlefield, following the audioguide, you'll pass by other **mass graves,** marked by small headstones, and ponder how entire clans fought, died, and were buried here.

Heading back to the parking lot, notice the wall of **protruding bricks.** Each represents a soldier who died. The handful of Hanoverian casualties are on the left (about 50); the rest of the long wall's raised bricks represent the multitude of dead Jacobites.

INVERNESS & LOCH NESS

CLAVA CAIRNS

Scotland is littered with reminders of prehistoric peoples—especially in Orkney and along the coast of the Moray Firth—but

the Clava Cairns, worth ▲, are among the best-preserved, most interesting, and easiest to reach. You'll find them nestled in the spooky countryside just beyond Culloden Battlefield. These "Balnauran of Clava" are Neolithic burial chambers dating from 3,000 to 4,000 years ago. Although they appear to be just some giant piles of rocks in a sparsely forested clearing, a closer look will help you appreciate the prehistoric logic behind them. (The site is explained by an information plaque near the entry.) There are three structures: a central "ring cairn" with an open space in the center but no access to it, flanked by two "passage cairns," which were once buried under turf-covered mounds. The entrance shaft in each passage cairn lines up with the setting sun at the winter solstice. Each cairn is surrounded by a stone circle, and the entire ensemble is framed by evocative trees—injecting this site with even more mystery.

Enjoy the mystery of the site: Were the stone circles part of a celestial calendar system? Or did they symbolize guardians?

Why were the clamshell-sized hollows carved into the stones facing the chambers? Was the soul of the deceased transported into the next life by the ray of sunlight on that brief moment that it filled the inner chamber? No one knows.

Cost and Hours: Free, always open; just after passing Culloden Battlefield on the B-9006 coming from Inverness, signs on the right point to *Clava Cairns.* Follow this twisty road a couple miles, over the "weak bridge" and to the free parking lot by the stones. Skip the cairns if you don't have a car.

CAWDOR CASTLE

Homey, intimate, and worth ▲, this castle is still the residence of the Dowager (read: widow) Countess of Cawdor, a local aristocratic branch of the Campbell family. While many associate the castle with Shakespeare's *Macbeth* (because "Cawdor" is mentioned more than a dozen times in the play), there is no actual connection with Shakespeare. *Macbeth* is set 300 years before the castle was even built. The castle is worth a visit simply because it's historic and beautiful in its own right—and because the woman who owns it flies a Buddhist flag from its tower. She is from Eastern Europe and was the Earl's second wife.

Cost and Hours: £11, good £5 guidebook explains the family and the rooms, May-Sept daily 10:00-17:30, closed Oct-April, tel. 01667/404-401, www.cawdorcastle.com.

Getting There: It's on the B-9090, just off the A-96, about 15 miles east of Inverness (6 miles beyond Culloden and Clava Cairns). In recent years, public transportation to the castle has been nonexistent—but ask at the Inverness TI just in case it has resumed.

Visiting the Castle: You'll follow a one-way circuit around the castle with each room explained with posted explanations written by the countess' late husband, the sixth Earl of Cawdor. His notes bring the castle to life and make you wish you'd known the old

chap. Cawdor feels very lived-in because it is. While the Dowager Countess moves out during the tourist season, for the rest of the year this is her home. You can imagine her stretching out in front of the fireplace with a good book. Notice her geraniums in every room.

The drawing room (for "with-drawing" after dinner) is lined with a family tree of portraits looking down. In the Tapestry Bedroom you'll see the actual marriage bed of Sir Hugh Campbell from 1662 and 17th-century tapestries warming the walls. In the Yellow Room, a flat-screen TV hides inside an 18th-century cabinet (ask a docent to show you). In the Tartan Passage, lined with modern paintings, find today's dowager—Lady Angelika—in a beautiful 1970 pastel portrait, staring at her late husband's predecessors. Notice how their eyes follow you creepily down the hall—but hers do not.

A spiral stone staircase near the end of the tour leads down to the castle's proud symbol: a holly tree dating from 1372. According to the beloved legend, a donkey leaned against this tree to mark the spot where the castle was to be built...and it was, around the tree.

The **gardens,** included with the ticket, are worth exploring, with some 18th-century linden trees and several surprising species (including sequoia and redwood). Note the hedge maze crowned by a minotaur (not open to the public) and surrounded by a laburnum arbor (dripping with yellow blossoms in May and June).

The nine-hole **golf course** on the castle grounds provides a quick and affordable way to have a Scottish golfing experience. The course is bigger than pitch-and-putt and fun even for non-golfers (£18/person with clubs). You're welcome to try the putting green for £4.

Nearby: The close but remote-feeling **village of Cawdor**—with a few houses, a village shop, and a tavern—is also worth a look if you've got time to kill.

Loch Ness

I'll admit it: I had my zoom lens out and my eyes on the water. The local tourist industry thrives on the legend of the Loch Ness monster. It's a thrilling thought, and there have been several seemingly reliable "sightings" (by monks, police officers, and sonar imaging). But even if you ignore the monster stories, the loch is impressive: 23 miles long, less than a mile wide, 754 feet deep, and containing more water than all of the freshwater bodies of England and Wales combined. It's essentially the vast chasm of a fault line, filled with water.

Getting There: The Loch Ness sights are a 20-minute drive southwest of Inverness. To drive the full length of Loch Ness takes about 45 minutes. Fort William-bound buses #19 and #919 make stops at Urquhart Castle and Drumnadrochit (8/day, 40 minutes).

Sights on Loch Ness

In July 1933, a couple swore they saw a giant sea monster shimmy across the road in front of their car by Loch Ness. Within days, ancient legends about giant monsters in the lake (dating as far back as the sixth century) were revived—and suddenly everyone was spotting "Nessie" poke its head above the waters of Loch Ness. Further sightings and photographic "evidence" have bolstered the claim that there's something mysterious living in this unthinkably deep and murky lake. (Most sightings take place in the deepest part of the loch, near Urquhart Castle.) Most witnesses describe a water-bound dinosaur (resembling the real, but extinct, plesiosaur). Others cling to the slightly more plausible theory of a gigantic eel. And skeptics figure the sightings can be explained by a combination of reflections, boat wakes, and mass hysteria. The most famous photo

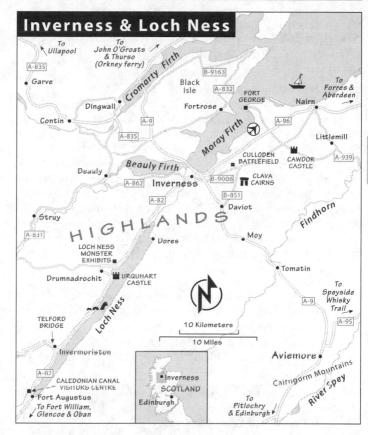

Inverness & Loch Ness

To Ullapool
To John O'Groats & Thurso (Orkney ferry)
A-835
Garve
Cromarty Firth
B-9163
Black Isle
A-832
FORT GEORGE
To Forres & Aberdeen
Nairn
Dingwall
Fortrose
Contin
A-9
Moray Firth
A-96
Littlemill
A-835
A-939
CULLODEN BATTLEFIELD
CAWDOR CASTLE
Beauly Firth
Deauly
A-862
Inverness
B-9006
CLAVA CAIRNS
B-851
A-82
Daviot
Findhorn
Struy
H I G H L A N D S
Moy
A-831
Dores
LOCH NESS MONSTER EXHIBITS
Tomatin
Drumnadrochit
URQUHART CASTLE
To Spayside Whisky Trail
A-9
A-95

10 Kilometers
10 Miles

TELFORD BRIDGE
Loch Ness
Invermoriston
Aviemore
Cairngorm Mountains
A-82
River Spey
CALEDONIAN CANAL VISITORS CENTRE
Fort Augustus
To Fort William, Glencoe & Oban
Inverness
SCOTLAND
Edinburgh
To Pitlochry & Edinburgh

of the beast (dubbed the "Surgeon's Photo") was later discredited—the "monster's" head was actually attached to a toy submarine. But

that hasn't stopped various cryptozoologists from seeking photographic, sonar, and other proof.

And that suits the thriving local tourist industry just fine. The Nessie commercialization is so tacky that there are two different monster exhibits within 100 yards of each other, both in the town of Drumnadrochit. Of the two competing sites, Nessieland is pretty cheesy while the Loch Ness Centre and Exhibition (described next) is surprisingly thoughtful. Each has a tour-bus parking lot and more square footage devoted to their kitschy shops than to the exhibits. While Nessieland is a tourist trap, the Loch Ness Centre may appease that small part of you that knows the *real* reason you wanted to see Loch Ness.

▲Loch Ness Centre & Exhibition

This exhibit has two parts: First you make six stops in a series of video rooms, and then you enter the exhibition explaining the history of the Great Glen and Loch Ness. It's spearheaded by Adrian Shine, a naturalist fond of saying "I like mud," who has spent many years researching lake ecology and scientific phenomena. With video presentations and special effects, this exhibit explains the geological and historical environment that bred the monster story, as well as the various searches that have been conducted. Refreshingly, it retains an air of healthy skepticism instead of breathless monster-chasing. It also has some artifacts related to the search, such as a hippo-foot ashtray used to fake monster footprints and the *Viperfish*—a harpoon-equipped submarine used in a 1969 Nessie search. You'll also learn how in 1952 record-seeker John Cobb died going 200 mph in his speedboat on the loch.

Cost and Hours: £8, ask about RS%, daily Easter-Oct 9:30-17:45, July-Aug until 18:45, Nov-Easter 10:00-16:15, last entry 45 minutes before closing, in the big stone mansion right on the main road to Inverness, tel. 01456/450-573, www.lochness.com.

▲Urquhart Castle

The ruins at Urquhart (UR-kurt), just up the loch from the Nessie exhibits, are gloriously situated with a view of virtually the entire lake and create a traffic jam of tourism on busy days.

The visitors center has a tiny exhibit with interesting castle artifacts and an eight-minute film taking you on a sweep through a thousand years of tumultuous history—from St. Columba's visit to the castle's final destruction in 1689. The castle itself, while dramatically situated and fun to climb through, is an empty shell. After its owners (who supported the crown) blew it up to keep the Jacobites from taking it, the largest medieval castle in Scotland (and the most important in the Highlands) wasn't considered worth rebuilding or defending, and was abandoned. Well-placed, descriptive signs help you piece together this once-mighty fortress. As you walk toward the ruins, take a close look at the trebuchet (a working replica of one of the most destructive weapons of English King Edward I),

The Caledonian Canal

Two hundred million years ago, two tectonic plates collided, creating the landmass we know as Scotland and leaving a crevice of thin lakes slashing diagonally across the country. This Great Glen Fault, from Inverness to Oban, is easily visible on any map.

British engineer Thomas Telford connected the lakes 200 years ago with a series of canals so ships could avoid the long trip around the north of the country. The Caledonian Canal runs 62 miles from Scotland's east to west coasts; 22 miles of it is man-made. Telford's great feat of engineering took 19 years to complete, opening in 1822 at a cost of one million pounds.

But bad timing made the canal a disaster commercially. Napoleon's defeat in 1815 meant that ships could sail the open seas more freely. And by the time the canal opened, commercial ships were too big for its 15-foot depths. Just a couple of decades after the Caledonian Canal opened, trains made the canal almost useless...except for Romantic Age tourism. From the time of Queen Victoria (who cruised the canal in 1873), the canal has been a popular tourist attraction. To this day the canal is a hit with vacationers, recreational boaters, and lock-keepers who compete for the best-kept lock.

The scenic drive from Inverness along the canal is entertaining, with Drumnadrochit (Nessie centers), Urquhart Castle, Fort Augustus (five locks), and Fort William (under Ben Nevis, with the eight-lock "Neptune's Staircase"). As you cross Scotland, you'll follow Telford's work—22 miles of canals and locks between three lochs, raising ships from sea level to 51 feet (Ness), 93 feet (Lochy), and 106 feet (Oich).

While Neptune's Staircase, a series of eight locks near Fort William, has been cleverly named to sound intriguing (see page 292), the best lock stop is midway, at Fort Augustus, where the canal hits the south end of Loch Ness. In Fort Augustus, the **Caledonian Canal Visitor Centre,** overlooking the canal just off the main road, gives a good rundown on Telford's work (described next). Stroll past several shops and eateries to the top for a fine view.

Seven miles north, in the town of **Invermoriston,** is another Telford structure: a stone bridge, dating from 1805, that spans the Moriston Falls as part of the original road. Look for a small parking lot just before the junction at A-82 and A-887, on your right as you drive from Fort Augustus. Carefully cross the A-82 and walk three minutes back the way you came. The bridge, which took eight years to build and is still in use, is on your right.

and ponder how this giant catapult helped Edward grab almost every castle in the country away from the native Scots.

Cost and Hours: £9, guidebook-£5, daily April-Sept 9:30-18:00, Oct until 17:00, Nov-March until 16:30, last entry 45 minutes before closing, café, tel. 01456/450-551, www.historic-scotland.gov.uk).

Loch Ness Cruises

Cruises on Loch Ness are as popular as they are pointless. The lake is far from Scotland's prettiest—and the time-consuming boat trips show you little more than what you'll see from the road. As it seems that Loch Ness cruises are a mandatory part of every "Highlands Highlights" day tour, there are several options, leaving from the top, bottom, and middle of the loch. The basic one-hour loop costs around £14 and includes views of Urquhart Castle and lots of legends and romantic history (Jacobite is the dominant outfit of the many cruise companies, www.jacobite.co.uk). I'd rather spend my time and money at Fort Augustus or Urquhart Castle.

▲Fort Augustus

Perhaps the most idyllic stop along the Caledonian Canal is the little lochside town of Fort Augustus. It was founded in the 1700s—before there was a canal here—as part of a series of garrisons and military roads built by the English to quell the Highland clansmen, even as the Jacobites kept trying to take the throne in London. Before then, there were no developed roads in the Highlands—and without roads, it's hard to keep indigenous people down.

From 1725 to 1733, the English built 250 miles of hard roads and 40 bridges to open up the region; Fort Augustus was a central Highlands garrison at the southern tip of Loch Ness, designed to awe clansmen. It was named for William Augustus, Duke of Cumberland—notorious for his role in destroying the clan way of life in the Highlands. (When there's no media and no photographs to get in the way, ethnic cleansing has little effect on one's reputation.)

Fort Augustus makes for a delightful stop if you're driving through the area. Parking is easy. There are plenty of B&Bs, charming eateries, and an inviting park along the town's five locks. You can still see the capstans, surviving from the days when the locks were cranked open by hand.

The fine little **Caledonian Canal Visitor Centre** tells the story of the canal's construction (free, daily Easter-Oct, tel. 01320/366-493). Also, consider the pleasant little canalside stroll out to the head of the loch.

Eating in Fort Augustus: You can eat reasonably at a string of eateries all lining the same side of the canal. Consider **The Little Neuk,** a good café serving filled rolls and homemade soups; **The**

Lock Inn, cozy and pub-like with great canalside tables, ideal if it's sunny; **The Bothy,** another pub with decent food; and the **Canalside Chip Shop** offering fish-and-chips to go (no seating, but plenty of nice spots on the canal). A small grocery store is at the gas station, next to the TI, which is a few steps from the canal just after crossing the River Oich (also housing the post office, a WC, and an ATM).

EASTERN SCOTLAND

*Pitlochry • Sights West of the Cairngorms • Loch Tay
• Speyside Whisky Trail • Balmoral Castle & the Royal
Deeside • Dunnottar Castle*

Between Edinburgh and Inverness, the eastern expanse of Scotland bulges out into the
North Sea. The main geological landmark is
Cairngorms National Park, with gently rugged Highland scenery and great hiking terrain. If your time is limited, Scotland is more
satisfying elsewhere. But this region is easily
accessible—you'll likely pass through at some point—and has a lot
to offer, especially for those with special interests.

This chapter is organized geographically: sights west and east
of the Cairngorms. Those in a hurry should focus on the west,
where the A-9 highway links up some fun choices. Pitlochry has a
green-hills-and-sandstone charm, a warm welcome, and a pair of
great distilleries linked by a nice hike, making it the region's best
overnight stop. Nearby you'll find a fascinating trip back to prehis-
tory (at the Scottish Crannog Centre on Loch Tay), a fun sheepdog
show, and an open-air folk museum.

East of the Cairngorms, the attractions require more of a
detour (most convenient for those connecting Inverness and St.
Andrews), but an even better look at rural Scotland. Whisky connoisseurs flock to Speyside, royalists visit Balmoral Castle and the
nearby home-base village of Ballater, and ruined-castle fans head
to Dunnottar.

West of the Cairngorms

The A-9 highway, connecting Inverness, Stirling, and Edinburgh, may be Scotland's most touristy road. Heading south on the A-9, soon after leaving Inverness, the highway begins to skirt around the curved west edge of Cairngorms National Park, which it follows almost all the way to Pitlochry. These bald, heather-covered hills are what many people picture when they imagine Highland scenery. The best look at the Cairngorms is on the east side of the park, around the village of Ballater and Balmoral Castle (see page 347); the A-939, connecting the valley of the River Spey to Ballater, is particularly dramatic. But you'll get a decent glimpse of scenery along the A-9.

As you follow the A-9, it seems every exit is stacked with

brown "tourist attraction" signs. For the most part, the options along here are more convenient than good; they tend to pale in comparison to alternatives elsewhere in the country. But if your trip to Scotland isn't taking you beyond this Highland corridor, some of these may be worth a stop. Pitlochry, described next, is the top town (particularly for those seeking a handy overnight); after that, I've listed more options in the order you'll reach them traveling from Inverness to Edinburgh.

Pitlochry

This likable tourist town, famous for its whisky and its hillwalking (both beloved by Scots), makes an enjoyable overnight stop. Just

outside the craggy Highlands, Pitlochry is set amid pastoral rolling hills that offer plenty of forest hikes. It seems that tourism is the town's only industry— with perhaps Scotland's highest concentration of woolens shops and outdoor outfitters. (The name "Pitlochry" comes from the old Pictish word for "tourist trap.") But Pitlochry also has the feel of a real community. People here are friendly and bursting with town pride: They love to chat about everything from the high-quality local theater to the salmon ladder at the hydroelectric dam. It's also a restful place, where— after the last tour bus pulls out—you can feel your pulse slow as you listen to gurgling streams.

Orientation to Pitlochry

Plucky little Pitlochry (pop. 2,500) lines up along its tidy, tourist-minded main street, Atholl Road, which runs parallel to the River Tummel. The train station is on Station Road, off the main street. Its two distilleries are a walk—or short drive—out of town (see my self-guided whisky walk). Navigate by following the black directional signs to Pitlochry's handful of sights.

TOURIST INFORMATION

The helpful TI, at one end of town, has free Wi-Fi and sells maps for local hill walks and scenic drives. Their good £1 *Pitlochry Path Network* brochure is handy (Mon-Sat 9:30-17:30, Sun 10:00-16:00, longer hours in summer, shorter hours and closed Sun Nov-March; 22 Atholl Road, tel. 01796/472-215).

HELPFUL HINTS

Special Events: In summer, a pipe band marches through town every Monday evening. In May and June, the salmon ladder at the dam comes to life (described later, under "Sights in Pitlochry"). Pitlochry's Highland Games are in early September (www.pitlochryhighlandgames.co.uk). And in October, the Enchanted Forest light-and-water show set to music illuminates Faskally Wood, just outside of town (www. enchantedforest.org.uk).

Bike Rental: Escape Route Bikes, located across the street and a block from the TI (away from town), rents a variety of bikes (£16/5 hours, £24/24 hours, includes helmet and lock if you ask, Mon-Sat 9:00-17:30, Sun 10:00-17:00, 3 Atholl Road, tel. 01796/473-859, www.escape-route.co.uk).

Parking: Drivers who aren't spending the night can park in the large pay-and-display lot next to the TI, in the center of town.

Sights in Pitlochry

DISTILLERIES

Pitlochry's two distilleries can be linked by a relaxing two-hour hike (described later, under "Whisky Walk.") For background on types of whiskies, how whisky is made, and tasting it like a pro, see page 464.

▲▲Edradour Distillery

This cute distillery (pronounced ED-rah-dower)—the smallest historic distillery in Scotland (est. 1825)—takes pride in mak-

ing its whisky with a minimum of machinery, and maintains a proud emphasis on tradition. Small white-and-red buildings are nestled in a delightfully green Scottish hillside. ("Edradour"—also the name of the stream that gurgles through the complex—means "land between two rivers.") With its idyllic setting and gregarious spirit, it's one of the most enjoyable distillery tours in Scotland. Unlike the bigger distilleries, they allow you to take photos of the equipment. If you like the whisky, buy some here and support the Pitlochry economy—this is one of the few independently owned distilleries left in Scotland.

Cost and Hours: £7.50 for a one-hour tour, departs 3/hour, April-Oct Mon-Sat 10:00-17:00, closed Sun and off-season, last

EASTERN SCOTLAND

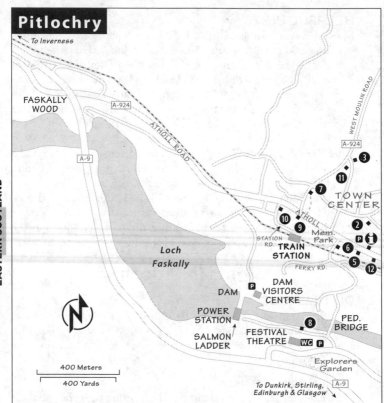

Pitlochry

To Inverness

FASKALLY WOOD

A-924

ATHOLL ROAD

A-9

WEST MOULIN ROAD

A-924

❸

⓫

❼

TOWN CENTER

❿
❾

ATHOLL

❷

STATION RD.

Mem. Park

TRAIN STATION

P

❻

❺

❶

⓬

FERRY RD.

Loch Faskally

DAM

P

DAM VISITORS CENTRE

POWER STATION

SALMON LADDER

FESTIVAL THEATRE

❽

PED. BRIDGE

WC P

Explorers Garden

400 Meters

400 Yards

To Dunkirk, Stirling, Edinburgh & Glasgow

A-9

tour departs one hour before closing, tel. 01796/472-095, www. edradour.com.

Getting There: Most come to the distillery by car (follow signs from the main road, 2.5 miles into the countryside), but you can also get there on a peaceful hiking trail that you'll have all to yourself (follow my "Pitlochry Whisky Walk," next page).

Visiting the Distillery: You'll watch a 10-minute orientation film, then enjoy a sit-down education while tasting two different drams. Then the guided tour proceeds through the facility: from the malt barn (where the barley is germinated and dried) to the still (where giant copper stills turn distiller's beer into whisky) to the warehouse (where 6,000 casks age in the darkness). Take a deep whiff of the rich aroma—you're smelling the so-called "angels' share," the tiny percentage of each cask that's lost to evaporation.

Bell's Blair Athol Distillery

This big, ivy-covered facility is conveniently located (about a half-mile from the town center) and more corporate-feeling, offering hour-long tours with a wee taste at the end. I'd tour this only if

Accommodations
1. The Poplars Guest House
2. Craigroyston House
3. Dunmurray Lodge
4. Beinn Bhracaigh B&B
5. The Buttonboss Lodge

Eateries & Other
6. Victoria's & Fern Cottage
7. The Old Mill
8. Port-na-Craig Inn
9. Just the Ticket Theater Box Office
10. John Muir Trust
11. Pitlochry Bowling Club
12. Bike Rental

you're a whisky completist, or if you lack the wheels or hiking stamina to reach Edradour.

Cost and Hours: £7.50, Easter-Oct tours depart 2/hour daily 10:00-17:00, July-Aug until 17:30, last tour departs one hour before closing; shorter hours, fewer tours, and closed Sat-Sun off-season; tel. 01796/482-003, www.discovering-distilleries.com/blairathol.

Pitlochry Whisky Walk

A fun way to visit the distilleries is to hill walk from downtown Pitlochry. The entire loop trip takes 2-3 hours, depending on how long you linger in the distilleries (at least an hour of walking each way). You'll see lush fern forests and a pretty decent waterfall. The walk is largely uphill on the way to the Edradour Distillery; wear good shoes, bring a rain jacket just in case, and be happy that you'll stroll easily downhill *after* you've had your whisky samples.

At the TI, pick up the *Pitlochry Path Network* brochure and follow along with its map. You'll be taking the **Edradour Walk** (marked on directional signs with yellow hiker icons; on the map it's a series of yellow dots). Leave the TI and head left along the busy A-924. The walk can be done in either direction, but I'll describe it counterclockwise.

Within 10 minutes, you'll walk under the railroad tracks and then come to **Bell's Blair Athol Distillery** on your left. If you're a whisky buff, stop in here. Otherwise, hold out for the much more atmospheric Edradour. You'll pass a few B&Bs and suburban homes, then a sign marked *Black Spout* on a lamppost. Just after this, you'll cross a bridge, then take the next left, walking under another stone rail overpass and away from the road. Following this path, you'll come to a clearing, and as the road gets steeper, you'll see signs directing you 50 yards off the main path to see the "Black Spout"—a wonderful waterfall well worth the few extra steps on your right.

At the top of the hill, you'll arrive in another clearing, where a narrow path hugs a huge field on your left. Low rolling hills surround you in all directions. It seems like there's not another person around for miles, with just the thistles to keep you company. From here it's an easy 20 minutes to the **Edradour Distillery.**

Leaving the distillery, to complete the loop, head right, following the paved road (Old North Road). In about 50 yards, a sign points left into the field. Take the small footpath that runs along the left side of the road. (If you see the driveway with stone lions on both sides, you've gone a few steps too far.) You'll walk parallel to the route you took getting to the distillery, hugging the far side of the same huge field. The trail then swoops back downhill through the forest, until you cross the footbridge and make a left. You'll soon reach Knockfarrie Road—take this downhill; you'll pass a B&B and hear traffic noises as you emerge from the forest. The trail leads back to the highway, with the TI a few blocks ahead on the right.

TOWN CENTER
Strolling the High Street

Pitlochry's main street is a pleasant place to wander and window-shop. As you stroll, consider this: The town exists thanks to the arrival of the train, which conveniently brought Romantic Age tourists from the big cities in the south to this lovely bit of Scotland. Queen Victoria herself visited three times in the 1860s, putting Pitlochry on the tourist map. The postcard-perfect Victorian sandstone architecture on the main street makes it clear that this was a delightful escape for city folks back in the 19th century.

Here are some things to look for, listed in order of how you'll reach them from the TI. The **memorial park** with the Celtic cross honors men from the local parish whose lives were lost fighting in World War I—a reminder of Scotland's disproportionate sacrifices in that conflict. Throughout Scotland, even many tiny villages have similar monuments.

Ferry Road, next to the park, branches off under the rail bridge and leads to a footbridge that takes you to the other side of the river—home to Pitlochry's spunky Festival Theatre, as well as a power station with a salmon ladder (a fun excuse for a lazy walk—described later).

Peek inside **The Hardware Centre.** In small towns like Pitlochry—without a Wal-Mart (I mean, Tesco)—shops like this serve

as catch-all general stores for the community. In addition to hardware, it carries a full range of kitchenware.

The **Love Your Sweets** shop, with a purple awning, stocks a staggering variety of uniquely Scottish candies in bulk. Step in to buy a mixed bag of some unusual flavors of hard candies, such as clove, rhubarb, or Irn-Bru. At the next little park on the right, a surging stream angles away from the main road and to the recommended Old Mill restaurant.

On the corner with Station Road is the headquarters of the **John Muir Trust.** John Muir (1838-1914) was born in Scotland, moved to the US when he was 10, and later helped establish the world's first national park system in the US. Inside is a free tiny exhibit called Wild Land, with a feel-good nature video and a small art gallery. They also sell books, maps, and other conservation-themed souvenirs (Mon-Sat 10:00-17:00, Sun 11:00-16:00, shorter hours and closed Tue off-season, tel. 01796/470-080, www.jmt.org).

Lawn Bowls
The **Pitlochry Bowling Club** lets outsiders rent shoes and balls and try their hand at the game (£3, generally Mon-Fri 10:00-12:00 & 14:00-16:00, 24 West Moulin Road, tel. 01796/473-459).

ACROSS THE RIVER
These sights lie along the largely undeveloped riverbank opposite Pitlochry's town center. While neither are knockouts, they're a fine excuse for a pretty stroll or drive. Walkers can reach this area easily in about 15 minutes: Head down Ferry Road (near the memorial park), cross the footbridge, and turn right.

Pitlochry Dam Visitors Centre and Salmon Ladder

Pitlochry's dam on the River Tummel provides a nice place to go for a stroll, and comes with a salmon ladder—a series of chambers that allow salmon to "step" their way upstream next to the dam (salmon generally run May-June).

The well-designed and family-friendly Visitors Centre celebrates hydroelectric power in the Highlands. Its fine nine-minute video, "Power from the Glens," explains the epic vision of generating clean power from—and for—the Highlands. You can also walk all the way across the top of the dam, pausing to read informational plaques and peer through windows into the hydroelectric plant (free, daily 9:30-17:30). Their cafeteria is delightful with a nice river view.

Pitlochry Festival Theatre

This theater company rotates its productions, putting on a different play every few nights. Most are classics, with a few musicals and new shows mixed in (£15-35; plays generally run May-Oct Mon-Sat). The theater hosts concerts on Sunday evenings—usually tribute acts—and a variety of other performances in winter (purchase tickets online or by phone; in person at Just the Ticket—Mon-Sat 9:00-17:00, closed Sun, 89 Atholl Road; or at the theater—same price, box office open daily 10:00-20:00, tel. 01796/484-626, www.pitlochryfestivaltheatre.com).

Nearby: Just above the theater's parking lot, the six-acre **Explorers Garden** features plants and wildflowers from around the world (£4, daily 10:00-17:00, closed Nov-March, last entry 45 minutes before closing, tel. 01796/484-626, www.explorersgarden.com).

Sleeping in Pitlochry

All of these have free parking.

$$ The Poplars Guest House, perched regally on a meticulously landscaped hill high above the main road, has been stylishly renovated by Jason and Nathalie. The huge home has a spacious lounge with views, and six rooms that combine modern comforts with a respect for tradition. Start the day off right with their whisky porridge (family room, closed in winter, at the end of Lower Oakfield at #27, tel. 01796/472-129, www.poplars-pitlochry.com, info@poplars-pitlochry.com).

$$ Craigroyston House, my sentimental favorite in Pitlochry, is a quaint, large Victorian country house with eight large and luxe bedrooms. Their terraced yard is a great place to sip some wine or play croquet. Vaughan and Susan, originally from Orkney, are welcoming and generous (family rooms, right above the TI parking lot at 2 Lower Oakfield, tel. 01796/472-053, www.craigroyston.co.uk, reservations@craigroyston.co.uk). Drivers can reach it on Lower Oakfield Road; walkers can walk up from the huge parking lot next to the TI on Atholl Road (find the small gate at the back of the lot).

$$ Dunmurray Lodge is a calming place to call home, with four springtime-colored rooms, and friendly hosts (family room, no kids under 5; breakfast includes gluten-free, vegetarian, and other options; 5-minute walk from town at 72 Bonnethill Road, mobile 0778-346-2625, www.dunmurray.co.uk, lorraine@dunmurray.co.uk, Lorraine and Mike).

$$ Beinn Bhracaigh (pronounced "benny vrackie," meaning "speckled mountain") is a guesthouse with a hotel feel. The 13 rooms are modern and tasteful, and they have a sitting room where you can serve yourself at the well-stocked honesty bar. Of my listings, it sits the highest above the main road—still within a (longish, steep) walk, but easier by car. The location comes with fine views across the town center and river to the hills beyond (minimum two-night stay in peak season and on weekends, no kids under 8, no elevator, 14 Higher Oakfield, tel. 01796/470-355, www.beinnbhracaigh.com, info@beinnbhracaigh.com, James and Kirsty).

$ The Buttonboss Lodge has a less idyllic setting, right along the busy main road across from the TI (expect some traffic noise). But it's affordable and convenient for train travelers. The eight rooms, managed by Cristian, are straightforward and a bit old-fashioned (25 Atholl Road, tel. 01796/472-065, mobile 0790-247-2065, www.buttonbosslodge.co.uk, info@buttonbosslodge.co.uk).

Eating in Pitlochry

Plenty of options line the main drag, including several bakeries selling picnic supplies.

$$ Victoria's restaurant and coffee shop, a local favorite, feels like a down-home diner, serving up an eclectic menu of comfort food (daily 10:00-21:00, patio seating, free Wi-Fi, at corner of memorial park, 45 Atholl Road, tel. 01796/472-670).

$$$ The Old Mill, tucked a block behind the main drag in an actual old mill, has good Scottish food, plus some pastas and salads. Sit in their popular, high-energy pub, calmer restaurant in back, or at picnic tables outside (food served daily 12:00-21:00, tel. 01796/474-020).

$$$ Fern Cottage, just behind Victoria's, has a darker, candlelit, dressier ambience and a Mediterranean spin on their menu (daily 12:00-15:00 & 17:00-20:30, Ferry Road, tel. 01796/473-840).

$$$ Port-na-Craig Inn, on the river just downhill from the theater, is a fancier option catering to theatergoers. For a calmer experience, go at 20:00, after the show has started (lunch specials, daily 11:00-21:00, tel. 01796/472-777).

Pitlochry Connections

The train station is open Monday to Saturday 8:00-18:30 and Sunday 10:30-18:00.

From Pitlochry by Train to: Inverness (almost hourly, 2 hours), **Stirling** (5/day direct, 1 hour, more with transfer in Perth), **Edinburgh** (8/day direct, 2 hours), **Glasgow** (9/day, 2 hours, some transfer in Perth). Train info: Tel. 0845-748-4950, www. nationalrail.co.uk.

By Bus to: Glasgow (1/day direct on National Express #588; 5/day on Citylink to Perth, then change to Megabus to Glasgow, 2.5 hours—train is faster), **Edinburgh** (3/day on Citylink #M90, 2.5 hours).

Sights West of the Cairngorms

ALONG THE A-9 HIGHWAY
▲▲Leault Working Sheepdogs

Each afternoon, Neil Ross presents a 45-minute demonstration of his well-trained sheepdogs. The experience is vividly real and fascinating. You'll hunker down in a natural little amphitheater in the turf while Neil describes his work. He'll demonstrate why shepherds have used a crook for thousands of years, and explain why farmers get frustrated when "fancy people with numbers after their names" try to tell them how to manage their land. Then the dogs get to work: With shouts and whistles, each dog follows individual commands, demonstrating an impressive mastery over the sheep. (Watching in awe, you can't help but think: Sheepdogs are smart... and sheep are idiots.) After the presentation, you'll meet (and pet) the border collie stars of the show, and may have the
chance to feed some lambs or to try your hand at shearing sheep. If they happen to have a litter of border collie puppies, even those who dislike dogs may find it hard to resist smuggling one home.

Cost and Hours: £5, demonstration only once per day, May-Oct Sun-Fri at 16:00, closed to the public at other times,

no demonstrations Sat or Nov-April, tel. 01540/651-402, www.
leaultworkingsheepdogs.co.uk.

Getting There: The entrance to the farm is a gravel road that
literally runs across the A-9. But since the little road sneaks up
on you, it's safer to exit for Kincraig, then follow the brown signs
around to a driveway that takes you (carefully) back across the A-9
and up to the farm.

▲Highland Folk Museum

Scotland doesn't have a top-notch open-air folk museum—but this
is close enough. Just off the highway on the outskirts of Newtonmore, the museum features re-creations of traditional buildings
from the surrounding area from the 1700s through the 1930s. The
buildings are a bit spread out, and it's quiet outside of frequent "activity days" (check the schedule online).

Cost and Hours: Free but donations welcome, daily April-
Aug 10:30-17:30, Sept-Oct 11:00-16:30, closed Nov-March, helpful £5 guidebook, tel. 01540/673-551, www.highlifehighland.
co.uk.

Getting There: Exit the A-9 in Newtonmore, then follow
brown signs for about five minutes through the village to the museum
(free parking).

Visiting the Museum: The highlight of the museum is a
circa-1700, thatched-roof Highland township called **Baile Gean,**
a gathering of four primitive
stone homes and three barns,
each furnished as it would
have been in the Jacobite era
(it's a 15-minute walk from
the entry—go to the right
through a pine forest and up
a small hill). Although built
for the museum, the township
was closely based on an actual

settlement a few miles away that was populated until the 1830s.
Costumed docents can explain traditional Highland lifestyles, and
you'll likely see—and smell—a peat fire filling one of the homes
with its rich smoke. (Because peat doesn't spit or spark, it was
much safer to burn than wood—which was too valuable to feed
fires anyway, as most tools were made of wood.) This area provided
an ideal backdrop for some of the rural-life scenes in the TV production of *Outlander* (see sidebar on page 498).

With more time, visit the other structures in the rest of the
open-air museum, such as the tweed shop; the schoolhouse, where
you'll learn about early-20th-century classrooms; or the Lochan-
hully House (look for the house with red eaves, past the play-

ground), which depicts a 1950s Scottish home. At the far end of the complex you may see some hairy "coos."

▲Blair Castle

If you like Scottish history, heritage, and antlers, you'll like Blair Castle. It's a convenient stop for those zipping past on the A-9. In Gaelic, a "blàr" or "blair" is a flat bit of land surrounded by hills. And sure enough, this stately, white palace rises up from a broad clearing. A stout fortress during the Jacobite wars, it was later renovated and expanded as a mansion in the Scottish Baronial style.

The former residence of the Dukes of Atholl (a.k.a. Clan Murray) is now owned and run as a business by a trust. It's filled with paintings, historic artifacts, Clan Murray mementoes, and grand, creaky staircases. Following the self-guided, one-way route, you'll enjoy a fine look at 19th-century aristocratic life. The WWI room recalls how the house was used as a hospital during that conflict. A highlight is the wood-paneled ballroom at the end, draped in tartan and bristling with antlers.

If time allows, explore the grounds—especially the walled Hercules Garden, where rugged plantings surround a lily-padded pond, overlooked by a statue of Hercules (accessed via the trail near the parking lot).

Cost and Hours: £11, April-Oct daily 9:30-17:30, closed Nov-March, last entry one hour before closing, tel. 01796/481-207, www.blair-castle.co.uk.

Getting There: From the town of Blair Atholl (just off of the A-9), drive down the long, tree-lined driveway to the free parking lot. From Pitlochry, you can take the more scenic B-8019/B-8079 instead of the A-9. Bus #87 runs from Pitlochry (5/day in summer, fewer off-season, 15 minutes, www.elizabethyulecoaches.co.uk).

Nearby: The **Atholl Country Life Museum** is a humble, volunteer-run museum literally across the street from Blair Castle. A local teacher created these exhibits, filling an old school to show the other side of the social and economic coin. Chatting with the volunteers makes a visit extra fun (£4, generally daily 13:30-17:00, July-Aug from 10:00, tel. 01796/481-232, www.athollcountrylifemuseum.org.uk).

▲Dunkeld

This charming wee town, just off the A-9, is worth a stretch-your-legs break. While the town center is pleasant—with flower boxes and cleverly named shops—its claim to fame is its partially ruined cathedral, which sits on the banks of the River Tay.

Pay-and-display parking is at both ends of town (the north end has a WC). The TI and cathedral are just down High Street from the main drag, Atholl Street.

The **Cathedral of St. Columba** was actually Scotland's leading church for a brief time in the ninth century, when that im-

portant saint's relics were being stored here during Viking raids. Later it blossomed into a large cathedral complex in a secluded, riverside setting. But it was devastated by the one-two punch of Reformation iconoclasts (who tore down most of the building) and Jacobites (who fought the Battle of Dunkeld near here). Duck inside to see the stony interior and its one-room museum (pick up the free info sheet or consider borrowing the good audioguide for a £1 donation). Outside, as you circle the entire complex, you'll discover that the current church is merely the choir of the original structure—a huge, ruined nave (currently undergoing restoration) stretches behind it.

The **$ Scottish Deli** is nice for a drop in, with soups, sandwiches, and salads (a few tables inside, corner of High Street and Atholl Street, tel. 01350/728-028).

ON LOCH TAY

A 30-minute drive west of the A-9, Loch Tay is worth visiting mostly for its excellent Scottish Crannog Centre—the best place in Scotland to learn about early Iron Age life. You can also drive along Loch Tay (and past the thundering Falls of Dochart) to connect Pitlochry and the A-9 corridor with the Trossachs and Loch Lomond.

▲▲Scottish Crannog Centre

Across Scotland, archaeologists know that little round islands on the lochs are evidence of crannogs—circular houses on stilts, dating to 500 years before Christ. Iron-Age Scots built on the water because in an age before roads, people traveled by

EASTERN SCOTLAND

boat, and because waterways were easily defended against rampaging animals (or people). Scientists have found evidence of 18 such crannogs on Loch Tay alone. One has been rebuilt, using mostly traditional methods, and now welcomes visitors. Guided by a passionate and well-versed expert, you'll spend about an hour visiting the crannog and learning about how its residents lived.

Cost and Hours: £10, family tickets available, daily 10:00-17:30, closed Nov-March, well-marked just outside Kenmore on the south bank of Loch Tay, tel. 01887/830-583, www.crannog.co.uk.

Visiting the Museum: The highlight is the two-part tour, led by guides dressed in prehistoric garb. Join whichever group is going next.

One part of the tour takes you out across the rustic wooden bridge to the crannog itself, where you'll huddle under the thatched roof and learn about Iron Age architecture. Your guide explains how families of up to 20 people lived in just one crannog—along with their livestock—and paints a vivid picture of what life was like in those rugged times.

In the other part of the tour, guides demonstrate Iron Age "technology"—turning a lathe, grinding flour, spinning yarn, and even starting a fire using nothing but wood and string. You'll then have a hands-on opportunity to try the tools yourself—and realize how easy the guides made it look.

A modest exhibit just off the gift shop explains the history of crannogs, excavation efforts, and the building of this new one.

Kenmore

Located where Loch Tay empties into the River Tay, Kenmore is a sleepy, one-street, black-and-white village with a big hotel, a

church, and a post office/general store. There's not much to do here, other than visit the nearby Scottish Crannog Centre, enjoy the Loch Tay scenery, and consider hiking through the woods to the Taymouth Castle (currently being renovated). With its classic old hotel, Kenmore can be a handy home base for this area.

Sleeping and Eating in Kenmore: $$ Kenmore Hotel,

dominating the village center, feels like a classic Scottish country hotel—it claims to be the oldest inn in Scotland (dating from 1572). The 39 rooms are old-fashioned but cozy, and welcoming lounges, terraces, and other public spaces sprawl through the building. Look for the Robert Burns poem above the fireplace in one of the bars (elevator, The Square, Kenmore, tel. 01887/830-205, www.kenmorehotel.com, reception@kenmorehotel.com). The **$$$** pub, dining room, and various outdoor dining areas all share the same menu.

Falls of Dochart

At the far end of Loch Tay from Kenmore, in the village of Killin, the road passes on a stone bridge over a churning waterfall where the peat-brown waters of the River Dochart tumble dramatically into the loch. The romantic bridge is busy with passing motorists enjoying a photo op; eateries and gift shops surround the scene. You can clamber down onto the flat stones for a closer look. From

the bridge, notice the stone archway marking the burial ground of the Clan Macnab.

East of the Cairngorms

While the A-9 corridor to the west is studded with touristy amusements, the area east of the Cairngorms (while hardly undiscovered) feels more rugged and lets you dig deeper into the countryside. In this area, I've focused on two river valleys with very different claims to fame: Speyside, curling along the top of the Cairngorms, is famous for its many distilleries; Royal Deeside, cutting through the middle of the Cairngorms, is the home of the Queen's country retreat at Balmoral and the neighboring village of Ballater. Overnighting in Ballater is an ideal way to linger in this region and sleep immersed in Cairngorms splendor.

Speyside Whisky Trail

Of the hundred or so distilleries in Scotland, half lie near the valley of the River Spey—a small area called Speyside. The ample waters of the river, along with generous peat deposits, have attracted distillers here for centuries. While I prefer some of the smaller, more intimate distillery tours elsewhere (including Oban Distillery in Oban, Talisker on the Isle of Skye, and Edradour near Pitlochry), Speyside is convenient to Inverness and practically a pilgrimage for aficionados. The distilleries here feel bigger and more corporate, but they also include some famous names (including the world's two best-selling brands of single malts, Glenfiddich and Glenlivet). And for whisky lovers, it's simply enjoyable to spend time in a region steeped in such reverence for your favorite drink.

PLANNING YOUR TIME

A quick car tour of Speyside takes about a half-day, and is a scenic way to connect Inverness to Royal Deeside (it also works as a side-trip from Inverness). Whisky aficionados will have their own list of distilleries they want to hit. But, for the typical traveler, here is an easy plan for the day:

Enjoy the scenic drive to Aberlour, tour the Speyside Cooperage, tour the Glenfiddich distillery, and finally have a short stop in Dufftown. These four stops are within about five miles of each other.

If driving south from Inverness, you could easily do these stops and then drive down to Balmoral Castle to tour it and sleep nearby in Ballater.

Orientation to Speyside

The A-95, which parallels the River Spey, is the region's artery (to reach it, take the A-9 south from Inverness and turn off toward Grantown-on-Spey). Brown *Malt Whisky Trail* signs help connect the dots. While several distilleries lie along the main road, even more are a short side-trip away. Three humdrum villages form the nucleus of Speyside: Aberlour (the biggest), Craigellachie (a wide spot in the road), and Dufftown (with a clock tower and a good dose of stony charm).

Because public transit connections aren't ideal, Speyside works best for drivers—though if you're determined, you could take the train from Inverness to Elgin and catch the "whisky bus" from there (Stagecoach bus #38, stops in Craigellachie and Aberlour on the way to Dufftown, about hourly, none Sun).

A word of caution: In Scotland, DUI standards are very low (0.05 percent) and strictly enforced. Go easy on the tastings, or bring a designated driver. Distilleries are often happy to give drivers their dram "to go" so they can enjoy it safely later.

Sights in Speyside

I've listed these roughly west to east, as you'll reach them approaching Speyside on the A-95. For a good primer on whisky and whisky tastings, see page 464.

Aberlour

Officially named "Charlestown of Aberlour" for its founder, this attractive sandstone town lines up along the A-95. It's famous both for its namesake whisky distillery (www.aberlour.com) and as the home of Walkers Shortbread, which you'll see sold in red-tartan boxes all over Scotland (you can get some at the factory store in town, but no tours). **$$ The Mash Tun,** just off the main road (next to a welcoming little visitors center), is an atmospheric whisky bar that serves lunch and rents rooms upstairs (tel. 01340/881-771, www.mashtun-aberlour.com).

Craigellachie

The blink-and-you'll-miss-it village of Craigellachie (craig-ELL-a-kee) is home to the landmark **$$ Craigellachie Hotel.** This classic, grand old hotel, a handy home base for whisky pilgrims, is famous for its whisky bar—stocking more than 800 bottles (opens daily at 17:00, the receptionist may let you in for a peek at other times, 26 rooms, tel. 01340/881-204 www.craigellachiehotel.co.uk). Just past the hotel on the A-941, keep an eye out on the left for the picturesque **Craigellachie Bridge,** built by the great Scottish industrial architect Thomas Telford.

Note that the A-95 takes a sharp turn to the right in Craigellachie (just before the hotel), leading to the cooperage described next, and beyond that, to the Glenfiddich Distillery and Dufftown; the main road (past the hotel and the bridge) becomes A-941.

▲Speyside Cooperage

Perhaps the single biggest factor in defining whisky's unique flavor is the barrel it's aged in. At this busy workshop on the outskirts

of Craigellachie, you can watch master coopers build or refurbish casks for distilleries throughout Scotland. The 14 coopers who work here—and who must first complete a four-year apprenticeship to get the gig—are some of the last of a dying breed; while just about everything used to be transported in barrels, today it's only booze. First you'll view an engaging, almost tear-jerking 15-minute film, then you'll follow your guide up to an observation deck peering down over the factory floor. Oak timber is shaped into staves, which are gathered into metal hoops, then steamed to make them more pliable. Finally the inside is charred with a gas flame, creating a carbonized coating that helps give whisky its golden hue and flavor. Because the vast majority of casks used in Scotland are hand-me-downs from the US (where bourbon laws only allow one use per barrel), you're more likely to see reassembly of old casks (with new ends) rather than from-scratch creation of new ones. But the process is equally fascinating. Apart from observing the barrel-making, it's also interesting to see the intensity of the workers—who are paid by the piece.

Cost and Hours: £3.50, tours depart every 30 minutes, Mon-Fri 9:00-15:30, closed Sat-Sun, Dufftown Road, Craigellachie, tel. 01340/871-108, www.speysidecooperage.co.uk.

Glenfiddich Distillery

As you enter Dufftown, keep an eye out on the left for the home of Scotland's top-selling single malt whisky. This sprawling but charming factory—with a name that means "Valley of the Deer" (hence the logo)—offers excellent tours and tastings. After a 15-minute promotional video, your kilted guide will walk you through the impressive plant, which includes a busy bottling hall. Your tour finishes with an extensive tasting session.

Cost and Hours: Basic £10 "Explorers" visit includes 1.5-hour tour and 4 tastings (departs every 30 minutes), more expensive options available, daily 9:30-16:00 (last tour), tel. 01340/822-373, www.glenfiddich.com.

Glenfiddich or Glenlivet? The two big distilleries of Speyside each offer £10 tours and tastings. Both tours are excellent, and they handle their crowds very well. I prefer Glenfiddich as it feels more historic and less corporate, and it's closer to other sights.

Dufftown

This charming, sleepy town has a characteristic crossroads street plan radiating from its clock-tower-topped main square. A few steps up Conval Street from the tower, the humble, one-room **Whisky Museum** doubles as the TI. You'll see a small selection of historical displays and tools from the whisky trade. Most importantly, you'll have a chance to chat with the fun retirees who run the place (free, daily 10:00-16:00 in summer, tel. 01340/821-591). **The Whisky Shop,** directly behind the tower, is a serious place selling 650 different types of whisky (daily

10:00-18:00, closed Sun in winter, 1 Fife Street, tel. 01340/821-097, www.whiskyshopdufftown.com).

Glenlivet Distillery

Sitting five miles south of the A-95 (turn off at Bridge of Avon), this is one of the area's most famous and popular distilleries to

tour. Their 75-minute tour spares you the gauzy video intro that comes with most tours and takes you right through the sprawling production facility—perched on a ridge overlooking Cairngorms National Park. The tour finishes with three tastings. If you're not taking the tour, you're welcome to enjoy their history exhibit room. Note: This is just a short detour for those connecting Speyside to Ballater on the scenic route through the mountains (B-9008/A-939).

Cost and Hours: £10, daily mid-March–mid-Nov 9:30-18:00, tours depart every 30 minutes 10:00-16:30, closed in winter, head to the village of Glenlivet and follow signs from there, tel. 01340/821-720, www.theglenlivet.com.

Balmoral Castle and Royal Deeside

Royal Deeside—the forested valley of the River Dee—is two sights in one: the Scottish home of the British royal family, wrapped in some of the most gorgeous scenery of Cairngorms National Park. Driving through the park you'll see pockets of Scots pine (Scotland's national tree). While no longer widespread, these once blanketed the Scottish countryside. In fact, 2,000 years ago the Romans must have been impressed. They called this land "Caledonia Silva," meaning "wooded land." Driving on, closer to Balmoral, you'll enter a high, treeless moorland with lots of broom plants (what we'd call Scotch broom) and wild thistles (Scotland's national flower). As you drive, cresting hills to meet vast views, you can imagine royals out on the hunt. (In fact, you'll see tiny huts used by hunters to hide out while they await the stag of their dreams.) The only game you'll likely see is hairy cows and lots of roadkill—mostly rabbit. (Hare today...)

▲Balmoral Castle

The Queen stays at her 50,000-acre private estate, located within Cairngorms National Park, from August through early October. But in the months leading up to Her Royal Highness' arrival, the grounds and the castle's ballroom are open to visitors. While royal-

EASTERN SCOTLAND

ists will enjoy this glimpse into the place where Liz, Chuck, Billy, and Katie unwind, cynics are disappointed that only one room (the ballroom) is open to the public. Some find the visit overrated and overpriced. Because this is a vacation palace (rather than a state residence), it lacks the sumptuous staterooms you'll see at Holyroodhouse in Edinburgh; this visit is about the grounds and the setting rather than the interior.

Cost and Hours: £11.50, includes audioguide, April-July daily 10:00-17:00, closed Aug-March, arrive at least an hour before closing, tel. 013397/42534, www.balmoralcastle.com.

Safaris: If you're caught up in the beauty of Balmoral, consider booking a ranger-led Land Rover safari through the grounds (£60, 3 hours, 2/day during the open season).

Background: Queen Victoria and Prince Albert purchased Balmoral in 1848. The thickly forested hills all around reminded Albert of his Thuringian homeland, but Victoria adored it as well—calling it her "Highland paradise." They remodeled the castle extensively in the Scottish Baronial style—a romantic, faux-antique look resembling turreted Scottish Renaissance castles from the 16th century—helping to further popularize that look. Ever since, each British monarch has enjoyed retreating to this sprawling property, designed for hunting (red deer) and fishing (salmon). The royal family was here when news broke of Princess Diana's death. (Their initial decision not to return to London or to mourn publicly was highly criticized, as depicted in the film *The Queen*.) Today Balmoral has a huge staff, 80 miles of roads, a herd of Highland cattle, and a flock of Highland ponies (stout little miniature horses useful for hauling deer carcasses over the hills).

Visiting the Castle: From the parking lot (with a TI/gift shop, WCs, and the royal church across the street—described later), walk

across the River Dee to reach the ticket booth. From here, you can either hike 10 minutes to the palace, or hop on the free trolley.

Once at the stables, pick up your included audioguide and peruse a few exhibits, including an 8-minute orientation film. In the main exhibit, you'll see a video of the kilts-

and-bagpipes welcome parade, plus a diorama of local wildlife, and lots and lots of historical photos of royals enjoying Balmoral—including about 60 years of royal family Christmas cards. Peek into the Queen's garage to see her custom Bentley.

Then follow your audioguide on a short loop through the grounds and gardens before arriving at the palace. (To cut to the chase, or if the weather is bad, you can shortcut from the exhibit directly to the palace and the one room open to the public.) As you walk through the produce and flower gardens, ponder the unenviable challenge of trying to time all of the flowers to bloom and the produce to ripen at the same time, coinciding with the royal family's arrival the first week of August (especially difficult given Scotland's notoriously uncooperative climate).

Finally you'll reach the single room in the palace open to the public: the palace ballroom. Display cases show off memorabilia (children's games played by royal tots, and a fully operational mini-Citroën that future kings and queens have enjoyed driving around). Near the exit, a touchscreen offers you a virtual glimpse at the tartaned private quarters that are off-limits to us commoners.

Nearby: For a free peek at another royal landmark, stop at **Crathie Kirk,** the small, stony, charming parish church where the royal family worships when they are at Balmoral, and where Queen Victoria's beloved servant John Brown is buried (£1 donation requested, daily 10:00-12:30 & 13:00-16:00, closed Nov-March). The church is just across the highway from the Balmoral parking lot.

The next town past Balmoral Castle (in the opposite direction from Ballater) is **Braemar** (bray-MAR). This tiny village hosts the most famous Highland Games in Scotland, as the Queen is almost always in attendance (first Sun in Sept, www.braemargathering. org). If you swing through town, you can take a look at its big games grandstand and its picturesque castle (not worth touring).

▲▲Ballater

Ballater (BAH-lah-tur) is the place where you'll feel as much royalist sentiment as anywhere in Scotland. For the people of Ballater (many of whom work, either directly or indirectly, with Balmoral Castle), the Windsors are, simply, their neighbors. Royal connections aside, Ballater is a pleasant, unpretentious, extremely tidy little town. Just big enough to have all the essential tourist services—but neatly nestled in the wooded hills of the Cairngorms, and a bit more "away from it all" than Pitlochry—Ballater is an ideal home base for those wanting to spend a night in this part of Scotland.

It was local springs—which bubbled up supposedly healing waters—that first put Ballater on the map. But there's no question the town is what it is today thanks to Queen Victoria and Prince Albert, who bought the nearby Balmoral Castle in 1848, then built a train station in Ballater to access it. Today, the town's best attraction may be its residents, who revel in telling tales of royal encounters. Prince Charles, who lives not at Balmoral but at Birkhall (not open to the public), has a particular affection for this part of the Cairngorms. He supports Ballater charities and has been known to show up unannounced at town events...and locals love him for it. ("Prince Charles is a really nice guy," one of them told me. "Not at all like the chap you see on TV.")

Sights in Ballater: The town's only real sight—the old **train station** built by Queen Victoria to more easily commute to her new summer home at Balmoral Castle—suffered a fire in 2015. The artifacts housed in its minimuseum were saved, and the station should be reopened by the time of your visit. (It will have the TI, library, and an exhibit of how Queen Victoria relied on trains to get to Balmoral.)

The town is also fun for a wander. Facing the station are two stately sandstone buildings honoring the couple that put this little village on the map: the Prince Albert Hall and the Victoria Hall. Exploring the streets nearby, with their characteristic little shops, you'll notice several boasting the coveted seals announcing "By Appointment of her Majesty the Queen" or "By Appointment of H.R.H. the Prince of Wales"—meaning that they're authorized to sell their wares directly to the gang at Balmoral.

A block from the station—past the Balmoral Bar, with its turrets that echo its namesake castle—the unusually fine parish church is surrounded by an inviting green, with benches, flower gardens, and royal flourishes...like everything in Ballater.

Sleeping in Ballater: The town has several fine B&Bs; given the royal proximity and generally touristy nature of Ballater, prices are high...but so is quality.

$$ Osborne House is a big and cozy home, with spacious rooms, a walled garden, and delightful hosts Heather and Neil (4 Dundarroch Road, tel. 013397/55320, www.osbornehousebedandbreakfast.

com, osbornehousebedandbreakfast@gmail.com). Just down the road past the Osborne House garden, look for the white fence surrounding the Victoria barracks—where soldiers tasked with guarding the Queen reside.

$$ Gordon Guest House, right in the center of town facing the historic train station, has five richly furnished rooms (Station Square, tel. 013397/55996, www.thegordonguesthouse.com, info@thegordonguesthouse.com, Martin and Amanda).

Eating in Ballater: If you're just passing through, consider grabbing lunch at the old-school café **$ The Bothy.** Farther along the main street (toward Aberdeen), near the end of the strip of shops, **$$ Rocksalt & Snails** is a hipper choice. There's also a handy, long-hours **Co-op grocery store** facing the parish church, and nice tables on the green. For a more serious dinner, Ballater has two good Indian restaurants (both facing the green) and a few hotel restaurants and pubs. **$$$$ Rothesay Rooms Restaurant,** sponsored by Prince Charles in 2016 as a charity project after the town suffered from devastating floods, has a good reputation (Wed-Sat 18:00-21:00, 3 Netherley Place near the church green, tel. 013397/53816, www.rothesay-rooms.co.uk). And **$$$ Clachan Grill,** serving modern Scottish cuisine, is about the most stylish and foodie place in town (Wed-Mon 17:00-21:00, closed Tue, tel. 013397/55999, look down a side lane near the bridge at 5 Bridge Square).

Scotland's East Coast

Scotland's inlet-slashed, island-speckled west coast gets all of the attention...and should. But if you're nearby, consider taking a peek at the east coast. While St. Andrews—with its links and beaches—is probably Scotland's finest east-coast town, one uniquely hulking castle ruin rises above other coastal choices: Dunnottar Castle. For those who enjoy hiking on coastal bluffs and exploring ruins, it's worth a detour on your way south from Ballater and Balmoral.

Dunnottar Castle

The mostly ruined, empty, and otherwise underwhelming castle of Dunnottar (duh-NAW-tur) owns a privileged position: clinging to the top of a bulbous bluff, flanked by pebbly beaches and surrounded nearly 360 degrees by the North Sea. It's scenic and strategic. From the parking lot, you'll walk five minutes to a fork: To the right, you'll come to a ridge with a panoramic view of the castle's fine setting; to the left, you'll hike steeply down (almost all the way to the beach), then steeply back up, to the castle itself. Inside, there's not much to see. The only important thing that happened here was the Battle for the Honours of Scotland, when the Scottish crown jewels were briefly hidden away in the castle from Oliver Cromwell's army, which laid siege to Dunnottar (unsuccessfully) for three days. But don't worry too much about the history, or the scant posted descriptions—just explore the stately ruins while enjoying the panoramic views, sea spray, and cry of the gulls.

Cost and Hours: The photo-op view is free (and enough for many); entering the castle costs £7, daily 9:00-17:30, shorter hours Oct-March, tel. 01569/762-173, www.dunnottarcastle.co.uk.

Getting There: It's just off the busy A-90 expressway, which runs parallel to the coast between Aberdeen and Dundee; exit for Stonehaven, and you'll find Dunnottar well-signed just to the south.

Nearby: Dunnottar sits just beyond **Stonehaven,** a pleasant, workaday seafront town that's a handy place to stretch your legs or grab some lunch (big pay parking lot right in the town center, ringed by eateries and grocery stores).

ISLE OF SKYE

Portree • Sights on the Isle of Skye

The rugged, remote-feeling Isle of Skye has a reputation for unpredictable weather ("Skye" comes from the Old Norse for "The Misty Isle"). But it also offers some of Scotland's best scenery, and it rarely fails to charm its many visitors. Narrow, twisty roads wind around Skye in the shadows of craggy, black, bald mountains, and the coastline is ruffled with peninsulas and sea lochs (inlets).

Skye is the largest of the Inner Hebrides, and Scotland's second-biggest island overall (over 600 square miles), but it's still manageable: You're never more than five miles from the sea. The island has only about 13,000 residents; roughly a quarter live in the main village, Portree. The mountain-like Cuillin Hills separate the northern part of the island (Portree, Trotternish, Dunvegan) from the south (Skye Bridge, Kyleakin, Sleat Peninsula).

Set up camp in Portree, Skye's charming, low-key tourism hub. Then dive into Skye's attractions. Drive around the appealing Trotternish Peninsula, enjoying Scotland's scenic beauty: sparsely populated rolling fields, stony homes, stark vistas of jagged rock formations, and the mysterious Outer Hebrides looming on the horizon. Go for a hike in (or near) the dramatic Cuillin Hills, sample a peaty dram of whisky, and walk across a desolate bluff to a lighthouse at the end of the world. Learn about the sordid clan history of Skye, and visit your choice of clan castles: the MacLeods' base at Dunvegan, the MacDonalds' ruins near Armadale, and—nearby but not on Skye—the postcard-perfect Eilean Donan fortress, previously a Mackenzie stronghold but today held by the Macraes. Or just settle in, slow down, and enjoy island life.

The most useful TI is in Portree; shops in smaller towns (including Dunvegan) host more basic "information points." At nearly every pullout you'll find an info post giving background on that stop.

PLANNING YOUR TIME

With two weeks in Scotland, Skye merits two nights, allowing a full day to hit its highlights: Trotternish Peninsula loop, Dunvegan Castle, the Fairy Pools hike (or another hike in the Cuillin Hills), and the Talisker Distillery tour. Mountaineers need extra time for hiking and hillwalking. Because it takes time to reach, Skye is skippable if you only have a few days in Scotland—instead, focus on the more accessible Highlands sights (Oban and its nearby islands, and Glencoe).

Situated between Oban/Glencoe and Loch Ness/Inverness, Skye fits neatly into a Highlands itinerary. To avoid seeing the same scenery twice, it works well to drive the "Road to the Isles" from Fort William to Mallaig, then take the ferry to Skye; later, leave Skye via the Skye Bridge and follow the A-87 east toward Loch Ness and Inverness, stopping at Eilean Donan Castle en route, or vice versa. With more time, take the very long and scenic route north from Skye, up Wester Ross and across Scotland's north coast, then down to Inverness (see the Northern Scotland chapter).

GETTING TO THE ISLE OF SKYE

By Car: Your easiest bet is the slick, free **Skye Bridge** that crosses from Kyle of Lochalsh on the mainland to Kyleakin on Skye (for more on the bridge, see page 379).

The island can also be reached by **car ferry.** The major ferry line connects the mainland town of Mallaig (west of Fort William along the "Road to the Isles"—see page 291) to Armadale on Skye (£15/car with 2 people, reservations required, April-late Oct 8/day each way, off-season very limited Sat-Sun connections, must check in at least 20 minutes before sailing or your place will be sold and you will not get on, can be canceled in rough weather, 30-minute trip, operated by Caledonian MacBrayne, toll-free tel. 0800-066-5000 or tel. 01475/650-397, www.calmac.co.uk).

By Bus: Skye is connected to the outside world by Scottish Citylink buses (www.citylink.co.uk), which use Portree as their Skye hub. From Portree, buses connect to **Inverness** (bus #917, 3/day, 3.5 hours) and **Glasgow** (buses #915 and #916, 3/day, 7 hours, also stops at **Fort William** and **Glencoe**). For **Edinburgh,** you'll transfer in either Inverness or Glasgow (4/day, 8 hours total). (For connections within the Isle of Skye, see later.)

More complicated **train-plus-bus** connections are possible for the determined: Take the train from Edinburgh or Glasgow to Fort William; transfer to the "Sprinter" train to Mallaig (4/day, 1.5

hours); take the ferry across to Armadale; then catch Stagecoach bus #52 to Portree (1 hour). Alternatively, you can take the train from Edinburgh or Glasgow to Inverness, take another train to Kyle of Lochalsh, then catch a bus to Portree.

GETTING AROUND THE ISLE OF SKYE
By Car
Once on Skye, you'll need a car to thoroughly enjoy the island. (Even if you're doing the rest of your trip by public transportation, a car rental is worthwhile here to make maximum use of your time; Portree-based car-rental options are listed on page 358.) If you're driving, the roads are simple and well signposted. But if you'll be exploring, a good map can be helpful. Sample driving times: Kyleakin and Skye Bridge to Portree—45 minutes; Portree to Dunvegan—30 minutes; Portree to the tip of Trotternish Peninsula and back again—2 hours (more with sightseeing stops); Portree to Armadale/ferry to Mallaig—1 hour; Portree to Talisker Distillery—40 minutes.

By Public Bus
Skye can be frustrating by bus (slow and limited). Portree is the hub for bus traffic. Most buses within Skye are operated by Stagecoach (www.stagecoachbus.com; buy individual tickets or, for longer journeys, consider the £8.85 all-day Dayrider ticket or the £33.30 weeklong Megarider ticket; buy tickets onboard). From Portree, you can loop around the **Trotternish Peninsula** on bus #57A (counterclockwise route) or bus #57C (clockwise route; Mon-Sat 4/day in each direction, limited on Sun). Bus #56 connects Portree and **Dunvegan Castle** (3/day, does not run on Sun, 40 minutes). From Portree to **Kyleakin,** take the Inverness-bound Citylink #917 (3/day, 1 hour) or local bus #50 (2/day, 1 hour, none on Sat-Sun); to reach **Eilean Donan Castle,** take any Citylink bus heading toward Fort William or Inverness (#915, #916, and #917; get off at Dornie and walk, 6/day, 1 hour).

By Tour
Several operations on the island take visitors to hard-to-reach spots. Figure £40-45 per person to join an all-day island tour (about 8 hours). Compare the offerings at the following companies, which use smaller 8- or 16-seat minibuses: **Skye Scenic Tours** (tel. 01478/617-006, www.skyescenictours.com), **Tour Skye** (tel. 01478/613-514, www.tourskye.com), and **SkyeBus** (tel. 01470/532-428, www.realscottishjourneys.com).

Portree-based **Michelle Rhodes** also does tours around the island (see page 358).

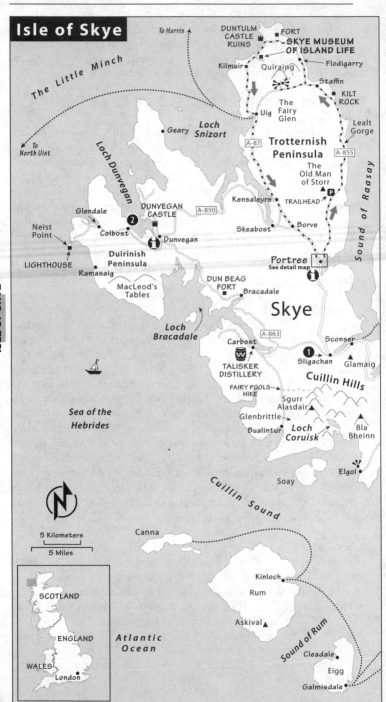

Isle of Skye

To Harris

DUNTULM CASTLE RUINS

FORT

SKYE MUSEUM OF ISLAND LIFE

The Little Minch

Kilmuir Quiraing Flodigarry

Staffin

KILT ROCK

Uig The Fairy Glen

Lealt Gorge

Loch Snizort

Geary

A-87

Trotternish Peninsula

To North Uist

Loch Dunvegan

Glendale

DUNVEGAN CASTLE

A-850

The Old Man of Storr

Neist Point

Colbost

Dunvegan

Kensaleyre TRAILHEAD

Sound of Raasay

LIGHTHOUSE

Ramasaig

Duirinish Peninsula

Skeabost Borve

MacLeod's Tables

DUN BEAG FORT

Bracadale

Portree
See detail map

Loch Bracadale

Skye

A-863

Carbost

Sconser

TALISKER DISTILLERY

Sligachan

Glamaig

Sea of the Hebrides

FAIRY POOLS HIKE

Cuillin Hills

Sgurr Alasdair

Glenbrittle

Bualintur

Loch Coruisk

Bla Bheinn

N

5 Kilometers

5 Miles

Soay

Elgol

Cuillin Sound

Canna

Kinloch

SCOTLAND

Rum

Sound of Rum

ENGLAND

Askival

Cleadale

WALES

London

Atlantic Ocean

Eigg

Galmisdale

ISLE OF SKYE

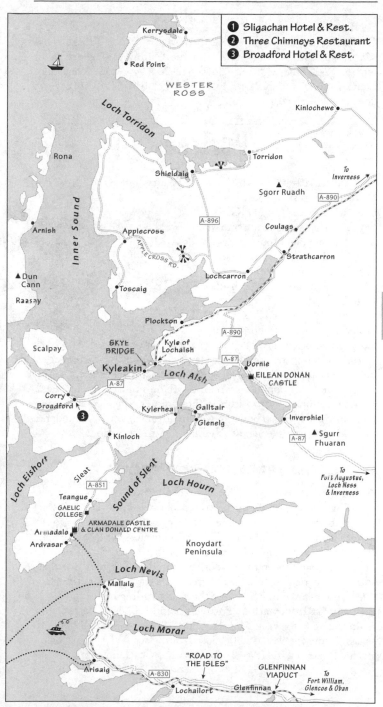

1 Sligachan Hotel & Rest.
2 Three Chimneys Restaurant
3 Broadford Hotel & Rest.

ISLE OF SKYE

By Taxi or Shuttle

GoSkye offers a shuttle service to the Fairy Pools, Talisker Distillery, the Old Man of Storr, and the Quiraing (single trips or return, £8-12 one-way, tel. 01470/532-264, www.go-skye.co.uk). **Don's Taxis** is available for private rides (tel. 01478/613-100, www. donstaxis.vpweb.co.uk).

Portree

Skye's main attraction is its natural beauty, not its villages. But of those villages, the best home base is Portree (pore-TREE), Skye's largest settlement, transportation hub, and tourism center—ideally located for exploring Skye's quintessential sights on the Trotternish Peninsula loop drive.

Portree is nestled deep in its protective, pastel harbor; overlapping peninsulas just offshore guard it from battering west coast storms. Most of today's Portree dates from its early-19th-century boom time as a kelp-gathering and herring-fishing center.

As the most popular town on Scotland's most popular island, Portree is jammed with visitors in the summer. There are lots of hotels and B&Bs (which book up well in advance) and an abundance of good restaurants (the best of which merit reservations).

Orientation to Portree

Although Portree doesn't have any real sights, it does boast a gorgeous harbor area and—in the streets above—all of the necessary tourist services: a good TI, fine B&Bs, great restaurants, a grocery store, a launderette, and so on. The main business zone of this functional town of about 3,000 residents is in the tight grid of lanes on the bluff just above the harbor, anchored by Portree's tidy main square, Somerled Square. From here, buses fan out across the island and to the mainland. B&Bs line the roads leading out of town.

Tourist Information: Portree's helpful TI is a block off the main square (June-Aug Mon-Sat 9:00-18:30, Sun until 17:00; off-season Mon-Sat 9:30-16:30, closed Sun; free Wi-Fi, just below Bridge Road, tel. 01478/612-137, www.visitscotland.com).

Portree

PLAY FIELDS

To Uig & Dunvegan

To Staffin, Portrush Peninsula & 🚩13

HOME FARM RD.
WINDSOR CRES.
STORMCHILL RD.
KILSON CRES.
STAFFIN RD.

PARK RD.
PARK LN.
YORK DRIVE
WENTWORTH ST.

MANSE IN
DUNVEGAN RD.
BRIDGE RD.

MARTIN CRES.
COOLIN DR.

To Scorrybreac Park

MILL RD.

SCHOOL

🚩12
🚩15
🚩7 Somerled Square 🅱
🚩6 LIGHTARRY COURT THE GREEN
🚩23

🚩17 🚩22
🚩4
🚩21
🚩18

🚩14 🚩5
🚩16
🚩3

Harbor
MEALE HOUSE

SEAFIELD PL.
VIEWFIELD RD.

P
P
Main Parking Lot

🚩1
🚩20

PORTREE MEDICAL CENTRE

BANK ST.
BAYFIELD RD.
BEAUMONT

SKYE GATHERING HALL

🚩2
🚩19
QUAY ST.

🚩11

🚩8

BAYFIELD RD.

APOTHECARY TOWER
"The Lump"

Loch Portree

🚩9

200 Meters
200 Yards

HIGHLAND GATHERING BOWL

To Sligachan & Kyle of Lochalsh
🚩10

ISLE OF SKYE

<u>Accommodations</u>
1 Rosedale Hotel
2 Pink Guest House
3 Marine House
4 The Portree Hotel
5 Ben Tianavaig
6 Youth Hostel
7 Independent Hostel & Launderette
8 Duirinish Guest House
9 Fishers Rock
10 To Greenacros Guest House
11 Seaforth Cottage

12 Easdale B&B
13 To Ballintoy B&B

<u>Eateries & Other</u>
14 Scorrybreac
15 The Isles Inn
16 Café Arriba & The Chippy
17 The Café
18 L'Incontro Pizza
19 Sea Breezes
20 Harbour Fish & Chips
21 Fat Panda
22 Co-op Grocery & Relish
23 Bike Rental

HELPFUL HINTS

WCs: Public WCs are across the street and down a block from the TI, across from the hostel.

Laundry: There's a **self-service launderette** below the Independent Hostel, just off the main square (usually 11:00-21:00, last load starts at 20:00, The Green, tel. 01478/613-737).

Bike Rental: Island Cycles rents bikes in the middle of town, just off the main square (£10/half-day, £20/24 hours, best to re-serve in advance in high season, Mon-Sat 9:00-17:00, closed Sun, shorter hours in winter, The Green, tel. 01478/613-121, www.islandcycles-skye.co.uk).

Car Rental: To make the most of your time on Skye, rent a car. Several options line up along the road to Dunvegan and charge around £40-60/day (most are closed Sun; smart to call sev-eral days ahead in peak season, but worth trying last-minute). The most user-friendly option is **M2 Motors,** which can pick you up at your B&B or the bus station (tel. 01478/613-344, www.m2-motors.co.uk). If they're booked up, try **Jansvans** (tel. 01478/612-087, www.jans.co.uk), **Highland Motors/ HM Hire** (based nearby in Borve but can pick up in Portree, tel. 01470/532-264, www.hm-hire.co.uk), or **Morrison** (tel. 01478/612-688, www.morrisoncarrental.com).

Parking: As you enter town, you'll see signs on the right directing you to a free parking lot below, at water level—after parking, just head up the stairs to the TI. You can also pay-and-display to park in the main town square (2-hour max, free after 18:00).

Town Walk: Michelle Rhodes leads guided one-hour town walks through Portree by request. While there's not a lot to say about the town, it's fun to have a local to explain things, and Michelle is a fine storyteller (£10 per person, call or email to set a time; mobile 07833-073-951, tel. 01478/611-915, www.skyehistoryandheritagetours.co.uk, michellelorrainerhodes@gmail.com). She also offers all-day guided driving tours around the island, tailored to your interests. Her specialty: clan battles, fairies, myths, and legends (£150 for two, £75/extra person).

Sights in Portree

There's not a turnstile in town, but Portree itself is fun to explore. Below I've described the village's three areas: the main square and "downtown," the harborfront, and the hill above the harbor.

Somerled Square and the Town Center

Get oriented to Portree on the broad main square, with its mercat cross, bus stops, parking lot, and highest concentration of public benches. The square is named for Somerled (Old Norse for "Sum-mer Wanderer"), the 12th-century ruler who kicked off the Mac-Donald clan dynasty and first united Scotland's western islands into the so-called Lordship of the Isles.

It seems every small Scottish town has both a mercat cross and a World War I memorial—and in Portree, they're combined into one. A mercat cross indicated the right for a town to host a market, and was the community gathering point for celebrations, public shamings, and executions. The WWI memorial is a reminder of the disproportionate loss of life that particular conflict exacted on Scotland. In the case of wee Portree, a band of 28 Gaelic-speaking brothers went to war...and eight came back. (Ten were killed in a single night of fighting.)

Much of present-day Portree was the vision of Sir James Mac-Donald, who pushed to develop the town in the late 18th century. City leaders imported the impressive engineer Thomas Telford (famous for his many great canals, locks, and bridges) to help design the village's harbor and the roads connecting it to the rest of the island.

Wentworth Street, running from this square to the harbor, is the main shopping drag. Several English-sounding streets in Portree (Wentworth, Bosville, Douglas, Beaumont) are named for aristocratic families that the MacDonalds married into, helping to keep the clan financially afloat. Window-shop your way two blocks along Wentworth Street. Turn right on Bank Street. The **Royal Hotel,** built on the site of MacNab's Inn, where Bonnie Prince Charlie bid farewell to Flora MacDonald following his crushing defeat at Culloden, then set sail, never again to return to Scotland.

Quay Street leads down the hill to...

▲▲Portree Harbor

Portree's most pleasant space (unless you've got food the seagulls

want) is its harbor, where colorful homes look out over bobbing boats and the surrounding peninsulas. As one of the most protected natural harbors on the west coast, it's the reason that Portree emerged as Skye's leading town. Find a scenic perch at the corner of the harbor and take it all in.

While tourism is today's main industry, Portree first boomed in the mid-18th century thanks to kelp. Seaweed was gathered here, sun-dried, and burned in kilns to create an ashy-blue substance that was rich in soda, an essential ingredient in the production of glass and soap. But with the defeat of Napoleon at Waterloo, international sources of kelp opened up, causing this local industry to crash. This economic downturn coincided with a potato famine (similar to the one across the sea in Ireland), and by the mid-1800s, many locals were setting sail from this harbor to seek a better life in North America. But Portree soldiered on, bolstered by its prime location for fishing—especially for herring. By the early 20th century, a nationwide herring boom had again buoyed Portree's economy, with hundreds of fishing boats crowding its harbor.

Notice the stone building with the sealed-off door at the base of the stairs leading up into town. This was the former **ice house,** which was in operation until the 1970s. The winch at the peak of the building was used to haul big blocks of ice into an enormous subterranean cellar, to preserve Atlantic salmon throughout the summer.

Survey the harbor, enjoying the **pastel homes**—which come with lots of local gossip. Rumor has it that these used to be more uniform, until a proud gay couple decided to paint their house pink (it's now a recommended B&B). What used to be a blue-and-white house next door (now an all-blue hotel) belonged to a fan of the West Ham United soccer team. Soon the other homeowners followed suit, each choosing their own color. Speaking of bright colors, look for the traffic-cone-orange boat floating in the harbor. This belongs to the Royal National Lifeboat Institution (RNLI), Britain's charity-funded answer to the US Coast Guard.

You may notice the busy fish-and-chips joint, with its customers standing guardedly against the nearby walls and vicious seagulls perched on rooftops ready to swoop down at the first sight of battered cod.

Go for a stroll along the Telford-built pier. Along here, a couple of different companies offer 1.5-hour excursions out to the sea-eagle nests and around the bay (ask the captains at the port, or inquire at the TI). At the far end of the pier is a BP gas station with huge, underwater tanks for fueling visiting boats. When big cruise ships are in port, they drop the hook and tender their passengers in to this pier.

Ascending "The Lump" (Hill Above the Harbor)

For a different perspective on Portree—and one that gets you away from the tourists—hike up the bluff at the south end of the harbor. From the Royal Hotel, head up Bank Street.

After a few steps, you'll spot the white **Meall House** on your left—supposedly Portree's oldest surviving home (c. 1800) and once the sheriff's office and jail. Today it's a center for the Gaelic cultural organization Fèisean nan Gàidheal, which celebrates the Celtic tongue that survives about as well here on Portree as anywhere in Scotland. Hiding behind the Meall House, along the harborview path, is the stepped-gable **Skye Gathering Hall** (from 1879). This is where Portree's upper crust throws big, fancy, invitation-only balls on the days before and after Skye's Highland Games. The rest of the year, it hosts cultural events and—on most days—a fun little market with a mix of crafts and flea-market-type items.

Back on Bank Street, continue uphill. Soon you'll approach the **Portree Medical Centre**—one of just two hospitals on the entire Isle of Skye. (Is it just me, or do those parking spots each come with a graveyard cross?)

Just before the hospital's parking lot, watch on the left for the

uphill lane through the trees. Use this to hike on up to the top of the hill that locals call "The Lump" (or, for those with more local pride, "Fancy Hill"). Emerging into the clearing, you'll reach a huge, flat **bowl** that was blasted out of solid rock to hold 5,000 people during Skye's annual Highland Gathering. (For more on Highland Games, see page 236.) In addition to the typical Highland dancing, footraces, and feats of strength, Skye's games have a unique event: From this spot, runners climb downhill, swim across Loch Portree, ascend the hill on the adjacent peninsula, then swim back again.

Walk left, toward the harbor, then head left again onto a path leading away from the bowl; you'll run into a crenellated **apothecary tower.** It was built in 1834, not as a castle fortification but to alert approaching sailors that a pharmacist was open for business in Portree. This tower was literally blown over by gale-force winds in a 1991 storm, but has since been rebuilt. It's usually open if you'd like to climb to the top for views over the harbor and

the region—on a clear day, you can see all the way to the Old Man of Storr (see page 368).

Walks and Hikes near Portree
The Portree TI can offer advice about hikes in the area; if either of the below options interests you, get details there before you head out.

One popular choice, which doesn't require a car, is called the

Scorrybreac Path. To get to the trailhead—three-quarters of a mile from Somerled Square—walk north out of Portree on Mill Road, veer right onto Scorrybreac Road when you're just leaving town (following the sign for *Budhmor*), then follow the coastline to the start of the hiking trail, marked by signs. From here, you'll walk along the base of a bluff with fine views back on Portree's colorful harborfront.

Drivers can tackle the more ambitious hike up to the **Old Man of Storr:** You'll drive about 15 minutes north of town (following the start of my Trotternish Peninsula Driving Tour) and park at the Old Man of Storr trailhead. Green trail signs lead you through a gate and up along a well-trod gravel path through a felled woodland. Once you've reached the top of the first bluff, take the right fork, and continue all the way up to the pinnacle. Plan on about two hours round-trip. (If you don't mind a longer drive, a better walk is at **The Quiraing**—see page 370.)

Sleeping in Portree

Portree is crowded with hikers and tourists in July and August: Book your room well in advance. You may need to check with several places. If you're late to the game, you might have better luck with a hotel, Airbnb, or one of the B&Bs lacking websites (of the ones I list, these include Marine House, Seaforth Cottage, and Easdale B&B). Spring and fall (March-June and Sept-Oct) are also busy, but a bit more manageable (and cheaper).

If looking last-minute, try the Facebook group "Skye Rooms," where hotels, B&Bs, and short-term apartments with late cancelations and random openings list their availability for the next day. Travelers looking for accommodations can also post their desired dates.

ON THE HARBOR

$$$ Rosedale Hotel fills three former fishermen's houses with mazelike hallways and 23 rooms (some modern, some more traditional). With-it Neil, a recent business school graduate, runs the hotel with the help of his family, including his mom, who cooks (family room and a few small, no-view, cheaper doubles available; no elevator, restaurant, bar for guests only, parking lot down the road; Beaumont Crescent, tel. 01478/613-131, www. rosedalehotelskye.co.uk, reservations@rosedalehotelskye.co.uk).

$$ At Pink Guest House, energetic Robbie and Fiona rent 11 bright, spacious rooms (8 with sea views) on the harbor. The rates include a full Scottish breakfast and the hosts' youthful enthusiasm (large family rooms, Quay Street, tel. 01478/612-263, www. pinkguesthouse.co.uk, info@pinkguesthouse.co.uk).

$ Marine House, a cozy, welcoming, delightful time warp run by sweet Skye native Fiona Stephenson, has three simple, homey rooms (two with a private bathroom down the hall) and fabulous views of the harbor. Breakfast is conversational, as you'll eat with the other guests at one big table (cash only, reserved parking right on harbor, 2 Beaumont Crescent, tel. 01478/611-557, stephensonfiona@yahoo.com).

UP IN TOWN

$$$$ The Portree Hotel is your basic, impersonal town-center accommodation (right on the main square) with 24 modernized rooms on three floors and no elevator (family rooms, bar/restaurant, no parking—must use public lots, tel. 01478/612-511, www.theportreehotel.com, contact@theportreehotel.com).

$$ Ben Tianavaig, on the busy road through town overlooking the harbor, offers four fresh and airy rooms (all with views). Charlotte and Bill are generous with travel tips, offer a breakfast special of the day, and foster a shoes-off tidiness (2-night minimum required, cash only, street parking out front; 5 Bosville Terrace, tel. 01478/612-152, www.ben-tianavaig.co.uk, info@ben-tianavaig.co.uk).

¢ Portree Youth Hostel, run by Hostelling Scotland (SYHA), is a modern-feeling, institutional, cinderblock-and-metal building with 54 beds in 16 rooms (private and family rooms available, continental breakfast extra, kitchen, laundry, tel. 01478/612-231, www.syha.org.uk, portree@syha.org.uk).

¢ Portree Independent Hostel, in the unmissable yellow building just off the main square, has 60 beds and equally bold colors inside (one double room and several 4-person rooms, no breakfast, kitchen, laundry, tel. 01478/613-737, www.hostelskye.co.uk, skyehostel@yahoo.co.uk).

JUST OUTSIDE TOWN
South of Portree, off Viewfield Road

Viewfield Road, stretching south from Portree toward the Aros Centre, is B&B central. All offer convenient parking and are within walking distance of town (figure 10-15 minutes). Some are on smaller side lanes that stretch down toward the water, but all are well marked from the main road.

$$ Duirinish Guest House feels homey, modern, and tidy. With four rooms, it sits across the main road from the water (only a few obstructed sea views) but comes with a spacious guest lounge and a warm welcome (2-night minimum, closed Nov-March, tel. 01478/613-728, www.duirinish-bandb-skye.com, ruth.n.prior@hotmail.co.uk, Ruth and Allan).

$$ Fishers Rock, a serene waterfront retreat with a glassy,

ISLE OF SKYE

contemporary, light-filled view breakfast room, has a soothing energy and three rooms (two-night minimum, closed in winter, tel. 01478/612-122, www.fishersrock.com, fishersrock@btinternet. com, Heather).

$$ Greenacres Guest House feels estate-like and a bit more formal, with fine china on the table, fountain and manicured hedges in the garden, and a glassed-in sunroom with views. The five rooms have different color schemes and styles, and some feature Ewen's handmade headboards, built from wood recycled from an old school (cash only, closed Oct-Easter, one of the farthest houses from town on Viewfield Road, about a 20-minute walk, tel. 01478/612-605, www.greenacres-skye.co.uk, greenacreskye@aol. com, Marie and Ewen).

$ Seaforth Cottage feels like a retired sea captain's home. Overlooking tidal flats, its garden is artfully littered with nautical flotsam and jetsam. The three simple rooms come with sea views and are a bit older, but priced accordingly (cash only, tel. 01478/612-040, ianskye48@hotmail.co.uk, gentle Ian).

$ Easdale B&B is another old-school place with three rooms, a bright breakfast room, and large, traditional lounge set just above the busy main road; it's a bit closer to town than the places listed above (cash only, no kids, Bridge Road, tel. 01478/613-244—call to reserve; spunky, plainspoken, and happily computer-free Chrissie).

North of Portree, off Staffin Road

$$ Ballintoy Bed and Breakfast, set back from the road and surrounded by a large field, has three immaculate ground-floor rooms accessorized with fun pops of color and artwork (family room, 2-night minimum preferred, includes continental breakfast, 15-minute walk from town on Staffin Road, tel. 01478/611-719, www.ballintoy-skye.co.uk, ballintoyskye@gmail.com, Gillian and Gavin).

SLEEPING BETWEEN PORTREE AND KYLEAKIN

$$$ Sligachan Hotel (pronounced SLIG-a-hin), perched at a crossroads in the scenic middle of nowhere (yet handy for road-tripping sightseers) is a compound of sleeping and eating options that is a local institution and a haven for hikers. The hotel's 21 rooms are comfortable, if a bit dated and simple for the price, while the nearby campground and bunkhouse offer a budget alternative. The setting—surrounded by the mighty Cuillin Hills—is remarkably scenic (closed Nov-Feb, on the A-87 between Kyleakin and Portree in Sligachan, hotel and campground tel. 01478/650-204, bunkhouse tel. 01478/650-458, www.sligachan.co.uk, reservations@sligachan. co.uk). For location, see the map on page 354.

Eating in Portree

Note that Portree's eateries tend to close early (21:00 or 22:00), and the popular places can merit reservations any evening in the high season.

UP IN TOWN

$$$$ Scorrybreac is Portree's best splurge, offering a delightful array of well-presented international dishes that draw from local ingredients and traditions. The cozy, modern, unpretentious dining room with eight tables fills up quickly, so reservations are a must (set multicourse menus only, Tue-Sun 17:30-22:30, closed Mon, 7 Bosville Terrace, tel. 01478/612-069, www.scorrybreac.com).

$$ The Isles Inn is a happening place, popular with hikers, with two halves serving the same menu—a brighter high-energy dining area and the darker pub—or you can sit at the bar. Offering a fun energy and warm service, they dish up simple, honest food one notch above pub grub. They have popular burgers, and their big slabs of salmon or haddock are served with fresh vegetables. While other places get stuffy, this has nice, fresh air circulation (daily 12:00-15:00 & 17:00-21:30, no reservations possible after 19:00, tel. 01478/612 129, facing the main square, Somerled Square). In summer, the Isles Inn hosts live music several nights a week from 21:30.

$$ Café Arriba is a fun and welcoming space offering refreshingly eclectic flavors in this small Scottish town. With a menu that includes local specialties, burgers, and Italian, this youthful, colorful, easygoing eatery's hit-or-miss cuisine is worth trying. Drop in to see what's on the blackboard menu today (lots of vegetarian options, daily 7:00-18:00, Quay Brae, tel. 01478/611-830).

$$ The Café, a few steps off the main square, is a busy, popular hometown diner serving good crank-'em-out food to an appreciative local crowd. It's family-friendly, with a good selection of burgers and fish-and-chips (daily 9:00-15:30 & 17:30-21:00, Wentworth Street, tel. 01478/612-553). Their homemade ice cream from the stand in front is a nice way to finish your meal.

$$ L'Incontro Pizza is Portree's favorite place for pizza. A sprawling, family-friendly place, it can merit reservations, too (open 17:00-21:00, closed Mon, The Green, tel. 01478/612-535).

DINING ON THE WATERFRONT

Portree's little harbor has a scattering of good eateries but none have actual waterfront seating. My hunch: It's because of the mean seagulls that hang out here.

$$$ Sea Breezes is a popular choice, with plain decor and a seafood-focused menu. At this basic, salty, no-nonsense eatery, you'll likely need reservations for dinner (daily 12:30-14:00 & 17:30-21:30 in summer, shorter hours off-season, closed Nov-Easter, tel. 01478/612-016, www.seabreezes-skye.co.uk).

EATING CHEAPER

Fish-and-Chips: Portree has two chippies: **$ The Harbour Fish & Chips Shop** is delightfully located on the charming harbor with good fish that's cheap and in big portions (daily 11:00-21:00, later in summer). The down side: Aggressive seagulls drive diners up against the wall. It's funny to watch. For a more relaxing meal, **$ The Chippy** sells very basic fish-and-chips and burgers, just up the harbor lane (on Bank Street) with peaceful-if-grungy tables and no seagulls.

Takeaway in Town: The **Fat Panda** Asian restaurant on Bayfield Road is satisfying, the **Co-op** grocery (daily 8:00-23:00) has a small selection of sandwiches and other prepared foods, and **Relish** is a deli serving good, fresh sandwiches (eat in or to go, end of Wentworth Street).

EATING ELSEWHERE ON THE ISLE OF SKYE

In addition to the following two destination restaurants, I've described some eateries in and near Kyleakin—where Skye meets the mainland—on page 379.

In Sligachan: The **Sligachan Hotel** (described earlier) is a grand and rustic old hotel in an extremely scenic setting, nestled in the Cuillin Hills. Its Harta Restaurant offers "casual dining with fine food" and a big and sloppy bar. Popular with campers and hikers, it's also family-friendly, with a zip-line for kids in the playground. The Seumas Bar has a Scotsman-pleasing range of whiskies. Choose between the lovely **$$$** dining room (nightly 18:30-21:00) and the big, open-feeling **$$** pub serving microbrews and mountaineer-pleasing grub (long hours daily, food served until 21:30, pub closed Oct-Feb; on the A-87 between Kyleakin and Portree in Sligachan, tel. 01478/650-204).

In Colbost, near Dunvegan: Out on a deserted road with just sheep for neighbors, the **$$$$ Three Chimneys Restaurant** is known throughout Scotland as a magnet for foodies. Its 16 tables fill an old three-chimney croft house, with a stone-and-timbers decor that artfully melds old and new—a perfect complement to the modern Scottish cuisine. It's cozy, classy, candlelit, and a bit dressy (do your best), but not stuffy. Reservations are essential (set multicourse menus only: £40 or £55 for lunch, £68 or £90 for dinner; daily 12:15-14:00 & 18:30-21:30, shorter hours off-season; tel. 01470/511-258, www.threechimneys.co.uk, Eddie and Shirley Spear). They also rent six swanky, pricey **$$$$** suites next door.

Getting There: It's in the village of Colbost, a 15-minute drive west of Dunvegan (about 45 minutes each way from Portree).

Sights on the Isle of Skye

I've organized these sights geographically, roughly from north (near Portree) to south.

PLANNING YOUR TIME

There is a well-trodden tourist path around Skye, and it's clearly the most memorable way for someone with a car to spend the day. The three big sights are Dunvegan Castle, Talisker Distillery, and Trotternish Peninsula, with its memorable Skye Museum of Island Life. It's possible—but rushed—to see all three in one day. (The challenge: The Skye Museum of Island Life closes at 17:00.) To see all three, start with the first distillery tour at 9:30, tour the castle, and get to the museum by about 16:30. This will rush the wonderful natural sights along the peninsula, but it might be worth it if time is short and you want to experience it all.

While you could drive directly from the castle to the museum and then tour the peninsula in a clockwise direction, it's far more scenic to drive it in a counterclockwise route as proposed here. Summer days are long, and the light can be wonderful in the early evening for the scenic west coast of the Trotternish Peninsula. Another option is to skip the distillery, do the castle first, and then have a leisurely tour of the peninsula as laid out in this chapter. Of course, if you have two days, do it all at your own pace.

TROTTERNISH PENINSULA

This inviting peninsula north of Portree is packed with windswept castaway views, unique geological formations, a few offbeat sights, and some of Scotland's most dramatic scenery. The following loop tour starts and ends in Portree, circling the peninsula counterclockwise (see map on page 354). Along the way, you'll explore a gaggle of old-fashioned stone homes, learn about Skye's ancient farming lifestyles, and pay homage at the grave of a brave woman who rescued a bonnie prince. In good weather, a spin around Trotternish is the best activity Skye offers and is worth ▲▲▲.

With minimal stops, the drive will take about two hours—but it deserves the better part of a day. Note that during several stretches, you'll be driving on a paved single-track road; use the occasional "passing places" to pull over and allow faster cars to go by.

ISLE OF SKYE

❍ Self-Guided Drive

• *Head north of Portree on the A-855, following signs for Staffin. About three miles out of town, you'll begin to enjoy some impressive views of the Trotternish Ridge. You'll be passing peat bogs and may notice stretches where peat has been cut from the fields by the roadside. As you pass the small loch on your right, straight ahead is the distinctive rock tower called the...*

Old Man of Storr

This 160-foot-tall tapered slab of basalt stands proudly apart from the rest of the Storr (as the mountain is called). The unusual land-scape of the Trotternish Peninsula is due to massive landslides (the largest in Britain). This block slid down the cliff about 6,500 years ago and landed on its end, where it has slowly been whittled by weather into a pinnacle. An icon of Skye, the Old Man of Storr has been featured in many films—from *Flash Gordon* to *Prometheus* to *Snow White and the Huntsman.* The lochs on your right supply drinking water for the town of Portree and have been linked together to spin the turbines at a nearby hydroelectric plant that once provided all of Skye's electricity.

If you'd like to tackle the two-hour hike to the Old Man, there's a parking lot directly below the formation (for details on the hike, see page 361).

• *After passing the Old Man, enjoy the scenery on your right, overlooking nearby islands and the mainland.*

As you drive, you'll notice that Skye seems to have more sheep than people. During the Highland Clearances of the early 19th century, many human residents were forced to move off the island to make room for more livestock. The people who remain are some of the most ardently Gaelic Scots in Scotland. While only about one percent of all Scottish people speak Gaelic (pronounced "gal-lic"), one-third of Skye residents are fluent. A generation ago, it was illegal to teach Gaelic in schools; today, Skye offers its residents the opportunity to enroll in Gaelic-only education, from primary school to college (Sabhal Mòr Ostaig, on Skye's Sleat Peninsula, is the world's only college with courses taught entirely in Scottish Gaelic; see page 382).

• *About four miles after the Old Man parking lot, you'll pass a sign for the River Lealt. Immediately after, the turnoff on the right is an optional stop at the...*

Lealt Gorge

Where the River Lealt tumbles toward the sea, it carves out a long and scenic gorge. To stretch your legs, you can walk about five

minutes along the lip of the gorge to reach a viewpoint overlooking a protected, pebbly cove and some dramatic rock formations. The formations on the left, which look like stacked rocks, are the opposite: They've been weathered by centuries of battering storms, which have peeled back any vegetation and ground the stones to their smooth state. Peering down to the beach, you'll see a smokestack

and some other ruins of a plant that once processed diatomite—a crumbly, clay-like substance made from algae fossils, which has hundreds of industrial uses. This factory, which closed in 1960, is a reminder of a time when tourism wasn't the island's main source of income. When this was functioning, no roads connected this point to Portree, so the factory's waterfront location made it possible to ship the diatomite far and wide.

• *Continue along the road. Just after the village of Valtos (about 2 miles after the Lealt Gorge viewpoint), you'll reach a loch (left), next to a parking lot (right). Park at the well-marked Kilt Rock viewpoint to check out...*

▲Kilt Rock

So named because of its resemblance to a Scotsman's tartan, this 200-foot-tall sea cliff has a layer of volcanic rock with vertical lava columns that look like pleats (known as columnar jointing), sitting atop a layer of horizontal sedimentary rock. The dramatic formations in the opposite direction are just as amazing.

• *Continuing north, as you approach the village of* **Staffin***, you'll begin to see interesting rock formations high on the hill to your left.*

Staffin's name, like that of the isle of Staffa (described on page 263), comes from Old Norse and means "the place of staves or pillars"—both boast dramatic basalt rock pillars. If you need a public WC, partway through town, watch on the left for the Staffin Community Hall (marked *Talla Stafainn*, sharing a building with a gro-cer). Or for a coffee or lunch break, you could visit (on the right) the Columba 1400 Centre, a Christian-run retreat for struggling teens from big cities. They run a nice cafeteria and shop to support their work (Mon-Sat 10:00-20:00, closed Sun, tel. 01478/611-400).

• *Just after you leave Staffin, watch for signs on the left to turn off and head up to the quintessential Isle of Skye viewpoint—a rock formation called...*

▲▲The Quiraing

You'll get fine views of this jagged northern end of the Trotternish Ridge as you drive up. Landslides caused the dramatic scenery in this area, and each rock formation has a name, such as "The Nee-dle" or "The Prison."

At the summit of this road, you'll reach a parking area. Even a short walk to a nearby bluff—to get away from the cars and alone with the wind and the island wonder—is rewarding. And there are several exciting longer hikes from here for a closer look at the formations. If you've got the time, energy, and weather for an unforgettable hike, here's your chance. You can follow the trail toward the bluff, and at the fork, decide to stay level (to the

base of the formations) or veer off to the left and switch back up (to the top of the plateau). Both paths are faintly visible from the park-ing area—if it's busy, you'll see hikers on each. Once up top, your reward is a view of the secluded green plateau called "The Table," another landslide block, which isn't visible from the road.

• *You could continue on this road all the way to Uig, at the other end of the peninsula. But it's more interesting to backtrack, then turn left onto the main road (A-855, now single-track), to see the...*

Tip of Trotternish

A few miles north, after the village of Flodigarry, you'll pass the **Flodigarry Hotel,** with a cottage on the premises that was once home to Bonnie Prince Charlie's protector, Flora MacDonald (the cottage is now part of the hotel and not open to the public).

Soon after, at the top of a ridge ahead, you'll see the remains of an old **fort** from World War II, when the Atlantic was monitored for U-boats from this position.

Farther down the road, at the tip of the peninsula, you'll pass (on the right) the crumbling remains of another fort, this one much older: **Duntulm Castle** (free, roadside parking, 5-minute walk

from road), which was the first stronghold on Skye of the influential MacDonald clan. It was from here that the MacDonalds fought many fierce battles against Clan MacLeod (for more on these clan battles, see the sidebar on page 381). The castle was abandoned around 1730 for Armadale Castle on the southern end of Skye (see page 380). While the castle ruins are fenced off, travelers venture in at their own risk. In the distance beyond, you can see the **Outer Hebrides**—the most rugged, remote, and Gaelic part of Scotland.
• *A mile after the castle, watch for the turnoff on the left to the excellent...*

▲▲Skye Museum of Island Life

This fine little stand of seven thatched stone huts, organized into a family-run museum, explains how a typical Skye family lived a century and a half ago.

Cost and Hours: £2.50, Easter-Sept Mon-Sat 9:30-17:00, closed Sun and Oct-Easter, tel. 01470/552-206, www.skyemuseum.co.uk, run by Margaret, Hector, and Dinah. Though there are ample posted explanations, the £1 guidebook is worth buying.

Visiting the Museum: The three huts closest to the sea are original (more than 200 years old). Most interesting is The Old Croft House, which was the residence of the Graham family until 1957. Inside you'll find three rooms: kitchen (with peat-burning fire), parents' "master bedroom," and a bedroom for the 10 kids. Nearby, The Old Barn displays farm implements, and the Ceilidh House (a gathering place for the entire community) contains dense but very informative displays about crofting (the traditional tenant-farmer lifestyle on Skye), the Gaelic language, and a fascinating wall of classic Skye postcards.

The four other huts, reconstructed here, house exhibits about weaving, the village smithy, and more. As you explore, admire the smart architecture of these humble but deceptively well-planned structures. Rocks hanging from the roof keep the thatch from blowing away, and the streamlined shape of the structure embedded in the ground encourages strong winds to deflect around the hut rather than hit it head-on.
• *After touring the museum, head out to the very end of the small road that leads past the parking lot, to a lonesome cemetery. Let yourself in through the gate to reach the tallest Celtic cross at the far end, which is the...*

ISLE OF SKYE

Monument to Flora MacDonald

This fine old cemetery, with mossy and evocative old tombs to ponder, features a tall cross dedicated to the local heroine who rescued the beloved Jacobite hero Bonnie Prince Charlie at his darkest hour. (After the original was chipped away by 19th-century souvenir seekers, this more modern replacement was placed here.) After his loss at Culloden, and with a hefty price on his head, Charlie retreated to the Outer Hebrides. But the Hanover dynasty, which controlled the islands, was closing in. Flora MacDonald rescued the prince, disguised him as her Irish maid, Betty Burke, and sailed him to safety on Skye. (Charlie pulled off the ruse thanks to his soft, feminine features—hence the nickname "Bonnie," which means "beautiful" or "handsome.") The flight inspired

a popular Scottish folk song: "Speed bonnie boat like a bird on the wing, / Onward, the sailors cry. / Carry the lad that's born to be king / Over the sea to Skye." For more on Bonnie Prince Charlie and the Battle of Culloden, see page 292.

• *Return to the main road and proceed about six miles around the peninsula. Soon after what was once a loch (now a giant depression), you'll drop down over the town of Uig ("OO-eeg"), the departure point for ferries to the Outer Hebrides (North Uist and Harris islands, 3/day) and a handy spot for services (cafés, a gas station, pottery shop, brewery, and WC).*

Continue past Uig, climbing the hill across the bay. To take a brief detour to enjoy some hidden scenery, consider a visit to the Fairy Glen. To find it, just after passing the big Uig Hotel, take a very hard left, marked for Sheadar *and* Balnaknock. *Follow this single-track road about a mile through the countryside. You'll emerge into an otherworldly little valley. Wind through the valley to just past the tiny lake and park below the towering Fairy Castle rock.*

▲The Fairy Glen

Whether or not you believe in fairies, it's easy to imagine why locals claim that they live here. With evocatively undulating terrain—ruffled, conical hills called "fairy towers" reflected in glassy ponds, rising up from an otherwise flat and dull countryside—it's a magical place. There's little to see on a quick drive-by, but hikers enjoy exploring these hills, discovering little caves, weathered stone fences, and delightful views. As you explore, keep an eye out for "Skye landmines" (sheep droppings). Hardy hikers enjoy clambering 10 minutes up to the top of the tallest rock tower, the "Fairy Castle." (By the way, the sheep are actually fairies until a human enters the valley.)

• *Head back the way you came and continue uphill on the main road (A-87), with views down over Uig's port. Looking back at Uig, you can see a good example of Skye's traditional farming system—crofting.*

Traditionally, arable land on the island was divided into plots. If you look across to the hills above Uig, you can see strips of de-marcated land running up from the water—these are crofts. Crofts were generally owned by landlords (mostly English aristo-crats or Scottish clan chiefs, and later the Scottish government) and rented to tenant farmers. The crofters lived and worked under very difficult conditions and were lucky if they could produce

enough potatoes and livestock to feed their families. Historically, rights to farm the croft were passed down from father to eldest son over generations, but always under the auspices of a wealthy landlord.

• *But you live in a more affluent and equitable world, and more Scot-tish memories await to be created here on Skye. This tour is finished. From here, you can continue along the main road south toward Portree (and possibly continue from there to the Cuillin Hills). Or you can take the shortcut road just after Kensaleyre (B-8036) and head west on the A-850 to Dunvegan and its castle. All of your Skye options are described in the following pages.*

NORTHWEST SKYE
▲▲Dunvegan Castle

Perched on a rock overlooking a sea loch, Dunvegan Castle is the residence of the MacLeod (pronounced "McCloud") clan.

One of Skye's preeminent clans, the MacLeods often clashed with their traditional rivals, the MacDonalds, whose castle is on the southern tip of the island (see page 381). The MacLeods claim that Dunvegan is the oldest continuously inhabited castle in Scotland. The current clan chief, Hugh Magnus MacLeod, is a film producer who divides his time

between London and the castle, where his noble efforts are aimed at preserving Dunvegan for future generations. Worth ▲▲▲ to people named MacLeod, the castle offers an interesting look at Scotland's antiquated clan system, provides insight into rural Scottish aristocratic lifestyles, and has fine gardens that are a delight to explore. Dunvegan feels rustic and a bit worse-for-wear compared to some of the more famous Scottish castles closer to civilization.

Cost and Hours: £13, daily 10:00-17:30, closed mid-Oct-March, café in parking lot, tel. 01470/521-206, www.dunvegancastle.com.

Getting There: It's near the small town of Dunvegan in the northwestern part of the island, well signposted from the A-850 (free parking). From Portree, bus #56 takes you right to the castle's parking lot.

Visiting the Castle: Follow the one-way route through the castle, borrowing laminated descriptions in each room—and don't hesitate to ask the helpful docents if you have any questions. You'll start upstairs and then make your way to the ground floor with its unforgettable exhibit on the people of St. Kilda.

Up the main staircase and looping left, you reach the **bedroom.** On the elegant canopy bed, look for the clan's seal and motto, carved into the headboard. The words "Hold Fast," which you'll see displayed throughout the castle, recall an incident where a MacLeod chieftain saved a man from being gored by a bull by literally taking the bull by the horns and wrestling it to the ground.

Beyond the bedroom, you'll ogle several more rooms, including the dining room. Here and throughout the castle, portraits of clan chieftains and the MacLeod family seem to be constantly looking down on you. The library's shelves are crammed with rich, leather-bound books.

Then you're routed back across the top of the stairs to the right wing, with the most interesting rooms. The 14th-century **drawing room** is the oldest part of the castle—it served as the great hall of the medieval fortress. But today it's a far cry from its gloomy, stony, Gothic-vaulted original state. In the 18th century, a clan chief's new bride requested that it be brightened up and modernized, so they added a drop ceiling and painted plaster walls. The only clue to its original bulkiness is how thick the walls are (notice that the window bays are nine feet thick). In the drawing room, look for the tattered silk remains of the Fairy Flag, a mysterious swatch with about a dozen different legends attached to it (explained by the handout).

Leaving the drawing room, notice the entrance to the **dungeon**—a holdover from that stout medieval fortress. Squeeze inside the dungeon and peer down into the deep pit. (Hey, is that a Mac-Donald rotting down there?)

At the end of this wing is the **north room,** a minimuseum of the clan's most prestigious artifacts. In the display case in the corner, find Rory Mor's Horn—made from a horn of the subdued bull that gave the clan its motto. Traditionally, this horn would be filled with nearly a half-gallon of claret (Bordeaux wine), which a potential heir had to drink in one gulp to prove himself fit for the role. Other artifacts include bagpipes and several relics related to Bonnie Prince Charlie (including his vest). In the center glass case, next to a lock of Charlie's hair, is a portrait of Flora MacDonald and some items that belonged to her.

From here a staircase leads to the ground floor, where you'll find some important exhibits in more utilitarian rooms. A glass case holds the Claymore Sword—one of two surviving swords made of extremely heavy Scottish iron rather than steel. Dating from the late 15th or early 16th century, this unique weapon is the bazooka of swords—designed not for dexterous fencing, but for one big kill-'em-all swing.

The MacLeods owned the rugged and remote St. Kilda islands (40 miles into the Atlantic, the most distant bit of the British Isles). They collected rent from the hardscrabble St. Kilda community of 100 or so (who were finally evacuated in 1930). The artifacts and dramatic photos of this community is a highlight of the castle visit. And, finally, you can watch a 12-minute video about the castle and the MacLeods, solemnly narrated by the 29th chief of the clan.

Between the castle and the parking lot are five acres of plush **gardens** to stroll through while pondering the fading clan system.

Circling down to the sea loch, you'll enjoy grand views back up to the castle (and see a dock selling 30-minute boat rides on Loch Dunvegan to visit a seal colony on a nearby island—£6, tel. 01470/521-500). Higher up and tucked away are some of the finer, hidden parts of the gardens: the walled garden, the woodland walk up to the water garden (with a thundering waterfall and a gurgling stream), and the wide-open round garden.

The flaunting of inherited wealth and influence in some English castles rubs me the wrong way. But here, seeing the rough edges of a Scottish clan chief's castle, I had the opposite feeling: sympathy and compassion for a proud way of life that's dissolving with the rising tide of modernity. You have to admire the way they "hold fast" to this antiquated system (in the same way the Gaelic tongue is kept on life support). Paying admission here feels more like donating to charity than padding the pockets of a wealthy family. In fact, watered-down MacLeods and MacDonalds from

ISLE OF SKYE

America, eager to reconnect with their Scottish roots, help keep the Scottish clan system alive.

The Giant Angus MacAskill Museum

This oddball museum fills a humble roadside barn in the town of Dunvegan. The pride of Peter Angus MacAskill (whose son, Danny, is a YouTube star for his extreme mountain biking on Skye) is happy to tell the story of "The Giant"—all seven feet nine inches of him—who teamed up with Tom Thumb to travel around the US in the circus and make Barnum and Bailey lots of money until he died in 1863 (£2, Apr-Oct daily 10:00-18:00, closed off-season).

▲Dun Beag Fort

If driving between the distillery and Dunvegan on A-863, you'll pass Skye's best-preserved Iron Age fort or "broch." This 2,000-year-old round stone tower caps a hill a 10-minute walk above its parking lot (just north of the village of Struan). The walk rewards you with an unforgettable chance to be alone in an ancient stone structure with a commanding view. Note all the stones scattered around Dun Beag and you can imagine it standing four times as tall—perhaps with three wood-framed floors inside protecting an entire community with their animals in times of threat—back before Julius Caesar sailed to Britannia.

▲Neist Point and Lighthouse

To get a truly edge-of-the-world feeling, consider an adventure on the back lanes of the Duirinish Peninsula, west of Dunvegan.

This trip is best for hardy drivers looking to explore the most remote corner of Skye and undertake a moderately strenuous hike to a lighthouse. Although it looks close on the map, give this trip 30 minutes each way from Dunvegan, plus at least 30 minutes to hike from the parking lot to the lighthouse (with a steep uphill return). After hiking around the cliff, the lighthouse springs into view, with the Outer Hebrides beyond.

Getting There: Head west from Dunvegan, following signs for *Glendale*. You'll cross a moor, then twist around the Dunvegan sea loch, before heading overland and passing through rugged, desolate hamlets that seem like the setting for a BBC sitcom about backwater Britain. After passing through Glendale, carefully track *Neist Point* signs until you reach an end-of-the-road parking lot.

Eating: It's efficient and fun to combine this trek with lunch or dinner at the pricey, recommended **Three Chimneys Restau-**

rant, on the road to Neist Point at Colbost (reservations essential; see page 366).

WESTERN SKYE
▲▲Talisker Distillery

Talisker, a Skye institution, has been distilling here since 1830 and takes the tours it offers seriously. This venerable whisky dis-

tillery is situated at the base of a hill with 14 springs, and at the edge of a sea loch—making it easier to ship ingredients in and whisky out. On summer days, the distillery swarms with visitors: You'll sniff both peated and unpeated grains; see the big mash tuns, washbacks, and stills; and sample a wee dram at the end. Island whisky tends to be smokier than mainland whisky due to the amount of peat smoke used during malting. Talisker workers describe theirs as "medium smoky," with peppery, floral, and vanilla notes.

Cost and Hours: £10 for one-hour tour with tasting and a £5 voucher toward a bottle; Mon-Fri 9:30-17:00, open Sat-Sun April-Oct only, Sun from 11:00, last tour one hour before closing; 30 tours/day in summer, 4/day in off-season; on the loch in Carbost village, tel. 01478/614-308, www.malts.com. Be sure to call for a reservation (and plan on a 40-minute drive from Portree). Designated drivers who need to skip the tasting can ask for a dram to go.

Nearby: Note that the **Fairy Pools Hike**—an easy walk that includes some of the best Cuillin views on the island—starts from near Talisker Distillery (see next section).

CENTRAL SKYE
▲▲Cuillin Hills

These dramatic, rocky "hills" (which look more like mountains to me) stretch along the southern coast of the island, dominating Skye's landscape. Unusually craggy and alpine for Scotland, the Cuillin ("cool-in") seem to rise directly from the deep. You'll see them from just about anywhere on the southern two-thirds of the island, but no roads actually take you through the heart of the Cuillin—that's reserved for hikers and climbers, who love this area. To get the best views with a car, consider these options.

Sligachan: The road from the Skye Bridge to Portree is the easiest way to appreciate the Cuillin (you'll almost certainly drive along here at some point during your visit). These mountains are all

ISLE OF SKYE

that's left of a long-vanished volcano. As you approach, you'll see that there are three separate ranges (from right to left): red, gray, and black. The steep and challenging Black Cuillin is the most popular for serious climbers; the granite Red Cuillin ridge is more rounded.

The crossroads of Sligachan has an old triple-arched Telford bridge—one of Skye's iconic views—and a landmark hotel (see page 366). The village is nestled at the foothills of the Cuillin, and is a popular launch pad for mountain fun. The 2,500-foot-tall cone-shaped hill looming over Sligachan, named Glamaig ("Greedy Lady"), is the site of an annual 4.5-mile hill race in July: Speed hikers begin at the door of the Sligachan Hotel, race to the summit, run around a bagpiper, and scramble back down to the hotel. The record: 44 minutes (30 minutes up, 13 minutes down, 1 minute dancing a jig up top). A Gurkha from Nepal did it in near record time...barefoot. The Sligachan Hotel feels like a virtual mountaineering museum with great old photos and artifacts throughout its ground floor (especially behind the reception desk). You're welcome to browse around.

Fairy Pools Hike: Perhaps the best easy way to get some Cuillin views—and a sturdy but manageable hike—is to follow the popular trail to the Fairy Pools. This is relatively near Talisker Distillery (in the southwestern part of the island, see page 377).

To reach the hike from the A-863 between Sligachan and Dunvegan, follow signs to *Carbost*. Just before reaching the village of Carbost, watch for signs and a turn-off on the left to *Glenbrittle*. Follow this one-track road through the rolling hills, getting closer and closer to the Cuillin peaks. The well-marked *Fairy Pools* turnoff will be on your right. Parking here, you can easily follow the well-tended trail down across the field and toward the rounded peaks. (While signs suggest a 9.5-mile, 4- to 5-hour loop, most people simply hike 30 minutes to the pools and back; it's mostly level.)

Very soon you'll reach a gurgling river, which you'll follow toward its source in the mountains. Because the path is entirely through open fields, you enjoy scenery the entire time (and you can't get lost). Soon the river begins to pool at the base of each waterfall, creating a series of picturesque pools. Although footing can be treacherous, many hikers climb down across the rocks to swim and sunbathe. This is a fun place to linger (bring a picnic, if not a swimsuit). As I overheard one visitor say, "Despite the fact that it's so cold, it's so invitin'!"

Elgol: For the best view of the Cuillin, locals swear by the drive from Broadford (on the Portree-Kyleakin road) to Elgol, at the tip of a small peninsula that faces the Black Cuillin head-on. While it's just 12 miles as the crow flies from Sligachan, give it a half-hour each way to drive to the tip (mostly on single-track roads). For even more scenery, take a boat excursion from Elgol into Loch Coruisk, a sea loch surrounded by the Cuillin (April-Oct, departures several times a day, fewer Sun and off-season, generally 3 hours round-trip including 1.5 hours free time on the shore of the loch).

SOUTH SKYE
Kyleakin

Kyleakin (kih-LAH-kin), the last town in Skye before the Skye Bridge, used to be a big tourist hub...until the bridge connecting it to the mainland enabled easier travel to Portree and other areas deeper in the island. Today this unassuming little village, with a ruined castle (Castle Moil), a cluster of lonesome fishing boats, and a forgotten ferry slip is worth a quick look but little more.

Eating in Broadford: Up the road in Broadford is the Broadford Hotel, part of an upscale Skye hotel chain (Torrin Road at junction with Elgol, tel. 01471/822-204, www.broadfordhotel.co.uk). Its **$$$$ restaurant** is attempting to bring classy cuisine to this small town in a nice contemporary setting with harbor views (set multicourse menu only, daily from 18:00). The hotel's **$$ Gabbro Bar** is a relaxed pub-grub bistro. It was at this hotel that a secret elixir—supposedly once concocted for Bonnie Prince Charlie—was re-created by hotelier James Ross after finding the recipe in his father's belongings. Now known as Drambuie, the popular liqueur—which caught on in the 19th century—is made with Scotch whisky, heather honey, and spices. With its wide variety of Drambuie drinks, the Broadford's **Spinaker Lounge** is the place to try it.

Skye Bridge

Connecting Kyleakin on Skye with Kyle of Lochalsh on the mainland, the Skye Bridge was Europe's most expensive toll bridge per foot when it opened to great controversy in 1995 amid concerns that it would damage B&B business in the towns it connects, and disrupt native otter habitat. Here's the Skye natives' take on things: A generation ago, Lowlanders (city folk) began selling their urban homes and buying cheap property on Skye. Natives had grown to enjoy the slow-paced lifestyle that came with living life according to the whim of the ferry, but these new transplants found their commute into civilization too frustrating by boat. They demanded a bridge be built. Finally a deal was struck to privately fund the bridge, but the toll wasn't established before construction began. So when the bridge opened—and the ferry line it replaced closed—locals were shocked to be charged upward of £5 per car each way to go to the mainland. A few years ago, the bridge was bought by the Scottish government, the fare was abolished, and the Skye natives were somewhat appeased. There's no denying that the bridge has been a boon for Skye tourism, making a quick visit to the island possible without having to wait for a ferry.

SKYE'S SLEAT PENINSULA
Clan Donald Center and Armadale Castle
Facing the sea just outside Armadale is the ruined castle of Clan Donald, also known as the MacDonalds (Mac/Mc = "son of"),

at one time the most powerful clan in the Scottish Highlands and Hebrides. Today it is the "spiritual home of clan Donald," a sprawling site with woodland walks, a ruined castle, and a clan history museum.

Armadale Castle—more of a mansion than a fortress—was built in 1790, during the rela-tively peaceful, post-Jacobite age when life at the MacDonalds' traditional home, Duntulm Castle at the tip of the Trotternish Peninsula, had become too rugged and inconvenient. Today the Armadale Castle ruins (which you can view, but not enter) anchor a sprawling visitors center that celebrates the MacDonald way of life. You'll explore its manicured gardens, ogle the castle ruins, and visit the Museum of the Isles. This modern, well-presented museum tells the history of Scotland and Skye through the lens of its most influential clan (only a few artifacts but good descriptions, includes 1.5-hour audioguide). While fascinating for people named Mac-Donald, it's pricey and not worth a long detour for anyone else. But because it's right along the main road near the Armadale-Mallaig ferry, it can be an enjoyable place to kill some time while waiting

The Feuding Clans of Skye

Skye is one of the best places to get a taste of Scotland's colorful, violent history of clan clashes. As the largest of the Inner Hebrides Islands, with easy nautical connections to Scotland's west coast and much of northern Ireland, it's logical that Skye was home to two powerful, rival clans: the MacDonalds and the MacLeods.

The MacDonalds (a.k.a. **"Clan Donald"**), with their base at Duntulm Castle, were the dominant clan of the Hebrides. In the 12th century, the MacDonalds' ancestral ruler Somerled first unified the disparate islands and western Highlands into a "Lordship of the Isles" that lasted for centuries. Throughout this period, they struggled to maintain control against rival clans—starting with the MacLeods.

Clan MacLeod, with its castle at Dunvegan (see page 373), controlled the western half of Skye. Another branch of the MacLeods was based on the Isle of Lewis, holding down the fort in the Outer Hebrides. The MacLeods' ancestor, Olav the Black, had been defeated by Somerled, pulling their territory in to the Lordship of the Isles. But over the centuries, the MacLeods frequently challenged the authority of the MacDonalds, clashing in countless minor skirmishes as well as major clan battles in 1411, 1480, and 1578.

Adding to the volatile mix was **Clan Mackenzie,** which controlled much of the northern Highlands from their base at Filean Donan Castle (see page 387). The Mackenzies waged battle against the MacDonalds in 1491 and again in 1497.

The epic 1578 clash featured a series of grievous offenses. First, the MacLeods invaded the MacDonald-controlled Isle of Eigg, and, upon finding the islanders huddled in a cave for protection, set a roaring fire at the mouth of the cave—killing virtually the entire population. In retaliation, the MacDonalds barred the door of a church on the MacLeod-controlled Isle of Uist and burned all of the worshippers alive. In the ensuing battle, the furious MacLeods massacred the MacDonalds and buried the dead on a turf dike—earning the conflict the name "Battle of the Spoiling Dike."

The final clan battle on Skye began with a strategic marriage designed to broker a peace between the warring clans. Donald MacDonald married Margaret MacLeod, following a tradition called a "handfast," in which the groom was allowed a "trial period" of one year and one day with his new bride. After Margaret injured her eye, Donald decided to "return" her. Adding insult to injury, he sent her back to Dunvegan Castle on a one-eyed horse, led by a one-eyed man with a one-eyed dog. And so began two years of brutal warfare between the clans (the War of the One-Eyed Woman). In 1601, the Battle of Coire Na Creiche decimated both sides, but the MacDonalds emerged victorious. It would be the last of the great clan battles between the MacDonalds and the MacLeods, and it's said to be the final battle fought in Scotland using only medieval weapons (swords and arrows), not guns.

for your ferry. At the parking lot is a big shop and café with free WCs.

Cost and Hours: £8.50, Easter-Oct daily 9:30-17:30, closed off-season, 2 minutes north of the Armadale ferry landing, tel. 01471/844-305, www.clandonald.com.

Nearby: Heading north on the A-851 from the Clan Donald Centre, keep an eye out for **Sabhal Mòr Ostaig** (a big complex of white buildings on the point). Skye is very proud to host this college, with coursework taught entirely in Scottish Gaelic. Named "the big barn" after its origins, its mission is to further the Gaelic language (spoken today by about 60,000 people).

ON THE MAINLAND, NEAR THE ISLE OF SKYE
▲Eilean Donan Castle

This postcard castle, watching over a sea loch from its island perch, is scenically (and conveniently) situated on the road between the Isle of Skye and Loch Ness.
While the photo op is worth ▲▲, the interior—with cozy rooms—is worth only a peek and closer to ▲. Famous from such films as Sean Connery's *Highlander* (1986) and the James Bond movie *The World Is Not Enough* (1999), Eilean Donan (EYE-lan DOHN-an) might be Scotland's most photogenic countryside castle (chances are good it's on that Scotland calendar you bought during your trip). Strategically situated at the confluence of three sea lochs, this was the stronghold of the Mackenzies—a powerful clan that was, like the MacLeods at Dunvegan, a serious rival to the mighty MacDonalds (see sidebar). Though it looks ancient, the current castle is actually less than a century old. The original castle on this site (dating from 800 years ago) was destroyed in battle in 1719, then rebuilt between 1912 and 1932 by the Macrae family as their residence. (The Macraes became bodyguards to the Mackenzies in the 14th century and later took over from their bosses as holders of the castle.)

Cost and Hours: £7.50, good £6 guidebook; March-Oct daily 10:00-18:00, July-Aug from 9:00, may open a few days a week Nov-Feb—call ahead, last entry one hour before closing; café, tel. 01599/555-202, www.eileandonancastle.com.

Getting There: It's not actually on the Isle of Skye, but it's quite close, in the mainland town of Dornie. Follow the A-87 about 15 minutes east of Skye Bridge, through Kyle of Lochalsh and toward Loch Ness and Inverness. The castle is on the right side of the road, just after a long bridge. Buses that run between Portree

ISLE OF SKYE

and Inverness (including #915, #916, and #917) stop at Dornie, a short walk from the castle (6/day, 1 hour from Portree).

Visiting the Castle: Buy tickets at the visitors center, then walk across the bridge and into the castle complex, and make your way into the big, blocky keep. You'll begin with some audiovisual introductory exhibits (left of main castle entry), then work through the historic rooms. While the castle is a footnote on a Scottish scale, the exhibits work hard to make its story engaging. Docents posted throughout can tell you more. First you'll see the claustrophobic, vaulted Billeting Room (where soldiers had their barracks), then head upstairs to the inviting Banqueting Room, with grand portraits of the honorable John Macrae-Gilstrap and his wife (who spearheaded the modern rebuilding of the castle). This room comes to life when you get a docent to explain the paintings and artifacts here. After the renovation, this was a sort of living room. Another flight of stairs takes you to the circa-1930 bedrooms, which feel more cozy and accessible than those in many other castles—and do a great job of evoking the lifestyles of the aristocrats who built the current version of Eilean Donan as their personal castle playset. Downstairs is a cute kitchen exhibit, with mannequins preparing a meal. Finally, you'll head through a few more humble exhibits (on old guns, bagpipes, and flags) to the exit.

NORTHERN SCOTLAND

Wester Ross • The North Coast • The Orkney Islands

Scotland's far north is its rugged and desolate "Big Sky Country"—with towering mountains, vast and moody moors, achingly desolate glens, and a jagged coastline peppered with silver-sand beaches. Far less discovered than the big destinations to the south, this is where you can escape the crowds and touristy "tartan tat" of the Edinburgh-Stirling-Oban-Inverness rut, and get a picturesque corner of Scotland all to yourself. Even on a sunny summer weekend, you may not pass another car for miles. It's just you and the Munro baggers. Beyond Orkney, there's no real "destination" in the north—it's all about the journey.

This chapter covers everything north of the Isle of Skye and Inverness, divided into three sections: the scenic west coast (called Wester Ross); the sandy north coast; and the fascinating Orkney archipelago just offshore from Britain's northernmost point.

Fully exploring northern Scotland takes some serious time. The roads are narrow, twisty, and slow, and the pockets of civilization are few and far between. With two weeks or less in Scotland, this area doesn't make the cut (except maybe Orkney). But if you have time to linger, and you appreciate desolate scenery and an end-of-the-world feeling, the untrampled north is worth considering.

Even on a shorter visit, Orkney may be alluring for adventurous travelers seeking a contrast to the rest of Scotland. The islands' claims to fame—astonishing prehistoric sites, Old Norse (Norwegian) heritage, and recent history as a WWI and WWII naval base—combine to spur travelers' imaginations.

PLANNING YOUR TIME

For a scenic loop through this area, try this four-day plan:

Day 1   From the Isle of Skye, drive up the west coast
        (including the Applecross detour, if time permits),
        overnighting in Torridon or Ullapool.
Day 2   Continue the rest of the way up the west coast, then
        trace the north coast from west to east, catching the
        late-afternoon ferry to Orkney. Overnight in tidy
        Kirkwall (2 nights).
Day 3   Spend all day on Orkney.
Day 4   Finish up on Orkney and take the ferry back to the
        mainland; with enough time and interest, squeeze in a
        visit to John O'Groats before driving three hours back
        to Inverness (on the relatively speedy A-9).

The above plan includes a borderline-unreasonable amount
of driving, on twisty, challenging, often single-track roads (especially on days 1 and 2). If you don't have someone to split the time
behind the wheel, or if you want to really slow down, consider
adding another overnight to break up the trip.

To reach **Orkney** most efficiently—without the slow-going
west coast scenery—consider zipping up on a flight (easy and frequent from Inverness, Edinburgh, or Aberdeen), or make good
time on the A-9 highway from Inverness up to Thurso (figure 3
hours one-way) to catch the ferry.

It's possible (but very slow) to traverse this area by bus, but I'd
skip it without a car. If you're flying to Orkney, consider renting a
car for your time here.

Wester Ross

North of the Isle of Skye,
Scotland's sparsely popu-
lated,   ruggedly   scenic
west coast is a big draw for
travelers seeking stunning
views without the crowds.
For casual visitors, the
views in Glencoe and on
the Isle of Skye are much
more accessible and just as
good as what you'll find farther north. But diehards enjoy getting
away from it all in Wester Ross. This section provides a quick out-
line of the most scenic route, from south to north.

This area, called Wester Ross (the western part of the region of
Ross), is remote, mountainous, and slashed with jagged "sea lochs."
(That's "inlets" in American English, or "fjords" in Norwegian.)

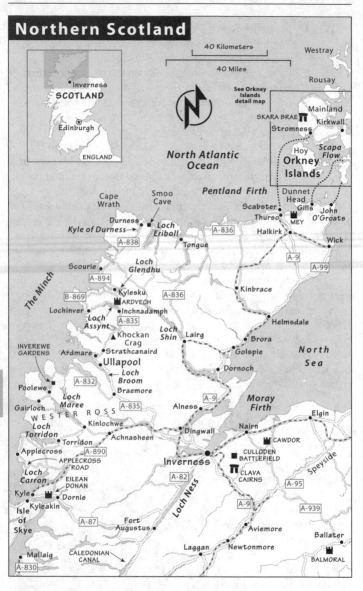

Northern Scotland

SCOTLAND

- Inverness
- Edinburgh
- ENGLAND

40 Kilometers

40 Miles

N

See Orkney
Islands
detail map

Westray

Rousay

Mainland

SKARA BRAE

Stromness

Kirkwall

Hoy

Scapa
Flow

Orkney
Islands

North Atlantic
Ocean

Pentland Firth

Dunnet
Head

Cape
Wrath

Smoo
Cave

Scrabster

Gills

John
O'Groats

Durness

Loch
Eriboll

Thurso

MEY

Kyle of Durness

A-838

A-836

Halkirk

Wick

Tongue

A-9

A-99

Scourie

Loch
Glendhu

A-894

Kinbrace

B-869

Kylesku

A-836

Lochinver

ARDVECH

Inchnadamph

Helmsdale

Loch
Assynt

A-835

Knockan
Crag

Loch
Shin

Lairg

Brora

North
Sea

INVEREWE
GARDENS

Ardmare

Strathcanaird

Golspie

Ullapool

Dornoch

The Minch

Loch
Broom

Poolewe

A-832

Braemore

A-9

Moray
Firth

Gairloch

Loch
Maree

A-835

Alness

Elgin

WESTER ROSS

Kinlochewe

Dingwall

Nairn

CAWDOR

Loch
Torridon

Achnasheen

Speyside

Applecross

Torridon

A-890

CULLODEN
BATTLEFIELD

APPLECROSS
ROAD

EILEAN
DONAN

Inverness

CLAVA
CAIRNS

A-95

Loch
Carron

Kyle

Dornie

A-82

A-939

Kyleakin

Loch Ness

A-9

Isle
of
Skye

A-87

Fort
Augustus

Aviemore

Ballater

Mallaig

Laggan

Newtonmore

BALMORAL

A-830

CALEDONIAN
CANAL

NORTHERN SCOTLAND

After seeing its towering peaks, you'll understand why George R.
R. Martin named the primary setting of his *Game of Thrones* epic
"Westeros."

There's a fine variety of scenery—but not many towns—on
the way north. Connecting Skye or Glencoe to Ullapool (the logical halfway point up the coast) takes a full day. It may not sound
like that many miles (figure 130 miles from Eilean Donan Castle

to Ullapool; the Applecross detour adds another 20 slow-going miles)—but they're twisty and often single-track. If you want to just get a taste of this rugged scenery—without going farther north—you can drive the Wester Ross coastline almost as far as Ullapool, then turn off on the A-835 for a quick one-hour drive to Inverness.

Sights in Wester Ross

▲▲Wester Ross Driving Tour, from Eilean Donan Castle to Ullapool

From the A-87, a few miles east of Kyle of Lochalsh (and the Skye Bridge), follow signs for the A-890 north toward *Lochcarron*. (Note that **Eilean Donan Castle** is just a couple of miles farther east from this turnoff; if coming from Skye, you could squeeze in a visit to that castle before backtracking to this turnoff.) From here on out, you can carefully track the brown *Wester Ross Coastal Trail* signs, which will keep you on track.

You'll follow the A-890 as it cuts across a hilly spine, then twists down and runs alongside **Loch Carron.** At the end of the loch, just after the village of Strathcarron, you'll reach a T-intersection that offers two choices. The faster route up to Ullapool—which skips much of the best scenery—takes you right on the A-890 (toward *Inverness*). But for the scenic route outlined here, instead turn left, following the A-896 (following signs for *Lochcarron*). From here, you'll follow the opposite bank of Loch Carron.

Soon after you pull away from the lochside, you'll cross over

a high meadow and see a well-marked turnoff on the left for a super-scenic—but challenging—alternate route: the **Applecross Road,** over a pass called Bealach na Bà (Gaelic for "Pass of the Cattle"). Intimidating signs suggest a much more straightforward alternate route that keeps you on the A-896 straight up to Loch Torridon (if doing this, skip down to the "Loch Torridon" section, later). But if you're relatively comfortable negotiating steep switchbacks, and have the time to spare (adding about 20 miles to the total journey), this road is drivable. You'll twist up, up, up—hearing your engine struggle up gradients of up to 20 percent—and finally over, with rugged-moonscape views over peaks and lochs. From the summit (at 2,053 feet), the jagged mountains rising from the sea are the Cuillin Hills on the Isle of Skye. Finally, you'll corkscrew back down the other side, arriving at the humble seafront town of Applecross.

Once in **Applecross,** you could either return over the same pass to pick up the A-896 (slightly faster), or, for a meandering but very scenic route, carry on all the way around the northern headland of the peninsula. This provides you with further views of Raasay and Skye, through a deserted-feeling landscape on single-track roads. Then, turning the corner at the top of the peninsula, you'll begin to drive above Loch Torridon, with some of the finest views on this drive.

Whether you take the Applecross detour or the direct route, you'll wind up at the stunning sea loch called **Loch Torridon—**

hemmed in by thickly forested pine-covered hills, it resembles the Rockies. You'll pass through an idyllic fjordside town, Shiel-daig, then cross over a finger of land and plunge deeper into Upper Loch Torridon. Near the end of the loch, keep an eye out for **The Torridon—**a luxurious lochfront grand hotel with gorgeous Victorian Age architecture, a café serving afternoon tea, and expensive rooms (www.thetorridon.com).

As you loop past the far end of the loch—with the option to turn off for the village of **Torridon** (which has a good youth hostel, www.syha.org.uk)—the landscape has shifted dramatically, from pine-covered hills to a hauntingly desolate glen. You'll cut through this valley—bookended by towering peaks and popular with hikers—before reaching the town of Kinlochewe.

At Kinlochewe, take the A-832 west (following *Ullapool* signs from here on out), and soon you'll be tracing the bonnie, bonnie

banks of **Loch Maree**—considered by many connoisseurs to be one of Scotland's finest lochs. You'll see campgrounds, nature areas, and scenic pull-outs as you make good time on the speedy two-lane loch-side road. (The best scenery is near the beginning, so don't put off that photo stop.)

Nearing the end of Loch Maree, the road becomes single-track again as you twist up over another saddle of scrubby land. On the other side, you'll get glimpses of Gair Loch through the trees, before finally arriving at the little harbor of **Gairloch.** Just beyond the harbor, where the road straightens out as it follows the coast, keep an eye out (on the right) for the handy Gale Center. Run as a charity, it has WCs, a small café with treats baked by locals, a fine shop of books and crafts, and comfortable tables and couches for taking a break (www.galeactionforum.co.uk).

True to its name, Gair Loch ("Short Loch") doesn't last long, and soon you'll head up a hill (keep an eye out for the pullout on the left, offering fine views over the village). The next village is Polewe, on **Loch Ewe.** Just after the village, on the left, is the **Inverewe Gardens.** These beautiful gardens, run by the National Trust for Scotland, were the pet project of Osgood Mackenzie, who in 1862 began transforming 50 acres of his lochside estate into a subtropical paradise. The warming Gulf Stream and—in some places—stout stone walls help make this oasis possible. If you have time and need to stretch your legs from all that shifting, spend an hour wandering its sprawling grounds. The walled garden, near

the entrance, is a highlight, with each bed thoughtfully labeled (£10.50, daily, www.nts.org.uk).

Continuing on the A-832 toward Ullapool, you'll stay above Loch Ewe, then briefly pass above the open ocean. Soon you'll find yourself following **Little Loch Broom** (with imposing mountains on your right). At the end of that loch, you'll carry on straight and work your way past a lush strip of farmland at the apex of the loch. Soon you'll meet the big A-835 highway; turn left and take this speedy road the rest of the way into Ullapool. (Or you can turn right to zip on the A-835 all the way to Inverness—just an hour away.) Whew!

Ullapool

A gorgeously set, hard-working town of about 1,500 people, Ullapool (ul-la-PEWL) is what passes for a metropolis in Wester Ross. Its most prominent feature is its big, efficient ferry dock, connecting the mainland with Stornoway on the Isle of Lewis (Scotland's biggest, in the Outer Hebrides). Facing the dock is a strip of cute little houses, today housing restaurants, shops, B&Bs, and residences. Behind the waterfront, the town is only a few blocks deep—you can get the lay of the land in a few minutes' stroll. Curving around the back side of the town—along a big, grassy campground—is an inviting rocky beach, facing across the loch in one direction and out toward the open sea in the other.

Orientation to Ullapool: Ullapool has several handy services for travelers. An excellent **bookshop** is a block up, straight ahead from the ferry dock. Many services line Argyle Street, which runs parallel to the harbor one block up the hill: the **TI** is to the right, while a Bank of Scotland **ATM** and the **post office** are to the left. On this same street, the town runs a fine little **museum** with well-done exhibits about local history (closed Sun and Nov-March, www.ullapoolmuseum.co.uk). This street, nicknamed "Art-gyle Street," also has a smattering of local art **galleries.**

Sleeping in Ullapool: Several guesthouses line the harborfront Shore Street, including **$ Point Cottage** (2 rooms, no breakfast, www.pointcottagebandb.co.uk), **$ Waterside House** (3 rooms, minimum two-night stay in peak season, www.waterside.uk.net), and the town's official **¢ youth hostel** (www.syha.org.uk). A block up from the water on West Argyle Street, **$ West House** has three rooms and requires a two-night minimum stay (no breakfast, www.westhousebandb.co.uk).

Eating in Ullapool: The two most reliable places are the **$$ Ceilidh Place,** on West Argyle Street a block above the harbor (www.theceilidhplace.com); and **$$$ The Arch Inn,** facing the water a half-block from the ferry dock (www.thearchinn.co.uk). Both have a nice pubby vibe as well as sit-down dining rooms with a focus on locally caught seafood. Both also rent rooms and frequently host live music. For a quick meal, two different **$ chippies** (around the corner from each other, facing the ferry dock) keep the breakwater promenade busy with al fresco budget diners and happy seagulls.

▲Northwest Scotland Driving Tour, from Ullapool to the North Coast

The scenery continues as you head north from Ullapool, all the way up to Scotland's northern coast. Leaving Ullapool, follow signs that read simply *North (A-835)*. You'll pass through the cute little beachside village of **Ardmair,** then pull away from the coast.

About 15 minutes after leaving Ullapool, just after you exit the village of Strathcanaird and head uphill, watch on the left for a pullout with a handy orientation panel describing the panorama of **towering peaks** that line the road. It looks like a mossy Monument Valley. Enjoy the scenery for about four more miles—surrounded by wee lochs and gigantic peaks—and watch for the **Knockan Crag** visitors center, above you on the right, with exhibits on local geology, flora, and fauna and suggestions for area hikes (unmanned and open daily 24 hours, WCs, www.nnr-scotland.org.uk).

Continuing north along the A-835, you'll soon pass out of the region of Ross and Cromarty and enter Sutherland. At the T-intersection, turn left for *Kylesku* and *Lochinver* (on the A-837). From here on out, you can start following the *North & West Highlands Tourist Route;* you'll also see your first sign for John O'Groats at the northeastern corner of Scotland (152 miles away).

You'll roll through moors, surrounded on all sides by hills. Just after the barely-there village of Inchnadamph, keep an eye

out on the left for the ruins of **Ardvrech Castle,** which sits in crumbled majesty upon its own little island in Loch Assynt, connected to the world by a narrow sandy spit. Just after these ruins, you'll have another choice: For the fastest route to the north coast, turn right to follow A-894 (toward *Kylesku* and *Durness*). If you have some time to spare, you could carry on straight to scenically follow Loch Assynt toward the sleepy fishing village of **Lochinver** (12 miles). After seeing the village, you could go back the way you came to the main road, or continue all the way around the little peninsula on the B-869, passing several appealing sandy beaches and villages.

Back on the main A-894, you'll pass through an almost lunar landscape, with peaks all around, finally emerging at the gorgeous, mountain-rimmed **Loch Glendhu,** which you'll cross on a stout modern bridge. From here, it's a serene landscape of rock, heather, and ferns, with occasional glimpses of the coast—such as at **Scourie,** with a particularly nice sandy beach. Finally (after the road becomes

A-838—keep left at the fork, toward *Durness*), you'll head up, over, and through a vast and dramatic glen. At the end of the glen, you'll start to see sand below you on the left; this is **Kyle of Durness,** which goes on for miles. You'll see the turnoff for the ferry to Cape Wrath, then follow tidy stone walls the rest of the way into **Durness.**

The North Coast

Scotland's north coast, which stretches a hundred miles from Cape Wrath in the northwest corner to John O'Groats in the northeast, is gently scenic, but less dramatic than Wester Ross—the jagged mountains loom far to the south, and your views are dominated by an alternating array of moors and jagged coastline. This is a good place to make up the long miles. I've described the driving route along the north coast from west to east.

NORTH COAST DRIVING TOUR
Durness to Thurso

Durness is a beachy village of cow meadows perched on a bluff above sandy shores. This area has a different feel from Wester Ross—it's less rugged and more manicured, with tidy farms hemmed in by neatly stacked stone walls. There's not much to see or do in the town, but there is a 24-hour gas station (gas up now—this is your last chance for a while...trust me) and a handy TI (by the big parking lot with the "Award Winning Beach," tel. 01971/509-005).

Head east out of the village on the A-838, watching for brown signs on your right to *Durness Village Hall.* Pull over here to stroll through the small **memorial garden for John Lennon,** who enjoyed his boyhood vacations in Durness.

Just after the village hall, on the left, pull over at **Smoo Cave** (free WCs in parking lot). Its goofy-sounding name comes from the Old Norse *smúga,* for "cave." (Many places along the north coast—which had a strong Viking influence—have Norse rather than Gaelic or Anglo-Saxon place names.) It's free to hike down the well-marked stairs to a protected cove, where an underground river has carved a deep cave into the bluff. Walk inside the cave to get a free peek at the waterfall; for a longer visit, you can pay for a 20-minute boat trip and guided walk (unnecessary for most; sign up at the mouth of the cave).

Back on the road, soon after Smoo Cave, on the left, is the gorgeous **Ceannabeinne Beach** (Gaelic for "End of the Mountains").

Of the many Durness-area beaches, this is the locals' favorite.

Heading east from the Durness area, you'll traverse many sparsely populated miles—long roads that cut in and out from the coast, with scrubby moorland and distant peaks on the other side. You'll emerge at the gigantic **Loch Eriboll,** which you'll circumnavigate—passing lamb farms and crumbling stone walls—to continue your way east. Leaving this fjord, you'll cut through some classic fjord scenery until you finally pop out at the scenic **Kyle of Tongue.** You'll cross over the big, modern bridge, then twist up through the village of Tongue and continue your way eastward (the A-838 becomes the A-836)—through more of the same scrubby moorland scenery. Make good time for the next 40 lonely miles. Notice how many place names along here use the term "strath"—a wide valley (as opposed to a narrower "glen"), such as where jagged mountains open up to the sea.

Finally—after going through little settlements like Bettyhill and Melvich—the moors begin to give way to working farms as you approach Thurso.

Thurso, John O'Groats, and Nearby

The main population center of northern Scotland (pop. 8,000), Thurso is a functional transit hub with a charming old core. As you face out to sea, the heavily industrialized point on the left is **Scrabster,** with the easiest ferry crossing to Orkney (for details, see "Getting to Orkney" on page 397).

• *Continuing east from Thurso (following brown* John O'Groats *signs on the A-836), it's about eight miles to the village of Dunnet. If you have time for some rugged scenery, turn off here to drive the four miles (each way) to...*

Dunnet Head

While John O'Groats is often mistakenly called "Britain's northernmost point," Dunnet Head pokes up just a bit farther. And, while it lacks the too-cute signpost marking distances to faraway landmarks, views from here are better than from John O'Groats. Out at the tip of Dunnet Head, a lonely lighthouse enjoys panoramic views across the Pentland Firth to Orkney, while a higher vantage point is just up the hill. Keep an eye out for seabirds, including puffins.

• *In the village of Dunnet, between the main road and Dunnet Head, look for the well-signed...*

Mary-Ann's Cottage

This little stone house explains traditional crofting lifestyles—left just as it was when 92-year-old Mary-Ann Calder moved out in 1990 (very limited hours).

• *Back on the main A-836, about four miles farther east is the turnoff for the...*

Castle of Mey

The Queen Mother grew up at Glamis Castle (see page 224), but after her daughter became Queen Elizabeth II, she purchased and

renovated this sprawling property as an escape from the bustle of royal life...and you couldn't get much farther from civilization than this. For nearly 50 years, the Queen Mum stayed here for annual visits in August and October. Today it welcomes visitors to tour its homey interior and 30 acres of manicured gardens (closed Oct-mid-May, www.castleofmey.org.uk).

• *From Mey, it's another six miles east to John O'Groats. About halfway there, in Gills Bay, is another ferry dock for cars heading to Orkney (see "Getting to Orkney" on page 397).*

John O'Groats

A total tourist trap that's somehow also genuinely stirring, John O'Groats marks the northeastern corner of the Isle of Britain—bookending the country with Land's End, 874 miles to the southwest in Cornwall. People enjoy traversing the length of Britain by motorcycle, by bicycle, or even by foot (it takes about eight weeks to trudge along the "E2E" trail—that's "End to End"). And upon arrival, whether they've walked for two months or just driven up for the day from Inverness, everyone wants to snap a "been there, done that" photo with the landmark signpost. Surrounding that is a huge parking lot, a souvenir stand masquerading as a TI, and lots of tacky "first and last" shops and restaurants. Orkney looms just off the coast.

Nearby: The real target of "End to End" pilgrims isn't the signpost, but the **Duncansby Head Lighthouse**—about two miles to the east, it's the actual northeasternmost point, with an even more end-of-the-world vibe. (By car, head away from the John O'Groats area on A-99, and watch for the Duncansby Head turnoff on the left, just past the Seaview Hotel.) If you have time for a hike, about a mile south of the lighthouse are the **Duncansby Stacks**—dramatic sea stacks rising up above a sandy beach.

• *You made it! Great job. Now to complete your journey, turn around and drive (or walk) 874 miles to Land's End.*

The Orkney Islands

The Orkney Islands, perched just an hour's ferry ride north of the mainland, are uniquely remote, historic, and—for the right traveler—well worth the effort.

Crossing the 10-mile Pentland Firth separating Orkney from northern Scotland, you leave the Highlands behind and enter a

new world. With no real tradition for clans, tartans, or bagpipes, Orkney feels not "Highlander" or even "Scottish," but Orcadian (as locals are called). Though Orkney was inhabited by Picts from the sixth century B.C., during most of its formative history—from 875 all the way until 1468—it was a prized trading hub of the Norwegian realm, giving it a feel more Scandinavian than Celtic. The Vikings (who sailed from Norway just 170 miles away) left their mark, both literally (runes carved into prehistoric stone monuments) and culturally: Many place names are derived from Old Norse, and the Orkney flag looks like the Norwegian flag with a few yellow accents.

There are other historic connections. In later times, Canada's Hudson's Bay Company recruited many Orcadians to staff its outposts. And given its status as the Royal Navy headquarters during both World Wars, Orkney remains one of the most pro-British corners of Scotland. In the 2014 independence referendum, Orkney cast the loudest "no" vote in the entire country (67 percent against).

Orkney's landscape is also a world apart: Aside from some dramatic sea cliffs hiding along its perimeter, the main island is mostly

NORTHERN SCOTLAND

flat and bald, with few trees, the small town of Kirkwall, and lots of tidy farms with gently mooing cows. While the blustery weather (which can change several times a day) keeps the vegetation on the scrubby side, for extra greenery each town has a sheltered community garden run by volunteers. Orkney's fine sandy beaches seem always empty—as if lying on them will give you hypothermia. Sparsely populated, the islands have no traffic lights and most roads are single lane with "passing places" politely spaced as necessary.

Today's economy is based mostly on North Sea oil, renewable energy, and fishing. The boats you'll see are creel boats with nets and cages to collect crabs, lobsters, scallops, and oysters. Unless a cruise ship drops by, tourism seems to be secondary.

For the sightseer, Orkney has two draws unmatched elsewhere in Scotland: It has some of the finest prehistoric sites in northern Europe, left behind by an advanced Stone Age civilization that flourished here. And the harbor called Scapa Flow has fascinating remnants of its important military role during the World Wars—from intentional shipwrecks designed to seal off the harbor, to muscular Churchill-built barriers to finish the job a generation later.

Orientation to Orkney

Orkney (as the entire archipelago is called) is made up of 70 islands, with a total population of 24,500. The main island—with the primary town (Kirkwall) and ferry ports connecting Orkney to northern Scotland (Stromness and St. Margaret's Hope)—is called, confusingly, Mainland. (It just goes to show you: One man's island is another man's mainland.)

PLANNING YOUR TIME

Orkney merits at least two nights and one full day. Some people (especially WWII aficionados) spend days exploring Orkney, but I've focused on the main sights to see in a short visit—all on the biggest island.

The only town of any substance, Kirkwall is your best home base. You can see its sights in a few hours (a town stroll, the fine Orkney Museum, and its striking cathedral). From there, to see the best of Orkney in a single day, plan on driving about 70 miles, looping out from Kirkwall in two directions: Spend the morning at the prehistoric sites (Maeshowe and nearby sites, Skara Brae), and the afternoon driving along the Churchill Barriers and visiting the Italian Chapel.

Cruise Crowds: Orkney is Scotland's busiest cruise port; on days when ships are in port, normally sleepy destinations can be jammed. Check the cruise schedule at www.orkneyharbours.com

and plan accordingly to avoid busy times at popular sights (such as Skara Brae, the Italian Chapel).

GETTING TO ORKNEY

By Car/Ferry: Two different car ferry options depart from near Thurso, which is about a three-hour drive from Inverness (on the A-9); for the scenic longer route, you could loop all the way up Wester Ross, and then along the north coast from Durness to Thurso (see earlier in this chapter). The two companies land at opposite corners of Orkney, at Stromness and St. Margaret's Hope; from either, it's about a 30-minute drive to Kirkwall.

Plan on about £60 one-way for a car on the Northlink ferry, or £40 on the Pentland ferry, plus £20 per passenger. For either company, reserve online at least a day in advance; check in at the ferry dock 30 minutes before departure.

For most, the best choice is the **Scrabster-Stromness** ferry, operated by NorthLink (3/day in each direction in summer, 2/day off-season, 1.5-hour crossing, www.

northlinkferries.co.uk). While it's a slightly longer crossing, it's also a bigger boat, with more services (including a good sit-down cafeteria—and famously tasty fish-and-chips), and it glides past the Old Man of Hoy, giving you an easy glimpse at one of Orkney's top landmarks. This ferry is coordinated with bus #X99, connecting Scrabster to Inverness (www.stagecoachbus.com).

The **Gills Bay-St. Margaret's Hope** route is operated by Pentland Ferries; its main advantage is the proximity of Gills Bay to John O'Groats, making it easy to visit Britain's northeasternmost point on your way to or from the ferry—but Gills Bay is also that much farther from Inverness (2-3/day in each direction, one-hour crossing, www.pentlandferries.co.uk).

There's also a **passenger-only boat** directly from John O'Groats to Burwick, which connects conveniently to an onward bus to Kirkwall (3/day July-Aug, 1/day May and Sept, none Oct-April, 40-minute crossing, www.jogferry.co.uk). While this works for those leaving their car at John O'Groats for a quick Orkney day trip, it's more weather-dependent.

By Plane: To get there fast, fly. Kirkwall's little airport has direct flights to Inverness, Edinburgh, Glasgow, and Aberdeen (www.flybe.com has good deals if you book ahead). Landing at the airport, you're four miles from Kirkwall; pick up a town map at the info desk. It's convenient to pick up a rental car at the airport. There

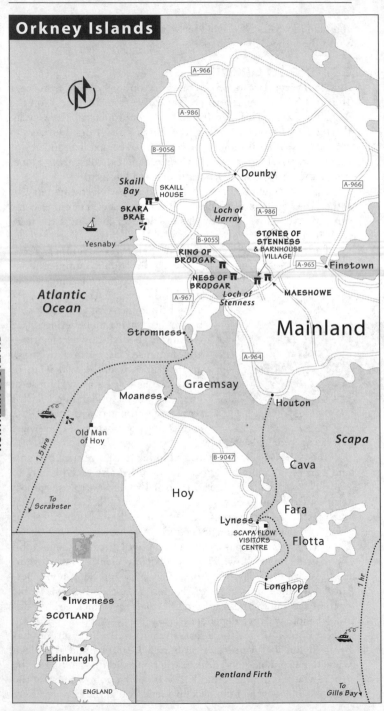

Orkney Islands

SCOTLAND

A-966

A-986

B-9056

Skaill Bay

SKAILL HOUSE

SKARA BRAE

Yesnaby

• Dounby

Loch of Harray

A-986

A-966

STONES OF STENNESS & BARNHOUSE VILLAGE

A-965

• Finstown

RING OF BRODGAR

B-9055

NESS OF BRODGAR

A-967

Loch of Stenness

MAESHOWE

Atlantic Ocean

Stromness

Mainland

A-964

Graemsay

Moaness •

Old Man of Hoy

• Houton

Scapa

B-9047

Cava

Hoy

Fara

Lyness •

SCAPA FLOW VISITORS CENTRE

Flotta

1.5 hrs

To Scrabster

Longhope •

1 hr

SCOTLAND

• Inverness

• Edinburgh

ENGLAND

Pentland Firth

To Gills Bay

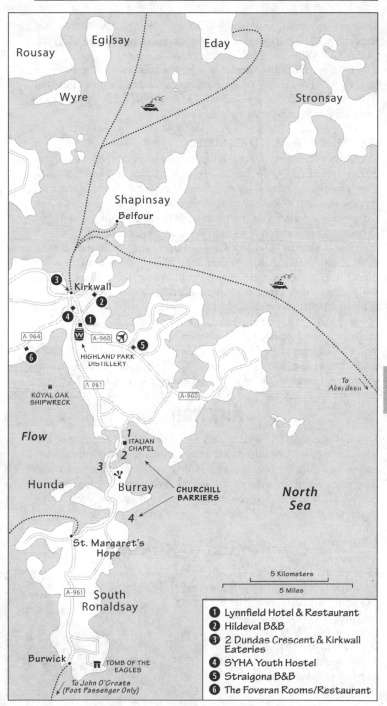

Rousay

Egilsay

Eday

Wyre

Stronsay

Shapinsay
Belfour

3 Kirkwall **2**
4 **1**
A-964 Ⓦ A-960 ✈ **5**
HIGHLAND PARK
DISTILLERY
6

A-961

Flow
A-960

ROYAL OAK
SHIPWRECK

1 ITALIAN CHAPEL
2
3

Hunda

Burray

CHURCHILL
BARRIERS

4

North
Sea

St. Margaret's
Hope

A-961

South
Ronaldsay

Burwick

TOMB OF THE
EAGLES

To John O'Groats
(Foot Passenger Only)

To Aberdeen

5 Kilometers

5 Miles

NORTHERN SCOTLAND

1 Lynnfield Hotel & Restaurant
2 Hildeval B&B
3 2 Dundas Crescent & Kirkwall Eateries
4 SYHA Youth Hostel
5 Straigona B&B
6 The Foveran Rooms/Restaurant

are not many taxis, so without a car your best bet is the bus that runs every 30 minutes—just pay the driver (airport code: KOI, tel. 01856/872-421, www.hial.co.uk/kirkwall-airport).

By Tour from Inverness: The John O'Groats foot ferry operates a very long all-day tour from Inverness that includes bus and ferry transfers, and a guided tour around the main sights (£72, daily June-Aug only, www.jogferry.co.uk).

GETTING AROUND ORKNEY

While this chapter is designed for travelers with a car (or a driver/guide—see next), **public buses** do connect sights on Mainland (operated by Stagecoach, www.stagecoachbus.com). From Mainland, **ferries** fan out to outlying islets (www.orkneyferries.co.uk); the main ports are Kirkwall (for points north) and Houton (for Hoy). If taking a car on a ferry, it's always smart to book ahead.

Local Guide: Orkney Uncovered is run by husband-and-wife team Kinlay (who guides) and Kirsty (who manages the office). Energetic and passionate about sharing their adopted home with visitors, their standard itinerary hits both prehistoric and wartime highlights (everything in this chapter—which Kinlay helped research). But they're happy to tailor an itinerary to your interests and offer a special price for Rick Steves readers (£300 for a full-day, 9-hour tour in a comfy van, more for 5 or more people, multiday tours and cruise excursions possible, tel. 01856/878-822, www.orkneyuncovered.co.uk, enquiries@orkneyuncovered.co.uk).

Kirkwall

Kirkwall (pop. 9,000) is tidy and functional. Like the rest of the island, most of its buildings are more practical than pretty. But it has an entertaining and interesting old center and is a smart home base from which to explore the island. Whether sleeping here or not, you'll likely pass through at some point (to gas up, change buses, use the airport, or stock up on groceries).

Orientation to Kirkwall

Historic Kirkwall's shop-lined, pedestrian-only main drag leads from the cathedral down to the harbor, changing names several times as it curls through town. It's a workaday strip, lined with a combination of humble local shops and places trying to be trendy. You'll pop out at the little harbor, where fishing boats bob and ferries fan out to the northern islets.

The handy **TI,** with free Wi-Fi, is at the bus station (on West Castle Street, daily 9:00-18:00, shorter hours off-season, tel. 01856/872-856, www.visitorkney.com). They produce a handy "breakfast bulletin" with the day's events and tourist news. The bus station stores bags for free (but not overnight). If you don't have a car, **Craigies Taxi** is reliable and responds quickly to a call (tel. 01856/878-787).

You're likely to find live music somewhere most nights. The **Reel Coffee Shop,** next to the cathedral, is passionate about music and hosts folk and "trad" evenings with an inviting vibe (generally Wed, Thu, and Sat at 20:00). Among the local craft beers on tap, the most popular, a pale ale, is Scapa Special. (They say it goes down better than the German fleet.)

Sights in Kirkwall

▲St. Magnus Cathedral

This grand edifice, whose pointy steeple is visible from just about anywhere in town, is one of Scotland's most enjoyable churches to visit (free, Mon-Sat 9:00-18:00, Sun from 14:00). The building dates from the 12th century, back when this was part of the Parish of Trondheim, Nor-

way. Built from vibrant red sandstone by many of the same stonemasons who worked on Durham's showpiece cathedral, St. Magnus is harmonious Romanesque inside and out: stout columns and small, rounded windows and arches. Inside, it boasts a delightful array of engaging monuments, all well-described by the self-guided tour brochure: a bell from the *Royal Oak* battleship, sunk in Scapa Flow in 1939 (explained later); a reclining monument of arctic explorer John Rae, who appears to be enjoying a very satisfying eternal nap; the likely bones of St. Magnus (a beloved local saint); and many other characteristic flourishes. But the highlight is the gravestones that line the walls of the nave, each one carved with reminders of mortality: skull and crossbones, coffin, hourglass, and the shovel used by the undertaker. Read some of the poignant epitaphs: "She lived regarded and dyed regreted."

Nearby: The **Bishop and Earl's Palaces** (across the street) are a pair of once-grand, now-empty ruined buildings—for most, they're not worth the admission fee.

▲▲Orkney Museum

Just across the street from the cathedral, this museum packs the old parsonage with well-described exhibits covering virtually every dimension of history and life on the island. A visit here (to see the Stone Age, Iron Age, and Viking arti-facts) can be good preparation before exploring the islands' archaeological sites. Poking around, you'll see a 1539 map showing how "Orcadia" was part of Scandinavia, an exhibit about the crazy annual brawl called The Ba', and lots of century-old photos of traditional life (free, Mon-Sat 10:30-17:00, closed Sun, fine book shop, tel. 01856/873-535).

Mercat Cross

In front of the cathedral stands Kirkwall's mercat cross (market cross), which is the starting point for the annual event called The Ba'. Short for "ball," this is a no-holds-barred, citywide rugby match that takes place every Christmas and New Year's Day. Hundreds of Kirkwall's rough-and-tumble young lads team up based on neighborhood (the Uppies and the Doonies), and attempt to deliver the ball to the opposing team's goal by any means necessary. The only rule: There are no rules. While it's usually just one gigantic scrum pushing back and forth through the streets, other tactics are used (such as the recent controversy when one team simply tossed the ball in a car and drove it to the goal). Ask locals about their stories—or scars—from The Ba'.

▲Highland Park Distillery

Outside the town center is a sprawling stone facility that's been distilling whisky since 1789 (legally). They give 75-minute tours similar to other distilleries, but this is one of only six in all of Scot-land that malts its own barley—you'll see the malting floor (where the barley is spread and stirred while germinating) and the peat-fired kilns. Guides love to explain how the distillery's well-regard-ed whiskies get their flavor from Orkney's unique composition of peat (composed mostly of heather on this treeless island) and its high humidity (which minimizes alcohol "lost to the angels" dur-ing maturation). While the distillery is "silent" for much of July and August, its tour is good even if the workers are gone (£10, tours Mon-Sat 10:00-16:00, Sun 12:00-16:00, fewer off-season, includes two tasty shots; on the edge of town to the south, toward the Scapa Flow WWII sites; tel. 01856/873-107, www.highlandpark.co.uk).

Sleeping in Kirkwall

These accommodations are in or near Kirkwall. Orkney's B&Bs are not well marked; get specific instructions from your host before you arrive.

In Kirkwall: $$$ Lynnfield Hotel rents 10 rooms that are a bit old-fashioned in decor, but with modern hotel amenities (on Holm Road/A-961, tel. 01856/872-505, www.lynnfieldhotel.com). High up in town, consider **$$ Hildeval B&B,** in a modern home with five contemporary-style rooms (on East Road, tel. 01856/878-840, www.hildeval-orkney.co.uk). With a handy location just behind the cathedral, **$ 2 Dundas Crescent** has three old-fashioned rooms rented by welcoming Ruth, in a big old house that used to be a manse—a preacher's home (tel. 01856/874-805, www.twodundas.co.uk). And ¢ the **SYHA Youth Hostel** rents both dorm beds and private rooms (Old Scapa Road, 15-minute walk from center, tel. 01856/872-243, www.syha.org.uk).

In the Countryside: Just past the airport, **$$ Straigona B&B,** about a five-minute drive outside of Kirkwall, has three rooms in a cozy modern home, run by helpful Julie and Mike (tel. 01856/861-328, www.straigona.co.uk). For more anonymity and grand views over Scapa Flow, the recommended restaurant **$$ The Foveran** has eight rooms, some with contemporary flourish and others more traditional (5 minutes from Kirkwall by car on the A-964, tel. 01856/872-389, www.thefoveran.com).

Eating in Kirkwall

The first three places are near the cathedral; the next two are on the harbor. The main pedestrian street connecting the harbor and cathedral is lined with other options. Hotels along the harbor are also a good bet for dinner.

$$ The Reel Coffee Shop is a music club, café, and pub popular for its light lunches (open daily 9:00-17:00, next to the cathedral). It reopens on many evenings to host live music (Wed, Thu, and Sat evenings from 20:00, 6 Broad Street, tel. 01856/871-000).

$$ Judith Glue Shop is a souvenir-and-craft shop across from the cathedral, with a cutesy café in the back (25 Broad Street, tel. 01856/874-225).

$ Strynd Tea Room, tucked down an alley near the cathedral (just behind The Reel), is a fine choice for coffee and cakes, afternoon tea, or a light lunch (Broad Street, tel. 01856/871-552).

$ The Harbour Fry is best place for fish-and-chips, with both

NORTHERN SCOTLAND

eat-inside or takeaway options (daily 12:00-21:00, half a block off the harbor at 3 Bridge Street, tel. 01856/873-170).

$$ Helgi's Pub, facing the harbor, serves quality food and is popular for its fun menu and burgers. Upstairs is boring, the ground floor is more fun, and you're welcome to sit at the bar if the tables are full. Reservations are smart for dinner (daily 12:00-14:00 & 17:00-21:00, 14 Harbor Street, tel. 01856/879-293, www.helgis. co.uk).

DESTINATION RESTAURANTS NEAR KIRKWALL

With talented chefs working hard to elevate Orcadian cuisine—using traditional local ingredients, but with international flourish, these are considered the best restaurants around.

$$$$ The Foveran, perched on a bluff with smashing views over Scapa Flow, has a cool, contemporary dining room with a wall of windows (dinner nightly May-Sept, weekends-only in winter, southwest of Kirkwall on the A-964, tel. 01856/872-389, www. thefoveran.com).

$$$$ Lynnfield Hotel, near the Highland Park Distillery on the way out of town, has a more traditional feel (open daily for lunch and dinner, reservations smart in the evening, on Holm Road/A-961, tel. 01856/872-505, www.lynnfieldhotel.com).

Sights in the Orkneys

PREHISTORIC SITES

Orkney boasts an astonishing concentration of 5,000-year-old Neolithic monuments worth ▲▲▲—one of the best such collections in Great Britain (and that's saying something). And here on Orkney, there's also a unique Bronze and Iron Age overlay, during which Picts, and then Vikings, built their own monuments to complement the ones they inherited. The best of these sites are easily toured along a single stretch of road, as described below.

Background: Five thousand years ago—centuries before Stonehenge—Orkney had a bustling settlement with some 30,000 people (a population larger than today's). The climate, already milder than most of Scotland thanks to the Gulf Stream, was even warmer then, making this a desirable place to live. Orkney's prehistoric residents left behind structures from every walk of life: humble residential settlements (Skara Brae, Barnhouse Village), mysterious stone circles (Ring of Brodgar, Stenness Stones), more than 100 tombs (Maeshowe, Tomb of the Eagles), and what appears to be a sprawling ensemble of spiritual buildings (the Ness of Brodgar). And, this being the Stone Age, all of this was accomplished using tools made not of metal, but of stone and bone.

Many more sites await excavation. (Any time you see a lump or a bump in a field, it's likely an ancient site—identified with the help of ground-penetrating radar—and protected by the government.) While you could spend days poring over all of Orkney's majestic prehistoric monuments, on a short visit focus on the following highlights. (Actual artifacts from these sites are on display only in the Orkney Museum in Kirkwall.)

Maeshowe

The finest chambered tomb north of the Alps, Maeshowe (mays-HOW) was built around 3500 B.C. From the outside, it looks like

yet another big mound. But inside, the burial chamber is remarkably intact. The only way to go inside is on a fascinating 30-minute tour. You'll squeeze through the entrance tunnel and emerge into a space designed for ancestor worship, surrounded by three smaller cells. At the winter solstice, the setting sun shines through the entrance tunnel, illuminating the entrance to the main cell. How they managed to cut and transport gigantic slabs of sandstone, then assemble this dry-stone, corbeled pyramid—all in an age before metal tools—still puzzles present-day engineers. Adding to this place's mystique, in the 12th century, a band of Norsemen took shelter here for three days during a storm, and entertained themselves by carving runic messages into the walls—many of them still readable (£6, tours daily 10:00-16:00, tel. 01856/761-606, www.historicenvironment.scot/maeshowe). Reservations are required (book in person or online, but not by phone).

Prehistoric Sites near Maeshowe

A narrow spit of land just a few hundred yards from Maeshowe is lined with several stunning, free-to-visit, always-"open" Neolithic sites (from Maeshowe, head south on the A-965 and immediately turn right onto the B-9056, following *Bay of Skaill* signs). Along this road, you'll reach the following sites, in this order (watch for the brown signs). Conveniently, these line up on the way to Skara Brae.

Stones of Stenness: Three-and-a-half standing stones survive from an original 12 that formed a

100-foot-diameter ring. Dating from around 3000 B.C., these are some of the oldest standing stones in Britain (a millennium older than Stonehenge).

Barnhouse Village: From the Stones of Stenness, a footpath continues through the field to the Barnhouse Village. Likely built around the same time as the Stones of Stenness, this was probably a residential area for the priests and custodians of the ceremonial monuments all around. Discovered in 1984, much of what you see today has been reconstructed—making this the least favorite site of archaeological purists. Still, it provides an illuminating contrast to Skara Brae (described later): While those Skara Brae homes were built underground, the ones at Barnhouse were thatched stone huts not unlike ones you still see around Great Britain today. The entire gathering was enclosed by a defensive wall.

Back on the road, just before the **causeway** between two lochs—saltwater on the left and freshwater on the right—two pillars flank the road (one intact, the other stubby). These formed a gateway of sorts to the important Neolithic structures just beyond.

Ness of Brodgar: On the left, look for a busy excavation site in action. The Ness of Brodgar offers an exciting opportunity to

observe an actual archaeological dig in progress (discovered only in 2003). The work site you see covers only one-tenth of the entire complex, which was likely an ensemble of important ceremonial buildings...think of it as the "Orkney Vatican." The biggest foundation, nicknamed "the Cathedral," appears to have been a focal point for pilgrimages. Don't be surprised if there's no action—due to limited funding, archaeologists are likely at work here only in July and August (at other times, it's carefully covered, with nothing to see). The archaeologists hope to raise enough funds to build a permanent visitors center. Free guided tours are sometimes available (July-Aug Mon-Fri at 11:00, 13:00, and 15:00, check www.nessofbrodgar.co.uk for details).

The Ring of Brodgat: Farther along on the left, look for stones capping a ridge above the road. The Ring of Brodgar is more than three times larger than the Stones of Stenness (and about 500 years newer). Of the original 60 or so stones—creating a circle as wide as a football field—25 still stand. The ring, which sits amidst a marshy moor, was surrounded by a henge (moat) that was 30 feet wide and 20 feet deep. Walking around the ring, notice that some are carved with "graffiti"—names of visitors from the late 19th century to the early 20th century, as well as some faint Norse runes carved by a Viking named Bjorn around A.D. 1150 (park 300 yards away, across the road).

Skara Brae

At the far-eastern reaches of Mainland (about a 20-minute drive from Maeshowe), this remarkable site illustrates how some Neolithic people lived like rabbits in warrens—hunkered down in subterranean homes, connected by tunnels and lit only by whale-oil lamps. Uncovered by an 1850 windstorm, Skara Brae (meaning roughly "village under hills") has been meticulously excavated and is very well presented (£7.50, open daily 9:30-17:30 year-round, café and WCs).

Begin your visit in the small exhibition hall, where you'll watch a short film and see displays on Neolithic life. Then head out and walk inside a reconstructed home from Skara Brae—with a hearth, beds, storage area, and live-bait tanks dug into the floor. Finally, walk across a field to reach the site itself. Museum attendants stand by to answer any questions.

The oldest, standalone homes at Skara Brae were built around 3100 B.C., a few centuries later, the complex was expanded and connected with tunnels. You'll walk

on a grassy ridge just above the complex, peering down into 10 partially ruined homes and the tunnels that connect them. For safety, all of this was covered with turf, with only two or three entrances and exits. Because sandstone is a natural insulator, these spaces—while cramped and dank—would have been warm and cozy during the frequent battering storms. If you see a grate, squint down into the darkness: A primitive sewer system, flushed by a rerouted stream, ran beneath all of the homes, functioning not too differently from modern sewers. And all of this was accomplished without the use of metal tools. They even created an ingenious system of giant stone slabs on pivots, allowing them to be opened and closed like modern doors.

Before leaving, look out over the nearby bay, and consider that this is only about one-third of the entire size of the original Skara Brae. What's now a beach was once a freshwater loch. But with the rising Atlantic, the water became unusable. About 800 years after it was built, the village was abandoned; since then, most of it has been lost to the sea. This area is called Skaill Bay, from the Old Norse *skål,* for "cheers!"—during Viking times, this was a popular place for revelry...but the revelers had no clue they were partying on top of a Neolithic village.

And now for something completely different: Your ticket to Skara Brae also includes the **Skaill House,** the sprawling stone mansion on the nearby hilltop. Here you can tour some lived-in rooms (c. 1950) and see a fascinating hodgepodge of items once important to a leading Orkney family. Some items illustrate Orkney's prime location for passing maritime trade: The dining room proudly displays Captain James Cook's dinner service—bartered by his crew on their return voyage after the captain was killed in Hawaii (Orkney was the first place they made landfall in the UK). You'll also see traditional Orkney chairs (with woven backs); in the library, an Old Norse "calendar"—a wooden stick that you could hold up to the horizon at sunset to determine the exact date; a Redcoat's red coat from the Crimean War; a Spanish chest salvaged from a shipwreck; and some

very "homely" (and supposedly haunted) bedrooms.

Nearby: Just south of Skara Brae, drivers can consider a quick visit to the sightseeing twofer of **Yesnaby** (watch for the turnoff on the B-9056). On a bluff overlooking the sea, you'll find an old antiaircraft artillery battery from World War II, and some of Orkney's most dramatic sea-cliff scenery.

SCAPA FLOW: WORLD WAR II SITES

For a quick and fascinating glimpse of Orkney's World War II locations, worth ▲▲▲, drive 10 minutes south from Kirkwall on the A-961 (leave town toward St. Mary's and St. Margaret's Hope, past the Highland Park Distillery)—to the natural harbor called Scapa Flow (see the sidebar). From the village of St. Mary's, you can cross over all four of the Churchill Barriers, with subtle reminders of war

all around. The floor of Scapa Flow is littered with shipwrecks, and if you know where to look, you can still see many of them as you drive by.

Barrier #1 crosses from St. Mary's to the Isle of Burray. This narrow channel is where, in the early days of World War II, the German

U-47 slipped between sunken ships to attack the *Royal Oak*—demonstrating the need to build these barriers. Notice that the Churchill Barriers have two levels: smaller quarried stone down below, and huge concrete blocks on top.

Just over the first barrier, perched on the little rise on the left, is Orkney's most fascinating wartime site: the **Italian Chapel** (£3, daily 9:00-18:30 in summer, shorter hours off-season). Italian POWs who were captured during the North African campaign (and imprisoned here on Orkney to work on the Churchill Barriers) were granted permission to create a Catholic chapel to remind them of their homeland. While the front view is a pretty Baroque facade, if you circle around you'll see that the core of the structure is two prefab Nissen huts (similar to Quonset huts). Inside, you can see the remarkable craftsmanship of the artists who decorated the church. In 1943, Domenico Chiocchetti led the effort to create this house of worship, and personally painted the frescoes that adorn the interior. The ethereal *Madonna*

e Bambino over the main altar is based on a small votive he had brought with him to war. An experienced ironworker named Palumbi used scrap metal (much of it scavenged from sunken WWI ships) to create the gate and chandeliers, while others used whatever basic materials they could to finish the details. (Notice the elegant corkscrew base of the baptismal font near the entrance; it's actually a suspension spring coated in concrete.) These lovingly crafted details are a hope-filled symbol of the gentility and grace that can blossom even during brutal wartime. (And the British military is proud of this structure as an embodiment of Britain's wartime ethic of treating POWs with care and respect.) Spend some time examining the details—such as the stained-glass windows, which are painted rather than leaded. The chapel was completed in 1944, just two months before the men who built it were sent home. Chiocchetti returned for a visit in the 1960s, bringing with him the wood-carved Stations of the Cross that now hang in the nave.

Continuing south along the road, you'll cross over two more barriers in rapid succession. You'll see the masts and hulls of **ship-**

Scapa Flow: Britain's Remote Wartime Naval Base

Orkney's arc of scattered islands form one of the world's largest natural harbors, called Scapa Flow (SKAH-pah flow). The Norsemen named this area *skalpai floi*—

"scabbard water," where a sword was sheathed—suggesting that they used this area to store their warships when not in use. And in the 20th century, Scapa Flow was the main base for Britain's Royal Navy.

During World War I, to thwart U-boat attacks, dozens of old ships and fishing vessels were requisitioned and intentionally sunk to block the gaps between the islets that define Scapa Flow. You can still see many of these "block ships" breaking the surface today.

At the end of World War I, a fleet of 74 German battleships surrendered at Scapa Flow. On the morning of June 21, 1919—days before the Treaty of Versailles was formally enacted—the British admiral took most of his navy out on a "victory lap" patrol. Once they were gone, the German commander ordered his men to scuttle the entire fleet, rather than turn them over. By the time the British fleet returned five hours later, 52 German ships littered the bottom of the bay. The British opened fire on the remaining German ships, killing nine Germans—the final casualties of World War I. While most of the ships were later salvaged for scrap, to this day, German crockery washes up on Orkney beaches after a storm. Seven ships remain at a depth of 150 feet, making this one of Eu-

wrecks (on the left) scuttled here during World War I to block the harbor. As you cross over the bridges, notice that these are solid barriers, with no water circulation—in fact, the water level on each side of the barrier varies slightly, since the tide differs by an hour and a half.

At the far end of **Barrier #3,** on the left, watch for the huge wooden boxes on the beach. These were used in pre-barrier times (WWI) for boom floats, which supported nets designed to block German submarines.

After Barrier #3, as you climb the hill, watch for the pull-rope's most popular scuba diving destinations.

Scapa Flow also played an important role in World War II. Even before Britain declared war on Germany, Luftwaffe reconnaissance flights had identified a gap in the sunken-ship barriers around the harbor. And on October 14, 1939—just weeks after war was declared—a Nazi U-47 slipped inside the harbor and torpedoed the HMS *Royal Oak,* killing 834 (including 110 seamen-in-training under the age of 15). To this day, the battleship—which had been fully loaded with fuel and ordnance—sits on the bottom of the bay, marked with a green warning buoy.

In April 1940, Luftwaffe planes flew from German-occupied Norway to bomb Orkney for three days straight in what's termed the "Battle of Orkney." But the islands were bulked up with heavy-duty gun batteries and other defenses, turning Orkney into a fortress. A sea of blimps called "barrage balloons"—designed to interfere with air attacks—clogged the air overhead. They even built a false fleet out of wood (also protected by barrage balloons) as a decoy for the Luftwaffe. The local population of 22,000 was joined by some 80,000 troops. Many surviving fragments from the Battle of Orkney can still be seen all over the island.

To ensure that no further surprises would sneak into the bay, First Lord of the Admiralty Winston Churchill visited here (just weeks before becoming prime minister) and hatched a plan to build sturdy barriers spanning the small distances between the islands south of Kirkwall. Throughout the wartime years, British workers and Italian prisoners of war labored to construct the "Churchill Barriers." The roads on top of the barriers opened just a few days after V-E Day, and today tourists use them to island-hop—and to learn about the dramatic history of Scapa Flow.

out on the right with an orientation board. From this **viewpoint,** you can see three of the Churchill Barriers in one grand panorama.

Carrying on south, the next barrier isn't a Churchill Barrier at all—it's an ayre, a causeway that was built during the Viking period.

Finally you'll reach **Barrier #4**—hard to recognize because so much sand has accumulated on its east side (look for the giant breakwater blocks). Surveying the dunes along this barrier, notice the crooked concrete shed poking up—actually the top of a shipwreck.

The far side of this sand dune is one of Orkney's best beaches—sheltered and scenic.

From here, the A-961 continues south past **St. Margaret's Hope** (where the ferry to Gills Bay departs) and all the way to Burwick, at the southern tip of South Ronaldsay. From here you can see the tip of Scotland. Nearby is the **Tomb of the Eagles,** a burial cairn similar to Maeshowe, but less accessible (time-consuming visit, www.tomboftheeagles.co.uk).

More WWII Sites: For those really interested in the World War II scene, consider a ferry trip out to the **Isle of Hoy;** the main settlement, Lyness, has the Scapa Flow Visitors Centre and cemetery (www.scapaflow.co.uk). Near Lyness alone are some 37 Luftwaffe crash sites. A tall hill, called Wee Fea, was hollowed out to hold 100,000 tons of fuel oil. Also on Hoy, you can hike seven miles round-trip to the iconic **Old Man of Hoy**—a 450-foot-high sea stack in front of Britain's tallest vertical sea cliffs. (Or you can see the same thing for free from the deck of the Stromness-Scrabster ferry.)

FERRY PORT TOWNS

With more time, check out these two towns with connections to northern Scotland. **Stromness** is Orkney's "second city," with 3,000 people. It's a stony 17th-century fishing town and worth a look. Equal parts fishing town and tourist depot, its traffic-free main drag has a certain salty charm. If driving, there's easy parking at the harbor. If catching the ferry to Scrabster, get here early to enjoy a stroll.

St. Margaret's Hope—named for a 13th-century Norwegian princess who was briefly Queen of Scots until she died en route to Orkney—is even smaller, with a charming seafront-village atmosphere. Ferries leave here for Gills Bay.

SCOTLAND:
PAST & PRESENT

Rugged and remote, Scotland has had a particularly hard-fought history. Split by the Highland Boundary Fault, which separates the flatter, more Anglo-Saxon, more London-looking Lowlands in the south from the craggy, deeply Celtic Highlands in the north, the two halves have distinct characters. Ringing the country are distant islands—the Hebrides, Orkney, and Shetland—each bringing its own local customs, history, and traditions to the table. Since ancient times, the feisty people of Scotland—Highlanders and Lowlanders alike—have fought to preserve their region's unique identity. Scotland's rabble-rousing national motto is *Nemo me impune lacessit*—"No one provokes me with impunity." In Scotland, perhaps more than most places, legends of national heroes abound.

PREHISTORIC ORIGINS, ROMAN REBELLION, AND HIGHLAND CLANS

Scotland's first inhabitants were hunter-gatherers who came north as the Ice Age receded (7000 B.C.). In Neolithic times (4500-2000 B.C.), a new wave of farmer-herders arrived from the south. They left us stone circles and passage graves (funeral mounds with a burial chamber inside, reached by a passage). While few Neolithic structures survive in Scotland, Orkney—which flourished during this age—has some of the UK's best and oldest (see page 404).

Also during the Stone Age, people began to settle on the waters of Scotland's many lochs, building igloo-shaped fortified islands called crannogs. Made of wood and built upon timber pilings driven deep into the loch's floor, they were linked to the shore only by a removable wooden plank. Crannogs were at once well-protected and easy to access (in an age when most travel was by boat), and they provided unobstructed views across the loch. Many circular "islands" you may notice in lochs today are likely grown-over, abandoned crannogs. (For more on crannogs, visit the excellent Crannog Centre on Loch Tay—see page 339.)

Around 500 B.C., the Celts moved in from Europe, bringing Iron-Age technology and the language that would develop into the Gaelic tongue. The Celts built hilltop forts, with large stone towers called brochs.

In A.D. 80, Roman legions—having already conquered England—marched north and established a camp near Edinburgh. They called today's Scotland "Caledonia" (a term you'll still see everywhere) and battled the fierce Celts, whom they dubbed Caledonii—or "Picts" ("painted"; for their war paint). But the Picts would not surrender. Eventually, the Romans decided they had expanded far enough—and Scotland just wasn't worth the effort. It was mountainous, wild, and dangerous—not just with Picts, but with predatory beasts such as bears, wolves, and lynx. The Romans sealed off Caledonia (and the pesky Picts) with two walls—the famous Hadrian's Wall (73 miles long and up to 20 feet high), running more or less along the modern-day border between Scotland and England, and the lesser-known Antonine Wall (from the Firth of Clyde to the Firth of Forth—essentially from today's Glasgow to Edinburgh). From then on, while England was forever stamped with a Roman/European perspective, Scotland was set on a course that was isolated and Celtic.

Medieval Scotland was a stew of peoples: Picts in the northern Highlands, Anglo-Saxons (Germanic invaders) in the south, and the "Scoti" (Celtic cousins from Ireland) on the west coast. (While little survives from this time, you can still see faint remains of some of the Scoti's important sites in Kilmartin Glen—see page 269.) The Scoti gradually overwhelmed and absorbed the Picts. In their kingdom of Alba (the Gaelic name for Scotland), they established Gaelic as the chief language and Christianity—brought from Ireland by St. Columba in the sixth century—as the dominant religion. Even at this early date, Scotland's geographical/ethnic boundary was already set: Gaelic/Celtic culture in the Highland north, English-friendly Anglo-Saxons in the Lowland south.

Vikings attacked from the north, and succeeded in capturing the northern islands, which remained Norse until the 15th century.

(To this day, Orkney and Shetland have a Norwegian flavor and a heritage of Old Norse rune carvings and place names.) But much of the Scottish realm united under a Gaelic warlord named Kenneth MacAlpin. In 843, in his capital at Scone (50 miles north of Edinburgh), MacAlpin was crowned atop the Stone of Scone—making him the first king of Scots.

But this "Scotland" was a tiny and troubled land. In the 11th century (as Shakespeare later recalled it), King Duncan was murdered by one of his own men: Macbeth. King Macbeth was, in turn, killed by Duncan's son, Malcolm Canmore—the man who would establish Edinburgh and bring remote Scotland onto the stage of the wider world.

Meanwhile, in the remote reaches of the Highlands and the Hebrides, communities were based on the clan system: tribes of people sharing a stretch of land managed by a chieftain, who served as a kind of caretaker for the people and future generations. In Gaelic, *clann* means "children"; the clan system was the traditional Scottish way of passing along power—similar to England's dukes, barons, and counts. Although clan members took the chief's name in solidarity, they were not necessarily related by blood. The patrilineal clan system eventually became further subdivided into septs—alliances of families who pledged allegiance to the same chieftain.

Most Highlanders were crofters (small, self-subsistence farmers) who lived in humble huts with dirt floors, dry-stone walls, and peat fires with heavy smoke that escaped through thatched roofs. (For a glimpse of this lifestyle—which persisted well into the 18th century—visit the Highland Folk Museum south of Inverness, described on page 337, or the Museum of Island Life on the Isle of Skye.) While it's not quite true that each clan had its own carefully designed tartan pattern, clan members did tend to live in a single geographical area, where certain natural dyes and weavers predominated—so they likely dressed in (somewhat) similar colors. (For more on the kilt tradition, see page 33.)

Some clans were allies, either through intermarriage or through shared interests. Others were sworn enemies. One of the most famous rivalries was a three-way struggle between Clan Donald (or MacDonald), Clan Mackenzie, and Clan MacLeod, who clashed in several epic battles (see sidebar on page 381).

WILLIAM WALLACE, ROBERT THE BRUCE, AND MEDIEVAL INDEPENDENCE

When King Malcolm III married the English Princess Margaret in 1070, it united the culture of the Highland Scots with that of the Lowland Anglo-Saxons. Margaret was exceptionally pious, and she fostered the Christian faith as never before. Increasingly, Scotland became ruled from the southern Lowlands and influenced by its southern neighbor, England. As English settlers moved north, they built castles and abbeys. They also brought with them a new social order—a hierarchical government that went beyond the small social unit of the Highland clan.

But in the far reaches of Scotland, the clan system still flourished. Clan Donald, based on the Isle of Skye's Sleat Peninsula, controlled its own sprawling kingdom: In the 12th century, a great warrior named Somerled took control of the Lordship of the Isles, which included most of Scotland's west-coast islands, and penetrated deep into the Highlands and present-day Northern Ireland (Antrim). This fully independent maritime state lasted until 1493, when its territory was finally folded into the holdings of the Stuart kings. (To this day, the British heir apparent carries the title "Lord of the Isles.")

In 1286, the king of Scotland died without an heir. To settle the battle over succession, the Scots invited King Edward I of England ("Longshanks") to arbitrate. Edward seized the moment to assert his power over Scotland. He invaded, defeated the chosen successor, and stole the revered coronation stone—the Stone of Scone—taking it back to London (where it remained, almost untouched, until 1996).

Enraged, the Scots rallied around nobleman William Wallace (see page 58). He defeated the English at Stirling Bridge (1297) and was named the "guardian of Scotland." Wallace marched his army into England, plundered its north, then returned to Scotland—where he was defeated at the Battle of Falkirk in 1298. Disgraced, Wallace retreated to the Highlands and waged guerrilla warfare against the English until he was finally betrayed, arrested, and brutally executed in 1305.

The torch was passed to the earl of Carrick, Robert the Bruce (see page 62), who united Scotland's many clans and defeated the English at the tide-turning Battle of Bannockburn (1314). Bruce was crowned King Robert, and his heirs would rule Scotland for the next four centuries under the Stewart family name. (Later, when Mary, Queen of Scots moved to France, she changed the spelling to "Stuart" because the French alphabet of the time lacked the letter "w"—for simplicity, I've used that spelling throughout this book.) Scotland had secured its independence.

Over the next two centuries, Scotland's kings ruled from their castle in Stirling, gradually asserting central control over local clans and expanding the country's boundaries into the modern nation. But the Stuart monarchy was still weak, beleaguered with infighting over succession. Fortunately, England was kept at bay, plagued by its own troubles fighting the French (Hundred Years' War) and each other (Wars of the Roses). Scotland's long-standing "Auld Alliance" with the French existed mainly to support its independence from England.

MARY, QUEEN OF SCOTS; JOHN KNOX; AND THE PROTESTANT REFORMATION

Everything changed when Henry VIII became king of England, sparking a border war with Scotland. In the Battle of Flodden (1513), Scotland was utterly defeated. Soon Scotland faced an even greater enemy. As the Reformation crept into Scotland (c. 1540-1560), it split the country in two. The Highlands remained Catholic, rural, pro-monarchy, and pro-French. The Lowlands grew increasingly Protestant, urban, anti-monarchy, and pro-English.

When the Scottish King James V died in 1542, his six-day-old daughter Mary was named Queen of Scots (r. 1542-1567). Mary grew up staunchly Catholic and was educated in France, where she married the French crown prince in 1558. By the time the newly widowed Mary arrived back home (in 1561) to rule her native Scotland, the teenage queen found a hostile country in the throes of a Protestant Reformation (for the full story, see the sidebar on page 208).

The leader of the movement was John Knox (1514-1572), who grew up poor outside of Edinburgh. At a young age, he was at the forefront of the Reformation and a disciple of early reformer George Wishart, who was burned at the stake. Knox was arrested and exiled for two years; he spent much of this time among reformers in England, and with John Calvin in Geneva. Upon his return to Scotland (1559), he brought with him crates full of English bibles, which he used to spread both the Word of God and the English language. Knox went on an evangelical kick, preaching fire and brimstone throughout the Lowlands. He spread the message of Protestantism, wrote a Declaration of Independence-type manifesto called the "Confession of the Faith," and (with the help of some powerful supporters) outlawed Catholicism under punishment of prison or even death.

Mary, Queen of Scots' homecoming came just as Reformation fever was at its peak. Mary summoned Knox for a series of debates, where they hashed out their differences. While they ultimately agreed to disagree on the larger points, they did come to some compromises: Mary insisted on her personal right to say Mass in private, despite the national ban on the Catholic faith.

The Scots soon became disgusted with Mary's messy personal life, starting with her 1565 remarriage. The groom was her first cousin, Lord Darnley—an English-Scottish prince whose claim to both crowns had made him many enemies. Their marriage soured, and rumors flew that Mary was getting fresh with her secretary. The secretary was brutally murdered at Edinburgh's Palace of Holyroodhouse in front of a horrified Mary, and suspicion fell on Darnley. Then Darnley himself was found strangled in his Edinburgh home, while Mary fled the country with the prime suspect—the earl of Bothwell—soon to be Mary's third husband. Amid all of the drama, Mary gave birth to a son—whether Darnley's or the secretary's, no one knows—who would grow up to be king of both Scotland and England.

PAST & PRESENT

KING JAMES VI/I, KING CHARLES I, AND CIVIL WAR

Following an uprising in 1567, Mary was forced to abdicate in favor of her infant son, who became King James VI of Scotland. Raised a Protestant, James assumed official duties at age 17 (1584) and brought a tentative peace to religiously divided Scotland. (Meanwhile, Mary was arrested on suspicion of the murder of Darnley, charged with an unrelated plot against her cousin, Queen Elizabeth I of England, and eventually beheaded in 1587.)

Typical Church Architecture

History comes to life when you visit a centuries-old church. Even if you wouldn't know your apse from a hole in the ground, learning a few simple terms will enrich your experience. Note that not every church has every feature, and a "cathedral" isn't a type of church architecture, but rather a designation for a church that's a governing center for a local bishop.

Aisles: The long, generally low-ceilinged arcades that flank the nave.

Altar: The raised area with a ceremonial table (often adorned with candles or a crucifix), where the priest prepares and serves the bread and wine for Communion.

Apse: The space beyond the altar, often bordered with small chapels.

Barrel Vault: A continuous round-arched ceiling that resembles an extended upside-down U.

Choir ("quire" in British English): A cozy area, often screened off, located within the church nave and near the high altar where services are sung in a more intimate setting.

Cloister: Covered hallways bordering a square or rectangular open-air courtyard, traditionally where monks and nuns got fresh air.

Facade: The front exterior of the church's main (west) entrance, usually highly decorated.

Groin Vault: An arched ceiling formed where two equal barrel vaults meet at right angles. Less common usage: term for a medieval jock strap.

Narthex: The area (portico or foyer) between the main entry and the nave.

Nave: The long, central section of the church (running west to east, from the entrance to the altar) where the congregation sits or stands through the service.

Transept: In a traditional cross-shaped floor plan, the transept is one of the two parts forming the "arms" of the cross. The transepts run north-south, perpendicularly crossing the east-west nave.

West Portal: The main entry to the church (on the west end, opposite the main altar).

In the 1592 Golden Act, Presbyterianism triumphed, and was made the rule of law. Scotland went forward as a predominantly Protestant nation. But even among Protestants, there were religious divisions. Scottish Protestants were Presbyterians, members of the newly reorganized Church (or "Kirk") of Scotland. Presbyterianism (from the Greek word *prebuteros,* "elder") championed a self-governing congregation with leaders they elected themselves. This was in stark contrast to historic Catholic and Church of England hierarchies, led by a bishop (from the Greek *episkopos*) appointed by the king. The religious divide had political implications: Naturally, monarchs wanted to retain the politically powerful right to appoint bishops and rule congregations, while Presbyterians insisted on separation of kirk and state. Presbyterians also tended to be anti-king and pro-parliament.

In 1603, Queen Elizabeth I—England's "virgin queen"—died without an heir. Her distant cousin, Scotland's King James VI, was

next in line for the English throne. Upon leaving Edinburgh and being crowned England's King James I in London (making him both King James VI and I), he united Scotland and England. The two nations have been tied together, however fitfully, ever since.

James' son Charles I (1600-1649) was born and crowned in Scotland, but otherwise spent most of his life in England. He continued his father's attempts to consolidate the many threads of Protestantism throughout his lands, favoring the English Episcopalian model. Charles I traveled to St. Giles' Cathedral in Edinburgh; appointed a bishop who, in turn, anointed him; and eventually introduced his own prayer book. This was a bridge too far for the Scots, who rioted and signed the National Covenant, proclaiming that the Scots had a special relationship with God that was outside the control of the crown. These "Covenanters" effectively declared their independence from the Church of England, and insisted that the Church of Scotland was under entirely Scottish control. A revolution was brewing.

The Covenanters went on military raids into northern England. King Charles attempted to quell the uprising with promises of reform, but became distracted by problems closer to home: Civil war broke out in England, pitting Charles (and the monarchy and Anglicanism) against Oliver Cromwell (with his supporters in parliament and the Puritans). Scotland was also divided. The Cov-

Typical Castle Architecture

Castles were fortified residences for medieval nobles. Castles come in all shapes and sizes, but knowing a few general terms will help you understand them.

Barbican: A fortified gatehouse, sometimes a stand-alone building located outside the main walls.

Crenellation: A gap-toothed pattern of stones atop the parapet.

Drawbridge: A bridge that could be raised or lowered using counterweights or a chain and winch.

Great Hall: The largest room in the castle, serving as throne room, conference center, and dining hall.

Hoardings (or Gallery or Brattice): Wooden huts built onto the upper parts of the stone walls. They served as watch towers, living quarters, and fighting platforms.

The Keep (or Donjon): A high, strong stone tower in the center of the castle complex; the lord's home and refuge of last resort.

Loopholes (or Embrasures): Narrow wall slits through which soldiers could shoot arrows.

Machicolation: A stone ledge jutting out from the wall, with holes through which soldiers could drop rocks or boiling oil onto wall-scaling enemies below.

Moat: A ditch encircling the wall, often filled with water.

Motte-and-Bailey: A form of early English castle, with a small hilltop fort (motte) and an enclosed, fortified yard (bailey).

Parapet: Outer railing of the wall walk.

Portcullis: A heavy iron grille that could be lowered across the entrance.

Postern Gate: A small, unfortified side or rear entrance from which to launch attacks or escape.

Towers: Tall structures with crenellated tops or conical roofs serving as lookouts, chapels, living quarters, or dungeons.

Turret: A small lookout tower rising up from the top of the wall.

Wall Walk (or Allure): A pathway atop the wall where guards could patrol and where soldiers stood to fire at the enemy.

The Yard (or Bailey): An open courtyard inside the castle walls.

enanters backed Cromwell, while many traditional Highlanders backed the king.

A Scottish army of 25,000 Covenanters invaded England, captured Charles I, and turned him over to Cromwell. On January 30, 1649, the English beheaded the king of Scotland.

ENGLAND'S ASCENDANCY AND THE ACT OF UNION

Left without a king, Scotland's landed gentry crowned Charles' son at Scone on January 1, 1651 (the last coronation at Scone). But Cromwell marched north and put a decisive end to any ideas of Scottish independence. It was clear that Scotland could never again be independent without the approval of England.

Charles II (1630-1685) escaped to France, where he spent the next nine years in exile. In 1660 he was invited back to London, and in 1661, the English parliament—suffering from Cromwell remorse—invited him to take the English throne. The monarchy was restored, with Charles II (a Stuart) ruling both England and Scotland.

But the two countries remained bitterly divided over religion. After Charles II died, his Catholic successor—James II (James VII of Scotland)—was ousted by England's parliament in a coup d'état (called the Glorious Revolution), and replaced by a Protestant noble from the Dutch House of Orange-Nassau and his English wife (King William III and Mary II).

In Scotland, the newly ascendant Lowland Protestants set about forcing Highland Catholics and Episcopalians to swear allegiance to the Protestant king. This culminated in the infamous Glencoe Massacre of 1692, where pro-William Protestants of the Campbell clan used the occasion as a pretext to slaughter their centuries-old enemy, the MacDonalds. (For more on Glencoe, see page 275.)

At the same time as Scotland's king was being forced into exile, the world was changing in other ways. England was on the rise as a naval and colonial superpower, and began encroaching on Scotland. Many Scots, particularly in the southern Lowlands, welcomed the English presence. These were people of Anglo-Saxon heritage, Calvinists and parliamentarians (who had like-minded counterparts in England), and traders and industrialists (who wanted to trade with wealthy England).

Due to a failed trading-post venture in Panama (the Darien Scheme), Scotland went bankrupt. Members of the Scottish parliament (some of whom were bribed) agreed to accept a bailout from England, which came with one major string attached: the Act of Union. So in 1707, Scotland's parliament (dominated by wealthy Lowlanders) voted itself out of existence, and the Scottish nation was officially joined with England, becoming part of "Great Britain." The independence of the Scottish nation—led by the Stuart family since the days of Robert the Bruce—was over.

JACOBITE RISINGS AND MASS EMIGRATIONS

Or was it? Many Scots, especially in the Highlands, clung loyally to their ousted King James II (VII of Scotland) and his successors. They were called Jacobites—after the Latin "Jacobus" for James—and saw the Stuarts as their best hope to regain Scotland's independence. On the other side was the ascendant Protestant/urban faction, who supported the British government and monarch.

In the first of two Jacobite "risings," a coalition of traditionalists, Highland clans, and Catholics rallied around James II's son in 1715. But English troops easily routed them at the Battle of Sheriffmuir (10 miles north of Stirling), the grand hopes of "The '15" rebellion sputtered, and James Junior was sent scurrying back to his home-in-exile in France.

In 1745, a second rebellion was led by James II's grandson, known as "Bonnie Prince Charlie." That summer, the exiled Prince

Charles sailed across the sea from France and landed in Scotland near Glenfinnan (see page 292), where he raised an army of Highlanders and set out to re-establish the Stuart monarchy. The terrified king put a price on Charles' bonnie head (the equivalent of £15 million today), but the outlaw prince succeeded in rallying many Scots to his cause. Within a few months, inspired by their charismatic leader, the Highlander forces had taken most of Scotland and even much of northern England. In their march toward London, they penetrated as far south as Derby—just 125 miles from the Tower of London. But the gains were ephemeral. Prince Charles' army was small (6,000 men) and disorganized; promised French support failed to materialize; and he had almost no popular support in the Lowlands, much less in England.

As better-equipped British troops advanced, Prince Charles pulled back to the Highlands. The two armies finally met in 1746 for one final, bloody conflict at Culloden Moor, just outside of Inverness, where Bonnie Prince Charlie's ragtag, kilted, bagpipe-bolstered army was routed and massacred. (For more on the prince and his defeat, see page 292.) Charles himself escaped the chaos, dressed as a female servant to sail "over the sea to Skye," and ulti-

Robert Burns (1759-1796)

Robert Burns, Scotland's national poet, holds a unique place in the heart of the Scottish people—a heart that still beats loud and proud, thanks, in large part, to Burns himself.

Born on a farm in southwestern Scotland, Robbie (or "Rabbie," as Scots affectionately call him) was the oldest of seven children. His early years were full of backbreaking farm labor, which left him with a lifelong stoop. Though much was later made of his ascendance to literary acclaim from a rural, poverty-stricken upbringing, he was actually quite well educated (per Scottish tradition), equally as familiar with Latin and French as he was with hard work.

He started writing poetry at 15, but didn't have any published until age 28—to finance a voyage to the West Indies. When that first volume, *Poems, Chiefly in the Scottish Dialect*, became a sudden and overwhelming success, he reconsidered his emigration. Instead, he left his farm for Edinburgh, living just off the Royal Mile. He spent a year and a half in the city, schmoozing with literary elites, who celebrated this "heaven taught" farmer from the hinterlands as Scotland's "ploughman poet."

His poetry, written primarily in the Scots dialect, drew on his substantial familiarity with both Scottish tradition and Western literature. By using the language of the common man to create works of beauty and sophistication, he found himself wildly popular among both rural folk and high society. Hearty poems such as "To a Mouse," "To a Louse," and "The Holy Fair" exalted the virtues of physical labor, romantic love, friendship, natural beauty, and drink—all of which he also pursued with vigor in real life. This further endeared him to most Scots, though considerably less so to Church fathers, who were particularly displeased with his love

mately died in exile in Rome. To this day, patriotic Scots lament the crippling blow dealt to the rebellion they call "The '45."

After Charlie's defeat, the authorities (aristocratic landowners with government assistance) came down brutally on those who had supported the Jacobites, targeting the Highland clans and their traditional way of life. Kilt-wearing was forbidden, the feudal clan system was dismantled, homes were burned, and valuables were plundered. Clan chieftains who hadn't been exiled took over formerly communal lands and treated them as their own.

Landowners decided to make more efficient use of their land, bringing about the so-called "Highland Clearances" (which escalife (of Burns' dozen children, nine were by his eventual wife, the others by various servants and barmaids).

After achieving fame and wealth, Burns never lost touch with the concerns of the Scottish people, championing such radical ideas as social equality and economic justice. Burns bravely and loudly supported the French and American revolutions, which inspired one of his most beloved poems, "A Man's a Man for A' That," and even an ode to George Washington—all while other writers were being shipped off to Australia for similar beliefs. While his social causes cost him some aristocratic friends, it cemented his popularity among the masses, and not just within Scotland (he became, and remains, especially beloved in Russia).

Intent on preserving Scotland's rich musical and lyrical traditions, Burns traveled the countryside collecting traditional Scottish ballads. If it weren't for Burns, we'd have to come up with a different song to sing on New Year's Eve—he's the one who found, reworked, and popularized "Auld Lang Syne." His championing of Scottish culture came at a critical time: England had recently and finally crushed Scotland's last hopes of independence, and the Highland clan system was nearing its end. Burns lent the Scots dialect a new prestige, and the scrappy Scottish people a reinvigorated identity. (The official Burns website, www.robertburns. org, features a full collection of his works.)

Burns died at 37 of a heart condition likely exacerbated by so much hard labor (all the carousing probably hadn't helped, either). By that time, his fortune was largely spent, but his celebrity was going strong—around 10,000 people attended his burial. Even the Church eventually overcame its disapproval, installing a window in his honor at St. Giles' Cathedral. In 2009, his nation voted Burns "Greatest Ever Scot" in a TV poll. And every January 25 (the poet's birthday), on Burns Night, Scots gather to recite his songs and poems, tuck into some haggis ("chieftain o' the puddin' race," according to Burns), and raise their whisky to friendship, and Scotland.

lated following The '45, and peaked in the early-19th century). They evicted their farming populations and transformed the agricultural model from croft (subsistence farming of locally used crops) to mass production (more profitable sheep). Many displaced farmers moved to cities for factory work (as this coincided with the burgeoning Industrial Revolution—see the next section). Many others sought a better life in the New World.

From the mid- to late-19th century, an estimated two million Scots emigrated, mostly to North America, Australia, and New Zealand. Many perished in the perilous four-month Atlantic crossing, on vessels so rife with disease they were nicknamed "coffin

Scottish Castles at a Glance

Scotland is a land of castles. But after seeing several, they start to blend together. To help you choose, here's a rundown of the defining characteristics of the castles listed in this book. These are listed roughly in order of worthiness.

▲▲▲**Edinburgh Castle** The granddaddy of them all, with good exhibits, historic chapels, royal apartments, the "Honours of Scotland" (crown jewels), a very big cannon, and lots of crowds. See page 32.

▲▲**Dunvegan Castle** (Isle of Skye) Remote, endearingly ragtag home of Clan MacLeod, with fine rugged gardens. See page 373.

▲▲**Palace of Holyroodhouse** (Edinburgh) Historic palace at the foot of the Royal Mile, with ties to Mary, Queen of Scots and still host to Queen Elizabeth II's annual Garden Party. See page 73.

▲▲**Stirling Castle** The historic home of Scotland's Stuart dynasty, with rebuilt rooms, fine exhibits, and a stunning and strategic location overlooking the site of many of Scotland's most important moments. See page 174.

▲**Balmoral Castle** (in eastern Scotland) The Queen's summer Highland home, with great Cairngorms scenery and fine gardens... but only one (ho-hum) room open to the public. See page 345.

▲**Blair Castle** (near Pitlochry, in eastern Scotland) Crenellated residence of Clan Murray, offering a glimpse of 19th-century aristocratic life. See page 338.

ships." Those who survived employed their Scottish work ethic and industriousness to help build their adopted nations (concentrated in places like Nova Scotia—"New Scotland"). Some 15 percent of today's Canadians cite Scottish heritage. In fact, the "Scottish" populations of both Canada and the United States rival the population of Scotland.

Meanwhile, back home, Highland culture all but died out. It was a bleak time for traditional life in Scotland.

SCOTLAND REBOUNDS: SCOTTISH ENLIGHTENMENT, INDUSTRIAL REVOLUTION, AND HIGHLAND REVIVAL

Despite the difficult times in the Highlands, Lowlands Edinburgh thrived. In the last half of the 1700s, the city had become one of Europe's (and the world's) most intellectual cities. Edinburgh ben-

▲**Cawdor Castle** (near Inverness) Charming castle with personality and purported ties to Macbeth. See page 318.

▲**Eilean Donan Castle** (near Isle of Skye) One of Scotland's most scenically set castles, on an islet in a loch. See page 382.

▲**Glamis Castle** (north of Dundee) The Queen Mother's home castle, with a striking exterior and an enjoyably idiosyncratic interior. See page 224.

▲**Inveraray Castle** (near Oban) Classic castle exterior and a cozy interior used to film scenes from *Downton Abbey*. See page 269.

▲**Urquhart Castle** (on Loch Ness) Mostly ruined castle perched over Loch Ness. See page 322.

Armadale Castle (Isle of Skye) Ruined Clan Donald mansion with fine gardens and a museum of clan history—fascinating to MacDonalds, dull to most others. See page 380.

Doune Castle (near Stirling) Otherwise underwhelming castle with ties to *Outlander* and Monty Python, and an entertaining Terry Jones-narrated audioguide. See page 193.

Dunnottar Castle Ruins stunningly set on a huge, bald rock towering over Scotland's east coast. See page 349.

St. Andrews Castle Ruined shell overlooking the beach and offering an explanation of castle warfare techniques. See page 209.

PAST & PRESENT

efited from a rich university tradition, a strong Protestant work ethic, an educated middle class, connections with a powerful England, and, simply, good genes. Edinburgh was a city of secular, rational thinkers who embraced the scientific method and empirical observation.

Scots of note from this period include philosopher David Hume (who applied cool rationality and a scientific approach to religion, morals, and philosophy); economist Adam Smith (who wrote about division of labor and the free market in *The Wealth of Nations*); James Watt (who developed better steam engines, propelling Great Britain—and the world—into a busy Industrial Age); and great names in virtually every discipline: geologist James Hutton, chemist Joseph Black, painter Allan Ramsay, and of course the literary greats Robert Burns (see the sidebar) and Sir Walter Scott (see page 68). It's fitting that the *Encyclopedia Britannica*—the pre-Wikipedia authority on all things—was first published in Edinburgh in 1768.

As the Industrial Revolution dawned, Scotland became a powerhouse: Textiles were woven in large factories, powered by Watt's steam engine, which were fueled by Lanarkshire coal, then exported on iron ships built in the Clyde shipyards. Scotland was a global leader in pig iron exports and shipbuilding. Glasgow—an industrial center—overtook genteel Edinburgh as Scotland's biggest city. Dundee boomed, thanks to its skill for processing jute, which could be turned into rope, sacks, sails, and other essential items for a seafaring culture (for more, visit Dundee's interesting Jute Museum—see page 223).

In the early 19th century, the Scottish civil engineer Thomas Telford (1757-1834)—nicknamed "The Colossus of Roads"—designed roadways, bridges, canals, and locks to tie together the remotest corners of Scotland, effectively shrinking the country for the modern era. (His masterpiece, the Caledonian Canal, is easy to see between Fort William and Inverness—see page 323.)

Meanwhile, just a few decades after the harsh post-Jacobite crackdown, Highland culture began to enjoy a renaissance. By the late 18th century, people were already romanticizing Bonnie Prince Charlie (further spurred by Sir Walter Scott's 1814 historical novel *Waverley*). In the Romantic Age of the 19th century, tartans, kilts, bagpipes, and other aspects of Highland culture made a big comeback. In 1852, Queen Victoria and Prince Albert purchased Balmoral Castle (in the shadow of the Highlands' Cairngorm Mountains—see page 345), and proceeded to renovate it in a fanciful interpretation of the Scottish Baronial style. This signaled not just an acceptance, but a nostalgic embrace, of traditional Highland culture, just a century after it had been dismantled by the same monarchy.

This Scottish Baronial style, popularized by Sir Walter Scott, was a Romantic, Neo-Gothic celebration of medieval Highland castles. It features a stout sandstone structure with pointy turrets, fanciful finials, round towers, crenellated battlements, and narrow windows—based on Scotland's 16th-century tower houses, which were in turn based on the châteaux of France.

In many ways, this is Scotland's signature architectural style: You'll see it everywhere, from the urban streets of Glasgow, to castles on the remotest fringes of Scotland, to a fictional school for witchcraft and wizardry.

THE 20TH CENTURY: SCOTLAND AT WAR

By the 20th century, Scotland was the workhorse of Great Britain. And as bastion of the working class, there's little wonder that the government was typically controlled by the Labour Party. James Ramsay MacDonald was PM of the UK from 1929 until 1935.

Scotland was also the workhorse of the British military—never more so than during World War I, when Scottish lads were disproportionately massacred on the battlefields of Europe. Scotland, with

about one-tenth of the UK's population, had double the per-capita deaths of other parts of Britain. One out of every four Scottish soldiers never came home. Earl Haig of Edinburgh commanded British troops—victoriously—through some of the most gruesome trench warfare in history, at Flanders Fields in Belgium. As you travel around Scotland, you'll find a WWI memorial in every tiny village—with unsettlingly long lists of local boys who sacrificed the utmost for Britain.

On most of these memorials, you'll find a little "addendum" plaque listing WWII deaths. While the Blitz was devastating to London and other English towns closer to the Continent (such as Coventry), the impact of World War II was felt less in the far-north reaches of Scotland—though Scapa Flow, a natural harbor surrounded by the Orkney Islands, was the remote headquarters of the British navy in both World Wars (see page 408).

(see page 408)

SCOTLAND TODAY: DEVOLUTION
AND SCOTTISH PRIDE

By the last decades of the 20th century, change was percolating in Scotland. Since the 1980s, the main topic of Scottish political debate has become "devolution": the push to "devolve" authority over Scottish affairs from London to Scotland proper. The general sea change in European culture over the last few generations of respecting smaller, underdog nations—even at the expense of big, historically dominant countries—has been felt here as much as anywhere.

For centuries—essentially ever since the crushed Jacobite up-

PAST & PRESENT

risings—the notion of Scottish independence was rarely taken seriously. That began to change in the mid- to late-20th century. The independence-minded Scottish National Party (SNP), which had been founded as a fringe movement in 1934, won its first seat in the UK parliament in 1967. The discovery of North Sea oil in the late 1960s gave this often-overlooked corner of the United Kingdom some serious economic clout, and with it, more political pull. Pro-independence factions gained traction with the slogan "It's Scotland's oil," proposing a windfall for Scots suffering through post-industrial rot and economic malaise.

The SNP gained seats in the UK parliament and pushed for a 1979 referendum on devolution. The measure won with 52 percent of the vote, but turnout was too low to legitimize the result. Through the 1980s and most of the 1990s, anti-independence UK prime ministers Margaret Thatcher and John Major downplayed devolution talk. But the SNP and other agitators ensured that the idea never completely faded.

When Prime Minister Tony Blair took office in May 1997, his Labour government (mindful of Scotland's strong working-class roots and long-standing support for the Labour Party) was more open to the idea of devolution. And in a referendum in September 1997, three out of every four Scots voted "yes" to the statement, "I agree that there should be a Scottish parliament." In response, the UK parliament passed the Scotland Act 1998, creating a Scottish parliament that convened to much fanfare in Edinburgh on May 12, 1999 (with Donald Dewar becoming the first-ever First Minister of Scotland). For the first time since the Act of Union in 1707, Scotland had its own parliament. The Scottish Parliament building—with mind-bending architecture and an inviting garden—opened in 2004 across the street from the Queen's residence at the Palace of Holyroodhouse (it's free to tour the interior—see page 45).

With devolution, Edinburgh once again has become the actual self-governing capital of Scotland. The Scotland Act 2012 further expanded the mandate of the Scottish parliament, and today, the list of "devolved" issues (under local Scottish control) includes education, the environment, health and social services, housing, and tourism. Other matters—including foreign policy, defense, energy policy, and social security—remain "reserved" for the central UK government.

Today the SNP is the most powerful party in Scotland (controlling 63 out of 129 seats in the Scottish parliament), and the third-largest party in the UK (controlling 35 out of 650 seats in the UK's House of Commons; there are only 59 House of Commons seats for Scotland). Its leader, Nicola Sturgeon of Glasgow, is the public face of the SNP, giving voice to independence-minded Scots.

Today's supporters of Scottish independence take up ballots, not broadswords. On September 18, 2014, the Scottish people went to the polls to vote on a simple question: "Should Scotland be an independent country?" Right up until the day of the referendum, many observers believed that Scotland was about to declare its independence, which would have opened up a whole range of questions about how two prosperous and powerful countries could peacefully disentangle themselves. But the results were clear: 55.3 percent of Scottish residents voted "no." While Scotland will remain part of the United Kingdom—for now—the referendum signaled to many in the greater UK that Scotland must be taken seriously. During the campaign, the opposition promised Scotland even more political autonomy if it voted "no." While Scottish nationalists want to fast-track these new powers, it's not clear how quickly it will happen. One thing is sure: The vote may be over, but the nationalists aren't done fighting yet.

In 2016, Britain voted to "Brexit" or leave the European Union. Most Scots voted to remain with the EU. Adding a new twist to the complicated political situation, it's likely that pro-EU Scotland would have voted for independence in 2014 had they known that the UK would vote to take them out of the EU two years later. Now, as the UK sorts out its messy situation with the EU, England's restless Celtic partners are wondering where their best future lies. And, at this point, nobody knows.

NOTABLE SCOTS

Throughout Scotland's history, the country has been a center of both scientific and creative thought. The 18th-century age of Scottish Enlightenment in particular was a hotbed of intellectual progress—I've listed the greats of that era earlier in this chapter (on page 426).

Famous artistic Scots include royal portraitist Henry Raeburn (whose 1790s ice-skating minister, *The Reverend Robert Walker Skating on Duddingston Loch,* still adorns modern-day Christmas cards); 20th-century landscape painter William MacTaggart; and Scotland's greatest architect Charles Rennie Mackintosh (see sidebar on page 140).

Scottish entertainers are everywhere, from the original James Bond (Sean Connery) and the young Obi-Wan Kenobi (Ewan McGregor), to two Dr. Whos (David Tennant and Peter Capaldi). Actors James McAvoy, Gerard Butler, Karen Gillan, Tilda Swinton, Billy Connolly, Craig Ferguson, Robert Carlyle, Robbie Coltrane, and Alan Cumming all hail from Scotland, as do musical artists the Proclaimers, Annie Lennox, Cocteau Twins, the Jesus and Mary Chain, Belle and Sebastian, and Franz Ferdinand; and sports stars Andy Murray (tennis), Catriona Matthews (golfer), and Jackie Stewart (auto racing). Scotland's literary tradition is particularly strong (see sidebar on page 68), with writers from Robert Burns to Sherlock Holmes creator Sir Arthur Conan Doyle making the country proud.

On the scientific front, Peter Higgs was researching at the University of Edinburgh in the 1960s when he speculated on the existence of a subatomic "God particle" that might tie together many other theories on the structure of the universe.

Great people of Scottish descent fill American and Canadian history books, among them James Monroe, Washington Irving, Andrew Carnegie, Alexander Graham Bell, Jack Daniel, Ronald Reagan, Neil Armstrong, and Bill Gates. Whether it's as part of the United Kingdom, or as its own increasingly independent nation, it's clear that Scotland's impact on the world has only just begun.

PRACTICALITIES

This chapter covers the practical skills of European travel: how to get tourist information, pay for purchases, sightsee efficiently, find good-value accommodations, eat affordably but well, use technology wisely, and get between destinations smoothly. To round out your knowledge, check out "Resources from Rick Steves." For more information on these topics, see www.ricksteves.com/travel-tips.

Tourist Information

Before your trip, start with the **Visit Scotland website,** which contains a wealth of knowledge on destinations, activities, accommodations, and transport in Scotland (www.visitscotland.com).

In Scotland, a good first stop is generally the tourist information office (abbreviated **TI** in this book). Officially called Visit Scotland Information Centres, these are all operated by the national tourist board (look for the purple signs). They're found even in very small and remote places, where they're called "information points."

TIs are in business to help you enjoy spending money in their

town. While this corrupts much of their advice—and you can get plenty of information
online—I still make a point to swing by to
confirm sightseeing plans, pick up a city map,
and get information on public transit, walking tours, special events, and nightlife. Prepare a list of questions and a proposed plan to
double-check. Some TIs have information on
the entire country or at least the region, so try
to pick up maps and printed information for
destinations you'll be visiting later in your trip.

Other Helpful Websites for Scotland:
To learn more about places around Scotland,
see www.undiscoveredscotland.co.uk. For hiking advice, see www.
walkhighlands.co.uk.

Travel Tips

Emergency and Medical Help: Dial 999 or 112 for police help
or a medical emergency. If you get sick, do as the locals do and go
to a pharmacy and see a "chemist" (pharmacist) for advice. Or ask
at your hotel for help—they'll know of the nearest medical and
emergency services.

Theft or Loss: To replace a passport, you'll need to go in person to a US embassy (see page 493). If your credit and debit cards
disappear, cancel and replace them (see "Damage Control for Lost
Cards" on page 439). File a police report, either on the spot or
within a day or two; you'll need it to submit an insurance claim for
lost or stolen rail passes or travel gear, and it can help with replac-
ing your passport or credit and debit cards. For more information,
see www.ricksteves.com/help.

Time Zones: Britain, which is one hour earlier than most of
continental Europe, is five/eight hours ahead of the East/West
Coasts of the US. The exceptions are the beginning and end of
Daylight Saving Time: Britain and Europe "spring forward" the
last Sunday in March (two weeks after most of North America), and "fall back" the last Sunday in October (one week before
North America). For a handy online time converter, see www.
timeanddate.com/worldclock.

Business Hours: Most stores are open Monday through Saturday (roughly 9:00 or 10:00 to 17:00 or 18:00). In cities, some
stores stay open later on Wednesday or Thursday (until 19:00 or
20:00). Sundays have the same pros and cons as they do for travelers in the US: Sightseeing attractions are generally open, many
street markets are lively with shoppers, banks and many shops are
closed, public transportation options are fewer (for example, no bus

service to or from smaller towns), and there's no rush hour. Friday and Saturday evenings are lively; Sunday evenings are quiet.

Watt's Up? Britain's electrical system is 220 volts, instead of North America's 110 volts. Most newer electronics (such as lap-

tops, battery chargers, and hair dry-ers) convert automatically, so you won't need a converter, but you will need an adapter plug with three square prongs, sold inexpensively at travel stores in the US. Avoid bringing older appliances that don't automatically convert volt-age; instead, ask to borrow one from your B&B or buy a cheap replacement locally. Low-cost hairdryers and other small appliances are sold at Superdrug and Boots (ask your hotelier for the closest branch). Or pop into a depart-ment store or grocery "superstore."

Discounts: Discounts (called "concessions" or "concs" in Brit-ain) for sights are generally not listed in this book. However, many sights, buses, and trains offer discounts to youths (up to age 18), students (with proper identification cards, www.isic.org), families, seniors (loosely defined as retirees or those willing to call them-selves seniors), and groups of 10 or more. Always ask. Some dis-counts are available only for British citizens.

Money

Here's my basic strategy for using money in Europe:
- Upon arrival, head for a cash machine (ATM) at the airport and load up on local currency, using a debit card with low in-ternational transaction fees.
- Withdraw large amounts at each transaction (to limit fees) and keep your cash safe in a money belt.
- Pay for most items with cash.
- Pay for larger purchases with a credit card with low (or no) international fees.

PLASTIC VERSUS CASH
Although credit cards are widely accepted in Europe, day-to-day spending is generally more cash-based than in the US. I find cash is the easiest—and sometimes only—way to pay for cheap food, taxis, tips, and local guides. Some businesses (especially smaller ones, such as B&Bs and mom-and-pop cafés and shops) may charge you extra for using a credit card—or might not accept credit cards at all.

Exchange Rate

1 British pound (£1) = about $1.30

Britain uses the pound sterling. The British pound (£), also called a "quid," is broken into 100 pence (p). Pence means "cents." You'll find coins ranging from 1p to £2 and bills from £5 to £50.

While the pound sterling is used throughout the UK, Scotland prints its own bills, which are decorated with Scottish landmarks and VIPs. These are interchangeable with British pound notes, which are widely circulated here. The coins are the same throughout the UK.

To convert prices from pounds to dollars, add about 30 percent: £20 = about $26, £50 = about $65. (Check www.oanda.com for the latest exchange rates.)

Having cash on hand helps you out of a jam if your card randomly doesn't work.

I use my credit card to book and pay for hotel reservations, to buy advance tickets for events or sights, and to cover major expenses (such as car rentals or plane tickets). It can also be smart to use plastic near the end of your trip, to avoid another visit to the ATM.

WHAT TO BRING

I pack the following and keep it all safe in my money belt.

Debit Card: Use this at ATMs to withdraw local cash.

Credit Card: Use this to pay for larger items (at hotels, larger shops and restaurants, travel agencies, car-rental agencies, and so on).

Backup Card: Some travelers carry a third card (debit or credit; ideally from a different bank), in case one gets lost, demagnetized, eaten by a temperamental machine, or simply doesn't work.

US Dollars: I carry $100-200 US as a backup. While you won't use it for day-to-day purchases, American cash in your money belt comes in handy for emergencies, such as if your ATM card stops working.

What NOT to Bring: Resist the urge to buy pounds before your trip or you'll pay the price in bad stateside exchange rates. Wait until you arrive to withdraw money. I've yet to see a European airport that didn't have plenty of ATMs.

BEFORE YOU GO

Use this pretrip checklist.

Know your cards. Debit cards from any major US bank will work in any standard European bank's ATM (ideally, use a debit card with a Visa or MasterCard logo).

Newer credit and debit cards have chips that authenticate and secure transactions. In Europe, the cardholder inserts the chip card into the payment machine slot, then enters a PIN. (In the US, you provide a signature to verify your identity.)

Any American card, whether with a chip or an old-fashioned magnetic stripe, will work at Europe's hotels, restaurants, and shops. I've been inconvenienced a few times by self-service payment machines in Europe that wouldn't accept my card, but it's never caused me serious trouble.

If you're concerned, ask if your bank offers a true chip-and-PIN card. Cards with low fees and chip-and-PIN technology include those from Andrews Federal Credit Union (www.andrewsfcu.org) and the State Department Federal Credit Union (www.sdfcu.org).

Report your travel dates. Let your bank know that you'll be using your debit and credit cards in Europe, and when and where you're headed.

Know your PIN. Make sure you know the numeric, four-digit PIN for each of your cards, both debit and credit. Request it if you don't have one and allow time to receive the information by mail.

Adjust your ATM withdrawal limit. Find out how much you can take out daily and ask for a higher daily withdrawal limit if you want to get more cash at once. Note that European ATMs will withdraw funds only from checking accounts; you're unlikely to have access to your savings account.

Ask about fees. For any purchase or withdrawal made with a card, you may be charged a currency conversion fee (1-3 percent), a Visa or MasterCard international transaction fee (1 percent), and— for debit cards—a $2-5 transaction fee each time you use a foreign ATM (some US banks partner with European banks, allowing you to use those ATMs with no fees—ask).

If you're getting a bad deal, consider getting a new debit or credit card. Reputable no-fee cards include those from Capital One, as well as Charles Schwab debit cards. Most credit unions and some airline loyalty cards have low-to-no international transaction fees.

IN EUROPE
Using Cash Machines

European cash machines work just like they do at home—except they spit out local currency instead of dollars, calculated at the day's standard bank-to-bank rate.

In most places, ATMs are easy to locate—in Britain ask for a "cashpoint." When possible, withdraw cash from a bank-run ATM located just outside that bank. Ideally, use it during the bank's opening hours; if your card is munched by the machine, you can go inside for help.

If your debit card doesn't work, try a lower amount—your request may have exceeded your withdrawal limit or the ATM's limit. If you still have a problem, try a different ATM or come back later—your bank's network may be temporarily down.

Avoid "independent" ATMs, such as Travelex, Euronet, Moneybox, Cardpoint, and Cashzone. These have high fees, can be less secure than a bank ATM, and may try to trick users with "dynamic currency conversion" (see later).

Exchanging Cash

Avoid exchanging money in Europe; it's a big rip-off. In a pinch you can always find exchange desks at major train stations or airports—convenient but with crummy rates. Banks in some countries may not exchange money unless you have an account with them.

Using Credit Cards

European cards use chip-and-PIN technology, while most cards issued in the US use a chip-and-signature system. But most European card readers can automatically generate a receipt for you to sign, just as you would at home. If a cashier is present, you should have no problems. Some card readers will instead prompt you to enter your PIN (so it's important to know the code for each of your cards).

At self-service payment machines (transit-ticket kiosks, parking, etc.), results are mixed, as US chip-and-signature cards aren't configured for unattended transactions. If your card won't work, look for a cashier who can process your card manually—or pay in cash.

Drivers Beware: Be aware of potential problems using a credit card to fill up at an unattended gas station, enter a parking garage, or exit a toll road. Carry cash and be prepared to move on to the next gas station if necessary. When approaching a toll plaza, use the "cash" lane.

Dynamic Currency Conversion

Some European merchants and hoteliers cheerfully charge you for converting your purchase price into dollars. If it's offered, refuse this "service" (called dynamic currency conversion, or DCC). You'll pay extra for the expensive convenience of seeing your charge in dollars. Some ATM machines also offer DCC, often in confusing or misleading terms. If an ATM offers to "lock in" or "guarantee" your conversion rate, choose "proceed without conversion." Other prompts might state, "You can be charged in dollars: Press YES for dollars, NO for pounds." Always choose the local currency.

PRACTICALITIES

Security Tips

Even in "Jollie Olde Britain," pickpockets target tourists. To safeguard your cash, wear a money belt—a pouch with a strap that you buckle around your waist like a belt and tuck under your clothes. Keep your cash, credit cards, and passport secure in your money belt, and carry only a day's spending money in your front pocket or wallet.

Before inserting your card into an ATM, inspect the front. If anything looks crooked, loose, or damaged, it could be a sign of a card-skimming device. When entering your PIN, carefully block other people's view of the keypad.

Don't use a debit card for purchases. Because a debit card pulls funds directly from your bank account, potential charges incurred by a thief will stay on your account while the fraudulent use is investigated by your bank.

While traveling, to access your accounts online, be sure to use a secure connection (see page 473).

Damage Control for Lost Cards

If you lose your credit or debit card, report the loss immediately to the respective global customer-assistance centers. Call these 24-hour US numbers collect: Visa (tel. 303/967-1096), MasterCard (tel. 636/722-7111), and American Express (tel. 336/393-1111). In Britain, to make a collect call to the US, dial 0-800-89-0011. Press zero or stay on the line for an operator. European toll-free numbers (listed by country) can be found at the websites for Visa and MasterCard. Diner's Club has offices in Britain (tel. 0845-862-29357) and the US (tel. 514/877-1577; call collect).

You'll need to provide the primary cardholder's identification-verification details (such as birthdate, mother's maiden name, or Social Security number). You can generally receive a temporary card within two or three business days in Europe (see www.ricksteves.com/help for more).

If you report your loss within two days, you typically won't be responsible for unauthorized transactions on your account, although many banks charge a liability fee of $50.

TIPPING

Tipping in Britain isn't as automatic and generous as it is in the US. For special service, tips are appreciated, but not expected. As in the US, the proper amount depends on your resources, tipping philosophy, and the circumstances, but some general guidelines apply.

Restaurants: If a service charge is included in the bill, it's not necessary to tip. Otherwise, it's appropriate to tip about 10-12 percent for good service. See page 455).

Taxis: For a typical ride, round up your fare a bit, but not more than 10 percent (for instance, if the fare is £7.40, pay £8). If the cabbie hauls your bags and zips you to the airport to help you catch your flight, you might want to toss in a little more. But if you feel like you're being driven in circles or otherwise ripped off, skip the tip.

Services: In general, if someone in the tourism or service industry does a super job for you, a small tip of a pound or two is appropriate...but not required. If you're not sure whether (or how much) to tip, ask a local for advice.

GETTING A VAT REFUND

Wrapped into the purchase price of your British souvenirs is a Value-Added Tax (VAT) of about 20 percent. You're entitled to get most of that tax back if you purchase more than £30 (about $40) worth of goods at a store that participates in the VAT-refund scheme (although individual stores can require that you spend more). Typically, you must ring up the minimum at a single retailer—you can't add up your purchases from various shops to reach the required amount. (If the store ships the goods to your US home, VAT is not assessed on your purchase.)

Getting your refund is straightforward...and worthwhile if you spend a significant amount on souvenirs.

Get the paperwork. Have the merchant completely fill out the necessary refund document (either an official VAT customs form, or the shop or refund company's own version of it). You'll have to present your passport at the store. Get the paperwork done before you leave the shop to ensure you'll have everything you need (including your original sales receipt).

Get your stamp at the border or airport. Process your VAT document at your last stop in the European Union (such as at the airport) with the customs agent who deals with VAT refunds. Arrive an additional hour early before you need to check in to allow time to find the customs office—and to stand in line. Some customs desks are positioned before airport security; confirm the location before going through security.

It's best to keep your purchases in your carry-on. If they're too large or dangerous to carry on (such as knives), pack them in your checked bags and alert the check-in agent. You'll be sent (with your tagged bag) to a customs desk outside security; someone will examine your bag, stamp your paperwork, and put your bag on the belt. You're not supposed to use your purchased goods before you leave. If you show up at customs wearing your new kilt, officials might look the other way—or deny you a refund.

Collect your refund. Many merchants work with a service that has offices at major airports, ports, or border crossings. These services, which extract their own fee (usually around 4 percent), can refund your money immediately in cash or credit your card (within two billing cycles). Other refund services may require you to mail the documents from home, or more quickly, from your point of departure (using an envelope you've prepared in advance or one that's been provided by the merchant). You'll then have to wait—it can take months.

CUSTOMS FOR AMERICAN SHOPPERS

You can take home $800 worth of items per person duty-free, once every 31 days. Many processed and packaged foods are allowed, including vacuum-packed cheeses, dried herbs, jams, baked goods, candy, chocolate, oil, vinegar, mustard, and honey. Fresh fruits and vegetables and most meats are not allowed, with exceptions for some canned items. As for alcohol, you can bring in one liter duty-free (it can be packed securely in your checked luggage, along with any other liquid-containing items).

To bring alcohol (or liquid-packed foods) in your carry-on bag on your flight home, buy it at a duty-free shop at the airport. You'll increase your odds of getting it onto a connecting flight if it's packaged in a "STEB"—a secure, tamper-evident bag. But stay away from liquids in opaque, ceramic, or metallic containers, which usually cannot be successfully screened (STEB or no STEB).

For details on allowable goods, customs rules, and duty rates, visit http://help.cbp.gov.

Sightseeing

Sightseeing can be hard work. Use these tips to make your visits to Scotland's finest sights meaningful, fun, efficient, and painless.

MAPS AND NAVIGATION TOOLS

A good map is essential for efficient navigation while sightseeing. The maps in this book are concise and simple, designed to help you locate recommended destinations, sights, and local TIs, where you can pick up more in-depth maps. Maps with even more detail are sold at newsstands and bookstores. The *Rick Steves Britain, Ireland & London City Map* is useful for planning ($9, www.ricksteves. com).

You can also use a mapping app on your mobile device. Be aware that pulling up maps or looking up turn-by-turn walking directions on the fly requires an Internet connection: To use this feature, it's smart to get an international data plan (see page 467). With Google Maps or City Maps 2Go, it's possible to download a map while online, then go offline and navigate without incurring data-roaming charges, though you can't search for an address or get real-time walking directions. A handful of other apps—including

PRACTICALITIES

Apple Maps, OffMaps, and Navfree—also allow you to use maps offline.

PLAN AHEAD

Set up an itinerary that allows you to fit in all your must-see sights. For a one-stop look at opening hours, see the "At a Glance" sidebars for Edinburgh (see page 26) and Scottish castles (page 426). Most sights keep stable hours, but you can easily confirm the latest by checking with the TI or visiting museum websites.

Don't put off visiting a must-see sight—you never know when a place will close unexpectedly for a holiday, strike, or royal audience. Many museums are closed or have reduced hours at least a few days a year, especially on holidays such as Christmas, New Year's, and Bank Holiday Mondays in May and August. A list of holidays is on page 493; check online for possible museum closures during your trip. Off-season, many museums have shorter hours.

Given how precious your vacation time is, I recommend getting reservations for any must-see sight that offers them (see page 9). Going at the right time helps avoid crowds. This book offers tips on the best times to see specific sights. Try visiting popular sights very early or very late. Evening visits (when possible) are usually peaceful, with fewer crowds.

If you plan to hire a local guide, reserve ahead by email. Popular guides can get booked up.

Study up. To get the most out of the self-guided tours and sight descriptions in this book, read them before you visit.

AT SIGHTS

Here's what you can typically expect:

Entering: Be warned that you may not be allowed to enter if you arrive less than 30 to 60 minutes before closing time. And guards start ushering people out well before the actual closing time, so don't save the best for last.

Many sights have a security check, where you must open your bag or send it through a metal detector. Some sights require you to check daypacks and coats. (If you'd rather not check your daypack, try carrying it tucked under your arm like a purse as you enter.)

At ticket desks, you may see references to "Gift Aid"—a tax-deduction scheme that benefits museums—but this only concerns UK taxpayers.

Photography: If the museum's photo policy isn't clearly posted, ask a guard. Generally, taking photos without a flash or tripod is allowed. Some sights ban selfie sticks; others ban photos altogether. Note that some whisky distilleries do not allow photos or photos with flash, supposedly because a spark from your camera could ignite the alcohol fumes. (It may have more to do with inter-distillery competition.)

Temporary Exhibits: Museums may show special exhibits in addition to their permanent collection. An extra fee, which may not be optional, might be assessed for these shows.

Expect Changes: Artwork can be on tour, on loan, out sick, or shifted at the whim of the curator. Pick up a floor plan as you enter, and ask museum staff if you can't find a particular item.

Audioguides and Apps: Many sights rent audioguides, which generally offer excellent recorded descriptions (about £5). If you bring your own earbuds, you can enjoy better sound. To save money, bring a Y-jack and share one audioguide with your travel partner. Museums and sights often offer free apps that you can download to your mobile device (check their websites). And, I've produced a free, downloadable audio tour for Edinburgh's Royal Mile; look for the 🎧 symbol in this book. For more on my audio tours, see page 10.

Guided tours are most likely to occur during peak season (either for free or a small fee—figure £5-10—and widely ranging in quality). Some sights also run short introductory videos featuring their highlights and history. These are generally well worth your time and a great place to start your visit.

Services: Important sights and cathedrals may have a reasonably priced on-site café or cafeteria (usually a handy place to rejuvenate during a long visit). The WCs at sights are free and generally clean.

Before Leaving: At the gift shop, scan the postcard rack or thumb through a guidebook to be sure that you haven't overlooked something that you'd like to see.

Every sight or museum offers more than what is covered in this book. Use the information in this book as an introduction—not the final word.

SIGHTSEEING PASSES

Many sights in Scotland are managed by either Historic Scotland or the National Trust for Scotland. Each organization has a combo-deal that can save some money for busy sightseers.

Historic Scotland's Explorer Pass covers its 77 properties, including Edinburgh Castle, Stirling Castle, and several sights on Orkney (£31/3 days out of any 5, £42/7 days out of any 14, www.historic-scotland.gov.uk/explorer). This pass allows you to skip the ticket-buying lines at Edinburgh and Stirling castles.

Membership in the **National Trust for Scotland** covers more than 350 historic houses, manors, and gardens throughout Great Britain, including 100 properties in Scotland. From the US, it's easy to join online through the Royal Oak Foundation, the National Trust's American affiliate (one-year membership: $65 for one person, $95 for two, family and student memberships, www. royal-oak.org). For more on National Trust for Scotland properties, see www.nts.org.uk.

Factors to Consider: An advantage to these deals is that you'll feel free to dip into lesser sights without considering the cost of admission. But remember that your kids already get in free or cheaply at most places, and people over 60 get discounted prices at many sights. If you're traveling by car and can get to the remote sights, you're more likely to get your money's worth out of a pass or membership, especially during peak season (Easter-Oct), when all the sights are open.

Sleeping

I favor hotels and restaurants that are handy to your sightseeing activities. In Britain, small bed-and-breakfast places (B&Bs) generally provide the best value, though I also include some bigger hotels. Rather than list accommodations scattered throughout a city, I choose places in my favorite neighborhoods. My recommendations run the gamut, from dorm beds to fancy rooms with all the comforts. Outside of pricey big cities, you can expect to find good doubles for £80-120 (about $105-155), including cooked breakfasts and tax. Bigger cities, swanky splurge B&Bs, and big hotels generally cost significantly more.

Extensive and opinionated listings of good-value rooms are a major feature of this book's Sleeping sections. I like places that are clean, central, relatively quiet at night, reasonably priced, friendly, small enough to have a hands-on owner and stable staff, and run with a respect for British traditions. I'm more impressed by a convenient location and a fun-loving philosophy than flat-screen TVs and a fancy gym. Most places I recommend fall short of perfection. But if I can find a place with most of these features, it's a keeper.

Britain has a rating system for hotels and B&Bs. Its stars are supposed to imply quality, but I find they mean only that the place is paying dues to the tourist board. Rating systems often have little to do with value.

Book your accommodations as soon as your itinerary is set, especially if you want to stay at one of my top listings or if you'll be traveling during busy times. See page 493 for a list of major holidays and festivals; for tips on making reservations, see page 448.

Some people make reservations as they travel, calling hotels and B&Bs a few days to a week before their arrival. If you anticipate crowds (worst weekdays at business destinations and weekends at tourist locales) on the day you want to check in, call hotels at

Sleep Code

Hotels are classified based on the average price of a typical en suite double room with breakfast in high season.

$$$$	**Splurge:** Most rooms over £160
$$$	**Pricier:** £120-160
$$	**Moderate:** £80-120
$	**Budget:** £40-80
¢	**Backpacker:** Under £40
RS%	**Rick Steves discount**

Unless otherwise noted, credit cards are accepted and free Wi-Fi is available. Comparison-shop by checking prices at several hotels (on each hotel's own website, on a booking site, or by email). For the best deal, *always book directly with the hotel.* Ask for a discount if paying in cash; if the listing includes **RS%,** request a Rick Steves discount.

about 9:00 or 10:00, when the receptionist knows who'll be checking out and which rooms will be available. Some apps—such as HotelTonight.com—specialize in last-minute rooms, often at business-class hotels in big cities.

RATES AND DEALS

I've categorized my recommended accommodations based on price, indicated with a dollar-sign rating (see sidebar). The price ranges suggest an estimated cost for a one-night stay in a typical en suite double room with a private toilet and shower in high season, and assume you're booking directly with the hotel (not through a booking site, which extracts a commission). Room prices can fluctuate significantly with demand and amenities (size, views, room class, and so on), but relative price categories remain constant. City taxes are generally insignificant (a dollar or two per person, per night). For most places, the rates I list include the 20 percent VAT tax—but it's smart to ask when you book your room.

While B&B prices tend to be fairly predictable, room rates are especially volatile at larger hotels that use "dynamic pricing" to set rates. Prices can skyrocket during festivals and conventions, while business hotels can have deep discounts on weekends when demand plummets. Of the many hotels I recommend, it's difficult to say which will be the best value on a given day—until you do your homework.

Once your dates are set, check the specific price for your preferred stay at several hotels. You can do this either by comparing prices on Hotels.com or Booking.com, or by checking the hotels' own websites. To get the best deal, contact my family-run places directly by phone or email. When you go direct, the owners avoid

PRACTICALITIES

the 20 percent commission, giving them wiggle room to offer you a discount, a nicer room, or a free breakfast if it's not already included (see sidebar). If you prefer to book online or are considering a hotel chain, it's to your advantage to use the hotel's website.

Some accommodations offer a discount to those who pay cash or stay longer than three nights. To cut costs further, try asking for a cheaper room (for example, with a shared bathroom or no window) or offer to skip breakfast (if included).

Additionally, some accommodations offer a special discount for Rick Steves readers, indicated in the listing by the abbreviation **"RS%."** Discounts vary: Ask for details when you reserve. Generally, to qualify you must book direct (that is, not through a booking site), mention this book when you reserve, show this book upon arrival, and sometimes pay cash or stay a certain number of nights. In some cases, you may need to enter a discount code (which I've provided in the listing) in the booking form on the hotel's website. Rick Steves discounts apply to readers with ebooks as well as printed books. Understandably, discounts do not apply to promotional rates.

Staying in B&Bs and small hotels can save money over sleeping in big hotels. Chain hotels can be even cheaper, but they don't include breakfast. When comparing prices between chain hotels and B&Bs, remember you're getting two breakfasts (about a £25 value) for each double room at a B&B.

When establishing prices, confirm if the charge is per person or per room (if a price is too good to be true, it's probably per person). Because many places in Britain charge per person, small groups often pay the same for a single and a double as they would for a triple. In this book, I've categorized hotels based on the per-room price, not per-person.

TYPES OF ACCOMMODATIONS
Hotels

In cities, you'll find big, Old World-elegant hotels with modern amenities, as well as familiar-feeling business-class and boutique hotels no different from what you might experience at home. But you'll also find hotels that are more uniquely European.

A "twin" room has two single beds; a "double" has one double bed. If you'll take either, let the hotel know, or you might be needlessly turned away. Some hotels can add an extra bed (for a small charge) to turn a double into a triple; some offer larger rooms for four or more people (I call these "family rooms" in the listings). If there's space for an extra cot, they'll cram it in for you. In general, a triple room is cheaper than the cost of a double and a single. Three or four people can economize by requesting one big room.

An "en suite" room has a bathroom (toilet and shower/tub)

Hotels vs. Booking Websites vs. Consumers

In the last decade it's become almost impossible for independent-minded, family-run hotels to survive without playing the game as dictated by the big players in the online booking world. Priceline's Booking.com and Expedia's Hotels.com take roughly 80 percent of this business. Hoteliers note that without this online presence, "We become almost invisible." Online booking services demand about a 20 percent commission. And in order to be listed, a hotel must promise that its website does not undercut the price on the third-party's website. Without that restriction, hoteliers could say, "Sure, sell our rooms for whatever markup you like, and we'll continue to offer a fair rate to travelers who come to us directly"—but that's not allowed.

Here's the work-around: For independent and family-run hotels, book directly by email or phone, in which case hotel owners are free to give you whatever price they like. Research the price online, and then ask for a room without the commission mark-up. You could ask them to split the difference—the hotel charges you 10 percent less but pockets 10 percent more. Or you can ask for a free breakfast (if not included) or free upgrade.

If you do book online, be sure to use the hotel's website (you'll likely pay the same price as via a booking site, but your money goes to the hotel, not agency commissions).

As consumers, remember: Whenever you book with an online booking service, you're adding a needless middleman who takes roughly 20 percent. If you'd like to support small, family-run hotels whose world is more difficult than ever, book direct.

attached to the room; a room with a "private bathroom" can mean that the bathroom is all yours, but it's across the hall. If you want your own bathroom inside the room, request "en suite." If money's tight, ask about a room with a shared bathroom. You'll almost always have a sink in your room, and as more rooms go en suite, the hallway bathroom is shared with fewer guests.

Note that to be called a "hotel," a place technically must have certain amenities, including a 24-hour reception (though this rule is loosely applied).

Modern Hotel Chains: Chain hotels—common in bigger cities all over Great Britain—can be a great value (£60-100, depending on location and season). These hotels are about as cozy as a Motel 6, but they come with private showers/WCs, elevators, good security, and often an attached restaurant. Branches are often

PRACTICALITIES

Making Hotel Reservations

Reserve your rooms as soon as you've pinned down your travel dates. For busy national holidays, it's wise to reserve far in advance (see page 493).

Requesting a Reservation: For family-run hotels, it's generally cheaper to book your room directly via email or a phone call. For business-class hotels, or if you'd rather book online, reserve directly through the hotel's official website (not a booking agency's site). For complicated requests, send an email.

Here's what the hotelier wants to know:

- type(s) of rooms you need and size of your party
- number of nights you'll stay
- your arrival and departure dates, written European-style as day/month/year (for example, 18/06/19 or 18 June 2019)
- special requests (such as en suite bathroom vs. down the hall, cheapest room, twin beds vs. double bed, quiet room)
- applicable discounts (such as a Rick Steves reader discount, cash discount, or promotional rate)

Confirming a Reservation: Most places will request a credit-card number to hold your room. If you're using an online reservation form, look for the *https* or a lock icon at the top of your browser. If you book direct, you can email, call, or fax this information.

Canceling a Reservation: If you must cancel, it's courteous—and smart—to do so with as much notice as possible, especially for smaller family-run places. Cancellation policies can be strict;

located near the train station, on major highways, or outside the city center.

This option is especially worth considering for families, as kids often stay for free. While most of these hotels have 24-hour reception and elevators, breakfast and Wi-Fi generally cost extra, and the service lacks a personal touch (at some, you'll check in at a self-service kiosk). When comparing your options, keep in mind that for about the same price, you can get a basic room at a B&B that has less predictable comfort but more funkiness and friendliness in a more enjoyable neighborhood.

Room rates change from day to day with volume and vary depending on how far ahead you book. The best deals generally must be prepaid a few weeks ahead and may not be refundable—read the fine print carefully.

The biggest chains are **Premier Inn** (www.premierinn.com, toll reservations tel. 0871-527-9222) and **Travelodge** (www.travelodge.co.uk, toll reservations tel. 0871-984-8484). Both have attractive deals for prepaid or advance bookings. Other chains op-

From:	rick@ricksteves.com
Sent:	Today
To:	info@hotelcentral.com
Subject:	Reservation request for 19-22 July

Dear Hotel Central,

I would like to stay at your hotel. Please let me know if you have a room available and the price for:
• 2 people
• Double bed and en suite bathroom in a quiet room
• Arriving 19 July, departing 22 July (3 nights)

Thank you!
Rick Steves

read the fine print or ask about these before you book. Many discount deals require prepayment, with no cancellation refunds.

Reconfirming a Reservation: Always call or email to reconfirm your room reservation a few days in advance. For B&Bs or very small hotels, I call again on my day of arrival to tell my host what time to expect me (especially important if arriving late—after 18:00).

Phoning: For tips on calling hotels overseas, see page 470.

erating in Britain include the Irish **Jurys Inn** (www.jurysinns.com) and the French-owned **Ibis** (www.ibishotel.com). Couples can consider **Holiday Inn Express,** which generally allows only two people per room. It's like a Holiday Inn lite, with cheaper prices and no restaurant (make sure Express is part of the name or you'll be paying more for a regular Holiday Inn, www.hiexpress.co.uk).

Arrival and Check-In: Many of my recommended hotels have three or more floors of rooms and steep stairs. Older properties often do not have elevators. If stairs are an issue, ask for a ground-floor room or choose a hotel with a lift (elevator). Air-conditioning isn't a given (I've noted which of my listings have it), but most places have fans. On hot summer nights, you'll want your window open—and in a big city, street noise is a fact of life. Bring earplugs or request a room on the back side. If you suspect night noise will be a problem (if, for instance, your room is over a noisy pub), ask for a quieter room on an upper floor.

If you're arriving in the morning, your room probably won't

PRACTICALITIES

be ready. Check your bag safely at the hotel and dive right into sightseeing.

In Your Room: More pillows and blankets are usually in the closet or available on request. Towels and linens aren't always replaced every day. Hang your towel up to dry.

TVs are standard in rooms, but may come with limited channels (no cable). Note that all of Britain's accommodations are nonsmoking. Most hotels have free Wi-Fi (although the Wi-Fi signal doesn't always make it to the rooms; sometimes it's only available in the lobby). There's sometimes a guest computer with Internet access in the lobby.

Electrical outlets may have switches that turn the current on or off; if your appliance isn't working, flip the switch at the outlet.

To guard against theft in your room, keep valuables out of sight. Some rooms come with a safe, and other hotels have safes at the front desk. I've never bothered using one and in a lifetime of travel, I've never had anything stolen from my room.

Breakfast: Your room cost usually includes a traditional full cooked breakfast (fry-up) or a lighter, healthier continental breakfast.

Checking Out: While it's customary to pay for your room upon departure, it can be a good idea to settle your bill the day before, when you're not in a hurry and while the manager's in. That way you'll have time to discuss and address any points of contention.

Hotelier Help: Hoteliers can be a good source of advice. Most know their city well, and can assist you with everything from public transit and airport connections to finding a good restaurant, the nearest launderette, or a late-night pharmacy.

Hotel Hassles: Even at the best places, mechanical breakdowns occur: Sinks leak, hot water turns cold, toilets may gurgle or smell, the Wi-Fi goes out, or the air-conditioning dies when you need it most. Report your concerns clearly and calmly at the front desk. For more complicated problems, don't expect instant results. Above all, keep a positive attitude. Remember, you're on vacation. If your hotel is a disappointment, spend more time out enjoying the place you came to see.

B&Bs and Small Hotels

B&Bs and small hotels are generally family-run places with fewer amenities but more character than a conventional hotel. They range from large inns with 15-20 rooms to small homes renting out a spare bedroom. Places named "guesthouse" or

"B&B" typically have eight or fewer rooms. The philosophy of the management determines the character of a place more than its size and amenities. I avoid places run as a business by absentee owners. My top listings are run by people who enjoy welcoming the world to their breakfast table.

Compared to hotels, B&Bs and guesthouses give you double the cultural intimacy for half the price. While you may lose some of the conveniences of a hotel—such as fancy lobbies, in-room phones, and frequent bedsheet changes—I happily make the trade-off for the personal touches, whether it's joining my hosts for afternoon tea or relaxing by a common fireplace at the end of the day. If you have a reasonable but limited budget, skip hotels and go the B&B way.

B&B proprietors are selective about the guests they invite in for the night. Many do not welcome children. If you'll be staying for more than one night, you are a "desirable." In popular weekend-getaway spots, you're unlikely to find a place to take you for Saturday night only. If my listings are full, ask for guidance. Mentioning this book can help. Owners usually work together and can call up an ally to land you a bed. Many B&B owners are also pet owners. If you're allergic, ask about resident pets when you reserve.

Rules and Etiquette: B&Bs and small hotels come with their own etiquette and quirks. Keep in mind that owners are at the whim of their guests—if you're getting up early, so are they; if you check in late, they'll wait up for you. Most B&Bs have set check-in times (usually in the late afternoon). If arriving outside that time, they will want to know when to expect you (call or email ahead). Most will let you check in earlier if the room is available (or they'll at least let you drop off your bag).

Most B&Bs and guesthouses serve a hearty cooked breakfast of eggs and much more (for details on breakfast, see the Eating section, later). Because the owner is often also the cook, breakfast hours are usually abbreviated. Typically the breakfast window lasts for 1 or 1.5 hours (make sure you know when it is before you turn in for the night). Some B&Bs ask you to fill in your breakfast order the night before. It's an unwritten rule that guests shouldn't show up at the very end of the breakfast period and expect a full cooked breakfast. If you do arrive late (or need to leave before breakfast is served), most establishments are happy to let you help yourself to cereal, fruit or juice, and coffee.

B&Bs and small hotels often come with thin walls and doors, and sometimes creaky floorboards, which can make for a noisy night. If you're a light sleeper, bring earplugs. And please be quiet in the halls and in your rooms at night...those of us getting up early will thank you for it.

Treat these lovingly maintained homes as you would a friend's house. Be careful maneuvering your bag up narrow staircases with fragile walls and banisters. And once in the room, use the luggage rack—putting bags on the bed can damage nice comforters.

In the Room: Every B&B offers "tea service" in the room—an electric kettle, cups, tea bags, coffee packets, and a pack of biscuits.

Your bedroom probably won't include a phone, but nearly every B&B has free Wi-Fi (if they don't, I'll generally note it in the listing). However, the signal may not reach all rooms; you may need to sit in the lounge to access it.

You're likely to encounter unusual bathroom fixtures. The "pump toilet" has a flushing handle or button that doesn't kick in unless you push it just right: too hard or too soft, and it won't go. (Be decisive but not ruthless.) Most B&B baths have an instant water heater. This looks like an electronic box under the shower-head with dials and buttons: One control adjusts the heat, while another turns the flow off and on (let the water run for a bit to moderate the temperature before you hop in). If the hot water doesn't work, you may need to flip a red switch (often located just outside the bathroom). If the shower looks mysterious, ask your B&B host for help...*before* you take your clothes off.

Paying: Many B&Bs take credit cards, but may add the card service fee to your bill (about 3 percent). If you do need to pay cash for your room, plan ahead to have enough on hand when you check out.

Short-Term Rentals

A short-term rental—whether an apartment (or "flat"), house, or room in a local's home—is an increasingly popular alternative, especially if you plan to settle in one location for several nights. For stays longer than a few days, you can usually find a rental that's comparable to—and even cheaper than—a hotel room with similar amenities. Plus, you'll get a behind-the-scenes peek into how locals live.

Many places require a minimum-night stay, and compared to hotels, rentals usually have less-flexible cancellation policies. Also you're generally on your own: There's no hotel reception desk, breakfast, or daily cleaning service.

Finding Accommodations: Aggregator websites such as Airbnb, FlipKey, Booking.com, and the HomeAway family of sites (HomeAway, VRBO, and VacationRentals) let you browse properties and correspond directly with European property owners or managers. If you prefer to work from a curated list of accommodations, consider using a rental agency such as InterhomeUSA.com or RentaVilla.com. Agency-represented apartments typically cost more, but this method often offers more help and safeguards than booking direct.

Before you commit, be clear on the details, location, and amenities. I like to virtually "explore" the neighborhood using the Street View feature on Google Maps. Also consider the proximity to public transportation, and how well connected the property is with the rest of the city. Ask about amenities (elevator, air-conditioning, laundry, Wi-Fi, parking, etc.). Reviews from previous guests can help identify trouble spots.

Think about the kind of experience you want: Just a key and an affordable bed...or a chance to get to know a local? There are typically two kinds of hosts: those who want minimal interaction with their guests, and hosts who are friendly and may want to interact with you. Read the promotional text and online reviews to help shape your decision.

Apartments and Rental Houses: If you're staying somewhere for four nights or longer, it's worth considering an apartment or house (shorter stays aren't worth the hassle of arranging key pickup, buying groceries, etc.). Apartments and rental houses can be especially cost-effective for groups and families. European apartments, like hotel rooms, tend to be small by US standards. But they often come with laundry machines and small, equipped kitchens, making it easier and cheaper to dine in. If you make good use of the kitchen (and Europe's great produce markets), you'll save on your meal budget. Also, determine how close the nearest public transit stop is, and factor transportation costs into the overall price.

Private and Shared Rooms: Renting a room in someone's home is a good option for those traveling alone, as you're more likely to find true single rooms—with just one single bed, and a price to match. Beds range from air-mattress-in-living-room basic to plush-B&B-suite posh. Some places allow you to book for a single night; if staying for several nights, you can buy groceries just as you would in a rental house. While you can't expect your host to also be your tour guide—or even to provide you with much info— some may be interested in getting to know the travelers who come through their home.

Other Options: Swapping homes with a local works for people with an appealing place to offer, and who can live with the idea of having strangers in their home (don't assume where you live is not interesting to Europeans). A good place to start is HomeExchange. To sleep for free, Couchsurfing.com is a vagabond's alternative to Airbnb. It lists millions of outgoing members, who host fellow "surfers" in their homes.

Confirming and Paying: Many places require you to pay the entire balance before your trip. It's easiest and safest to pay through the site where you found the listing. Be wary of owners who want to take your transaction offline to avoid fees; this gives you no re-

The Good and Bad of Online Reviews

User-generated review sites and apps such as Yelp, Booking. com, and TripAdvisor can give you a consensus of opinions about everything from hotels and restaurants to sights and nightlife. If you scan reviews of a hotel and see several complaints about noise or a rotten location, it tells you something important that you'd never learn from the hotel's own website.

But as a guidebook writer, my sense is that there is a big difference between the uncurated information on a review site and a guidebook. A user-generated review is based on the experience of one person, who likely stayed at one hotel in a given city and ate at a few restaurants there (and who doesn't have much of a basis for comparison). A guidebook is the work of a trained researcher who, year after year, visits many alternatives to assess their relative value. I recently checked out some top-rated user-reviewed hotel and restaurant listings in various towns; when stacked up against their competitors, some were gems, while just as many were duds.

Both types of information have their place, and in many ways, they're complementary. If something is well-reviewed in a guidebook, and also gets good ratings on one of these sites, it's likely a winner.

course if things go awry. Never agree to wire money (a key indicator of a fraudulent transaction).

Hostels

Britain has hundreds of hostels of all shapes and sizes. Choose your hostel selectively. Hostels can be historic castles or depressing tenements, serene and comfy or overrun by noisy school groups.

A hostel provides cheap beds in dorms where you sleep alongside strangers for about £20-30 per night. Travelers of any age are welcome if they don't mind dorm-style accommodations and meeting other travelers. Most hostels offer kitchen facilities, guest computers, Wi-Fi, and a self-service laundry. Hostels almost always provide bedding, but the towel's up to you (though you can usually rent one for a small fee). Family and private rooms are often available.

Independent hostels tend to be easygoing, colorful, and informal (no membership required; www.hostelworld.com). You may pay slightly less by booking directly with the hostel. A few chains have multiple locations around Scotland, including **MacBackpackers** (www.scotlandstophostels.com); others are listed on the **Scottish Independent Hostels** website, with a fun variety of well-established places (www.hostel-scotland.co.uk).

Official hostels are part of Hostelling International (HI) and share an online booking site (www.hihostels.com). In Scotland, these official hostels are run by the Scottish Youth Hostel Association (SYHA, also known as Hostelling Scotland, www.syha.org. uk). HI hostels typically require that you be a member or pay extra per night.

Eating

These days, the stereotype of "bad food in Britain" is woefully dated. Britain has caught up with the foodie revolution, and I find it's easy to eat very well here.

British cooking has embraced international influences and local, seasonal ingredients, making "modern British" food quite delicious. While some dreary pub food still exists, you'll generally find the cuisine scene here innovative and delicious (but expensive). Basic pubs are more likely to dish up homemade, creative dishes than microwaved pies, soggy fries, and mushy peas. Even traditional pub grub has gone upmarket, with gastropubs that serve locally sourced meats and fresh vegetables.

All of Britain is smoke-free. Expect restaurants and pubs to be nonsmoking indoors, with smokers occupying patios and doorways outside. You'll find the Brits eat at about the same time of day as Americans.

When restaurant hunting, choose a spot filled with locals, not tourists. Venturing even a block or two off the main drag leads to higher-quality food for a better price. Locals eat better at lower-rent locales. Rely on my recommendations in the various eating sections throughout this book.

Tipping: At pubs and places where you order at the counter, you don't have to tip. Regular customers ordering a round sometimes say, "Add one for yourself" as a tip for drinks ordered at the bar—but this isn't expected. At restaurants and fancy pubs with waitstaff, it's standard to tip about 10-12 percent; you can add a bit more for finer dining or extra-good service. Occasionally a service charge is added to your bill, in which case no additional tip is necessary—but this is rare in Scotland. Tip only what you think the service warrants (if it isn't already added to your bill), and be careful not to tip double.

RESTAURANT PRICING

I've categorized my recommended eateries based on price, indicated with a dollar-sign rating (see sidebar). The price ranges suggest the average price of a typical main course—but not necessarily a complete meal. Obviously, expensive items (such as steak and seafood), fine wine, appetizers, and dessert can significantly increase your final bill.

PRACTICALITIES

Restaurant Code

I've assigned each eatery a price category, based on the average cost of a typical main course. Drinks, desserts, and splurge items (steak and seafood) can raise the price considerably.

$$$$	**Splurge:** Most main courses over £20
$$$	**Pricier:** £15-20
$$	**Moderate:** £10-15
$	**Budget:** Under £10

In Scotland, carryout fish-and-chips and other takeout food is **$**; a basic pub or sit-down eatery is **$$**; a gastropub or casual but more upscale restaurant is **$$$**; and a swanky splurge is **$$$$**.

The dollar-sign categories also indicate the overall personality and "feel" of a place:

$ Budget eateries include street food, takeaway, order-at-the-counter shops, basic cafeterias, bakeries selling sandwiches, and so on.

$$ Moderate eateries are typically nice (but not fancy) sit-down restaurants, ideal for a straightforward, fill-the-tank meal. Most of my listings fall in this category—great for getting a good taste of the local cuisine on a budget.

$$$ Pricier eateries are a notch up, with more attention paid to the setting, service, and cuisine. These are ideal for a memorable meal that's still relatively casual and doesn't break the bank. This category often includes affordable "destination" or "foodie" restaurants.

$$$$ Splurge eateries are dress-up-for-a-special-occasion-swanky—Michelin star-type restaurants, typically with an elegant setting, polished service, pricey and intricate cuisine, and an expansive (and expensive) wine list.

I haven't categorized places where you might assemble a picnic, snack, or graze: supermarkets, delis, ice-cream stands, cafés or bars specializing in drinks, chocolate shops, and so on.

BREAKFAST (FRY-UP)

The traditional fry-up, or full Scottish breakfast—generally included in the cost of your room—is famous as a hearty way to start the day. Also known as a "heart attack on a plate," your standard fry-up comes with your choice of eggs, Canadian-style bacon and/or sausage, a grilled

Haggis and Other Traditional Scottish Dishes

Scotland's most unique dish, **haggis,** began as a peasant food. Waste-conscious cooks wrapped the heart, liver, and lungs of a sheep in its stomach lining, packed in some oats and spices, and then boiled the lot to create a hearty, though barely palatable, meal. Traditionally served with "neeps and tatties" (turnips and potatoes), haggis was forever immortalized thanks to Robbie Burns' *Address to a Haggis.*

Today, haggis has been refined almost to the point of high cuisine. You're likely to find it on many menus, including at breakfast. You can dress it up with anything from a fine whisky cream sauce to your basic HP brown sauce. To appreciate this iconic Scottish dish, think of how it tastes—not what it's made of.

The king of Scottish **black puddings** (blood sausage) is made in the Hebrides Islands. Called Stornoway, it's so famous that the European Union has granted it protected status to prevent imitators from using its name. A mix of beef suet, oatmeal, onion, and blood, the sausage is usually served as part of a full Scottish breakfast, but it also appears on the menus of top-class restaurants.

Be on the lookout for other traditional Scottish taste treats. **Cullen skink** is Scotland's answer to chowder: a hearty, creamy fish soup, often made with smoked haddock. A **bridie** (or Forfar bridie) is a savory meat pastry similar to a Cornish pasty, but generally lighter (no potatoes). A **Scotch pie**—small, double-crusted, and filled with minced meat, is a good picnic food; it's a common snack at soccer matches and outdoor events. **Crowdie** is a dairy spread that falls somewhere between cream cheese and cottage cheese.

And for dessert, **cranachan** is similar to a trifle, made with whipped cream, honey, fruit (usually raspberries), and whisky-soaked oats. Another popular dessert is the **Tipsy Laird,** served at "Burns Suppers" on January 25, the annual celebration of national poet Robert Burns. It's essentially the same as a trifle but with whisky or brandy and Scottish raspberries.

tomato, sautéed mushrooms, baked beans, and often haggis, black pudding, or a dense potato scone. Toast comes in a rack (to cool quickly and crisply) with butter and marmalade. Other options include porridge and sometimes pancakes or waffles. The meal is typically topped off with tea or coffee. Many B&B owners offer vegetarian, organic, gluten-free, or other creative variations on the traditional breakfast.

Much as the full breakfast fry-up is a traditional way to start the morning, these days most places serve a healthier continental breakfast as well—with a buffet of yogurt, cereal, fruit, and pastries. At some hotels, the buffet may also include hot items, such as eggs and sausage.

LUNCH AND DINNER ON A BUDGET

Even in pricey cities, plenty of inexpensive choices are available: pub grub, daily lunch and early-bird dinner specials, ethnic restaurants, cafeterias, fast food, picnics, greasy-spoon cafés, cheap chain restaurants, and pizza. On menus, adding "supper" to an item means it comes with fries (so "fish supper" is fish-and-chips).

I've found that portions are huge, and with locals feeling the economic pinch, **sharing plates** is generally just fine. Ordering two drinks, a soup or side salad, and splitting a £10 meat pie can make a good, filling meal. If you're on a limited budget, share a main course in a more expensive place for a nicer eating experience.

Pub grub is the most atmospheric budget option. You'll usually get hearty lunches and dinners priced reasonably at £8-15 under ancient timbers (see "Pubs," later). Gastropubs, with better food, are more expensive.

Classier restaurants have some affordable deals. Lunch is usually cheaper than dinner; a top-end, £30-for-dinner-type restaurant often serves the same quality two-course lunch deals for about half the price.

Many restaurants have **early-bird** or **pre-theater specials** of two or three courses, often for a significant savings. They are usually available only before 18:30 or 19:00 (and sometimes on weekdays only), but are good for bargain hunters willing to eat a bit earlier.

Ethnic restaurants add spice to Britain's cuisine scene. Eating Indian, Bangladeshi, Chinese, or Thai is cheap (even cheaper if you do takeout). Middle Eastern shops sell gyro sandwiches, falafel, and *shwarmas* (grilled meat in pita bread). An Indian samosa (greasy, flaky meat-and-vegetable pie) costs about £2 and makes a very cheap, if small, meal. (For more, see "Indian Cuisine," later.)

Fish-and-chips is a heavy, greasy, but tasty British classic. Every town has at least one "chippy" selling takeaway fish-and-chips in a cardboard box or (more traditionally) wrapped in paper for about £5-7. You can dip your fries in ketchup, American-style, or "go British" and drizzle the whole thing with malt vinegar and fresh lemon.

Most large **museums** (and many historic **churches**) have handy, moderately priced cafeterias with forgettably decent food.

Picnicking saves time and money. Fine park benches and polite pigeons abound in most towns and city neighborhoods. You can easily get prepared food to go. The modern chain eateries on nearly every corner often have simple seating but are designed for take-out. Bakeries serve a wonderful array of fresh sandwiches and pasties (savory meat pastries—sometimes called bridies in Scotland). Street markets, generally parked in pedestrian-friendly zones, are fun and colorful places to stock up for a picnic.

Open-air markets and supermarkets sell produce in small quantities. The corner grocery store has fruit, drinks, fresh bread, tasty British cheese, meat, and local specialties. Supermarkets often have good deli sections, even offering Indian dishes, and sometimes salad bars. Decent packaged sandwiches (£3-4) are sold everywhere. Munch a relaxed "meal on wheels" picnic during your open-top bus tour or river cruise to save 30 precious minutes for sightseeing.

PUBS

Pubs are a fundamental part of the British social scene, and whether you're a teetotaler or a beer guzzler, they should be a part of your travel here. "Pub" is short for "public house." It's an extended common room where, if you don't mind the stickiness, you can feel the local pulse. Smart travelers use pubs to eat, drink, get out of the rain, watch sporting events, and make new friends. Unfortunately, many city pubs have been afflicted

with an excess of brass, ferns, and video slot machines. The most traditional atmospheric pubs are in the countryside and in smaller towns.

It's interesting to consider the role pubs filled for Britain's working class in more modest times: For workers with humble domestic quarters and no money for a vacation, a beer at the corner pub was the closest they'd get to a comfortable living room, a place to entertain, and a getaway. And locals could meet people from far away in a pub—today, that's you!

Though hours vary, pubs generally serve beer daily from 11:00

to 23:00, though many are open later, particularly on Friday and Saturday. (Children are served food and soft drinks in pubs, but you must be 18 to order a beer.) As it nears closing time, you'll hear shouts of "Last orders." Then comes the 10-minute warning bell. Finally, they'll call "Time!" to pick up your glass, finished or not, when the pub closes.

A cup of darts is free for the asking. People go to a public house to be social. They want to talk. Get vocal with a local. This is easiest at the bar, where people assume you're in the mood to talk (rather than at a table, where you're allowed a bit of privacy). The pub is the next best thing to having relatives in town. Cheers!

Pub Grub: For £8-15, you'll get a basic budget hot lunch or dinner in friendly surroundings. For something more refined, try a **gastropub,** which serves higher-quality meals for £12-20.) The *Good Pub Guide* is an excellent resource (www.thegoodpubguide.co.uk). Pubs that are attached to restaurants, advertise their food, and are crowded with locals are more likely to have fresh food and a chef—and less likely to sell only lousy microwaved snacks.

Pubs generally serve traditional dishes, such as fish-and-chips, roast beef with Yorkshire pudding (batter-baked in the oven), and assorted meat pies, such as steak-and-kidney pie or shepherd's pie (stewed lamb topped with mashed potatoes) with cooked vegetables. Side dishes include salads, vegetables, and—invariably—"chips" (French fries). "Crisps" are potato chips. A "jacket potato" (baked potato stuffed with fillings of your choice) can almost be a meal in itself. A "ploughman's lunch" is a traditional British meal of bread, cheese, and sweet pickles. These days, you'll likely find more pasta, curried dishes, and quiche on the menu than traditional fare.

Meals are usually served from 12:00 to 14:00 and again from 18:00 to 20:00—with a break in the middle (rather than serving straight through the day). Since they make more money selling beer, many pubs stop food service early in the evening—especially on weekends. There's generally no table service. Order at the bar, then take a seat. Either they'll bring the food when it's ready or you'll pick it up at the bar. Pay at the bar (sometimes when you order, sometimes after you eat). It's not necessary to tip unless it's a place with full table service. Servings are hearty, and service is quick. A beer, cider, or dram of whisky adds another couple of pounds. Free tap water is always available. For details on ordering beer and other drinks, see the "Beverages" section, later.

GOOD CHAIN RESTAURANTS

I know—you're going to Britain to enjoy characteristic little hole-in-the-wall pubs, so mass-produced food is the furthest thing from your mind. But several excellent chains with branches across the UK offer long hours, reasonable prices, reliable quality, and a nice break from pub grub. My favorites are Pret and Eat. Expect to see these familiar names wherever you go:

Pret (a.k.a. Pret à Manger) is perhaps the most pervasive of these modern convenience eateries. Some are takeout-only, and others have seating ranging from simple stools to restaurant-quality tables. The service is fast, the price is great, and the food is healthy and fresh. Their slogan: "Made today. Gone today. No 'sell-by' date, no nightlife."

Côte Brasserie is a contemporary French chain serving good-value French cuisine in reliably pleasant settings (early dinner specials).

Byron Hamburgers, an upscale hamburger chain with hip interiors, is worth seeking out if you need a burger fix. While British burgers tend to be a bit overcooked by American standards, Byron's burgers are your best bet.

Wagamama Noodle Bar, serving pan-Asian cuisine (udon noodles, fried rice, and curry dishes), is a noisy, organic slurpathon. Portions are huge and splittable. There's one in almost every mid-size city in Britain, usually located in sprawling halls filled with long shared tables and busy servers who scrawl your order on the placemat.

Loch Fyne Fish Restaurant is a Scottish chain that raises its own oysters and mussels. Its branches offer an inviting, lively atmosphere with a fine fishy energy and no pretense (early-bird specials).

Marks & Spencer department stores have inviting deli sections with cheery sit-down eating (along with their popular sandwiches-to-go section). M&S food halls are also handy if you're renting a city flat and want to prepare your own meals.

Ask and **Pizza Express** serve quality pasta and pizza in a pleasant, sit-down atmosphere that's family-friendly. **Jamie's Italian** (from celebrity chef Jamie Oliver) is hipper and pricier.

Yo! Sushi lets you pick your dish off a conveyor belt and pay according to the color of your plate.

Carry-Out Chains: While the following may have some seating, they're best as places to grab prepackaged food on the run.

Major supermarket chains have smaller, offshoot branches that specialize in sandwiches, salads, and other prepared foods to go. These can be a picnicker's dream come true. Some shops are stand-alone, while others are located inside a larger store. The most prevalent—and best—is **M&S Simply Food** (an offshoot of Marks & Spencer; there's one in every major train station). **Sainsbury's**

Local grocery stores also offer decent prepared food; **Tesco Express** and **Tesco Metro** run a distant third.

Eat is a "cheap and cheery" chain providing office workers with good, healthful sandwiches, salads, and pastries to go.

INDIAN CUISINE

Eating Indian food is "going local" in cosmopolitan, multiethnic Britain. You'll find Indian restaurants in most cities, and even in small towns. Take the opportunity to sample food from Britain's former colony. Indian cuisine is as varied as the country itself. In general, it uses more exotic spices than British or American cuisine—some hot, some sweet. Indian food is very vegetarian-friendly, offering many meatless dishes.

For a simple meal that costs about £10-12, order one dish with rice and naan (Indian flatbread). Generally, one order is plenty for two people to share. Many Indian restaurants offer a fixed-price combination that offers more variety, and is simpler and cheaper than ordering à la carte. For about £20, you can make a mix-and-match platter out of several shareable dishes, including dal (simmered lentils) as a starter, one or two meat or vegetable dishes with sauce (for example, chicken curry, chicken *tikka masala* in a creamy tomato sauce, grilled fish tandoori, chickpea *chana masala*, or a spicy vindaloo dish), *raita* (a cooling yogurt that's added to spicy dishes), rice, naan, and an Indian beer (wine and Indian food don't really mix) or chai (cardamom/cinnamon-spiced tea, usually served with milk). An easy way to taste a variety of dishes is to order a thali—a sampler plate, generally served on a metal tray, with small servings of various specialties.

AFTERNOON TEA

While more of an English custom, afternoon tea is served in Scottish tearooms and generally includes a pot of tea, small finger foods (like sandwiches with the crusts cut off), homemade scones, jam, and thick clotted cream. A lighter "cream tea" gets you tea and a scone or two. Tearooms, which often serve appealing light meals, are usually open for lunch and close at about 17:00, just before dinner.

DESSERTS (SWEETS)

To the British, the traditional word for dessert is "pudding," although it's also referred to as "sweets" these days. Sponge cake, cream, fruitcake, and meringue are key players.

Trifle is the best-known British concoction, consisting of sponge cake soaked in brandy or sherry (or orange juice for children), then covered with jam and/or fruit and custard cream.

Whipped cream can sometimes put the final touch on this "light" treat.

The British version of custard is a smooth, yellow liquid. Cream tops most everything that custard does not. There's single cream for coffee. Double cream is really thick. Whipped cream is familiar, and clotted cream is the consistency of whipped butter.

Fool is a dessert with sweetened pureed fruit (such as rhubarb, gooseberries, or black currants) mixed with cream or custard and chilled. Elderflower is a popular flavoring for sorbet.

Flapjacks here aren't pancakes, but are dense, sweet oatmeal cakes (a little like a cross between a granola bar and a brownie). They come with toppings such as toffee and chocolate.

Scones are tops, and many inns and restaurants have their secret recipes. Whether made with fruit or topped with clotted cream, scones take the cake.

BEVERAGES

Beer: The British take great pride in their beer. Many locals think that drinking beer cold and carbonated, as Americans do, ruins the taste. Most pubs will have **lagers** (cold, refreshing, American-style beer), **ales** (amber-colored, cellar-temperature beer), **bitters** (hop-flavored ale, perhaps the most typical British beer), and **stouts** (dark and somewhat bitter, like Guinness).

At pubs, long-handled pulls (or taps) are used to draw the traditional, rich-flavored "real ales" up from the cellar. These are the connoisseur's favorites and often come with fun names. Served straight from the brewer's cask at cellar temperature, real ales finish fermenting naturally and are not pasteurized or filtered, so they must be consumed within two or three days after the cask is tapped. Naturally carbonated, real ales have less gassiness and head; they vary from sweet to bitter, often with a hoppy or nutty flavor.

Short-handled pulls mean colder, fizzier, mass-produced, and less interesting keg beers. Mild beers are sweeter, with a creamy malt flavoring. Irish cream ale is a smooth, sweet experience. Try the draft cider (sweet or dry)...carefully.

Order your beer at the bar and pay as you go, with no need to tip. An average beer costs about £4. Part of the experience is standing before a line of hand pulls, and wondering which beer to choose.

As dictated by British law, draft beer and cider are served by the pint (20-ounce imperial size) or the half-pint (9.6 ounces). (It's almost feminine for a man to order just a half; I order mine with quiche.) In 2011, the government sanctioned an in-between serving size—the schooner, or two-thirds pint (it's become a popular size for higher alcohol-content craft beers). Proper Scottish ladies like a **shandy** (half beer and half 7-Up).

PRACTICALITIES

Whisky 101

Whisky is high on the experience list of most visitors to Scotland—even for teetotalers. Whether at a distillery, a shop, or a pub, be sure to try a few drams. (From the Gaelic word for "drink," a dram isn't necessarily a fixed amount—it's simply a small slug.) While touring a distillery is a ▲▲▲ Scottish experience, many fine whisky shops (including Cadenhead's in Edinburgh) offer guided tastings and a chance to have a small bottle filled from the cask of your choice.

Types of Whisky

Scotch whiskies come in two broad types: **"single malt,"** meaning that the bottle comes from a single batch made by a single distiller; and **"blends,"** which master blenders mix and match from various whiskies into a perfect punch of booze.

While single malts get the most attention, blended whiskies represent 90 percent of all whisky sales. They tend to be light and mild—making them an easier way to tiptoe into the whisky scene. Overseen by a master blender (a prestigious job, like a "nose" in the French wine industry), a neutral base of grain whisky (usually made from corn or wheat) is merged with a variety of single malts, and then aged in oak casks for just six months to a year of "marriage."

There are more than 100 distilleries in Scotland, each one proud of its unique qualities. The **Lowlands,** around Edinburgh, produce light and refreshing whiskies—more likely to be taken as an aperitif. Whiskies from the **Highlands** and **Islands** range from floral and sweet (vanilla or honey) to smoky (peaty) and robust. **Speyside,** southeast of Inverness, is home to half of all Scottish distilleries. Mellow and fruity, Speyside whiskies can be the most accessible for beginners. The **Isle of Islay** is just the opposite, specializing in the peatiest, smokiest whiskies—not for novices. Only a few producers remain to distill the smoky and pungent **Campbeltown** whiskies in the southwest Highlands, near Islay.

Making Whisky

Single-malt whisky has three ingredients: water, malted barley, and yeast.

To malt (or germinate) the barley, it's spread out on a floor, watered, and periodically turned. In about a week, when the barley starts to sprout, it's dried in an oven. Some distilleries (especially on the islands) use peat in their kilns, giving their whisky a distinctive smoky flavor.

Once malted, the barley is milled into a fine grist that's mixed with hot water to create mash. A sugary solution called wort is extracted from the mash, then cooled and mixed with yeast. For three or four days, the wort fizzes and ferments in big "washback" tubs as the yeast turn sugar into alcohol.

To boost the alcohol content, the wash is then double-distilled in tall, copper stills. First, in the "wash still," the liquid is heated, to allow the alcohol to evaporate. Those gases are sent through coiled tubes to recondense them into a liquid called "low wines." That liquid flows through a second spirit still to create "spirit." No two stills are the same, and the copper in each brings about unique qualities in the spirit.

Distillers keep only the "heart" of the run; it has the most consistent alcohol levels and flavor profile. They snip off the "head" and "tail" (collectively called "feints") to be redistilled.

At the end of the distillation process, you have a concentrated, colorless liquid called "new make spirit"—but not yet "whisky." For that, the liquid must be aged for at least three years (more commonly eight or more years; the final product must register at least 40 percent alcohol by volume). This maturation typically takes place in casks made of American white oak, often recycled from the US. (American laws permit each cask to be used only once—but no such regulation exists in Scotland.) It's increasingly in vogue to use casks that have previously aged sherry, port, wine, or cognac, in order to infuse the whisky with faint echoes of those flavors.

During maturation, about 1 to 3 percent of the alcohol is lost to evaporation—what's poetically described as "the angel's share." For a long-aged whisky, it's more like the lion's share: A 25-year-old cask of whisky can end up being just over half full.

Finally, the aged whisky is bottled—or, in some cases, entire casks are sent to specialty stores

Tasting Whisky

Tasting whisky is like tasting wine; you'll use all your senses. First, swirl the whisky in the glass and observe its color and "legs"—the trail left by the liquid as it runs back down the side of the glass (quick, thin legs indicate light, young whisky, slow, thick legs mean it's a heavier and older one). Then take a deep sniff—do you smell smoke and peat? And finally, taste it (sip!). What's the dominant first punch? The smooth middle? The "finish"? Swish it around and let your gums taste it, too. Adding a few drops of water is said to "open up the taste"—look for a little glass of water with a dropper standing by, and try tasting your whisky before and after.

A whisky's flavor is most influenced by three things: whether the malt is peat-smoked; the shape of the stills; and the composition of the casks. Even local climate can play a role; some island distilleries tout the salty notes of their whiskies, as the sea air permeates their casks.

Whisky: While bar-hopping tourists generally think in terms of beer, many pubs are just as enthusiastic about serving whisky. If you are unfamiliar with whisky (what Americans call "Scotch" and the Irish call "whiskey"), it's a great conversation starter. Many pubs have dozens of whiskies available. Lists describe their personalities (peaty, heavy iodine finish, and so on), which are much easier to discern than most wine flavors.

A glass of basic whisky generally costs around £2.50. Let a local teach you how to drink it "neat," then add a little water. Make a friend, buy a few drams, and learn by drinking. Keep experimenting until you discover the right taste for you.

Consider going beyond the single-malt whisky rut. Like microbrews, small-batch, innovative Scottish spirits are trendy right now. Blends can be surprisingly creative—even for someone who thinks they're knowledgeable about whisky—and non-whisky alternatives are pushing boundaries. For example, you'll find gin that's aged in whisky casks, taking off the piney edge and infusing a bit of that distinctive whisky flavor.

Distilleries throughout Scotland offer tours, but you'll often only learn about that one type of whisky. At a good whisky shop, the knowledgeable staff offer guided tastings (for a fee and typically by pre-arrangement), explaining four or five whiskies to help you develop your palate. If you don't care for a heavy, smoky whisky, ask for something milder. Some shops have several bottles open and will let you try a few wee drams to narrow down your options. Be aware: If they're providing samples, they're hoping you'll buy a bottle at the end.

But the easiest and perhaps best option for sampling Scotland's national drink is to find a local pub with a passion for whisky that's filled with locals who share that passion.

For much more about whisky, see the "Whisky 101" sidebar.

Other Alcoholic Drinks: Many pubs also have a good selection of wines by the glass and a fully stocked bar for the gentleman's "G and T" (gin and tonic).

Non-Alcoholic Drinks: Teetotalers can order from a wide variety of soft drinks—both the predictable American sodas and other more interesting bottled drinks, such as ginger beer (similar to ginger ale but with more bite), root beers, or other flavors (Fentimans brews some unusual options that are stocked in many pubs). The uniquely Scottish soft drink called Irn-Bru (pronounced "Iron Brew") is bright orange and tastes like bubble gum. Note that in Britain, "lemonade" is lemon-lime soda (like 7-Up).

PRACTICALITIES

Staying Connected

One of the most common questions I hear from travelers is, "How can I stay connected in Europe?" The short answer is: more easily and cheaply than you might think.

The simplest solution is to bring your own device—mobile phone, tablet, or laptop—and use it just as you would at home (following the tips below, such as connecting to free Wi-Fi whenever possible). Another option is to buy a European SIM card for your mobile phone—either your US phone or one you buy in Europe. Or you can use European landlines and computers to connect. Each of these options is described next, and more details are at www.ricksteves.com/phoning. For a very practical one-hour talk covering tech issues for travelers, see www.ricksteves.com/mobile-travel-skills.

USING A MOBILE PHONE IN EUROPE

Here are some budget tips and options.

Sign up for an international plan. Using your cellular network in Europe on a pay-as-you-go basis can add up (about $1.70/minute for voice calls, 50 cents to send text messages, 5 cents to receive them, and $10 to download one megabyte of data). To stay connected at a lower cost, sign up for an international service plan through your carrier. Most providers offer a simple bundle that includes calling, messaging, and data. Your normal plan may already include international coverage (T-Mobile's does).

Before your trip, call your provider or check online to confirm that your phone will work in Europe, and research your provider's international rates. Activate the plan a day or two before you leave, then remember to cancel it when your trip's over.

Use free Wi-Fi whenever possible. Unless you have an unlimited-data plan, you're best off saving most of your online tasks for Wi-Fi. You can access the Internet, send texts, and even make voice calls over Wi-Fi.

Most accommodations in Europe offer free Wi-Fi, but some—especially expensive hotels—charge a fee. Many cafés (including Starbucks and McDonald's) have free hotspots for customers; look for signs offering it and ask for the Wi-Fi password when you buy something. You'll also often find Wi-Fi at TIs, city squares, major museums, public-transit hubs, airports, and aboard trains and buses. In Britain, another option is to sign up for Wi-Fi access through a company such as BT (one hour-£4, one day-£10, www.btwifi.co.uk) or The Cloud (free though sometimes slow, www.skywifi.cloud).

Minimize the use of your cellular network. Even with an international data plan, wait until you're on Wi-Fi to Skype, down-

The Language Barrier?

Yes, Scots speak English, but it has distinct qualities. Scottish people are known for their inimitable burr, and they're proud of their old Celtic language, Gaelic.

Scottish Gaelic thrives only in the remotest corners of Scotland—the Highlands and the Hebrides. In major towns and cities, virtually nobody speaks Gaelic on an everyday basis, but the language is kept alive by a Scottish population keen to remember its heritage. New Gaelic schools open all the time, and Scotland has replaced many road signs with new ones listing both English and Gaelic spellings (*Edinburgh/Dùn Èideann*).

Scotland has another language of its own, called Scots. Aye, you're likely already a wee bit familiar with a few Scots words, ye lads and lassies. A generation or two ago, Scots was denigrated in favor of the Queen's English. But in today's age of regionalism, Scots is enjoying a renaissance. Schoolchildren from Scots-speaking families once faced punishment for saying "youse" to mean "you all." Now a new generation of kids is being taught Scots. As you travel, you'll begin to collect Scots words (see next page)...and enjoy the lovely musical lilt as well. One popular Scots saying is "Whit's fur ye'll no go by ye"—you'll get what's coming to you, good or bad.

As the old joke goes, "A language is just a dialect with an army and a flag." So Scots is halfway there. Linguists who argue that Scots is technically an ancient English dialect have clearly never heard a Scot read aloud the poetry of Robert Burns. He wrote in unfiltered (and often unintelligible) Scots, as in this opening line of "To a Louse": "Ha! Whaur ye gaun, ye crowlin ferlie?"

Fortunately, you're unlikely to meet anyone quite that hard to understand. Most Scottish people switch easily as the need arises, toggling between Scots (when they're hanging out with the lads or lassies) and the Queen's English (in professional settings). If you have a hard time understanding someone, ask them to translate: You may take home some new words as souvenirs.

Even within Scotland, there's a lot of regional variation. Lowland Scots is the most widespread dialect, although the language has evolved since Burns popularized it, and many of the poet's words are unfamiliar even to Lowland Scots today. Some cities have their own, very specific accents. For example, people in Dundee speak Dundonian, while in Aberdeen, they speak Doric, which replaces the word "what" with "fit." So a Doric speaker visiting a shoe store might say something that sounds like, "Fit fit fits fit fit?" (What foot fits what foot?) To sample the various regional dialects around Scotland, visit www.ayecan.com.

Scots Words

Scotch may be the peaty drink the bartender serves you, but the nationality of the bartender is Scottish; you could also call him a Scot, and the language he speaks is Scots. A sharp intake of breath (like a little gasp), sometimes while saying "aye," means "yes." And many Scots greet you with a cheery, "Aright!" (a compressed version of "Are you all right?").

Here are some Scots words that may come in handy during your time here:

auld	old
aye	yes
bairn, wean	child
blether	talk
bonnie	beautiful, handsome, good
braw	good, fine
cairn	pile of stones
close	an alley leading to a courtyard or square
ken	to know
kirk	church
nae	no (as in "nae bother"—you're welcome)
neeps	turnips
pend	arched gateway
ree	king, royal (*righ* in Gaelic)
tattie	potato
wee	small
wynd	tight, winding lane connecting major streets

Many Scots (or Gaelic) words relate to geography, and turn up often in place names:

aber	confluence or mouth of a river
bal	town
ben	mountain
blair	clearing
brae	slope, hill
burn	creek or stream
crag or craig	cliff, rocky ground, sea rock
dun or dum	hill fort
eilean	island
fell	hill
firth	estuary
glen	narrow valley
innis or inch	island
inver	confluence or mouth of a river
kyle	strait
loch	lake
sea loch	inlet
strath	wide valley

How to Dial

International Calls

Whether phoning from a US landline or mobile phone, or from a number in another European country, here's how to make an international call. I've used one of my recommended Edinburgh hotels as an example (tel. 0131/667-5806).

Initial Zero: Drop the initial zero from international phone numbers—except when calling Italy.

Mobile Tip: If using a mobile phone, the "+" sign can replace the international access code (for a "+" sign, press and hold "0").

US/Canada to Europe

Dial 011 (US/Canada international access code), country code (44 for Britain), and phone number.

▶ To call the Edinburgh hotel from home, dial 011-44-0131/667-5806.

Country to Country Within Europe

Dial 00 (Europe international access code), country code, and phone number.

▶ To call the Edinburgh hotel from Germany, dial 00-44-0131/667-5806.

Europe to the US/Canada

Dial 00, country code (1 for US/Canada), and phone number.

▶ To call from Europe to my office in Edmonds, Washington, dial 00-1-425-771-8303.

Domestic Calls

To call within Britain (including Scotland), from one British landline or mobile phone to another, simply dial the phone number, including the initial zero if there is one.

▶ To call the Edinburgh hotel from Glasgow or from London, dial 0131/667-5806.

More Dialing Tips

British Phone Numbers: Numbers beginning with 074 through 079 are mobile numbers, which are more expensive to call than a landline.

load apps, stream videos, or do other megabyte-greedy tasks. Using a navigation app such as Google Maps over a cellular network can take lots of data, so do this sparingly or use it offline.

Limit automatic updates. By default, your device constantly checks for a data connection and updates apps. It's smart to disable these features so your apps will only update when you're on Wi-Fi, and to change your device's email settings from "auto-retrieve" to "manual" (or from "push" to "fetch").

When you need to get online but can't find Wi-Fi, simply turn on your cellular network just long enough for the task at hand.

Toll and Toll-Free Calls: Numbers starting with 0800 and 0808 are toll-free, but those beginning with 084, 087, and 03 are generally inexpensive toll numbers (£0.15/minute maximum from a landline, £0.20-.40/minute from a mobile). Numbers beginning with 09 are pricey toll lines. If you have questions about a prefix, call 100 for free help. International rates apply to US toll-free numbers dialed from Great Britain—they're not free.

More Phoning Help: See www.howtocallabroad.com.

European Country Codes		Ireland & N. Ireland	353 / 44
Austria	43	Italy	39
Belgium	32	Latvia	371
Bosnia-Herzegovina	387	Montenegro	382
Croatia	385	Morocco	212
Czech Republic	420	Netherlands	31
Denmark	45	Norway	47
Estonia	372	Poland	48
Finland	358	Portugal	351
France	33	Russia	7
Germany	49	Slovakia	421
Gibraltar	350	Slovenia	386
Great Britain	44	Spain	34
Greece	30	Sweden	46
Hungary	36	Switzerland	41
Iceland	354	Turkey	90

When you're done, avoid further charges by manually turning off data roaming or cellular data (either works) in your device's Settings menu. Another way to make sure you're not accidentally using data roaming is to put your device in "airplane" mode (which also disables phone calls and texts), and then turn your Wi-Fi back on as needed.

It's also a good idea to keep track of your data usage. On your device's menu, look for "cellular data usage" or "mobile data" and reset the counter at the start of your trip.

Use Wi-Fi calling and messaging apps. Skype, Viber, Face-

Time, and Google+ Hangouts are great for making free or low-cost voice and video calls over Wi-Fi. With an app installed on your phone, tablet, or laptop, you can log on to a Wi-Fi network and contact friends or family members who use the same service. If you buy credit in advance, with some of these services you can call any mobile phone or landline worldwide for just pennies per minute.

Many of these apps also allow you to send messages over Wi-Fi to any other person using that app. Be aware that some apps, such as Apple's iMessage, will use the cellular network if Wi-Fi isn't available: To avoid this possibility, turn off the "Send as SMS" feature.

USING A EUROPEAN SIM CARD

With a European SIM card, you get a European mobile number and access to cheaper rates than you'll get through your US carrier. This option works well for those who want to make a lot of voice calls or needing faster connection speeds than their US carrier provides. Fit the SIM card into a cheap phone you buy in Europe (about $40 from phone shops anywhere), or swap out the SIM card in an "unlocked" US phone (check with your carrier about unlocking it).

SIM cards are sold at mobile-phone shops, department-store electronics counters, some newsstands, and vending machines. Costing about $5-10, they usually include prepaid calling/messaging credit, with no contract and no commitment. Expect to pay $20-40 more for a SIM card with a gigabyte of data. If you travel with this card to other countries in the European Union, there should be no extra roaming fees.

I like to buy SIM cards at a phone shop where there's a clerk to help explain the options. Certain brands—including Lebara and Lycamobile, both of which are available in multiple European countries—are reliable and especially economical. Ask the clerk to help you insert your SIM card, set it up, and show you how to use it. In some countries, you'll be required to register the SIM card with your passport as an antiterrorism measure (which may mean you can't use the phone for the first hour or two).

Find out how to check your credit balance. When you run out of credit, you can top it up at newsstands, tobacco shops, mobile-phone stores, or many other businesses (look for your SIM card's logo in the window), or online.

PUBLIC PHONES AND COMPUTERS

It's possible to travel in Europe without a mobile device. You can make calls from your hotel (or the increasingly rare public phone), and check email or browse websites using public computers.

Most **hotels** charge a fee for placing calls—ask for rates before

Tips on Internet Security

Make sure that your device is running the latest versions of its operating system, security software, and apps. Next, ensure that your device and key programs (like email) are password- or passcode-protected. On the road, use only secure, password-protected Wi-Fi hotspots. Ask the hotel or café staff for the specific name of their Wi-Fi network, and make sure you log on to that exact one.

If you must access your financial info online, use a banking app rather than accessing your account via a browser. A cellular connection is more secure than Wi-Fi. Avoid logging onto personal finance sites on a public computer.

Never share your credit-card number (or any other sensitive information) online unless you know that the site is secure. A secure site displays a little padlock icon, and the URL begins with *https* (instead of the usual *http*).

you dial. You can use a prepaid international phone card (available at post offices, newsstands, street kiosks, tobacco shops, and train stations) to call out from your hotel. Dial the toll-free access number, enter the card's PIN code, then dial the number.

If there's no phone in your **B&B** room, and you have an important, brief call to make, politely ask your hosts if you can use their personal phone. Use a cheap international phone card with a toll-free access number, or offer to pay your host for the call.

Public pay phones are hard to find in Britain, and they're expensive. To use one, you'll pay with a major credit card (minimum charge-£1.20) or coins (minimum charge-£0.60).

Most hotels have **public computers** in their lobbies for guests to use; otherwise you may find them at Internet cafés or public libraries (ask your hotelier or the TI for the nearest location). On a European keyboard, use the "Alt Gr" key to the right of the space bar to insert the extra symbol that appears on some keys. If you can't locate a special character (such as @), simply copy it from a Web page and paste it into your email message.

MAIL

You can mail one package per day to yourself worth up to $200 duty-free from Europe to the US (mark it "personal purchases"). If you're sending a gift to someone, mark it "unsolicited gift." For details, visit www.cbp.gov, select "Travel," and search for "Know Before You Go."

The British postal service works fine, but for quick transatlantic delivery (in either direction), consider services such as DHL (www.dhl.com). For postcards, get stamps at the neighborhood post office, newsstands within fancy hotels, and some minimarts and card shops.

Transportation

If you're debating between using public transportation and renting a car, consider these factors: Cars are best for three or more traveling together (especially families with small kids), those packing heavy, and those delving into the countryside—a tempting plan for this region. Trains and buses are best for solo travelers, blitz tourists, city-to-city travelers, and those who don't want to drive. While a car gives you more freedom, trains and buses zip you effortlessly and scenically from city to city, usually dropping you in the center, often near a TI. Cars are an expensive headache in places like Glasgow, but necessary for remote destinations not well-served by public transport.

In Scotland, my choice is to connect big cities by train or bus and to explore rural areas (including most of the Highlands) footloose and fancy-free by rental car. The mix works quite efficiently (e.g., Edinburgh and Glasgow by train or bus, with a rental car for the rest).

TRAINS

Regular tickets on Britain's great train system (15,000 departures from 2,400 stations daily) are the most expensive per mile in all of Europe. For the greatest savings, book online in advance and leave after rush hour (after 9:30 weekdays).

Since Britain's railways have been privatized, a single train route can be operated by multiple companies. However, one website covers all train lines (www.nationalrail.co.uk), and another covers all bus and train routes (www.traveline.org.uk for information, not ticket sales). Another good resource, which also has schedules for trains throughout Europe, is German Rail's timetable (www.bahn.com).

As with airline tickets, British train tickets can come at many different prices for the same journey. A clerk at any station can figure out the cheapest fare for your trip.

While not required, reservations are free and can normally be made well in advance. They are an especially good idea for long journeys or for travel on Sundays or holidays. Make reservations at any train station, by phone, or online when you buy your ticket. With a point-to-point ticket, you can reserve as late as two hours before train time, but rail-pass holders should book seats at least 24 hours in advance (see later for more on rail passes).

Public Transportation Routes in Scotland

50 Kilometers

50 Miles

- —·— Rail
- — — Bus
- ······ Ferry

Orkney Islands

Mainland Stromness

St. Marg. Hope
Burwick
Scrabster
Gills Bay
Thurso
John O' Groats
Wick

North Sea

Stornoway

Lewis

Ullapool

Harris
Tarbert
Dingwall

Lochmaddy
Uig

Elgin

Dunvegan
Portree
Inverness
Ulst
Lochboisdale
Skye
Kyle of Lochalsh
Culloden

Loch Ness
(Urquhart Castle)

Aviemore
Aberdeen

Arm.
Mallaig
Glen-finnan
SCOTLAND
Ballater
Stone-haven

Fort William
Pitlochry

Ballachulish
Glencoe
Dundee
Arbroath

Craig-nure
Perth
Leuchars

Staffa
Mull
Crian-larioh
St. Andrews

Iona
Fionn-phort
Oban
Crail
Anstruther

Balloch
Stirling

Glasgow
Edinburgh

Largs
Holy Island

Arran
Berwick

Ard.
Kilmarnock

Troon
Prestwick

Cairnryan
Dumfries
To York & London

Larne
Hexham

Stranraer
Carlisle
ENGLAND

NORTHERN IRELAND
Penrith

Belfast
Irish Sea
Keswick

To Dublin
To Liverpool
Isle of Man
Windermere
To Liverpool & London

Rail Passes

There are three different Scotland-only passes: Spirit of Scotland (covers most trains in Scotland), Central Scotland (Edinburgh/Glasgow area), and Scottish Highlands (Glasgow and points north). But for a Scotland-only itinerary, these probably won't save you money over point-to-point tickets (especially if you buy tickets in advance or use a discount Railcard).

Rail Passes and Train Travel in Scotland

A **BritRail Pass** lets you travel by train in Scotland, England, and Wales for three to eight days within a one-month period, fifteen days within two months, or for continuous periods of up to one month. In addition, BritRail sells three different regional Scotland passes that are good for three to eight days of train travel within three, eight, or fifteen-day periods. Discounted rates are offered for children, youths, seniors, or for three or more people traveling together.

BritRail passes are sold only outside Europe (through travel agents or Rick Steves' Europe). For more on the ins and outs of rail passes, including prices, download my **free guide to Eurail Passes** (www.ricksteves.com/rail-guide) or go to www.ricksteves.com/rail.

If you're taking just a couple of train rides, individual **point-to-point train tickets** may save you money over a pass. Use this map to add up approximate pay-as-you-go fares for your itinerary, and compare that to the price of a rail pass. Keep in mind that significant discounts on point-to-point tickets may be available with advance purchase.

Map shows approximate costs, in US$, for one-way, second-class tickets at off-peak rates.

Particularly if you travel between London and Scotland, consider the BritRail Pass (covers England, Scotland, and Wales). A rail pass offers hop-on flexibility and no need to lock in reservations, except for overnight sleeper cars. Passes come in "consecutive day" and "flexi" versions, with price breaks for youths, seniors, off-season travelers, and groups of three of more. Most allow one child under 16 to travel free with a paying adult. If you're exploring the backcountry with a BritRail pass, second class is a good choice since many of the smaller train lines don't even offer first-class cars.

BritRail passes cannot be purchased locally; buy your pass through an agent before leaving the US. Make sleeper reservations in advance; you can also make optional, free seat reservations (recommended for busy weekends) at staffed train stations. For specifics, see www.ricksteves.com/rail.

Buying Tickets

In Advance: The best fares go to those who book their trips well in advance of their journey. Savings can be significant. For an Edinburgh-Inverness round-trip (standard class), the peak "anytime" fare is about £62 (£52 for "off-peak"). An "advance" fare for the same ticket booked a couple of months out can cost as little as £25. If traveling longer distances, such as from Scotland to England, expect higher fares but greater advance discounts.

The cheapest fares (minimum 7-day advance purchase) sell out fast. Especially in summer, it's often necessary to book six to eight weeks ahead. Keep in mind that "return" (round-trip) fares are not always cheaper than buying two "single" (one-way) tickets—but National Rail's website will automatically display this option if it's the lowest fare. Cheap advance tickets often come with the toughest refund restrictions, so be sure to nail down your travel plans before you reserve.

To book ahead, go in person to any station, book online at www.nationalrail.co.uk, or call 0345-748-4950 (from the US, dial 011-44-20-7278-5240, phone answered 24 hours) to find out the schedule and best fare for your journey; you'll then be referred to the appropriate vendor—depending on the particular rail company—to book your ticket. If you order online, be sure you know what you want; it's tough to reach a person who can change your online reservation. You'll pick up your ticket at the station, or you may be able to print it at home. (BritRail pass holders, however, cannot make online seat reservations.)

A company called **Megabus** (through their subsidiary Megatrain) sells some discounted train tickets well in advance on a few specific routes, though their focus is mainly on selling bus tickets (info tel. 0871-266-3333, www.megatrain.com).

Buying Train Tickets as You Travel: If you'd rather have the flexibility of booking tickets as you go, you can save a few pounds by buying a round-trip ticket, called a "return ticket" (a same-day round-trip, called a "day return," is particularly cheap); buying before 18:00 the day before you depart; traveling after the morning rush hour (this usually means after 9:30 Mon-Fri); and going standard class instead of first class. Preview your options at www.nationalrail.co.uk.

Senior, Youth, Partner, and Family Deals: To get a third off the price of most point-to-point rail tickets, seniors can buy a Senior Railcard (ages 60 and up), younger travelers can buy a 16-25 Railcard (ages 16-25, or full-time students 26 and older), and two people traveling together can buy a Two Together Railcard (ages 16 and over). A Family and Friends Railcard gives adults about 33 percent off for most trips and 60 percent off for their kids ages 5 to 15 (maximum 4 adults and 4 kids). Each Railcard costs £30; see www.railcard.co.uk.

BUSES

Although buses are about a third slower than trains, they're also a lot cheaper. And buses go many places that trains don't, including destinations in the Highlands and the islands. For details on bus connections in the Highlands—where buses are the most useful—see page 235.

Most long-haul domestic routes in Scotland are operated by **Scottish Citylink.** In peak season, it's worth booking your seat on popular routes at least a few days in advance (at the bus station or TI, online at www.citylink.co.uk, or by calling 0871-266-3333). At slower times, you can just hop on the bus and pay the driver. If you're taking lots of buses, consider Citylink's Explorer pass (£49/3 days in 5-day period, £74/5 days in 10-day period, £99/8 days in 16-day period).

Some regional routes are operated by Citylink's **Stagecoach** service (www.stagecoachbus.com). If a Stagecoach bus runs the same route as a Citylink one—such as between Glencoe and Fort William—it's likely cheaper (and maybe slower).

Longer-distance routes (especially those to England) are operated by **National Express** (tel. 0871-781-8181, www.nationalexpress.com) or **Megabus** (book far ahead for best discounts, toll tel. 0900-160-0900, www.megabus.com).

RENTING A CAR

Rental companies in Britain require you to be at least 21 years old and to have held your license for one year. Drivers under the age of 25 may incur a young-driver surcharge, and some rental companies will not rent to anyone 75 or older. If you're considered too young or old, look into leasing (covered later), which has less-stringent age restrictions.

Research car rentals before you go. It's cheaper to arrange most car rentals from the US. Consider several companies to compare rates. Most of the major US rental agencies (including Avis, Budget, Enterprise, Hertz, and Thrifty) have offices throughout Europe. Also consider the two major Europe-based agencies, Europcar and Sixt. It can be cheaper to use a consolidator, such as Auto Europe/Kemwel (www.autoeurope.com—or the often-cheaper www.autoeurope.eu), which compares rates at several companies to get you the best deal—but because you're working with a middleman, it's especially important to ask in advance about add-on fees and restrictions.

Always read the fine print or query the agent carefully for add-on charges—such as one-way drop-off fees, airport surcharges, or mandatory insurance policies—that aren't included in the "total price."

For the best deal, rent by the week with unlimited mileage. I normally rent the smallest, least expensive model with a stick shift (generally cheaper than automatic). Almost all rentals are manual by default, so if you need an automatic, request one in advance. An automatic makes sense for most American drivers: With a manual transmission in Britain, you'll be sitting on the right side of the car, and shifting with your left hand...while driving on the left side of the road. When selecting a car, don't be tempted by a larger model, as it won't be as maneuverable on narrow, winding roads.

Figure on paying roughly $250 for a one-week rental. Allow extra for supplemental insurance, fuel, tolls, and parking. For trips of three weeks or more, leasing can save you money on insurance and taxes.

Picking Up Your Car: Big companies have offices in most cities, but small local rental companies can be cheaper. If you pick up your car in a smaller city or at an airport (rather than downtown), you'll more likely survive your first day on the road. Be aware that Brits call it "hiring a car," and directional signs at airports and train stations will read *Car Hire*.

Compare pickup costs (downtown can be less expensive than the airport) and explore drop-off options. Always check the hours of the location you choose: Many rental offices close from midday Saturday until Monday morning and, in smaller towns, at lunchtime.

When selecting a location, don't trust the agency's description of "downtown" or "city center." In some cases, a "downtown" branch can be on the outskirts of the city—a long, costly taxi ride from the center. Before choosing, plug the addresses into a mapping website. You may find that the "train station" location is handier. Returning a car at a big-city train station or downtown agency can be tricky; get precise details on the car drop-off location and hours, and allow ample time to find it.

When you pick up the rental car, check it thoroughly and make sure any damage is noted on your rental agreement. Rental agencies in Europe tend to charge for even minor damage, so be sure to mark everything. Before driving off, find out how your car's lights, turn signals, wipers, radio, and fuel cap function, and know what kind of fuel the car takes (diesel vs. unleaded). When you return the car, make sure the agent verifies its condition with you. Some drivers take pictures of the returned vehicle as proof of its condition.

The AA: The services of Britain's Automobile Association are included with most rentals (www.theaa.com), but check for this when booking to be sure you understand its towing and emergency road-service benefits.

Car Insurance Options

When you rent a car, you are liable for a very high deductible, sometimes equal to the entire value of the car. Limit your financial risk with one of these three options: Buy Collision Damage Waiver (CDW) coverage with a low or zero deductible from the car-rental company, get coverage through your credit card (free, if your card automatically includes zero-deductible coverage), or get collision insurance as part of a larger travel-insurance policy.

Basic **CDW** includes a very high deductible (typically $1,000-1,500), costs $15-30 a day (figure roughly 30-40 percent extra) and reduces your liability, but does not eliminate it. When you reserve or pick up the car, you'll be offered the chance to "buy down" the basic deductible to zero (for an additional $10-30/day; this is sometimes called "super CDW" or "zero-deductible coverage").

If you opt for **credit-card coverage,** you'll technically have to decline all coverage offered by the car-rental company, which means they can place a hold on your card (which can be up to the full value of the car). In case of damage, it can be time-consuming to resolve the charges with your credit-card company. Before you decide on this option, quiz your credit-card company about how it works.

If you're already purchasing a **travel-insurance policy** for your trip, adding collision coverage is an option. For example, Travel Guard (www.travelguard.com) sells affordable renter's collision insurance as an add-on to its other policies; it's valid everywhere in

British Radio

Local radio broadcasts can be a treat for drivers sightseeing in Britain. Many British radio stations broadcast nationwide; your car radio automatically detects the local frequency a station plays on and displays its name.

The BBC has five nationwide stations, which you can pick up in most of the country. These government-subsidized stations have no ads.

BBC **Radio 1:** Pop music, with youthful DJs spinning top-40 hits and interviewing big-name bands.

BBC **Radio 2:** The highest-rated station nationwide, aimed at a more mature audience, with adult contemporary, retro pop, and other "middle of the road" music.

BBC **Radio 3:** Mostly classical music, with some jazz and world music.

BBC **Radio 4:** All talk—current events, entertaining chat shows, special-interest topics such as cooking and gardening, and lots of radio plays.

BBC **Radio 5 Live:** Sporting events as well as news and sports talk programs.

You'll encounter regional variations of BBC stations, such as BBC London, Radio York, BBC Scotland, and BBC Gaelic. At the top of the hour, many BBC stations broadcast the famous "pips" (indicating Greenwich Mean Time) and a short roundup of the day's news.

Beyond the BBC offerings, several private stations broadcast music and other content with "adverts" (commercials). Some are nationwide, including **XFM** (alternative rock), **Classic FM** (classical), **Absolute Radio** (pop), and **Capital FM** (pop).

Traffic Alerts: Ask your rental-car company about turning on automatic traffic alerts that play on the car radio. Once these are enabled (look for the letters *TA* or *TP* on the radio readout), traffic reports for the area you are driving in will periodically interrupt programming.

Europe except the Republic of Ireland, and some Italian car-rental companies refuse to honor it, as it doesn't cover you in case of theft.

For more on car-rental insurance, see www.ricksteves.com/cdw.

Leasing

For trips of three weeks or more, consider leasing (which automatically includes zero-deductible collision and theft insurance). By technically buying and then selling back the car, you save lots of money on tax and insurance. Leasing provides you a brand-new car with unlimited mileage and a 24-hour emergency-assistance program. You can lease for as little as 21 days to as long as five and a

PRACTICALITIES

Driving in Scotland

To Orkney Islands

Scrabster   John O'Groats

Durness   20m .75h

70 m · 2.25 h

120m·3h

m = miles
h = hours

Not exactly to scale

105 m· 3h

120 m· 3h

70 m · 2.25 h

60 m · 1.25h

Ullapool

85m · 2h

85m · 2h

Skye   Apple-   Inverness   105 m · 2.75 h
Portree   cross

35m   40m   60 m · 1.5h   Dufftown
1h   1.5 h   20m   (Speyside)
.5h

45m   75m   45m
1h   1.75h   1.5h   55m · 1.25h

Kyle of   90m
Armadale   Lochalsh   Loch   1.75h   75m · 2h   40m · 1.25h   Aberdeen
Mallaig   45m · 1.5h   Ness
(Urquhart
Castle)   SCOTLAND   Ballater   20m
50m · 1.25h   (Balmoral   .5h
Ft. William   Castle)   45m
20m ·.5h   1h   Dunnottar
Glencoe   90m · 2.75h   55m · 1.75h   Castle
Mull   35m· 1h   Pitlochry
Iona   80m · 1.75h   50m · 1h
35m· 1.25h   Oban   45m · 1.25h   Dundee
Fionn-   Craig-   85m · 2.25h   60m · 1.25h   70m   25m
phort   nure   75m · 2h   · 1.5h   .5h   St.
30m   50m · 1.5h   Andrews
.75h   Stirling
Loch Lomond
(Balloch)   25m
75h   40m · 1h   Edinburgh
25m·.75h   50m · 1h   Holy
Glasgow   75m · 2h   Island

90m · 2.25h   135m · 2.5h   130m · 3h   100m · 2.5h   125m · 2.75h   80m·1.75h

To
Larne & Belfast
(Northern Ireland)   Hadrian's Wall
Cairnryan   145m · 3h   65m · 1.5h   50m · 1h   75m · 1.5h

Note: Your times   Keswick   Durham   ENGLAND
may vary based on   100m
traffic, sheep,   2.5h
construction   120m   To York
& road conditions.   · 3h
To
Liverpool

120m·3h (via Gairloch)

50m· 2h (Trotternish Loop)

PRACTICALITIES

half months. Car leases must be arranged from the US. One of the many companies offering affordable lease packages is Auto Europe.

Navigation Options

If you'll be navigating using your phone or a GPS unit from home, remember to bring a car charger and device mount.

Your Mobile Device: The mapping app on your mobile phone works fine for navigation in Europe, but for real-time turn-by-turn directions and traffic updates, you'll generally need Internet access. And driving all day while online can be very expensive. Helpful exceptions are Google Maps, Here WeGo, and Navmii, which provide turn-by-turn voice directions and recalibrate even when they're offline.

Download your map before you head out—it's smart to select a large region. Then turn off your cellular connection so you're not charged for data roaming. Call up the map, enter your destination, and you're on your way. View maps in standard view (not satellite view) to limit data demands.

GPS Devices: If you prefer the convenience of a dedicated GPS unit, known as a "satnav" in Britain, consider renting one with your car ($10-30/day). These units offer real-time turn-by-turn directions and traffic without the data requirements of an app. Note that the unit may only come loaded with maps for its home country; if you need additional maps, ask.

A less-expensive option is to bring a GPS device from home. Be aware that you'll need to buy and download European maps before your trip.

Maps and Atlases: Even when navigating primarily with a mobile app or GPS, I always make it a point to have a paper map. It's invaluable for getting the big picture, understanding alternate routes, and filling in when my phone runs out of juice. Several good road atlases cover all of Scotland. Ordnance Survey, Collins, AA, and Bartholomew editions are all available at tourist information offices, gas stations, and bookstores. The tourist-oriented Collins Touring maps do a good job of highlighting the many roadside attractions you might otherwise drive right past. Before you buy a map, look at it to be sure it has the level of detail you want.

DRIVING IN BRITAIN

Driving here is basically wonderful—once you remember to stay on the left and after you've mastered the roundabouts. Every year, however, I get a few notes from traveling readers advising me that, for them, trying to drive in Britain was a nerve-racking and regrettable mistake. If you want to get a little slack on the roads, drop by a gas station or auto shop and buy a green *P* (probationary driver with license) sign to put in your car window (don't get the red *L* sign, which means you're a learner driver without a license and thus prohibited from driving on motorways).

Many Yankee drivers find the hardest part isn't driving on the left, but steering from the right. Your instinct is to put yourself on the left side of your lane, which means you may spend your first day or two constantly drifting into the left shoulder. It can help to remember that the driver always stays close to the center line.

PRACTICALITIES

Road Rules: Be aware of Britain's rules of the road. Seat belts are mandatory for all, and kids under age 12 (or less than about 4.5 feet tall) must ride in an appropriate child-safety seat. It's illegal to use a mobile phone while driving—pull over or use a hands-free device. In Britain, you're not allowed to turn left on a red light unless a sign or signal specifically authorizes it. For more information about driving in Britain, ask your car-rental company, read the Department for Transport's *Highway Code* (www.direct.gov.uk—click on "Driving and transport" and look for "The Highway Code" link), or check the US State Department website (www. travel.state.gov, click on "International Travel," then specify your country of choice and click "Traffic Safety and Road Conditions").

AND LEARN THESE ROAD SIGNS

Speed Limit (mph) / Yield / No Passing / End of No Passing Zone

One Way / Intersection / Roundabout Ahead / Expressway

Danger / No Entry / Cars Prohibited / All Vehicles Prohibited

No Through Road / Restrictions No Longer Apply / Yield to Oncoming Traffic / No Stopping

Parking / No Parking / Road Narrows / Peace

Speed Limits: Speed limits are in miles per hour: 30 mph in town, 70 mph on the motorways, and 60 or 70 mph elsewhere (though, as back home, many British drivers consider these limits advisory). The national sign for the maximum speed is a white circle with a black slash. Motorways have electronic speed limit signs; posted speeds can change depending on traffic or the weather. Follow them accordingly.

Note that road-surveillance cameras strictly enforce speed limits. Any driver (including foreigners renting cars) photographed speeding will get a nasty bill in the mail. (Cameras—in foreboding gray boxes—flash on rear license plates to respect the privacy of anyone sharing the front seat with someone he or she shouldn't.) Signs (an image of an old-fashioned camera) alert you when you're entering a zone that may be monitored by these "camera cops." Heed them.

Roundabouts: Don't let a roundabout spook you. After all,

How to Navigate a Roundabout

NOTE:

- TRAFFIC IN ROUNDABOUTS FLOWS IN A CLOCKWISE DIRECTION.
- WHITE CARS ARE ENTERING THE ROUNDABOUT, GRAY CARS ARE EXITING.
- VEHICLES ENTERING A ROUNDABOUT MUST YIELD TO VEHICLES IN THE ROUNDABOUT.
- LOOK TO YOUR RIGHT AS YOU MERGE! ☺

you routinely merge into much faster traffic on American highways back home. Traffic flows clockwise, and cars already in the roundabout have the right-of-way; entering traffic yields (look to your right as you merge). You'll probably encounter "double-roundabouts"—figure-eights where you'll slingshot from one roundabout directly into another. Just go with the flow and track signs carefully. When approaching an especially complex roundabout, you'll first pass a diagram showing the layout and the various exits. And in many cases, the pavement is painted to indicate the lane you should be in for a particular road or town.

Freeways (Motorways): The shortest distance between any

two points is usually the motorway (what we'd call a "freeway"). In Britain, the smaller the number, the bigger the road. For example, the M-8 is a freeway, while the B-8000 is a country road.

Motorway road signs can be confusing, too few, and too late. Miss a motorway exit and you can lose 30 minutes. Study your map before taking off. Know the cities you'll be lacing together, since road numbers are inconsistent. British road signs are rarely marked with compass directions (e.g., *A-9 North*); instead, you need to know what major town or city you're heading for *(A-9 Inverness)*. The driving directions in this book are intended to be used with a good map. Get a road atlas, easily purchased at gas stations in Britain, or download digital maps before your trip (see page 483).

Unless you're passing, always drive in the "slow" lane on motorways (the lane farthest to the left). The British are very disciplined about this; ignoring this rule could get you a ticket (or into a road-rage incident). Remember to pass on the right, not the left.

Rest areas are called "services" and often have a number of amenities, such as restaurants, cafeterias, gas stations, shops, and motels.

Fuel: Gas (petrol) costs about $5.50 per gallon and is self-serve. Pump first and then pay. Diesel costs about the same. Diesel rental cars are common; make sure you know what kind of fuel your car takes before you fill up. Unleaded pumps are usually green. Note that self-service gas pumps and automated tollbooths and parking garages often accept only cash or a chip-and-PIN credit card (see page 437).

Driving in Cities: Whenever possible, avoid driving in cities. Most cities have modern ring roads to skirt the congestion. Follow signs to the parking lots outside the city core—most are a 5- to 10-minute walk to the center—and avoid what can be an unpleasant grid of one-way streets or roads that are restricted to public transportation during the day.

Driving in Rural Areas: Outside the big cities and except for the motorways, British roads tend to be narrow. In towns, you may have to cross over the center line just to get past parked cars. Adjust your perceptions of personal space: It's not "my side of the road" or "your side of the road," it's just "the road"—and it's shared as a cooperative adventure. If the road's wide enough, traffic in both directions can pass parked cars simultaneously, but frequently you'll have to take turns—follow the locals' lead and drive defensively.

Narrow country lanes are often lined with stone walls or woody hedges—and no shoulders. Some are barely wide enough for one car. Go slowly, and if you encounter an oncoming car, look for the nearest pullout (or "passing place")—the driver who's closest to one is expected to use it, even if it means backing up to reach it. If another car pulls over and blinks its headlights, that means, "Go ahead; I'll wait to let you pass." British drivers—arguably the most courteous on the planet—are quick to offer a friendly wave to thank you for letting them pass (and they appreciate it if you reciprocate). Pull over frequently—to let faster locals pass and to check the map.

Parking: Pay attention to pavement markings to figure out where to park. One yellow line marked on the pavement means no parking Monday through Saturday during work hours. Double yellow lines mean no parking at any time. Broken yellow lines mean short stops are OK, but you should always look for explicit signs or ask a passerby. White lines mean you're free to park.

In towns, rather than look for street parking, I generally just pull into the most central and handy pay-and-display parking lot I can find. To pay and display, feed change into a machine, receive a timed ticket, and display it on the dashboard or stick it to the driver's-side window. Rates are reasonable by US standards, and locals love to share stickers that have time remaining. If you stand by the machine, someone on their way out with time left on their sticker will probably give it to you. Most machines in larger towns accept credit cards with a chip, but it's smart to keep coins handy for machines and parking meters that don't.

In some municipalities, drivers will see signs for "disc zone" parking. This is free, time-limited parking. But to use it, you must obtain a clock parking disc from a shop and display it on the dashboard (set the clock to show your time of arrival). Return within the signed time limit to avoid being ticketed.

Some parking garages (a.k.a. car parks) are totally automated and record your license plate with a camera when you enter. The Brits call a license plate a "number plate" or just "vehicle registration." The payment machine will use these terms when you pay before exiting.

FERRIES

Ferries link the Scottish mainland to its many islands. For most west-coast routes, including the isles of Mull and Skye, you'll take a ferry run by Caledonian MacBrayne (tel. 0800-066-5000 or 01475/650-397, www.calmac.co.uk). Ferries to Orkney are operated by

NorthLink (www.northlinkferries.co.uk) and Pentland Ferries (www.pentlandferries.co.uk); Orkney Ferries runs the interisland routes (www.orkneyferries.co.uk).

Ferries can fill up in peak season—especially car spaces. During the summer, it's smart to reserve at least a day or two ahead (possibly more for popular routes). Check in at least 30 minutes ahead of your departure. Walk-on passengers don't need to reserve. Most car ferries have some kind of eatery on board.

TAXIS AND UBER

Most British taxis are reliable and cheap. In many cities, couples can travel short distances by cab for little more than two bus or subway tickets. Taxis can be your best option for getting to the airport for an early morning flight or to connect two far-flung destinations. Ride-booking services like Uber usually work in Britain just like they do in the US: You request a car on your mobile device and the fare is automatically charged to your credit card.

FLIGHTS

The best comparison search engine for both international and intra-European flights is Kayak.com. An alternative is Google Flights, which has an easy-to-use system to track prices. For inexpensive flights within Europe, try Skyscanner.com.

Flying to Europe: Start looking for international flights about four to six months before your trip, especially for peak-season travel. Off-season tickets can usually be purchased a month or so in advance. Depending on your itinerary, it can be efficient to fly into one city and out of another. If your flight requires a connection in Europe, see my hints on navigating Europe's top hub airports at www.ricksteves.com/hub-airports.

Flying Within Europe: Several cheap, no-frills airlines affordably connect Scotland with with other destinations in the British Isles and throughout Europe. If you're considering a train ride that's more than five hours long, a flight may save you both time and money. When comparing your options, factor in the time it takes to get to the airport and how early you'll need to arrive to check in.

Well-known cheapo airlines that serve Scotland include **EasyJet** (www.easyjet.com), **Ryanair** (www.ryanair.com), **Thomson** (www.thomsonfly.com), and **Flybe** (www.flybe.com). All serve Edinburgh and Glasgow; easyJet and Flybe also serve Inverness.

But be aware of the potential drawbacks of flying with a discount airline: nonrefundable and nonchangeable tickets, minimal or nonexistent customer service, pricey and time-consum-

PRACTICALITIES

ing treks to secondary airports, and stingy baggage allowances with steep overage fees. If you're traveling with lots of luggage, a cheap flight can quickly become a bad deal. To avoid unpleasant surprises, read the small print before you book. These days you can also fly within Europe on major airlines affordably—and without all the aggressive restrictions—for around $100 a flight.

Flying to the US and Canada: Because security is extra tight for flights to the US, be sure to give yourself plenty of time at the airport. It's also important to charge your electronic devices before you board because security checks may require you to turn them on (see www.tsa.gov for the latest rules).

Resources from Rick Steves

Begin your trip at www.ricksteves.com: My mobile-friendly **website** is *the* place to explore Europe. You'll find thousands of fun articles, videos, photos, and radio interviews organized by country; a wealth of money-saving tips for planning your dream trip; monthly travel news dispatches; a practical video library of my travel talks; my travel blog; and my latest guidebook updates (www.ricksteves.com/update).

Our **Travel Forum** is an immense yet well-groomed collection of message boards where our travel-savvy community answers questions and shares their personal travel experiences—and our well-traveled staff chime in when they can be helpful (www.ricksteves.com/forums).

Our **online Travel Store** offers travel bags and accessories that I've designed specifically to help you travel smarter and lighter. These include my popular carry-on bags (which I live out of four months a year), money belts, totes, toiletries kits, adapters, other accessories, and a wide selection of guidebooks and planning maps (www.ricksteves.com/shop).

Choosing the right **rail pass** for your trip—amid hundreds of options—can drive you nutty. Our website will help you find the perfect fit for your itinerary and your budget: We offer easy, one-stop shopping for rail passes, seat reservations, and point-to-point tickets (www.ricksteves.com/rail).

Small Group Tours: Want to travel with greater efficiency and less stress? We offer more than 40 itineraries and have over 900 departures annually reaching the best destinations in this book...and beyond. We cover the best of Britain with our seven-day in-depth London city tour, our 14-day England tour, our 13-day South England tour, our 10-day Scotland tour, and our 13-day Family Europe: London to Florence tour. You'll enjoy great guides, a fun bunch of travel partners (with small groups of 24 to 28 travelers), and plenty of room to spread out in

PRACTICALITIES

a big, comfy bus when touring between towns. You'll find European adventures to fit every vacation length. For all the details, and to get our Tour Catalog, visit www.ricksteves.com or call us at 425/608-4217.

Books: *Rick Steves Scotland* is one of many books in my series on European travel, which includes country and regional guidebooks (including Great Britain, Scotland, and England), city guidebooks, Snapshot guidebooks (excerpted chapters from my country guides), Pocket guidebooks (full-color little books on big cities, including London), "Best Of" guidebooks (condensed country guides in a full-color, easy-to-scan format), and my budget-travel skills handbook, *Rick Steves Europe Through the Back Door.* Most of my titles are available as ebooks.

My phrase books—for Italian, French, German, Spanish, and Portuguese—are practical and budget-oriented. My other books include *Europe 101* (a crash course on art and history designed for travelers); *Mediterranean Cruise Ports* and *Northern European Cruise Ports* (how to make the most of your time in port); and *Travel as a Political Act* (a travelogue sprinkled with tips for bringing home a global perspective). A more complete list of my titles appears near the end of this book.

TV Shows: My public television series, *Rick Steves' Europe,* covers Europe from top to bottom with over 100 half-hour episodes, and we're working on new shows every year. We have 11 episodes on Britain—that's over five hours of vivid video coverage of one of my favorite countries. To watch full episodes online for free, see www.ricksteves.com/tv.

Travel Talks on Video: You can raise your travel I.Q. with video versions of our popular classes (including talks on travel skills, packing smart, cruising, tech for travelers, European art for travelers, travel as a political act, and individual talks covering most European countries). See www.ricksteves.com/travel-talks.

Radio: My weekly public radio show, *Travel with Rick Steves,* features interviews with travel experts from around the world. It airs on 400 public radio stations across the US, and you can also listen to it as a podcast on iTunes, iHeartRadio, Stitcher, Tune In, and other platforms. A complete archive of programs (over 400 in all) is available at www.soundcloud.com/rick-steves.

Audio Tours on My Free App: I've also produced dozens of free, self-guided audio tours of the top sights in Europe, including sights in Edinburgh. My audio tours and other audio content are available for free through my **Rick Steves Audio Europe app,** an extensive online library organized into handy geographic playlists. For more on my app, see page 10.

APPENDIX

Useful Contacts

Emergency Needs
Police, Fire, and Ambulance: 112 (Europe-wide in English)
Police and Ambulance: Tel. 999
US Consulate in Edinburgh: Tel. 020/7499-9000, no walk-in passport services; Mon-Fri 8:30-17:00, closed Sat-Sun; 3 Regent Terrace; https://uk.usembassy.gov/embassy-consulates/edinburgh
Canadian Consulate in Edinburgh: Mobile 0770-235-9916 (business hours); after hours call the High Commission of Canada in London at tel. 020/7004-6000, www.unitedkingdom.gc.ca

Holidays and Festivals

This list includes selected Scottish festivals plus national holidays observed throughout Scotland (and Great Britain). Many sights and banks close on national holidays—keep this in mind when planning your itinerary. Before planning a trip around a festival, verify the dates with the festival website, the Visit Scotland website (www.visitscotland.com), or my "Upcoming Holidays and Festivals in Scotland" webpage (www.ricksteves.com/europe/scotland/festivals).

During July and August, book as far ahead as possible; Edinburgh is particularly jammed up in August during its festival season. Hotels also get booked up during Easter week; over the early May, spring, and summer Bank Holidays; and during Christmas, Boxing Day, and New Year's Day. On Christmas, virtually everything shuts down. Museums also generally close December 24 and 26.

Throughout the summer, communities small and large across Scotland host their annual Highland Games (like a combination track meet/county fair). These are a wonderful way to get in touch with local culture and traditions. For more on this phenomenon, see page 236.

Some Scottish towns have holiday festivals in late November and early December, with markets, music, and entertainment in the Christmas spirit (for instance, Stirling's Hogmanay party).

Jan 1	New Year's Day (closures)
Jan 2	New Year's Holiday (closures)
Jan 25	Burns Night (poetry readings, haggis)
April	Easter Sunday-Monday: April 1-2, 2018; April 21-22, 2019
May	Early May Bank Holiday: May 7, 2018; May 6, 2019; Spring Bank Holiday: May 28, 2018; May 27, 2019
June	Edinburgh International Film Festival (www.edfilmfest.org.uk)
Mid-June	Royal Highland Show, Edinburgh (Scottish-flavored county fair, www.royalhighlandshow.org)
July	Edinburgh Jazz and Blues Festival (www.edinburghjazzfestival.com)
Early Aug	Summer Bank Holiday: August 6, 2018; August 5, 2019
Aug	Edinburgh Military Tattoo (massing of military bands, www.edintattoo.co.uk)
Aug	Edinburgh Fringe Festival (offbeat theater and comedy, www.edfringe.com)
Aug	Edinburgh International Festival (music, dance, shows, www.eif.co.uk)
Late Aug	Cowal Highland Gathering, west of Glasgow in Dunoon
Early Sept	Braemar Gathering, north of Pitlochry (first Sat)

Oct	Royal National Mòd (Gaelic cultural festival, http://ancomun.co.uk)
Nov 5	Guy Fawkes Night (fireworks, bonfires, effigy-burning of 1605 traitor Guy Fawkes)
Nov 30	St. Andrew's Day (dancing and other cultural events)
Dec	St. Andrew's Day Bank Holiday: Dec. 2, 2019 only
Dec 24-26	Christmas holidays
Dec 31-Jan 2	Hogmanay (music, street theater, carnival, www.hogmanay.net)

Books and Films

To learn more about Scotland past and present, check out a few of these books or films.

Nonfiction

Crowded with Genius (James Buchan, 2003). This account of Edinburgh's role in the Scottish Enlightenment details the city's transformation from squalid backwater to marvelous European capital.

Edinburgh: Picturesque Notes (Robert Louis Stevenson, 1879). One of the city's most famous residents takes readers on a tour of his hometown.

The Emperor's New Kilt (Jan-Andrew Henderson, 2000). Henderson deconstructs the myths surrounding the tartan-clad Scots.

The Guynd (Belinda Rathbone, 2005). The marriage of an American woman and a Scottish man endures through cultural gaps and household mishaps.

How the Scots Invented the Modern World (Arthur Herman, 2001). The author explains the disproportionately large influence the Scottish Enlightenment had on the rest of Europe.

The Life of Samuel Johnson (James Boswell, 1790). Scottish laird Boswell's portrait of his contemporary is so admired that it inspired the use of Boswell's name to mean a close and companionable observer (Sherlock Holmes, for instance, at times refers to Watson as "my Boswell").

Scotland: The Autobiography: 2,000 Years of Scottish History by Those Who Saw It Happen (Rosemary Goring, 2007). Extracts from primary sources let a diverse cast of real-life characters, from Tacitus to Muriel Spark, tell the story of the nation.

Sea Room (Adam Nicolson, 2001). The owner of three tiny islands in the Hebrides contemplates their magical appeal and dramatic history.

A Traveller's History of Scotland (Andrew Fisher, revised 2009). Fisher probes Scotland's turbulent history, beginning with the Celts.

Fiction

For the classics of Scottish drama and fiction, read the "Big Three": Sir Walter Scott, Robert Louis Stevenson, and poet Robert Burns.

44 Scotland Street (Alexander McCall Smith, 2005). The colorful residents of an Edinburgh apartment house bring Scottish society to life.

Complete Poems and Songs of Robert Burns (Robert Burns, 2012, featuring work from 1774–1796). This collection showcases the work of a Scottish icon who wrote in the Scots language, including that New Year's classic "Auld Lang Syne."

The Cone Gatherers (Robin Jenkins, 1980). A staple of British secondary-school reading lists, this tragic novel about two brothers is set on a Scottish country estate during World War II.

Consider Phlebas (Iain M. Banks, 1987). In this first book in the popular *The Culture* science fiction series, Scottish author Banks describes a galactic war.

The Heart of Midlothian (Sir Walter Scott, 1818). This novel from one of Great Britain's most renowned authors showcases the life-and-death drama of lynchings and criminal justice in 1730s Scotland. Other great reads by Sir Walter include *Waverley* (1814), *Rob Roy* (1818), and *Ivanhoe* (1819).

Knots and Crosses (Ian Rankin, 1987). The Scottish writer's first Inspector Rebus mystery plumbs Edinburgh's seamy underbelly.

Lanark (Alasdair Gray, 1981). This eccentric, sprawling four-part novel set in Glasgow (and a fictional alt-Glasgow) tackles huge themes—capitalism, power, love—and earned Gray a reputation as a great Scottish writer.

Macbeth (William Shakespeare, 1606). Shakespeare's "Scottish Play" depicts a guilt-wracked general who assassinates the king to take the throne.

Outlander (Diana Gabaldon, 1991). This genre-defying series kicks off with the heroine time-traveling from the Scotland of 1945 to 1743. A popular TV adaptation began airing in 2014 (see page 498).

The Prime of Miss Jean Brodie (Muriel Spark, 1961). The story of an unconventional young teacher who plays favorites with her students is a modern classic of Scottish literature. (The film adaptation from 1969 stars Maggie Smith.)

The Strange Case of Dr. Jekyll and Mr. Hyde (Robert Louis Stevenson, 1886). This famous Gothic yarn by a Scottish author chronicles a fearful case of transformation in London, exploring Victorian ideas about conflict between good and evil.

Sunset Song (Lewis Grassic Gibbon, 1932). Farm girl Chris Guthrie is rudely confronted by adolescence, modernity, and war in this lauded Scottish classic, the first book in the trilogy "A Scots Quair."

Film and TV

The 39 Steps (1935). This Alfred Hitchcock classic about a London man wrongly accused of murder is set in Edinburgh, Glencoe, and other parts of the Scottish countryside.

The Angels' Share (2012). In this working-class comedy, a Glaswegian ne'er-do-well discovers he has a great nose for whisky.

Braveheart (1995). Mel Gibson stars in this Academy Award-winning adventure about the Scots overthrowing English rule in the 13th century.

Brigadoon (1954). In this classic musical, an American couple visiting Scotland discover a magical village.

Highlander (1986). An immortal swordsman remembers his life in 16th-century Scotland while preparing for a pivotal battle in the present day.

A History of Scotland (2010). This BBC series presented by Neil Oliver offers a succinct, lightly dramatized retelling of Scottish history.

Local Hero (1983). A businessman questions his decision to build an oil refinery in a small Scottish town once he gets a taste for country life.

Loch Ness (1996). A skeptical American scientist is sent to Scotland to investigate the existence of the Loch Ness monster.

Mary, Queen of Scots (2018). Saoirse Ronan stars in this portrayal of Mary upon her return to Scotland (from France) and her complicated relationship with cousin Elizabeth I. (A 1971 movie of the same name stars Vanessa Redgrave and Glenda Jackson.)

Monarch of the Glen (2000). Set on Loch Laggan, this TV series features stunning Highland scenery and the eccentric family of a modern-day laird.

Mrs. Brown (1997). A widowed Queen Victoria (Dame Judy Dench) forges a very close friendship with her Scottish servant, John Brown (Billy Connolly).

One Day (2011). Two University of Edinburgh students meet and fall in love on their graduation day, and their story continues to be told at each anniversary.

The Queen (2006). Helen Mirren expertly channels Elizabeth II at her Scottish Balmoral estate in the days after Princess Diana's death.

Rob Roy (1995). The Scottish rebel played by Liam Neeson struggles against feudal landlords in 18th-century Scotland.

Outlander Locations in Scotland

American novelist Diana Gabaldon's *Outlander* series spans continents and centuries, but the origin story—that of a High-lands laird and an English combat nurse caught up in the Jacobite rebellion—is grounded in Scotland. Much of the Starz television adaptation was filmed here. *Outlander* fans may enjoy seeing some of the following landmarks.

Outlander begins with Claire Randall on her honeymoon in 1945 **Inverness** (see page 296)—played on TV by **Falkland** village, near St. Andrews. Claire is mysteriously transported back in time to 1743 at **Craig na Dun,** a fictional stone circle inspired by **Clava Cairns** near Inverness (page 318). The TV version was filmed at **Dunalastair Estate,** between Pitlochry and Loch Rannoch.

Claire is rescued by the MacKenzie clan and tends to injured Highlander Jamie Fraser. They travel to the fictional **Castle Leoch,** seat of the Clan Mackenzie (the real-life Mackenzie home is Castle Leod, near Strathpeffer). Exterior scenes at Castle Leoch were filmed at **Doune Castle** near Stirling (page 193); the grounds—where Claire gathers herbs—were filmed in **Pollok County Park** (near Glasgow's Burrell Collection; page 159).

Claire meets the "witch" Geillis Duncan in fictional **Cranesmuir** village, but **Culross,** with its distinctive mercat cross (page 192) is a fine onscreen stand-in. The stone-and-thatched village where the MacKenzies collect rents was filmed at the **Highland Folk Museum** (page 337). Claire and Jamie visit the fictional Fraser family homestead, **Lallybroch** (on TV the deserted country estate of **Midhope Castle**—closed to the public).

In the books, Black Jack Randall's stout stone fortress is at **Fort William** (page 286); for TV those scenes were filmed at **Blackness Castle** on the Firth of Forth. Nearby, **Linlithgow Palace** is the filming location for the fictional **Wentworth Prison** (where Black Jack imprisons—and Claire rescues—Jamie), and **Aberdour Castle** plays the monastery where Jamie recovers. Scenes at **Ardsmuir Prison,** where Jamie is interned after the Battle of Culloden, were filmed at **Craigmillar Castle,** on the outskirts of Edinburgh. **Carfax Close,** where A. Malcolm has his print shop is fictional—and played on TV by Edinburgh's very real **Tweeddale Court** and **Bakehouse Close.**

Many of the show's interior scenes are filmed at **Wardpark Studios,** a former factory converted into Scotland's first permanent film studio for *Outlander.* For more *Outlander* locations, see www.visitscotland.com/outlander.

Skyfall (2012). In this James Bond film, we learn that 007 grew up in the Scottish Highlands, with a climactic scene at his childhood home (filmed near Glencoe).

Trainspotting (1996). Ewan McGregor stars in this award-winning, wild, gritty picture about Edinburgh's drug scene in the 1980s. In *T2 Trainspotting* (2017), McGregor's character returns to Edinburgh 20 years later to reconnect with his buddies.

FOR KIDS

Always Room for One More (Sorche Nic Leodhas, 1965). This Caldecott Medal-winning picture book presents a Scottish folktale with evocative illustrations.

Bagpipes, Beasties and Bogles (Tim Archbold, 2012). This whimsical story about spooky creatures and bagpipes serves up Scottish culture in a package perfect for young readers.

Brave (2012). This Disney flick follows an independent young Scottish princess as she fights to take control of her own fate.

Greyfriars Bobby (2005). Based on a true story, this family-friendly film is about a terrier in Edinburgh who became a local legend after refusing to leave his master's gravesite.

An Illustrated Treasury of Scottish Folk and Fairy Tales (Theresa Breslin, 2012). Kelpies, dragons, brownies, and other inhabitants of the Scottish Isles come to life in this lovely volume of traditional lore.

Kidnapped (Robert Louis Stevenson, 1886). This fantastic adventure story is based on events in 18th-century Scotland.

The Luck of the Loch Ness Monster (A. W. Flaherty, 2007). A picky American girl on a boat to Scotland throws her oatmeal out the porthole every morning, unwittingly feeding the Loch Ness monster that follows her.

Queen's Own Fool (Jane Yolen and Robert Harris, 2008). A historical novel for 10-and-ups based on the girl who was a jester in the court of Mary, Queen of Scots, the first of the "Stuart Quartet" books.

The Story of Scotland (Richard Brassey and Stewart Ross, 1999). This humorous, comic-book style history book will engage young travelers.

This Is Edinburgh (Miroslav Sasek, 1961, updated 2006). Vivid illustrations bring the Scottish capital to life in this classic picture book.

The Water Horse (2007). In this film based on a book of the same name, a young boy in 1940s Scotland discovers an egg, which later hatches into the fabled Loch Ness monster.

Conversions and Climate

NUMBERS AND STUMBLERS

- In Europe, dates appear as day/month/year, so Christmas 2019 is 25/12/19.
- What Americans call the second floor of a building is the first floor in Scotland.
- On escalators and moving sidewalks, Scots keep the left "lane" open for passing. Keep to the right.
- To avoid the Scottish version of giving someone "the finger," don't hold up the first two fingers of your hand with your palm facing you. (It looks like a reversed victory sign.)
- And please...don't call your waist pack a "fanny pack" (see the British-Yankee Vocabulary list at the end of this appendix).

METRIC CONVERSIONS

Scotland uses the metric system for nearly everything. Weight and volume are typically calculated in metric: A kilogram is 2.2 pounds, and one liter is about a quart (almost four to a gallon). Temperatures are generally given in Celsius, although some newspapers also list them in Fahrenheit.

1 foot = 0.3 meter	1 square yard = 0.8 square meter
1 yard = 0.9 meter	1 square mile = 2.6 square kilometers
1 mile = 1.6 kilometers	1 ounce = 28 grams
1 centimeter = 0.4 inch	1 quart = 0.95 liter
1 meter = 39.4 inches	1 kilogram = 2.2 pounds
1 kilometer = 0.62 mile	32°F = 0°C

IMPERIAL WEIGHTS AND MEASURES

Scotland hasn't completely gone metric. Driving distances and speed limits are measured in miles. Beer is sold as pints (though milk can be measured in pints or liters), and a person's weight is measured in stone (a 168-pound person weighs 12 stone).

1 stone = 14 pounds
1 Scottish pint = 1.2 US pints
1 schooner = 2/3 pint
1 imperial gallon = 1.2 US gallons or about 4.5 liters

CLOTHING SIZES

When shopping for clothing, use these US-to-UK comparisons as general guidelines (but note that no conversion is perfect).

Women: For pants and dresses, add 4 (US 10 = UK 14). For blouses and sweaters, add 2. For shoes, subtract 2½ (US size 8 = UK size 5½)

Men: For clothing, US and UK sizes are the same. For shoes, subtract about ½ (US size 9 = UK size 8½)

SCOTLAND'S CLIMATE

First line, average daily high; second line, average daily low; third line, average days without rain. For more detailed weather statistics for destinations in this book (as well as the rest of the world), check www.wunderground.com.

J	F	M	A	M	J	J	A	S	O	N	D

EDINBURGH

42°	43°	46°	51°	56°	62°	65°	64°	60°	54°	48°	44°
34°	34°	36°	39°	43"	49°	52°	52°	49°	44°	39°	36°
14	13	16	16	17	15	14	15	14	14	13	13

Fahrenheit and Celsius Conversion

Europe takes its temperature using the Celsius scale, while we opt for Fahrenheit. For a rough conversion from Celsius to Fahrenheit, double the number and add 30. For weather, remember that 28°C is 82°F—perfect. For health, 37°C is just right. At a launderette, 30°C is cold, 40°C is warm (usually the default setting), 60°C is hot, and 95°C is boiling. Your air-conditioner should be set at about 20°C.

Packing Checklist

Whether you're traveling for five days or five weeks, you won't need more than this. Pack light to enjoy the sweet freedom of true mobility.

Clothing

- [ ] 5 shirts: long- & short-sleeve
- [ ] 2 pairs pants (or skirts/capris)
- [ ] 1 pair shorts
- [ ] 5 pairs underwear & socks
- [ ] 1 pair walking shoes
- [ ] Sweater or warm layer
- [ ] Rainproof jacket with hood
- [ ] Tie, scarf, belt, and/or hat
- [ ] Swimsuit
- [ ] Sleepwear/loungewear

Money

- [ ] Debit card(s)
- [ ] Credit card(s)
- [ ] Hard cash ($100-200 in US dollars)
- [ ] Money belt

Documents

- [ ] Passport
- [ ] Tickets & confirmations: flights, hotels, trains, rail pass, car rental, sight entries
- [ ] Driver's license
- [ ] Student ID, hostel card, etc.
- [ ] Photocopies of important documents
- [ ] Insurance details
- [ ] Guidebooks & maps
- [ ] Notepad & pen
- [ ] Journal

Toiletries Kit

- [ ] Basics: soap, shampoo, toothbrush, toothpaste, floss, deodorant, sunscreen, brush/comb, etc.
- [ ] Medicines & vitamins
- [ ] First-aid kit
- [ ] Glasses/contacts/sunglasses
- [ ] Sewing kit
- [ ] Packet of tissues (for WC)
- [ ] Earplugs

Electronics

- [ ] Mobile phone
- [ ] Camera & related gear
- [ ] Tablet/ebook reader/media player
- [ ] Laptop & flash drive
- [ ] Headphones
- [ ] Chargers & batteries
- [ ] Smartphone car charger & mount (or GPS device)
- [ ] Plug adapters

Miscellaneous

- [ ] Daypack
- [ ] Sealable plastic baggies
- [ ] Laundry supplies: soap, laundry bag, clothesline, spot remover
- [ ] Small umbrella
- [ ] Travel alarm/watch

Optional Extras

- [ ] Second pair of shoes (flip-flops, sandals, tennis shoes, boots)
- [ ] Travel hairdryer
- [ ] Picnic supplies
- [ ] Water bottle
- [ ] Fold-up tote bag
- [ ] Small flashlight
- [ ] Mini binoculars
- [ ] Small towel or washcloth
- [ ] Inflatable pillow/neck rest
- [ ] Tiny lock
- [ ] Address list (to mail postcards)
- [ ] Extra passport photos

APPENDIX

BRITISH-YANKEE VOCABULARY

While Scotland has its own unique lexicon (see "The Language Barrier?" on page 468), most Scottish people also speak "British." Here are some words that may be unfamiliar. For a longer list, plus a dry-witted primer on British culture, see *The Septic's Companion* (Chris Rae). Note that instead of asking, "Can I help you?" many Brits offer a more casual, "You alright?" or "You OK there?"

advert: advertisement

afters: dessert

anticlockwise: counterclockwise

Antipodean: an Australian or New Zealander

aubergine: eggplant

banger: sausage

bangers and mash: sausage and mashed potatoes

Bank Holiday: legal holiday

bap: small roll, roll sandwich

bespoke: custom-made

billion: a thousand of our billions (a million million)

biro: ballpoint pen

biscuit: cookie

black pudding: sausage made with onions, pork fat, oatmeal, and pig blood

bloody: damn

blow off: fart

bobby: policeman ("the Bill" is more common)

Bob's your uncle: there you go (with a shrug), naturally

boffin: nerd, geek

bollocks: all-purpose explective (a figurative use of testicles)

bolshy: argumentative

bomb: success or failure

bonnet: car hood

boot: car trunk

braces: suspenders

bridle way: path for walkers, bikers, and horse riders

brilliant: cool

brolly: umbrella

bubble and squeak: cabbage and potatoes fried together

candy floss: cotton candy

caravan: trailer

car-boot sale: temporary flea market, often for charity

car park: parking lot

cashpoint: ATM

casualty: emergency room

cat's eyes: road reflectors

ceilidh (KAY-lee): informal evening of song and folk fun (Scottish and Irish)

cheap and cheerful: budget but adequate

cheap and nasty: cheap and bad quality

cheers: good-bye or thanks; also a toast

chemist: pharmacist

chicory: endive

Chinese whispers: playing "telephone"

chippy: fish-and-chips shop

chips: French fries

chuffed: pleased

chunter: mutter

cider: alcoholic apple cider

clearway: road where you can't stop

coach: long-distance bus

concession: discounted admission

concs (pronounced "conks"): short for "concession"

coronation chicken: curried chicken salad

cos: romaine lettuce
cot: baby crib
cotton buds: Q-tips
courgette: zucchini
craic (pronounced "crack"): fun, good conversation (Irish/Scottish and spreading to England)
crisps: potato chips
cuppa: cup of tea
dear: expensive
digestives: round graham cookies
dinner: lunch or dinner
diversion: detour
dogsbody: menial worker
donkey's years: ages, long time
draughts: checkers
draw: marijuana
dual carriageway: divided highway (four lanes)
dummy: pacifier
elevenses: coffee-and-biscuits break before lunch
elvers: baby eels
face flannel: washcloth
fag: cigarette
fagged: exhausted
faggot: sausage
fancy: to like, to be attracted to (a person)
fanny: vagina
fell: hill or high plain (Lake District)
first floor: second floor
fiver: £5 bill
fizzy drink: pop or soda
flutter: a bet
football: soccer
force: waterfall (Lake District)
fortnight: two weeks (shortened from "fourteen nights")
fringe: hair bangs
Frogs: French people

fruit machine: slot machine
full Monty: whole shebang, everything
gallery: balcony
gammon: ham
gangway: aisle
gaol: jail (same pronunciation)
gateau (or gateaux): cake
gear lever: stick shift
geezer: "dude"
give way: yield
glen: narrow valley (Scotland)
goods wagon: freight truck
gormless: stupid
goujons: breaded and fried fish or chicken sticks
green fingers: green thumbs
half eight: 8:30 (not 7:30)
hard cheese: bad luck
heath: open treeless land
hen night (or hen do): bachelorette party
holiday: vacation
homely: homey or cozy
hoover: vacuum cleaner
ice lolly: Popsicle
interval: intermission
ironmonger: hardware store
jacket potato: baked potato
jelly: Jell-O
jiggery-pokery: nonsense
Joe Bloggs: John Q. Public
jumble (sale): rummage sale
jumper: sweater
just a tick: just a second
kipper: smoked herring
knackered: exhausted (Cockney: cream crackered)
knickers: ladies' panties
knocking shop: brothel
knock up: wake up or visit (old-fashioned)
ladybird: ladybug
lady fingers: flat, spongy cookie
lady's finger: okra

lager: light, fizzy beer

left luggage: baggage check

lemonade: lemon-lime pop like 7-Up, fizzy

lemon squash: lemonade, not fizzy

let: rent

licenced: restaurant authorized to sell alcohol

lift: elevator

listed: protected historic building

loo: toilet or bathroom

lorry: truck

mack: mackintosh raincoat

mangetout: snow peas

marrow: summer squash

mate: buddy (boy or girl)

mean: stingy

mental: wild, memorable

mews: former stables converted to two-story rowhouses

moggie: cat

motorway: freeway

naff: tacky or trashy

nappy: diaper

natter: talk on and on

neep: Scottish for turnip

newsagent: corner store

nought: zero

noughts & crosses: tic-tac-toe

off-licence: liquor store

on offer: for sale

OTT: over the top, excessive

panto, pantomime: fairy-tale play performed at Christmas (silly but fun)

pants: (noun) underwear, briefs; (adj.) terrible, ridiculous

pasty (PASS-tee): crusted savory (usually meat) pie from Cornwall

pavement: sidewalk

pear-shaped: messed up, gone wrong

petrol: gas

piccalilli: mustard-pickle relish

pillar box: mailbox

pissed (rude), **paralytic, bevvied, wellied, popped up, merry, trollied, ratted, rat-arsed, pissed as a newt:** drunk

pitch: playing field

plaster: Band-Aid

plonk: cheap, bad wine

plonker: one who drinks bad wine (a mild insult)

prat: idiot

publican: pub owner

public school: private "prep" school (e.g., Eton)

pudding: dessert in general

pukka: first-class

pull, to be on the: on the prowl

punter: customer, especially in gambling

put a sock in it: shut up

queue: line

queue up: line up

quid: pound (£1)

randy: horny

rasher: slice of bacon

redundant, made: laid off

Remembrance Day: Veterans' Day

return ticket: round-trip

revising; doing revisions: studying for exams

ring up: call (telephone)

rubber: eraser

rubbish: bad

satnav: satellite navigation, GPS

sausage roll: sausage wrapped in a flaky pastry

Scotch egg: hard-boiled egg wrapped in sausage meat

Scouser: a person from Liverpool
self-catering: accommodation with kitchen
Sellotape: Scotch tape
services: freeway rest area
serviette: napkin
setee: couch
shag: intercourse (cruder than in the US)
shambolic: chaotic
shandy: lager and 7-Up
silencer: car muffler
single ticket: one-way ticket
skip: Dumpster
sleeping policeman: speed bumps
smalls: underwear
snap: photo (snapshot)
snogging: kissing, making out
sod: mildly offensive insult
sod it, sod off: screw it, screw off
sod's law: Murphy's law
soda: soda water (not pop)
soldiers (food): toast sticks for dipping
solicitor: lawyer
spanner: wrench
spend a penny: urinate
spotted dick: raisin cake with custard
stag night (or **stag do**): bachelor party
starkers: buck naked
starters: appetizers
state school: public school
sticking plaster: Band-Aid
sticky tape: Scotch tape
stone: 14 pounds (weight)
stroppy: bad-tempered
subway: underground walkway
sultanas: golden raisins
surgical spirit: rubbing alcohol

suspenders: garters
suss out: figure out
swede: rutabaga
ta: thank you
take the mickey/take the piss: tease
tatty: worn out or tacky
tattie scone: potato pancake
taxi rank: taxi stand
telly: TV
tenement: stone apartment house (not necessarily a slum)
tenner: £10 bill
tick: a check mark
tight as a fish's bum: cheapskate (watertight)
tights: panty hose
tin: can
tip: public dump
tipper lorry: dump truck
toad in the hole: sausage dipped in batter and fried
top hole: first rate
top up: refill (a drink, mobile-phone credit, petrol tank, etc.)
torch: flashlight
towel, press-on: panty liner
towpath: path along a river
trainers: sneakers
treacle: golden syrup
Tube: subway
twee: quaint, cutesy
twitcher: bird-watcher
Underground: subway
verge: grassy edge of road
verger: church official
way out: exit
wee (adj.): small (Scottish)
wee (verb): urinate
Wellingtons, wellies: rubber boots
whacked: exhausted
whinge (rhymes with hinge): whine

wind up: tease, irritate
witter on: gab and gab
wonky: weird, askew
yob: hooligan
zebra crossing: crosswalk
zed: the letter Z

INDEX

Children: books for, 499
Church Street (Inverness): 303
Churches: architecture, 419;
 Canongate Kirk (Edin-
 burgh), 44; Crathie Kirk
 (Balmoral), 347; Old High
 Church (Inverness), 304–305;
 Rosslyn Chapel (Roslin Vil-
 lage), 89–90; St. Andrew's
 and St. George's Church
 (Edinburgh), 50–51; St.
 Andrews Cathedral, 211–213;
 St. Giles' Cathedral (Edin-
 burgh), 39–40, 65–69; St.
 Magnus Cathedral (Kirkwall),
 401–402; St. Oran's Chapel
 (Iona), 260–262; Tolbooth
 Church (Edinburgh), 36
Cinema: 161, 249
Clan Donald: 381
Clan Donald Center (Skye):
 380–382
Clan Mackenzie: 381
Clan MacLeod: 381
Clans: 381, 415–416
Clava Cairns: 318, 498
Climate: 501
Clock Tower (Inverness): 302
Clothing sizes: 500
Clyde-built ships: 130
Cockburn Street (Edinburgh):
 41–42
Coffin Cairn: 280
Commando Memorial (Fort
 William): 289
Concessions: 435
Consulates: 493
Costs: 3–5
Covenanters: 79
Craig na Dun. *See* Clava Cairns
Craigellachie: 343
Craigmillar Castle: 498
Cranachan & Crowdie (Edin-
 burgh): 101
Cranesmuir. *See* Culross

Crannog Centre: 199
Crathie Kirk (Balmoral): 347
Credit cards: 9, 436–438, 439;
 vs. cash, 435–436. *See also*
 money
Cresswell Lane (Glasgow): 146,
 160
Crown jewels: 57–59
Cruises: 324. *See also* ferries
Cuillin Hills: 377–379
Cuisine: 457. *See also* eating
Culloden Battlefield: 313–317
Culross: 192–193, 498
Culture: connecting with, 11
Currency: 15–16; exchange rate,
 436. *See also* money
Customs and duty: 441

D

Da Vinci Code, The (Brown): 89
Dalkeith Road (Edinburgh): 21
Dancing: 237, 248–249
David I: 176
Day trips: from Edinburgh, 30,
 127–128; to the Highlands,
 134; from Inverness, 300–301
Deacon Brodie's Tavern (Edin-
 burgh): 37–38
Deanston Distillery (Doune):
 194, 200
Debit cards: 9, 436–438, 439.
 See also money
Department stores. *See* shop-
 ping
Devil's Staircase: 280, 283
Dewar, Donald: 139
Dining. *See* eating
Discounts: 435
Discovery Point (Dundee):
 221–223
Distilleries: 194, 245–246,
 329–332, 344, 345, 377,
 402–403. *See also* whisky
Distraining for Rent (Wilkie):
 84

INDEX

MAP INDEX

Start your trip at

Our website enhances this book and turns

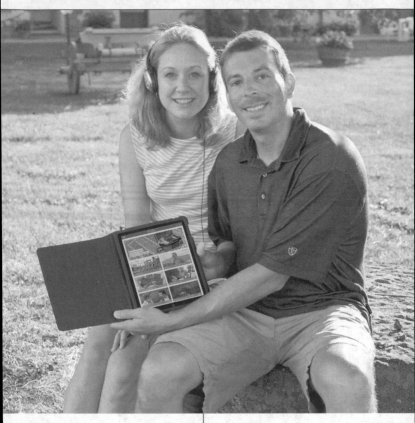

Explore Europe

At ricksteves.com you can browse through thousands of articles, videos, photos and radio interviews, plus find a wealth of money-saving travel tips for planning your dream trip. And with our mobile-friendly website, you can easily access all this great travel information anywhere you go.

TV Shows

Preview the places you'll visit by watching entire half-hour episodes of Rick Steves' Europe (choose from all 100 shows) on-demand, for free.